Praise for *Stalin's War*

"*Stalin's War* is above all about strategy: the failure of Roosevelt and Churchill to make shrewd choices as World War II played out. McMeekin brilliantly argues that instead of weighting the European and Pacific theaters to favor their own interests—and to weaken the inevitably antagonistic Soviet Union—FDR and Churchill left the most critical parts of Asia unguarded while they ground down the German army, a decision that favored Stalin's interests far more than their own. Roosevelt's 'Germany first' strategy and the trillion dollars of Lend Lease aid he poured into Stalin's treasury would underwrite Soviet control of China and East Central Europe after 1945 and hatch a Cold War whose dire effects are with us still."

 —Geoffrey Wawro, author of *Sons of Freedom* and director of the
  University of North Texas Military History Center

"A sweeping reassessment of World War II seeking to 'illuminate critical matters long obscured by the obsessively German-centric literature' on the subject. . . . Yet another winner for McMeekin, this also serves as a worthy companion to Niall Ferguson's *The Pity of War*, which argued that Britain should not have entered World War I. Brilliantly contrarian history."

 —*Kirkus*

"Historian McMeekin (*The Russian Revolution*) draws from recently opened Soviet archives to shed light on Stalin's dark reasoning and shady tactics. . . . Packed with incisive character sketches and illuminating analyses of military and diplomatic maneuvers, this is a skillful and persuasive reframing of the causes, developments, and repercussions of WWII."

 —*Publishers Weekly*

MAY - - 2021

ALSO BY SEAN McMEEKIN

The Russian Revolution: A New History

*The Ottoman Empire: War, Revolution, and the
Making of the Modern Middle East, 1908–1923*

July 1914: Countdown to War

The Russian Origins of the First World War

*The Berlin-Baghdad Express:
The Ottoman Empire and Germany's Bid for World Power*

*History's Greatest Heist:
The Looting of Russia by the Bolsheviks*

*The Red Millionaire:
A Political Biography of Willy Münzenberg*

STALIN'S WAR

A NEW HISTORY OF WORLD WAR II

SEAN McMEEKIN

BASIC BOOKS

New York

Basic Books
Hachette Book Group
1290 Avenue of the Americas, New York, NY 10104
www.basicbooks.com

Printed in the United States of America

First Edition: April 2021

Published by Basic Books, an imprint of Perseus Books, LLC, a subsidiary of Hachette Book Group, Inc. The Basic Books name and logo is a trademark of the Hachette Book Group.

The Hachette Speakers Bureau provides a wide range of authors for speaking events. To find out more, go to www.hachettespeakersbureau.com or call (866) 376-6591.

The publisher is not responsible for websites (or their content) that are not owned by the publisher.

Print book interior design by Trish Wilkinson.

Library of Congress Cataloging-in-Publication Data

Names: McMeekin, Sean, 1974- author.
Title: Stalin's war : a new history of World War II / Sean McMeekin.
Other titles: New history of World War II
Description: First edition. | New York City : Basic Books, 2021. | Includes
    bibliographical references and index.
Identifiers: LCCN 2020038843 | ISBN 9781541672796 (hardcover) |
    ISBN 9781541672772 (epub)
Subjects: LCSH: World War, 1939-1945--Soviet Union. | World War,
    1939–1945—Diplomatic history. | World War, 1939-1945--Pacific Area. |
    Stalin, Joseph, 1878–1953.
Classification: LCC D764 .M3825 2021 | DDC 940.53/47--dc23
LC record available at https://lccn.loc.gov/2020038843

ISBNs: 978-1-5416-7279-6 (hardcover), 978-1-5416-7277-2 (ebook)

LSC-C

Printing 1, 2021

For the Victims

Contents

Photo sections appear after pages 216 and 432

A Note on Dates, Names, Translation, and Transliteration

THE SECOND WORLD War, like the First, wrought havoc with place names, as cities and regions changed hands between empires, from empires to nation-states, and sometimes back into empires again. Moscow somehow escaped the nomenclature revolution, but this is one mercy among endless headaches. With most other cities, I have used the common contemporary form with modern usage in parentheses, thus Danzig (Gdańsk). In more politically sensitive cases, I have offered three or even four versions on first usage, as in Cernâuti (Chernovitsyi/Chernivtsi) or Lwów (Lemberg/Lvov/Lviv).

For Russian-language words, I have used the Library of Congress transliteration system in the source notes, with a somewhat simplified version in the main text, in which I avoid most "hard" and "soft" signs (e.g., Kharkov not Khar'kov) and make certain exceptions for common spellings of surnames (e.g., Trotsky not Trotskii, Rokossovsky not Rokossovskii, Belyaev not Beliaev). The idea is to make it as easy as possible for English readers to sound out Russian names, and also to remember them. For Bulgarian names and sources, I have followed the Library of Congress system for Cyrillic to the extent this was possible, with a few exceptions where Bulgarian differs from Russian, in which case I have done my best to capture the sound of the words. It is impossible to be consistent in all these things; may common sense prevail.

All translations from the French, German, Russian, Bulgarian, and Turkish, unless I am citing another translated work or note otherwise, are my own.

Introduction

Whose War?

FOR AMERICANS, AUSTRALIANS, Britons, Canadians, and Western Europeans, the global conflict of 1939–1945 has always been Hitler's war. Depending on taste, the story begins with the Versailles Treaty of 1919, or Hitler's accession to power in 1933 based on German resentment of that treaty, or the German remilitarization of the Rhineland in 1936, or the Munich conference of 1938, or Kristallnacht in November 1938, or Hitler's invasion of rump Czechoslovakia in March 1939 and the British guarantee to Poland, or, in the most literal version, the German invasion of Poland on September 1, 1939. But it always centers on Hitler as the villain who gives the struggle meaning. In popular culture, the Nazis are the perennial foils in an unbroken sequence of movies, from those produced during the war itself, such as *Casablanca* (1942), to modern films such as *Inglourious Basterds* (2009). In politics, the Nazis are cudgels used to beat political opponents: to compare someone to Hitler is the ultimate insult. No one actually defends Hitlerian Germany, outside of parodies like Mel Brooks's *The Producers* (1967 and much revived), but Hitler still haunts our nightmares as an all-purpose bogeyman, with remembrance of the horrors he unleashed uniting us in denunciation of Fascism, anti-Semitism, racism, and other evils of Nazism.

There has always been something missing, though, in this Hitler-centric view of World War II, which rings hollower the further east one travels from Berlin to Beijing. In Eastern Europe, German aggression left behind much less of a trace than the

1

Stalinist variety, which outlasted it by decades. East of the Volga, it left virtually no trace at all. In Asia, where Hitler's Germany was not even an active belligerent, the Soviet legacy of the war lives on in the Communist governments of China, North Korea, and Vietnam, countries on which Hitler's short-lived Reich left not even a shadow. Nor did Hitler play a role in the Pearl Harbor attack in December 1941 that brought the United States into the war— even if Hitler made it easier for the Roosevelt administration to choose a "Germany first" strategy when he foolishly declared war on the United States after Pearl Harbor in solidarity with Japan. In Putin-era Russia, although Communism has been repudiated, Stalin and the Great Patriotic War loom larger than ever in popular memory as a hard-fought Russian victory against Fascism in which Hitler himself, unlike in Western histories, is often out of focus. Viewed from Beijing, Pyongyang, Hanoi, Moscow, Budapest, or Bucharest, the conflict we call World War II was not Hitler's war at all. It did not begin in September 1939 and end in May 1945, with victory parades and flowers and kisses for the victors. In Eastern Europe, the war lasted until 1989, in the form of Soviet military occupation. On the Korean Peninsula, in China and Taiwan, questions arising from the conflict remain unresolved.[1]

It has always been a stretch to lump together all the wars on the globe between the Japanese invasion of Manchuria in September 1931 and Japan's final capitulation in September 1945, as many historians are now conceding. Victor Davis Hanson's recent general history *The Second World Wars* illustrates the point, as does Antony Beevor when he opens his own history, *The Second World War*, by conceding that it was "an amalgamation of conflicts." It is even more of a stretch to blame them all on one man—a man who was not even in power in Germany when the Manchurian conflict erupted, and who had been dead for four months when Japan surrendered. Still, if we do wish to find a common thread linking the on-and-off global wars lasting from 1931 to 1945, it would make far more sense to choose someone who was alive and in power during the whole thing, whose armies fought in both Asia and Europe on a regular (if not uninterrupted) basis for the entire period, whose empire spanned the Eurasian continent that furnished the theater for most of the fighting and nearly all of the casualties, whose territory was coveted by the two main Axis aggressors, and who succeeded in defeating them both and massively enlarging his empire in the process—emerging, by any objective evaluation, as the victor inheriting the spoils of war, if at a price in Soviet lives (nearly thirty million) so high as to be unfathomable today. In all these ways, it was not Hitler's, but Stalin's, war.[2]

If Stalin's imprint on this global conflict is most obvious in the broad lens, it is no less visible in narrow focus. The Japanese incursion into Manchuria in September 1931 was an escalation in a long-running struggle with Russia—first Tsarist, then Soviet—over control of Manchuria and its key ports and railways. Stalin had deployed one hundred thousand troops in Manchuria as recently as 1929 to secure the main railway lines and would maintain troops on and sometimes inside the borders of occupied Japanese Manchukuo all the way until August 1945, when Soviet troops invaded Manchuria and expelled Japan for good. Even in the critical days of late August and early September 1939, Stalin was driving events. It is widely known that the Molotov-Ribbentrop Pact of August 23 gave Hitler a free hand to invade Poland without fear of hostile Soviet intervention. It is less commonly known that the Germans were expecting the Red Army to invade Poland simultaneously to claim Stalin's share of the country—or that Stalin's share was larger than the Germans'. Instead, Stalin waited until Poland's armies had been destroyed before authorizing the Red Army to move in, even then denying that the USSR was at war with Poland to escape the odium of being Hitler's cobelligerent. Nor was the resulting partition of Poland Hitler's idea; it was Stalin's, floated as a trial balloon in 1938 to lure Germany to the negotiating table.

The European war that broke out in September 1939—pitting Britain, France, and Poland against Germany, with the USSR claiming to be neutral—did not have Hitler's planned or desired lineup of belligerents. He had sincerely believed that France and Britain would back down, as they had done when he had confronted them over Czechoslovakia. Nor did this war serve genuine French or British interests, as was made clear both in the dilatory approach to fighting it these powers took—which left Poland alone on the battlefield in 1939—and in the final reckoning six years later, which left the French and British empires in ruins and Poland under Soviet domination. But it was precisely the war Stalin wanted, even if, owing to German operational élan and Western ineptitude, it did not turn into an indecisive war of attrition—bleeding both sides equally, as in 1914–1918—that the Soviet dictator would have preferred to see.

To argue this, as I do in the book that follows, is not mere speculation. Stalin's dialectical view of Soviet foreign policy—in which metastasizing conflict between warring capitalist factions would enable Communism to advance to new triumphs—was firmly rooted in Marxism-Leninism, based on the precedent of Russia's own experience in the First World War, and clearly and consistently stated on many occasions, both verbally and in print. To understand Stalin's approach to the world does not require fancy ideological footwork or special insight, but simply to read his words and evaluate his actions in light of them. It asks us to spend a small fraction of the energy historians have devoted to divining Hitler's ideology, strategic thinking, and war aims to those of Stalin, the man who bested him decisively. Now that the Russian archives are (mostly) open, including the Politburo "Special Files"; with dozens of Soviet document collections in print, full of original material and priceless revelations; and with a growing body of secondary literature based on this new material, there is no longer an excuse for the enduring Hitlerian hypermnesia in the historical literature on World War II and the concomitant neglect of the enormous Soviet part in the drama. We have all the information we need to reevaluate Stalin's role in the conflict from its origins, through the years in which it tilted ever more favorably to Soviet interests in Europe and Asia, to its grim conclusion for millions of people.[3]

The story that emerges in these pages is not cheerful or edify-
ing, but it should help illuminate critical matters long obscured by
the obsessively German-centric literature on World War II, from
the misleading Soviet touting of "collective security" in the late
1930s, to Soviet manipulation of Britain and France after Stalin's
invasion of Poland, to Stalin's actions at his most dangerous moment during the so-called Phony War—when the Soviet invasion
of Finland nearly provoked a broad British-French-led coalition
into declaring war on the USSR—to the German-Soviet showdown in the Balkans and Stalin's diplomatic blackmail, which led
to Hitler's decision to move ahead with the German-led attack
on the Soviet Union (Operation Barbarossa). We will examine
the controversy surrounding the Soviet military posture in spring
1941 and the myth of Stalin's alleged emotional breakdown after a German invasion, which came as far less of a shock to him
than has often been claimed, and explore the "war for aluminum"
on the eastern front, which nearly halted the Soviet war effort in
1941. We will then assess the damage from the first six months of
Barbarossa, which had seen the invaders all but destroy the lavishly outfitted Red Army, upend Stalin's well-laid plans, and put
the USSR squarely on the back foot. Then we will pull back to examine the series of diplomatic coups that allowed Stalin to recover
the strategic initiative by 1943 and press on to Berlin and Beijing,
from the role of Soviet agents in pushing the United States toward
war with Japan in 1941—a top priority of Stalin's foreign policy
for years—and in helping set the "Germany first" priorities of the
American war; to the success of Soviet diplomats, sympathizers,
and agents of influence in shaping US-British policy on Yugoslavia,
Poland, China, and postwar Germany; to the unheralded role of
cascading lend-lease aid in restoring Soviet industrial capacity and
providing the armor, fuel, and mobile striking power that enabled
Stalin's ultimate victories in both Europe and Asia.

Eastern-front aficionados may be surprised that Hitler does not
invade the USSR until Chapter 17, but they will learn more about
what Stalin was up to in the years before this invasion wrought a

public-relations miracle, turning Stalin from Hitler's fellow aggressor into the Uncle Joe of Roosevelt-administration fantasy, whose manifold crimes and armed invasions of seven neighboring countries between 1939 and 1941 were conveniently forgotten once it appeared that the Soviet armies could serve as a battering ram to destroy the German Wehrmacht. Churchill's admirers may be floored to learn how Stalin-friendly, and Poland-unfriendly, his views were as early as 1939, and how badly this supposedly hardheaded realist fell for Soviet agitprop in Yugoslavia—but they will be pleasantly surprised to see him defended over the Mediterranean gambit of 1943, which turned out to be Churchill's last stand, his last effort to shape the war in a direction preserving British power and influence.

The story that follows is not a biography of Stalin, of whom there are fine new studies available based on archival research, including some by Russian historians translated into English. Nor is it a military history of the eastern front, of which there are now many very good ones. Still less is this a comprehensive history of the Second World War. What I have tried to do in these pages, rather, is to reexamine the conflict as a whole in light of newly available Russian documents covering the war in Europe and Asia and material seldom examined by Western historians in Poland and the Balkans. Even better-trodden archives in Germany, France, Britain, and the United States yield surprising revelations when one asks new questions. Some of my discoveries are brand new. Others come from older collections or studies neglected or forgotten because they do not fit the prevailing narratives of the Second World War(s). No conflict has to happen, nor endure as long as this one did. It cost tens of millions of people their lives, homes, property, and livelihoods, and forced hundreds of millions more to live for decades under totalitarian rule, foreign domination, or the threat of nuclear obliteration. Whether or not everyone is convinced by my interpretation of the course of events, it is my hope that every reader learns something new and thinks deeply about the war's legacy and meaning. We owe this much to the victims.[4]

Prologue
May 5, 1941

THE NIGHT STARTED out innocuously enough. Addressing an elite audience of two thousand military academy graduates in the Andreevsky Hall in the Moscow Kremlin, flanked by party luminaries and the secretary of the Communist International, Josef Stalin "proposed a toast to the executive personnel of the academies, to the chief officers, and to the professors, for bridging the gap in teaching modern equipment." There followed predictable bromides about the formidable Red Army, mailed fist of the global proletariat. Stalin recalled the crushing Soviet victories over Japan's Kwantung Army in Manchuria (Manchukuo) in August 1939—triumphs now embodied in the world-altering Soviet-Japanese Neutrality Pact, which he had just signed three weeks earlier—while glossing over the Red Army's less glorious performance in the Finnish war of 1939–1940, a struggle that had, at least, taught bitter lessons about modern warfare.

Since the Soviet-Finnish war, Stalin noted, the USSR had "reconstructed our army and armed it with modern military equipment." The Red Army had grown from 120 to more than 300 divisions, of which one-third, he noted with pride, were now mechanized. Soviet armored vehicles, too, had "changed their appearance." Easily blown up in 1939 by the Finns' Molotov cocktails, Soviet tanks were now stouter, with armor "3–4 times thicker." Heavy Soviet KVs and medium-weight models like the T-34, Stalin pointed out, were "tanks of the first line, which could break through the front." Soviet artillery, he observed further, "has been transformed, with more cannon and fewer howitzers." The Red Army, unlike in 1939 or 1940, now had ample stocks of anti-tank and anti-aircraft guns, capable of firing shells up to one thousand meters per second.[1]

As for aviation, the Red Air fleet had been thoroughly modernized in the last two years, with the speed of Soviet fighters rising from an average of 400 to 500 kilometers per hour (about 250 to 300 miles per hour) to 600 to 650 kilometers per hour (around 400 miles per hour) for newer I-15, I-16, and I-153 (Chaika) planes and state-of-the-art Mig-3 fighters. The air force also had light Soviet bombers designed for the attack and for close infantry support during an offensive. "In the case of war," Stalin vowed, "these warplanes will be deployed in the first line."[2]

Stalin admitted that the German Wehrmacht was "dizzy with success" after Hitler's heady triumphs over Poland in 1939, over France and the Low Countries in spring 1940, and over British forces everywhere from Norway and Belgium to, more recently, Libya and Greece. Even so, Stalin scoffed, "there is nothing special about the German army with regard to its tanks, artillery, or air force." German tanks, Stalin noted, were inferior to the new Soviet models in both armor and striking power. The vaunted German Luftwaffe, moreover, had not only failed to knock out the Royal Air Force (RAF) during the Battle of Britain in 1940, but was now being "overtaken even by the Americans," who were turning out superior warplanes, despite not being at war. The very successes of the Wehrmacht, Stalin argued, were breeding complacency, as the German high command had "lost its taste for further improvements in military technology." No matter how good the Germans were, Stalin thundered with a note of defiance, "there is not now and has never been an invincible army in the world."[3]

Interesting as Stalin's soliloquy on Soviet military technology might have been to foreign military attachés (who were not allowed in the room), it was old hat to the academy graduates, who had heard much of it before. Still, it was an impressive performance. Stalin spoke without notes for forty minutes before concluding with rousing toasts to the health of Red Army tank crews, aviators, artillerymen, and "modern infantry." "It was a fantastic speech," wrote a government notetaker in his diary, which "radiated confidence in our military people, in our strength, and dispersed the 'aura of glory' that enveloped the German army." Satisfied, Stalin yielded the floor to his host, the head of the Frunze Military Academy, Lieutenant General M. S. Khozin.[4]

What transpired next was so dramatic, so unexpected, that no one present ever forgot it. Khozin, parroting the *Pravda* propaganda line of the day, saluted Stalin for the success of his "peace policy," which had kept the Soviet Union out of the "capitalist war" raging in Europe and Asia. Before he could finish his platitudes, Stalin leapt to his feet, cut off the poor lieutenant general, and reproached him for pushing an "out of date policy." Stalin then moderated his tone, reassuring the officers and party bosses present that the "Soviet peace policy"—a thinly veiled allusion to the Molotov-Ribbentrop Pact signed with Nazi Germany in August 1939—had indeed bought the Red Army time to modernize and rearm, while also allowing the USSR to "push forward in the west and north, increasing its population by thirteen millions in the process." But the days of peaceful absorption of new territory, Stalin stated forthrightly, "had come to an end. Not another foot of ground can be gained with such peaceful sentiments."[5]

The Red Army, Stalin told its future commanders, "must get used to the idea that the era of the peace policy is at an end and that the era of widening the socialist front by force has begun." Anyone "who failed to recognize the necessity of offensive action," Stalin admonished, "was a bourgeois and a fool." The defensive doctrine that had animated strategic planning and war-gaming for a European conflict prior to 1941, he explained, was appropriate only for a weak, unprepared Red Army. "But today, now that our army has been thoroughly reconstructed, fully outfitted for fighting a modern war, now that we are strong—now we must shift from defense to offense." The transformation was not merely material, but philosophical, a policy shift that would require the Red Army's officers and political commissars to "transform our training, our propaganda, our agitation, the imprinting of an offensive mentality on our spirit."[6]

Issuing a veiled threat to Hitler, his erstwhile alliance partner in Berlin, Stalin declared that the time had come to "put an end, once and for all, to the adulation of the German Wehrmacht." "There's going to be war," he vowed. According to some witnesses, he stated explicitly that "the enemy will be Germany." Warming to his theme, Stalin compared the USSR to a "rapacious predator, coiled in tense anticipation, waiting for the chance to ambush its prey." And that day, Stalin concluded, "was not far away."[7]

Showing that he meant business, Stalin left the shadows from which he usually operated and assumed the presidency of the Council of People's Commissars on May 6, replacing Vyacheslav Molotov as the USSR's head of state for the first time. From this moment forward, all responsibility for Soviet foreign policy, for peace or war, for victory or defeat, lay in Stalin's hands alone. The time for subterfuge was over. War was imminent.

I.

BEFORE THE STORM

The Main Currents of Soviet Foreign Policy,
1917–1938

1

World Revolution

THE UNION OF Soviet Socialist Republics was a state like no other. From its earliest days, the "world's first proletarian government" defined itself in opposition to the existing capitalist states of the world. By repudiating all of the sovereign treaty and debt obligations of formerly Tsarist Russia in February 1918, Vladimir Lenin's revolutionary government effectively set itself up as an outlaw, outside—or above—the entire international system, bound only by its devotion to the global proletariat and the world revolution, not to shopworn, bourgeois concepts such as treaties and the rule of law. As Lenin explained with characteristic bluntness in his pamphlet denouncing the now-outmoded "petty bourgeois mentality" in May 1918, "If war is waged by the proletariat after it has conquered the bourgeoisie in its own country, and is waged with the object of strengthening and extending socialism, such a war is legitimate and 'holy.'"[1]

Understandably, the Western capitalist powers against whom Lenin's vituperation was directed—Britain, France, and the United States—responded in kind to the Bolshevik default, freezing Russian assets abroad and refusing to recognize Lenin's outlaw regime. This subtraction from the international system of what had, before 1914, been one of the world's largest and most dynamic economies would in itself have a profound impact on the financial frailty of the post-1918 world, capping off the economic devastation of the First World War, from damage to infrastructure and trade to debt-fueled inflation. Before the October Revolution of 1917, Russia had been allied to these Western nations, which held the bulk of its foreign debt, in the Great War and had been bound by the

London convention of September 1914 not to sign a separate peace treaty with the Central powers (Germany and Austria-Hungary, later joined by the Ottoman Empire and Bulgaria). When Lenin's diplomats signed just such a treaty with the victorious Germans at Brest-Litovsk in March 1918, this provided still more confirmation for the Allies of the lawless nature of Lenin's regime. By sending troops to aid Lenin's opponents in the nascent Russian Civil War, the Western Allies also provided confirmation for the binary, us-against-them mentality of Bolshevik foreign policy.

Of course, despite mutual antipathy between Bolshevik Russia and the capitalist powers, the conduct of diplomacy often had to be tempered by practical considerations. Such was certainly the case at Brest-Litovsk, where Lenin had authorized his diplomats to sign a punitive treaty with Germany and the other Central powers with scarcely concealed contempt for those capitalist regimes. (En route to the negotiations, Russians were witnessed throwing propaganda leaflets from the train at German soldiers.) To force Lenin's hand, German warplanes even bombed Petrograd in early March 1918, prompting the commissar of foreign affairs, Leon Trotsky, to petition the Western Allies for help against the invading Germans—first asking France for logistical assistance in relocating the capital from Petrograd to Moscow, then issuing a conditional invitation for British marines to land at the northern Arctic port of Murmansk to protect war supplies, and finally broaching the idea, soon dropped, that British and American officers might help train the new Red Army. The Brest-Litovsk agreement between the early Soviet government and the Central powers was marked by cynicism on both sides.[2]

Despite the confusing twists and turns of early Bolshevik diplomacy necessitated by the weakness of Lenin's regime in 1918, a telltale pattern of Soviet diplomatic practice was emerging. There may have been a temporary convergence of interest between Lenin and the Western Allies after Brest-Litovsk, which led to Trotsky's conditional olive branches to the Allies, but the fundamental hostility between the two sides was revealed as soon as these circumstances changed. The same was true of relations between Lenin and the Central powers. Far from being a loyal German agent (as many Allied critics believed because of his acceptance of German funds and logistical support prior to the October Revolution), Lenin agreed to German terms at Brest-Litovsk in March 1918 only to win time, and he repudiated those terms with perfect impunity as soon as he learned of the German collapse on the western front at the end of September. The Brest-Litovsk Treaty, a German diplomat reported from Moscow on October 10, "is a dead letter. Our influence with the Bolsheviks is completely exhausted. They do with us now what they wish." With schadenfreude, Bolshevik diplomats celebrated Germany's comeuppance by confiscating German diplomatic bags in Moscow and Petrograd; in the bags, they found (and helped themselves to) 250 million Tsarist rubles. The same was true of Soviet encouragement of autonomy for national minorities, such as Finns, Poles, and Ukrainians. This policy was embodied in a decree on the "Rights of the Peoples of Russia to Self-Determination" signed by Lenin and his nationalities commissar, Josef Stalin, in November 1917, when the Bolsheviks still wished to break up the Tsarist empire. Once his government was strong enough, Lenin fought to bring these peoples back under Soviet control—succeeding in the case of Ukraine, although not with Finland, which preserved its independence in the Russian Civil War, or with Poland, which defeated the Red Army in 1920 and expanded its borders eastward into Soviet Ukraine, well past the Curzon Line endorsed by the Entente powers at Versailles in 1919.[3]

Treaties signed with capitalist powers, such as the diktat peace imposed by Germany at Brest-Litovsk, were seen as temporary truces, valid only so long as they served Soviet interests, or when the Soviets were too weak to break them. This was equally true of Soviet agreements with the Western Allies, such as Trotsky's invitation for Allied troop landings in March 1918, which was later expunged from memory as the Bolsheviks mythologized a conspiratorial "Allied intervention" to strangle Lenin's infant regime.

As early as June 27, 1918, Georgii Chicherin, Trotsky's successor as commissar of foreign affairs, issued a formal protest against the "invasion of the English armed force" at Murmansk, notwithstanding the fact that the English had been invited there by Trotsky as a result of the German military occupation of western Russia.[4]

The same pattern of opportunistically playing hostile capitalist factions against each other could be observed in Soviet diplomatic practice after the Allies withdrew from Russia. As Lenin explained to a party congress in late November 1920, shortly after the rout of the last White forces in the Russian Civil War: "If we are obliged to tolerate such scoundrels as the capitalist thieves, each of whom is preparing to plunge a knife into us, it is our direct duty to make them turn their knives against each other." Thus, the Anglo-Soviet Trade Agreement, which a Bolshevik team signed in London in March 1921, seemed to signal a long-awaited thaw in relations between Moscow and the victorious Western powers. Keen to open up the Soviet market to English exports of wool and weapons after Britain had sunk into a postwar industrial depression, Prime Minister David Lloyd George had forfeited his leverage up front by refusing to demand repayment of the Russian loan and equity obligations that Lenin had repudiated in the 1918 default. Exports were indeed stimulated, until the Bolsheviks spent the last of the Tsarist gold bullion they had seized in the revolution, leaving the Soviet government effectively broke. But when the Allies refused to extend Moscow new loans at a conference in Genoa in April 1922, the Bolsheviks reached a more favorable deal with Germany at a hotel in nearby Rapallo, in which Berlin extended a credit line to the Soviets while allowing Lenin to repudiate outstanding Western debt claims for good. The Treaty of Rapallo, which included a secret clause allowing German industrialists to manufacture and test new weapons on Soviet Russian territory, evading the prohibition on German rearmament imposed by the Versailles Treaty, exacerbated tensions between the Germans and the Allies yet again.[5]

While many Western statesmen were shocked by such duplicitous Soviet behavior, Lenin never really made a secret of the ruthless hostility driving Communist relations with the outside world. "As long as capitalism and socialism exist," he proclaimed at a Moscow party congress on November 26, 1920, "we cannot live in peace: in the end, one or the other will triumph—a funeral dirge will be sung either over the Soviet Republic or over world capitalism." The lesson for Soviet foreign policy was clear. "Until the final victory of socialism in the whole world," Lenin explained, "we must exploit the contradictions and opposition between two imperialist power groups, between two capitalist groups of states, and incite them to attack each other." Soviet statesmen should strive to increase tensions between rival coalitions in the capitalist world: a new "rift between the Entente and Germany" would surely open at some point. No less promising, in Lenin's view, was the "future Japanese-American war" for capitalist "supremacy" in the Pacific, for the "right to loot": "They want to fight, they will fight." In the initial stages of a global capitalist war breaking out in Europe or Asia, it would be best for Communists to stay on the sidelines while the belligerents exhausted themselves. "As soon as we are strong enough to defeat capitalism as a whole," Lenin vowed, "we shall immediately take it by the scruff of the neck."[6]

As Lenin's brutal remarks suggest, the true face of Soviet foreign policy was revealed not in the day-to-day activity log of the foreign and trade commissariats, where officials could be as pragmatic as they pleased so long as the agreements they signed served short-term Soviet interests, but in the machinations of the Third International, or Communist International (Comintern), formed in March 1919. Following the lead of Marx's own First International (1864–1876), and the better-organized yet ultimately ineffectual Second International (1889–1914), which had failed to prevent the outbreak of the "imperialist war" of 1914–1918, the Comintern was explicitly devoted to world revolution and the overthrow of existing capitalist governments. The twenty-one conditions of membership, imposed on national Communist parties functioning as sections of the Executive Committee of the Communist International (ECCI) in Moscow, divided up party organizations into legal and illegal branches, with the latter functioning as shadow Communist governments ready to take power, come the revolution (condition two). With an eye on the Bolsheviks' own hostile takeover of the Russian Imperial Army via Lenin's defeatist "peace platform" in 1917, condition four required Communist parties to carry out "persistent and systematic propaganda and agitation among the armed forces, and Communist nuclei must be formed in every military unit." Another critical condition (number fifteen) required national Communist parties to "render selflessly devoted assistance" to the USSR (and to any future Communist governments) "in its struggle against counter-revolutionary forces," to urge workers to sabotage any efforts by their governments to "transport war materials to [the Soviet Union's] enemies," and to "carry on legal or illegal propaganda among the armed forces that are sent to strangle the workers' republic."[7]

In this way, a dangerous virus was injected into the international system, with political parties in every significant country in the world devoted to routinely sabotaging (and ultimately overthrowing) their own governments while in the paid service of a foreign power, the USSR. Making Soviet influence operations still more explosive, the Bolsheviks had inherited Europe's largest gold reserves from the Tsarist regime—until they were depleted in February 1922 to pay for English wool and high-end military imports—along with a bottomless supply of looted jewelry and diamonds in the vaults of the Moscow Gokhran, or central treasury of valuables.[8]

Although the Communist-subversion virus remained latent in most countries, most of the time, it spread quickly in the ravaged lands of the defeated powers of the First World War. It spread to Hungary, where a copycat Soviet regime was installed in 1919 by Bela Kun, a veteran of the Russian Civil War, and to Germany, where Communist or Communist-inspired uprisings erupted in early 1919 in Berlin and in Munich in March 1921 and again in October 1923. Although these uprisings ultimately failed, they had the important side effect of inspiring the *völkisch*-nationalist reaction (especially in Bavaria), which culminated in Nazism. In this way, Communist subversion of foreign governments, by fueling political extremism on both left and right, drove the dialectical process that (in the Marxist-Leninist view) would lead to the inevitable triumph of Communism. As Lenin's nationalities commissar, Josef Stalin, explained in an important treatise in 1919:

> The world has definitely and irrevocably split into two camps: the camp of imperialism and the camp of socialism. Over there, in *their* camp, are America and Britain, France and Japan, with their capital, armaments . . . and experienced administrators. Here, in *our* camp, are Soviet Russia and the young Soviet republics and the growing proletarian revolution in the countries of Europe, without capital, without . . . experienced administrators, but, on the other hand, with experienced *agitators* capable of firing the hearts of working people. . . . The struggle between these two camps constitutes the hub of present-day affairs.[9]

To the disappointment of Lenin and Stalin, the revolutionary mood in Europe slowly dissipated after the failure of the Communists' "German October" and of Hitler's Beer Hall Putsch in November 1923, owing in part to a new arrangement on German war reparations payments (the Dawes Plan), which helped curb the hyperinflation plaguing Germany and Central Europe and thereby lessened the appeal of extremist parties and groups. On the bright side, the reduction of international tensions helped make possible a political rapprochement between Moscow and several of the former Entente powers after the first-ever Labour government in Britain, led by Ramsay MacDonald, recognized the Soviet Union in February 1924, a move followed swiftly by Italy and later that year by France. Even inside the Soviet Union, the radical, maximalist-socialist policies of War Communism (c. 1918–1921)— which abolished all private economic exchange, including the use of money—were abandoned under Lenin's New Economic Policy in 1921, which allowed the re-legalization of private grain trade, retail, and even small-scale manufacturing. By the mid-1920s, the life-and-death struggle between the "two camps," as Stalin had called them, seemed quiescent, if not abandoned entirely.

Still, despite the appearance of Communist moderation at home and the regularization of diplomatic relations, there was no genuine reconciliation between the Soviet regime and the capitalist governments it was devoted to destroying. Even in Britain, the country that had led the way in normalizing relations with Moscow—first on de facto terms in Lloyd George's Anglo-Soviet Trade Agreement of March 1921 and then in the recognition by MacDonald's Labour government—suspicion of Soviet motives ran high. Neither Lloyd George nor MacDonald had insisted on debt repayment, or on a binding commitment not to interfere in domestic British politics, as a condition of a deal with Moscow, and their failure to demand such concessions rankled British conservatives. In May 1927, a Tory-led government authorized a raid on the Soviet trade agency Arcos in London, which turned up enough evidence of Communist subversion in British politics to justify the breaking off of diplomatic relations for the next three years. Other capitalist powers that had seen the property of their citizens confiscated by the Communists, such as the Netherlands, Switzerland, Yugoslavia, and the United States, remained aloof from the USSR, refusing to recognize the Bolsheviks' outlaw regime all through the 1920s.[10]

In a sign of intent, Comintern propagandists spent much of 1927—a relatively peaceful and prosperous year, during which it seemed that the miseries of the postwar years had been overcome even in Germany, where voters had lost interest in Nazi and Communist extremism—drumming up hysteria about the "Menacing War Danger Against the Soviet Union," a war scare used to justify the massive rearmament drive of the first Five-Year Plan, launched in 1928.* Without a hint of subtlety, the Comintern's propaganda

---

* The only evidence of foreign "designs" that year was the breaking off of diplomatic relations by Great Britain and the crackdown by Chiang Kai-shek's Kuomintang on the Chinese Communist Party. In both cases,

mastermind, a Lenin comrade from wartime Switzerland named Willi Münzenberg, launched a Comintern periodical called, simply, *The Coming War*.[11]

This belligerent line was wholly to the liking of Josef Stalin, the nationalities commissar who had emerged, after Lenin's death in January 1924, as general secretary of, and the dominant figure in, the Soviet Communist Party. More cautious in temperament than the mercurial Lenin, a man who preferred operating in the shadows, Stalin was a born street fighter, a veteran of countless skirmishes and brawls in which he had always come out on top.

Although a political animal who, like Lenin, was willing to adjust his policies to evolving circumstances, Stalin was just as certain of his fundamental worldview. Far from abandoning his "two camps" theory of international relations after the fall of Bela Kun's Hungarian Soviet Republic in August 1919 and the failure of the German Communists to take power in 1919, 1921, and 1923, Stalin doubled down. In his first major work after Lenin's death, *Foundations of Leninism* (1924), Stalin endorsed Lenin's theory of "revolutionary defeatism," by which Lenin had predicted that proletarian revolution would occur not because of the inexorable growth of class contradictions, as prophesied in Marx's *Das Kapital*, but as a byproduct of "imperialist war," as "the first of the countries to be vanquished" would then be the first to fall. Though a less elegant theoretician than Lenin, Stalin was just as clearheaded about the circumstances that enabled the improbable Bolshevik triumph in 1917. "Had the two chief coalitions of capitalist countries not been engaged in mortal combat during the imperialist war in 1917," he wrote in January 1925, "had they not been clutching at each other's throats . . . it is doubtful whether the Soviet power would have survived."[12]

---

the paranoid rhetoric of Soviet agitprop was not only overblown but upside down, in that it was plainly Soviet influence operations in Britain and China that had sparked countermoves in London and Shanghai, rather than any putative British or Chinese designs on Soviet territory.

The lesson for the future of Communism was clear. Europe might have been calm in the mid-1920s, but any Marxist student of history knew that the peace between the "imperialist factions" was a precarious one. The losers of the last war, such as Germany, and even winners jealous of others' greater winnings, such as Italy and Japan, were smoldering with resentment over the terms imposed by the victors at Versailles. "If war breaks out," Stalin told the Central Committee of the Communist Party of the Soviet Union in 1925, "we shall not be able to sit with folded arms. We will have to take action, but we shall be the last to do so. And we shall do so in order to throw the decisive weight on the scales, the *weight* that can turn the scales."[13]

2

Stalin Makes His Mark

STALIN, BORN JOSEF Vissarionovich "Soso" Djugashvili in the Georgian village of Gori in 1878, was a man who usually knew what he wanted. He was caricatured by jealous rivals like Trotsky as a bland bureaucrat, a "grey blur," or "Comrade Card Index," but Stalin was a more interesting personality than this. Materials that became available after the fall of the Soviet Union show the young Stalin to have been intelligent and charismatic, even an accomplished poet, who wrote well-regarded verse in his native Georgian under the pen name Soselo. Although he was short (about five feet, five inches) and his face was flawed by pockmarks, Stalin cut a dashing figure as a Caucasian bandit chieftain whom many women found attractive. Above all, Stalin was ambitious and ruthless, a born Bolshevik in temperament who made his bones by organizing violent Caucasian robberies, most famously the great Tiflis heist of June 1907, when Stalin's gang threw ten grenades at an armored cash convoy in broad daylight. According to Tsarist secret police (Okhrana) files, forty were killed and another fifty wounded in Stalin's terrorist "spectacular," which impressed Lenin and made Stalin's name in the Bolshevik movement.[1]

In the jostling for power that followed Lenin's death in January 1924, Stalin also proved an astute politician. Although some Western observers were surprised by the eclipse of the more famous Trotsky, who had been much better liked in European socialist circles than the fanatical Lenin, it was less than shocking for Soviet insiders, who knew that Trotsky, despite his fame and flamboyance, had little real constituency in the party. Trotsky's CV was impressive, comprising high-profile public roles as commissar of foreign affairs and then of war, but he had made little effort to build a network of loyalists in the party, perhaps feeling that he did not need to. Trotsky was also a recent convert to Bolshevism, joining the party only in July 1917. As a perennial exile, he also had less experience in Russian politics than Stalin, who had toiled away inside the country during the war, doing battle with the Tsarist secret police.

The truth was that Trotsky was something of a dilettante. He was so out of touch with political currents that he failed to show up for Lenin's funeral in 1924, a catastrophic error that allowed Stalin to reap the reward for organizing the elaborate rite, the embalming of the body, and the cult of personality that turned Lenin into a Communist deity, second only to Marx in the pantheon of Marxism-Leninism. By 1925, Trotsky was on the path to oblivion. Owing to his control of promotions and firings in the party's Organizational Bureau (Orgburo), Stalin needed only two more years to sideline rivals in the Political Bureau (Politburo)— from Trotsky's "left Communist" allies, Moscow and Leningrad party bosses Lev Kamenev and Grigory Zinoviev, to the "right" deviationist Nikolai Bukharin, who wanted to abandon Trotsky's doctrine of "permanent revolution" and grow gradually into "socialism in one country." By the end of 1927, Stalin was supreme as general secretary of the Communist Party, if not yet a dictator.

With no rivals left, Stalin was now free to realize the promise of Lenin's revolution while putting his own indelible stamp on Communism. Addressing the Fifteenth Communist Party Congress in December 1927, Stalin reminded his now-cowed comrades that Lenin had never intended his proto-capitalist compromises of the early 1920s to be permanent. The essential question of the Marxist dialectic, Stalin argued, was *kto-kogo* (who whom): Who would vanquish whom, socialism or capitalism? To resume the socialist offensive, Stalin proposed the forcible collectivization of agriculture at a Central Committee plenum in July 1928, as the first step toward a fully planned socialist economy. Significantly, the primary rationale he offered was to secure the USSR against military attack by building up a state-controlled grain reserve. A second was to sell grain abroad to finance imports of industrial equipment. In his speech launching the first Five-Year Plan in November 1928, Stalin thundered, "We are fifty or a hundred years behind the advanced countries. We must make up this gap in ten years. Either we do it, or they will crush us."[2]

The foreign policy corollary of Stalin's forced march to industrialization at home was the new "class against class" doctrine proclaimed at the congress of the Comintern in Moscow in summer 1928, which inaugurated the so-called Third Period. After the calm years of the mid-1920s, it was expected that "world capitalism" would enter a period of heightened contradictions and class struggle, which brought with it new dangers for Soviet Russia but also new opportunities for Communist expansion. As Stalin had argued back in 1926, "No matter what our successes . . . we cannot consider the land of the proletarian dictatorship guaranteed against dangers from without. So, in order to win conclusively, *we must bring it about that the present capitalist encirclement is replaced by a socialist encirclement*, that the proletariat is victorious in at least several more countries. Only then can our victory be considered final."[3]

In policy terms, this meant that Communist parties all over the world would adopt a hard left line, supporting constant strikes and organizing militias and paramilitary forces to engage political enemies in street combat. Instead of cooperating with other leftists, Communists were expected to denounce Europe's socialist parties—those who had refused to adopt the twenty-one conditions—as "social fascists," even in Germany, where real Fascists were on the scene in the form of Adolf Hitler's National Socialist German Workers' Party.[4]

The "Third Period" turned out to be just as turbulent as Stalin had hoped. The onset of a worldwide Depression in the wake of the Wall Street crash of October 1929 and a string of bank failures on both sides of the Atlantic in 1931 produced mass unemployment and widespread social misery in the United States and

Europe. The collapse of demand in the advanced economies in turn ruined the economies of the primary producers around the world. In Germany, Communist and Nazi paramilitaries battled in the streets when they were not cooperating against the tottering Weimar democratic government, as in several demagogic plebiscite campaigns and the notorious Berlin public transport strike of November 1932. Although, in the short run, the descent of Germany's cities into conditions of virtual civil war helped the Nazis at the polls more than the Communists, Stalin continued pushing "class against class" policies, on the logic of *chem khuzhe, chem luchshe* (the worse the better)—the better for Communism, that is.

Back at home, Stalin's socialist offensive reached its climax just as the capitalist world was succumbing to the Depression. The timing was more than incidental. Stalin's industrialization drive was conceived, sold, and executed like a military operation targeting the capitalist world. As he told the graduates of the new Industrial Academy in Moscow in April 1930, "The 50,000 tractors you are going to give the country each year are 50,000 shells blowing up the old bourgeois world." These future industrialists were the "shock brigades" of the "Red offensive" against capital, foot soldiers in a forced march to socialism, with the targets of each year's march—seventeen million tons of pig iron! One hundred seventy thousand tractors! Two hundred thousand cars and trucks!—set, raised, and then raised again. The pace of production was never enough for Stalin, who proposed the slogan "Five Years in Four." Whenever onerous production targets went unmet, capitalist saboteurs were blamed, as if they had been spies in an army camp.[5]

Stalin's collectivization of Soviet agriculture followed a similar template of military mobilization, but was still more murderous in execution. In January 1930, the Politburo passed a resolution "On Measures for the Elimination of Kulak Households in Districts of Comprehensive Collectivization." For Ukrainians and others victimized by it, this document has acquired the same notoriety in the history of Soviet famine as the Wannsee Protocols of January 1942 has in the history of the Holocaust. Stalin's intentions in stipulating various categories of kulak (capitalist) peasant households fit for deportation may not have been as explicitly murderous as the Wannsee Protocols (though many Ukrainians, and some historians, now believe they were), but the results were unquestionably genocidal. By singling out the most productive peasant smallholders for "elimination" and confiscating their land and produce, the decree had catastrophic effects on the food situation in Ukraine and other grain-producing areas—from the predictable sabotage resulting from peasants slaughtering horses, cattle, and pigs before they were seized by requisitioners, to the no-less-predictable collapse in grain yields after millions of Russia's most industrious peasants, and their families, were deported or simply shot. By the winter of 1932–1933, a terrible famine had descended on the areas of comprehensive collectivization, affecting more than seventy million people from Ukraine to the North Caucasus to Central Asia. Cannibalism is commonly noted in the Soviet secret-police reports from the period. The worst (and best-known) famine occurred in Ukraine, where at least three or four million starved to death in an epic story of woe remembered by Ukrainians as the Holodomor (hunger-extermination). Owing to lack of access to relevant archives, historians are only now reckoning with the catastrophic results elsewhere in the Soviet Union, such as in Kazakhstan, where as many as 1.5 or 2 million Kazakhs starved to death in 1932 and 1933. Stalin's collectivization drive destroyed the entire nomadic way of life in Soviet Central Asia, as had been the policy's express intention.[6]

A welcome side effect of the mass deportations of kulaks, Kazakh nomads, and other rural traditionalists, from Stalin's perspective, was that it furnished an almost bottomless supply of forced labor for his industrialization drive. Thrown together in crowded cattle cars (some marked "white coal" or "meat") and shipped off to labor camps in the Arctic far north or the frigid east of Siberia, peasants and nomads were fortunate to survive the journey; many thousands did not. Those who reached Stalin's network of forced-labor camps alive were put to work at backbreaking tasks, ill-fed and driven to exhaustion by heavily armed camp guards. Many of the most famous public-works projects in the USSR, from the 155-mile-long White Sea–Baltic Canal to the Moscow Metro, were built by slave labor. The Siberian goldfields at Kolyma and Chukotka were notorious for horrendous work conditions. Death rates in Kolyma approached 50 percent. As an eyewitness observed, "A man pushing a wheelbarrow up the high runway . . . would suddenly halt, sway for a moment, and fall down. . . . And that was the end. Or a man, loading a barrow, prodded by the shouts of a foreman or a guard . . . would sink to the ground [and] blood would gush from his mouth." Even free Soviet workers, the proletarians in whose name the Communist regime supposedly governed, were bound to their factories by internal passports, introduced in 1932.[7]

Brutal as labor conditions were in Stalin's merciless planned economic system, the results were encouraging, in material terms at least. The Siberian goldfields yielded about 100 million rubles per year of ready capital. Great new electric utilities and mining combines soon dotted the landscape of eastern Ukraine, while gigantic tractor and auto factories dominated the industrial suburbs of Moscow, Leningrad, and Chelyabinsk. Magnitogorsk, a planned industrial city near Orenburg, soon housed the largest iron- and steelworks in the world, employing nearly a quarter of a million people. Yekaterinburg in the Ural Mountains, recently famous as the last residence of Tsar Nicholas II and his family before the Romanovs were murdered in July 1918, was now better known for housing Uralmash (Ural'skii Zavod Tyazhelogo Mashinostroyenia), the world's largest complex for the construction of heavy machinery.

For all the propaganda about "building socialism," the truth was that most of Stalin's great new industrial works were modeled on, and in many cases directly imported from, Western capitalist firms, especially American ones. The construction of Stalin's huge iron and steel combines, in theory planned by the State Institute for the Design of Metallurgical Factories (Gipromez) of Leningrad (as Petrograd was renamed in 1924), was overseen by the Freyn Engineering Company of Chicago, Illinois, hired in May 1927. Magnitogorsk was designed from top to bottom by Arthur G. McKee and Company of Cleveland, Ohio, based on the prototype of a US Steel plant in Gary, Indiana. In similar fashion, American experts from the MacDonald Engineering Company of Chicago had overseen the construction of four of the world's largest cement combines, one at Kerch on the Black Sea, two outside Moscow, and another just east of the Ural Mountains. The gigantic new hydroelectric plant on the Dniepr River in Ukraine was designed and built by the Hugh L. Cooper firm, based in New York City. Even sensitive Soviet industries such as gold, copper, lead, zinc, and aluminum mining were dependent on American knowhow, with two hundred American engineers working in Russian nonferrous metals production by 1933. The main copper-smelting plant in the USSR, the Karabash Combinat in the Urals, employed eleven Yankee engineers. The Soviet bauxite-mining and aluminum-smelting industry, critical in the construction of tanks and warplanes, was designed from scratch by the American expert Frank E. Dickie, hired from the Alcoa corporation in 1930 (though French aluminum experts were later imported too). Small wonder a Soviet chronicle of the first Five-Year Plan, *Za industrializatsiiu*, was forced to admit in 1933 (in a passage later purged from official accounts of the period) that it was "a combination of American business and science with Bolshevik wisdom" that had "created these industrial giants in three or four years."[8]

So ubiquitous were American specialists in Stalin's planned economy that they had their own expatriate newspaper, the *Moscow News*, whose articles and ads targeted "American engineers, specialists and miners working in the USSR." Even that ubiquitous emblem of Stalinist central planning, the state-run, mechanized, collective farm, or *kolkhoz*—inspired by Marx's exhortation in *The Communist Manifesto* to unleash "industrial armies in the countryside"—was modeled on an American capitalist operation. This was the family farm of one Thomas D. Campbell, the "wheat king" of Montana, who happened to own a sprawling estate of 95,000 acres—large enough to satisfy Stalin's notion of mechanized gigantism in the countryside. Campbell visited Soviet Russia on Stalin's invitation in both 1928 and 1930 to teach Soviet collectives the latest techniques in mechanized wheat production.[9]

Stalin also resolved to model the evolving Red Air Force (*Voenno-vozdushnie sili* or VVS) on American aviation technology. So critical was this priority for Stalin—increasingly referred to simply as the *Vozhd* (leader)—that he dispatched a massive espionage team of seventy-five "students" in summer 1931 to enroll in US universities such as MIT and take jobs in aviation firms. The most important of these agents, Stanislav Shumovsky (code name BLÉRIOT), would remain in the United States for over a decade, overseeing a spying operation so successful that, by the mid-1930s, his men had placed agents or recruited sources in all the main US aviation firms, from the Douglas plant in Southern California, manufacturer of the DC series of huge, dual-engine passenger planes, transports, and bombers; to Bell Aircraft in Buffalo, New York, a leader in fighter design; to Wright Aeronautical in Paterson, New Jersey, the largest manufacturer of aeroengines in the entire world. Shumovsky became more brazen the longer he stayed, escorting Andrey Tupolev, Sergei Ilyushin, and Pavel Sukhoi—three of Stalin's top military aircraft designers—around several dozen American universities, research labs, and aviation plants, allowing them to reverse engineer American fighters, light bombers, and transport planes into Soviet versions.[10]

While many of Stalin's new *kolkhozi* and factories did not meet production targets (failures for which a series of industrial and agricultural "wreckers" were scapegoated and put on trial), the growth trend line from 1929 onward was solid in the aggregate, ramping up more dramatically every year. So powerful was the whiff of progress that thousands of Americans, thrown out of work by the Great Depression, voluntarily emigrated to the USSR in the early 1930s, enticed by the promise of Stalin's supposed worker's paradise, or at least by the full employment allegedly produced by a rapidly industrializing planned economy.[11]

Still, there remained a thorny problem. The real goal of Stalin's Five-Year Plan was to mass manufacture modern military hardware. In September 1930, Marshal M. N. Tukhachevsky, the hero of the Russian Civil War and Stalin's foremost military planner, stated that a modern army would require the annual production of fifty thousand tanks and forty thousand warplanes. And yet, as suggested by his hiring of Americans to design and run his factories and his dispatch of spies to American universities and aviation firms in 1931, Stalin remained at the mercy of the capitalist world he hoped desperately to overcome. Relations with the Western European powers were still frosty. Despite the cooperation born of the Rapallo agreement of 1922, German firms had soured on Russia after a series of Soviet defaults. The firm most heavily involved in the Rapallo arms trade, Junkers, had gone bankrupt in 1925. Moreover, after Hitler came to power in January 1933, and particularly after his government blamed and cracked down on German Communists for the Reichstag fire that February, the Germans could not really be trusted. Industrial espionage could help Soviet engineers and aircraft designers, but only up to a point. In order to modernize the armies of Communism, it might be necessary to strike a deal with the capitalist devils in the United States of America.[12]

3

Strategic Coup in Washington

DESPITE WINNING RECOGNITION from most European and Asian powers, the USSR's diplomatic position remained precarious in the early 1930s. Some of the countries that had taken the lead in recognizing Moscow later reversed course. After opening relations in 1924, Britain severed them in 1927 in retaliation for Communist meddling in British domestic politics. So, too, had China broken off relations after egregious Soviet interference in the country's internal affairs, in the form of the violent Communist Canton (or Ghangzhou) Uprising of 1927. Mexico bravely resisted diplomatic pressure from Washington by recognizing the Soviets in 1924 and made headlines again in 1926 with Stalin's appointment of the world's first-ever female ambassador to Mexico City, but later broke off relations with Moscow in 1930 over "ideological differences." Japan had recognized the USSR in 1925, but the invasion of Manchuria in September 1931 threw relations with Moscow into the deep freeze, with both sides arming heavily along the Siberia-Manchuria border. Japan's ambassador to the USSR wrote to Tokyo (in a message intercepted by Soviet intelligence) that Japan "must be ready to declare war at any moment and to adopt a tough policy towards the Soviet Union." As Stalin told his advisers in June 1932, "The Japanese are certainly (certainly!) preparing for war against the USSR, and we have to be ready for anything."[1]

The most important diplomatic holdout was the United States. It had not escaped Stalin's attention that American and Japanese troops had intervened against the Red Army in Siberia in 1918–1919, or that relations between those two powers had become increasingly strained. Japanese statesmen resented the construction limits for capital ships (battleships and cruisers) dictated by the Washington Naval Treaty of 1922, which imposed a tonnage ratio of three to five for Japan against both the United States and Britain. The US Immigration Act of 1924 had barred Japanese nationals (along with other Asians) from emigrating to America on racial grounds, an obvious insult. American officials led the way in condemning the Japanese occupation of Manchuria, now styled Manchukuo by the occupiers. US secretary of state Henry Stimson fumed against this "aggressive act by Japan."[2]

In view of the growing antipathy between Washington and Tokyo, the prospect of American recognition of the USSR took on geopolitical importance. Although Russian moves in the Far East garnered little international attention, the truth was that the Soviets, despite their "anti-imperialist rhetoric," were no less active interventionists in China than the Japanese. In 1926, Red Army troops had occupied the Tannu Tuva—an area of northwest Mongolia almost as large as Britain that had belonged to China since the early eighteenth century—to seize its plentiful gold mines (it remains Russian territory today). The botched, Soviet-supported Canton Uprising of 1927 was an outrage to Chinese nationalists. In 1929, after rejecting a Chinese request to evacuate Manchuria, Stalin deployed nearly one hundred thousand Soviet troops to secure the Chinese Eastern Railway there. After the Japanese invasion of Manchuria in 1931, the Red Army remained poised at the border for years, ready to reinvade if Moscow sensed weakness from Japan. Consistent with this pattern of imperialist opportunism in China, in January 1932 Stalin cynically offered to sell the Chinese Eastern Railway to Japanese Manchukuo over Chinese objections. (Japan said no.)[3]

With an eye on the tense situation in Manchuria, Secretary of State Stimson commissioned a study of the "pros and cons" of US recognition of the USSR by the Far Eastern division of the State Department in spring 1932. Interestingly, Stimson concluded that recognition of Communist Russia during the ongoing Manchurian

34

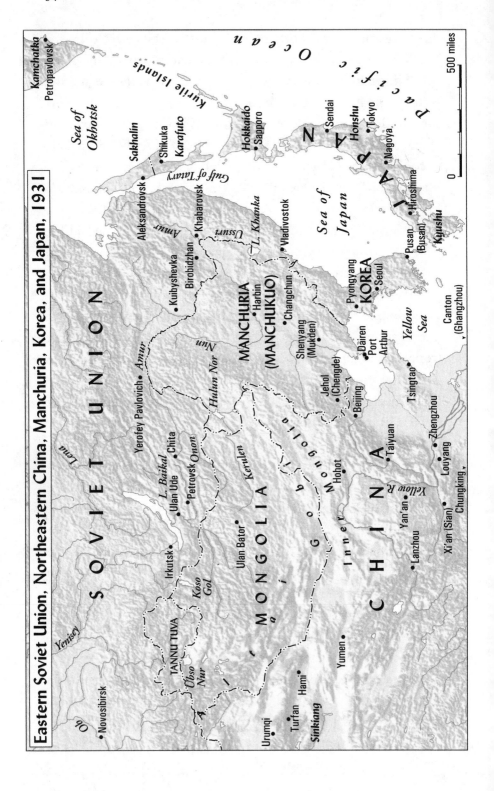

Eastern Soviet Union, Northeastern China, Manchuria, Korea, and Japan, 1931

crisis was undesirable precisely because "the whole world, and particularly Japan, would jump to the conclusion that our action had been dictated solely by political expedience," as "a maneuver to bring forceful pressure upon Japan."[4]

The lack of recognition restricted Soviet access to American capital. Many American firms and engineers had taken on commissions in the Soviet economy, but these deals were all done under the table, financed on the fly by Soviet gold exports and by illicit Soviet sales of artwork and antiquities in European and American auction houses. But the deepening of the Depression after 1931 severely dented the Soviet art-laundering business. Coupled with the Japanese threat in Manchuria and the galloping anti-Communism of Germany after Hitler came to power, the pinch in Soviet art sales left Moscow low on foreign reserves. So desperate was Stalin for outside support that he signed a nonaggression pact with Mussolini's Fascist Italy in 1933.[5]

A glimmer of hope for Stalin had appeared in Washington in the presidential inauguration of Franklin Delano Roosevelt on March 4, 1933. Roosevelt, despite dropping hints, had made no firm commitment to recognize Russia during an election campaign that had focused mostly on domestic economic issues. Still, the mere fact that Roosevelt had won, and decisively at that (472 to 59 in the Electoral College, winning all but six states), was significant. Following twelve years in the political wilderness under Republican presidents, the Democrats were primed to shake things up in Washington. The nadir of the Great Depression, which hit the United States in the months preceding FDR's inauguration, produced a compelling mandate for change.

Nonetheless, Roosevelt needed to tread carefully. While the handful of American industrialists who had signed concessions in Soviet Russia, along with most Democratic and pro-Roosevelt media organizations (like the *New York Times* and *New York Herald Tribune*), tended to favor recognition, most Republicans and the conservative press (notably the *Chicago Tribune*) remained opposed, lending the issue a partisan air that did not appeal to a president-elect trying to broaden his coalition. The outgoing president, Herbert Hoover, had warned Roosevelt of the "Moscow counterfeiting of millions of dollars in American currency," an operation exposed in the *New York Times* on February 24, 1933. Most State Department professionals remained wary of Stalin. As the head of the Eastern European division, Robert F. Kelley pointed out to Roosevelt on July 27, 1933, "so long as the Communist regime continues to carry on in other countries activities designed to bring about . . . the overthrow of the Government and institutions of these countries, the establishment of genuine friendly relations between Russia and those countries is out of the question." Before considering recognition, Kelley argued, the United States must demand "the abandonment by Moscow of direction, supervision, control, financing, et cetera, through every agency utilized for the purpose, of communist and other related activities in the United States."[6]

Refraining from Comintern-directed revolutionary agitation was—or should have been—only the first essential precondition for recognition of the Soviet Union. As Kelley reminded Roosevelt, there was also the "question of repudiated debts and confiscated property" dating back to the Bolshevik default of 1918. The American share of annulled Russian state loans alone amounted to $298 million in principal, not including interest or inflation adjustment, of which $192,601,297 was owed to the US government and another $106,884,157 owed to private American citizens. American-owned property nationalized (that is, confiscated) by the Bolsheviks made up another $336,691,771. A conservative estimate would thus put Soviet obligations to expropriated American property and bondholders, circa 1933, at well over $600 million in principal—the equivalent of perhaps $60 billion today. Aside from the moral imperative of recovering some of these losses for Americans at a time of crippling economic hardship and suffering, Kelley reminded President Roosevelt that "the Government of the United States has a profound interest in the maintenance of the sanctity of international obligations."[7]

Of course, it was unrealistic to expect American bondholders to get full value on the dollar. Nonetheless, the recognition question gave Roosevelt substantial leverage, as Soviet diplomats realized. While Russian estimates of American losses in the default were lower than Kelley's, the Soviet foreign affairs commissar, Maxim Litvinov, was willing to concede, in a memorandum circulated to the Politburo, $284 million in defaulted state loans and $60.5 million in expropriated property, which might justify an American claim, including fifteen years of interest, of about $500 million. It was not that Stalin wanted to pay this sum. Rather, Litvinov wanted Soviet diplomats to be prepared for what he expected would be Roosevelt's baseline demand.[8]

Litvinov need not have fretted so much. In a replay of the dynamic behind the Anglo-Soviet Trade Agreement of 1921, Roosevelt was blinded by the chimera of economic stimulus, thinking that the Soviet Union would provide a major new export market for American firms. As he boasted to his Treasury secretary, Henry Morgenthau, "If I could only, myself, talk to some one man representing the Russians, I could straighten out this whole question." In Roosevelt's mind, all it would take was the right meeting "in order to break the ice between the two countries and in that way gradually get the people of the United States used to doing business with Russia."[9]

Like Lloyd George in 1921, Roosevelt mistakenly believed that irrational political tensions were holding up Russian imports of American goods, rather than the more prosaic explanation that Communism had so impoverished Russia that the Soviets had limited means to pay for them. There were plenty of American firms already operating in Russia: Soviet demand for US technology was almost insatiable. What the Soviets were after, as Morgenthau explained to Roosevelt, was access to the US bond market to obtain "large loans" to enable substantial purchases of American raw materials and industrial inputs. The real issue in 1933 was not "breaking the ice," but deciding whether or not to demand a serious quid pro quo in exchange for recognition of Stalin's tyrannical regime and for extending it new loans.[10]

All the leverage, in other words, was enjoyed by the United States. The Soviets desired recognition to win international prestige, enhance access to Western capital, and open new embassies and consulates offering legal protections for Soviet agents and Communists operating in North America. By contrast, US firms already had access to the Soviet market—limited, but only by the ability of the Soviets to pay. Any new loans to Stalin that the US government would guarantee might stimulate demand for US exports, but they would also come with a substantial risk of default, based on a clear pattern of Soviet behavior dating back to 1918. There were more serious risks too, evident in the record of Communist subversion of countries that had allowed Soviet agents to operate out of embassies, such as Germany, Britain, and China. The advantages of recognition were so lopsided in Stalin's favor that Roosevelt could have set terms as steep as he liked, demanding repayment of the entire $600 million in lost principal, along with ironclad guarantees that the Soviet government cease subsidizing the Communist Party of the United States of America (CPUSA) and other agents on US soil. Litvinov came to Washington in November 1933 to plead for recognition, fully expecting that he would have to agree to repay, if not the $500 million he expected Roosevelt to ask for, then "at the very least a substantial sum of money."[11]

Roosevelt, alas, did not have any idea how much leverage he enjoyed. Remarkably, his opening bid was not $600 million, nor the $500 million Litvinov expected, but $150 million, a mere fourth of the principal owed—and even that, he let Litvinov know, was not so much his own claim but the smallest sum that he "could persuade Congress to accept." With the president signaling that he thought $150 million unreasonable, it was an easy trick for Litvinov to barter him down to a noncommittal figure "between $75 and $150 million." With chutzpah, Litvinov then commissioned a study by the Soviet Ministry of Finance on Tsarist assets seized inside the United States in retaliation for the 1918 default, coughing up the figure of $143 million, which—after being adjusted for interest—allowed Litvinov to issue a counterclaim for $161 million. If accepted, it would nullify FDR's own watered-down claim entirely.[12]

To twist the knife in, Stalin invited the *New York Times* correspondent in Moscow, Walter Duranty—notorious among more honest foreign journalists for his blanket denials of the Ukrainian famine earlier that year—to the Kremlin for a sympathetic Christmas Day interview. With sycophancy impressive even by his own abysmal standards, Duranty neglected to ask a single question about Soviet obligations to deposed American bondholders, instead lofting Stalin softballs such as "What do you think is the potential for Soviet-American trade?" and "How can you reassure foreign creditors about Soviet means to pay?" Stalin nearly slipped here, admitting that the Soviets had defaulted on German loans, but he claimed that this was not relevant, as "we are no longer dependent on German industry, but can manufacture our own equipment now." An intelligent interviewer would have probed here to learn why—if the Soviets really no longer needed foreign imports or technology transfers for Stalin's industrialization drive—they were so keen on securing American recognition and new loans from Wall Street. Instead, Duranty meekly asked, "So, what is your opinion of America?" Reeling in his target with flattery, Stalin replied that the new president was "a decisive and masculine leader."[13]

By the time Litvinov and Stalin were done manipulating him, Roosevelt had agreed to reduce US claims, after subtracting Soviet claims of compensation for seized Tsarist assets, to a mere $75 million. And even this modest sum—in a trick the Germans were now painfully familiar with—would not be paid off immediately, but rather in a rolling installment plan via "excessive" interest due on a new $200 million US-government-guaranteed loan from the Export-Import Bank to Moscow, payable over twenty or twenty-five years. Rather than secure relief for American investors and

bondholders robbed blind by the Bolsheviks at a time of great economic hardship, Roosevelt had instead promised Stalin a vast store
of ready American capital, which would allow him to resume his
rearmament drive at full blast.[14]

The only demands the president's negotiating team, headed by
Henry Morgenthau, levied in exchange for the diplomatic recognition they granted the USSR on November 16, 1933, was this nonbinding promise to pay off old debts via a large new loan, a vague
understanding that the Soviets use this loan to purchase American
products, and a nonbinding promise to "refrain from interfering
in any manner in the internal affairs of the United States." Except for the Soviet promise to buy US wares with Export-Import
credits—that is, to enjoy the privilege of importing desperately
needed goods with no cash down—there was never any intention,
on Stalin's part, of being true to the letter of Litvinov's carefully
worded declarations. Soviet officials haggled for months over repayment terms on American loans, threatening to place orders
in Europe instead of the United States if interest rates were not
reduced. As late as May 1935, the Soviets were still insisting on
easy terms and a twenty-year loan, while promising nothing about
paying old debts.[15]

Although they succeeded in burying American debt claims, the
Soviets did not get everything they wanted. Negotiations over
Russian debt repayment and new American loans were mooted
when Congress enacted the Johnson Act on April 13, 1934, which
prohibited foreign nations in default from marketing their bonds
in US markets (this law remains in force today).* Instead of es-
tablishing mutual trust, the financial impasse helped to poison

---

* The USSR was not the only country affected by the Johnson Act. Brit-
ain suspended repayment of its colossal World War I debts to the United
States in June 1934, thereby forfeiting access to the US loan market.
Combined with the Neutrality Acts passed by the US Congress in 1936,
1937, and 1939, the Johnson Act would have serious consequences for
US-British relations and the ability of Britain to import arms.

US-Soviet diplomatic relations from the start. As Roosevelt's first ambassador to the USSR, William Bullitt, informed the president soon after arriving in Moscow that April, "The honeymoon atmosphere has evaporated completely before I arrived. . . . Their underlying hostility to all capitalist countries now shows through the veneer of intimate friendship."[16]

Litvinov and Stalin also did not obtain a binding agreement from Roosevelt on Japan, which helped explain why Bullitt received such a cold welcome in Moscow. At one point, Litvinov had asked Roosevelt what he thought "of an agreement with us [the USSR] on joint action in the event of a danger to peace," only to be put off. But Litvinov's coup in Washington did allow the USSR to escape diplomatic isolation at a dangerous time. Although Stalin crowed that US recognition was an act of "the most serious significance" for the international system, it did not entail bilateral security cooperation against the Japanese in Asia, if that was what the Soviets wanted. As Bullitt reported to Roosevelt on April 24, 1934, "The Russians are convinced that Japan will not attack this spring or summer," and thus "they no longer feel that they need our immediate help."[17]

As for Litvinov's pie-crust promise to refrain from interfering in American politics, this was immediately broken. According to the American Communist D. H. Dubrowsky, Litvinov arrived at a CPUSA meeting after leaving the White House in November 1933 "all smiles" and stated, "Well, it is all in the bag; we have it. They wanted us to recognize the old debts that we owed them and I promised we were going to negotiate . . . but they did not know *we were going to negotiate until doomsday*." Litvinov's pledge not to interfere in US domestic affairs, he informed CPUSA leaders, did not bind the party, but only the Soviet government, and was anyhow "a scrap of paper which will soon be forgotten in the realities of Soviet-American relations." Given a green light by Litvinov, the CPUSA published a statement reaffirming its commitment to revolutionary principles in the *New York Times* on November 19, 1933.[18]

This was no idle threat. In the years after Roosevelt recognized the USSR, dozens of Soviet agents and CPUSA members infiltrated the US government, helped along by the vigorous (and almost entirely un-vetted) bureaucratic expansion of FDR's New Deal. Key targets for infiltration included the Agricultural Adjustment Administration (AAA), where a Communist cell run by Harold Ware provided entrée for notorious Soviet agents such as Whittaker Chambers, Elizabeth Bentley, and Nathan Silvermaster. Ware, though American born, had lived in Soviet Russia in the early 1920s, overseeing an experiment in mechanized-collectivist agriculture (Russian peasants mostly remembered him chasing them around threateningly with a baseball bat). Communists also infiltrated the Works Progress Administration, the National Labor Relations Board, and the Justice Department. The State Department, meanwhile, was honeycombed with Soviet agents such as Laurence Duggan (code name FRANK), Michael Straight (NIGEL), and Alger Hiss.[19]

The Communist penetration of the FDR administration after 1933 was noteworthy, because the public line of the CPUSA was harshly critical of the New Deal, suggesting that it was not enthusiasm for the president's policies that motivated Communists to work for him. In July 1933, CPUSA head Earl Browder publicly denounced FDR's Industrial Recovery Act as the "Industrial Slavery Act" and the labor-union-legalizing Wagner Act as "Roosevelt's company-union club against the workers." The CPUSA's annual "May Day Manifesto" of 1934, in accordance with the Comintern doctrine that socialists were the real Fascists, denounced Rooseveltian "New Deal Fascism and War." Recognizing the USSR in 1933 was not enough for Roosevelt to escape this kind of vituperation, until American Communists received instructions from Moscow to cease abusing him after Stalin's new Popular Front doctrine, which instructed Communists to stop attacking socialists and cooperate with them, was promulgated in October 1935.[20]

What drove Communist penetration of the US government in the mid-1930s was not ideological affinity (at least until Stalin's doctrinal about-face in 1935) but Soviet opportunism, enabled by the Roosevelt administration's lax security. The most critical factor was the stamp of legitimacy the president had placed on the USSR by recognizing Stalin's regime, which removed the stigma from Communist Party membership. Between recognition, in November 1933, and 1938, the ranks of card-carrying CPUSA members exploded from thirteen thousand to over eighty thousand. A large part of the reason there were so many Communists in the US government by the late 1930s was simply that there were so many more Communists around to draw on. By sheer critical mass, CPUSA members were able to throw their weight around in Washington.[21]

More important than all these party members put together was the rise of sympathizing agents of influence into the upper reaches of the Roosevelt administration. Among these were Hiss, who was whisked up from Harold Ware's cell in the AAA (in 1933) to the Senate committee investigating the munitions industry (1934), the Office of the Solicitor General (1934–1936), and finally the Office of Special Political Affairs in the State Department (1936–1947), where he had access to classified material relating to US military strategy and substantial influence over policy. Though Hiss had plenty of defenders against the charges of espionage laid against him by Elizabeth Bentley and Whittaker Chambers after the war (Hiss was sentenced for perjury in 1950), decrypted Soviet telegrams (the Venona files) released to the public in the 1990s have confirmed that Hiss collaborated closely with Soviet military intelligence (the GRU), even if he never joined the CPUSA.[22]

More highly placed still was Harry Dexter White, a Harvard-educated economist who went to work for the Treasury Department in 1934 and rose rapidly to become the right-hand man of Henry Morgenthau, Roosevelt's powerful secretary of the Treasury. Venona decrypts show that White began working for the GRU as early as 1935 under the Soviet spy code name KASSIR (later changed to JURIST), reporting initially to CPUSA members Whittaker Chambers and Nathan Silvermaster, and later directly to Soviet functionaries working for the People's Commissariat of Internal Affairs (NKVD), including successive Washington NKVD *rezidenti* (bureau chiefs) Iskhak Akhmerov, Boris Bazarov, and Vitaly Pavlov. Although White's motivation for spying remains unclear—however sympathetic to Communism, he appears never to have joined the CPUSA—there is no longer any doubt that White regularly met with Soviet agents and shared sensitive information with them (in addition to the Venona decrypts, Pavlov later published a tell-all memoir about his work with White).[23]

By the end of the 1930s, there were hundreds of paid Soviet agents working inside the US government (either 221, according to contemporary Soviet records, or 329, according to the Venona decrypts), from the Departments of Agriculture and State to the Treasury and the US Army. Then there were the seventy-five-plus spies and informants working under Stalin's spy leader, Shumovsky, who stepped up his activities still further after US recognition of the USSR allowed many Soviet nationals to operate perfectly legally under diplomatic cover. In 1935, Shumovsky brought a team of Soviet aviation experts large enough to occupy seven cars—led by Stalin's most brilliant aircraft designer, Andrey Tupolev—on an open buying expedition of US aviation factories; Stalin gave Tupolev $600,000 to spend as he saw fit. Shumovsky's penetration of US aviation was so thorough that, by 1938, a disgruntled American aeronautical engineer informed the US air attaché in London that "the Russian government has agents in practically all American [aircraft] factories." There were hundreds more soft sympathizers like Hiss and White, placed highly enough to directly shape policies that affected the USSR, from technology transfer and bilateral trade protocols to US relations with Japan, with whose Kwantung Army in occupied Manchukuo Stalin's regime remained in a state of undeclared hostilities all through the 1930s. A Soviet espionage ring in Tokyo led by Richard Sorge (code name RAMZAI)—a German correspondent with the *Frankfurter Zeitung* whose pose as a vociferously anti-Communist Nazi gave him entrée with both the German embassy and the Japanese government—furnished Stalin with invaluable intelligence about Japanese intentions vis-à-vis the Soviet Far East and the United States. As Whittaker Chambers's Soviet handler reported proudly to Moscow, "We have agents at the very center of government, influencing policy." The Soviet embassy in Washington was a critical strategic foothold for Stalin as he prepared his Communist empire for war.[24]

4

Behind the Popular Front

DIPLOMATIC RECOGNITION IN Washington was an important milestone in Soviet efforts to improve the position of Communism abroad. The advent of a rival totalitarian regime in Berlin after Hitler's ascension to power in January 1933, followed by the brutal Nazi crackdown against Communists in the wake of the Reichstag fire of February 28, offered Stalin an ideological foil to polish his own image. A symbiotic relationship developed between Nazi Germany and Communist Russia, with both sides exploiting the other's atrocities for propaganda while quietly collaborating behind the scenes on matters of mutual interest, as in the turning over of political opponents for arrest or the exchange of VIP prisoners. In a striking episode of cooperation, Hitler's government arranged a special plane out of Germany for Giorgi Dimitrov, one of the Communist defendants charged with setting the Reichstag fire, after Dimitrov was acquitted in a Leipzig court in December 1933. Exonerated by the Nazis after a courtroom clash with Hitler's Prussian minister-president and Gestapo chief, Hermann Göring (which some suspect to have been staged), Dimitrov returned in triumph to Moscow in 1934, whereupon Stalin promoted him to general secretary of the Comintern.[1]

There was much for each dictator to learn from the other. Hitler shocked world opinion by having leading members of his party's paramilitary *Sturmabteilung* murdered on the Night of the Long Knives of June 30, 1934, in order to reassure the commanders of the German Army that he would respect its preeminence. Stalin then unleashed his own terror in the wake of the murder of Leningrad Communist Party boss Sergei Kirov on December 1,

1934, which ultimately engulfed the upper ranks of the Communist Party leadership and secret police. Hitler and Stalin also quietly revived trade ties in May 1933, renewing the Berlin treaty of April 1926, which ensured that the Soviets would continue to pay down bills incurred for German imports during the Rapallo era.[2]

In the battle for world opinion, the relationship was less evenly balanced. The Nazis made little effort to conceal their crimes against human decency—from the notorious book burnings of May 1933 to the post-Reichstag-fire mass internments of Communists and socialists, to increasingly overt Nazi attacks on Jews and Jewish-owned businesses, to the creation of the first concentration camp to house Hitler's political enemies at Dachau. Hitler even voluntarily withdrew Germany from the League of Nations in October 1933 in defiance of its refusal to allow Germany to rearm on equal terms with other Great Powers. Germany was replaced, in a sense, by the USSR, which joined the league in September 1934 on the strength of US diplomatic recognition and French lobbying to rope Stalin into a mutual assistance pact against Hitler.[3]

By contrast, the Soviet government made no public acknowledgment of the concentration camps in which it had been interning enemies of the people since 1918, much less of the burgeoning Gulag forced-labor network—which dwarfed the embryonic Nazi camps in scale and economic importance—or of the Ukrainian or Kazakh famine-genocides, or, at first, of Stalin's post-Kirov-affair purges (until the public show trials began in August 1936).* While some Russians lucky enough to escape Stalin's prison state, and a few Western visitors brave enough to question the claims of their regime-provided minders, published probing critiques of the Soviet famine-genocide of the early 1930s and the Great Terror,

---

* There was one exception. In April 1935, the Soviet government made public a decree extending the death penalty for "offenses against the state" to minors as young as twelve years old. This allowed Stalin to threaten his political opponents with the murder of their children.

these accounts were overshadowed by the lies of Stalin-friendly journalists like the *New York Times*' Walter Duranty and fellow travelers such as George Bernard Shaw. There was a double standard when it came to public exposure of the crimes of Hitler and Stalin that began in 1933 and continues on, in the historical literature, to this day.[4]

The contrast in perceptions of Nazi and Soviet foreign policy was just as extreme. As with domestic repression, Hitler scarcely bothered to conceal his designs: overturning the Versailles Treaty of 1919 and the reparations burden it imposed on Germany, pursuing German rearmament, and revising Germany's truncated post–World War I borders in the East. Combined with Nazi brutality at home, Hitler's rearmament drive and assertive foreign policy allowed Stalin and his commissar of foreign affairs, Maxim Litvinov, to pose as principled opponents of German aggression, winning broad international sympathy despite scant evidence of any real change in Soviet behavior abroad. Remarkably, despite the frequent boasting of American and European Communists that they were the most principled anti-Fascist opponents of Nazi Germany, it was not until more than two years after Hitler's ascension to power that Stalin finally jettisoned the Comintern's "class against class" doctrine, which had been imposed in 1928, and instructed Communists everywhere to impugn socialists as "social fascists," more dangerous than real Fascists like Mussolini and Hitler.[5]

Nonetheless, when Stalin finally did change the doctrine, at the Seventh Comintern Congress held in Moscow in July and August 1935, the impact was dramatic. The new Popular Front strategy enabled socialists and Communists to cobble together winning anti-Fascist electoral coalitions in France and Spain in 1936, which brought Moscow-loyal Communist Party members into the cabinets of both countries for the first time ever. The new doctrine proved a political gold mine for Stalin. In the United States, the dubious idea that Stalin's anti-Fascist USSR was the most principled opponent of Hitler's Germany seduced thousands into joining the movement, whether as sympathizers who might attend a few meetings or as paid informants.[6]

Even for those in the political mainstream, such as President Roosevelt himself, it was hard not to see the Soviet Union as a like-able protagonist once Hitler started throwing his weight around Europe. Although the president's hands were tied, owing to strong congressional and public opposition, from deepening strategic ties with Moscow, Roosevelt did everything he could to improve relations with Stalin. In November 1936, he appointed a Soviet sympathizer, Joseph Davies, as his ambassador in Moscow, after Bullitt had become too openly critical of Stalin. Davies warmed US-Soviet relations during the Popular Front era, largely because he stopped criticizing Stalin's policies, whether out of ideological sympathy for Communism or, as some critics suspected, because of the favored access Stalin gave Davies's breakfast-cereal-heiress wife, Marjorie Merriweather Post, to looted Russian artworks she acquired in Moscow at steep discounts (these paintings now grace the walls of the Hillwood museum in Washington, DC).[7]

It is worth pausing here to examine the views that cost Bullitt his position as ambassador. Whereas Roosevelt wanted to believe that the shift in Comintern doctrine and the opening of Soviet talks of an anti-German alliance with France signaled a genuine desire on Stalin's part for reconciliation with the capitalist world, Bullitt reported in July 1935, when the Popular Front was being announced, that "contrary to the comforting belief which the French now cherish, it is my conviction that there has been no decrease in the determination of the Soviet Government to pro-duce world revolution." Bullitt based this conclusion on the fact that every single Soviet and Comintern official he had spoken to had "expressed his belief in the necessity of world revolution." For this reason, Stalin's diplomatic overtures toward "friendly states" such as (in the current instance) France were, in Bullitt's view, "a merely tactical policy" akin to "armistice relations"—a temporary cease-fire in the battle between Communism and capitalism. As for the prospect of a new European war, Bullitt did not doubt that current Soviet policy was "peaceful," but this was only because Stalin had not yet completed his armament drive. "It is the primary object of the Soviet Foreign Office," Bullitt concluded, "to maintain peace . . . until the strength of the Soviet Union has been built up to such a point that it is entirely impregnable to attack and ready, should Stalin so desire, to intervene abroad."[8]

Where Ambassador Bullitt had seen deception and guile in Stalin's foreign policy, his successor saw unicorns. In a typical Kremlin encounter in June 1938, Joseph Davies fawned over Stalin with compliments ("You are a greater leader than Catherine the Great, than Peter the Great, a greater leader even than Lenin"), informed him that "I know you are a man of peace," and offered to share sensitive intelligence about American naval deployments in the Pacific. Inviting Stalin to intervene in US politics, Davies warned the Vozhd that, although Roosevelt was favorably disposed toward him and the Soviet Union more generally, the president was "surrounded by reactionary elements" in Washington, who would, Davies hoped, be sidelined.[9]

Davies took the lead for Stalin, urging the president to clean house in the State Department. Roosevelt had been suspicious of the division of Eastern European affairs ever since its head, Robert F. Kelley, had written long memoranda opposing recognition of the USSR back in 1933. Whereas the Western European division was marked by the dilettantism of America's well-born diplomatic establishment, Kelley's division conducted actual research. Budding Soviet experts such as Loy Henderson, Ray Atherton, Charles "Chip" Bohlen, and George Kennan—all of whom served tours of duty in Moscow—had put together what Henderson proudly called "the best Soviet library in the United States." Unhappy with the diligent reporting of these experts on the Moscow show trials and Great Terror, which sat awkwardly with Davies's courtship of Stalin, Roosevelt had his trusted undersecretary of state Sumner Welles, a school friend who had attended Groton and Harvard with the president, conduct a thorough purge in 1937. The East

European affairs division was subordinated into the West European division, and Kelley was shipped off to Turkey. Even the division's library, which contained incomparable material on Soviet history and government, including editions of *Pravda* and *Izvestiya* going all the way back to the Russian Revolution, was dismantled—an act of virtual book burning that did away with two decades' worth of institutional knowledge of Soviet affairs in Washington.[10]

In Britain, despite the suspicious, Bullitt-esque posture toward the USSR of the conservative-led governments of Stanley Baldwin (1935–1937) and Neville Chamberlain (1937–1940)—US ambassador Davies denounced the latter to Stalin as "reactionary"— Popular Front–style agitprop still provided fertile ground for the recruitment of Soviet spies. The most famous were the "Cambridge five": Anthony Blunt, Guy Burgess, John Cairncross, Kim Philby, and Donald Maclean. Another Cambridge man, James Klugmann, was the head of the British Communist Party's propaganda and education department, in effect Stalin's recruiter in chief at Cambridge and Oxford. Modern research has established that the Cambridge five numbered nine at least. These elites, accompanied by less glamorous recruits, infiltrated the top ranks of the British government and media establishment, including the Foreign Office (Donald Maclean); the Secret Intelligence Service, or MI6 (Kim Philby and Guy Burgess); the BBC (Burgess again); and British Army intelligence (James Klugmann). An Oxford recruit, Tom Wylie (code name MAX), supplied classified information from the War Office to Burgess and Philby. By decade's end, as MI6 historian Christopher Andrew writes, "the volume of high-grade intelligence these men supplied was to become so large that Moscow sometimes had difficulty coping with it." In a typical year, more than nine thousand classified British government documents were passed on to Moscow.[11]

The diplomatic catchword after 1935 was "collective security." The idea, assiduously promoted by Maxim Litvinov and swallowed uncritically by apologists like Joseph Davies, was that the USSR must be an essential part of any coalition to contain Hitler. France, the country most directly threatened by Hitler's rearmament campaign, fell hardest for Stalin's propaganda. Despite skepticism in the French high command about the value of a military alliance with Stalin, French diplomats negotiated a Franco-Soviet Pact of Mutual Assistance even before the election of a Popular Front government in June 1936. A draft was signed as early as May 1935 and ratified by the French parliament in February 1936. In the case of the "threat or the danger of aggression on the part of a European state," the pact stated with Germany in mind, France and the USSR would proceed to "an immediate mutual consultation" and "lend each other reciprocal aid and assistance."[12]

The repercussions of the Franco-Soviet Pact were serious, though unintended. The agreement bore resemblance to the Franco-Russian Alliance of 1894, which had confirmed the division of Europe into two hostile military blocs and lent credence to German fears of encirclement. Still, the agreement of 1894, however dangerous in its provocation of Germany, had real teeth: France and Russia had committed themselves to mobilize simultaneously in case of war, with tight coordination. In theory, this could have deterred the Germans, even if, in practice in 1914, it did not. The Franco-Soviet Pact brought with it all the sorry diplomatic consequences of the earlier one—confirming Hitler's complaints about the unjustness of the Versailles system—while containing no binding military clauses whatsoever. It was all provocation and no deterrence, as Hitler showed within days of its ratification when, on March 7, 1936, citing the Franco-Soviet Pact as pretext, he ordered German troops to march into the Rhineland—overturning that region's demilitarization mandated by the Versailles Treaty—and nothing happened.

In defense of France's beleaguered diplomats, there was a good reason the Franco-Soviet Pact had been left militarily toothless. If the Quai d'Orsay had signed a genuine military accord with Stalin, this would have complicated France's defense agreements with Hitler's eastern neighbors. True, Czechoslovakia had signed its own (equally toothless) mutual assistance pact with the USSR in May 1935, but there were reasons to doubt that the Czechs truly wanted to invite in the Red Army to deter German aggression and that the Soviets would be able to get there if Prague asked. Because the USSR shared no land borders with Czechoslovakia or Germany, any military collaboration with France or Czechoslovakia against Hitler, as the French General Staff observed in January 1936, would require the Red Army to transit Poland and Romania, two countries that had active border disputes with Soviet Russia. Poland, at the time, had more reason to fear the USSR than Germany, as shown in the nonaggression pact it had signed with Hitler in January 1934. As the French General Staff report noted ruefully, "[Our] military alliance with Poland [which dated to 1921] would appear to be incompatible with a Russian military alliance. One must choose between them."* By refusing to make a clear choice between Poland and Stalin's Russia, France simultaneously provoked German aggression and estranged key allies in Eastern Europe. By affixing a seal of approval to Stalin's totalitarian regime, the Franco-Soviet Pact also alarmed the conservative-led government of France's ally Great Britain. For these reasons, the French General Staff hated the Franco-Soviet Pact, but was forced to swallow it anyway.[13]

There was clearly an element of buyer's remorse on the French side. As Pierre Laval, the slippery statesman responsible for negotiating the pact, confessed to Soviet diplomats in July 1936, he had been "basically alone" in the French government in favoring a genuine Soviet alliance. The ratification of the pact, which Moscow had hoped that France would sign in summer 1935 to publicize the Popular Front, was delayed for months. There were even ominous signs, picked up by Soviet intelligence, that Laval—a later Vichy collaborator—was meeting regularly with Hitler's right-hand

---

* In a sign of the gulf between France's generals and politicians, this report conceded that German objections that the Franco-Soviet pact violated the 1925 Locarno Treaty were "basically justified."

Europe, circa 1936

NORWAY

Oslo

SWED

IRELAND

Dublin

North

Sea

DENMARK

Copenhagen

UNITED

NETHERLANDS

KINGDOM

Hamburg

Atlantic

Amsterdam

Berlin

London

Ocean

Brussels

Cologne

Brest

BELGIUM

GERMANY

Paris

RI.*

Prague

LUX.

CZE

Munich

Bern

Vienna

SWITZ.

AUSTRIA

FRANCE

Milan

ANDORRA

Marseille

Lisbon

Madrid

Barcelona

Corsica

ITALY

PORTUGAL

SPAIN

Rome

Adriatic Sea

Sardinia

Tarant

Tangier

Gibraltar

(Br.)

Sp. Morocco

Casablanca

Algiers

Sicily

Morocco

Algeria

Tunis

Malta

(Fr.)

(Fr.)

(Br.)

Tunisia

(Fr.)

Medi

RI.* Rhineland remilitarized by Hitler in 1936

0   500 Miles

Libya

(It.)

man, Hermann Göring, while the Franco-Soviet Pact was still on hold in the French Senate. Soviet diplomats had genuine grounds for doubting French good faith.[14]

Compounded by the failure of the West to stand up to Hitler when he remilitarized the Rhineland, France's reluctance to enter into a real military alliance with the USSR played into Stalin's pose as the only counterweight to Hitler in Europe. Litvinov, who was Jewish, was a perfect front man for Stalin's charm offensive, talking up collective security in every capital he visited. Abused in Nazi anti-Semitic screeds as "Finkelstein," Litvinov was recognized in the West as a sincere, principled opponent of Hitler. After Hitler absorbed Austria into the German Reich in the Anschluss of March 1938, Litvinov issued a public statement demanding that "the Great Powers . . . take a firm and unambiguous stand." This is exactly what those powers famously failed to do at Munich in September 1938, when Neville Chamberlain leaned on French premier Édouard Daladier to appease Hitler by offering him the Czech Sudetenland. Litvinov, uninvited to Munich, could only fume from the sidelines.[15]

Genuine as Litvinov's hatred of Hitler may have been, there are good reasons to doubt Stalin's sincerity about collective security. In the *Short Course*, a kind of bible of Communism published in 1938 as the Czechoslovakia crisis was breaking, the term "collective security" does not appear. Stalin instead spoke of a "new period" in European and world affairs, declaring that the "Second Imperialist War has actually begun." The loose mutual assistance pacts Litvinov had signed with Czechoslovakia and France, as more perceptive ambassadors like Bullitt had intuited, entailed no genuine Soviet obligation to defend these countries against aggression by declaring war on Germany. Litvinov himself stated plainly to the director general of the Czechoslovak Foreign Office, Arnost Heidrich, shortly before the Munich conference of 1938, that

Soviet Russia would not repeat the mistake of Czarist Russia in 1914. . . . We know that the Western Powers would like to have Hitler liquidated by Stalin and Stalin by Hitler, but in that they will not succeed. While in 1914–1917 the Western Powers, sparing their forces, watched the bloody struggle between Germany and Russia, this time we shall observe the contest between Germany and the Western Powers and shall not intervene in the conflict *until we ourselves feel it fit* to do so *in order to bring about the decision.*[16]

Despite the public fanfare, Soviet foreign policy had not magically changed in 1935 from fanatical hostility toward the capitalist world to principled cooperation based on shared antipathy toward Hitler. Nor did the USSR stand in any way alongside Britain, France, and France's Eastern European partners against territorial revisionism, as the Czechoslovaks had convinced themselves when they signed a pact with Moscow in 1935. The Soviet Union had been born in armed hostility to the Entente powers after World War I and had lost huge swaths of formerly Russian land—from newly independent Finland and the Baltic states, to former Ukrainian and Belorussian territory in what was now eastern Poland, to Romanian Bessarabia along the Black Sea littoral. The USSR was just as revisionist as Italy and Nazi Germany in seeking to overturn the postwar settlement. For now, though, Stalin was artfully concealing his own territorial ambitions.[17]

Stalin provided clues about these ambitions in 1937 and 1938, although few Western diplomats were paying close attention. In May 1937, Litvinov was quietly removed from the European desk in the Soviet Foreign Ministry and replaced by Vice Commissar of Foreign Affairs V. P. Potemkin, even while Litvinov remained foreign affairs commissar—that is, front man. In February 1938, Potemkin hinted to the Bulgarian minister in Moscow that Stalin might be interested in a partition of Poland. In April 1938, Potemkin wrote ominously in a Soviet theoretical journal, *Bol'shevik*, that "Hitler aims to let Poland loose against the Soviet Union. . . . Let the Polish army be shattered. Let [Poland] again, as in 1920, begin to tremble under the hooves of the Soviet columns. . . . [Hitler] is

preparing [Poland's] fourth partition. Let history be repeated." So
blatant were Potemkin's hints about dismembering Poland in tan-
dem with Germany that they reached the French ambassador in
Moscow, Robert Coulondre, in October 1938. The next month, another mouthpiece of the Kremlin, *Izvestiya*, openly mooted the idea
of partitioning Poland—the northeastern section joining Soviet Belorussia, eastern Galicia being annexed to Soviet Ukraine, and the
area west of the Vistula (Weichsel) being assigned to Germany.[18]

Stalin had dropped another hint about his revisionist foreign
policy aims in April 1938, between the Anschluss and Munich,
when he sent a special envoy, Boris Yartsev, to Helsinki without
Litvinov's knowledge to demand the right to build Soviet military bases on Finnish territory. After Yartsev was rebuffed, Stalin
sent an NKVD officer to Helsinki to demand a thirty-year Soviet
lease on the island of Suursaari and four smaller islets in the Gulf
of Finland. The only difference between this and Hitler's moves
in Austria and Czechoslovakia that year was that Stalin's Finnish
gambit failed. Pushing neighbors around and dropping hints about
partitioning Poland was a far cry from "collective security."[19]

The ultimate aim of Soviet foreign policy—the weakening of
capitalist regimes by any means necessary and the concomitant
global expansion of Communism—remained the same. War between Hitler and the Western democracies might break out over
Hitler's claims on the Czech Sudetenland, or it might not; in either
case, it was best not to intervene militarily until it served Soviet
interests to do so. As Stalin privately told his military intelligence
chiefs, "There are immediate enemies and potential enemies,"
and the Czechs were, at the time, "the enemies of our enemies,
nothing more." Far from fearing that the Sudetenland crisis would
lead to European war, Stalin was disappointed that the Western
betrayal at Munich on September 30 deprived him of "a pretty
little war which others would fight," as the German ambassador
in Moscow, Count Friedrich-Werner von der Schulenburg, reported to Berlin on October 3, adding that such a war "would have
brought so much joy to Moscow." After observing that Poland,

too, had exploited Munich to slice off bits of Czech territory, Soviet propagandists cackled in *Pravda* on October 1 that "the Poles [are] digging a grave for Poland's independence."[20]

Stalin's purging of the Soviet armed forces in 1937–1938 had seriously hampered Soviet military credibility in the short run, whatever his intentions were at the time of Munich. Although the Communist Party and secret police had been targeted soon after the Kirov murder in December 1934, it was the spectacular downfall of M. N. Tukhachevsky, Russian Civil War hero and marshal of the Soviet Union, after the May Day parade in 1937 that truly marked the onset of Stalin's Great Terror. Tukhachevsky—a dashing ex-nobleman officer resented by Stalin ever since the two had crossed swords in the Polish-Soviet War in August 1920—was a perfect foil for jealous rivals such as Communist Party hack Kliment "Klim" Voroshilov, a crony of Stalin's who had teamed up with him to do away with ex-Tsarist officers appointed by Trotsky at Tsaritsyn (the future Stalingrad) in 1918. In November 1938, Voroshilov boasted that he had personally purged forty thousand Soviet officers, including three of five field marshals, fifteen of sixteen field army commanders, sixty of sixty-seven corps commanders, and thousands of lower-ranking officers. Meanwhile, he had promoted nearly one hundred thousand new men to replace them. During this time of violent churn in the officer corps, the USSR was hardly ready to fight a major European war. Despite all Litvinov's talk of collective security, the refusal of the Western powers to invite him to Munich shows that responsible statesmen had a more realistic appraisal of Soviet war readiness and the real nature of Stalin's foreign policy.[21]

We can get a better idea of genuine, rather than professed, Soviet foreign policy priorities from Stalin's actions in the two armed conflicts of the Popular Front era, the Spanish Civil War (1936–1939) and the Sino-Japanese War, which erupted in 1937. On the surface, the advent of a Popular Front government in Madrid in February 1936 offered a proving ground for Soviet anti-Fascism after General Francisco Franco's nationalist forces rebelled in July

1936. But the guiding principle of Stalin's intervention in Spain, historians discovered after the opening of the Soviet archives, was not so much anti-Fascism as opportunism. The Madrid government possessed, in 1936, the fourth-largest gold reserve in the world. Unlike Hitler and Mussolini, who allowed Franco to purchase arms on credit, thus giving them a vested interest in him winning the war (so that they could recoup payment), Stalin insisted on payment up front. By the end of 1936, Stalin had secured $518 million in Spanish gold, or 463 tons of bullion. In exchange, the Soviets sent to Spain 320 warplanes, 350 tanks, 1,900 guns, 15,000 machine guns, 500,000 rifles, 250 grenade launchers, and ammunition.[22]

This was not nothing, but it was hardly the kind of all-out commitment Spanish Republican forces might have expected after handing the country's gold reserves over to Moscow. Soviet supplies largely dried up after the first war winter of 1936–1937. A better idea of Stalin's real commitment to the Republican cause can be gleaned from his sending to Madrid only 2,082 Soviet troops and military technicians—a mere fraction of the military manpower that Hitler's Germany (16,000) and Mussolini's Italy (70,000) devoted to Spain. As the head of the Soviet military mission in Madrid, the former chief of Soviet Army intelligence Jan Berzin (code name DONIZETTI or STARIK, meaning "old man"), complained to Stalin on December 12, 1936, that he did not have "enough rifles to equip 12 brigades," he was short of "tanks, bombers, fighters, and artillery."[23]

Meanwhile, the $518 million in gold Stalin wrested from Madrid gave him his pick of promising new aviation technology in France, Germany, Italy, and the United States. The Soviet DB-3 bomber was developed in a million-dollar deal by the Glenn L. Martin Company of Baltimore. Stalin also purchased a Soviet license to build both DC-2 and DC-3 transport planes from the Douglas Aircraft Company for $130,000 and $207,500, respectively. The DC-3, when redesigned by Boris Pavlovich Lisunov, became the Soviet Li-2 transport. Because of the lack of US government contracts in an era when Congress was reluctant to authorize military spending, some American aviation firms, such as Vultee Aircraft of Los Angeles, which specialized in light dive-bombers designed for infantry support in ground attack, became positively dependent on Soviet orders; the Il-2 Shturmovik, designed by Sergei Ilyushin, was based on Vultee prototypes. Stalin also ordered a sixty-two-thousand-ton American aircraft carrier and a number of other capital ships in 1938 (although these orders were later blocked, owing to US obligations to Britain under the London Naval Treaty) and placed lucrative orders with leading European firms such as Renault (warplanes and aviation engines), Ratier-Figeac (aviation propellers), and Hotchkiss (machine guns).[24]

It was not that Stalin did not want his side to win the war in Spain. Rather, in exchange for material support, Stalin demanded political control of the government fighting the war—a higher priority than military victory. Coinciding with the violent purges in the Soviet Union, Spain furnished Stalin a tableau to expand the Great Terror to Europe. This was the era of the middle-of-the-night knock on the door by NKVD brute squads, of death quotas and deportations of suspicious foreigners to Soviet concentration camps. Although the Moscow show trials and Red Army purges generated the most attention outside Russia, some nine-tenths of Great Terror victims were targeted as ethnic minorities, predominantly Ukrainians and Poles. The bizarre notion advanced by Soviet apologists—that a regime undergoing a genocidal paroxysm of xenophobia at home was devoted to international law, the sanctity of borders, and principled collective security abroad—has distorted the diplomatic history of the period.[25]

Likewise, the cause of Republican anti-Fascism in Spain, however appealing to volunteers from Europe and North America, is hard to reconcile with Stalin's use of the civil war as a killing ground for alleged enemies of the USSR. In May 1937, an NKVD team, led by the ruthless Aleksandr Orlov, arrived in Barcelona to carry out a bloody sectarian purge—a searing episode first chronicled by George Orwell in *Homage to Catalonia*. After sending "Old Man" Berzin back to Moscow to be executed—STARIK had complained that Stalin was not sending enough arms to help the Republicans win the war—Orlov established a tribunal of espionage and high treason in Barcelona, which was soon working at full blast. Orlov's victims included foreign volunteers too.[26]

Soviet-directed purges significantly undermined Republican morale. Even as Stalin's agents tightened the political corkscrew, more Soviet advisers returned home every month. By 1938, the Soviet military presence in Spain had fallen to 250 men and Soviet arms shipments had slowed to a trickle. The fallout was predictable. Franco's forces went from triumph to triumph, reaching the Mediterranean in April 1938 and splitting Republican Spain in two. Stalin responded not by cutting Madrid off but by recalling fifty more Soviet officers and doling out just enough aid to keep Juan Negrín's government on life support. A cynic might conclude that Stalin's goal in the Spanish Civil War had been not so much winning it as prolonging the fighting for as long as possible.[27]

In the case of China, we can say this without hesitation. New research in Soviet archives has unearthed the critical role Stalin played in reigniting the Sino-Japanese War in 1937. Tensions between Japan's Kwantung Army and the Russians in the Far East had eased during the cease-fire years since 1933, despite periodic border incidents and covert Soviet support for anti-Japanese partisans in Manchukuo (occupied Manchuria). In March 1935, Stalin even agreed to sell Japan Russia's old Manchurian Railway concession (which dated back to Tsarist times) for 140 million yen. The pause in fighting on the Japanese front had allowed Chiang Kai-shek's nationalists to concentrate their fire on the Chinese Communist Party (CCP) forces, with the Kuomintang's fifth encirclement campaign of September 1933 pushing the Communists into their Long March, which, though weakening Communist forces in the short run, made the reputation of Mao Zedong. In November 1935, Mao was named the new leader of the CCP, now based deep in the interior at Yan'an. The Manchurian war that had dominated the headlines in the early 1930s seemed, by 1936, to have devolved into a debilitating Chinese civil war—a war both the Soviets and the Japanese were content to observe from the sidelines.[28]

Then Stalin took a hand. On the surface, the Comintern's new Popular Front doctrine offered the prospect of an Asian realignment, with Moscow brokering a truce between Chiang and Mao to unite China against Japanese aggression. Mao, weaker and more isolated, was willing to parley. He wrote to Chiang on August 25, 1936, proposing an "all-Chinese united government of national defense." But Chiang, a former Soviet client who had broken with Stalin in 1927, rejected Mao's olive branch. On December 12, 1936, Chiang was arrested (or kidnapped) by his own officers at Xi'an (Sian), who held him hostage and opened negotiations with Mao's envoy, Zhou Enlai. Informed of Chiang's capture, Mao sent a telegram to Moscow rejoicing at news of "the arrest of the mother of all criminals." On December 15, the CCP requested that the Kuomintang mutineers "hand Chiang over to a people's tribunal." But Stalin insisted on Chiang's release after Chiang agreed to release Communist prisoners and open a "second united front" against Japanese Manchukuo. In a pointed rejoinder to the Anti-Comintern Pact signed by Germany and Japan on November 25, 1936 (Italy would sign the following year), Stalin's coup ensured, as S. C. M. Paine argues in a new study, that "Chinese not Russian soldiers would die fighting Japan."[29]

If this was Stalin's objective in December 1936, he succeeded brilliantly. Japan took the bait, responding to the united front—which appeared, in Japanese eyes, to herald a Communist takeover of China—by invading the Chinese mainland after a bloody skirmish at the Marco Polo Bridge on the outskirts of Beijing on July 7, 1937. By November, Japan had incurred 40,000 casualties (9,115 dead and 31,257 wounded). Chinese losses were heavier still, amounting to 187,200 in the first four months, including 70 percent of Chiang's officers. Just as Stalin had hoped, it was the nationalists who did the fighting and dying against Japan, not Mao's Communists.

Both Mao and Chiang had expected, reasonably enough, that the Red Army—250,000 strong in Mongolia and the Soviet Far East—would intervene after Stalin had helped reignite the war. But they badly misread Stalin's foreign policy. His aim in opening a Chinese united front was not to waste his own strength fighting Japan, but to preserve it by prolonging the Sino-Japanese War. As Nelson T. Johnson, the US ambassador in China, observed in February 1938, with a far keener grasp of Soviet foreign policy than his gullible counterpart in Moscow, "Communist Russia expects to profit by the chaos that Japan is creating, and sees safety for itself in a Japan that is exhausting itself in China."[30]

Just as in Spain, Stalin sent just enough arms and supplies to China to keep the war going. These included expendable Soviet-made fighters, heavy guns, machine guns, trucks, and even eighty-two light and medium tanks. But a more substantial commitment to Chiang, let alone outright Soviet military intervention, was not to be. By the time Shanghai fell to Japan in November 1937, Chiang's diplomats in Moscow had grown desperate, demanding that Stalin intervene before it was too late. But the Vozhd, who had his own sleeper agent in Chiang's camp (Commander General Chang Chih-Chung), saw no cause for desperate measures. On November 18, 1937, Stalin promised to send troops only if the collapse of the Chinese government was imminent.[31]

He was good to his word. Whenever nationalist forces were on the run, the Red Army would draw off enough Japanese forces to allow Chiang to recover; then Stalin would withdraw and let the Chinese and Japanese go back to slaughtering each other. Thus, after the Japanese swept up the Yangtze and threatened Wuhan, forcing Chiang to withdraw his headquarters and government upriver to Chungking, Stalin authorized an incursion south of Vladivostok, at the Soviet-Korean border town of Zhanggufeng. The Zhanggufeng incident of July 1938 spiraled into a real battle, pitting twenty-one thousand Red Army troops against three thousand Japanese. The Japanese held out for a month, long enough to force a postponement of their Yangtze campaign, before ceding

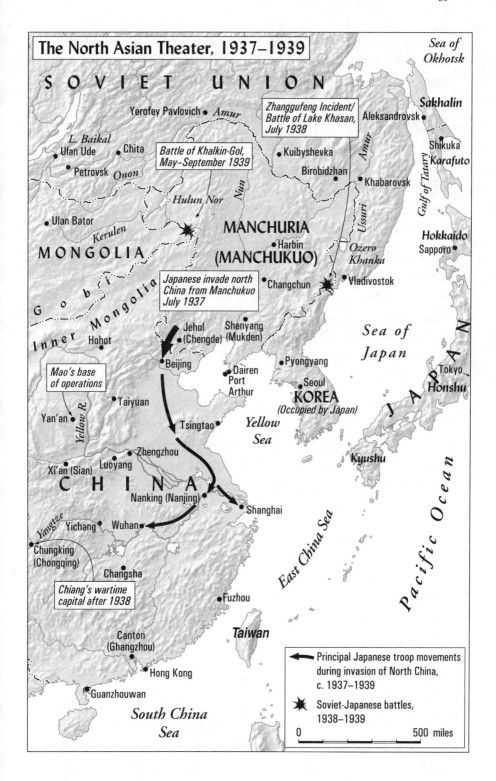

The North Asian Theater, 1937–1939

Sea of Okhotsk

S O V I E T   U N I O N

Yerofey Pavlovich • *Amur*

Zhanggufeng Incident/ Battle of Lake Khasan, July 1938

Aleksandrovsk •

Sakhalin

L. Baikal
Ulan Ude •   • Chita

Battle of Khalkin-Gol, May–September 1939

• Kuibyshevka

Birobidzhan

Shikuka
Karafuto

• Petrovsk   *Onon*

Amur

• Khabarovsk

Gulf of Tatary

Hulun Nor

Nun

MANCHURIA

• Ulan Bator

Kerulen

Ozero Khanka

Ussuri

Hokkaido
Sapporo •

M O N G O L I A

(MANCHUKUO)
• Harbin

Gobi

Inner Mongolia

Japanese invade north China from Manchukuo July 1937

Changchun •   • Vladivostok

Sea of Japan

Hohot •

Jehol
• (Chengde)

Shenyang
(Mukden)

Mao's base of operations

• Beijing

• Dairen
Port
Arthur

Pyongyang •

Seoul •

Tokyo •
Honshu

J A P A N

• Taiyuan

KOREA
(Occupied by Japan)

Yan'an •

Yellow R.

Tsingtao •

Yellow Sea

Xi'an (Sian) •   Luoyang
Zhengzhou •

C H I N A

Nanking (Nanjing) •

• Shanghai

Kyushu

Pacific Ocean

Yangtze   Yichang •   Wuhan •

Chungking
(Chongqing)

Changsha •

East China Sea

Chiang's wartime capital after 1938

• Fuzhou

Taiwan

Canton
(Ghangzhou)

• Hong Kong

• Guanzhouwan

South China Sea

← Principal Japanese troop movements during invasion of North China, c. 1937–1939

※ Soviet-Japanese battles, 1938–1939

0   500 miles

the town. Stalin celebrated his victory at Lake Khasan, as the Russians called the battle, by deporting two hundred thousand Koreans from the region to Kazakhstan.[32]

The same pattern emerged the following spring, after a series of Japanese victories threatened to open new flanks threatening Chungking from the north and south. Once again, Stalin authorized a limited incursion against Japanese Manchukuo in May 1939, this time on the western side of Soviet Mongolia.* The initial Soviet provocation was small: a Mongolian cavalry regiment crossed the Khalkin-Gol River to graze their horses on the steppe, advancing twenty kilometers to the village of Nomonhan, before the Kwantung Army forced it back to the river. Before crossing back over to Soviet territory, the Mongolians opened fire. The Red Army's Fifty-Seventh Special Corps brought in tanks and warplanes and, before long, a real firefight was underway.[33]

The border clash the Russians refer to as the Battle of Khalkin-Gol raged all summer 1939, though it was largely ignored by the Western press. Stalin took the battle seriously enough that he entrusted command to a brilliant young Tukhachevsky protégé, Georgii Zhukov. By late July, Zhukov had assembled a lethal mechanized force of fifty-eight thousand men, including hardened veterans of the Spanish Civil War, which deployed 500 tanks (mostly T-26s used in Spain and a few prototypes of modern Soviet BT-7 and T-34 tanks), 385 armored cars, and 400 warplanes. The Kwantung Army, commanded by General Michitarō Komatsubara, attacked Zhukov's forces on July 1 and 23, both times failing. Zhukov then launched his own assault on August 20. Although the Japanese defenders inflicted heavy losses, Komatsubara had no

---

* Soviet diplomats claimed to be responding to a Japanese violation of the "Mongolian People's Republic." There was an element of unreality here: neither country officially claimed (or was recognized as legitimate ruler of) the territory violated by the other. The Soviet position was that Mongolia was independent, just as Tokyo denied responsibility for Manchukuo.

anti-tank guns and little armor (one Japanese battalion commander tried to mount a Soviet BT-7 tank, kamikaze-style, with a sword; he did not succeed). In all, the Kwantung Army suffered 20,000 dead and 41,000 injured or captured out of 75,000 deployed—a casualty rate of 79 percent—against heavy but lesser Soviet losses of 7,974 killed and 15,251 wounded. Although war had never been declared, on September 15, 1939, Tokyo sued for peace. Zhukov was summoned to Moscow and awarded the "gold star of Hero of the Soviet Union."[34]

Zhukov's victory achieved a number of critical strategic objectives for Stalin. First, by providing relief to Chiang's nationalist forces, it ensured that the Sino-Japanese War would continue. Chiang even launched a new offensive along the Yangtze River that winter (with predictable cynicism, after Zhukov's victory Stalin curtailed Soviet arms shipments to China). Second, Komatsubara's humiliating defeat all but finished off the Japanese Army faction that favored a northern strategy focused on Soviet Russia as the main enemy. The army's "strike north" scheme, its main operational plan since the 1920s, had envisioned a "rapid conquest of Siberia as far west as Lake Baikal" in order to "eliminate the Communist threat to Asia." This plan was now moot. The Japanese cabinet responsible for the Khalkin-Gol debacle fell on September 3, 1939.[35]

With Stalin disengaging, the Sino-Japanese War drew in other powers concerned about Japanese expansion, including Britain and the United States. This, in turn, strengthened the case of the Japanese Navy faction favoring a "strike south" strategy targeting British, Dutch, and American colonies in Southeast Asia. As Bullitt had written Roosevelt before being sacked, "It was the heartiest hope of the Soviet Government that the United States will become involved in a war with Japan." By making obvious the failure of the army's northern strategy and strengthening the hand of the navy faction in Tokyo, Zhukov's triumph made such a war far more likely.[36]

By removing the Japanese threat to Siberia, Zhukov's triumph also allowed Stalin to concentrate his forces in the west as war clouds gathered over Europe. Even as Soviet Russia and Nazi

Germany had been fighting a proxy war in Spain and exchanging ideological salvos in public, Stalin and Hitler had maintained contact through back-channel intermediaries. At the Eighteenth Party Congress in Moscow on March 10, 1939, Stalin mocked the passive nonintervention policy of the Western capitalist powers in what he called the "Second Imperialist War." The real reason Britain and France had offered Hitler the Sudetenland at Munich, Stalin argued, was "as the price for [Germany] to wage war against the Soviet Union." A great "hullaballoo" was being raised in the Western press that Nazi Germany would soon be "marching on Soviet Ukraine." But the Germans, Stalin guffawed, "are refusing to meet their bills [i.e., to invade the USSR] and are sending them to Hades." To Hitler, Stalin declared defiantly that "we are not afraid of the threats of aggressors." But to the Western capitalist powers—Britain, France, and the United States, which were all trying, in Stalin's view, to maneuver him into war against Hitler—he issued a pointed warning that the USSR would not be "drawn into conflicts by warmongers who are accustomed to have others pull the chestnuts out of the fire for them."[37]

Five days after Stalin's "chestnuts" speech, Hitler ordered German troops to occupy Prague and the rest of Czechoslovakia. Enraged by Hitler's betrayal of his Munich promise not to move beyond the Sudetenland, British opinion turned decisively against appeasement. On March 31, 1939, Chamberlain extended a security guarantee to Poland, endorsed by France. Just as Lenin had foretold, the rival capitalist blocs stood on the precipice of war. It would not be difficult for Stalin to make them turn their daggers against each other.

II.

"HUGE AND HATEFUL"

The Molotov-Ribbentrop Pact

5

Courting Hitler

It was no accident that Stalin distanced himself from collective security in March 1939, just as Britain got serious about it. The closer the Western powers and Hitler drew toward war over Poland, the harder it would be for Stalin to pretend that bringing about such a conflict was not his most cherished foreign policy objective. Litvinov's collective security chatter had served a diplomatic purpose, but only as long as Stalin had not had to pledge the Soviets to intervene in a real armed conflict against Hitler—as Britain would surely now demand that he do—and to help Poland, one of Russia's traditional enemies and a serious Soviet military opponent as recently as 1920.

A hint of the true face of Soviet foreign policy was provided immediately after Prime Minister Chamberlain proclaimed his fateful guarantee of "Polish independence" in the House of Commons on March 31, 1939—not, that is, of Poland's territorial integrity, as neighbors with designs on Polish territory noticed. Chamberlain's statement has received opprobrium over the years, much of it deserved. Hitler read the loose guarantee of Polish "independence" as a green light for adjusting Poland's borders, even as Poland's foreign minister, Józef Beck, took Chamberlain's declaration as a "British blank check"—a solemn vow to intervene militarily if Germany threatened Poland's independence. Both interpretations suffered from wishful thinking, enabled by Chamberlain's poor choice of words. The upshot was the simultaneous encouragement of German diplomatic bullying and the stiffening of Polish resistance to it, which ratcheted up the odds of war.[1]

In fairness to Chamberlain, there were good reasons for the subtle wording. To have guaranteed the entirety of Polish territory—as Chamberlain's critics have often insisted he should have done—would have been to recognize the opportunistic Polish seizure of Teschen from the Czechs two days after Munich—an act of territorial larceny that, like Hungary's seizure of southern Slovakia, had played a role in the destruction of Czechoslovakia that Hitler had just completed.* Poland, as Chamberlain knew, had signed a nonaggression pact with Nazi Germany in January 1934 as a hedge against Soviet aggression. Foreign Minister Beck had visited the Führer's mountain retreat at Berchtesgaden as recently as January 5, 1939, where Hitler had proposed a deal to compensate Warsaw with more territory at Czech expense (Carpatho-Ruthenia, in today's Ukraine) in exchange for Poland turning over Danzig (Gdańsk) and the Polish corridor to Germany. Beck, though happy to pocket Teschen in the wake of Munich, was now having second thoughts, and he refused. However alarming Hitler's recent behavior had been—from his bullying of Chamberlain at Munich, to the brutal, state-enabled Kristallnacht pogrom against Jews and Jewish-owned businesses carried out across Germany on November 9–10, 1938, to the occupation of Prague on March 15—Poland was not blameless in the Czechoslovakian tragedy.[2]

Personally affronted as he was by Hitler's move into Prague, Chamberlain had to consider opinion in the cabinet and the Commons. The Liberal and Labour opposition, however wary of Hitler and Nazism, were reluctant to be drawn into war against Germany by a Tory government. The Tories in Chamberlain's cabinet, including the foreign secretary, Viscount Halifax, were no less leery. An unconditional guarantee of Poland's integrity would have pleased the gung-ho Winston Churchill, but his belligerent

---

*Citing alleged abuses of Polish nationals, Warsaw sent an ultimatum to Prague at 11:45 p.m. on September 30, 1938—the evening after the Allied betrayal of Czechoslovakia at Munich—demanding an answer by 12 p.m. the following day. It was not Poland's finest moment.

Europe, c. 1936–1939

German territory in 1936

Territory occupied by Germany in 1938

Territory occupied by Germany in 1939

Czechoslovakian territory occupied by Hungary

Poland annexes Teschen, Nov. 1938

anti-Hitler stance was still a minority position in the party, as had been made clear by Churchill's exclusion from the last two Tory cabinets (including this one). Moreover, a commitment to defend Poland at all costs would—like an invitation for Churchill to join the cabinet—have been understood by Hitler as a virtual commitment to fight. For this reason, Chamberlain could not have issued one without risking the collapse of his government.

Seeking political and diplomatic cover, Chamberlain had tried to enlist not only French but also Soviet support for a statement guaranteeing Polish independence. Despite his own misgivings about Stalin, Chamberlain had arranged a meeting with Ivan

Maisky, the Soviet ambassador to London, in the hope of extracting a Soviet endorsement. Carefully, Maisky had told Chamberlain that he might say "on his own authority" that the USSR "appreciated the principles" embodied in a statement regarding Poland, so long as he did not quote Maisky, Litvinov, or Stalin as having done so on the record. But even this qualified endorsement of Chamberlain's Polish guarantee was rescinded when Litvinov informed the British ambassador to Moscow, Sir William Seeds, on April 1, 1939, that Maisky had been "misunderstood" and that Chamberlain's statement on Poland was "not at all appreciated." Britain, Litvinov told Seeds, "could pursue [its] own policy: the Soviet Government would stand aside." As if to underscore Moscow's distance from the Western powers over Poland, three days later the Soviet news agency TASS emphatically denied a French news report "that the Soviet Union has undertaken or promised to undertake to supply Poland in the event of war with war materials and to deny its raw materials market to Germany." The truth was that "the Soviet Union has given no such promise and assumed no such obligation." So much for the supposed Soviet commitment to collective security.[3]

Still, despite his own deep-seated hostility toward Poland, for diplomatic reasons Stalin could not simply cast off all disguise. On April 17, 1939, he authorized Litvinov to discuss the possibility of a mutual assistance pact with Britain and France. Significantly, however, Litvinov instructed Maisky to "leave the initiative to the British and French." In a sign of the bad faith with which he viewed the Western powers, Stalin that very same day authorized his ambassador in Berlin, A. F. Merekalov, to visit the German Foreign Ministry in order to reassure the German state secretary, Richard von Weizsäcker, that Stalin's foreign policy was in no way anti-German. Weizsäcker assured Merekalov that there was "no reason why [Russia] should not live with us on a normal footing. And from normal [our] relations might become better and better."[4]

For all that Neville Chamberlain has been abused for naiveté in his reading of Hitler, it is worth noting here that the British prime minister was perfectly justified in his wariness of Stalin. Soviet Russia, Chamberlain wrote his sister on March 26, was "both hated and respected by many of the smaller States, notably by Poland, Romania, and Finland." After the Russians disowned his March 31 statement on Poland, the prime minister concluded, with justification, that the USSR did not have "the same aims and objects as we have, or any sympathy with democracy as such. She is afraid of Germany and Japan, and would be delighted to see other people fight them."[5]

The beleaguered Édouard Daladier government in Paris received no better treatment in Moscow. France's military attaché in the city, Colonel August Antoine Palasse, had been trying to cultivate contacts in the Soviet high command for two years. Although France had been, theoretically, a Soviet ally since 1935, Palasse was not even allowed to attend Red Army maneuvers. As a disgruntled Colonel Palasse reported to Paris, Stalin's spy chief Lavrenty Beria had placed him under "round the clock NKVD surveillance" in June and July 1938 because, to furnish intelligence requested in Paris as the Czechoslovak crisis was breaking, he had been asking too many questions about the Soviet military posture. On April 13, 1939, as the showdown over Poland was heating up, Palasse visited the Soviet Defense Ministry to request an urgent audience. He was rebuffed without explanation. After being rebuked by his superiors for failing to furnish decent intelligence on the Red Army, Palasse reminded the French high command, in a plaintive report filed on April 19, that "I assumed my post here in an atmosphere of revolutionary terror, a terror which has still not ceased today, and which renders it all but impossible to enter into genuine relations with Soviet military personalities." Palasse added drily that "relations between our two countries have not been, in general, of a nature tending to facilitate my mission."[6]

Although Stalin's government had been dropping lumps of coal into French and British laps all winter, the first sign of a genuine revolution in Soviet foreign policy came on April 27, 1939, when Litvinov and Maisky were summoned to Moscow for consultation.

A dramatic scene was enacted in the Kremlin, as Litvinov came in for vicious abuse at the hands of Vyacheslav M. Scriabin (Bolshevik name Molotov, meaning "hammer"), the chairman of the Council of People's Commissars. The hammer to Stalin's "steel" during the Great Terror years, Molotov had worked closely with the Vozhd, drawing up purge lists and death quotas: they cosigned 3,167 execution orders on a single day (November 12, 1938). "The atmosphere," Maisky later recalled, was "as tense as it could get. Molotov became violent, colliding with Litvinov incessantly, accusing him of every kind of mortal sin." Stalin "puff[ed] at his pipe" during Molotov's tirade, making clear to Maisky that Molotov, an Old Bolshevik and unsentimental foreign policy opportunist, was now in favor.[7]

Next week, the hammer came down. On the night of May 3, 1939, the Soviet Foreign Ministry on Kuznetsky Most was surrounded by NKVD troops in a blunt coup that saw Litvinov and his top appointees physically removed from the premises, along with virtually all Jewish employees. As Molotov recalled, Stalin had ordered him to "purge the [Foreign] Ministry of Jews." Not only was Stalin jettisoning Litvinov's policy of anti-Hitler collective security, but he was extending an anti-Semitic olive branch to the Nazis by purging Jews from the Soviet foreign policy establishment and turning it over to a gentile, Molotov. Stalin was courting Hitler.[8]

Hitler got the message. On May 5, Hitler's propaganda chief, Joseph Goebbels, issued instructions that Nazi journalists should suspend their "sharp attacks on the Soviet Union until they received new instructions." Addressing his army commanders on May 23, Hitler hinted at a possible deal with Stalin but warned that "economic relations with Russia would only be possible, once political relations have improved." Ideally, Hitler wanted an improvement in political relations without having to give away anything in return, such as a renunciation of the Anti-Comintern Pact with Italy and Japan. Yet, as the German ambassador in Moscow, Schulenburg, informed State Secretary Weizsäcker on May 22, Molotov had already made clear to him that merely reopening trade talks "was not a sufficient political gesture and that he wanted a thorough-going offer of a political nature from us."[9]

Stalin was careful not to seem too eager. Meeting Hitler halfway, Molotov declared himself willing to open talks, so long as they appeared to be purely economic—and thus should be conducted by Stalin's trade commissar, the Armenian Old Bolshevik Anastas Mikoyan—rather than political, which would have been his own responsibility. In this way, Molotov could preserve plausible deniability that he was dealing with Hitler and maintain flexibility vis-à-vis Britain and France. Far from welcoming Molotov's hot potato, Mikoyan was even cooler to the Germans, laying down strict conditions before he would open state-level trade negotiations. These conditions, he informed Stalin on June 19, 1939, the Germans had yet to satisfy.[10]

German-Soviet trade discussions were no mere red herring. In economic terms, both countries needed each other, and the stakes were high. Stalin's armament drive had stimulated voracious demand for machine tools and engineering know-how, areas in which German firms excelled. Hitler's own armament efforts had ratcheted up German demand for oil, manganese, cotton, and grain, all of which the Soviets produced in abundance. Rubber stocks were perilously low in Germany, sufficient for only two to three months in case of war. Although Russia did not produce rubber, it had ready access to Asian supplies, which might prove critical in the case of a British blockade of Germany. It was the same story with steel and nickel: if supplies of iron ore from the Gällivare mines of Sweden and the Petsamo nickel combines in Finland were disrupted across the Baltic, German mass production of panzers and warplanes would be impossible. Little wonder the German Office for Economic Development concluded that "making our greater economic sphere blockade-proof can only be achieved through close economic cooperation with Russia."[11]

Mikoyan and Molotov were playing hard to get. Behind the scenes, though, Stalin was moving toward a genuine political realignment with Berlin. Molotov instructed his diplomats to drop hints that Stalin might be interested in territorial changes after all. Thus on June 15, Georgi Astakhov, the Soviet chargé d'affaires in Berlin, mooted a Polish partition to the Bulgarian minister in Berlin, Parvan Draganov, who was known to be friendly with the Germans. On several occasions that June, Soviet diplomats asked their British and French counterparts about their attitude toward Soviet encroachment into the three Baltic states—Estonia, Latvia, and Lithuania—the idea being that sending in the Red Army might help deter Hitlerian aggression. On June 2, Molotov handed the British and French ambassadors a draft agreement, under which the Soviets might provide mutual assistance to smaller European states under "threat of aggression by a European power." To deter Stalin, on June 7, Latvia and Estonia signed nonaggression treaties with Germany, joining Lithuania, which had signed one back in March. On three separate occasions that June, Soviet officials in the Berlin embassy broached the subject of Bessarabia—the area of coastal Romania abutting the Danube delta that had belonged to Tsarist Russia—with German diplomats. The hint was not subtle: Stalin was in the market for territory.[12]

Still, he was in no rush. As summer wore on, it became clear that Germany's ardor for a deal was much stronger than Russia's. Every day brought a possible armed clash with Poland closer for Hitler, and dry summer weather would not last forever (the Wehrmacht's ideal launch date was August 26). Hitler's Polish war plans, along with his acute economic vulnerability, were well known to Stalin, who had a highly placed mole in the German embassy in Warsaw. Meanwhile, although the battle raging at Khalkin-Gol kept Soviet forces tied down all summer, the dramatic failure of Japan to break through on July 23 eased the strategic pressure on Moscow. The longer the diplomatic picture in Europe was unclear, the greater leverage Stalin enjoyed over Hitler.[13]

Emboldened by Zhukov's stand in Manchuria, Stalin authorized a tentative approach to the Germans in Berlin. On July 26, Astakhov, the Soviet chargé d'affaires, met with the German legation counselor and trade expert Karl Schnurre at a Berlin restaurant.

Astakhov became animated as he assailed German forward policy in "the Baltic states, Finland, and Romania," which "left the Soviet government with the feeling of being under threat." As Schnurre reported, the Russian had shown "especially strong interest in the Romanian question." Astakhov also asked if Germany had designs on the "Galician and Ukrainian" parts of Poland. Schnurre assured Astakhov that Germany had "no policy on the Ukrainian question which threatened Soviet interests." Schnurre proposed a three-stage plan: a new commercial treaty, followed by "the normalization and improvement of political relations," and then a Rapallo-style alliance treaty. Astakhov promised that he would "report this to Moscow."[14]

The Germans interpreted Astakhov's remarks as an invitation. With Stalin expecting to receive a British-French delegation in August, the clock was ticking. The stakes were high enough that Hitler's trusted Nazi foreign minister, the former champagne salesman Joachim von Ribbentrop, stepped in to speed things along. If Stalin negotiated with Hitler in good faith, Ribbentrop told Astakhov over dinner on August 2, "there was no problem from the Baltic to the Black Sea that could not be solved between the two of us." Unlike the democratic powers, Ribbentrop boasted, Nazi Germany "did not need to pay heed to vacillating public opinion" and could settle foreign affairs "on solid ground." In this spirit, Ribbentrop assured the Russian that "there was room for two of us on the Baltic." Ribbentrop also "dropped a gentle hint at coming to an agreement with Russia on the fate of Poland." The next move was up to Stalin.[15]

In a sign of the convergence of thinking in Berlin and Moscow, Molotov called on Ambassador Schulenburg the next day, even before Schulenburg had learned of Ribbentrop's meeting with Astakhov in Berlin. Schulenburg, a career diplomat, was less frank than Ribbentrop, promising simply that Soviet interests in Poland would be respected, along with the "integrity" of the Baltic states. This time, it was Molotov's turn to be blunt. "At the mention of the Baltic states," Schulenburg reported to Ribbentrop, "Molotov was interested in learning what States we meant by the term and whether Lithuania was one of them." Molotov and Ribbentrop were both mooting a carve up of Eastern Europe.[16]

Even so, Stalin was in no hurry. With the German desperation for a deal now clear, the Russians could use Paris and London to ratchet up pressure on Berlin. Although rumors were swirling around the Moscow embassy circuit, the evidence we have suggests that the Chamberlain and Daladier governments had no idea how close the two dictators were to working out a deal. If they had, they would surely have shown more urgency in dispatching their joint diplomatic mission to Russia, headed by the British admiral Reginald Drax and French general Joseph Doumenc. Significantly, Drax and Doumenc did not fly to Moscow, traveling instead aboard an old steamer called the *City of Exeter*, which took six days to reach Russia.[17]

Because the Allied mission was unhurried and relatively low-level, it is usually dismissed by historians as unserious, with its amateurishness confirming Stalin's contemptuous view of the Western powers and giving him strategic (if deeply amoral) grounds for negotiating with Hitler. But this is not really fair to the Allies, and certainly not to the French, who took the mission more seriously than the British did. Unlike his British counterpart Drax, Doumenc was given full legal authority by the French government to negotiate a binding military agreement with Moscow. Prior to leaving for Russia on August 5, Doumenc was briefed by Prime Minister Daladier, Foreign Minister Georges-Étienne Bonnet, and the chief of the General Staff, General Maurice Gamelin. What France needed in case war broke out with Germany over Poland, Gamelin informed Doumenc, was for the USSR to "undertake nothing against Poland [or] Romania . . . but rather to aid these, our allies, or rather our future allies, if they request [this aid]—that is, by offering aerial support, fuel, and logistical support." In other words, France wanted Stalin to help Russia's neighbors instead of invading them. That he felt the need to emphasize this point suggests that Gamelin suspected Stalin was more likely to exploit a conflict by invading Poland and Romania than to aid them.[18]

These suspicions were brutally confirmed after Doumenc and Drax arrived in Moscow on August 12, when Stalin and Molotov refused even to receive them. The task was left instead to Stalin's defense commissar, Marshal Kliment Voroshilov, a political hack who had personally signed 185 death lists during the Great Terror. Voroshilov approached the talks in bad faith but good humor. Abandoning any pretense about collective security, Voroshilov demanded, over and over, permission to send Soviet troops into northern and southern Poland and into Romania if the French and British declared war on Germany because Hitler invaded Poland— basically to invade the USSR's western neighbors. Doumenc tried to finesse things by predicting that Poland and Romania, if invaded by Germany, "would readily assent if you came to their aid." At this, Voroshilov scoffed that "it is not at all clear that [Poland and Romania] will consent." When Drax conceded that Stalin would indeed need permission from the Poles before invading Poland, Voroshilov said he was "very sorry to learn that the military missions of Britain and France did not pose these questions themselves and have not brought us a definitive answer." Doumenc was game enough to send an envoy to Warsaw on August 17 to ask if the Poles would permit Stalin to invade Poland if Germany attacked (the answer was no). The unfortunate fact, Doumenc reported to Gamelin, was that Stalin would not "consider any military agreement" until permission was granted for Soviet troops "to enter Polish and Romanian territory."[19]

Exploiting his visitors' desperation, Voroshilov pumped them for information on Allied military dispositions. Drax and Doumenc dutifully shared with the Russian marshal a detailed map of France's Maginot Line and the mobilization timetable of England's underwhelming expeditionary force to Europe. When Doumenc asked, on August 14, for reciprocal intelligence about Soviet dispositions, Voroshilov refused unless the Allies told him whether

Stalin would "be allowed to send troops through the Vilensky corridor"—by which he meant the diagonal strip of the Vilna (Vilnius) district in northeastern Poland, although claimed by Lithuania—"and through Galicia [into southern Poland], and into Romania." Absent such guarantees, the discussion would remain "of no immediate importance," giving no cause for Voroshilov to volunteer sensitive military information.[20]

So uninterested were the Russians in what Drax and Doumenc were offering that as early as August 14, on the second day of talks with the British and French, Molotov issued instructions for his diplomats to open talks with the Germans on not only "the pending economic negotiations" but also "the Polish question." Significantly, he insisted that these talks take place in Moscow.[21]

Molotov's proposal to open political talks shows that Stalin was just as interested in a deal as Hitler, even if the latter was more pressed for time by his military timetable. At 8 p.m. on August 15, Ambassador Schulenburg called on Molotov. His instructions from Berlin were blunt and broad. In addition to what Ribbentrop had told the Russians earlier about German willingness to settle questions pertaining to "the Baltic Sea, the Baltic area, Poland," Ribbentrop added the hint of an agreement on Romania (under the heading "Southeastern questions, etc.") and asked that Molotov request "an audience with Stalin" for the German foreign minister. To all this Molotov assented, while adding a twist. With an eye on the influence Germany might be able to exert on Japan, whose forces were locked in battle with Zhukov at Khalkin-Gol, Molotov asked "where things stood with the idea of [the USSR] concluding a Non-Aggression Pact [with Japan]? Was the German government sympathetically inclined towards the idea?" Schulenburg reported these remarks verbatim to Ribbentrop in Berlin.[22]

Hitler was delighted. On August 16, Ribbentrop wired Schulenburg that "Germany is ready to conclude a nonaggression pact with the Soviet Union, and, if the Soviet Government so desires, one which would be irrevocable for a term of twenty-five years." Ribbentrop promised to settle Baltic questions to Stalin's satisfaction and to "exercise influence for an improvement . . . of Russian-Japanese relations." He was ready to "come by plane to Moscow any time after Friday, August 18, to deal on the basis of full power from the Führer with the entire complex of German-Russian questions and, if the occasion arises, to sign the appropriate treaties."[23]

Stalin needed only Hitler's word to move forward. After receiving a preliminary German draft on August 18 for a nonaggression pact lasting twenty-five years, Molotov prepared a counter draft on August 19 that, in a sign of Stalin's strategic restlessness, shortened the duration to five years. Hinting at possible Soviet designs on neighboring countries, Molotov added a clause stipulating that Germany and the USSR must refrain from supporting any "third country" pressed into hostilities with either power. Molotov concluded his counter draft by stipulating that the nonaggression treaty must be made conditional on the signing of a "special protocol . . . covering the points in which the High Contracting Parties are interested in the field of foreign policy."[24]

In Molotov's August 19 draft lies a critical clue to Stalin's thinking. Whereas Hitler, with a Polish war on the horizon, wanted as simple and sweeping a nonaggression pact as possible, Stalin wanted to keep his foreign policy options open, by shortening the pact's duration (by a factor of five) while also demanding a heavy price up front. Far from wishing to forestall a European war between Germany and the Western powers, Stalin's aim was to ensure that it would break out. According to a controversial transcript of Stalin's remarks on this very day, first published in translation in 1939 and later discovered in the Russian archives, the Vozhd told Molotov that, if he cut a deal with England and France, "Germany will back off and seek a *modus vivendi* with the Western Powers." By contrast, if Molotov "accept[ed] Germany's proposal and conclude[d] a nonaggression pact with her," Stalin predicted that Germany "will certainly attack Poland, and the intervention of England and France is then unavoidable." From the Communist perspective, the latter scenario—a bloody war in which the capitalist power blocs sought to destroy each other—was much better than peace. It was, Stalin explained, "in the interests of the USSR, the Land of the Toilers, that war breaks out between the Reich and the capitalist Anglo-French bloc." The only danger was that one bloc might defeat the other too quickly, before they had bled each other sufficiently. "Everything should be done," Stalin continued, "so that [the war] drags out as long as possible with the goal of weakening both sides." Viewing the Western capitalist powers, led by arch-imperialist Britain, as the stronger side, Stalin argued that the "task" of Soviet foreign policy, for now, "consists in helping Germany"—that is, signing a pact with Berlin. With the Japanese conflict in the Far East still unsettled, the USSR should strive to stay out of the European war for as long as possible, "while being able to hope for our own timely entrance into war."*[25]

With Molotov having given the green light for Ribbentrop to come to Moscow, all that remained to work out was the timing. True to Molotov's formula, a German-Soviet economic agreement was inked first, at 2 a.m. on Sunday, August 20, under which the Soviets would supply Hitler with at least 240 million Reichsmarks' worth of raw materials over the next two years (mostly oil, cotton, manganese, and rubber), in exchange for an equivalent value in German manufactures and technology transfer. This sum was a mere baseline: the goal was to ramp up bilateral trade to 1 billion Reichsmarks per year. Sunday afternoon, Hitler requested that Ribbentrop be received in Moscow on either Tuesday or the following day. In a wire to "the Chancellor of the German Reich" sent Monday evening, Stalin welcomed "the assent of the German

---

*After a version of Stalin's August 19 remarks was published by the French *Havas* news agency in December 1939, Stalin denounced the text as a forgery, a denial accepted by nearly all historians. But Russian historians unearthed a virtually identical transcript after the Soviet archives were opened in 1991. Of course this version may not be any more genuine than the *Havas* script. Nonetheless, the ideas expressed are uncannily consistent with Stalin's pronouncements on Soviet foreign policy going back to 1925, and subsequently.

Government to the conclusion of a non-aggression pact" and agreed to receive Ribbentrop on Wednesday, August 23.[26]

The scene at Moscow's Khodynka Aerodrome that day was striking. Along the runway, swastikas fluttered alongside the ubiquitous hammer and sickle banners of the Soviet Union. The swastikas had been requisitioned, as Roger Moorhouse notes in *The Devils' Alliance*, from "local film studios, where they had recently been used for anti-Nazi propaganda films." No less jarring was the musical accompaniment, with a Soviet military band serenading Ribbentrop with "Deutschland über alles," before switching over to the socialist "Internationale." More ominous were the handshakes of secret policemen. As one German diplomat observed, "Look how the Gestapo officers are shaking hands with their counterparts of the NKVD and how they are all smiling at each other. They're obviously delighted finally to be able to collaborate. But watch out! This will be disastrous, especially when they start exchanging files."[27]

The Russians spared no expense laying out the welcome mat for Ribbentrop. The greatest honor was the presence of Stalin, who almost never received foreign visitors. In a revealing contrast with the feeble show put on for the British and French envoys, still cooling their heels up the road,* Soviet-German talks began immediately after the Germans arrived at the highest level, with Stalin and Molotov receiving Schulenburg and Ribbentrop. Hitler, camped out by the phone in Berchtesgaden and planning to move against Poland within days, needed a deal as soon as possible. Stalin, knowing the leverage was his, was inclined to give it to Hitler—for a price.[28]

Booze flowed freely as the four men worked out the details of their pact. Molotov drank to Ribbentrop's health, Ribbentrop to

---

*The last round of negotiations between Drax, Doumenc, and Voroshilov had concluded at midnight on Tuesday, August 22. With Ribbentrop en route for Moscow, that morning Stalin told Voroshilov to tell the French and British visitors he had gone "duck hunting."

Stalin's, and Stalin proposed a toast to Hitler, assuring his guests that "I know how much the German people loves its Führer." In a revealing aside, Molotov traced the diplomatic revolution of the present moment back to Stalin's "chestnuts" speech to the Eighteenth Party Congress in March—a speech that, he realized now, had been "well understood in Germany." Everyone agreed heartily with Stalin's cynical jibe that the Anti-Comintern Pact had "frightened principally the City of London and the small British merchants." Ribbentrop chimed in that "Stalin will yet join the Anti-Comintern Pact." As to the conclusion of a nonaggression pact, the only disagreement was over the duration, with Ribbentrop angling for a symbolic number like one hundred years and Stalin whittling him down to a more plausible ten.[29]

As for the fate of Poland and Eastern Europe, there was surprisingly little friction. Molotov and Stalin raised no objection when Ribbentrop informed them ominously that "the German people would no longer put up with Polish provocation." All the Russians wanted was their fair share of territory "in the event of a territorial and political rearrangement of the areas belonging to the Polish state," with the dividing line "bounded approximately by the line of the rivers Narew, Vistula, and San." Far from a token sliver of Poland, the Soviet zone was larger than the German one (although the share of Poland's population was smaller). The Baltic area was divided, in the pact's "secret protocols," into "spheres of influence." In a sign of Stalin's superior leverage, the Soviet sphere included all of Finland, Estonia, and Latvia; the German one had only Lithuania. Stalin and Molotov declared a Soviet "interest" in Bessarabia. "The Führer accepts," Ribbentrop declared, "that the eastern part of Poland and Bessarabia as well as Finland, Estonia, and Latvia, up to the river Dvina, all fall within the Soviet sphere of influence." There was some haggling over the Soviet-German frontier on the Baltic; Stalin insisted he needed Libau (Liepāja) and Windau (Ventspils). Hitler, by telephone from Berchtesgaden, agreed. The only discord came when Ribbentrop proposed a flowery expression of Nazi-Soviet friendship. "Do you not think we should take a little more account of public opinion in both our countries?" Stalin asked, reminding Ribbentrop that "for many years now, we have been pouring buckets of shit over each other's heads."[30]

In this way, the destinies of millions of people, from the Arctic Ocean to the Danube delta, were settled by four tipsy men in the Kremlin. Seldom has a nonaggression pact been more transparent in furthering armed aggression. The territorial protocols of the Moscow Pact signed by Molotov and Ribbentrop on August 23, 1939, to be sure, remained secret. But the nonaggression clauses were published proudly in *Pravda* the next morning and trumpeted aloud in Berlin, suggesting that Poland was in serious danger—although only from German attack; the idea that Stalin might also invade was scarcely suspected, least of all in Warsaw.* While Hitler kept Britain and France occupied after they declared war on Germany and vice versa, the USSR could expand its borders westward, at small risk of outside intervention, while enjoying immense economic leverage over the Germans. Small wonder Stalin told Zhukov that he "had twisted Hitler around his finger."[31]

It was true that the price of Stalin's strategic coup was an unsightly agreement with Hitler, which Molotov was now enjoined to justify. In a speech before the Supreme Soviet on August 31, 1939, laying down the Comintern line, Molotov blamed the European war about to break out on the British, who had tried—but, mercifully, failed—to "embroil Germany and Soviet Russia in war, in order to kill two birds with one stone." Instead, the Soviets had turned the table on the Western imperialist powers with their "peaceful" nonaggression pact. Anyone who criticized this pact, Molotov instructed Communists all over the world to say, was a "warmonger, trying to bring about a global bloodbath."[32]

Despite the degree of difficulty involved in dissembling like this, the benefits of the Moscow Pact for Communism were obvious.

---

* Poland's foreign minister Józef Beck actually petitioned the Soviet government for help after the German invasion on September 1.

The capitalist world would soon be embroiled in a terrible war, and the USSR would be able to spread its territory substantially westward against seemingly helpless foes. All Stalin needed to do was ensure that neither Germany nor its opponents secured a decisive advantage. Once the two sides had exhausted themselves in a death struggle, the path would be clear for the armies of Communism to march in and seize the capitalist world by the throat.

6

Gangster Pact, Part I
Poland

SECRET THOUGH ITS territorial clauses were, there was little doubt in the West about Hitler's reasons for agreeing to the Moscow or Molotov-Ribbentrop Pact. By lifting the threat from the East, the pact enabled Hitler to contemplate an invasion of Poland with relative equanimity. Of course, there was still a grave risk that Britain and France would declare war on Nazi Germany in response. In the short run, however, this was a much lesser danger to the German Wehrmacht than hostile Soviet armed intervention would have been. As neither Britain nor France shared a border with Poland, they would be hard pressed to assist it, short of a French invasion of Germany's western frontier or a British blockade of the Baltic—neither of which would much slow down a German war machine able, owing to Poland's unfavorable geography, to invade from multiple directions simultaneously. France's chief of staff, General Maurice Gamelin, had promised the Polish government that he would hurl "the bulk of the French army" across the Maginot Line within fifteen days if Hitler invaded Poland, but there were good reasons to doubt this would happen. There was little sign of war readiness, much less enthusiasm, in Paris, where the political temperature was best captured in the famous question posed on the cover of *L'oeuvre* on May 4, 1939: Were Frenchmen truly ready to "die for Danzig"?[1]

Nor was it clear that Britain would go to war on Poland's behalf. Although Chamberlain's government responded to news of the Moscow Pact by signing a mutual assistance treaty with

Poland on August 25, 1939, valid for five years, its clauses regarding military cooperation were slippery, as the Poles would soon discover. Britain did not promise to make war, but rather "at once [to] give the Contracting Party engaged in hostilities [i.e., Poland] all the support and assistance in its power." In practice, this might mean anything from a full-scale invasion of the country attacking Poland to the dispatch of military aid or the disbursement of war loans. Even those less helpful options were not ironclad, in view of Britain's poor track record on Polish arms requests since Chamberlain's supposed guarantee of March 31.* Nor did the mutual assistance treaty specify which country Britain expected to invade Poland. As worded, the treaty could apply to the USSR as much as to Nazi Germany.[2]

Nonetheless, the renewed British overture to Warsaw was enough to give Hitler pause. Insofar as his agreement with Stalin eliminated the immediate danger of a two-front war of the kind Germany had faced in 1914, the Moscow Pact was a coup. But the pact, as Hitler would now learn, had left as many questions open as it had answered. What it stated was that each party must decline to "lend its support to" or "participate in any grouping" of powers fighting the other. Diplomatically speaking, all Molotov and Stalin had really done was declare neutrality in the war they hoped would now break out between Germany, Poland, and the Western powers. But such a war was not the kind Hitler wanted, even if it was obviously better than one that would pit Germany against those Western powers, Poland, and the Soviet Union too. If Britain and France, unfazed by Hitler's diplomatic coup in Moscow, chose

---

*On a visit to Warsaw in July 1939, General Edmund Ironside, chief of the Imperial General Staff, expressed his regret that Britain, stretched to the limit because of obligations to France and the empire, would not be able to contribute any Royal Air Force squadrons to Poland's defense, although he hoped to send bombers and "a modest contingent of Hurricane fighters" once a loan was secured. Negotiations over loan terms then bogged down, getting nowhere before the war started. It was not the last time Britain would disappoint Poland.

to go to war with him over Poland anyway, then all Ribbentrop had really accomplished was to reduce the enemy coalition facing Germany by one. In the supposed partnership between Berlin and Moscow, Hitler was running all the risk, while Stalin could simply sit back and wait for the capitalist powers to attack each other.[3]

Small wonder that Hitler hesitated in the last days of August 1939, postponing his original launch date for the invasion of Poland (August 26) and opening back-channel diplomatic communications with London through a Swedish businessman friendly with the Prussian minister-president Hermann Göring, known to the British as "Mr. G." What Hitler had in mind after learning of the Polish-British agreement of August 25, according to Mr. G, was a compromise settlement assigning both Danzig (Gdańsk) and the Polish corridor to the German Reich, while Warsaw would be compensated with a new Polish corridor to Gdynia, the more ethnically Polish port city northwest of Danzig (Gdańsk). While unwilling to accept such terms and justifiably wary of Hitler's motives, Chamberlain agreed on August 27 to send Mr. G back to Berlin to feel out the Germans about more direct negotiations. If Hitler agreed to an "international guarantee" to balance out German and Polish claims (e.g., Danzig/Gdańsk given to Germany, with Polish rights guaranteed, and the Polish corridor retained by Warsaw, with German right of way) and the prospects for a diplomatic compromise looked favorable, then Göring might be invited to "come to London to deal with the concluding stages."[4]

Over the next three days, a series of high-stakes diplomatic proposals were exchanged between Berlin, Warsaw, and the Western capitals. Even US president Roosevelt took a hand when he informed Whitehall on August 28 that Poland had agreed to direct talks with Germany—a report immediately contradicted by Hitler. The upshot of these probes was a telegram from Berlin, deciphered by the British Foreign Office on August 30, to the effect that (as Foreign Secretary Halifax interpreted the message) "Hitler accepted discussion with the Polish government, but said that the discussion must start at once in Berlin. . . . He accepted our proposal in regard to an international guarantee [of Germanified Danzig/Gdańsk and German transit rights in the Polish corridor], but *subject to the consent of the U.S.S.R.*" Aside from the novelty of Hitler appealing to Stalin and the ominous demand that a Polish emissary be sent to Berlin to be presented with a fait accompli—the kind of cynical maneuver that had preceded German moves against Austria and Czechoslovakia—the impression Hitler's message left on Halifax was that of a "man who was trying to extricate himself from a difficult position." Chamberlain, too, dismissed suggestions that war was imminent and rejected a proposal mooted in the House of Commons to evacuate children from London (a precaution already undertaken in Paris). Chamberlain reassured the cabinet, in words curiously lacking concern over the fate of Poland, that "there was no reason to think that Herr Hitler would start operations against us, but would wait for us to attack him."[5]

Meanwhile, Mr. G reported later on August 30 that, while Hitler had been insisting on recovering "all Polish territories which had been within the pre-war boundaries of Germany," Göring had badgered him down into settling for only Danzig (Gdańsk) and the Polish corridor. Of course, this was still more than Polish leaders—bolstered by the new pact of August 25 and their understandable, if misguided, conviction that Britain and France would support them with genuine military action against Germany—were willing to give up. Britain's good-faith approach to Hitler's entreaties had, for now, stayed his hand. "But for our reply," Mr. G told Halifax and Chamberlain, "war would have broken out on Tuesday morning [August 29]."[6]

In view of Hitler's well-known plans to invade Poland, last-minute diplomatic machinations such as these are often dismissed as irrelevant. According to this view, all they may truly have done was postpone the clash of arms between Germany and Poland by a few days. By the last week of August 1939, the Wehrmacht was fully mobilized and on high alert. Polish general mobilization had been declared on August 28, rescinded the following day, and then resumed, confusingly, on August 30. Border violations on the German-Polish frontiers were occurring every day. Despite Hitler's blustering, the intimidation was not just on the German side. The Polish government, print press, radio stations, and Polish diplomats were full of big talk about thumping the Wehrmacht, drawing on the confidence that Poland had, after all, defeated the Soviet Union only nineteen years before. On August 31, Poland's ambassador to the Reich, Josef Lipski, reported to Warsaw that if war began, "riots would break out in Germany and Polish troops would march successfully to Berlin."[7]

We must remember that no war is inevitable. It is significant that Hitler displayed cold feet in the last days of August 1939, sensing that he was leading Germany into a larger conflict than he had bargained for. Although willing to assume the risk of British and French intervention over Poland, Hitler did not desire this intervention. As he had told his generals on May 23, in the case of a war with Poland, "there must be no simultaneous conflict with the West." Still less was there a sign of war lust in the German public, whatever Hitler's mood. Nor was there a breath of war enthusiasm in Paris and London. After learning of the German invasion of Poland the morning of September 1, it took the British and French governments two days to respond, and even then their ultimatums were not coordinated (the British one, delivered at 9 a.m. on September 3, expired two hours later, one hour before France's own ultimatum was delivered to Berlin). Chamberlain's attitude remains difficult to fathom. At one point in late August, the prime minister expressed alarm at the lack of news from Warsaw on the progress of German-Polish negotiations, though not because he was afraid silence pointed to war. Rather, Chamberlain was disturbed at the "possible, but very distasteful explanation . . . that Polish negotiators were, in fact, giving way to Germany"—depriving Britain of a casus belli. The mood in Poland, despite the defiant boasting of Ambassador Lipski in Berlin, was far more anxious than belligerent, in view of Germany's obvious advantages in strategic geography and the order of battle.[8]

There was only one statesman in Europe who truly relished the prospect of a general war breaking out over Poland: Stalin. As Molotov boasted to the Supreme Soviet on August 31, Stalin had outmaneuvered the "ruling classes of Britain and France" who had tried to goad the Soviet Union into a war with Germany. Instead, it was Western capitalist powers who now stood on the brink of war with the Reich—a war in which the USSR would maintain "absolute neutrality." Molotov reserved special opprobrium for France's socialists and Britain's Labour Party, those on the left who had been so enthusiastic about collective security. "If these gentlemen," he scoffed, "want with such impregnable desire to wage war, then let them wage this war themselves, without the Soviet Union. We will then see what kind of warriors they are."[9]

Safe from German hostility, with Hitler's promises of territory in his pocket, Stalin was ideally placed to profit from a European war. News of the German invasion of Poland was greeted warmly in the Kremlin. No less welcome was the news that Britain and France declared war on Germany two days later. As Stalin told the Comintern's general secretary, Giorgi Dimitrov, on September 7, "A war is on between two groups of capitalist countries. . . . We see nothing wrong in their having a good hard fight and weakening each other. It would be fine if at the hands of Germany the position of the richest capitalist countries (especially England) were shaken. Hitler, without understanding it or desiring it, is shaking and undermining the capitalist system." For now, Germany—opposed by Poland, Britain, and France—appeared to be weaker. Stalin told Dimitrov, "We can maneuver, pit one side against the other to set them fighting with each other as fiercely as possible. The nonaggression pact is to a certain degree helping Germany. Next time, we'll urge on the other side."[10]

The only danger, from Stalin's perspective, was if he displayed too obviously his partiality for Hitler in the conflict, which might convince Britain or France to declare war on him too. On September 3, Ribbentrop wired Ambassador Schulenburg in Moscow, requesting that he ask Molotov whether the USSR would participate in the Polish war as promised and provide "relief" to the hard-pressed Wehrmacht. Did not Stalin, Ribbentrop asked, "consider it desirable for Russian forces to move at the proper time against Polish forces in the Russian sphere of interest and, for their part, to occupy this territory?" Carefully, Molotov replied on September 5 that "the time has not yet come." True, he admitted, the Soviet delay meant that the Germans might "be forced temporarily to cross the line of demarcation between the two spheres of interest of the two parties." But this was fine by Stalin, so long as the Germans (after doing all the work against the Polish armies) turned over this Polish territory to the USSR. Stalin wished, Molotov explained cryptically, to avoid "excessive haste," which might "injure our cause and promote unity among our opponents"—that is, risk incurring the wrath of Britain and France against the USSR. The Red Army did mobilize on September 5, yet it did so in all western Soviet military districts—from Finland through the Baltic states, White Russia, Western Ukraine, and Romania—not just against Poland. On September 10, to reassure the Germans, Molotov informed Schulenburg that the Soviets had mobilized three million troops, although he left unsaid why they had been mobilized.[11]

For the Germans, it was a maddening performance. Hitler's Polish war was going reasonably well so far, although at a heavy human price. Hitler's vacillation at the end of August had allowed the German high command (OKW) an extra week to prepare the invasion force, which was reinforced by an extra twenty-one infantry and two motorized divisions. In the end, the Wehrmacht was able to muster a million and a half troops for a five-pronged invasion of Poland, with the Third Army sweeping down in the north from East Prussia, the Fourth Army targeting Danzig (Gdańsk) along the Baltic coast from northwest Pomerania, the Eighth Army crossing east from Breslau, the Tenth Army coming from Silesia, and the Fourteenth Army invading from Slovakia in the south, aiming at Cracow. Over the skies of Poland, the Luftwaffe had seized control of the air, knocking out much (though not all) of the Polish Air Force, outnumbered five to one, on the ground. Having achieved clear sky dominance, the Luftwaffe conducted brutal air raids on Warsaw, Lódz, Czestochowa, Cracow, and Poznan (Posen)—on 158 towns and cities in all—introducing the world to the terrifying screams of the Stuka dive-bomber. The German advantage in tanks was more lopsided still: about 2,600 to 150.[12]

The Poles fought bravely, but there was little they could do to slow down the Luftwaffe or the Wehrmacht's mechanized divisions. As early as September 4, just three days into the war, the Polish Council of Ministers ordered the evacuation of the government and the foreign diplomatic corps to Nałęczów, on the eastern bank of the Vistula (Weichsel) southeast of Warsaw—the only direction from which Germany had not invaded the country. But after Cracow fell on September 6, even Nałęczów was vulnerable, and so the Polish government, along with the British, French, and US ambassadors, fled further east into Podol'ye, east of Tarnopol (Ternopil) in formerly Russian Ukraine, believing this extremity of eastern Poland was safe from the Germans. Foreign Minister Beck stayed on in Warsaw for now.[13]

The blitzkrieg continued. On September 7, the Polish military base on the Westerplatte peninsula, guarding Danzig (Gdańsk), surrendered after a furious bombardment from the Luftwaffe and the German Baltic fleet. Fifty miles west of Warsaw, two Polish armies were trapped in a fork between the rivers Bzura and Vistula (Weichsel). Poland's cities were devastated by Luftwaffe bombers, with twenty-five thousand civilians killed in Warsaw alone. Columns of refugees fleeing urban infernos were strafed by German fighter planes. To the rear of the advancing armies, German SS divisions terrorized Poles and Jews accused of sabotage or sniping, or in retaliation for Polish attacks on ethnic Germans behind the lines. While such atrocities were not imaginary—some five or six thousand Polish-German civilians were killed behind Polish lines—the numbers were wildly exaggerated by Nazi propaganda. German countermeasures were pitiless. More than five hundred Polish towns and villages were put to the torch; the local synagogue often providing the first kindling. Captured war prisoners

The Invasion of Poland, 1939

Lithuania, Latvia, and Estonia occupied by the Soviet Union

- Pskov
- LATVIA
- Riga
- Velikie Luki
- "Vilensky Corridor"
- Copenhagen
- Baltic Sea
- DEN.
- Memel
- LITHUANIA
- Kaunas (Kovno)
- Vitebsk
- Danzig (Gdańsk)
- Königsberg
- East Prussia
- Wilja
- Vilna (Vilnius)
- GERMANY
- 4
- 3
- Grodno
- Niemen
- Minsk
- Jedwabne
- Bialystok
- Belorussia
- Berlin
- Vistula (Weichsel)
- Narew
- Posen/ Poznan
- Bzura
- Warsaw
- Pinsk
- Pripet
- SOVIET
- Warta
- POLAND
- Brest-Litovsk
- UNION
- 8
- Oder
- Łódź
- Szack
- Dresden
- Breslau
- Naleczów
- Lublin
- Bug
- Rovno
- Zhitomir
- 10
- Częstochowa
- Prague
- Cracow
- Galicia
- Lwów (Lemberg/Lvov/Lviv)
- Ukraine
- PROTECTORATE OF BOHEMIA & MORAVIA
- Tarnopol (Ternopil)
- Brünn
- 14
- Stanislawów
- Podol'ye
- Bug
- SLOVAKIA
- Kolommy
- Dniestr
- Danube
- Vienna
- Bratislava
- Ruthenia
- Kuty
- Prut
- HUNGARY
- 0   250 Miles
- ROMANIA

→ Axis of German advance   **10** German army   → Soviet occupation of eastern Poland

- - - 1939 boundaries   ∘∘∘∘∘∘∘∘ Line agreed to by the Molotov-Ribbentrop Pact. August 23, 1939

▪▪▪▪ Poland 1939

were used as human shields or stripped of their uniforms and gunned down as illegal partisans. Even German sources concede that sixteen thousand Polish civilians were executed in September 1939, surely a gross underestimate. Another three thousand Polish war prisoners were dispatched that month. Polish Jews predictably fared worst of all, with tens of thousands expelled from their homes and at least forty-five thousand executed by year's end.[14]

The campaign so far was just as rapid—and ruthless—as Hitler could have hoped. True, he had not secured the neutrality of Britain and France, which put Germany's long-term strategic position at risk. But there was little sign of decisive military action from London and Paris. The Royal Air Force made a few desultory raids on the German Baltic coastal area, but dropped mostly propaganda leaflets, not bombs. The British Expeditionary Force began a slow-motion deployment across the Channel, which impressed neither Britain's French allies nor the Germans. The French armies crossed the German frontier near Saarbrücken, then stopped. It was a shameful performance from Poland's Western allies, all but ensuring defeat.

The most serious consequence of British and French passivity lay in its impact on Stalin's decision-making. Far from hiding the jackal-like opportunism of the Soviet position, Molotov told Schulenburg point-blank on September 10 that Stalin would only move after Warsaw fell. The pretext would be that, when Poland ceased to exist, the Red Army was acting to protect "endangered Ukrainians and Belorussians." "Please let us know," Molotov told Schulenburg, "when you expect to capture Warsaw—for appearances' sake we should not cross Poland's border until the capital had fallen." And yet the Poles refused to give in, to Stalin's frustration and Molotov's embarrassment. Just as the brave Poles defending Warsaw highlighted the fecklessness of Britain and France, they exposed Soviet duplicity and cowardice. With Poland largely beaten and no sign of Western intervention, what were the Russians waiting for?[15]

Wehrmacht commanders could not make heads or tails of Soviet intentions. "Since the beginning of September," German Army intelligence reported on September 13, "we have observed the movement of vehicles, horses, and reserves in Russia," but "the extent of the mobilization remains unclear." The German high command reckoned that the Russians had concentrated about six hundred thousand troops on the western borders of the Soviet Union, but these were not all on the Polish frontier. The Soviet mobilization pattern showed equal strength north and south of the Pripyat marshes, with a Belorussian Army focused on central Poland and a Ukrainian one that might move into southeastern Poland, but which might equally well be poised to invade Romania.[16]

So effective was Stalin's camouflaging of the Soviet military posture that, when the Red Army finally crossed the Polish frontier early in the morning of September 17, 1939, the move came as a surprise to both Polish and German commanders on the ground. The timing was opportune. On September 12, German troops had crossed the Molotov-Ribbentrop demarcation lines into "Soviet" Poland, suggesting that there would soon be little left of Poland's carcass to occupy. On September 15, Stalin agreed to Tokyo's armistice request in the wake of Zhukov's crushing victory at Khalkin-Gol, which reassured him that the Japanese threat in the Far East was receding. Finally, on September 16, a German communiqué announced the fall of Warsaw—erroneously, but no one knew this yet. Stalin decided he could wait no longer to seize his Polish prize.[17]

What followed was one of the ugliest episodes in modern diplomatic history. With his countrymen locked in a bitter struggle for their existence, Poland's ambassador in Moscow, Wacław Grzybowski, was summoned to the Kremlin at 3 a.m. on September 17 and handed an ersatz declaration of war. Because "the Polish state no longer exists" and was unable to protect Russia's "brothers of the same blood, Ukrainians and Belorussians," Molotov informed the bewildered ambassador, Stalin had ordered the Red Army to "cross the border and take under their protection the lives and property of the inhabitants of Western Ukraine and Western Belorussia." Because Poland had forfeited its existence, Grzybowski was told his diplomatic immunity had expired: he was promptly arrested by the NKVD, along with the Polish consul in Kiev, Janusz Matuszynski.*

---

* As penance for his own role in Poland's destruction, Schulenburg intervened to secure Grzybowski's release. The less fortunate Kiev consul, Matuszynski, vanished into the Gulag.

The statesmen, diplomats, and command officers inside Poland fared little better. Having evacuated southeast from Warsaw, then further east, Poland's leaders found themselves directly in the path of the Soviet advance. Far from an afterthought, the Soviet invasion was the defining moment, the critical catalyst in Poland's destruction. Until the Soviet pincers closed in, the Polish high command had gamely regrouped in eastern Poland to fight on, even while Warsaw was conducting a heroic defense. But now "in practical terms resistance [was] hopeless," as Marshal Edward Smigly-Rydz, Poland's commander in chief, informed Poland's civilian leaders at Kolommy (in today's southwestern Ukraine) at 11:30 a.m. on September 17. The meeting had to break up after the Red Army grew near and chased everyone southwest toward the Romanian border. In the frontier town of Kuty, a council was held at which Marshal Smigly-Rydz, Foreign Minister Beck, Poland's premier and president, and the French, Turkish, and Romanian ambassadors huddled to determine if Poland might continue the war from abroad and, if so, from where. At 8 p.m., word came that the Red Army had closed within eighteen miles. And so Poland's leaders gave up the ghost, fleeing into Romania without securing permission to continue the war; in effect, they were hostages.* In his last directive to the Polish Army, Smigly-Rydz announced that "the Soviets have crossed the border. I hereby order a total withdrawal to Romania and Hungary via shortest available routes. Do not fight the Bolsheviks unless they attack first or attempt to disarm our forces."[18]

The Soviet invasion also cut off the best escape route to neutral Romania for Poles, Jews, and other civilian refugees fleeing Nazi terror. The bewildered residents of eastern Poland, abandoned by their commander in chief and their government, had

---

*Beck was forced by Romania to sign a humiliating agreement stipulating that "the Polish government has renounced all its constitutional, political, and administrative functions." It was not the last indignity Poland would suffer in the war.

no idea where the "grey army decorated with red stars" was going, or whether it came as friend or foe. In Tarnopol (Ternopil), Stanislawów, and Rovno, city officials urged residents to welcome the Soviet invaders. Many Jews rejoiced in the news that the Red Army had arrived. At Jedwabne, a large banner was raised, reading, "We welcome you." A young, Communist-sympathizing Pole fleeing east from the Germans and stopped by a patrol near Rovno later recalled his astonishment "to see Soviet military uniforms and hear the Russian language" so far from the Soviet frontier. Had the "mighty Red Army," he wondered, "come to fight the Nazis and expel them from Poland?" Hoping to "express [his] joy at seeing them," the Pole was surprised when he and his companions were instead "ordered to put up our hands," whereupon they were placed under arrest and deported east into the Soviet Union.[19]

Illusions about the benign intentions of the invader were quickly dashed. Soviet leaflets instructed Polish enlisted men to "kill your officers and generals" and "drive them from your land." Red Army gunners, tank crews, and riflemen opened fire on Polish forces at Grodno, Szack (near Brest-Litovsk), and in forty other locations. None of these battles lasted very long, but they were not mere skirmishes either. An idea of the ferocity of this forgotten war can be gleaned from Soviet casualty figures in what was supposed to be a mop-up peacekeeping operation: 246 killed and 503 wounded on the Belorussian front, plus 491 dead and 1,359 wounded on the Ukrainian front; in all, 737 dead and 1,862 wounded, or 2,599 casualties. Losses among the Polish defenders were, predictably, higher, amounting to between six and seven thousand killed and ten thousand wounded.[20]

Bloody as this Soviet war of aggression was, for Stalin this was a small price to pay in exchange for acquiring half of Poland along with colossal war booty. As Molotov boasted in a speech to the Supreme Soviet in October 1939, the Red Army, in Stalin's undeclared war against an undefended country, had captured 900 Polish guns and 1 million artillery shells, 10,000 machine guns, 300,000 rifles, 150 million rounds, and 300 Polish warplanes. Stalin's territorial

haul was more impressive still, with Western Belorussia extended
by 108,000 square kilometers, on which lived 4.8 million people,
and Western Ukraine by 88,000 square kilometers, on which lived
8.4 million. In this way, Stalin expanded his Communist empire
by nearly two hundred thousand square kilometers (seventy-eight
thousand square miles) and acquired 13.2 million new subjects,
including Poles (40 percent), Ukrainians (34 percent), Belorussians
(8.5 percent), Jews (8.45 percent), and some Russians, Germans,
Lithuanians, and Czechs. Stalin's share of occupied Poland was no
mere token slice: it was five thousand square miles larger than the
German share.[21]

Generally speaking, the Russians and Germans respected the
demarcation line. Both sides also shared crucial intelligence on
Polish deployments, and the Soviets broadcast radio signals from
Minsk to help Luftwaffe pilots navigate (and avoid shooting Red
formations). A kind of pidgin occupation slang evolved, with soldiers from each army saluting their counterparts with the curious
(and, from the Polish perspective, grotesque) greeting, "Germanski und Bolsheviki zusammen stark" (Germans and Bolsheviks are
strong together). East of Lwów—as the Poles called the capital
city of Galicia, fought over so bitterly in World War I and in the
Polish-Soviet War of 1920—Soviet and German tanks did briefly
exchange fire on September 19, until Soviet officers reminded the
Germans that, according to the Moscow Pact, Lvov (Lemberg to
the Germans and Lviv to Ukrainians) fell in the Soviet zone. But
there were no significant casualties. The German commander
promptly turned over his Polish war prisoners to Soviet captivity
and withdrew his troops westward in good order.[22]

Nonetheless, there was predictable friction as the armies of Hitler and Stalin divided up the Polish spoils. Many German commanders resented being forced to surrender hard-won gains to a
Red Army that had done little more than move its men forward,
often against light or nonexistent opposition. This was particularly true in Lwów (Lemberg/Lvov/Lviv), where there was a
strong pro-German element, dating to the time when the city had

belonged to Austria-Hungary. Portraits of the late Habsburg emperor Franz Josef were ubiquitous, and 80 percent of the books on sale in the city were in German. The city's Polish commander, Wladyslaw Langner, spoke German. A delegation of local property owners had begged Langner to surrender the city to the Wehrmacht—which he had done, until the Germans were obliged to hand these unfortunate souls over to the mercies of the NKVD. This betrayal, a former rector of the University of Lemberg told a German officer in November 1939, "was bewildering to the local population and it remains so today."[23]

Although Lemberg was ceded, so overwhelming was Hitler's victory that it was impossible for the Germans to cough up all of the territory promised to Stalin without causing disruption in transport and logistics. The rapidity of the Nazi advance meant that the Wehrmacht had overstepped the demarcation line not only in Lemberg, but also in Lublin province and the entire area between the Vistula (Weichsel) and Bug Rivers. On September 27, after the defiant Poles finally ran up the white flag in Warsaw, Ribbentrop flew to Moscow to settle the disposition of Polish territory. Demonstrating the superior leverage Stalin enjoyed, Hitler was still the diplomatic supplicant, even though the Germans had done all the work. Cleverly, Molotov conceded German gains in central Poland (including "the province of Lublin and parts of the province of Warsaw"), pressing a Soviet counterclaim on Lithuania. By agreeing to this, Ribbentrop unwittingly played into Stalin's hands, handing over the rich farmland and industry of partly Germanic Lithuania and concentrating Germany's gains in the most ethnically Polish areas of Poland. The Soviet-occupied zone, by contrast, was less Polish, with Ukrainians, Belorussians, and Jews outnumbering the Polish minority, which made up, at most, 40 to 50 percent of the population. All this reinforced the impression in the West that Hitler was the primary aggressor in Poland and Stalin a mere interested bystander.[24]

In a crowning touch of Soviet diplomacy, the new Soviet-German frontier largely tracked the Curzon Line proposed at

The Soviet-German Division of Poland, 1939

Riga

LATVIA

LITHUANIA

Memel

Kaunas (Kovno)

Wilja

Vilna (Vilnius)

Minsk

Danzig (Gdańsk)

Königsberg

East Prussia

Niemen

"Vilensky Corridor"

Belorussia

Baltic Sea

Jedwabne

Bialystok

Narew

G

Vistula (Weichsel)

Posen (Poznan)

Bzura

Warta

Warsaw

Bug

Pinsk

Pripet

E

Łódź

P O L A N D

R

Breslau

Oder

Line agreed to by the Molotov-Ribbentrop Pact

Nałęczów

Lublin

Peace Boundary of September 28, 1939

M

Czestochowa

Vistula

Lwów (Lemberg/ Lvov/Lviv)

Zhitomir

A

Cracow

A

Tarnopol (Ternopil)

Ukraine

Boryslav

B

Brünn

Drohobych

Galicia

SLOVAKIA

Kolommy

Bratislava

Ruthenia

Vienna

Kuty

Dniestr

HUNGARY

Budapest

Prut

N

O

I

N

U

T

E

I

V

O

S

ROMANIA

0   250 Miles

═══════ 1939 boundary of Poland   ▬ ▬ ▬ ▬ 1939 boundaries   ▲ Oil fields

---------- The Curzon Line (1920) with extensions (A & B) into E. Galicia

ooooooo Line agreed to by the Molotov-Ribbentrop Pact. August 23, 1939

▬▬ ▬▬ Peace boundary established by the German-Soviet Treaty of Friendship, Cooperation and Demarcation, September 28, 1939

Versailles, neatly reversing the verdict of the 1920 Polish-Soviet War (which had allowed Poland to expand its borders further eastward). All Stalin had done, Molotov could and did claim, was restore the old borders of Tsarist Russia—borders once acceptable to the Western powers. David Lloyd George, the former British prime minister who had been in power then, parroted Molotov's line in the *Sunday Express* on September 24, 1939, arguing that Stalin's conquests "did not really amount to a fourth partition of Poland," as he had only seized "Ukraine and White Russia," annexed by Poland in 1920 "against the wishes of the Supreme Allied War Council." (How, Poland's London ambassador Count Edward Raczynski objected, did Lloyd George "reconcile his endorsement of Stalin's dismemberment of Poland with Britain's security guarantee," on which grounds it had gone to war?) By October 1939, Molotov had worked out the talking point that "9/10 of the new Soviet territory" was "former Soviet territory" (that is, it had been Soviet for a few months in winter 1919–1920, in between the Russian Civil War and the Polish-Soviet War).*[25]

Significantly, however, the new Soviet border lines contained two non-Curzon deviations westward, which both Hitler and the Western Allies might have found alarming had they been paying closer attention. At Bialystok and Lvov/Lemberg, Soviet salients now thrust out like fists. The southern salient also contained oil fields in east Galicia at Drohobych and Boryslav, which Molotov had insisted on having over Ribbentrop's strenuous objections. It also provided a strategic glacis for the Red Army and Red Air Force to threaten Romania and its oil fields and refineries, on which Germany, with all of its North Sea ports blockaded by the British fleet since the start of the war, depended for most of its petroleum. On

---

* Later in the war, after Stalin had occupied still more territory, Molotov exaggerated this line further, claiming that "19/20" of Stalin's newly conquered territory was "formerly Soviet." In the case of Finland, the Baltic states, and Romanian Bessarabia, this was a bald-faced lie: although former Tsarist possessions, these areas had never belonged to Soviet Russia.

this, and every other significant point of contention, Stalin got his way.[26]

For now, though, it was all smiles. In the German-Soviet Treaty of Friendship, Cooperation and Demarcation signed in Moscow on September 28, Hitler and Stalin boasted that they had "created a sure foundation for a lasting peace in Eastern Europe" and that they aimed "to put an end to the state of war existing between Germany on the one hand, and England and France on the other" (why those countries had declared war on only one of the states invading Poland was left unsaid). If the Western powers did not yield, they continued with a hint of menace, "the governments of Germany and the U.S.S.R. shall engage in mutual consultations with regard to necessary measures."[27]

Still more ominous was a "secret supplementary protocol" to the treaty. This stated that neither Stalin nor Hitler would "tolerate in their territories" any "Polish agitation which effects the territory of the other party. They will suppress in their territories all beginnings of each agitation and inform each other concerning suitable measures for this purpose." An additional "confidential protocol" laid down principles for a forcible population exchange, with the Soviets allowing "Reich nationals and other persons of German descent" to migrate westward, and the German government agreeing to turn over (or expel) "persons of Ukrainian or White Russian descent residing in the territories under its jurisdiction."[28]

What these secret protocols meant for the unfortunate people of occupied Poland soon became clear. In the German zone, Hitler's SS Einsatzgruppen moved in, arresting and interrogating thousands of Jews and Polish elites, from civil servants to doctors, Catholic priests, and university professors. Although some Ukrainians and Belorussians were allowed to migrate into the USSR, the vast majority of Polish, and especially Jewish, detainees were sent to concentration camps or simply shot, as were nearly fifty thousand victims by year's end.[29]

In the Soviet zone of eastern Poland, Stalin's NKVD wasted no time rounding up "enemies of the proletariat," such as merchants, aristocrats, Catholic priests, and, above all, military officers. Although in theory Polish civilians were deported only if they were found guilty of crimes such as belonging to the wrong social class, in practice basically anyone captured in Poland by the invading Red Army—with the exception of certain Ukrainians, Germans, and Belorussians, separated out by ethnicity—was subject to deportation as a prisoner of war. On the principle of collective guilt, already familiar to Gulag victims, the NKVD made sure, on arresting Polish class enemies, to arrest their entire families too. The first trains of deportees left eastern Poland on September 20, 1939. A hint of the rationale for the deportations came five days later, when Stalin's NKVD chief, Lavrenty Beria, ordered that twenty-five thousand Polish war prisoners be put to work building the Novograd-Volynskii-Rovno-Dubno-Lvov road—an order swiftly approved by the Politburo. An idea of the immense scale of the operation can be gleaned from a Politburo resolution from December 1939, which stipulated that captured Polish slave laborers assigned to work in forestry would be distributed in Siberia on the basis of "100 to 500 families per village."[30]

Conditions facing Stalin's Polish deportees were abysmal. One typical train car, into which thirty-six Polish prisoners had been crammed, took six weeks to reach Moscow, during which time, as one survivor recalled, "bread and water had been given to the prisoners at only a few regular intervals." All but three perished on the journey. Once a week, the survivor continued, "the truck door had been opened just enough to enable the dead to be dropped out. Corpses of children froze in the snow and their mothers, vainly striving to restore them to life, covered them with their own bodies and felt the same deathly chill creep up their own limbs and touch their own hearts."[31]

The Sovietization of occupied Poland also brought with it theft on a massive scale. A German liaison officer reported on October 28, 1939—before the Soviet frontier was "hermetically sealed" and he was forced to leave—that "plunder and forced evacuations went hand in hand." It was not the seizure of valuable items that struck the German officer, but the pilfering of common goods that were rare or unknown under Communism, such as "watches, rings, and cigarettes," "bed linens and household tools," and even "nails, needles, string, [and] paper." In a replay of the Bolshevik Revolution in Russia, the NKVD emptied Polish prisons of genuine criminals, urged them to rob the rich, and then filled the prisons with bourgeois victims stubborn enough to resist their own expropriation. Peasants were urged to kill their landlords, employees their employers. As one witness observed, "Mass murders with axes suddenly became frequent." One horrific incident saw a man "tied to a stake" before "his skin [was] peeled off and his wound salted before [he was] forced to watch the execution of his family."[32]

Piggybacking on the Polish class war cynically encouraged by the NKVD, Soviet planning ministers arrived on the scene to nationalize property—that is, to transfer title of Polish real estate, industrial, and commercial property to the Soviet state. Just as in Russia in 1917, the first priority was the banks, where the money was. In ex-Polish Galicia (now Western Ukraine) alone, *Pravda* reported with Communist pride in March 1940, the Soviet occupiers had laid claim to 414 banks and 1,500 other credit institutions. In each bank, they "opened the vaults and helped themselves to the greater part of the contents deposited there." In the more rural-agricultural area of ex-Polish Western Belorussia, the Soviet occupation brought with it a smaller-scale reenactment of the Ukrainian Holodomor of the early 1930s, as private landholdings were divided up into 605 collective farms, onto which hundreds of thousands of farmers were herded like cattle.[33]

To counter the popular resistance that inevitably greeted such policies, the NKVD established special occupation tribunals. In the upside-down moral world of Stalinism, the Politburo resolution creating them, dated October 3, 1939, authorized occupation judges in Western Ukraine and Western Belorussia to try offending locals for "war crimes"—an interesting legal concept in view of the fact that the USSR had never declared war on the country it was now occupying. The pretext was that these provinces had never justly belonged to Poland in the first place, and so anyone resisting the Soviet occupation authorities was not a foreign subject, nor a war prisoner protected under the Geneva Conventions (which the Soviet Union had never ratified anyway), but a mere "counter-revolutionary." And yet, awkwardly, the resolution hinted at the ghost-like existence of some legal entity known as Poland when it authorized tribunals to try "crimes committed by . . . serving soldiers of the former Polish army."[34]

Despite the show of solidarity between the totalitarian powers, there was already a rough division of loyalties on the ground, reflected in the way targeted populations voted with their feet. By the end of 1939, nearly 350,000 Polish Jews, caught in the German zone, had been expelled or fled east to Soviet-occupied towns such as Lwów (Lemberg/Lvov) and Bialystok, where they were initially welcomed; many discovered the horrors of privation and forced labor in Soviet Gulag camps only later. Ukrainian nationals in Galicia and eastern Poland, in turn, fled west into German arms. Because it was initially conquered by the Germans, Lemberg/Lvov emerged as a key transit point for groups trying to flee the Red Army, such as the Ukrainian People's Republic, a successor government-in-exile to the short-lived Ukrainian Republic of 1918–1920. Although Ukrainian activists who escaped west into the German zone—such as the head of the radical wing of the Organization of Ukrainian Nationalists, Stepan Bandera—were kept under close surveillance, they were not turned over to the Russians either. Many Polish elites in Lemberg/Lvov, too, had welcomed the Germans, hoping for better treatment than they would receive under Stalin. Enough did, at any rate, to justify a horrific crackdown against Ukrainian and Polish nationalists by the NKVD after the Reds arrived. In ironic Communist homage to Nazi racial politics, only those able to demonstrate German ethnicity in the Soviet zone were allowed to migrate westward into the Reich. With black humor, Stalin in October 1939 appointed as his representative on the "Soviet-German commission on the evacuation of Germans from Soviet-occupied Poland" Maxim Litvinov, the

Jewish foreign minister he had sacked five months earlier to extend his olive branch to Hitler.[35]

In these ethnic prisoner swaps, the Soviets generally got the better end of the deal, as with everything else related to the Molotov-Ribbentrop Pact. In exchange for allowing tens of thousands (ultimately about 150,000) of German nationals to enter the Reich, Stalin acquired hundreds of thousands of bodies to fill his labor camps, with some estimates running as high as 1.5 million Polish and Jewish deportees by early 1941, a figure larger than German repatriations by a factor of ten. The number of victims murdered by Soviet authorities in occupied Poland by June 1941—about five hundred thousand—was likewise three or four times higher than the number of those killed by the Nazis. Amazingly—despite his own war of conquest against Poland being, if not as deadly as Hitler's during its military phase, then marked by a geometrically larger number of executions and deportations and far more destruction in economic terms—the Vozhd received not even a slap on the wrist from the Western powers for his crimes. Some of this discrepancy in Western reaction to the German and Soviet invasions owed to Molotov's outwitting of Ribbentrop in his central-Poland-for-Lithuania swap, which created the diplomatic illusion that Germany had conquered "Polish Poland" and the Russians merely a small, ex-Soviet, not-altogether-Polish sliver of it. For neither the first nor the last time in the twentieth century, Germany's diplomats had proved just as inept as its generals had been competent.[36]

Still, we should not let Western statesmen off the hook. British and French leaders chose to swallow Molotov's lies about Stalin reclaiming former Soviet territory not because the lies were clever, but because they wanted to believe them, so as to avoid armed entanglement with the USSR at a time when they were already having trouble figuring out how to defeat Germany alone. As Foreign Minister Halifax explained to the British war cabinet on September 17, 1939, he and the French ambassador, Charles Corbin, had earlier agreed that the "provisions of the Anglo-Polish Agreement would not come into operation as a result of Soviet aggression against

Poland, since the Agreement provided for action to be taken by His Majesty's Government only if Poland suffered aggression from a *European* power." In their grasping for legal straws to avoid entanglement with Stalin, Halifax and Corbin had adopted the view of Slavophile intellectuals that Russia was not really a European country. Realizing how absurd this sounded, Halifax informed the war cabinet that, whatever the text of the agreement may have said, there was an unwritten "understanding between the two governments" of Britain and France "that the European power in question was Germany." "On this interpretation," Halifax concluded in his odd legal briefing, "Great Britain was not bound by treaty to become involved in war with the U.S.S.R. as a result of their invasion of Poland. M. Corbin has indicated that the French Government took the same view." The Allied cause was not one of principled objection to armed aggression as such, but to German aggression specifically. Hitler's invasion of Poland, less cynically camouflaged than Stalin's, was easier to grandstand against.[37]

Halifax was not the only moral relativist in Whitehall. The British war cabinet refused to issue even a mild diplomatic protest at the Soviet invasion of Poland or to withdraw the British ambassador from Moscow. (The French ambassador to the USSR did, at least, submit a formal note of protest.) The furthest the war cabinet would go was to temporarily delay the release of critical strategic exports to the USSR, including copper, tin, and machine tools sent to Russia's Arctic ports of Archangel and Murmansk. In an astonishing act of diplomatic blackmail, Molotov threatened that if Britain did not cough up these supplies, Stalin would intern the crews of all British ships in Archangel and Murmansk; he even prevented Britain's ambassador from communicating with the captains. Stalin need not have worried. He would get his copper and tin from London.[38]

Strengthening the hand of the Stalin appeasers in Whitehall was Chamberlain's addition of Winston Churchill to the war cabinet as first lord of the Admiralty on September 3. For all his principled bellicosity, Churchill was, perhaps because of his strong anti-Hitler stance, a curiously soft touch on Stalin—a neat reversal of the positions underlying Chamberlain's appeasement policy in 1938. Churchill saw the Soviet dictator as a potential ally in the war against Hitler, the current alliance between Berlin and Moscow notwithstanding. On October 1, 1939, in the first of a series of wartime radio addresses on the BBC, Churchill defended the USSR's invasion of eastern Poland "in the interests of its own safety" and pointed out that the forward Soviet position there posed a roadblock to German expansion. This address was welcomed by the Soviet ambassador in London, Ivan Maisky, who called on Churchill at the Admiralty to thank him. Churchill assured Maisky that Britain would also view Soviet expansion into the Baltic region favorably as a counterweight to German influence.[39]

In a meeting of the war cabinet on November 16, 1939, Churchill went still further in endorsing Stalinist aggression. "No doubt it appeared reasonable to the Soviet Union," Churchill argued, "to take advantage of the present situation to regain some of the territory which Russia had lost as a result of the last war, at the beginning of which she had been the ally of France and Great Britain." That Hitler had used the same justification for Germany's territorial claims on Poland either did not occur to Churchill or did not bother him. Nor did it trouble him that, as he predicted, Stalin would shortly apply the same rationale "not only to the Baltic territories, but also to Finland." Far from being opposed to Soviet aggression, Churchill argued that "it was in our [British] interests that the USSR should increase their strength in the Baltic, thereby limiting the risk of German domination of this area." The imperative for British policy in the short term, he argued, was to avoid making the "mistake" of trying to "stiffen the Finns against making concessions to the USSR."[40]

The fate of Poland was only the beginning of a heady period of Communist expansion made possible by the Molotov-Ribbentrop Pact. With a permission slip from Berlin and a green light from London, Stalin could now proceed to Sovietize the Baltic countries and Finland.

7

Gangster Pact, Part II
Finland

WHILE RIBBENTROP, BECAUSE of Hitler's haste, had been flexible on the fine print of the Moscow Pact and the German-Soviet Treaty of Friendship, Cooperation and Demarcation, Molotov and Stalin had been meticulous with their own territorial claims. By insisting on Soviet predominance in Finland and the Baltic states (now including Lithuania too), Stalin could not only recover Russia's old Tsarist borders in the northwest but also acquire naval bases to project Soviet power further into the Baltic Sea, whence came numerous stores vital to Hitler's war effort, from Swedish iron ore and timber to Finnish nickel. Compounding the economic leverage Stalin enjoyed over his partner in Berlin—owing to Hitler's need for Soviet oil, manganese, cotton, and grain, as well as rubber transshipments from Asia—Soviet domination of the Baltic would turn Nazi Germany into a virtual economic vassal of the USSR, with the Wehrmacht's every forward movement dependent on Stalin's goodwill. With his keen grasp of geopolitics, Churchill had hinted at this German vulnerability in the war cabinet, drawing from it the strategically plausible if morally questionable conclusion that Britain should therefore encourage Soviet aggression against Russia's Baltic neighbors.

The one thing Stalin had not reckoned on was that any of these neighbors might object. Certainly he did not expect resistance from the Baltic states. As early as September 24, 1939, Molotov had advised the Estonian foreign minister, Karl Selter, to "yield to the wishes of the Soviet Union in order to avoid something worse."

The next day, Selter was informed what those wishes amounted to: a mutual assistance pact allowing the Soviets to establish military bases on Estonian soil. When Selter pointed out that such a pact was incompatible with the nonaggression treaty Estonia had signed with Germany in June, Molotov replied, "I can assure you that Germany will give her consent. . . . If you wish, I can procure this consent." Selter returned to Tallinn to feel out the German minister, only to discover, to his horror, that Molotov was right about the Germans. After Selter returned to Moscow on September 27, Stalin stepped in to finish him off. Citing a spurious "provocation" having to do with a Polish submarine that had "escaped" from Tallinn harbor and allegedly sunk a Soviet merchant ship, the Vozhd demanded the right to station twenty-five thousand Red Army troops in Estonia, a Soviet Army base in Tallinn, naval bases in Paldiski and on the Estonian islands of Saaremaa and Hiiumaa, and to build "a number of [Soviet] aerodromes" in the country. Were all this not granted, Stalin warned, Estonia would endure "what happened to Poland. Where is Poland now?" With Soviet troops and tanks massing on the Estonian border to make good on Stalin's threat, Selter was forced to sign the treaty at midnight on September 28.[1]

Latvia was next in line. After witnessing the humiliation of his Estonian counterpart, Latvia's foreign minister, Vilhelm Munters, could have had no illusions about what lay in store when he was summoned to the Kremlin on October 2, 1939. Nonetheless, Munters must have been shaken by Molotov's threat that he would not be allowed to leave Moscow until he signed an agreement. The unfortunate foreign minister was further jolted by Stalin's jocular tone when the Vozhd boasted, "I tell you frankly: a division of spheres of interest has already taken place. As far as Germany is concerned, we can occupy you." This Stalin proposed to do with thirty thousand troops. He also demanded four aerodromes on Latvian territory, along with Soviet naval bases in the port cities of Libau (Liepāja), Windau (Ventspils), and Pitrags. He got them.[2]

Lithuania, Stalin's newest prize and the most strategically located—it made up the new borderland between Nazi Germany and the Sovietized Baltic region—would be flattered with the largest occupying force, fifty thousand Red Army troops. When informed of this, Lithuania's foreign minister, Juozas Urbsys, objected that such an occupation would "reduce Lithuania to a vassal state." Stalin replied brutally, "You talk too much." Still, Urbsys, unlike his Estonian and Latvian counterparts, held firm enough to barter Stalin down from his initial demand for a dozen Soviet Army bases on Lithuanian territory to four. Urbsys also secured the transfer of the disputed province of Vilna (Vilnius, or what the Soviets called the "Vilensky Corridor") to Lithuania from what had been eastern Poland, with Soviet recognition fixed for fifteen years. Of course, it may have been that, as Urbsys suspected, Stalin agreed to this only because he planned to incorporate all of Lithuania into the USSR eventually. For the time being, though, it was Lithuania, not the USSR, that incurred the odium of Poland's government-in-exile, which launched protests against the Lithuanian annexation in London.* Once more, Soviet troops massed on the border to press the point. On October 10, Urbsys signed, and Lithuania became Stalin's newest satellite.[3]

Wasting little time, the next day Stalin signed a sweeping order, no. 001223, authorizing the "deportation of anti-Soviet elements from Lithuania, Latvia, and Estonia." Although this was a standing order, valid indefinitely, in practice only a small number of Lithuanians, Latvians, and Estonians were rounded up in October 1939. Stalin's more urgent goal, judging from a series of Politburo resolutions over the coming weeks, was to track down Polish officers who had fled to the Baltic states. In early November, two entire NKVD divisions—12,824 agents—were assigned to blanket the railways and rail stations in districts bordering German

---

*Poland's minister in Lithuania left the country in protest, an act of pique that later saved him from falling into Stalin's hands when the Soviets occupied the country in force.

Poland in a great manhunt for Polish officers and elites who had escaped Stalin's clutches so far. For now, rounding up renegade Poles remained a higher priority for Stalin than punishing the Baltic peoples.[4]

Stalin also had designs on Finland, which had an even greater strategic importance for Russia than the Baltic states. Finland's southern borders crept dangerously close to Leningrad (formerly Petrograd and Saint Petersburg), birthplace of the Bolshevik Revolution of 1917 and Russia's former capital. At one point, the frontier ran only twenty miles from the city outskirts across the flat plains of the Karelian Isthmus, a distance easily covered in hours by infantry, an hour by motorized divisions, or in mere minutes by warplanes. Finland's southern coastline also dominated the Baltic Sea and Gulf of Finland approaches to Leningrad. The Russian Imperial Navy had once placed its headquarters in the Finnish port of Helsinki (then Helsingborg). While Finland, with a tiny population of scarcely 3.5 million—not much larger than Lithuania's 2.9 million—could hardly have threatened the Soviet colossus, it had fought fiercely for independence during the Russian Civil War, conquering Helsinki in April 1918 and dealing the Reds a series of painful blows. The Finnish White Guards—as the Bolsheviks referred to the forces then commanded by the redoubtable Gustav Mannerheim—had also, Stalin remembered, worked with German troops and collaborated with the British Baltic fleet. Had Mannerheim's connections with the Germans not been so strong, the British might have lent his Finnish guards more support in the critical days of fall 1919, when Petrograd nearly fell to the Whites. All this was small consolation to Stalin, who mostly remembered the humiliation of losing Finland and Finnish double-dealing with outside powers. The fear that Finland might once again invite in a power hostile to the USSR, whether Britain or Germany, was never far from Stalin's mind.

It was to counter this threat that Stalin had sent his special envoy Boris Yartsev to Helsinki in April 1938. The scenario Yartsev proposed to the Finns was that a hostile Germany might use

Finland as a springboard to invade Russia, or that Hitler's agents might install a pro-Nazi government in Helsinki that would invade the Soviet Union. Not unnaturally, Yartsev's demand for Soviet basing rights struck Finnish leaders as a violation of Finland's sovereignty. After these proposals were rejected, Stalin's envoy had demanded "positive guarantees" that Finland would not allow in German troops in case of a war between Germany and the USSR. This demand, too, was turned down, along with the new Soviet request, lodged by Stalin's NKVD man in March 1939, for a thirty-year Soviet lease on Suursaari and four smaller islands in the Gulf of Finland.[5]

The Molotov-Ribbentrop Pact altered the strategic equation. Wherever Germany's sympathies might have lain, it had looked the other way as Stalin bullied the tiny Baltic states. This suggested that Hitler might leave Finland in the lurch too, despite the role played by German troops liberating Finland from Communist rule in 1918 and the popularity of the Finnish national cause in Germany. Although Finland's leaders had no knowledge of the secret protocols assigning their country to Stalin's sphere of influence, they may have suspected what lay in store when Molotov summoned a Finnish delegation to the Kremlin on October 12, 1939. Once again Stalin made a personal appearance to heighten the intimidation factor, and he handed the Finns a brutal ultimatum demanding "that the frontier between Russia and Finland in the Karelian Isthmus region be moved westward to a point only 20 miles east of Viipuri, and that all existing fortifications on the Karelian Isthmus be destroyed; that the Finns cede to Russia the islands of Suursaari, Lavansaari, Tytarsaari, and Koivisto in the Gulf of Finland, along with most of the Rybachi peninsula on the Arctic coast." Stalin's ultimatum also insisted on a lease on the peninsula of Hanko, protruding outward from Finland's Baltic coast west of Helsinki, and that Finland permit the Soviets to "establish a base there, manned by 5,000 troops and some support units."[6]

In exchange for these concessions, Stalin offered Soviet land in eastern Karelia; there, the Soviet interior was already guarded by

Lake Ladoga. The territory Stalin was offering comprised 5,500 square kilometers, nearly twice as large as the land he was demanding (about 2,700 square kilometers). And yet the difference in strategic importance was plain. Eastern Karelia was mostly uninhabited marshland and swamps. The western Karelian Isthmus, where Stalin's claims were focused, guarded the approaches to Leningrad and was an invasion highway to Viipuri (Vyborg) and Helsinki. Likewise, a Sovietized Hanko would threaten Helsinki from the other direction. Shifting the frontier from Leningrad toward Helsinki and turning over Hanko and the islands, Stalin made clear, was the price that Finland had to pay to avoid the fate of Poland.[7]

Aggressive and insulting as the Soviet demands on Finland were, Stalin and Molotov fully expected them to be accepted. As the Ukrainian party boss and future general secretary Nikita Khrushchev later recalled, the mood in the Politburo at the time was that "all we had to do was raise our voice a little bit and the Finns would obey. If that didn't work, we could fire one shot and the Finns would put up their hands and surrender." Stalin ruled, after all, a heavily armed empire of more than 170 million that had been in a state of near-constant mobilization since early September and that had recent campaign experience in Poland, even if it was in a haphazard mop-up operation. In armor, the order of battle was almost absurdly lopsided. Well into the second Five-Year Plan of Stalin's armament drive, the Red Army had already deployed twenty-one thousand modern tanks, while the tiny Finnish Army did not possess an anti-tank gun (though it would acquire 37 mm Bofors anti-tank guns from Sweden before the war broke out). Most of these Soviet tanks were light T-26 models, but hundreds of them had been outfitted with a "compressed-air-operated thrower," designed to spray poisonous chemicals, gases, or burning liquids. The Finnish Air Force had maybe a dozen fighter planes, facing a Red Air armada of 15,000, with 10,362 brand-new warplanes built in 1939 alone. Finnish artillery dated to the 1904–1905 Russo-Japanese War. The Finnish Army had a few 1914-era water-cooled heavy machine guns, a few light machine guns (the twenty-three-pound Lahti/Saloranta), and handheld submachine guns or *koonipistolit* (machine pistols, known as the Suomi). But Finnish Army reserves still mostly drilled with wooden rifles dating to the nineteenth century. By contrast, the Red Army was, in November 1939, the largest in the world, the most mechanized, the most heavily armored, and the most lavishly armed, even if surely not—because of Stalin's purges—the best led.[8]

One can imagine, therefore, Stalin's shock when the Finns said no. Surely they were joking? As Stalin pointed out, he was offering more land than he was demanding: "Would any other great power do that?" When the Finns demanded to know why the Russians were insisting on Hanko and Finland's Baltic islands, Stalin replied that "the mouth of the Finnish Gulf must be closed to prevent any nation from entering there." And who, the Finnish envoy asked, "would attack Russia?" Molotov-Ribbentrop Pact or no, Stalin said it might be either "Germany or England." Still hopeful of an easy win, Stalin offered a six-day extension. "We'll sign an agreement on October 20," Molotov proposed, "and the following evening, we'll throw a party for you."[9]

Showing impressive stubbornness, the Finnish delegation returned to Moscow only on October 23, three days after Molotov's deadline. This time, the Finnish government dispatched the higher-ranking Väinö Tanner, shortly to be named foreign minister. Over the preceding week, Finnish diplomats had canvassed opinion among Finland's Scandinavian neighbors and the Western powers. Remarkably, although not a single country had offered to intervene on Finland's behalf if it came to blows with the Soviet colossus, the Finnish answer to Stalin's ultimatum remained a firm no. "Is it your intention to provoke a conflict?" Molotov asked, only for Tanner to reply, "We want no such thing, but you seem to." The only concession Molotov and Stalin made was to reduce the proposed Soviet occupation garrison at Hanko from five thousand to four thousand. For the Finns, this was a nonstarter. Hanko was so close to Helsinki that giving it up would amount to a surrender of sovereignty. With remarkable bravery, the Finns refused Stalin's terms once again.[10]

Stunned by this unexpected resistance, Stalin and Molotov did not, at first, know quite what to do. On the bright side, the timetable for opportunistic Soviet expansion no longer seemed as pressing as it had back in late September and the first days of October 1939, when the Baltic states had been bullied into submission. On October 6, Hitler had given an address to the Reichstag, announcing victory over Poland and offering Britain a peace settlement that would include German acceptance of Polish statehood, though sharply truncated. The Führer had also warned sharply that, if Chamberlain's government refused his terms and continued the war, the conflict would lead to the destruction of the British Empire. Nevertheless, Hitler's Reichstag speech had raised the hopes of many Europeans that peace was in sight and corresponding fears in Moscow that the window of opportunity for Communist expansion might now be closing. In his diary, Neville Chamberlain conceded that Hitler had made a "very attractive series of proposals," and that "his tone had been surprisingly friendly to Great Britain." In public, however, Chamberlain defiantly rejected Hitler's peace feeler on October 12, and declared that "the German government, and the German government alone, stands in the way of peace."[11]

Despite the welcome news that the European war would go on, ensuring more opportunities for Soviet expansion, Stalin would have to tread carefully in Finland, lest he risk awakening the ghost of British anti-Communism from its long slumber. Chamberlain and Halifax may have declined to back Finland—and Churchill might have proposed conceding the entire Baltic region to the Soviet sphere as a counterweight to Germany—but there were still hard-liners in the British Foreign Office. The British ambassador in Finland, Thomas Snow, was a fire-breathing anti-Communist who did his best to remind Whitehall, as the Red Army mobilized on the Finnish frontier, that Stalin was as much of an aggressor as Hitler was. The British ambassador in Moscow, Sir William Seeds, was less firm in his political convictions, but he was no Joseph Davies–

style appeaser either. Seeds was cool enough toward Stalin that he has been blamed by some diplomatic historians for the failure of British-French-Soviet alliance talks in summer 1939 (unfairly, in light of materials now available from the Soviet archives). The first secretary of Britain's Moscow embassy, John Le Rougetel, was a man in Thomas Snow's line. These diplomats were Chamberlain's appointees, and they shared their prime minister's wariness of Stalin. Even Churchill, despite his recent remarks advocating that the Baltic become a Soviet sphere of influence, was known to Stalin as a devoted anti-Communist from Russian Civil War days, when indeed he had been one.[12]

With his highly placed spies in London, Stalin must have known that the mood was becoming agitated by Soviet moves in the Baltic region. On October 31, 1939, the British war cabinet took up the question of "Soviet Aggression Against Finland or Other Scandinavian Countries." The subtext was that Britain's reputation had been compromised by the hypocrisy of its refusal to stand up to Soviet aggression in Poland. "Most neutral states," Britain's Chiefs of Staff concluded, "regard the spread of Bolshevism as worse than Hitlerism, against which we have set our face. There is, therefore, some danger that, if we fail to stand up to Russia, we may lose the sympathy of neutral states to an extent which may have dangerous military implications." It had not escaped Whitehall's notice that US president Roosevelt had written a letter to the president of the USSR, M. I. Kalinin, on October 12, demanding clarification of the Soviet posture on Finland in language alarming enough that Molotov had composed a reply (in Kalinin's name) on October 15, assuring Roosevelt carefully that the talks underway in Moscow had no aim other than "improving mutual relations between the Soviet Union and Finland." Molotov was less diplomatic in his speech to the Supreme Soviet on October 31, when he declared that "it was hard to reconcile America's meddling in these questions with her profession of neutrality."[13]

It was true that intervening against the USSR, if Stalin invaded Finland, would expand the war and strain Britain's stretched military resources. But if Britain took a stand and the Americans joined the Allied cause, the British Chiefs of Staff predicted, "there is no doubt that the open support of the United States would decide the attitude of Japan and probably also that of Italy and Spain. The resulting accretion of our military strength would far outweigh the additional commitments we should undertake in going to war with Russia." Here was a flash of strategic insight. The Finnish cause had the potential to transform the so-far desultory and hypocritical British-French resistance to Hitler alone into a principled war against armed aggression by *both* totalitarian regimes. It therefore could remake the strategic landscape, possibly even turning Fascist Italy, Franco's Spain, and Japan into Western Allies while bringing the huge weight of the United States onto the Allied scales, if not as a full belligerent then perhaps with financial support and arms deliveries. But, rather than pursuing this intriguing line of thought, the war cabinet changed the subject. To avoid assuming "additional military burdens," it was resolved that Britain and France should go to war against Stalin only if the USSR invaded Finland and Sweden too (despite there being no evidence of a Soviet intention to do so). And so, the idea of a grand alliance against the totalitarian dictatorships of Hitler and Stalin was stillborn, for now.[14]

Stalin had dodged a bullet. Even so, the signs from Helsinki were not promising. On November 3, after yet another encounter in the Kremlin had gone sour over the Hanko question, Molotov warned the Finnish delegates that "we civilians can't seem to do any more. Now it seems to be up to the soldiers. Now it is their turn to speak." Still not quite ready to give up, Molotov and Stalin called the Finns in one last time on November 4. Stalin was not willing to give up Hanko, but perhaps the question could be finessed, with the Finns calling the new Soviet base there "a concession, a rental, an exchange, a trade . . . anything they want to." Still the Finns said no.[15]

With diplomacy having broken down, it was indeed time for the soldiers to speak. But the truth was that, in November 1939, neither side was ready to wage war. Having expected the Finns to come around, Stalin had issued no orders to begin invasion preparations until after talks had finally broken down on November 3 and 4. The daunting task of preparing what was now a winter campaign fell to Kirill Meretskov, commander of the Leningrad military district. Meretskov did his best, but time was short and it was not easy to bring units up to combat strength on short notice. The most critical task would be undertaken by the strongly mechanized Seventh and Thirteenth Armies, composed of nine rifle divisions, four tank brigades, and several heavy artillery regiments. These would advance across the Karelian Isthmus to try to break through the Mannerheim Line, a series of reinforced-concrete pillboxes, log-roofed bunkers, and earthworks guarded by Finland's best troops. Meanwhile, the Eighth Army—with five rifle divisions, a light tank brigade, and several more heavy artillery regiments—would advance northwest from Lake Ladoga against a second, slightly less imposing Mannerheim defensive line. Further north, the Ninth Army, spearheaded by the mechanized 163rd Division, would advance westward into central Finland toward Suomussalmi, with the goal of cutting the country in two. Finally, the much smaller Fourteenth Army was to coordinate an attack with the Soviet northern fleet on Petsamo to secure the city's critical nickel supplies and establish an Arctic perimeter against possible British naval encroachment. On paper at least, Meretskov was able to throw over a million (in practice, more like six hundred thousand) troops into this four-pronged invasion of Finland, along with thousands of warplanes offering close infantry support and blitzkrieg-style terror by bombing Finland's cities. The overmatched Gustav Mannerheim, recalled to command the Finnish defense, would have less than 150,000 troops to oppose this armored Soviet invasion, and many of his soldiers were older reservists and teenagers.[16]

Still, however overwhelming the Soviet advantage would be in the order of battle, wars are not won on paper. As Meretskov wrote on the eve of hostilities in late November 1939, "The terrain

The Soviet-Finnish War, 1939–1940

Legend:
- Soviet forces (armies)
- Axis of Soviet attacks
- Finnish forces (corps or larger formation)

Arctic Ocean

NORWAY

Barents Sea

Narvik

Petsamo

Murmansk

14

NORTH FINLAND GROUP

Imandra Oz

Kola Peninsula

SWEDEN

Kandalaksha

Salla

Pya Oz

9

White Sea

Tornia

Top Oz

Kestenga

Pongoma

Archangel

Molotovsk

Oulu (Uleåborg)

Suomussalmi

Kunto Oz

Kem

Sotkamo

Parandovo

FINLAND

Seg Oz

GROUP TALVELA

Povenets

Vaasa

Joensuu

IV Tolvajärvi

SOVIET

Kristinestad

Vartsilä

8

L. Onega

Pori (Björneborg)

SUPREME COMMAND

Karelian Isthmus

UNION

Husikaupunki (Nystad)

Mannerheim

KANNAS

Lake Ladoga

Vidlitsa

Lahti

Viipuri (Vyborg)

Svir

Beloe Oz.

Tarku (Åbo)

Kotka

Taipale

Terijoki (Zelenogorsk)

Helsinki

13

Hanko

Gulf of Finland

Leningrad

Cherepovets

Tallinn

Narva

7

Mannerheim Line

ESTONIA

Lake Peipus

Novgorod

Volkhov

Tartu (Dorpat)

Pskov

Luga

- –·–·– Prewar boundaries
- ░░ Areas occupied by the Soviet Union

0   50   100   150 Miles

of coming operations is split by lakes, rivers, swamps, and is almost entirely covered by forests." It was unsuitable terrain for motorized vehicles, and this would likely neutralize the effectiveness of Meretskov's tanks and heavy armor, if not render them entirely superfluous. "It is criminal to believe," he concluded his report, with a note of realism, "that our task will be easy, or only like a march, as it has been told to me by officers in connection with my inspection."[17]

One of the biggest problems facing Meretskov was how to motivate Red Army grunts—training in the cold, snowy wastes of Karelia—to fight what was plainly just a war of aggression, in winter, no less. This was the job of PURKKA, the Red Army's political department, headed by another of Stalin's hatchet men, the former editor of *Pravda* Lev Mekhlis. Mekhlis had overseen the agitprop side of the Red Army purges in 1937–1938, "descending on the army," Simon Sebag Montefiore writes, "like a galloping horse of the Apocalypse." By November 1939, Mekhlis ruled over a vast propaganda army inside the army, subjecting soldiers to several hours of ideological indoctrination every day by *politruks* (political commissars), during which the men were not training with firearms or practicing combat maneuvers. On November 23, Mekhlis reported to Stalin that "7th Army is not yet politically oriented enough." To remedy the lack of war enthusiasm, Mekhlis promised to "mass-print" a new daily newspaper for Seventh Army. Mekhlis also created an occupation daily called *The Voice of the Finnish People* and hired translators to churn out Finnish editions of *Pravda*. Mekhlis dispatched another trusted Stalin workhorse, the Leningrad party boss and NKVD chieftain Andrei Zhdanov— who had signed hundreds of execution lists during the Great Terror—to indoctrinate the Soviet Ninth Army, which would invade central Finland.[18]

At the center of the Soviet agitprop scheme for the Finnish invasion was a plan—cooked up by Mekhlis, Molotov, and Stalin— to erect a Finnish Communist puppet government just over the border in Terijoki, thirty miles northwest of Leningrad (today's

Russian Zelenogorsk). The idea was that this new "Democratic Government of Finland," headed by the fifty-eight-year-old Finnish politician Otto Kuusinen (a Stalin stooge and resident of Moscow since 1920), would invite in the Red Army in order to, as Molotov's communiqué put it, "establish good relations between our countries and, with united forces, protect the security and inviolability of our nations." Kuusinen's program for communizing Finland was dated, calling for an eight-hour workday—something Finnish workers had enjoyed for their country's entire two-decade existence—along with the breaking up of the great landowner estates from Tsarist times, of which there were now very few left. More to the point, Kuusinen's propaganda leaflets advised Finns not to shoot at the invading Russian army, but instead at "the White Guard government of Tanner and Mannerheim!"[19]

Other than the transparent ruse of Kuusinen's expensively endowed puppet government,* the Soviet invasion of Finland followed the Nazi template from Poland closely. On November 26, 1939, a border incident was arranged. Red Army gunners fired shells at the Mainila border outpost on the Karelian Isthmus, or the Finns fired shells at the Soviet border garrison, as Molotov claimed in his "protest" filed with the Finnish government—believed by no one outside, or indeed inside, the Kremlin. (It was later confirmed by neutral observers that the Finns did not even have artillery at Mainila.) Molotov demanded that the Finns withdraw all of their armed forces twenty-five kilometers behind the border with the USSR, a demand Mannerheim refused. With Stalin's wafer-thin casus belli arranged, the Soviet invasion could proceed. In another homage to Hitler's methods, there was no declaration of war. Just past dawn on November 30, Stalin's undeclared war against Finland began with a furious artillery barrage on all fronts, followed by the scream of warplanes overhead.[20]

---

* Its operations, mostly the printing of propaganda leaflets, were paid for out of a special NKVD fund of 35 million Finnish markka.

The only difference between the bald acts of territorial aggression in Finland and Poland was that the Soviet blitzkrieg was less efficient than the German one. Soviet medium bombers—mostly SB-2s dropping one-thousand-kilogram payloads from cautious heights of three thousand feet or more—were not especially accurate. In Helsinki, Russian bombers failed to knock out a single docking bay, airfield runway, Finnish warplane, or oil tank (although one airport hangar was destroyed). A stray bomb hit the Soviet legation building. According to eyewitnesses, Red fighter pilots strafed Helsinki suburbs as well, "machine-gunning women and children who had fled their houses to the fields." Similar scenes of horror were repeated in Viipuri (Vyborg), as well as in provincial towns such as Lahti, Enso, and Kotka. While early estimates of civilian casualties were inflated, it was later confirmed that, in the first two days of Soviet bombing, at least 87 Finnish civilians were killed and 270 wounded.[21]

Meretskov's landward assault on the Karelian Isthmus fared little better than the air campaign. During the interval between the border incident of November 26 and the Russian onslaught early on November 30, Mannerheim had wisely evacuated most of the civilian population. A series of clever booby traps were set for the invaders, including "pipe mines"—steel tubes crammed with explosives buried in snowdrifts and set off by hidden trip wires. The most effective defense of all was the Molotov cocktail, first used in Spain but ingeniously updated by the Finns, who would fill liquor bottles with a blend of gasoline or kerosene, tar, and potassium chloride. In fits of derring-do, Finnish soldiers on skis would drop these into the turrets of advancing tanks, ram branches or crowbars into the tank treads, or slice holes in the ice to sink them. At least eighty Soviet tanks were destroyed in the initial border clashes on the isthmus, fatally slowing down Meretskov's advance before the Seventh Army even reached the fortifications of the Mannerheim Line. Despite boasts in the Russian high command that the campaign would be over in twelve days (Klim Voroshilov was overheard saying it would take only four), by mid-December

1939 most of the Soviet Seventh and Thirteenth Armies were still blundering along short of the Mannerheim Line. On December 17, the Thirteenth Army actually went into reverse, retreating after bloody losses in a clash at Taipale. By then, even the tiny Finnish Air Force of old Dutch Fokker fighters (162 strong) had joined the rout, knocking down Soviet bombers—one Finnish ace took out six in four minutes—and doing wonders for the morale of the Finns below. Further north, the Soviet Ninth Army was nearly destroyed in a battle near the burned-out village of Suomussalmi on December 9. One Finnish ski sniper, a farmer named Simo Häyhä, personally killed, according to legend, more than five hundred Russians. Soviet losses in December 1939 were positively appalling, as high as 70 percent in many units. Wounded Russians overwhelmed the hospitals of Leningrad. One overworked Soviet surgeon complained in early December that he was dealing with nearly four hundred wounded Red Army soldiers every day.[22]

In a sign of growing alarm in the Soviet high command, Mekhlis suspended even carefully edited press reports from the front on December 5. (In what may not have been a coincidence, the next day the Finnish high command reported the first use of Soviet chemical weapons at the front, an episode mercifully not repeated.) A week later, purplish accounts in *Pravda* about Kuusinen's puppet Terijoki government—allegedly six thousand Finnish proletarians had volunteered to fight in his "Finnish National Army"—were abandoned as too ludicrous for even devoted Communists to believe. Mekhlis and Zhdanov informed Stalin on December 19 that all advancing units had sustained "heavy losses" and that the men would need "rest time"—though all they were willing to grant was two days' leave, barely enough time to get to Leningrad and back. By December 28, the mood on the isthmus was bad enough that commanders of the Thirteenth Army began requesting leave time of "six to eight days" for their exhausted men. By early January 1940, morale was so atrocious, with Russian soldiers deserting in droves, that Mekhlis's PURKKA agitprop commissars abandoned euphemism and began reporting the truth. In the first two weeks of 1940 alone, Stalin received twenty-two summary reports from the NKVD on army discipline problems.[23]

So abysmal was the Red Army's performance that Stalin felt the need to intervene. Voroshilov took Stalin's abuse in one notorious shouting match in the Kremlin, famously toppling a platter of suckling pig before storming out (a gesture that amused the Vozhd enough that Voroshilov survived as a kind of court jester of the Soviet high command). Meretskov, too, came in for withering criticism. "The whole world is watching us," Stalin admonished him on January 7. "The authority of the Red Army is the guarantor of the security of the USSR. If we get stuck in the face of such a weak opponent, that will arouse the anti-Soviet forces of imperialist circles." To assist Meretskov, Stalin appointed Semyon Timoshenko, a loyal and competent career officer who had come up through the ranks, to command a new Northwestern Army Group on December 26, 1939. With this reshuffling of the Finland command, Stalin was tacitly admitting that a real war was underway, not some protection mission launched from Leningrad to assist Kuusinen's puppet government in Terijoki.[24]

The most important change came in January 1940, when Mekhlis and Stalin responded to cascading reports of morale problems by forming disciplinary NKVD battalions, called *kontrolno-zagraditel'nyie otryadyi* (control detachments), inside each Red Army unit, with powers of life and death over the soldiery. The creation of these punitive battalions, made public on January 24 in order to terrorize Red Army soldiers into compliance, ultimately stiffened (or at least stopped the bleeding away of) Soviet fighting morale in Finland.* In the short run, though, the practice had the unfortunate effect of exacerbating the already frightful reputation of Stalin's regime abroad. "At one place," a Swedish volunteer told a British journalist, "the Russian soldiers were being driven forward like

---

* According to German liaison officers, it was Mekhlis who advised Stalin, on January 19, 1940, to make the terror battalions public in order to cut off an epidemic of "self-wounding."

cattle with machine guns behind them, and they were stumbling forward hiding their faces with their arms and the Finns just mowed them down with machine guns. He said that the Finnish machine gunners were half of them in tears at having to do it; but what could you do. You couldn't just let thousands of Russians . . . go into the country." Many Finnish soldiers felt pity for their opponents, prodded into battle by merciless commissars. "The Russians," one Finn noted, "have no nurses, no doctors, and no Red Cross equipment. . . . They pour petroleum over their dead (and probably over a great many wounded too) and burn them." Another Finnish soldier told a British interviewer that

> it is like killing helpless children to fire on these poor Russians who are forced to fight, who are so hungry and in cold clothing. One of the prisoners said when our soldiers gave him food "what a pity I did not take my wife with me so that she could also have some of this lovely food." What shall we do with all our prisoners, they need such a lot of food? Shall we wash them and clothe them and send them to America?[25]

Perhaps the most damning verdict on Soviet morale came from an anecdote, widely repeated around Helsinki, in which "three Russians, taken prisoner, ask for a last meal before they are shot. The Finns say: we're not going to shoot you. So two of the prisoners said, 'Well at least you are going to shoot this one' pointing to the third, 'he's a commissar [i.e., a politruk].' When the Finns said no they said, 'Well for heaven's sake let us shoot him then.'"[26]

By January and February 1940, stories like these were pouring out of Finland, uniting the civilized world in horrified opposition as Stalin, like Hitler, stood exposed as a bald aggressor. Even in Germany, despite a press ban on the Soviet invasion, public opinion was as emphatically pro-Finnish as in Western capitals. In a fitting coda to the now-dead Popular Front, the USSR was expelled from the League of Nations on December 13, 1939, the first nation to suffer this ignominy. As the League's general secretary caustically observed, "Germany, Italy and Japan had at least the decency to resign from the League before committing flagrant aggressions."[27]

Across Europe, young men and women were mobilizing to help the Finns. Swedes and Norwegians arrived first, but they had plenty of company. Soviet spies in Bucharest reported to Stalin that Romania had mobilized on the Soviet borders and that plans were in place for mass arrests of Communists. No less worrying were intelligence reports that Turkey was mobilizing troops on the Caucasian border. In Italy, enthusiasm for the Finns was almost universal. Hitler's ally Mussolini—still neutral in the European conflict—had withdrawn his ambassador in Moscow and was on the verge of declaring war on the USSR, offering the tantalizing prospect of a split in the Fascist coalition. Quietly, Britain and France began to allow Italian volunteers and arms shipments to pass through their territory and ports en route to Helsinki (Nazi Germany had denied permission in obeisance to the Moscow Pact). Generally pro-German Hungary—the people of which were related by kinship and language to the Finns—was also sending weapons and volunteers to Finland. By early February 1940, thousands of tons of war matériel from Hungary and Italy were being transshipped through France to Finland. Britain, despite its need to defend the home islands against the Luftwaffe, agreed to send several dozen fighter planes—Gladiators and long-nosed Blenheims, with promises of Hurricanes to come—to Helsinki. Hundreds of Polish exile pilots were training in England, keen to strike a blow against the Russians in Finland. As Chamberlain told the war cabinet on January 31, 1940, "Events seemed to be leading the Allies towards open hostilities with Russia." The French were even more gung ho, proposing an amphibious landing at Petsamo on January 16.[28]

More dangerous still to Stalin was the sharpening moral stance of the US president. Roosevelt's only domestic political rival of similar stature, former president Herbert Hoover, had gotten under his skin by organizing the high-profile Finnish Relief Fund, which raised nearly $4 million for the plucky Finns after receiving public endorsements from 1,400 American newspapers. His blood up, Roosevelt cast aside his earlier sympathies for Soviet Russia, which had seen him purge the State Department of anti-Communists in 1937. While careful not to alarm Stalin with formal sanctions, in early January 1940 the president encouraged US firms working in the Soviet oil sector to recall skilled American employees from the USSR (though leaving this up to their "conscience and discretion"). All but forcing the president's hand, a resolution was introduced in the House of Representatives to withdraw the US ambassador from Moscow and break off diplomatic relations, and it nearly passed (losing by just 108 to 105).[29]

In a speech to the American Youth Congress on February 10, Roosevelt thundered that the USSR "is run by a dictatorship as absolute as any . . . in the world. It has allied itself with another dictatorship, and it has invaded a neighbor so infinitesimally small that it could do no conceivably possible harm to the Soviet Union, a neighbor which seeks only to live in peace as a democracy." The president declared a "moral embargo" of strategic exports to Moscow, opened a $10 million credit line to Helsinki, and authorized the dispatch of forty-three Brewster Buffalo fighters. Congress soon tripled this figure, committing $30 million to Finland. If the Western Allies and previously pro-Axis Hungary and Italy, along with other resentful Soviet neighbors such as Romania and Turkey—all encouraged by the burgeoning groundswell of support in the United States—ganged up against the USSR, Stalin's harassed and terrorized Red Army would find itself in very serious trouble.[30]

The Vozhd was nothing, though, if not a political survivor. Like a caged animal, he was most dangerous when cornered. As shown in his creation of terror battalions to machine-gun down his own soldiers if they retreated, wavered in attack, or tried to surrender to the enemy, Stalin, when his back was up against the wall, was capable of ruthlessness that would make even Hitler blush.

8

Maximum Danger

Finland, Baku, and the Katyn Massacre

AFTER BEGINNING SO well with the carve up of already-defeated Poland and the helpless Baltic states, Stalin's war had taken a perilous turn in Finland. It was not only in the Karelian Isthmus sector that his armies had failed. North of Lake Ladoga, two entire Soviet rifle divisions were nearly obliterated at the battle of Tolvajärvi in December 1939 by a few lightly armed Finnish battalions. Further north, the story was worse still. In a series of battles near Suomussalmi in late December and early January 1940, which saw Finnish ski troops at their lethal best, the Soviet Forty-Fourth and Sixty-Third Divisions were basically annihilated. After the last Russian resistance was "snuffed out" on January 8, William Trotter writes in *Frozen Hell*, Finnish spotters counted "the stone-stiff bodies of 27,500 Russian soldiers," along with the remains of 43 tanks and 270 trucks. Finnish war booty included forty-eight artillery pieces, three hundred machine guns, and "a motley but welcome assortment of trucks and armored cars." Suomussalmi was a Soviet humiliation.[1]

Only in the far north, on the Arctic front, had Red Army troops performed well, and this was largely because Finnish defenses there were weakest, consisting of only a single company and artillery battery. The Soviet 104th Division, supported by the guns of the Soviet Arctic fleet, conducted a smooth amphibious strike against Petsamo. Although the town was of strategic importance because of the nearby deposits of high-grade nickel and its port on the Barents Sea, its capture by the Russians in early December 1939 did Stalin little immediate good. After the port froze over, it was all the Fourteenth Army could do to hole up and wait for spring, even while Finnish and Lapp (Sámi) ski snipers picked off hundreds of unfortunate Russians guarding the supply road to Murmansk. Meanwhile, the Soviet capture of Petsamo, though a lone bright spot for the Red Army in a depressing winter, alarmed both Stalin's German allies, who relied on Petsamo nickel for panzer production, and the British and French, who feared Soviet encroachment against Norway.[2]

On February 5, 1940, the Anglo-French Supreme War Council met in Paris. With Poland lost and little appetite in the British and French high command for a frontal assault on the Germans' heavily fortified Siegfried Line in the west, the Soviet-Finnish war seemed to offer the best chance for the Allies to strike a blow against Hitler—and Stalin. If Norway allowed in British or French troops, the Allies could cut off Hitler's supplies of iron ore from the Gällivare mines in northern Sweden, along with nickel from Petsamo, the latter now controlled by Hitler's Soviet allies, who were holding on for dear life. The British Admiralty, on Churchill's orders, had begun contingency planning for a Norwegian operation (Catherine) as early as September 1939. But Norway had not given permission. The French favored a more direct approach, landing fifty thousand Allied troops, including a Polish expeditionary force, at Petsamo to strike a dual blow at Stalin and Hitler. But Churchill and the British Admiralty, which would be providing the naval transports and escorts, remained cool to a Barents Sea operation at Petsamo, favoring a Norwegian operation instead.[3]

Significant as Petsamo was, the most vulnerable spot for both dictators lay south at Baku, whence came three-quarters of Soviet petroleum production—oil that was also fueling Hitler's war machine. On January 6, 1940, the British war cabinet discussed bombing the Soviet Caucasus. Many of Britain's area experts—such as Fitzroy Maclean, the colorful ex-diplomat who had explored Soviet

Central Asia while posted to Moscow in the late 1930s*—were hostile to the idea because of the possibility of provoking Russian moves against Iran or Afghanistan. Though noting Maclean's dissent, the war cabinet resolved on January 30, 1940, that "the closeness of Soviet-German cooperation . . . may lead us to send an expedition to Finland in the near future. In the circumstances it is clearly of importance that we should know what prospects we have of taking effective action against the Soviet Union." British air chiefs were instructed to look into an aerial strike on Baku.[4]

By February 1940, loose talk of Allied plans to go to war with the Soviet Union was all over London and Paris, and spreading through the bazaars of the Middle East too. In Ankara, the British military attaché, Sir Hughe Knatchbull-Hugessen, opened "unofficial conversations" with the Turkish foreign minister, Mehmet Şükrü Saraçoğlu, about the "possibility of starting subversive activities in the Soviet Union." On February 13, the British consul in Teheran reported that the Iranian prime minister had sought him out and "threw out hints about staff conversations" about the possibility of striking Russian oil interests in the Caucasus. The Iranian war minister had called in the British military attaché and told him that "the time had come for Iran and Britain to coordinate plans for war against Russia." Iran's position, at least, was thus clear. To cover possible repercussions in South Asia in the case of a British war against Soviet Russia, Knatchbull-Hugessen also sought out the Afghan ambassador to Ankara, Faiz Muhammad Khan. Khan told him that if Stalin's troubles in Finland continued much longer, "Bokhara, Khiva, Samarkand and Ferghana were all disaffected and ripe for trouble: in fact the whole Moslem element in Russia was ready for revolt if Russia's present difficulties continued long."[5]

No doubt much of this was just idle talk. Even so, it is significant that British diplomats opened discussions with Iran and Turkey about air strikes against the Soviet Caucasus, because any such air

---

* Adventures recounted in Maclean's memoir *Eastern Approaches*, still in print today.

strikes—whether carried out from French bases in Syria or British air bases in Iraq—would have to cross Turkish or Iranian airspace. Nor was the Afghan connection irrelevant to the prospect of an Allied agreement with Turkey and Iran. Turkey had signed an alliance agreement in 1937 with Iran, Iraq, and Afghanistan—the Saadabad Pact—that could easily be activated against the USSR in case of war. Such multilateral negotiations may have been tentative and noncommittal, but they were a necessary preliminary to armed action against Stalin.[6]

The idea of Turkey joining a war against the USSR was far from fanciful. Republican Turkey, breaking the traditional Ottoman pattern of enmity, had been friendly with Soviet Russia in the 1920s and 1930s out of shared antipathy to the Western powers dating to the British-French carve up of the Ottoman Empire after World War I. Relations had, however, cooled considerably in recent years. The Molotov-Ribbentrop Pact had alarmed Ankara enough that Turkey began negotiating a mutual assistance pact with Britain and France in September 1939 (concluded on October 19), which Stalin—having hitched the Soviet star to Nazi Germany, the country at war with those powers—interpreted as a hostile act. Stalin summoned Turkey's foreign minister to a rude dressing-down in the Kremlin on October 1, 1939, after making him cool his heels waiting for a week. Was the British-French-Turkish pact, Stalin asked Saraçoğlu, directed against the USSR? Were Turkey's agreements with Romania, Yugoslavia, and Greece dating to 1934—the Balkan Entente—designed to counter German aggression, or Soviet? The Vozhd bluntly reminded Saraçoğlu of the sad fate of Poland (Warsaw had fallen just three days earlier), observed that "Romania, like Poland, has too much territory," and asked whether Turkey's commitments "would require her to go to war against the USSR" if "Romania refused to give us Bessarabia" and Stalin went to war with Bucharest.* Ominously, Stalin reminded

---

*Stalin thus baldly revealed his Moscow Pact–approved designs on Romanian territory to Turkey's foreign minister, possibly because, in Ankara

Saraçoğlu that Britain and France—Turkey's proposed partners—
had chosen "to declare war on Germany and not on Russia," even
though "we had carved up Poland together." But, as Stalin pointed
out, "they might do so at any time, and then we would have to
fight Britain and France." In that case, where would Turkey stand?
Molotov demanded a Turkish pledge that any military obligations undertaken toward Paris and London must "be immediately
voided in case Britain and France attack the USSR." Saraçoğlu assured Molotov that Turkey would comply—and he did, inserting
a "secret opt-out clause" in the final pact with Britain and France in
case those powers went to war with the Soviet Union.[7]

In view of this diplomatic bullying in Moscow, it is unsurprising
that Saraçoğlu responded to the British attaché's overture in Ankara by begging for the chance to settle scores with Stalin. As early
as October 1939, the Turkish foreign minister had mischievously
informed the French military attaché in Ankara that Stalin was terrified of "a British aerial assault from bases in Iraq on the oil installations of the Caucasus." On January 2, 1940, the British Communist
paper the Daily Worker ran a cover story on "Plans Hatching to Extend War to Near East," which claimed to have information from
"reliable sources" that France and Britain were plotting to attack
the Soviet Union with a half million Turkish troops, four hundred
thousand French troops based in Syria, and a token British force,
consisting mostly of air support. While these numbers were fanciful, the Daily Worker story shows that there was serious concern in
Moscow about Stalin's vulnerable Caucasian underbelly.[8]

In mid-February 1940, these plans took on a more serious aspect when Turkey's military attaché in London broached the
subject with the director of British military intelligence. "The Allies," the Turkish attaché proposed, "could cripple Russia and it
was a matter on which our staffs should get together and form a
plan." In view of "indications which the Turks have given lately of

---

and most of the Balkan capitals, they were already being discussed—
even if few statesmen in Western Europe were paying attention.

awakening interest in the future of the Turkish elements in Caucasia," the War Office concluded, it was likely "that the Turkish Military Attaché's remarks . . . were not made without some sort of suggestion from Ankara." Saraçoğlu was the likely source.[9]

Such talks were carried out in secret, but the mere volume of conversation on the subject sparked press leaks. On February 22, 1940, the London *News Chronicle* ran a provocative cover story on the "Siegfried Line in the Caucasus," claiming that "Allied and German engineers" were "racing to complete fortifications on the Russian and Turkish sides of the mountains before the spring." The London *Times* reported that Turkish and Soviet troops had exchanged fire in Caucasian border clashes, and that the Germans, concerned for Hitler's Caucasian oil supplies, had dispatched engineers to Batumi. The *Telegraph* speculated that "Allied reinforcements in the Middle East portended an attempt to capture the Caucasus oil fields." So damaging were these (exaggerated, but basically true in the last case) stories that the Foreign Office lodged complaints with the editors of the *Times* and *Telegraph*.[10]

However dubiously reported, Stalin took rumors of Allied (and Turkish) intervention against vital Soviet oil supplies very seriously. On January 21, 1940, the Vozhd had informed the Politburo that "it is not us, but the Turks, who are ruining themselves. We are quite satisfied that we have freed ourselves from any sort of friendship with Turkey." Even if the French were more enthusiastic about attacking the USSR, Stalin was more terrified of British intervention, in view of both Britain's genuine naval and aerial capacity and his own recollection, however distorted by time and ideology, of the British intervention against the Reds in the Russian Civil War, especially in the Baltic region but also, briefly, in Baku and Azerbaijan in 1918. Stalin and Molotov asked the Soviet ambassador to London, Ivan Maisky, to call Britain's bluff.[11]

On February 24, 1940, Maisky relayed a request from the Soviet government to Britain's undersecretary of state, R. A. "Rab" Butler, that London pass on Stalin's proposed peace terms to Finland. If Britain refused Stalin's request, Maisky told Butler—in a manner

Butler found "both ridiculous and sinister"—"the attitude taken up by H.M.G. in this question might have unforeseen consequences." Maisky admonished Butler with a Russian proverb: Britain "should be content to seize a titmouse when you had the opportunity and not look upwards in the sky for a crane," the idea being that Britain was refusing to "bring our two countries closer together." In view of the fact that the British people had been "deeply stirred by the unprovoked attack of the Soviet Union upon a small and friendly country," Butler replied, what Maisky was actually asking Britain to do—endorse Stalin's territorial demands on Finland—was to "swallow a crane and hope later for a titmouse." Butler concluded that Stalin's motive was "to try to prove that it is we who are and always have been egging on the Finns and trying to sabotage the theater of war."[12]

If this was Stalin's intention, then Butler and his colleagues were doing nothing to dissuade him. In Moscow, Britain's embassy secretary, John Le Rougetel, had made arrangements to have the US embassy take over diplomatic functions in case Britain declared war. In London, the War Office commissioned reports in February 1940 on the Soviet oil industry and its vulnerabilities; on the geography of the Transcaucasus, including the location of oil wells, refineries, and pipelines; on public opinion inside the Soviet Union; and on morale in the Red Army.[13]

The most imaginative British move was the decision by the War Office, in early February 1940, to send two Russian-speaking English officers, Major R. O. A. Gatehouse and Captain C. H. Tamplin, to Finland to visit prisoner-of-war camps and debrief captured Soviet troops. In the end they spoke to 2,075 men. The resulting report provides an astonishing snapshot of Red Army morale during the Finnish war, and of the state of public opinion across a broad cross section of the Soviet population in the first winter of the Second World War. The overwhelming impression was of a common experience of horror. These war prisoners were men who, Gatehouse and Tamplin concluded, "had undergone, in most cases, undescribable hardship and privation, who had been

warned that they would be shot or tortured to death if captured."
They were "still in terror of their own 'command personnel' Politruks. . . . They had been browbeaten, bullied, starved, frozen,
half-killed and mutilated, and some of them still did not believe
they were not going to be shot." Some of the Soviet war prisoners "had been shot and left for dead by their own commanders,
or seen their friends shot; others had 'liquidated their superiors.'"
Most had been shocked by the "humanity and kindness" extended
to them by their captors; they had been told by Mekhlis's politruks
that the Finns would torture and murder them. They found this
gentle behavior so surprising that it had left them "disillusioned
about their home country."[14]

Disillusionment with Communism did not necessarily portend
a political awakening, however. Nearly all of those interviewed
refused to be returned home "as exchanged prisoners of war," as
they were "confident of being instantly shot" and terrified that
"dire retribution would fall on their families." The basic attitude of
a Soviet soldier-citizen toward life, Major Gatehouse and Captain
Tamplin concluded, was that of an "obvious fatalism." "They accept the persecution in civil life and the brutal discipline of military
life, the permanent shortage of food and clothes, and the ordering,
herding and hectoring by the Soviet state as being the dictate of an
unkind fate."[15]

The War Office's rationale for sending Gatehouse and Tamplin
to Finland was to gauge the odds that an internal rebellion might
destabilize Stalin's regime, in case Britain went to war with the
USSR. But those odds did not look good. The ignorance of the
average Red Army soldier was "abysmal," with a "large number
hardly literate," despite the Soviet regime's vaunted literacy campaign of the 1920s. "Twenty years of underfeeding," Gatehouse
and Tamplin observed, had resulted in "a very low standard of
physique and lack of stamina." The two hours of atheist agitprop
Red Army grunts endured from their politruks every day produced apathy. "The Russian marches to war with a revolver at his
back, and prefers the chance of death at the hands of the enemy to

the certainty of death if he refuses," they explained. "Patriotism as such," the authors wrote, "was dead."

The only thing that seemed to inspire enthusiasm among the Soviet peoples was religion, "in which they showed a lively interest." In a negative sense, resentment of Stalin's collectivization drive lingered. The kolkhoz, or collective farm, was, "from end to end of Russia, the most hated institution in the land." For this reason, Ukrainians, who had suffered the most under collectivization and retained something of a national consciousness, seemed the most promising for recruiting agents provocateurs. In sum, Gatehouse and Tamplin concluded, "the overthrow of the [Soviet] government can only be achieved by foreign military intervention."[16]

Whether or not an internal rebellion was in the offing, the British were getting serious about intervening against the Soviet Union. On March 5, 1940, Field Marshal Edmund Ironside, chief of the Imperial General Staff, called in his subordinate officers. Ironside did not think Britain was prepared for war with Russia, but he was under pressure from the war cabinet, where—Churchill aside—sentiment against the Russians was increasingly belligerent.* "The War Cabinet would like to force it on," Ironside informed his staff. They should work on the assumption that "if Russia comes into the war we shall at once begin bombing the Baku oil fields probably some time in April." It was expected that bombing sorties, if carried out twice a week from Iraqi bases by two squadrons of Blenheims, would require five to twelve weeks to knock out the major Soviet oil installations, pipelines, and refineries in Baku and Batumi.[17]

Anti-Soviet war fever was running high in London. Even the skeptical Fitzroy Maclean had begun to come around. Once Baku's petroleum "supplies were cut off," Maclean wrote on March 6,

---

* From his speeches in the Commons, Churchill's reticence about antagonizing Stalin was well known, and resented, in Paris. As *Le Petit Parisien* asked, "No one will think that Mr. Churchill is under any illusions as regards Hitler, but is he sufficiently mistrustful of Moscow?"

"the industrial and agricultural effort of the Soviet Union would be paralysed and there could be no question of any further Soviet help to Germany." Maclean had been floored by a report submitted in February by an American petroleum engineer returning from a stint in Baku, who "said that there were no real defenses against any serious attack. There were no anti-aircraft guns and refineries at Baku would be easily occupied or destroyed even though they were in three totally independent units. Equally Baku-Batoum pipe lines could not be defended against a determined attack." The "best hope of making trouble in the Soviet Union," Maclean concluded, "was in Transcaucasia," so long as Britain and France—the French had sixty thousand troops in Syria under the command of General Maxime Weygand—obtained "the active support of Turkey."[18]

Turkey remained the wild card. Saraçoğlu had expressly promised Stalin that Ankara would not be dragged into a British-French war against the Soviet Union. Turkey still had not authorized British or French warships to transit the straits into the Black Sea, which ruled out the Admiralty's planned naval strike on Batumi. On the other hand, Saraçoğlu was dropping hints that he would welcome an Allied aerial strike against Baku, though while maintaining Turkish deniability. The tricky part was that a British strike on Baku would likely be carried out from RAF bases in northern Iraq over Iranian airspace, which would require connivance from Baghdad and Teheran, whereas a French strike must originate in Syria, requiring the use of Turkish airspace.

For this reason, the French were pressing harder in Ankara than the British. In early March 1940, Saraçoğlu dropped a tantalizing hint to the French ambassador, René Massigli, that Turkey might look the other way if the Allies violated its airspace. Massigli had noted to Saraçoğlu that Allied bombers targeting Soviet oil installations in Transcaucasia "would have to fly over either Persian or Turkish territory, both of whom might be neutral." Saraçoğlu "immediately replied," Massigli told his British counterpart, "So you fear a protest from Iran"—implying, to Massigli, that "there need be no special need to fear a protest from Turkey."* This is certainly how Massigli's report was interpreted in Paris, where Commander in Chief Gamelin, who had previously expressed concerns about diverting troops away from France, was now arguing that "there are other places than the Western front where the war may be fought."[19]

Lending a frisson to these Allied intrigues in Ankara was a Caucasian exile organization known as Prometheus, which also had branches in Istanbul and Paris. As if to roll all of Stalin's nightmares into one great conspiracy, Prometheus—with Ukrainian, Muslim Caucasian, and even Georgian branches—had been subsidized by the Polish government (its first headquarters was in Warsaw) and still maintained contact with the Poles' exile government in London. Fitzroy Maclean, already on Stalin's radar after he had sought to evade his NKVD minders in the late 1930s, was on friendly terms with Prometheus leaders, including Said Shamyl. Shamyl was the grandson of the legendary Imam Shamyl, who had tormented the Russians in a Caucasian holy war lasting from 1832 to 1859 (Imam Shamyl's son had also fought for Turkey in the Russo-Ottoman war of 1877–1878). Said Shamyl sought out General Weygand in Beirut, asking for French arms and logistical support for a new jihad against Stalin. Shamyl also met with Maclean in London to discuss the idea.[20]

Of course, Stalin could not have known every detail of these plots and plans against him. He knew an impressive amount, though, and not just from leaks in British newspapers. Soviet archives have revealed the existence of a double agent, number fifty-nine in the NKVD files, who regularly met with ranking French,

---

*After the Germans captured the French archives and leaked them to the press, this exchange became a notorious centerpiece of the "Massigli affair," implying a violation of Saraçoğlu's neutrality pledge to Stalin. Massigli publicly denied this conversation took place—a denial belied by his boastful account of it delivered to the British ambassador right after it happened.

British, and Polish officers and provided Stalin's NKVD intelligence chief, Beria, with reliable reports on Allied strategic planning. Agent fifty-nine was almost certainly a Georgian Mingrelian former Menshevik named Michael Kedia, well known personally to Beria and Stalin since childhood. Kedia so thoroughly penetrated the Allied military establishment that General Weygand hired him in Beirut as his principal adviser on Caucasian affairs. With the help of agent fifty-nine, Beria was able to provide Stalin access to, as a Russian historian discovered after Soviet archives were opened in 1991, "verbatim texts of high-level documents within the French and British General Staff, as well as internal communications between key French and British officers." Weygand's plans to strike at Baku were so well known in Moscow that Soviet consuls casually discussed them with friendly colleagues (Bulgarian diplomats, for example) as early as February 14, 1940.[21]

Facing an ongoing military debacle in Finland and the possibility of Allied aerial intervention in Transcaucasia—or Allied naval strikes on Soviet-occupied Petsamo—Stalin responded with ruthless vigor. The first task was to shore up Soviet frontline positions in Finland, whatever the human cost. Timoshenko, who had overseen the eastern Polish campaign in September 1939, proved an inspired appointment. Basically giving up on the northern fronts, Timoshenko packed the main front with everything he had, massing nearly six hundred thousand troops on the narrow Karelian Isthmus, 2,800 guns, and new tanks, including heavy KV models that were almost invulnerable to Finnish tactics (Molotov cocktails in particular). Timoshenko's watchword for the assault was the uninspiring but realistic "gnawing through."[22]

This the Russians proceeded to do, and not quickly. Timoshenko's Karelian Isthmus assault, launched on February 1 with an initial artillery barrage of three hundred thousand shells, lasted a month. Taipale, scene of a Russian humiliation in December, was pounded with fifty thousand shells on February 13 alone; somehow the Finns held on. By February 15, the Red Army had broken through the Mannerheim Line, only for the Finns to pull back to an "intermediate line" of fortifications by February 18, where they held out for another two weeks. On February 28, Timoshenko ordered an all-out offensive on the intermediate line, only for Mannerheim to preempt him by pulling back to a *third* defensive line, such that the Red Army succeeded in conquering little but empty trenches. Thus far, the Russians had lost nearly two hundred thousand dead in Finland, and there was no sign the enemy was beaten. The state of Finnish morale was summed up in a radio order on February 21: "If no relief comes, we will fight to the last man." The logic of attrition in this war between numerically mismatched opponents meant that, if it continued on into spring and summer, Mannerheim would run out of warm bodies to man his trenches even if morale did not crack. Timoshenko might not have won the war for Stalin, but he had removed the stain of humiliation.[23]

Salutary though Timoshenko's victories were, they did little to relieve Stalin's mind about the dangers of Allied intervention if the Finnish war lasted into spring. By the end of February 1940, British-French plans for sending an expeditionary force to Finland, composed of six British divisions alongside fifteen thousand French and Polish troops, were nearly complete: the first echelon was scheduled to leave France on March 2 and arrive in Finland by March 12 or 13. Allied planning for Operation Catherine—the amphibious operation in Norway that would be undertaken in early April—was also conducted all through February and March 1940, along with German counterpreparations that were, in their own way, just as alarming to Stalin, because they made a British-French move into Norway or Finland still more likely. Narvik, a northern Norwegian port targeted in both Allied and German plans, was only 360 flying miles from Petsamo and just 400 miles from Murmansk. The last thing Stalin wanted to see was the encroachment of Britain's formidable navy into Arctic waters anywhere near Petsamo and Murmansk—or British, French, or Polish boots on the ground in Scandinavia. We know today that the Allies' Finnish deployment fizzled out, and how the Norwegian campaign turned out, but no one knew this in February and March

1940, when the most likely scenario, in view of Britain's storied naval tradition, was a series of successful British-escorted Allied amphibious landings in Norway to cut Hitler off from Sweden's Gällivare iron mines, and in Finland to seize the nickel of Petsamo, then held by Soviet troops just miles from the critical Soviet naval and supply base at Murmansk.[24]

Meanwhile, bazaar talk about Baku was reaching fever pitch. With his vast intelligence apparatus, it was easy for Stalin to pick up the scent. In early March 1940, the Vozhd instigated queries at the US embassy in Moscow—the neutral Americans being viewed by all sides as the best informed on petroleum logistics—about the potential impact on Soviet oil production of an Allied bombing raid on Baku. Word of Stalin's query got out after American diplomats informed the Turks, who leaked the story to none other than the loose-tongued French ambassador in Ankara. "The Russians," René Massigli told the British ambassador in turn, "are in a great panic about a possible bombardment of Baku from the air and had asked American advice as to what exactly would happen in such an event and how great the damage would be. The Americans had replied that as the whole district was simply saturated with oil there would be a blaze unequalled in the history of the world and probably the damage would take a great many years to repair."[25]

The timing of this pessimistic American report delivered to Stalin, coinciding as it did with the imminent dispatch of an Allied expeditionary force to Finland and the peaking of Allied chatter about Baku, is significant. On March 3, the US ambassador in Moscow who had delivered this report to Stalin, Laurence Steinhardt, warned the British embassy that "Stalin is hypnotized by the bogey of Allied intervention in the Caucasus while he is still entangled in Finland." In this state of nervous anxiety, Stalin made two critical decisions in sequence, the ramifications of which resonate to this day. The first came on March 5, a date that should resonate in the catalog of twentieth-century crimes against humanity. All winter, there had been rumblings about a great Stalinist purge of Polish prisoners, both in sensitive areas near the new German frontier and in Gulag camps in the Soviet rear. On February 10, the NKVD had conducted a new series of raids in frontier districts, yielding thousands more Polish prisoners. By this point, there were hundreds of thousands of Poles scattered around the labor camps of the Gulag, including more than twenty thousand military officers. Whereas laborers for Beria's road-building projects in Western Ukraine were drawn from ordinary Poles or enlisted men, captured officers and Polish government officials were being held further back from the old Polish frontier in the labor camps at Starobel'sk, near Kharkov (11,262 Polish war prisoners); at Ostashkov, near Kalinin (Tver), northeast of Moscow (15,991); in Kozelsk, southeast of Smolensk (2,284); and at more obscure sites like Yuzha, near Vologda. Most of these labor camps for Polish elites were located in forests, far from rail connections, in order to guard against escape or communication with neighboring camps.[26]

One might think that this geographic dispersion and isolation of Polish officers and officials had effectively neutralized any organized Polish resistance movement inside the USSR. This was not, however, to reckon with Stalin's hypersensitive precautionary mindset, nor with his almost preternatural loathing of Poles, dating back to Russian Civil War days. Like Hitler's anti-Semitism, Stalin's hatred of Poles was a perverse compliment, born of a grudging respect for their strength as a people—a people whom he genuinely feared. Stalin once told the Yugoslav Communist Milovan Djilas that "nations which had been ruled by powerful aristocracies, like the Hungarians and the Poles, were strong nations." Stalin's "fear of the Hungarians and Poles," Djilas concluded, "was a revealing back handed recognition of stamina." In view of the increasing numbers of Polish exile soldiers and pilots training in England and France for possible deployment on the western front against Hitler or in either Finland or Transcaucasia against the USSR, Stalin may not have been entirely wrong in his fearful assessment of the Polish threat to the Soviet regime.[27]

On February 28, 1940, the first shoe dropped when Beria commissioned a study of the labor camps at Ostashkov and Kozelsk,

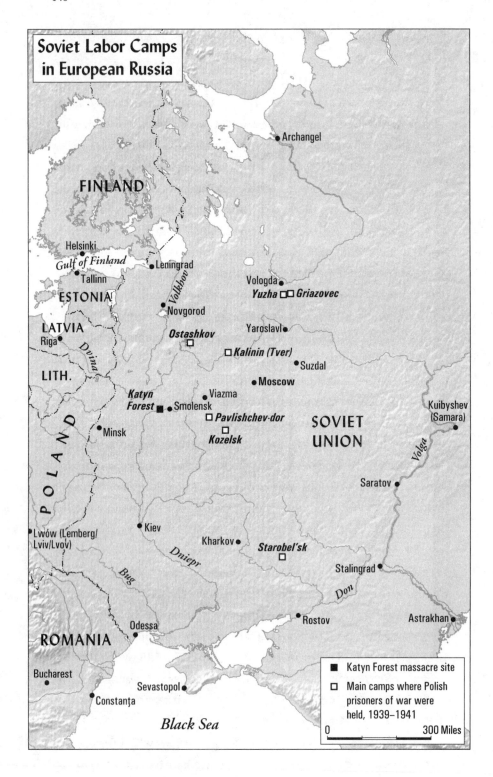

Soviet Labor Camps in European Russia

Archangel

FINLAND

Helsinki

Gulf of Finland
Tallinn
Leningrad

ESTONIA

Novgorod

Vologda
Yuzha □□ *Griazovec*

Volkhov

LATVIA
Riga

Ostashkov
□

Yaroslavl

Dvina

□ *Kalinin (Tver)*

LITH.

Suzdal

Moscow

Viazma

*Katyn
Forest* ■ Smolensk

□ *Pavlishchev-dor*
□
Kozelsk

SOVIET
UNION

Kuibyshev
(Samara)

Minsk

POLAND

Volga

Saratov

Kiev

Lwów (Lemberg/
Lviv/Lvov)

Kharkov
Starobel'sk
□

Dniepr

Stalingrad

Bug

Don

Rostov

Astrakhan

Odessa

ROMANIA

Bucharest

Sevastopol

Constanța

Black Sea

■ Katyn Forest massacre site

□ Main camps where Polish
prisoners of war were
held, 1939–1941

0   300 Miles

demanding to know how many "Polish policemen, gendarmes, and officers" were held in each location. A flurry of sinister NKVD directives followed, targeting categories such as "soldiers and young noncommissioned officers of the former Polish army, located in industrial labor camps"; Polish officers of ranks of captain and above, including naval ones (8,362); and "Polish government officials, regime elements, and merchants" (another 148). In all, Beria counted up 14,736 "former Polish officers, officials, [regime] *pomeshchikov* [freeloaders], policemen, gendarmes, [and] jailers" detained in interior Gulag camps, of whom 97 percent were ethnically Polish. Beria totted up another 18,632 prisoners in occupied Western Belorussia and Western Ukraine, of which 6,348 fell in the categories listed above, augmented by 12,284 prisoners deemed to be "spies, saboteurs, counterrevolutionary elements, and defectors." Because this second lot of "dangerous elements" had been captured in the contested multiethnic border regions, Beria allowed that only 10,685 of these 18,632 were Poles. All of the Polish ex-officers, aristocrats, and bourgeois ex-regime officials, Beria informed Stalin, were "lethal enemies of Soviet power" who were "carrying on, even in prison, with anti-Soviet agitation and counterrevolutionary work." "Every one of these [Poles]," Beria warned, "is just waiting to be liberated in order to be allowed to actively participate in the battle against Soviet power." Making exception for ethnic Germans and others protected by one of the few other regimes still friendly to Moscow, Beria recommended to Stalin, in the top-secret NKVD directive no. 794/B dated March 5, 1940, that 14,700 prisoners from the first interior camp list and another 11,000 prisoners from the second list—in all 25,700 Polish officers and elites—be rearrested and subjected to the "highest measure of punishment—execution."[28]

While, owing to the operation's geographical breadth and complexity, it would take weeks for the NKVD to translate Beria's murderous directive into action, once the order was given there was no going back. Meanwhile, Stalin and Molotov cut the legs off Allied plans for military intervention in Finland or the Caucasus by suing for peace with Helsinki on terms far milder than anyone had expected—especially Mannerheim, who informed his French liaison officer on March 12 that, absent Allied reinforcements, his men were too exhausted to fight on for more than two more weeks. Stalin did gain a bit more than he had demanded before the war. In addition to Petsamo, Hanko, and various Baltic ports, Stalin acquired the entire Karelian Isthmus, where the most bitter fighting had taken place, now styled the "Karelo-Finland SSR." Soviet gains neutralized the Mannerheim Line and provided strategic depth for Leningrad, though, as one Soviet officer lamented, "we have won just about enough ground to bury our dead." But Viipuri (Vyborg) and Helsinki were still Finnish, and there would be no Soviet military occupation. In the biggest climbdown of all, the Soviet-Finnish armistice, signed on March 12, made no mention of the Terijoki puppet government. In view of the exhaustion of Mannerheim's reserves, the armistice terms were the best the Finns could have hoped for. Finland had held out, preserving its independence (although Stalin did insist Finland not be allowed to sign a defensive pact with Sweden and Norway) and preventing the worst.[29]

For all his manifold cruelties, the Vozhd had his moments, and this was one of them. His peace initiative in Finland may have been the most critical decision Stalin made in his entire career. At the time, Soviet diplomatic isolation was complete. Virtually the entire civilized world had united to condemn Stalin's war of aggression, and four major powers—Britain, France, Italy, and Spain—were on the cusp of armed intervention against the USSR, along with five smaller ones in their wake: Hungary, Turkey, Iraq, Iran, and Afghanistan. Even the arch-neutral United States had declared a moral embargo on strategic exports to Stalin and raised money and arms, both privately and in Congress, for the Finnish defense. In view of what we now know about Stalin's superlative spy network, it is not likely a coincidence that Stalin made peace with Finland on March 12, 1940—the very day the first echelon of British-French-Polish troops were scheduled to arrive in Finland, at least in Allied planning documents. Stalin's relations with his German pact partners, too, had gone ice-cold after he rejected an officious German offer to mediate a settlement with Finland in February. With the world against him, Stalin swallowed his pride, signed a disappointing peace treaty, and cut the legs out from under Allied intervention plans. The prospect of a grand alliance against the totalitarian dictators was moribund. Somehow, Stalin had escaped French and British hostility once again, leaving Hitler alone to fight the world's two largest empires. Stalin knew when to fold when holding a weak hand.[30]

Although the Finnish war was over, the wounds to the psyches of Soviet leaders had not healed. The paranoia in Moscow was palpable. In a brutal speech before the Supreme Soviet on March 30, Molotov lashed out at Chamberlain, Daladier, and their Labour-socialist supporters in Britain and France. He decried "the Attlees and Blums," these "lackeys of capitalism," who had unleashed the "barbarity and bestiality of the White Finns." Dripping with sarcasm, Molotov described a series of (mostly imaginary) Finnish atrocities against Soviet prisoners of war as "the fruits of so-called Western civilization." Chamberlain's efforts to "prolong the war in Finland," Molotov thundered, had "given the world a glimpse of the dark side of his 'peace-loving imperialistic soul.'" But Molotov's deepest anger was reserved for Roosevelt and the "so-called peace-loving USA," who, he claimed with some justification, had armed the Finns to fight Communism—even if only with a few dozen Brewster Buffalo fighters and some cash.[31]

Allied intervention or no intervention, the moment of maximum danger had provided Stalin with an excuse to do away with an entire hated class of aristocratic-bourgeois Polish officers and elites, and he was not going to miss it. In the first week of April 1940, thousands of Polish prisoners at the camps on Beria's list were rounded up and told that they were being returned to Poland. At Ostashkov, there was even a band to serenade prisoners as they were sent off to their deaths. Shipped in special trains "in batches of a few hundred at a time," the men had "not the slightest suspicion," one witness recalled, "that they were in the shadow of Lady Death." One by one, the unsuspecting victims were escorted to soundproof cellars and then shot in the back of the head. Although most of the bodies were dumped in the Katyn Forest—about twenty kilometers west of Smolensk, the area gave its name to the crime after corpses were discovered there by the Germans in 1943—the executions were mostly carried out in cities. The bodies were then shipped for disposal in rural pits unlikely to be found. In Kalinin (Tver), the city northwest of Moscow nearest Ostashkov, Stalin's trusted NKVD butcher, Vasily Blokhin, oversaw a team of fifty who shot hundreds of Poles each day. Thousands more Poles were murdered in Kharkov, located between the Polish prisoner camps at Kozelsk and Starobel'sk. In all, 21,892 Polish war prisoners were slaughtered by Stalin's executioners in April 1940, including more than 15,000 army officers, 5,000 policemen, and nearly 2,000 government officials and business leaders. All but one of the victims were men. Roughly 8 percent were Polish Jews. For good measure, Beria had his NKVD squads track down the wives and children of executed Poles—of whom 60,667 were counted—and deport them all to special labor camps in Kazakhstan.[32]

Parallel to the Katyn Massacre, Beria ordered yet another Polish mass deportation. This time, the seventy-eight thousand victims were Polish nationals, absorbed into the USSR in 1939 and 1940, who were so loyal to Poland that they had refused to accept Soviet identity papers and were thus easy to round up for deportation. In one of the myriad terrible injustices of the Molotov-Ribbentrop Pact, the vast majority of these patriotic Poles, about 84 percent, were Jewish refugees who had fled the German occupation zone to escape persecution, only now to disappear into the Soviet Gulag.[33]

Meanwhile, Allied war planning against the USSR continued out of sheer bureaucratic momentum. On the French side, this momentum was buttressed by the fall of Daladier's government on March 21—in large part because of the premier's failure to do anything to save Finland, for which he was pilloried in the French Chamber of Deputies. Neville Chamberlain received similarly

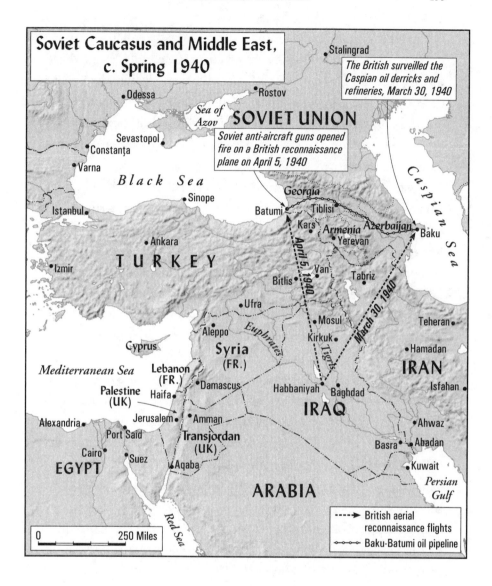

Soviet Caucasus and Middle East, c. Spring 1940

The British surveilled the Caspian oil derricks and refineries, March 30, 1940

Soviet anti-aircraft guns opened fire on a British reconnaissance plane on April 5, 1940

----→ British aerial reconnaissance flights
◇—◇—◇—◇ Baku-Batumi oil pipeline

0 250 Miles

harsh criticism in a grueling seven-hour session in the House of Commons on March 19. Chamberlain, chastened, resolved to plot against Stalin more vigorously.[34]

However illogical in diplomatic terms, the Allies came closest to waging war on the Soviet Union in the weeks *after* the Soviet-Finnish armistice of March 12, 1940. Plans for bombing Soviet oil installations in Baku, later code-named Operation Pike, were hashed out in Paris at the Supreme War Council on March 28. One

of the most notorious documents of the "Massigli affair" dates to
April 1, 1940, when Massigli reported that the Turkish government was willing to consider a "defensive war" against the USSR,
but not an offensive one. Massigli thought the Allies should not
even ask Turkey for formal permission before bombing Baku. If
they had to violate Turkish airspace, the Turks could protest and
deny responsibility.[35]

In late March and early April 1940, just as Beria's NKVD thugs
began rounding up Stalin's Polish Gulag prisoners for shooting,
the British Air Ministry's long-planned surveillance of Soviet oil installations at Baku and Batumi was carried out by a daredevil pilot
named Hugh Macphail, taking off from northern Iraq in a twin-
engine Lockheed 14 Super Electra called the *Cloudy Joe*. To provide
political cover, Macphail and his copilot wore civilian clothing
and carried civilian passports, and RAF markings were removed
from the plane. *Cloudy Joe* penetrated Soviet airspace over Baku at
11:45 a.m. on March 30, 1940, and circled the city for over an hour
while a brave photographer named Alan "Tubby" Dixon dangled
himself through an emergency panel in the plane's floorboard to
snap pictures of Baku's oil installations and the city's—mercifully
still minimal—Soviet air defenses. The photos suggested that, because the wooden oil derricks along the Caspian were placed only
seventy yards apart, incendiary bombs could easily ignite a general
conflagration of the entire petroleum-saturated area. Encouraged
by this intelligence, on April 1 the British Air Ministry ordered four
squadrons of Bristol Blenheim Mk IV bombers, forty-eight in all,
to reinforce Britain's Middle East command in Iraq.[36]

There was no causative connection between Macphail's mission and the Katyn Massacre, but the specter of British armed intervention must have steeled Stalin's nerve as he carried out one
of his greatest crimes. In fact, Soviet anti-aircraft guns in Batumi,
on stricter alert after the failure in Baku, opened fire on Macphail's
Cloudy Joe on April 5, launching three salvos that came successively
closer to the aircraft (although all missed). This was the day Poles
were rounded up at Starobel'sk, the second-largest officer camp

on Beria's target list; the NKVD emptied out the largest of the camps, Ostashkov, the following day.

Macphail's surveillance photographs can still be found in the British archives, providing a glimpse into an alternative world in which the war machines of Stalin and Hitler might have slowly ground to a halt for lack of oil in the weeks after May 15, 1940. On that date, the French Middle Eastern command in Syria had hoped to deliver the hammer blow against the Soviet petroleum industry, if the dithering Chamberlain and the half-hearted British government he headed had ever given the go-ahead. But the Allies missed their chance. Just when it seemed that powerful forces were gathering to put Stalin's murderous tyranny out of commission, Beria's massacres decapitated a potential internal Polish-led resistance movement, while Stalin's astute climbdown in Finland had denied the Allies—along with Italy, Hungary, the United States, and other neutral powers—cause for going to war with him.[37]

It had been a close call for Communism in its existential struggle with the capitalist world, but Stalin's wiles had seen off real and potential threats and restored the Soviet position. With a timely assist from his alliance partner in Berlin, Stalin would soon resume the offensive.

9

Stalin Strikes

The Baltic, Bessarabia, and Bukovina

DIPLOMATIC AND STRATEGIC logic would suggest that the nearer the Allies came to open conflict with the USSR, the closer Stalin would draw to Hitler to stave off encirclement. And yet German leaders had been nearly as disturbed by the Soviet invasion of Finland as the Allies were, though not without a hint of schadenfreude about Russian reverses. At the end of December 1939, when the Soviet position looked bleakest, the German General Staff concluded that the Red Army, although "a gigantic military instrument," would be "no match for an army with modern equipment and superior leadership." The German Admiralty did offer Stalin quiet support, coordinating a few naval operations out of a joint German-Soviet Arctic base at Zapadnaya Litza Bay. The German Foreign Office had also prevented the transit across German territory of any war matériel from Italy, Hungary, or Belgium to Finland, while German diplomats warned Sweden that intervention on Finland's side would be regarded by Hitler as a hostile act. Ribbentrop's trade officials signed a sweeping new commercial agreement with Moscow on February 11, 1940, which expanded trade targets for Russian commodities such as grain, oil, cotton, manganese, iron ore, nickel, chrome, platinum, and other metals in exchange for German deliveries of tank, light bomber, and helicopter prototypes, aeroengines and blueprints, artillery pieces, armored vehicles, gun sights, and a battle cruiser under construction, the *Lützow*, which the Germans promised to tow to Leningrad. Despite these gestures, German diplomats annoyed Stalin by offering to mediate an end to the Finnish war, offers Stalin continually and firmly rejected.[1]

Resenting the slight, after signing his own peace treaty with Finland, Stalin ordered Soviet diplomats and trade officials to retaliate against Hitler's people in ways petty (denying or slow-walking visas for German trade officials), political (refusing to release German nationals captured by the Russians in Poland, of whom 129,000 had been registered to date), and truly consequential (holding up promised shipments to Germany of Caucasian oil and Ukrainian wheat). On April 5, 1940, Ambassador Schulenburg protested these flagrant violations in a meeting with Stalin's trade commissar Anastas Mikoyan, who responded in what Schulenburg considered a "very negative" manner. On April 8, Schulenburg demanded an audience with Molotov, only to be put off with a flimsy excuse. Stalin appeared to be souring on his strategic marriage with Hitler.[2]

Then, suddenly, as if a switch had been thrown, all tensions between Moscow and Berlin vanished. On April 10, Molotov agreed to see Schulenburg and apologized for the recent "suspension of petroleum and grain shipments," a mistake he attributed to the "excessive zeal of subordinate agencies." "Amazed at the change," Schulenburg thought of a likely explanation: Germany's lightning invasions of Denmark and Norway on April 8 and 9, 1940. By landing troops at Kristiansand, Stavanger, Bergen, Trondheim, Narvik, and Oslo, the Germans had beaten Britain to the punch and foiled Allied plans to cut Hitler off from his Scandinavian iron, timber, and nickel supplies, neutralizing the British threat to Soviet interests in the far north. "Our Scandinavian operations," Schulenburg wrote to Ribbentrop on April 11, "must have relieved the Soviet Government enormously." Stalin, Schulenburg noted, was "always extraordinarily well informed" and must therefore have known of the Allied plans to "occupy Norway and Sweden" and was "terrified of them." "The Soviet Government," the ambassador surmised, "saw the English and French appearing on the

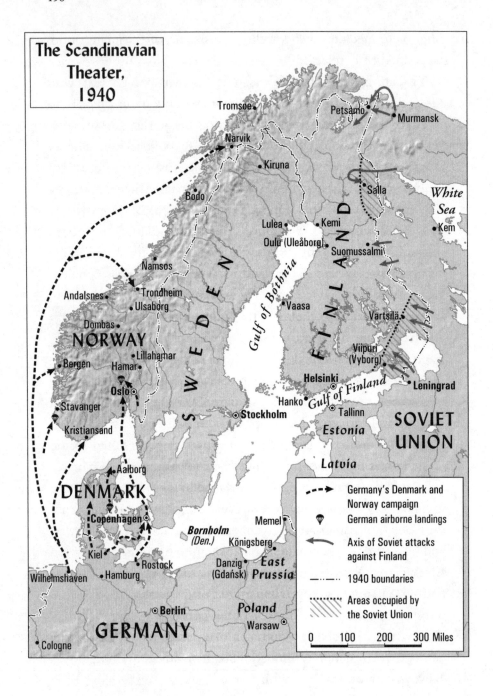

The Scandinavian Theater, 1940

Tromsoe

Narvik

Kiruna

Bodo

Petsamo

Murmansk

Salla

White Sea

Kem

Namsos

Andalsnes

Trondheim

Ulsaborg

Dombas

NORWAY

Bergen

Lillahamar

Hamar

Oslo

Stavanger

Kristiansand

Lulea

Oulu (Uleåborg)

Kemi

Suomussalmi

FINLAND

Vaasa

Vartsilä

Viipuri (Vyborg)

Helsinki

Hanko

Gulf of Finland

Leningrad

Gulf of Bothnia

S W E D E N

Stockholm

Tallinn

Estonia

SOVIET UNION

Latvia

Aalborg

DENMARK

Copenhagen

Bornholm (Den.)

Memel

Kiel

Rostock

Königsberg

Danzig (Gdańsk)

East Prussia

Wilhelmshaven

Hamburg

Berlin

Poland

Warsaw

GERMANY

Cologne

- - - ➤ Germany's Denmark and Norway campaign

⛉ German airborne landings

⟵ Axis of Soviet attacks against Finland

— · — · — 1940 boundaries

⋯⋯⋯ Areas occupied by the Soviet Union

0   100   200   300 Miles

shores of the Baltic Sea, and they saw the Finnish question re-opened. . . . Finally they dreaded the danger of becoming involved in a war with two Great Powers." Apparently, Schulenburg noted with satisfaction, "this fear was relieved by us."[3]

In one month, the strategic landscape had been transformed in Stalin's favor by Allied delay and indecision, Stalin's guile in ending the Finnish war, and the German strike in Norway. Of course, the Allies did not give up hope even after the Germans occupied the capital, Oslo, on April 9 and installed a puppet government led by Vidkun Quisling. Under British naval cover, the Allies expelled the Germans from Narvik, installing a mixed force of French Foreign Legion troops, Scots and Irish guards, and Polish exile forces there, only a few hundred miles from Petsamo. All but joining the Norwegian battle on Hitler's side, Stalin authorized Hitler to use the shared German-Soviet Arctic naval base to resupply the German destroyers that cleared the British flotilla from Narvik in June. Meanwhile, the British and French Communist parties were mobilized in a press campaign denouncing the Allies' "imperialist aggression" in Scandinavia.[4]

As if celebrating Hitler's Norwegian victory as his own, on May 5 Stalin promoted Semyon Timoshenko to marshal of the Soviet Union and named him commissar of defense. With the threat of Allied intervention receding, Stalin gave his new defense commissar license to undertake genuine military reforms. Marshal Timoshenko extended the training period for recruits from forty-five to ninety days, reintroduced old Tsarist ranks such as admiral and general, smartened up uniforms, and restored the spit-and-polish discipline the politicized Red Army had been lacking. A Politburo decree abrogated the clause in the notorious order no. 1 of 1917 forbidding the saluting of officers. Timoshenko also promoted officers, such as Zhukov, who had proved themselves in battle at Khalkin-Gol or in Finland. Stalin used the strategic pause born of the Finnish armistice and the German victory in Norway to give Timoshenko a virtually unlimited credit line for modernizing the Red Army, via ramped-up production of tanks, including the heavy KVs that had proved their worth in the Karelian Isthmus and an equally durable (but faster) state-of-the-art medium tank, the T-34 (of which six hundred were ordered); capital investment in the extension of railways in European Russia; and the construction of new aerodromes and tank parks.[5]

The danger of Allied intervention had not disappeared entirely. On April 9, British air command, having received Macphail's surveillance reports on Baku and Batumi, shared these with General Weygand of France's Middle Eastern command in Syria and began collaborative planning of an Allied strike in Transcaucasia. "We shall shortly be in a position," Colonel Leslie Hollis of the Air Ministry reported to the War Office on April 9, 1940, "to put forward a co-ordinated plan for consideration by the French and British High Commands." To reassure the French that the British had not given up hope, the War Office's joint intelligence subcommittee sent Fitzroy Maclean to France en route to Ankara and Damascus, where he was to meet with General Weygand. Maclean arrived in Paris on May 13, in time to have a front-row seat as the Germans launched their invasion of France and the Low Countries. On May 15, Maclean returned to London, his aborted mission having fallen victim to superior German military initiative. Maclean's post-Paris memorandum, like the Allied intervention plans that lay behind his trip, was memory holed, thus depriving British policymakers of his perceptive observation that Stalin's abiding aim was "to prolong the war between the Allies and Germany in the hope of weakening both sides."[6]

Not until the Germans launched their long-expected western offensive on May 10, 1940, were Stalin's anxieties about Allied intervention against him put to rest. Hitler's offensive promised to satisfy Stalin's principal objective in signing the Moscow Pact. Somehow, France and Britain had so far wiggled out of fighting a real war of attrition between the capitalist Great Powers, leaving Poland to its fate and then sitting on their heels during the long Phony War (which the Germans had mocked as a *Sitzkrieg*). So passive had the Western Allies been, that Russia, despite being neutral in the European war, had done more fighting than they had so far, in Finland. This had not been Stalin's plan. But now British and French soldiers, too, would fight, bleed, and die. Finally, Communists could enjoy watching "two groups of capitalist countries . . . having a good hard fight and weakening each other," as Stalin had boasted to Comintern's general secretary Dimitrov in September 1939.[7]

It did not turn out quite the way Stalin had hoped, however. In a series of brilliant coups, German parachute troops seized bridges and fortresses all over Belgium and Holland, while the panzer divisions of generals Paul Ludwig Ewald von Kleist and Heinz Guderian smashed through the Ardennes Forest, outflanked France's defensive Maginot Line, isolated the main Allied forces to the north, and raced toward the Channel. By May 15, when Maclean returned from Paris, the Netherlands had already surrendered, the Allied high command was in a panic, and Premier Paul Reynaud had telephoned London to announce (prematurely, if understandably) that France had been "defeated." In five days, Hitler's audacious offensive had transformed the strategic landscape beyond anyone's imagining.

Initially, Stalin and Molotov had been pleased when they learned of the German offensive. When Schulenburg shared the news, Molotov could scarcely conceal his "delight," the ambassador reported to Berlin on May 10. Stalin, Molotov told Schulenburg, "fully understood" Hitler's need to protect Germany from the predations of British-French imperialism and "has no doubt that we will be successful." The rapidity of the German victories was alarming, however. Stalin and Molotov would have preferred a slow, grinding, bloody battle of attrition—a German victory, yes, but one that weakened Hitler almost as much as his enemies. According to Khrushchev's later recollection, after learning the extent of the Allied debacle later in May, Stalin "cursed the French and he cursed the British, asking how they could have let Hitler smash them like that."[8]

Nonetheless, the news was not all bad from the Soviet perspective. In a flash, the Allied threat to Stalin's southern flank, via British air command in Iraq and Weygand's French Middle Eastern Army in Syria, was erased—literally, in that Weygand was recalled to Paris on May 20 to take over the wavering French high command. Whether or not the British expeditionary force, fighting a rearguard battle while retreating to the English Channel at Dunkirk, survived to fight another day, the British had been thrown squarely on the defensive. Simultaneous with the retreat in France and the Low Countries, the Allied position at Narvik was abandoned, with the last troops (along with the Norwegian ex-government and royal family) evacuated between June 2 and 7. The Germans were now supreme in Scandinavia. Once France fell as expected, London would face the prospect of German air raids and the threat of an amphibious invasion. The idea of a British offensive in the Soviet Arctic, or against Baku, was now fantastic.

Meanwhile, the political shake-up in London following the debacles in Norway and France, which brought the sixty-five-year-old Winston Churchill to power in Downing Street, was also tailor-made for Stalin's purposes. With a well-earned reputation for being tougher on Hitler than his predecessor had been, Churchill was also correspondingly softer on Stalin. That Churchill viewed Finland and the Baltic region as a Soviet sphere of influence was well known in Paris, if not fully trusted in Moscow, where he was still remembered as an arch anti-Communist from the Russian Civil War days. High hopes were expressed in the British *Daily Worker* and pro-Soviet front organizations in London, such as the Russia Today Society, that Churchill would purge the cabinet of Stalin-phobes like Chamberlain and Halifax and put an end to "the previous government's policy of hostility towards the U.S.S.R." Although his political position was not strong enough to get rid of Chamberlain and Halifax, Churchill did bring in the Labour Party leader, Clement Attlee, and appoint, on Attlee's recommendation, a Soviet-sympathizing Labour MP, Stafford Cripps, as ambassador to Moscow. It was a clear olive branch to Stalin: Cripps had also been recommended to Churchill by Maisky, the Soviet ambassador in London. The days of Sir William Seeds and John Le

Rougetel rooting for the Finns to rout the Russians were over. When Stalin received him on July 1, Cripps promised to forward any confidential message the Vozhd wished to get through to Churchill. Although Stalin remained wary, Churchill was clearly a huge improvement over Chamberlain. The Vozhd could not have asked for a better advocate in Whitehall.[9]

A further coup for Soviet interests came on June 10, 1940, when Mussolini's Italy, piggybacking on Germany's victories, opportunistically declared war on Britain and France. Italy's woeful military performance in southeastern France left much to be desired. Nonetheless, the transformation of the diplomatic firmament was revolutionary. Just three months before, Stalin had faced the prospect of a British-French-Italian intervention against him in Finland. Now, France was spent, and Italian intervention against the Allies would keep the British busy in the Mediterranean for the foreseeable future, fending off threats to Egypt and the Suez Canal. With the relatively sympathetic Churchill in power in London and Soviet-sympathizing Cripps in Moscow, mighty Britain had almost been turned from Soviet adversary to ally.

For these and other reasons, Soviet officials were wholly supportive, in public at least, of the German invasion of France and the Low Countries. The Comintern line laid down in Moscow even instructed French men and women—via both print propaganda and the soon-notorious radio broadcasts of French Communist Party (PCF) leader Maurice Thorez—not to resist the Germans, however absurd this sounded to more patriotic party members (many hundreds of whom, including twenty-one of the PCF's seventy-three parliamentary deputies, tore up their party cards in disgust). In retaliation for the party's support of the invading enemy, 3,000 French Communists were arrested, and another 2,500 party members were deprived of their posts in city and town governments. Despite the crackdown, French Communists sabotaged French munitions factories and passed out propaganda leaflets to French soldiers with defeatist slogans like "Down with the imperialist war." Thorez later crowed, in a radio broadcast from Moscow on

June 17, that "French imperialism has just suffered its greatest defeat in history."[10]

The importance of Soviet economic support for Hitler's war of conquest should not be discounted. Although it is difficult to calculate what exact percentage of the petrol used by German panzers in their thrust to the English Channel came from Russian sources, figures of Soviet energy and food exports to Germany are now available. In May and June 1940, roughly the period of the invasion of France and the Low Countries, the USSR supplied the Reich with 163,000 tons of petroleum and 243,000 tons of Ukrainian wheat. During the crucial days of late May and early June 1940, when the Wehrmacht chased down and trapped the British expeditionary force at Dunkirk, Soviet oil deliveries ramped up to nearly four thousand tons per day in order to meet galloping German demand. In a literal sense, Stalin fueled Hitler's conquest of Western Europe.[11]

The only downside of the German victories in the West, from Stalin's perspective, was that they happened far too fast. Just as Mussolini needed, like a jackal, to tear into France's corpse while it was still warm, Stalin would have to stake his own claims while the Battle of France provided a media smokescreen. He would also have to move before France's capitulation allowed Hitler to move troops back east, where they might contest Soviet territorial claims in the Baltic states or Romania. As early as May 16, an article in Izvestiya claimed ominously that the crushing German victories in the Low Countries "proved that the neutrality of the small states, which do not have power to support [them], is a mere fantasy." On May 25, Molotov called in the Lithuanian ambassador, alleged that Red Army soldiers had been abducted in Lithuania, and warned that if Lithuania did not halt such "provocations," Stalin would "take other measures." On June 7, the Lithuanian prime minister, Anastas Merkys, was summoned to the Kremlin for a vicious tirade by Molotov, which suggested, to Merkys, that a Soviet invasion was imminent.[12]

Still, if Stalin struck too soon, he might awaken opposition in London, as he had done by invading Finland. The enigmatic Churchill, inspired by the successful evacuation of nearly 340,000 Allied troops from Dunkirk, gave his "we shall never surrender" speech to the Commons on June 4, 1940, suggesting that his cabinet, unlike that of the ever-hesitant Chamberlain, would not look kindly on dictatorial aggression (though Churchill was speaking of surrendering to Hitler, not Stalin). If Stalin moved too slowly, however, he might encounter opposition of a different kind from a triumphant Hitler, reluctant to cede him yet another Soviet conquest won by German arms.

When the French capital fell on June 14, Stalin decided that he could wait no longer. With the world mesmerized by the drama in Paris, Molotov wired ultimatums to Tallinn, Riga, and Vilna (Vilnius), accusing all three governments of making "war preparations" against the USSR. Just before midnight, Lithuania's foreign minister, Juozas Urbsys, was summoned to the Kremlin. "Pora prekratit' shutit'" (It's time to stop joking around), Molotov admonished the Lithuanian. Gamely, Urbsys asked, "With how many troops do you propose to occupy us?" "Three or four corps," Molotov replied. Meaning how many divisions? the foreign minister asked. "Nine to twelve," came the reply. This was enough for Lithuania's president, Antanas Smetona, who fled to Germany. The next day, three hundred thousand Soviet troops entered Lithuania, to occupy a country of two million people. By midnight on June 15, the Soviet Baltic fleet had enveloped the entire Baltic coastline between Lithuania and Latvia, sealing off the ports in case anyone tried to flee the coming invasion.[13]

At 2 p.m. on June 16, Molotov summoned the Latvian ambassador for similar abuse. Latvia was denounced as the ringleader of a Baltic Entente that had proved its hostility to the Soviet Union. Asked again to specify how many corps Stalin proposed to invade Latvia with, Molotov answered, with ennui, "Probably two." They would arrive, he added, "presently." Next, it was the turn of the

Estonian ambassador, who arrived in the Kremlin at 2:30 p.m., just as his shell-shocked Latvian colleague was leaving. When the Estonian ambassador protested that his country, unlike Lithuania, had not been accused of provocations against Soviet citizens, Molotov retorted that the Estonian government "maintained a hostile attitude." Estonia had been singled out for abuse in *Pravda* because of the mentality of its "intelligentsia," which "preaches a loyal attitude towards England and expresses its hatred of Germany and everything German." In retaliation for the anti-German Anglophilia of Estonia's elite citizens, Molotov informed the bewildered ambassador, Stalin proposed to occupy "the main cities of Estonia, including the capital, Tallinn."[14]

Over the next forty-eight hours, the Red Army poured into Latvia and Estonia as Molotov had promised, crushing everything and everyone that stood in its path. Latvian president Karlis Ulmanis vowed in one last radio broadcast to his people, "I will stay in my place, you stay in yours." He bravely stood duty in the presidential palace until he was seized by the NKVD and deported to a labor camp. The commander of the Latvian border guards, General Ludvigs Bolsteins, killed himself rather than submit to this "alien power" that "wants to force us to tear down ourselves," as he wrote in a plaintive suicide note. The Estonian president, Konstantin Päts, was carted off into the Gulag, vanishing without a trace (he died in Soviet captivity in 1956). Only the Lithuanian president, Smetona, survived, fleeing into the German Reich by "turning up his trousers" and "wading across a brook," as the Soviet press cruelly taunted.[15]

In a bizarre coda to Stalin's brutal conquest of three tiny countries that had not even resisted, Molotov called in the German ambassador, Schulenburg, on the evening of June 17—the day the Red Army bludgeoned its way into Riga and Tallinn—and expressed "the warmest congratulations of the Soviet Government on the splendid successes of the German Armed Forces," who had just completed their rout of France. The timing was no coincidence. With the new French government of Marshal Philippe

Baltic States, c. 1940

Pori (Björneborg)

FINLAND

Gulf of Bothnia

Finnish territory occupied by the Soviet Union

Lake Ladoga

Viipuri (Vyborg)

Tarku (Åbo)

Helsinki

Leningrad

Hanko

Gulf of Finland

Stockholm

Tallinn

Narva

Paldiski

Lake Peipus

Novgorod

Hiiumaa

Estonia

Lake Ilmen

Saaremaa

Soviet Union occupies Estonia, Latvia, and Lithuania in June 1940

Pskov

Velikaya

Volkhov

Lovat

Gotland

Pitrags

Baltic Sea

Windau (Ventspils)

Latvia

Velikie Luki

Jalgava (Mitau)

Riga

Dvina

Liepája (Libau)

Siauliai (Shavli)

Memel

Lithuania

Vitebsk

Wilja

Smolensk

Königsberg

Kaunas (Kovno)

Vilna (Vilnius)

SOVIET

Danzig (Gdańsk)

East Prussia

"Vilensky Corridor"

Minsk

Dnieper

Niemen

UNION

GERMANY

Vistula

Narew

Bug

Russo-German Border September 1939

Belorussia

Soviet-occupied Poland

Gomel

Warsaw

Pinsk

Łódź

Poland

Pripet

Ukraine

Chernigov

GENERAL

Lublin

GOVERNMENT

Cracow

Lwów (Lemberg Lviv/Lvov)

‑‑‑‑‑‑‑‑‑	Boundaries of Poland in 1939
▬▬▬	Boundaries in 1939
▬ ▬ ▬	Russo-German border after September 1939
‑·‑·‑	Boundaries in 1940
⚓	Soviet Baltic naval bases

0   50   100   150 Miles

Pétain having sued Hitler for an armistice that morning, Molotov hoped that the Germans would be in a generous mood as he shared the alarming news of Stalin's invasion. Stalin, Molotov explained, had been forced to occupy the three Baltic countries in order to "prevent them from becoming a launching pad for Anglo-French intrigues" (this on the day that France surrendered to Germany). By neutralizing the threat posed to both Berlin and Moscow by the pro-Allied machinations in Tallinn, Riga, and Vilna (Vilnius), Molotov concluded, Stalin's move would also prevent the Baltic Entente from "quarreling with Germany."[16]

The German ambassador listened impassively to this imaginative hogwash. Delicately, he asked Molotov if it was acceptable for the Germans to hold on to Lithuania's exiled president, who had just requested asylum in Berlin. With totalitarian chivalry, Molotov replied it was "the position of the Soviet government" that the Germans could "do with him as they wished." Interpreting Schulenburg's calm reaction to Molotov's justification of the Baltic invasions as a green light from Berlin, Stalin had Marshal Timoshenko, now defense commissar, write up orders on June 21 instructing commanders of the Red Army's new Baltic military district to "disarm the population" and to "shoot anyone who resists." Stalin then assigned three trusted NKVD chiefs who had "blooded" themselves in the Great Terror to rule these ex-countries. The loyal Stalin stooge Andrei Zhdanov arrived in Estonia. Latvia would be purged by A. Y. Vishinsky, the chief public prosecutor of the Moscow show trials. Lithuania, the largest and most strategically significant of the countries, would be disciplined into submission by Beria's Georgian comrade Vladimir Dekanozov.[17]

What followed was drearily predictable for anyone familiar with Soviet history. The presidents of Estonia and Latvia were the first of tens of thousands of unfortunate Baltic nationals deported into Stalin's network of slave labor camps that summer by the NKVD for the crime of belonging to the wrong social category, opposing Communism, or being perceived as hostile to the occupiers. A typical NKVD directive of July 7, 1940, targeted Lithuanians: "Preparatory to liquidation. Active abolition of the leading influence of parties hostile to the State: Nationalists, Voldemarists, Populists, Christian Democrats, Young Lithuanians, Trotskyists, Social Democrats, National Guardsmen and others." "Night after night," one Latvian survivor recalled, "the dreaded black vans of the secret police raced through the streets. . . . Hundreds upon hundreds of men, women and children were spirited away into the vastnesses of the Soviet Union."[18]

Since 1917, "expropriation" had followed the imposition of Soviet Communism on a region as predictably as night follows day, and the Baltic states were no exception. As always, the banks were the first target, with the state reserves of Estonia, Latvia, and Lithuania nationalized as soon as the Red Army secured the capitals. With extraordinary arrogance, Molotov laid claim to the foreign holdings of the three occupied countries as well, issuing a protest to the US ambassador that the Americans were not turning over to Stalin the Baltic gold reserves held at the Federal Reserve Bank in New York. Despite the risk of provoking Hitler, German property holdings in the Baltic region, too, were seized, as much as 330 million Reichsmarks' worth, as German military intelligence reported to Berlin. Meanwhile, an "acute shortage" of consumer goods was soon reported in the Baltic region, a mystery explained by the flooding of party stores in Moscow with what one shopper noticed were "unfamiliar foreign items; suits, dresses, shoes, cigarettes, chocolate, crackers, cheese, canned goods, a hundred other items obviously of non-Soviet origin." All this "was the overflow of goods from the frontier areas taken over by the Red Army," as Soviet officials admitted, boasting to their comrades about "the good things to which the Soviet liberators helped themselves in the conquered areas."[19]

Horrible as all this was, expropriated Baltic deportees were, in a way, the lucky ones. Near Kaunas (Kovno), Lithuania, Dekanozov's NKVD shot 450 arrestees and dumped the bodies in a mass grave. Other Baltic elites were tortured for information. According to surviving eyewitnesses, victims were "bound to trees with iron hoops before being burned alive." Others had "their testicles kicked to pulp, were seated on red-hot stoves, had needles rammed under their fingernails," "had their jaws ripped down to their necks," or "had their eyes gouged and their tongues cut out."[20]

Now that the Baltic states had been occupied, purged, and expropriated, Romania was next in line. For months, the Soviet press had dropped unsubtle hints about Stalin's hostile intentions toward Romania, with party organs criticizing Romania's absorption of "Russian" Bessarabia in the post–World War I treaties. (Why the Romanian claim on Bessarabia, inhabited by virtually no Russians, was "imperialist" but the Soviet one was not was not explained.) In a particularly sinister touch, on April 24, 1940—as Beria's executioners were mass murdering thousands of Polish prisoners— Molotov warned the Romanian ambassador, Georghe Davidescu, that "Romania's sheltering of Polish refugees had made an unfortunate impression on the Soviet Union."[21]

The alleged harboring of Poles in Bucharest was, of course, a red herring justifying Stalin's plainly imperialist hunger for Romanian territory.* Soviet designs on formerly Russian Bessarabia were no secret, even if they had not been acknowledged in the public sections of the Moscow Pact. For years, Soviet bureaucrats had been beavering away, preparing mouthwatering reports on the dimensions (44,422 square kilometers), population (3 million proletarians!), and economic resources of Bessarabia, even as Bolshevik propagandists hammered home the theme that Bessarabia had been "stolen" from Russia by "White Guardists in league with the Entente." More ambitiously, and without telling Ribbentrop, Molotov had authorized Soviet diplomats to make the case for the Soviet absorption of Romanian Bukovina as well, despite this territory never having belonged to Russia. Here, the argument would

---

*The Germans had lodged similar complaints about the "sheltering of Poles" in Bucharest, in another sign of the curious mirroring of the Molotov-Ribbentrop Pact. Still, unlike Molotov and Stalin, Hitler had not threatened to invade the country in retaliation.

depend on ethnography, the idea being that Bukovina, despite having no Russians to speak of, had a slight plurality of Ukrainians (346,178, or 38 percent), who were allegedly oppressed by a minority of Romanians (309,733, or 34 percent).[22]

Moving more gingerly now that the drama in France was over, Molotov summoned Schulenburg to the Kremlin on June 23 to sound out the Germans about Soviet claims on Bessarabia. If the Romanians did not agree to cede this former Tsarist province to Stalin, Molotov warned the ambassador, "then the Soviet Union will resolve the question by force of arms." Probing the ambassador for weakness, Molotov pressed Soviet claims on Bukovina too, because it was "populated by Ukrainians." Why this justified a Soviet claim on Bukovina—a region never before ruled by Russia and nowhere mentioned in the Moscow Pact or in any subsequent agreements—Molotov did not explain, beyond saying that he thought it would be "reasonable" if the Germans said yes. Alas, the ambassador did not agree. Any Soviet move into Romania, Schulenburg warned Molotov politely but firmly, would excite the jealous attention of other neighbors like Hungary and Bulgaria. If not properly adjudicated in advance, a preemptive Soviet move "might throw Romania into chaos," which would threaten German access to "Romanian products, especially oil." He could agree to nothing regarding the disposition of Romanian territory, Schulenburg said, before consulting with Ribbentrop—that is, with Hitler.[23]

Though coming up empty, Molotov had confirmed for Stalin how vulnerable Germany's strategic position remained, in spite of its thumping victories in Western Europe. Other than Baku and the Caucasus, which Stalin controlled, Romanian Ploeşti, just north of Bucharest, was Hitler's only source for the petrol the Luftwaffe and the Wehrmacht's panzers and motorized divisions ran on. The only other option was synthetic fuel extracted from coal, a hugely expensive process that could supply, at best, only a small fraction of the Reich's needs. Romanian oil—which accounted for more than 50 percent of German petroleum imports, totaling 1.865 million tons in 1940 (against a Soviet share of 32.5 percent)—was Hitler's Achilles' heel, and Stalin was not about to pass up an opportunity to exploit this vulnerability if he could.[24]

In a sign of Stalin's ever-growing appetite for territory, Molotov summoned the Italian ambassador, Signor Augusto Rosso, to the Kremlin later that same day to broach a possible Italian-Soviet carve up of Turkey. So long as Italy supported Soviet claims at the Ottoman Straits, Soviet "primacy in the Black Sea," and, most importantly, the "enlargement of the Soviet Union in the area south and southeast of Batumi [i.e., eastern Turkey]," Molotov promised Ambassador Rosso that Stalin would not oppose Italian claims "in other regions of Turkey," whatever they might turn out to be.* Although intrigued by the prospect of a Turkish partition agreement, updated from the notorious Sykes-Picot Agreement of 1916 for the Fascist-Communist age, Rosso could only reply that, like his German counterpart Schulenburg, he needed to consult higher authorities.[25]

On June 25, 1940, after Schulenburg had consulted Ribbentrop and Hitler, Molotov and the German ambassador got down to business. Ribbentrop, Schulenburg informed Molotov, had agreed to Stalin's claim on Bessarabia, as promised in the Moscow Pact, as long as this claim was "settled peacefully." But when Molotov repeated his talking point that Bukovina was Ukrainian, Schulenburg whipped out an ethnographic encyclopedia. He informed Molotov that many other peoples besides Ukrainians—including Romanians, Hungarians, Jews, and even Germans—lived in Bukovina. Molotov, annoyed, retorted that Schulenburg was using "an old Romanian encyclopedia" that was not to be trusted. After a heated debate about the ethnography of the sub-Carpathian

---

* Molotov's idea of exploiting Turkish-Italian tensions was not groundless. Earlier in 1940, the French ambassador in Ankara, Massigli, had proposed that Turkey could regain the Dodecanese Islands from Italy if it supported an Allied strike on the USSR.

region, Molotov finally proposed a crude quid pro quo, with the Soviets taking over Romanian Bukovina and Bessarabia and allowing the Germans to occupy Ploești, with its critical oil wells and refineries. "Don't worry," Molotov promised the German, "we will take over these territories peacefully—but not slowly." Schulenburg replied that Ribbentrop had given him diplomatic leeway on Bukovina and proposed a compromise: the Soviets could have the province's northern half, abutting their zone of occupied Poland. German diplomats in Bucharest, he assured Molotov, would tell the Romanians to give way.[26]

It was now the turn of Romania's ambassador to receive the Stalin treatment. Just before midnight on June 26, 1940, Molotov handed Davidescu an ultimatum giving Romania twenty-four hours to accede to a rash of onerous demands, from pulling troops back ten kilometers from the Soviet border to ceding Bessarabia and northern Bukovina. When Davidescu said he needed more time, Molotov responded bluntly that what Stalin had demanded was "the ceding of territory to the Soviet Union, not a negotiation." He then added that, in order to facilitate an immediate occupation of these territories by the Red Army, he expected Romania, by June 28, to finish clearing out troops from "Chernovitsyi [Cernâuti, or today's Chernivtsi], Khotyn, Soroki [Soroca], Kishinev [Chisinau], Benderyi [Bender], and Akkerman [today's Bilhorod-Dnistrovskyi]" and to evacuate all Romanian soldiers from the provinces of Bessarabia and northern Bukovina "within three to four days" (soon reduced to three). As for unarmed Romanian citizens and officials, Molotov agreed, as if being generous, that they would be allowed to stay in the occupied provinces, so long as they promptly "turned over all government property to the [Soviet] military authorities." Among the property claimed were the rail networks of Bessarabia and northern Bukovina, including all locomotive engines (157 and 117, respectively), first-class railway wagons (256 and 295), ordinary passenger wagons and rolling stock (4,109 and 2,435), and cisterns and storage tanks (312 and 120).[27]

Territorial Changes in Romania, 1940

SOVIET UNION

POLAND

Western Poland occupied by Germany, Sept. 1939

Eastern Poland occupied by the Soviet Union, Sept. 1939

•Kowel

Bug

Kiev•

•Zhitomir

Dniepr

Ukraine

•Vinnitsa

SLOVAKIA

•Lwów (Lemberg/ Lvov/Lviv)

Ruthenia

Munkács•

Cernăuti (Chernovitsyi/ Chernivtsi)

Khotyn•

Dniestr

Soroki (Soroca)

Bug

Transnistria

•Satu Mare

Carpathian

Bukovina

Bessarabia

•Budapest

HUNGARY

Danube

Transylvania

Oradea•

Cluj (Klausenburg)•

Mountains

Moldova

Roman•

Prut

Kishinev (Chisinau)

Benderyi (Bender)

Odessa•

•Targu-Mures

Siret

Akkerman• (Bilhorod-Dnistrovski)

•Arad

Kilia Arm

Novi Sad•

•Timisoara

Transylvanian Alps

ROMANIA

Galati• Braila•

Danubian Delta

Belgrade•

Pitesti•

Ploesti•

Danube

Dobruja

•Bucharest

Constanța•

Wallachia

Black Sea

YUGOSLAVIA

Danube

•Varna

Sofia•

BULGARIA

Burgas•

Romanian territory occupied by the Soviet Union, 1940

Romanian territory occupied by Hungary, 1940

Romanian territory occupied by Bulgaria, 1940

Czechoslovakian territory occupied by Hungary, 1938

Ploesti oil field and refineries

Istanbul

GREECE

TURKEY

0   100   200 Miles

On June 28, the Soviet invasion of Romania began on schedule—actually ahead of schedule, as the first troops crossed the Bessarabian frontier at 4 a.m., despite the Romanian military authorities having been assured they had until 10 a.m. to evacuate. Adding to the helplessness of the Romanian position, Hungarian troops had mobilized on the Transylvanian frontier, and Bulgarian troops were massing near the southern Dobruja (which Bucharest had wrested from Sofia in the postwar treaties). Britain, though theoretically a guarantor of Romania's borders, was too far away to offer military assistance and had not promised to do so. Italy was sympathetic too, but Mussolini could promise nothing without Berlin's approval. Only the German government was in a position to help, and the Germans, worried about possible disruption of their oil supplies, had warned Bucharest not to resist Soviet demands. Diplomatically isolated and massively overmatched by incoming Soviet forces, there was little for the Romanians to do but comply with Stalin's brutal ultimatum and withdraw. Even in complying, Romanian troops—given three days to withdraw and denied even the final six-hour grace period—found themselves harried by the invaders, "who took," one Romanian official complained, "the course of jostling the Romanians and cutting their retreat in order to possess themselves of large quantities of provisions, munitions, and war material." The humiliation would not be forgotten.[28]

In this way, Stalin achieved yet another cheap victory for Communism. As Molotov boasted before the Supreme Soviet, the "peaceful" occupation of Bessarabia expanded the Soviet frontiers by forty-five thousand square kilometers on which lived 3.2 million souls; the acquisition of northern Bukovina brought in another six thousand square kilometers and a half million people. In less than two weeks, counting the Baltic annexations, Stalin had acquired ten million new subjects for Communism. Added to the thirteen million acquired the previous fall in Poland, the Soviet population had expanded by twenty-three million (minus, though Molotov neglected to mention this, those unfortunate souls crushed underfoot in the Soviet invasions or executed by the NKVD). Stalin had seized coastal Bessarabia up to the mouth of the Danube, giving the USSR, as Molotov boasted, control of "the mightiest river in Europe, whence flows the commercial production of many European lands." The Soviet move into Bukovina split Transylvania in two, effectively surrounding the Wallachian plain and its rich farmland and the oil wells and refineries that fueled Hitler's war machine. Meanwhile, the "Ukrainian and Moldavian inhabitants" of the new province known as the Moldavia SSR, Molotov added, would now enjoy "the blessings of Communism."[29]

These blessings included the by-now-familiar litany of Soviet outrages, from the looting of banks and private businesses to the mass deportation of objectionable classes of people. The only difference between the Sovietization of occupied Romania and that of eastern Poland and the Baltics was that there were no more illusions about what Soviet occupation meant. Despite being given scarcely a day's notice, locals rapidly loaded up whatever moveable property they could carry and fled as fast as they could. As one evacuee from Cernâuti (Chernovitsyi/Chernivtsi) recalled, "Churches rang their bells, as if tolling a death-knell. People were running. Some knelt down to pray. Many were in a state of shock. A low wail was running down the streets." The last train left Cernâuti at 2 p.m. on June 28, packed with people and whatever they could stuff into the rail cars.[30]

Those left behind were less fortunate. As in every other Soviet occupation, banks and private businesses were nationalized—including substantial German holdings, in another hostile Soviet move with serious implications for the Moscow Pact. In the first two weeks after the Soviet invasion, 51,391 ex-Romanian citizens were taken into custody by the occupation authorities. By August 2, 1940, the total had surpassed two hundred thousand. By year's end, three hundred thousand Romanians had been deported from Moldavia SSR to Gulag camps in the Soviet interior.[31]

With his opportunistic moves against the Baltic states, Bessarabia, and northern Bukovina in the wake of the German humiliation of France, Stalin was wringing every last drop of nectar out of his honeyed partnership with Hitler while still, somehow, escaping the hostility of Hitler's opponents. Britain, in what Churchill called the country's "finest hour," now stood alone against Nazi Germany. For some reason, though, Britain had not declared war on Berlin's alliance partner, despite Stalin having invaded the same number of sovereign countries since August 1939 as Hitler had (seven).* But there were limits to Hitler's patience, and Stalin had just about reached them.

---

*Hitler's seven consisted of Poland, Denmark, Norway, Luxembourg, the Netherlands, Belgium, and France. Stalin had invaded Japanese (or Chinese) Manchuria, Poland, Finland, Lithuania, Latvia, Estonia, and Romania.

10

Showdown at the Danube Delta

DESPITE ULTIMATELY AGREEING to Soviet territorial demands in Romania, Hitler and Ribbentrop had clearly done so under duress. In strategic terms, Stalin had Hitler over a barrel. Not only was the German war machine dependent on the flow of Russian petroleum from Baku, but this oil was being sent across the Black Sea from Batumi to Odessa and then transshipped into Central Europe via Romania. All this Russian oil, along with Romanian petrol refined at Ploeşti, would now have to transit Soviet-controlled territory to reach the German Reich. So dependent was the German war effort on the petroleum supply route through former Galicia that German diplomats insisted the Soviets leave the critical stretch of the double-tracked railway running from Odessa through Cernâuti (Chernovitsyi/Chernivtsi) to Cracow on the European standard gauge, even while Soviet sappers converted other lines in eastern Poland to the wider Russian gauge. By opening up the resources of the East to Berlin, the Moscow Pact had enabled Hitler to circumvent the British blockade—which had ultimately doomed Germany in the last war—at the price of turning Germany into an economic vassal of the Soviet Union.[1]

So long as Britain stayed in the war, it seemed that Hitler had to swallow his pride and smile through his teeth, despite Stalin's increasingly onerous demands. It was not that the Führer wanted to continue the war with the British Empire. As Hitler remarked upon learning that France had sued for peace on June 17, "The war in the West is over. France is defeated, and I will shortly come to an agreement with England." German peace offers were extended to London via intermediaries in the Vatican, Stockholm, and even the US embassy in Berlin. It was Churchill's principled refusal to parley, not Hitler's hubris, that ensured the European war would continue. As a frustrated Hitler confessed to Franz Halder, chief of the German General Staff, in Berchtesgaden on July 13, Britain was unwilling to seriously discuss peace terms because Churchill was "placing her hopes in Russia and the United States." Neither of those continent-size powers were in the war yet, but Churchill was convinced that they would join him against Hitler eventually.[2]

Although German U-boats operating in the Atlantic had to respect it, American neutrality was largely illusory. True, a series of Neutrality Acts passed in 1936, 1937, and 1939 strictly limited the ability of the president to help London with military aid.* But Roosevelt sent clear signals to Churchill via back-channel correspondence (to frustrate any of the president's critics who obtained copies, Churchill wrote under the bland pseudonym of "former naval person") that he was strongly on England's side against Germany. On May 26, once it had become clear that the Allied armies in Europe were collapsing (and before the Dunkirk evacuation had saved the British Army), Roosevelt had even offered to open US ports "for repair to the British fleet" if there was a danger it might fall into German hands. Although appreciating the gesture, Churchill declined this American gift horse, perhaps fearing that, if he surrendered the British fleet to Roosevelt, Britain would never get it back.[3]

Nineteen forty was a presidential election year, and Roosevelt, using the European war as a pretext, was seeking an unprecedented third term. In his nomination-acceptance speech at

---

* So strict were these regulations that Britain had begun shipping gold bullion across the Atlantic to pay for arms purchases in May 1939, even before the war broke out. This bullion, along with gold shipments during the war, was sent to Fort Knox, where it would remain an unmistakable marker of the transfer of wealth from the British Empire to the United States.

the Democratic convention on July 19, Roosevelt was careful to
say that the United States would stay out of the war "except in
the case of attack." But he also declared that the United States regarded the "totalitarian states" as a strategic adversary, and that
his government would emphatically defend the "western hemisphere" against outside aggression. This speech buttressed Churchill's hopes of US intervention, helping doom the final German
peace feeler, issued earlier that day, when Hitler had appealed in
the Reichstag "once more to reason and common sense in Great
Britain. . . . I can see no reason why this war need go on." When
Roosevelt sidestepped Congress and agreed, on August 13, to
send Britain fifty mothballed World War I–vintage destroyers in
exchange for ninety-nine-year leases on British naval and air bases
in the Caribbean, on Bermuda, and in Newfoundland, Churchill's
refusal to entertain Hitler's peace offers seemed vindicated, if at an
extortionate price.[4]

The Soviet case was more frustrating still to Berlin. Nominally,
Stalin was Hitler's ally and partner in aggression, and yet because
Britain refused to declare war on the USSR, Soviet neutrality and
Churchill's hopes for a Soviet intervention against Nazi Germany
blocked a possible deal between Berlin and London. Annoyed
as he was with Stalin, for now Hitler had no better option than
to stick with him. In his Reichstag address of July 19, Hitler reaffirmed his commitment to the Moscow Pact, proclaiming to the
world that "neither Germany nor Russia has made one step, to this
time, outside their zone of interest."[5]

By similar logic, Stalin saw no reason to break with Hitler, however alarmed he was by the German victories in Western Europe.
Stalin's adroit maneuvering to end the Finnish war in March, and
the fall of France in June, had erased the threat of British-French
intervention in the Caucasus. But the confirmation of these plans
in captured documents shared with Moscow by the Germans also
made unthinkable the idea that the USSR might cooperate with
the conniving imperialists of London. The Massigli affair—as it

was styled after German newspapers published incriminating documents captured in France between July 5 and 12—gave Stalin and Molotov good reason to cold-shoulder Churchill and his new ambassador, Cripps, even if the Baku plots dated to the Chamberlain era. Conveying Stalin's reply to Hitler's Reichstag speech, Molotov announced before the Supreme Soviet on August 1 that the Moscow Pact had "done away with the possibility of friction" in what he euphemistically called "the application of Soviet measures of security along our western frontiers," while "guaranteeing to Germany tranquility in the East." The "course of recent events in Europe," Molotov concluded, "have not only not weakened the strength of the [Moscow] Pact, but have proven its importance and the need for its further development."[6]

In contrast to his profession of equanimity with Berlin, Molotov peppered his speech with jibes at Britain and France—understandably, in light of the Germans' exposure of their plots to bomb Baku. Molotov blamed France's military humiliation on the stubborn refusal of "her leaders, unlike their German counterparts, to properly appreciate the weight of the Soviet Union in the affairs of Europe." As for Britain, rather than dwell on the British pilots' Caucasian overflights, which Molotov blamed on Turkey and Iran—easy and less dangerous targets—he gently mocked Churchill's decision to continue the war against Italy and Germany because he was "counting on assistance from the United States." Showing that this was no mere aside, Molotov attacked the Americans with more venom than he had the British, singling out Washington for its refusal to hand over the foreign reserves of the Baltic countries that Stalin had just erased from existence, or, as Molotov cynically put it, "gold which our State Bank recently purchased from the Banks of Lithuania, Latvia, and Estonia." President Roosevelt's "well advertised 'concern' for the interests of the entire 'Western Hemisphere,'" Molotov sneered, was a mask for American "imperialist plans" to take over European colonies, as had already happened in the Western Hemisphere with the

bases-for-destroyers deal. Roosevelt's rhetorical support for Churchill, Molotov thundered, "harbors the danger of a further extension and kindling of war and its conversion into a world imperialist
war." Even so, despite what he mocked as Churchill's pathetic re-
liance on the Americans and "all of England's hostile acts against
the USSR," Molotov allowed that his appointment of Labour MP
Stafford Cripps as ambassador "brought the possibility, at least, of
better relations."[7]

From his precarious perch in London, facing a seemingly un-
beatable German war machine encamped across the English
Channel, Churchill could only fume at the apparently unbreach-
able solidarity of the Molotov-Ribbentrop gangster pact. In late
June 1940, Churchill sent a personal letter to Stalin—the first of
many—to ascertain if there was anything to the rumors of tensions between Moscow and Berlin. "You became friends with
Hitler," Churchill wrote, as if observing a startling coincidence,
"at almost the same time as we became his enemy." Perhaps, he
suggested, Britain and the USSR could find common ground in
opposing "German hegemony in Europe" while also deepening
economic ties via commodity trading. Although Stalin agreed to
receive Cripps, who handed him Churchill's letter on July 1, the
Vozhd remained "formal and frigid" during the meeting. Stalin
even defended Hitler's conquests, disputing Churchill's character-
ization of a fully Nazified continent after the fall of France. To
"achieve hegemony in Europe," the Vozhd objected, "would require mastery of the seas, and Germany has no such mastery and
will not likely achieve it." True to the letter of the Moscow Pact,
Stalin informed Hitler immediately about his conversation with
Cripps and made no reply to Churchill's letter.* As Sir Orme Sargent, a wizened Foreign Office expert, minuted on Cripps's report,

---

* Stalin did not respond to any of Churchill's letters until July 18, 1941,
four weeks after Hitler had invalidated the Moscow Pact by invading the
Soviet Union.

"Stalin has . . . got Sir S. Cripps exactly where he wants him, that is to say, as a suppliant on his doormat holding his pathetic little peace offerings of tin in one hand and rubber in the other."[8]

Despite his frustrations, Churchill was impressed by the audacity of Soviet foreign policy. On July 3, he called in Ambassador Maisky to learn what he could about Stalin's intentions. Might not Soviet aggression in Romania, Churchill asked, represent "a return to the imperialism of the Tsars?" Maisky, a good Communist, pretended to be shocked by the question, which prompted Churchill's retort: "Perhaps you are right, instead it is a new Soviet imperialism." Probing further, Churchill asked if "the Soviet incursion into Romania might not be viewed entirely favorably in Berlin?" Maisky replied coldly that "the views of the German government are unknown to me." Persisting in his line of attack, Churchill cited a quote attributed to France's collaborationist Vichy minister, Pierre Laval, that Hitler "had no real hostility towards France," as his real ambition was "to deal a death blow . . . to Bolshevism." Maisky replied that the Soviet Union was "ready for all eventualities." Maisky's elliptical remark buttressed Churchill's hopes for "a possible *Russian* attack against Germany," as he mused aloud in a closed session of the Commons later in July.[9]

Behind the scenes, relations between Berlin and Moscow were just as frosty as Churchill hoped, even if he was unable to confirm this on the record. After the fall of France and the Soviet invasion of the Baltic countries in the days after June 17, 1940, rumors had swirled around Europe that the Red Army, capitalizing on the Wehrmacht's concentration in the West, was preparing to march from Lithuania into virtually undefended East Prussia and German-occupied Poland. These rumors were serious enough that, on June 23, the Soviet TASS news agency issued an official denial of press reports "appearing almost every day in the American, Japanese, English, French, Turkish and Swedish press" that Stalin had "concentrated 100 or as many as 150 divisions on the [Soviet] Lithuanian-German border," preparatory to invading the

Reich. Revealing as much as it denied, the TASS communiqué announced that the Red Army had invaded the Baltic countries "not with 100 or 150 but instead not more than 18 or 20 divisions, which are moreover not all concentrated on the Lithuanian-German border, but are spread out across many districts of the [former] Baltic Republics." Those troops, the report concluded, had not been massed in Estonia, Latvia, and Lithuania "with the aim of applying pressure against Germany, but rather in order to guarantee the fulfillment of the USSR's mutual assistance pacts with these Baltic countries."[10]

Hitler could hardly have been reassured by Stalin's assurance that only twenty Red Army divisions now threatened basically un-defended East Prussia. On June 19, a German spy reported from Estonia that the Soviets had informed the departing British ambas-sador in Tallinn that Stalin planned to deploy three *million* troops in the Baltic region "to threaten Germany's eastern borders." Whatever the truth about Red Army troop strength in the Bal-tics, Soviet military intelligence was well aware of the favorable order of battle in June and July 1940. As an internal memorandum prepared by the Soviet General Staff at the time noted, "The path between Kaunas and Berlin lies completely open for our air force, as is the stretch of land from Vilkovsky-Königsberg-Berlin for our armored divisions and motorized infantry."[11]

The same possibility occurred to the Polish exile government in London, headed—after the self-dissolution of the previous gov-ernment when it fled to Romania in September 1939—by General Wladyslaw Sikorski. On June 19, 1940, Sikorski requested that Vis-count Halifax appoint a Polish liaison diplomat to Britain's Mos-cow embassy. (Having been destroyed by Stalin alongside Hitler, Poland had no embassy of its own in Moscow.) In his memoran-dum to Halifax, Sikorski proposed that this Polish liaison diplomat work with Stafford Cripps to "make use of the valuable reserves of trained [Polish] men and officers, both in Soviet-occupied terri-tory and in the Soviet Union itself (i.e., deported prisoners of war), in order to create, with the assistance of the Soviet authorities, a

Polish army of some 300,000 men for service against Germany."*
Although Halifax declined Sikorski's proposal and the episode
is forgotten today, in the days after the fall of France there was
considerable chatter in London about an opportunistic Soviet invasion of the vulnerable eastern borders of Hitler's Reich, with
Polish veterans joining the fight.[12]

The Germans also heard rumors that the Soviets were contem-
plating an invasion. In early July, German military intelligence
picked up an intriguing story from "a reliable source" in Lithuania,
who had overheard a conversation between "two drunken Soviet
officers" and a local resident. When the Lithuanian asked "why was
it necessary to send so many Soviet troops in to occupy the Baltic states," the Soviet officers "answered spontaneously, that their
main task was [to prepare for] an invasion of Germany." Asked
to specify who had sent them into Lithuania with this purpose,
the Russians gave a stunning answer: "Cripps." The much-touted
meeting between Stalin and Churchill's new Soviet-sympathizing
ambassador to Moscow on July 1, 1940, had sparked talk in the
Soviet officer corps of a reversal of alliances, with a British charm
offensive helping convince Stalin to turn against Hitler before the
German armies could shift eastward from France.[13]

Whatever he may have said in public, in private Hitler was
aghast at Stalin's effrontery in taking such bald advantage of the
feats of German arms in the West to conquer new territory—
not to mention his aggressive moves near the Reich's frontiers in
Lithuania and occupied Poland. As early as July 21, 1940, Hitler
broached the idea of a possible invasion of the USSR with the German Army commander in chief, General Walter von Brauchitsch.
In the wake of the Soviet invasion of Romania, German diplomats began dropping hints with friendly Balkan powers, such as

---

*Helping to explain why this abortive plot was memory holed was the
fact that, unbeknownst to Sikorski and Cripps, Stalin had murdered virtually the entire cadre of Soviet-captured Polish officers they had hoped
would lead armies into battle against Hitler.

Bulgaria, that it was time to choose sides in the coming eastern war. On June 28—the day the Russian invasion of Bessarabia and northern Bukovina began—Ribbentrop promised the Bulgarian minister in Berlin, Parvan Draganov, that Germany would support Bulgaria's claim on the southern Dobruja, abutting the Black Sea coast below Romania, as a counterweight to the Soviet push southward from Bessarabia into the Danube delta.[14]

As Ribbentrop's Bulgarian trial balloon suggested, Stalin's invasion of Romania had reopened the entire postwar settlement in the Balkans. By virtue of having joined the winning side in the last war, despite an inept military performance, Romania had massively enlarged its territory at the expense of three now-jealous neighbors, with Russia losing Bessarabia, Bulgaria the southern Dobruja, and Hungary most of Transylvania. Just as the Nazis had thundered against the Versailles Treaty for truncating Germany, so did Hungarians wish to tear up the Treaty of Trianon and Bulgarians the Treaty of Neuilly-sur-Seine. By seizing Bessarabia and northern Bukovina, Stalin had given Hitler a golden opportunity to win new, revisionist allies for the Axis keen to share in the carve up of Romania.

Of course, if Ribbentrop backed Hungarian and Bulgarian claims on Romanian territory, this might easily prejudice German relations with Romania itself, which were important and delicate because of the oil wells and refineries of Ploești. And yet Russian behavior during the invasion of Bessarabia and northern Bukovina was so offensive that Romanian diplomats were desperate to counter further Soviet encroachment. As early as July 12, 1940, NKVD spies in Bucharest picked up rumors that the Romanian government had quietly asked Rome and Berlin for military aid to expel the Russian invaders, on the understanding that Bessarabia would be returned to Romania. Nothing concrete was promised yet, but Hitler invited Romania's prime minister, Ion Gigurtu, to Berchtesgaden and showered him with attention before returning to Salzburg for more formal discussions on July 27. The next day, Hitler and Ribbentrop received the Bulgarian premier, Bogdan

Filov. Although no communiqués were issued, it was obvious that some kind of German settlement of Balkan questions was afoot. Now it was Stalin's turn to be annoyed. On July 29, Molotov called in the German ambassador for an explanation of the Salzburg summits.[15]

Owing to the combination of German victories in the West and the bad impression left by cheap Soviet aggression in the East, Hitler was at the height of his power and influence. True, the German chancellor was a despised figure in England after Germany launched the aerial bombing raids of the Battle of Britain in late July 1940, especially after the Luftwaffe switched from military targets to indiscriminate raids on London on September 7, 1940.* He was only a bit less hated in Washington, DC, where the terrors of the Blitz dominated the news cycle, owing to the soon-legendary radio broadcasts of Edward R. Murrow of CBS News. But in Europe, Hitler's favor was being courted everywhere—from Scandinavia, where Finland was desperate for a counterweight to Stalin, to the Balkans, where Romania was smarting for revenge against the Russians and both Bulgaria and Hungary were in the market for recovering lost territory. Even Vichy France had become a supplicant of Hitler's Reich, with the new collaborationist government of Marshal Philippe Pétain clamoring for a military alliance with Germany against Britain, especially after Churchill ordered the destruction of a good part of the French fleet at Mers-el-Kébir on the Algerian coast on July 3, 1940, to prevent it from falling into German hands, killing 1,297 Frenchmen in the process. On the Continent, only neutral Spain remained aloof from the Reich, owing to national exhaustion, Franco's stubborn streak, and his

---

* After, it should be noted, the Royal Air Force had begun bombing Berlin on August 25—in retaliation for the German air raids over England—staging sorties at night, which all but guaranteed civilian casualties. Hitler thundered against these "nighttime pirate raids" in the Berlin Sportpalast on September 4, vowing that Germany would retaliate by raining bombs down on London.

abiding fear of the British naval threat to Spain's coastline. Otherwise, German influence reigned supreme from the Arctic to the Mediterranean, while Britain and France were, for once, frozen out.

So often undermined by the haste of German military planners for action, German diplomats were, for once, riding high and given the time they needed to court, cajole, and mediate. Of course, German military planners were far from idle in the months after France's capitulation. The Luftwaffe was ramping up production to support the Battle of Britain, even while troops and armor were withdrawn from the West to Eastern Europe, movements noted with alarm by Soviet military intelligence. But even if Hitler chose to tear up the Moscow Pact and invade the USSR, as he had begun hinting to his aides that he might eventually do, it was far too late in the year to start such a campaign. Unlike in the Luftwaffe, the trend in the Wehrmacht and the German Economic Ministry after the fall of France was toward demobilization, with thousands of troops released from duty and many munitions factories returning, for now, to civilian production. The earliest realistic launch date for an eastern war against Stalin, Hitler told General Franz Halder on July 31, 1940, was spring 1941. With no major land campaigns in Europe at hand for the rest of 1940, there was plenty of time for German diplomats to work out a Balkan settlement.[16]

All roads in European diplomacy now led through Berlin—or rather, Salzburg and Vienna, where Hitler (in a nod to his Austrian origins) preferred to receive distinguished visitors. The essentials of the Romanian settlement to come were worked out quietly at Salzburg in late July, when Ribbentrop gave assurances to both Bulgaria and Hungary that their claims would be satisfied so long as their diplomats kept them within "reasonable boundaries." To goad Romania into going along, Ribbentrop had the German General Staff share intelligence with Bucharest of "suspicious concentrations of Russian troops on the Romanian frontier" on August 24, and he suggested that the Romanian government demand an explanation from Moscow. The report was not fictitious either. In the last days of August 1940, a number of border clashes ensued in the Danube delta, with Romanian soldiers suffering casualties from Soviet gunfire. Soviet-Romanian tensions were peaking when, on August 29, Romania's foreign minister arrived in Vienna in order to, he hoped, petition Hitler for restitution and protection.[17]

Instead, the Germans presented Romania with a fait accompli. In order to receive a German-Italian guarantee of its frontiers against future Soviet encroachment, Romania had to surrender the southern Dobruja to Bulgaria and the western half of Transylvania to Hungary. After the news of this brutal "Vienna Award" was relayed to Bucharest, the shock was severe enough that the Romanian government fell on September 4, and the beleaguered sovereign, King Carol, fled the country in disgrace. But even this worked to Hitler's advantage, as it brought to power a Fascist "National Legionary" government under Ion Antonescu. Although no Germanophile, Antonescu was so ferociously anti-Communist that he accepted Hitler's guarantee of Romania's new borders against Stalin,* in spite of Germany's role in truncating those borders.[18]

After a rough go in the first months of the Moscow Pact, German diplomats were now running rings around their Soviet counterparts. After hearing rumors of the Vienna Award—at a conference to which his own diplomats had not been invited—Molotov called in Schulenburg for an explanation. Revealingly, neither Molotov nor Stalin was concerned about the German-brokered truncation of Romania. Rather, the Vozhd was upset that Germany had guaranteed whatever Romanian territory was left. With visible annoyance, Molotov asked Schulenburg, "Why have you given this guarantee? You knew that we had no intention of attacking Romania." Schulenburg retorted, "That is just why

---

*Antonescu's government forbade the showing of Soviet movies and even suppressed the distribution of Romanian-Russian language dictionaries.

we gave the guarantee. You have often told us that you have no further claim on [Romania]; our guarantee can, therefore, be no source of annoyance to you."[19]

Giving the lie to his disavowal of interest in Romanian territory, Molotov on September 9 called Schulenburg in again and pressed a Soviet claim on southern Bukovina. On September 14, Molotov, citing Germany's presumptive attempt to redraw the Balkan map in Vienna, went further, proposing a new International Commission on the Danube River to replace the old one, on which Britain and France had seats. Molotov's proposal for a Sovietized Danube commission revealed baldly that Stalin's real aims in the region were not limited to Bessarabia and Bukovina; he wanted to control the entire lower Danube to safeguard Soviet naval dominance in the Black Sea. With their own interests in riverine commerce on the Danube and the free flow of Romanian oil into the Reich, the Germans could hardly let Stalin have this. The impasse was serious enough that Schulenburg returned to Berlin on September 23 for consultation with Ribbentrop and Hitler.[20]

Rather than give in to Molotov's demands, Hitler pressed forward. In October 1940, German troops, engineers, and advisers began blanketing the Wallachian plain around Bucharest and along the Danube. The official explanation given to Molotov was that these were "units of instruction" sent at Romania's request. This was not entirely untrue: Antonescu had invited German troops in and even insisted that he pay their expenses. (The Germans, after initially objecting that they were happy to pay, agreed to charge Bucharest 100 million lei per month for "protecting Romania's oil fields and refineries.") Molotov issued a public denial that Stalin had agreed to this German move into Romania. Although Berlin issued a communiqué reaffirming that "the relations between the Reich and the USSR are, and will remain, very good," few informed observers believed this. Tensions were serious enough that Ribbentrop wrote a long letter to Stalin on October 13 suggesting that he or Molotov come to Berlin personally to clear the air.[21]

In the meantime, Ribbentrop invited Molotov to send a delegation to Bucharest to establish a new International Commission on the Danube. Adding tension to the Bucharest conference, it opened on October 28, 1940, the day Mussolini's Italy, having already occupied Albania back in 1939, opportunistically declared war on Greece, making official the spread of the European war into the Balkans. Stalin's diplomats, led by Molotov's trusted deputy Arkady Sobolev, were as blunt as ever, demanding that powers other than Soviet Russia and Romania be excluded from administration of the lower "maritime" Danube that fed into the Black Sea via the delta, with naval vessels of all other powers forbidden from using these waters. The Russians also claimed exclusive possession of the "Kilia Arm," the only channel in the Danube delta deep enough to allow in seagoing ships, including a chain of islands on the Romanian side of the demarcation line agreed to back in June. Already, Russian torpedo boats were probing the delta for weaknesses in the Romanian defenses and landing parties of commandos on the Kilia Islands. Border clashes were now happening almost daily, as were violations of Romanian airspace by Soviet pilots. Usually, incidents involved mere warning shots, but not always. On September 13, a Romanian woman was shot and killed sowing hay near the frontier; the guilty NKVD border guards pulled her corpse onto Soviet territory to conceal the evidence.[22]

Romanian troops also regularly violated the border. It was inevitable that both sides would do so along a fiercely contested, ill-defined frontier in a vast river delta dotted with islands. Prisoners were often taken. By the time of the Danube conference in November and December 1940, both sides had arrested enough enemy nationals in the delta that, in order to maintain diplomatic appearances, a prisoner exchange was hastily arranged, with sixteen Romanian detainees exchanged for eight Soviet subjects. Increasingly assertive Soviet behavior in the delta, and at the conference table, left "no doubt," as a Romanian diplomat complained, about Stalin's aim of "assuring the U.S.S.R. of absolute mastery of the mouths of the Danube," thus asserting Soviet "sovereignty over the gates to the Black Sea."[23]

Still hopeful of avoiding an open breach with Stalin, German diplomats stalled for time in Bucharest, raising endless points of order and allowing the conference to drag into December without agreeing to Soviet claims. By then, the spread of the war into the Balkan theater and the eastern Mediterranean, because of the Italian invasion of Greece, had brought still more explosive questions into play. Tensions between Berlin and Moscow were now serious enough that only intervention from on high could dissipate them. As Ribbentrop had already visited Moscow twice to honor Stalin, it was Molotov's turn to pay homage to Hitler in Berlin.

11

Summit in Berlin
The Four-Power Pact?

AT A CEREMONY in Berlin on September 27, 1940, the foreign ministers of Italy and Japan, Galeazzo Ciano and Saburo Kurusu, affixed their signatures alongside Ribbentrop's to a new Tripartite Pact. Although trumpeted to the world as a formidable military alliance, in truth the agreement was more symbolic than substantial, as it contained no binding provisions regarding military cooperation. The symbolism, however, was significant. The Tripartite Pact represented a repudiation, ideologically or at least semantically, of the previous agreement between the three powers, the Anti-Comintern Pact of 1936. This time, the signatories were declaring their opposition not to Soviet Communism, but to the "Anglo-Saxon world order," with the subtext that the signatories were devoted to peace, whereas the British Empire and, by extension, the United States wished to prolong the war. Japan agreed to acknowledge "the leadership of Italy and Germany in the establishment of a new order in Europe," and the Axis powers recognized, in turn, Japanese supremacy over "Greater East Asia."

This much was clear, but the role of both hostile and friendly third parties, such as the United States and the USSR, was up for interpretation. Ideally, the Germans would have liked for the Tripartite Pact to intimidate the United States into staying neutral. The November presidential election was imminent, and Roosevelt's pro-British stance was under increasing scrutiny, owing to isolationist sentiments embodied in the huge "America First" movement. So carefully was Roosevelt treading in his campaign for a third term that he promised American mothers and fathers at a rally in Boston on October 30, just days before the election, that "your boys are not going to be sent into any foreign wars." Whether or not Roosevelt was intimidated by the Tripartite Pact, the pacifist line this arch-interventionist president took in the heat of an election campaign suggested that most Americans remained desperate to stay out of the European war.[1]

As for the Soviets, suspicions about the Tripartite Pact were natural. Was it a mere cosmetic touch-up of the Anti-Comintern Pact, and thus still inspired by opposition to Communism? Was it meant to replace the Moscow Pact of August 1939 or to complement it? As a courtesy, Ribbentrop authorized Ambassador Schulenburg to inform Molotov about the impending pact a day early on September 26. Schulenburg reassured Molotov that the pact "in no way prejudices the political status of agreements between the three signatory powers and the USSR." In an official editorial in *Pravda* on September 30, Molotov declared that the Tripartite Pact was merely a restatement of the already existing state of hostilities between "Italy, Germany, and Japan, on the one side, and Britain and the United States, on the other." As for the division of Europe and Asia into spheres of interest, Molotov declared that this arrangement would ultimately depend "on the relations of the warring powers and . . . the outcome of the war." Challenging German claims that the war with Britain was all but won, Molotov noted that America's capitalist might had not been brought to bear yet. "Although the United States," he wrote, "has not yet formally entered the war on the side of England against Germany, Italy, and Japan, it is abundantly clear that, in reality, the USA finds itself in the same war camp as the opponents of these powers in both the European and Asian hemispheres." The USSR, Molotov concluded, remained committed to "peaceful neutrality" in any ongoing Great Power conflicts, "so long as this stance of neutrality depends solely on her."[2]

It was a clever response, full of the usual Soviet obfuscation. In view of the history of the previous twelve months, in which the Red Army had entered Manchurian territory to fight Japanese troops and had invaded six other sovereign countries, Molotov's assertion that the USSR was devoted to "peaceful neutrality" was risible on its face, although this did not mean it would not be believed by Communist sympathizers in Britain and the United States. What Molotov had really done was declare Stalin's distance from Hitler's war aims. However unlikely this was to happen in view of the bellicose anti-German stance of both Churchill and Roosevelt, Hitler and Ribbentrop clearly hoped, by publicizing the Tripartite Pact, to bring an end to the war out of sheer intimidation of London and Washington. Stalin, by contrast, wanted the war to go on, so that he would not have to face Hitler's triumphant armies alone, and also in the hope that the United States would be drawn into the war alongside Britain to counterbalance Germany in Europe and Japan in Asia. In July 1940, Japan had bullied Britain into closing down the Burma Road used to supply Chiang Kai-shek's Chinese Army overland from Southeast Asia, an illustration of both Japanese strength and Britain's strategic isolation after the fall of France. With the United States still formally neutral and the Luftwaffe and Wehrmacht poised threateningly across the Channel, Churchill was loath to risk going to war against Japan. But a Japanese war would suit Stalin's purposes admirably. The best chances for further Soviet expansion lay in a global conflict, which would fatally weaken both of the warring capitalist camps. It would then be up to Stalin to choose the moment to strike.

Back in Europe, Hitler was unsure how to fit the Soviet Union into his "new order." Neutralizing Stalin had been necessary to avoid a two-front war, while access to Soviet raw materials had enabled Germany to circumvent the British blockade. But this was an awkward relationship at best, and it was becoming more awkward all the time. Previously separated by a belt of buffer states, the USSR and Nazi Germany now shared a border thousands of miles long—a frontier now bristling with heavily armed sentries and spies. In Finland and Romania, Soviet encroachment had been threatening enough to German economic interests that the

Germans were blanketing both countries with military advisers. On September 27, the same day Ribbentrop signed the Tripartite Pact, German diplomats in Helsinki signed a military defense agreement with Finland. At least 430 German troops had arrived in Romania by October 1940, and two fighter squadrons by early November. Antonescu's government, in turn, promised not only to pay the expenses of these German detachments but also to step up oil deliveries to the Reich.[3]

Compounding Hitler's frustration, Stalin, though cold-shouldering Churchill and Ambassador Cripps, maintained the pretense of neutrality in the world war, even while happily pocketing territory in the slipstream of Hitler's military victories. Molotov might hint at dissatisfaction at being excluded from the Tripartite Pact, but then Stalin had adamantly refused to declare war on Britain. German diplomats stressed their cooperation with Russia; Russian diplomats played this down at every turn. Soviet duplicity was mind-boggling.

It was time, Hitler decided, to force the Soviets to put up or shut up. Clearly not wanting to be pinned down, Stalin waited eight days before responding to Ribbentrop's invitation of October 13 to come to Berlin to iron out Soviet-German differences, agreeing to send Molotov in his stead in November.* The delay did allow Hitler time to meet with Franco at Hendaye on the Spanish border on October 23, although this turned out to be a mixed blessing. Sensing that Hitler's diplomatic options were narrowing, Franco demanded an exorbitant price for entering the war alongside Germany, including large territorial gains in France, and denied Hitler permission to send German troops through Spain to attack the British base at Gibraltar. The failure of the Franco summit was a poor omen for Molotov's visit to Berlin. It also raised the stakes, as Franco's stubborn stand at the western end of the

---

* In fairness to Stalin, Ribbentrop's letter was nineteen pages long. Simply translating it into Russian was a lot of work.

Mediterranean accentuated the urgency of the Balkan questions at the eastern end.

To heighten the propaganda impact of the Berlin meeting, the news was kept secret until the eve of Molotov's departure on November 10. Stafford Cripps heard the news on the radio and was—according to his dinner host that evening, US ambassador Laurence Steinhardt—"not only surprised but shocked by the news." Cripps, who had not been allowed to see Molotov (let alone Stalin) for months, lodged a feeble protest at "the peculiar Soviet interpretation of the word neutrality." Privately, Cripps told Steinhardt that he was afraid a new diplomatic accord between the dictators would shake the foundations of Churchill's government. "Should Molotov's visit to Berlin result in more extensive collaboration between the Soviet Union and Germany," Cripps warned Steinhardt, "influential circles in Great Britain might begin to press for peace with Germany on an anti-Soviet basis." In Berlin, the German press gushed over the "wise and strong policy" of that "great and realistic statesman, Stalin." The stage was set for what could be argued was the single most important diplomatic encounter of the war.[4]

In a sign of the high hopes Hitler and Ribbentrop had for the summit, the Germans spared no expense in rolling out the red carpet for Molotov at the Belorusski train station in Moscow. The red carpet was flanked by a "dozen German officers, in full dress," along with Schulenburg and the Italian and Japanese ambassadors. To the strains of the "Internationale," Molotov marched to the train, observers noted, "with a pistol his pocket," accompanied by fifty Germans who would travel with the Soviet delegation and sixty-five Russian aides, including "sixteen secret policemen, three servants, and a doctor." The NKVD alone had asked for three entire train cars, and the Germans obliged.[5]

Just past 11 a.m. on November 12, 1940, Molotov's entourage arrived at Berlin's Anhalter Bahnhof. It was a cold, rainy morning, but the Germans had done all they could to provide a proper welcome. An honor guard of the army stood "to immaculate attention," flanked by Ribbentrop; Hitler's SS chief, Reichsführer Heinrich Himmler; and the supreme commander of the Wehrmacht, Field Marshal Wilhelm Keitel. The heavy cloud cover accentuated the visual effect as searchlights lit up the Soviet flags hoisted along the platform, carefully blended in with the swastikas. A Nazi band struck up the "Internationale" (played at double time, just in case any nearby Communists might have been tempted to sing), and Ribbentrop gave a welcoming address. All the Nazi notables then shook Molotov's hand, though observers noted that the Soviet statesman spent the longest time huddled with Himmler. The immense Soviet delegation was then escorted into a sixty-vehicle convoy and whisked off to Bellevue Palace, where the Russians would be staying. Trying to interpret the mood, an American journalist noticed that, despite the proper welcome at the station, the streets were mostly empty. But this could have owed merely to the rain.[6]

However ambiguous the mood might have been in the streets of Berlin, at the Bellevue there was no doubt that the Germans wanted to impress. Molotov's interpreter, Valentin Berezhkov, recalled being amazed by "the ostentation of the rooms," with the walls "decorated with tapestries and paintings in heavy gilt frames" and all the servants and waiters "garbed in gold-braided livery." The contrast with the Soviet delegation, everyone outfitted in "identical dark blue suits, grey ties, and cheap felt hats," was striking. Even so, the Russians must have enjoyed the "opulent lunch" they were served by "white-gloved staff" in surroundings more elegant than they could find anywhere in the USSR, even in the Kremlin. Others noted strange incongruities. Vladimir Dekanozov, one of Stalin's more diminutive executioners, amused everyone when he mounted a "gilded Bismarckian chair," which was so huge that his feet "barely touched the floor."[7]

Molotov, his interpreter Berezhkov, and Dekanozov were then driven over to Wilhelmstrasse, where the real business began. Ribbentrop, in his opening monologue, ranged broadly over the war but with particular emphasis on Japan. Just as it had been possible to "delimit the mutual spheres of interest between Soviet Russia and Germany," Ribbentrop proposed that "a delimitation of interests could also be achieved between Japan and Russia." The "Lebensraum [living space] policy" of Tokyo, Ribbentrop argued, was "now oriented not toward the East and North" against the Soviet Union, but "toward the South"—against Britain and the United States. "England," Ribbentrop proposed in a nod to Soviet anti-imperialism, "no longer had the right to dominate the world," and it was time for Russia to claim its share in the Near East and on the Indian Ocean. Ribbentrop then brought up Turkey, reminding Molotov that Ankara had signed a defense agreement with Britain and France. "We know," Ribbentrop continued, "that the Soviet Union is unsatisfied with the Montreux Convention [on the Turkish Straits]. We, too, are dissatisfied with this Convention." Perhaps, he suggested, Germany, Italy, and the USSR could work out a new convention to "guarantee that the Soviet Union will have access to the Straits and the Mediterranean Sea."[8]

Molotov listened politely but said little. "All that you have said is very interesting," he finally chimed in. Nonetheless, "any delimitation of spheres of influence" between the Tripartite Pact and the USSR, Molotov replied carefully, would require "precise negotiations over a long period of time." A bit less carefully, Molotov said that the "division of spheres of influence between Russia and Germany in 1939 had been *ischerpano* [exhausted] by the events of 1939–1940, with the exception of Finland, a matter still far from settled and to which I will return here in Berlin." So far, Molotov had given away little other than Stalin's concern over Finland. It was the impression of Ribbentrop's translator that Molotov was "keeping his powder dry" for Hitler.[9]

Molotov was then whisked over to the German Chancellery and escorted "past an honor guard of the SS-Leibstandarte" to meet the Führer. With his taste for theatrics, Hitler had arranged an over-the-top welcome as "two tall blond SS men in black tightly-belted uniforms with skulls on the caps clicked their heels and threw open the tall, almost ceiling-high doors" to reveal a hall

ninety feet long and fifty feet wide. Molotov, dour as usual, did
not seem particularly impressed, but he did recall being greeted by
Hitler in a "surprisingly gracious and friendly manner." Hitler was
a picture of affability as he expounded on geopolitics, his favorite
subject. "Germany," Hitler told his Russian guest, "has gained, as a
result of this war, enough land to keep her occupied for a hundred
years." The Germans, happy with dominating Europe, had no interest in Asia or the Black Sea. Any troops Germany was sending
to the Balkans, the Führer explained, were only there to oppose
British encroachment. Knowing that Stalin was upset about the
German deployment in Romania, Hitler promised that Germany
would withdraw these troops "as soon as the war was over" and
the British threat to Germany's oil lifeline thus neutralized. The
overriding problem of geopolitics, Hitler argued, was that Italy,
Germany, and Russia were denied fair access to the sea by the British. Common ground could surely be found in overturning this,
especially now that "the war with England is 99% won." Even if
the United States was officially neutral, it was on England's side,
which showed that the "Anglo-Saxon powers" were bent on world
domination.

Molotov, once Hitler had finished his monologue, agreed with
this critique of British imperialism, declaring it "intolerable and
unjust" that one "miserable island" should rule "half the world."
But he wanted to know more about the Tripartite Pact, and about
German intentions in Finland. Moreover, there are "important
issues to be clarified," Molotov insisted, "regarding Russia's Balkan and Black Sea interests with regard to Bulgaria, Romania, and
Turkey." Just as the discussion was getting down to the really contentious issues, it was interrupted by an air-raid alarm, the arrival
of British bombers overhead giving the lie to Hitler's foolish boast
that the war was 99 percent won.[10]

Returning to his suite at the Bellevue after a dinner reception at
the Hotel Kaiserhof—at which he met the Reich air marshal, Hermann Göring, and Hitler's deputy Führer, Rudolf Hess—Molotov
sat down with his translator, Berezhkov, to write up a transcript

of the Hitler meeting to be wired to Stalin. Berezhkov had, at first, tried to dictate a version out loud to a lower-ranking typist, a mistake he would not make again after Molotov brutally rebuked him for his carelessness (the Germans having presumably bugged their rooms). Molotov was also discomfited by his receipt of a telegram from Stalin around midnight, in which the Vozhd rebuked him for vagueness in his earlier meeting with Ribbentrop (of which a short transcript had been wired to Moscow at 4:20 p.m., in between the two sessions). Stalin was perturbed that Molotov had implied, in his remarks to Ribbentrop about the territorial settlement of 1939 being "exhausted with the exception of Finland," that the entire nonaggression pact might be up for discussion. The Vozhd warned that Molotov had better be more careful when he spoke to Hitler—a warning that would have been less alarming had Molotov not received it after already speaking with Hitler that afternoon.[11]

Both men now on their guard, Berezhkov and Molotov stayed up the whole night working on the Hitler transcript. To reassure Stalin, Molotov sent a brief summary of the Hitler meeting just past 5 a.m. on November 13, declaring himself satisfied so far. Although the talk with Hitler had been "general," he informed Stalin, the Führer had promised to evacuate troops from Romania at the end of the war with Britain. "Hitler's big interest," he said, "lies in agreeing with the USSR on spheres of influence. [He] wants us to focus on Turkey." On Finland, Molotov noted that Hitler had "remained silent," but he promised Stalin that "he would raise the matter and force the Germans to discuss it" the next day.[12]

Upon waking, Molotov paid a visit to Göring at the Air Ministry, where he tried to glean inside information about the Battle of Britain. He was then handed yet another alarming telegram from Stalin, dispatched at 11 a.m., which spelled out in detail exactly what line the Vozhd wanted him to take in his second meeting with Hitler. His thin patience already exhausted by Molotov's vague reports from Berlin, Stalin laid down the law. He instructed Molotov to remind Hitler that, in light of Britain's aggressive moves in the eastern Mediterranean, Russia had a vital interest not only in its own access to the Turkish Straits, but in preventing hostile powers "such as England from attacking her Black Sea coastline." In order to ensure this vital national interest, Stalin insisted that Hitler sign off on a Soviet occupation of Bulgaria and the garrisoning of Soviet troops at the Bosporus, in order to fulfill the "vital Soviet interest of defending access to the Straits." Molotov had no difficulty grasping the Vozhd's meaning. Shortly before departing the Bellevue for his final meeting with Hitler, Molotov sent off an urgent wire to the Kremlin, assuring Stalin, "I got your message. . . . I will hone in on the Black Sea, the Straits, and Bulgaria."[13]

Arriving at the Chancellery just past 2 p.m., Molotov, his translator Berezhkov, Dekanozov, and the Soviet ambassador, V. N. Merkulov, were given a rather "austere" luncheon consisting of "beef tea, pheasant and fruit salad." Hitler explained that, in addition to being a vegetarian (the pheasant was for the others), he was abstaining from coffee during the war. He was also a teetotaler, and did not smoke either. If this was a way of putting the Russian off his guard, it did not work. Still, Molotov was forced on the defensive when Hitler began the discussion by invoking his remark about the Moscow Pact of 1939 being "fulfilled"—recognizing the same sore point that Stalin had.* The Russian was forced to agree that Germany had lived up to its obligations during the Finnish war, and that it had gone beyond what had been promised in the pact by allowing the Soviets to occupy northern Bukovina along with Bessarabia. But Molotov objected that the German security guarantee to Romania (the Vienna Award) had "completely violated the interests of the USSR" in the "southern Bukovina." Hitler reminded Molotov that Bukovina had not even been mentioned in the Moscow Pact or in any subsequent written agreements. Germany, the Führer confessed in a tirade belying his claims that the

---

*With subtle differences. Stalin had objected to the word "exhausted" (ischerpano), whereas Hitler heard "fulfilled" (abgeleistet or erfüllt, retranslated into Russian as vyipolneno).

war with Britain was nearly over, was "engaged in a life and death struggle," and the Reich needed to secure "certain economic and military resources" to continue the fight. Recovering himself, Hitler proposed that it was better if Germany and Russia recognized which areas were most critical to each other and worked together. "I believe," Hitler said grandly, "that our successes will be greater if we stand back to back and fight together against the outside world, than if we face each other down breast to breast." To this, Molotov could only agree, although Hitler's airy stab at solidarity could not hide the obvious tensions over Romania.[14]

A more serious break occurred on the Finnish question. Ominously, Molotov said that the ongoing dispute over the German presence there could be "resolved without war," but only if Stalin was given a firm assurance that "there must be neither German troops in Finland nor political demonstrations in Germany or Finland against the interests of the Soviet Russian government." Hitler patiently explained that Germany was only interested in Finland because of its production of "nickel and timber" and had no designs on its territory. Any German troops dispatched to Finland were there only to guard those supplies, and this deployment "would be finished in a few days." As for "political demonstrations," Hitler objected that Berlin had consistently advised Finland to comply with Stalin's demands. Unsatisfied, Molotov said that he was referring not to diplomacy but to "the dispatch of Finnish delegations to Germany," the reception of prominent Finns in Berlin, the publication of patriotic Finnish slogans criticizing the March peace treaty with the USSR, and so on. Taken aback by the aggressive nature of Molotov's demands, Hitler asked him point-blank whether "the Soviet Union had the intention of resuming the war with Finland." Molotov's answer was not reassuring: "Not if the constant anti-Soviet agitation in Finland ceases." Thrown on the defensive, Hitler spluttered that Germany's only real interest was that Finland remain at peace, repeating that this was to ensure Germany's supplies of nickel and timber. To close the subject, the Führer reaffirmed that Finland "belonged to the Russian sphere of influence," and vowed that Germany would send "no more troops to Finland" nor maintain a permanent military presence there.[15]

Trying to regain the initiative, Hitler changed the subject to the British Empire, hoping to reorient Soviet attention south, or at least to agree on some joint communiqué decrying Anglo-Saxon imperialism. But Molotov, with Stalin's instructions in mind, wanted none of these anti-imperialist platitudes. "Let us talk of matters closer to Europe," he said, "such as Turkey." After a disquisition on the importance of the Turkish Straits for Russia as the "preeminent Black Sea power" and the need to overturn the Montreux Convention, Molotov asked Hitler "what Germany would say if Russia gave Bulgaria, that is, the independent country located closest to the Straits, a guarantee under the same conditions that Germany and Italy had given to Romania?" Annoyed by the question, Hitler objected that Romania had requested a guarantee from Rome and Berlin, whereas "it was unclear that Bulgaria has made any such request of the Soviet Union." Still, Hitler assured Molotov that he was certain the Italians would favor revising the Montreux Convention in order to secure Soviet access to the straits. Moreover, he added, because the Romania guarantee involved Italy, it, too, would have to be consulted on Bulgaria.

Following Stalin's firm guidelines on the straits question, Molotov was not going to be put off so easily. With the British fleet now active in the eastern Mediterranean because of Italy's invasion of Greece, and the Massigli affair in recent memory, Soviet security concerns about the straits were not idle. "We need one thing above all," Molotov insisted to the Führer: "To be guaranteed against any attack through the Straits." "If need be," he added, "we will make arrangements with Turkey" to prevent the British from "using Greek or Turkish territory for an attack on the Straits." Once more, and then a third time, Molotov asked Hitler to express an opinion—even "a provisional one"—"regarding a guarantee to Bulgaria." Hitler, each time, repeated his answer: he would need to know whether Bulgaria had requested a Soviet guarantee and he would have to consult Mussolini. Tiring of the charade, Hitler alluded to the late hour, praised Stalin as a "man who will be remembered by history forever," and suggested (after enduring this unpleasant encounter with Molotov) that next time, the Vozhd himself should come to Berlin.[16]

That evening, Molotov hosted a farewell reception at the Soviet embassy. Unsurprisingly, in view of the unpleasant three-and-a-half-hour grilling Hitler had endured from Molotov—never, Hitler's translator recalled, "had any foreign visitor spoken to him like this before"—the Führer declined to attend, although Ribbentrop, Göring, and Hess did join the large Soviet delegation for drinks. Lubricated by vodka and caviar, the party was just starting to liven up when the Royal Air Force was again heard overhead. Trying to put a brave face on, Ribbentrop joked, after everyone was safely underground, that "our British friends are complaining that they have not been invited to the party." In reality, he tried wanly to reassure Molotov, Britain was "finished." If that was the case, Molotov is said to have retorted, "then why are we in this shelter and whose bombs are falling on us?"[17]

Before Molotov left Berlin, Ribbentrop was game enough to write up and hand over to him a draft agreement transforming the Tripartite Pact into a "Four-Power Pact" devoted to "the early restoration of world peace" (that is, to pressuring Britain into ending the war against the Axis). The four powers would agree to "respect each other's sphere of influence," with the boundaries of those influence spheres "to be valid for ten years." As a sop to Stalin, the Germans put revision of the Montreux Convention front and center, committing the four powers to write up a new convention that "would accord to the Soviet Union the unrestricted right of passage through the Straits for her warships at any time," while denying such access to other powers, such as the British. Molotov promised to respond after he had consulted with Stalin in Moscow.[18]

The mood in the German camp was cautiously optimistic. "Agreement on all questions of mutual interest," Hitler's propaganda chief, Joseph Goebbels, wrote in his diary on November 15, the day after Molotov left Berlin. "A cold shower for the 'friends of the Soviet Union' in London. We can be satisfied. Everything else depends on Stalin. We shall have to wait for his decision."[19]

Molotov must have shown skill in fooling Ribbentrop, for he had already made up his mind that there was little hope of an agreement. As he wired Stalin just past midnight on the night of November 13–14, "Neither meeting [with Hitler] produced desirable results." The Führer had shown teeth on the Finnish question, which they "had spent the bulk of their time discussing." Hitler had swatted Stalin's "Bulgarian guarantee" away by deferring to Italy. On the Turkish Straits, Hitler had again deferred to his alliance partner in Rome, with talk of overturning Montreux, but no approval of a Soviet occupation. When Molotov had raised this question again with Ribbentrop at the farewell dinner, Ribbentrop had insisted that Germany, Italy, Turkey, and the USSR together write up a post-Montreux convention. But "neither Italy nor Germany," Molotov had retorted, "is a Black Sea power." The only "concession" Hitler was willing to give to Soviet Russia, Molotov warned Stalin, "was recognition of the Indian Ocean as our sphere of influence"—a prospect so surreal and unrealistic that it seemed to indicate contempt.[20]

Stalin's formal reply to Ribbentrop's invitation to join the Tripartite Pact was a blunt no. All but confessing its offensive nature, Molotov delivered the rejection to Schulenburg in person on November 25, 1940, in a handwritten note. The Soviet Union would not join the Tripartite Pact, Stalin declared, until five conditions were met. First, "all German troops must be withdrawn from Finland without delay." In exchange, Stalin vowed "to safeguard German economic interests in Finland (the export of nickel and timber)." The second condition was that the Soviet Union be permitted, "in the coming months," to station "naval and land forces [in Turkey] at the Bosporus and the Dardanelles." Third, the signatory powers must recognize "a Soviet sphere of influence south of Baku and Batumi, towards the Persian Gulf." Fourth, Japan must "renounce her claim on the coal and oil reserves of north Sakhalin [island]." Finally, Stalin demanded "a fifth secret protocol . . . recognizing Bulgaria as a security zone of the USSR's Black Sea borders, pursuant to the signing of a mutual assistance pact between the Soviet Union and Bulgaria." Unless these five conditions were satisfied in binding "secret protocols," there would be no Four-Power Pact.[21]

Stalin had made it perfectly clear where he stood. The next move was up to Hitler.

12

Hitler Bars the Door

FROM HITLER'S PERSPECTIVE, Stalin's effrontery had gone beyond all bounds of reason. It was not simply Molotov's aggressive manner in Berlin that had shocked the German dictator, but the concrete dangers posed by Stalin's demands to German interests. The German war effort was dependent enough on Soviet petroleum, grain, cotton, manganese, and other raw materials; now Stalin wanted a stranglehold over Finnish nickel and timber as well. If the Soviets were allowed to take over southern Bukovina and occupy Bulgaria, the oil fields and refineries of Ploești would be effectively surrounded, leaving nearly every drop of natural oil available to the Reich at Stalin's mercy—roughly 83 percent based on 1940 figures, including Caucasian oil shipped across the Black Sea to Odessa and then transshipped by rail via ex-Polish Galicia in Soviet Western Ukraine. Were Red Army troops to garrison the Bosporus and Dardanelles, while Soviet sappers secured the lower Danube and delta, Germany would be cut off from the Black Sea at a time when Britain was already blockading Europe's North Sea, Baltic, Atlantic, and Mediterranean coastlines.

Heightening the shock of Stalin's refusal to join the Tripartite Pact on any but the most insulting terms, the Vozhd's message was delivered just as Hitler was at the height of his power and nearly everyone else who mattered in Europe was coming to pay homage to the great conqueror. In a clear declaration of intent, King Boris III of Bulgaria visited Hitler at Berchtesgaden, just three days after Molotov left Berlin on November 14, 1940. (Although Boris, with a wary eye on Stalin, did not sign a pledge to join Germany just yet.) Over the next ten days, three more countries sent delegations to Salzburg and signed on to the Tripartite Pact: Hungary, Slovakia, and Romania. Meanwhile, the opportunistic Italian invasion of Greece was going ahead. Even if the Italians foundered, the Wehrmacht could easily sweep in via Romania, where German troops were already gathering—and possibly through Bulgaria, if permission was forthcoming—to clean up Mussolini's mess. In a clear expression of intent, Hitler issued directive no. 18 on November 12, 1940—the day of his first meeting with Molotov in Berlin—which strengthened the military mission in Romania with an eye to a future Greek deployment. After the German conquest of Western Europe, the Balkans looked ripe to fall.[1]

Ribbentrop made no formal reply to Molotov's insulting counterproposal of November 25, but we can get a sense of Hitler's reaction from the way he unloaded on the Bulgarian minister to Berlin, Parvan Draganov, in a three-and-a-half-hour monologue on December 3. Returning from a triumphant round of receptions in Salzburg, Hitler was floored by the aggressive tone of Stalin's response to Ribbentrop's invitation to join the Tripartite Pact; it had the ring of an ultimatum. After acquainting his listener with Stalin's proposals, Draganov reported to Sofia, Hitler "said that he now well understood Russia's real intentions and reacted strongly." Germany, the Führer continued, "has already had an unpleasant experience with the Bolshevization of the Baltic countries, from which we are now frozen out and can receive nothing." The loss of Estonia, Latvia, and Lithuania to Communism was bad enough, but this would be nothing compared to the spread of Soviet influence south of the Danube, where "Germany has huge and vital economic interests." This was true, and not only of Romanian oil and petrol refineries: mines dotting the southern Balkans supplied Germany with copper, bauxite (for aluminum), lead, zinc, and molybdenum. Then there was chrome, the alloy used to strengthen steel and improve its resistance to rust and acid, critical in the production of tanks, warplanes, armor plates, and projectiles. The German war economy needed 5,500 tons of chrome each month to function, of which 2,200 came from the southern Balkans (Serbia, Albania, Bulgaria, and Greece) and the other 3,300 tons was shipped through the Balkans from Turkey. For this reason, Hitler told Draganov, he "could not permit the Bolshevization of the Balkans." Showing that these were not mere words, Hitler promised on the spot, in a written pledge scribbled on a notepad, to send Bulgaria by the end of December 1940 "coastal mines, two naval batteries with 17 cm and 24 cm guns, 9,700 kilometers of underwater cable, and an order of rubber dinghies and pontoon bridges." Hitler promised to ship to Sofia, by February, "10,000 shells for 15 cm howitzers, 10,000 shells for 105 cm Polish cannon, 26,000 for 10.5 cm light howitzers, and . . . 40,000 mortars and mines." True to Hitler's word, on December 12, 1940, Germany dispatched a military mission to Bulgaria headed by Colonel Kurt Zeitzler, under the command of Field Marshal Wilhelm List's Twelfth Army. Bulgaria may not have joined the Tripartite Pact, but it was at the top of Hitler's priority list for winter.[2]

Sofia was in Stalin's sights too. Just as Hitler suspected, the idea of a Soviet guarantee of Bulgaria had not originated with the Bulgarians. On November 20, a week after the conclusion of the Berlin meeting, the well-informed Bulgarian Foreign Ministry sent a circular to its diplomats abroad, warning them of the impending Soviet demand for a "security guarantee" or a "mutual assistance pact." On November 22, Molotov summoned the Bulgarian ambassador in Moscow, Ivan Stamenov, to demand clarification of Bulgaria's intentions regarding the Tripartite Pact. Molotov's trusted deputy, Arkady Sobolev, took a break from the ongoing Danube conference in Bucharest to pop in to Sofia on November 25, the same day Molotov was dictating Stalin's quasi ultimatum to the German ambassador in Moscow. Taking a friendlier tone, Sobolev promised Bulgaria's prime minister that "the Soviet Union would support Bulgaria's national aspirations not only in the West" (for example, against Yugoslavia, which had sliced off territory from Bulgaria as a result of the Treaty of Neuilly-sur-Seine), "but also in eastern Thrace" (that is, at Turkey's expense).[3]

Meanwhile, in Moscow that same day, Molotov and Stalin met with Giorgi Dimitrov, the Bulgarian secretary of the Comintern. Hitler may have handed the southern Dobruja over to Bulgaria—receiving for his intervention an effusive letter of praise from Prime Minister Filov and the salutations of the Sofia press—but the Vozhd could play that game too. Molotov got things rolling, informing Dimitrov that, during his visit to Berlin, "we concluded no agreement and assumed no obligations towards the Germans." In view of the Balkan impasse with Berlin, he warned Dimitrov that "immediate measures must be taken to prevent Bulgaria from falling under the exclusive influence of Germany and being used by Germany as a willing instrument." Dimitrov chimed in that the Comintern was already doing all it could in "following a course of demoralizing German troops in the various countries" and offered to "intensify these operations still further." That, Molotov agreed, "is what we must do. We would not be Communists if we did not do this. Only it must be done quietly."[4]

Stalin then summoned Dimitrov to the Kremlin and unloaded on him in a manner eerily similar to the treatment Hitler had given the Bulgarian minister in Berlin. Unless the Bulgarians accepted his offer of a "mutual assistance pact," the Vozhd warned, "they will fall into the clutches of the Germans and Italians and so perish." To sweeten his ultimatum, Stalin proposed to support all of Sofia's remaining territorial claims, some dating back to the Balkan Wars of 1912–1913, from the Turkish-held "Midia-Enos line" and "the Adrianople [Edirne] region of western Thrace," to Greek-held "Dedeagatch, Drama, and Kaválla," and to "render aid to the Bulgarians in the form of loans of grain, cotton, and so forth, as well as our navy." As for Turkey, the intended victim of many of these territorial adjustments, Stalin told Dimitrov that "we need a base to ensure that the Straits cannot be used against us. . . . *We shall drive the Turks into Asia.*" Still, he wanted Dimitrov to know that "the main thing at present is Bulgaria." In a sign of the priority Stalin now accorded Bulgaria, he informed Dimitrov that Arkady Sobolev was in Sofia as they spoke, and that Molotov would shortly summon Bulgaria's ambassador, Ivan Stamenov, to speak in the same vein.[5]

The Soviets may not have been as swift as the Germans in dispatching troops and war matériel, but they excelled in propaganda. Scarcely had Dimitrov left the Kremlin than he fired off a missive to Bulgarian Communist leaders in Sofia, informing them of the territorial promises Stalin had made to Bulgaria if they signed a pact with Moscow, and instructing them to "mobilize our [parliamentary] deputies, and initiate a vigorous nationwide campaign in favor of this proposal; demand its immediate and unconditional acceptance. The destiny of the Bulgarian people for many years to come rests on this decision."[6]

It would be an exciting winter in Sofia. Relegated by the punitive treaties of 1913 and 1919 to the status of a Balkan backwater, Bulgaria was suddenly at the heart of geopolitics. Some of this was owed to spillover from the German-Soviet showdown in Romania and the Italian campaign in Greece, but it was no less heady for that. Fate, and the fortunes of war, had decreed that the two most powerful dictators on earth were battling toe to toe for supremacy in Sofia, of all places—an accidental capital born of Great Power diplomacy at the 1878 Congress of Berlin. Dimitrov's agents in Sofia salted their agitprop with an uncharacteristic appeal to pan-Slavism, accompanied by a classic Communist fake letter-writing campaign, with six hundred "Bulgarian proletarians" from across the country wiring telegrams to Premier Filov—all of which, to the premier's bewilderment, demanded that he invite Soviet troops into his country. (Noticing the identical rhetorical style of the telegrams, Filov concluded, reasonably enough, that they had all been written by a single person.)[7]

Meanwhile, hundreds of German soldiers, camouflaged in civilian clothing, began spreading out across Bulgaria in December 1940, gathering intelligence, scouring for supplies, and preparing the way for a German deployment. In a curious mirroring, both sides claimed, with surface plausibility, that their moves in Sofia aimed to thwart British military plans. And yet neither Hitler nor Stalin could have doubted for a moment who the real opponent in Bulgaria was.

Filov and the Bulgarians were clearly enjoying the sudden attention in this political war between Berlin and Moscow. So, too, were the Germans, once it became clear they were winning. To be sure, King Boris III and Premier Filov were careful not to declare partiality just yet, lest they provoke Stalin into an amphibious strike on Bulgaria's Black Sea coastline before Hitler's promised coastal mines and shore batteries had arrived to secure it. But they signaled their intentions by allowing German troops into the country in early December, and then dithered for days before responding to Stalin's offer of a mutual assistance pact. On December 19, the Soviet ambassador in Sofia lodged a complaint with the German embassy that Stalin's proposal was left dangling (the Germans responded blandly that they had heard Bulgaria's foreign minister was ill). Warned by the Germans that he must not give in to Moscow, Filov on December 20 sent a wire to Molotov politely declining Stalin's offer. By year's end, so many German soldiers had poured in that it was difficult to conceal the truth, whatever Sofia's official position. In a plaintive admission of defeat, TASS announced on January 12, 1941, that press rumors that "the Government of the U.S.S.R. has agreed to this penetration into Bulgaria by German troops" were false.[8]

The playing field was more even in Romania. The Germans were blanketing the country with troops, nearly a half million by the end of 1940. Hitler, by drawing a line in the wet sand of the delta at the Danubian commission conference in Bucharest, had barred the door to further Soviet encroachment into the Balkans. But it should not be forgotten that the Russians were also investing occupied Romania—that is, the Moldavia SSR—with troops, tanks, and fourteen new aerodromes for the Soviet Air Force, with their construction overseen by the NKVD. As in Bulgaria, the Russians did not move as quickly as the Germans, but they were just as thorough in their military preparations. By early 1941, German intelligence was picking up reports of "monstrous numbers of Soviet troops concentrated in Bessarabia and Bukovina."[9]

In Finland, the Russians were holding their own. Although the Germans had signed a defense agreement with Helsinki in September, Stalin had the country positively surrounded. The Red Army had flooded the Karelian Isthmus guarding the approach to Helsinki with troops, and the NKVD was overseeing the construction of four new aerodromes on the territory of Soviet-occupied Finland (that is, the Karelo-Finland SSR). The Hanko Peninsula, which guarded Helsinki from the Baltic in the other direction, was now a massive Soviet forward base behind enemy lines, occupied by an advance echelon of eight "special infantry brigades" that guarded NKVD construction battalions sent to build new bases and modernize the coastal batteries. On November 5, 1940, the Politburo appropriated 45 million rubles for fortifying Hanko.[10]

In view of these aggressive Soviet moves, it was with understandable trepidation that the Finnish ambassador to Moscow received Molotov's warning on December 6, 1940, that, if Finns voted into power any one of four "anti-Soviet" (that is, patriotic) candidates in Finland's upcoming presidential elections, Stalin would interpret this as a "rejection of the Soviet-Finnish peace treaty of 12 March 1940" and act accordingly. Lending credence to Stalin's threat, Molotov recalled the Soviet military attaché from Helsinki. Most ominously of all, from the German perspective, was the arrival in Petsamo, that same week in December, of a large Soviet team of engineers and trade experts, seeking—the Germans feared—to wrest control over Finland's nickel exports.[11]

From the Arctic to the Dardanelles, a phony war had descended on Eastern Europe, just as uneasy as the Sitzkrieg in the West during the first war winter—and, in view of the scale of armor on both sides, far more dangerous to life and limb for anyone unlucky enough to be trapped near the borderlands. While the movement of German troops east from France and southeast into the Balkans was generating the most headlines, Soviet military preparations on the other side of the frontier were on an even larger scale, if not as ruthlessly efficient in logistical execution.

It was not only Hitler and his generals who were beginning to feel an itchy trigger finger. As early as June 1940, German agents had reported from Soviet-occupied Galicia that "the view is universally held in Soviet military circles" that "war between the Soviet Union and Germany is unavoidable, and that the Soviets will be the aggressors." The mood in the NKVD—according to a pro-Axis businessman captured near the Romanian border and interrogated by Beria's agents before being let go—"was not at all friendly to Germany." In "Soviet leadership circles," he continued, "they know exactly what to expect from Germany"—that is, war. "After the Western powers and Germany have bloodied themselves, the [Russians] hope to be in Berlin by 1941 and in Rome by 1942." In July 1940, Molotov himself had coldly informed Stalin's puppet prime minister of Soviet-occupied Lithuania, Vincas Kreve-Mickevicius, that "the decisive battle between the proletariat and the degenerate bourgeoisie will take place in the vicinity of the Rhine, and will decide the future of Europe for all time." Soviet pilots were showing increasing boldness surveilling Hitler's defenses. On December 9, 1940, the German embassy in Moscow filed a complaint about nine recent violations of German and Romanian airspace by Soviet pilots photographing German military installations and, alarmingly, the oil refineries of Ploești.[12]

The timing of that German protest note is significant. It was after reading Stalin's ultimatum of November 25 that Hitler called in Draganov and vowed, on December 3, to go all in on Bulgaria. The departure of Molotov's envoy from the Bucharest Danube conference on November 25 to make a similar push for Stalin in Sofia marked the end of any real effort to mediate the differences between the Romanian-German and Soviet sides on the delta. According to a Western news correspondent, the increasingly fractious Bucharest conference saw "a fistfight break out between the Italian and Soviet delegations" on December 17, just three days before Bulgaria defied Stalin by declining his oppressive offer for a

mutual assistance pact. On December 21, the Bucharest meetings
broke up for good. The Danube conference was thus flaming out
when Hitler issued his secret order no. 21 on December 18, 1940,
declaring that "the German army must be ready, even before the
end of the war with England, to crush Russia in a rapid campaign."
The "end goal of the operation," Hitler's order continued, "is the
creation of a protective barrier against Asian Russia along the line
Volga-Astrakhan. In this manner, in case of need the last industrial
region the Russians have left in the Urals could be paralyzed using
aviation." Order no. 21 represented a critical escalation in Hitler's
planning for a war of conquest in the East.[13]

Having wrung what he could out of the Moscow Pact, Hitler
was now clearing the decks for war. But so, too, was Stalin gearing
up for a showdown with his partner in Berlin. If German intelligence reports about the alarming concentration of armor on the
Soviet side of the border were accurate, the hitherto undefeated
Wehrmacht would have a real fight on its hands.

Josef Stalin and Nikita Khrushchev confer in 1936, as the Great Terror is unleashed. (*Pravda.*)

US ambassador to the USSR, Joseph Davies, while visiting the White House in 1937 (Library of Congress.)

Red Army infantry on the attack at Zhanggufeng (Lake Khasan), near the Korean frontier, July 1938 (Viktor Antonovich Tyomin.)

Soviet troops march toward Khalkin-Gol, circa August 1939. (Ministry of Defense of the Russian Federation, mil.ru.)

Ribbentrop and Stalin share a joke in the Kremlin as Molotov (left) and German ambassador Schulenburg (in rear) look on, August 23, 1939. (Bundesarchiv, Bild 183-H27337.)

A Red Army soldier guards a captured Polish PWS-26 aircraft, shot down near the city of Rovno (Rivne) in eastern Poland on September 18, 1939, the day after the Soviet invasion. (Photograph number HU 87205 of the Imperial War Museums in London.)

Soviet soldiers stand behind a captured Polish armored car in Brest-Litovsk on September 20, 1939, with German officers visible in background. (Photograph number HU 106367 of the Imperial War Museums in London.)

The Red Army occupies Estonia after Stalin secures Soviet military basing rights, October 1939. (Public domain.)

The Russian Army enters formerly Polish Wilno (Vilna/ Vilnius) after the German-Soviet invasion of Poland, October 6, 1939. (Photograph number 87199 of the Imperial War Museums in London.)

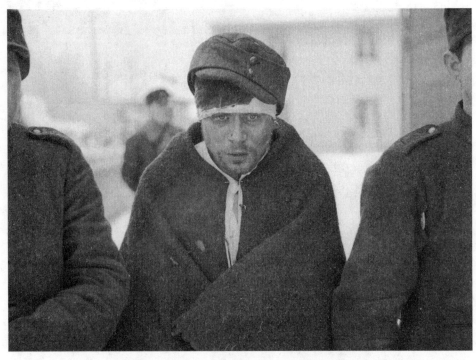

A Soviet war prisoner captured by the Finns, January 1940 (Military Museum of Finland.)

The Red Army marches into Romanian Bessarabia, June 1940. (Romanian National Archives, ANRM, Fototeca, 43928.)

Hitler greets Molotov in Berlin, November 1940. (*Pravda* front page, November 18, 1940.)

Soviet tanks produced by Factory No. 183. From left to right: a BT-7, an A-20, a T-34 from 1940 model year with the L-11 gun, and a T-34 from 1941 model year with the F-34 gun. Both the T-34 and the BT-7 deployed the revolutionary suspension design of the American engineer J. Walter Christie. (Russian government.)

The Il-2 Shturmovik, a Soviet light bomber named after designer Sergei Ilyushin and based on an American Vultee prototype. Stalin initially asked that Ilyushin remove the rear machine-gunner hold in order to make room for a larger bombload and fuel tank, only to relent after Barbarossa was launched, allowing the gunner hold to be restored so the plane could function tactically as a fighter. (San Diego Air & Space Museum.)

The twin-engine Pe-2 was redesigned by Vladimir Petlyakov, to Stalin's specifications, into a low-altitude dive-bomber for close infantry support. (Photo by author.)

A restored Su-2, a Soviet light bomber designed prior to Barbarossa—by Pavel Sukhoi, a veteran of Stanislav Shumovsky's US aviation tours—for the attack. To improve its speed, the plane's steel armor was only 9 mm thick. It proved a disappointment in the defensive war the Soviets were forced to conduct in 1941. (Alan Wilson of Hawkeye UK.)

A BT-7 fast tank captured by the Germans on the eastern front in 1941. Sporting a five-hundred-horsepower diesel engine and riding on the revolutionary suspension designed by the American engineer J. Walter Christie, the BT-7 could shed its caterpillar tracks to run on wheels if traveling on a paved road. But there were few paved roads in European Russia in 1941. (Wehrmacht operational photograph.)

A Soviet T-34 tank captured by the Wehrmacht during Operation Blau in 1942. Like the BT-7, the T-34 rode on a "Christie suspension." (Bundesarchiv Bild number 169-0017.)

Soviet war stores captured by the Finnish Army east of Ketenga, c. November 1941 (SA-Kuva [Finnish Wartime Photograph Archive].)

Jewish victims of a mass pogrom in Kaunas (Kovno) at the Lietukis garage after the German invasion, June 27, 1941 (Vilna Gaon State Jewish Museum of Lithuania.)

Bodies of those murdered by the NKVD prior to the Soviet evacuation of Lwów (Lemberg/ Lvov/Lviv), photographed on July 6, 1941 (Österreichiche Nationalbibliothek.)

A German soldier sifts through clothing and belongings of Jewish victims of the Babi Yar massacre, 1941. (Waralbum.ru.)

Harry Dexter White, assistant secretary of the US Treasury and Soviet spy (Alamy.)

Harry Hopkins meets with Stalin in the Kremlin, July 1941. (Alamy.)

British MK-2 Matilda tanks are loaded at the Liverpool docks for shipment to the USSR, October 17, 1941. (Photograph H 14786 from the collections of the Imperial War Museums.)

III.

PREPARING FOR ARMAGEDDON

13

Mobilizing the Proletariat

By December 1940, Hitler was feeling boxed in by the Moscow Pact, which had left the entire German war effort against Britain hostage to Soviet goodwill. But Stalin, too, saw only diminishing returns. The pact's primary strategic benefit, from the Communist perspective, had already been achieved: embroiling Europe in the "second imperialistic war," as *Pravda* put it on New Year's Eve 1940–1941, thereby "aggravating the internal inconsistencies of the capitalistic order." The idea had been for Germany and the Western powers to destroy each other, as they had nearly done in World War I, leaving the ruins of capitalist Europe ripe for the Communist picking. Instead, Hitler had pulled off a series of miracles. The Wehrmacht had hardly been weakened in the German conquest of western and northern Europe (aside from Luftwaffe losses in the Battle of Britain), and Hitler was now deploying troops in the southeast, too close for Soviet comfort. Hitler's firm stand in Romania and Bulgaria had ended the period of "peaceful" Communist expansion inaugurated in 1939—that is, the forcible Sovietization of countries too weak to resist.[1]

Despite the peace platitudes of Soviet communiqués, Stalin's actions pointed increasingly to war, however and whenever it would start. Since the first Five-Year Plan was inaugurated in 1928, the Soviet economy had been on a war footing. The production targets of the third Five-Year Plan, launched in 1938, were breathtaking, envisioning the production of 50,000 warplanes annually by the end of 1942, along with 125,000 air engines and 700,000 tons of aerial bombs; 60,775 tanks, 119,060 artillery systems, 450,000 machine guns, and 5.2 million rifles; 489 million artillery shells, 120,000 tons of naval armor, and 1 million tons of explosives; and, for good measure, 298,000 tons of chemical weapons. While not all of these targets were realistic or met, progress in the most critical areas—such as tanks, anti-tank guns, and warplanes—was striking. By the end of 1940, the Red Army deployed 23,307 operational tanks, 15,000 45 mm anti-tank guns, and 22,171 warplanes, with thousands more state-of-the-art models of each coming on line in 1941. In these areas, the Red Army was the world's most formidable. The Wehrmacht, by comparison, had only 3,387 panzers on hand prior to the invasion of France in May 1940 (although this was then augmented with French war booty, including 2,170 captured tanks). Göring's vaunted Luftwaffe deployed only 1,800 warplanes in the Battle of Britain—and the RAF had even fewer fighters and bombers. The Red Air Force deployed more warplanes in the supposedly minor campaign in Finland (3,885, including 1,732 bombers) than did the British and Germans combined in the most famous aerial campaign of the war. Soviet pilots flew more than 101,000 sorties in Finland, demonstrating the vast technological potential of the supposedly backward Red Army. Stalin's fighter pilots may have been less well trained and skilled, and his bombers less accurate, than Hitler's and Churchill's. But for sheer mass of pilots, planes, and tanks, the USSR was in its own league, and no one else was close. This was true even of military submarines. By 1941, the Red fleet had 267. Germany, despite its desperate need to destroy Allied shipping, had begun the new war in 1939 with all of fifty-seven U-boats.[2]

Soviet superiority in manpower was more obvious still. The purges of 1937 and 1938 had scarcely dented growth in the raw size of the peacetime Red Army, which expanded from 1.2 million in 1936 to 1.9 million in 1939, 3.75 million in 1940, and over 5 million by spring 1941. The Red Army's projected wartime strength, in case of general mobilization, rose from 5.3 million in 1937 to 6.5 million by 1939, before ramping up to 8.682 million in the mobilization plan for 1941 (as of December 1940). By contrast, the Tsarist army—the "Russian steamroller" of legend that had panicked the German General Staff into (allegedly) launching a preventive war in 1914—had numbered a bit over one million in peacetime and three million after mobilization, both figures one-third the size of Stalin's mechanized (and airborne) steamroller by the end of 1940. As Stalin himself boasted at the sixtieth birthday celebration of Marshal Klim Voroshilov in February 1941, "The Tsarist government dreamt of having in peacetime an army of 1,700,000 and was able to bring the army up to 1,100,000. We have an army of over 4,000,000 and it is well equipped. It is a force that cannot be ignored. . . . We can achieve success in the realm of foreign relations, because we have a mighty army!"[3]

In fact, although German Army intelligence grievously underestimated the scale and quality of Soviet armor in 1941, their estimates of Soviet troop reserves stood at "11 or 12 million," suggesting the German high command had a good idea of the scale of Stalin's mobilization drive. While Germany, being at war since 1939, was (unlike in 1914) already mobilized, the overall strength of the Wehrmacht, as of spring 1941, stood at about 6.7 million men, of which less than half were available on the eastern front against the USSR. Stalin's mobilization plan for 1941 ensured that the Red Army would have a decisive edge in manpower of at least three to one.[4]

These figures do not account for the millions of Soviet subjects—many of them recently acquired via conquest—deployed in Beria's NKVD construction battalions near the German frontier, building roads and rail lines, tank parks, petrol stations, and military airfields. Even free Soviet laborers (that is, those not imprisoned or deported to camps) were already working under the kind of all-out-war conditions that Hitler's own production commissar, Albert Speer, would not impose until 1943. On June 26, 1940, in the hectic period after the fall of France, when Stalin ordered the invasion of four countries, Gosplan, the state ministry of economic planning, extended the Soviet workweek from six to seven days—that is, all of them. On October 2, 1940, Gosplan established a "strategic labor reserve" of Soviet teenagers between the ages of fourteen and seventeen, with an annual target of "800,000 to 1 million" young workers, who would all be trained in advanced military-production techniques. Each of these teenage labor draftees was conscripted for four years of service in Soviet war industry. In every sense of the word, Stalin was mobilizing his people—Gulag and war prisoners, Red Army conscripts and reserves, teenage labor draftees, and ordinary workers—for war.[5]

Raw numbers tell only part of the story of Stalin's ferocious mobilization drive. The Red Army was not only the world's largest and most mechanized force. In many critical areas, it was now the most technologically advanced. Rapallo-era cooperation had allowed the Soviets to copy from and improve on German tank and bomber prototypes, and Stanislav Shumovsky's long-form espionage mission, along with US diplomatic recognition in 1933, allowed Soviet engineers to study and often openly purchase blueprints of the latest American designs as well. By 1940, the Red Army had deployed an impressive variety of Soviet-manufactured tanks, like the BT-7 *bystrokhodnyi tank* (fast tank), which sported a five-hundred-horsepower diesel engine. With a revolutionary suspension designed by American engineer J. Walter Christie and sold to the Soviet trading agency Amtorg in 1930, the BT-7 could shed its "caterpillar" tracks to run on wheels if traveling on a paved road. Then there were the slower but heavily armored forty-five-ton KV models that were almost invulnerable to standard anti-tank guns and had no real equivalent in any other European army (the acronym honored Stalin's crony, Klim Voroshilov).* The most famous Soviet tank was the twenty-nine-ton T-34, which also deployed the efficient "Christie suspension" of the BT-7, mounted the same 76 mm gun as the KV, and was invulnerable to anti-tank shells smaller than 50 mm (and then only at short range). In its

---

*Although the BT track shedding was impressive, it was not useful inside the USSR, which had abysmal roads. The KV tanks faced a similar problem: they were too heavy to cross many Russian bridges. Still, the KV tanks had fared well on frozen ground in Finland.

armor-to-weight ratio and its versatility, the T-34 was superior to anything the Germans had. Since the deficiencies of the light T-26 had been exposed in Finland, Stalin ordered production shifted toward the better-armored T-34 and KV series. Whereas the cheaper T-26 had accounted for half of Soviet tank production in 1939–1940 (3,000 of 5,900 produced), only 102 were built in 1941. The T-34, still in prototype phase in 1939, would see production ramp up from 115 in 1940 (the Politburo had ordered 600) to an impressive 3,027 in 1941. Production of KV tanks for 1941 ramped up to 1,370, a 550 percent increase over 1940. Rounding out Soviet tank priorities was the T-40, a sturdier and more lethal version of the light-amphibious 3.5-ton T-37. The T-40 was still light at 5.5 tons and amphibious, but mounting two armor-piercing machine guns and a 20 mm automatic cannon. Two thousand T-40s were ordered for 1941.[6]

The shift in Soviet tank production toward the T-34 and KV models in 1940 may have demonstrated little more than recognition in the Soviet high command of the inadequacy of the T-26's armor, exposed by the Finns earlier that winter, not any intention of going on the offensive in Europe (at least beyond Finland, Romania, and the Baltics). Had offensive warfare on the better-paved roads of Germany and German-occupied Central Europe been the main consideration in procurement, one would have expected the Soviet high command to order more of the BT rapid tanks after talks with Hitler broke down in November 1940. Instead, production of the road-enabled BT tanks was discontinued after the last 779 rolled off the line in 1940 (although the Red Army possessed, by then, 6,456 of these speedy technological marvels—6,456 more than any other army possessed). The ramped-up production of KVs in 1941, likewise, suggests little more than that Timoshenko had been pleased with the strength of their armor in the Karelian Isthmus offensive of February 1940. Organizationally speaking, the Soviet high command did create nine new mechanized corps in the Red Army in July 1940, each to consist of two entire tank divisions, along with motorized, motorcycle, and logistical elements. But this renewed strategic emphasis on tanks and motorized divisions, coming as it did right after the German Wehrmacht had demonstrated their importance in France, was hardly surprising. With 23,000 operational tanks on hand already by the end of 1940, and another 6,500 tanks ordered in 1941—split roughly three ways between light amphibious T-40s, versatile medium T-34s, and heavily armored KVs—Red Army tank commanders would be, in any case, well-prepared for all possible contingencies.[7]

The spike in T-40 production in 1941, nonetheless, represented something new in Soviet military doctrine and planning, and the timing of the shift is significant. On November 5, 1940—just a week before Molotov arrived in Berlin—the Politburo ordered the formation of *vozdushno-desantnoi brigadyi* (airborne brigades) in the Red Army. Each airborne brigade would consist of 2,900 troops, including four battalions of trained parachutists (each with 546 men), with the airplanes also carrying light and handheld machine guns, eight 45 mm and four 76 mm guns, 50 and 82 mm mortars, 24 motor vehicles, 73 motorcycles, and 11 amphibious T-40 tanks. While modified heavy bombers (such as the TB-3) and cargo aircraft (such as the Soviet PS-84, a copy of the American Douglas DC-3) would carry this equipment, the Soviets were also experimenting with winged military gliders, which would be released after initially being towed by an engine plane. Some of these, like the KT-20, were capable of carrying as many as twenty men. For now, though, the emphasis remained on using the heavier aircraft to transport parachutists, machine guns, and light amphibious tanks. In view of the demands Molotov lodged with Hitler the next week in Berlin, the most likely scenario Stalin had in mind for these airborne-amphibious-tank brigades was a rapid landing along Bulgaria's Black Sea coastline or at the Turkish Straits.[8]

The role of paratroops in the new airborne assault brigades would be paramount. At first glance, it might seem that Soviet military planners were simply trying, as in the emphasis on tanks and motorized divisions, to keep pace with the Germans, who had deployed parachute troops to such devastating effect in Denmark,

Norway, and especially Belgium in 1940. And yet here, as with its tanks, the Red Army was far more advanced than we might expect based on its checkered performance in Finland, where the frontal-assault nature of the campaign and the ferocious hostility of locals behind the front lines had presented few good opportunities for paratroopers. All through the 1930s, the Red Army had been training parachutists, many first jumping off from parachute towers erected in cities before graduating to airborne drops. According to a possibly inflated boast in *Pravda* on August 18, 1940, there were a million trained parachutists in the USSR. Whatever the real number, the Soviet high command made full use of this resource, with thousands of trained parachutists spread out across six airborne brigades.[9]

Stalin's choices regarding air power were still more suggestive of strategic intent. The Soviet high command shifted massive resources into aviation, with the number of both personnel and pilot training schools tripling between 1939 and 1941, to 476,000 men and 111 schools. This was not to count the 100 construction battalions working for Beria's NKVD, numbering 25,000 men each, tasked with building new aerodromes for the rapidly growing Red Air fleet—already the world's largest in 1939, before 10,362 new warplanes were built in 1940 and 20,150 more ordered by the Politburo for 1941. Stalin's aviation priorities can be gleaned from the shift away from the long-range Soviet "strategic" heavy bomber, the TB-7, toward cheaper, mass-produced, low-flying light bombers. The most promising of these were the Su-2 (named after its lead designer-inventor, Pavel Sukhoi, a veteran of Shumovsky's US aviation tours), of which 1,150 were ordered by the Politburo on December 7, 1940, and the Il-2 Shturmovik (named after designer Sergei Ilyushin, although based on an American Vultee prototype), with 1,750 ordered. A third light bomber, designed in prison by Vladimir Petlyakov, was given a radical redesign on Stalin's orders after Petlyakov was freed, transforming a slow, high-altitude heavy bomber (the PB-100) into a faster, low-altitude dive-bomber, mounting an all-metal fuselage bomb bay and a machine gun. The resulting Pe-2 was promising enough that the Politburo ordered 1,700 for 1941. In a Politburo plan approved in November 1940, the Soviet Air Force would be expanded by dozens of new fighter regiments, spearheaded by a high-altitude Mig-3 fighter (of which 3,600 were ordered) that would replace the Polikarpov I-16s used in Spain and Manchuria, and 23 new light-bomber regiments led by the Su-2s, Il-2s, and Pe-2s, charged with providing tactical support for advancing infantry.* By contrast, the Politburo ordered only two strategic bomber regiments composed of TB-7, TB-3 and DB-3s.[10]

The Su-2, Il-2, and Pe-2 were Stalin's answers to the German Ju-87 Stuka dive-bomber and the Japanese Nakajima B-5N, later used at Pearl Harbor. The point of these clear-sky bombers was neither strategic bombing of enemy war-industrial capacity (their range was too limited for this) nor close-order dogfighting (they were too slow and clumsy to outmaneuver fighters); it was to provide close infantry support and conduct bombing raids in essentially uncontested air, as the Germans had done in Poland and France and the Soviets had done (though less successfully) in Finland. The Su-2, mounting the new M-88 engine, had a bombload capacity of four hundred to six hundred kilograms, could fire ten rocket-propelled shells of either 82 mm or 132 mm caliber, and mounted five ShKAS machine guns. To improve its speed, the Su-2's armor was light, with the pilot and gunner protected by a steel skin that was just 9 mm thick. The slower Il-2 was nearly as lethal, with the same bombload capacity, chambers to launch eight rocket missiles, two 23 mm automatic cannons capable of firing 550 rounds per minute, and two machine guns—but it was also

---

*The Mig-3 would prove a disappointment in combat, as it was given no real chance to function at high altitude and was slower than German Messerschmitt fighters at low altitudes. Likewise, the Su-2 struggled in the tactical, often defensive war the USSR found itself in after June 1941, and production was later discontinued. But these disappointments tell us little about how Stalin and the Soviet air command *intended* these planes to be used.

better protected from enemy fighter or ground fire, with cabin, engine, and fuel tanks covered with thick riveted steel armor. The twin-engine Pe-2, after Petlyakov's redesign to Stalin's specifications, was faster and less heavily armed, which gave it versatility. With its speed and ShKAS machine gun, the Pe-2 could even function as a kind of heavy fighter, in addition to its primary function as a light, clear-sky bomber. These were all warplanes designed for the attack, especially so in the case of the Il-2, after Stalin expressly asked that Ilyushin remove the rear machine gunner hold in order to make room for a larger bombload and fuel tank.*[11]

No less significant than the changing composition of Stalin's motorized and tank divisions and the Red Air Force was their rapidly evolving deployment. Since the Siberian-Japanese front had quieted down after August 1939, and Stalin and Hitler had plunged Europe into war, Stalin had concentrated his armed forces in European Russia. As early as summer 1940, after the Germans had rolled up France and the Low Countries and begun redeploying Wehrmacht divisions east—and Stalin had made his own moves in Poland, Finland, the Baltics, Bessarabia, and Bukovina—the Soviet mobilization plan, submitted by Timoshenko on August 18, assumed a European war pitting the USSR against a German-led coalition including Finland, Romania, "possibly Hungary," and, after hostilities had commenced, Turkey and maybe Italy too. Significantly, Germany was assumed to be the most likely European opponent, not Britain, as had been the case during the Finnish war and the Baku crisis in spring 1940. At this stage, Timoshenko was expecting to fight a defensive war, on the assumption that "the Germans' main strike will be directed towards the north of the San

---

* Unlike the Su-2, for which Stalin had such high hopes, the Il-2 would prove its worth in tactical combat—after Stalin relented and allowed the rear-gunner hold to be restored. Again, we find a gap between the kind of war Stalin was planning for and the war the Soviets were forced to fight after June 1941. Of the three light bombers, the Pe-2 proved to be the most effective *as designed*, because its speed allowed it to function as a "heavy fighter" when needed.

River's mouth" from Poland and East Prussia toward Moscow. The invading coalition, Timoshenko estimated, would be able to deploy—with Hungary but not Italy and Turkey included—233 infantry divisions, 10,550 tanks, and 13,900 warplanes against a Red Army numbering, on all fronts, 270 infantry divisions, 11,750 tanks, and 16,400 warplanes. As it would be difficult to fight off a German invasion if these forces were split equally between Asia and Europe, Timoshenko argued that "we must concentrate our main forces in the West." His August 1940 mobilization plan envisioned a western deployment of 143 infantry, 8 motorized, and 18 tank divisions, along with 172 aviation regiments flying 10,320 warplanes.[12]

In view of the deterioration of Soviet-German relations over Balkan issues in fall 1940, Timoshenko's plan, however Europe-focused, was not tilted enough westward to satisfy Stalin. In late September, Timoshenko shifted still more resources to the southwestern front, where Western Ukraine bordered pro-Axis Romania. This front alone would now be blanketed with seventy-five Red infantry divisions, nine tank and four motorized divisions, five special tank brigades, and eighty-eight aviation regiments—nearly as much armor as Timoshenko had proposed to mobilize in the entire European sector north of the Pripyat marshes.[13]

The Soviet mobilization plan was honed further in talks between Timoshenko, Stalin, and the chief of the General Staff, Kirill Meretskov,* held in the Kremlin from October 3 to 5, 1940. In addition to reaffirming that the "main grouping" would occur on the "southwestern front," the October 5 Soviet mobilization plan assumed, for the first time, that the Red Army would ultimately

---

*In a pattern consistent with Stalin's fickle use and abuse of his generals, Meretskov had been imprisoned after his humiliating defeat on the Karelian Isthmus in the Finnish War—only to be let go and promoted to General, then Deputy Commissar of Defense, then chief of the General Staff. To say that such treatment kept Stalin's generals on edge is an understatement.

take the offensive against Germany and its allies. The goal was to concentrate sufficient armor on the southwestern front—80 infantry, 11 tank, and 5 motorized divisions, plus 20 special tank brigades and 140 aviation regiments—to make possible "a powerful strike in the direction of Lublin," with the objective of cutting Germany off from Romania and the Balkans. Of course, to launch such a massive mechanized force onto enemy territory would require a huge investment in logistics and infrastructure in Western Ukraine. To this end, Timoshenko and Meretskov asked that Stalin appropriate whatever funds were necessary to "develop the rail network and build aerodromes" on the western and southwestern fronts, the latter expected shortly to house twenty thousand warplanes. Overall, the new mobilization plan demanded that the Soviet Air Force aim for a balance of 60 percent bombers and 40 percent fighters for 1941, "with *all of them to be used in the West.*"[14]

In mid-December 1940, after Stalin's demands were rejected and German countermoves had begun in Romania and Bulgaria, the Balkan situation was threatening enough that Stalin ordered a detailed "Plan for Southwestern Front Deployment" from the commander of the Kiev military district, General M. A. Purkaev. Purkaev's report outlined his district's available force pool and armor (twenty infantry and five mechanized corps, including eleven tank and five motorized divisions, thirteen special tank and seven motorized brigades, eighty-one aviation regiments, and two airborne assault brigades); measured the carrying capacity of the railroads running west toward the frontier; summarized the state of aerodrome construction in Western Ukraine, Bessarabia, and northern Bukovina; and proposed a mobilization timetable for each "echelon" of the force that would invade Romania and the Reich, including how long it would take them to reach the enemy border.[15]

The most dramatic material evidence of more offensive Soviet intent was the construction of forward air bases abutting the new frontier separating Stalin's empire from Hitler's. The "Main Soviet Administration of Aerodrome Construction," run by the NKVD, ordered the construction of 251 new Red Air Force bases in 1941, of which fully 80 percent (199) were located in western districts abutting the German Reich—and not just any districts either. They were built in territories Stalin had acquired since the Moscow Pact, including sixty-one in Western Belorussia (the northern sector of occupied Poland), fifty-four in Western Ukraine (the southern sector of occupied Poland), five in Soviet Moldavia (occupied Bessarabia and northern Bukovina), eleven in Sovietized Latvia, seven in Lithuania, five in Estonia, four on the Karelian Isthmus of occupied Finland, and four in the Soviet border district abutting East Prussian Königsberg. There were also eighteen new aerodromes being built in the military districts of Kiev and Odessa—essential to operations on the southwestern front, including surveillance and bombing runs into Romania—but recessed further from the enemy frontier than the other aerodromes. The cost of each of these new Soviet air bases, even with the use of NKVD slave labor, averaged 16 to 17 million rubles. Stalin thus spent 3.3 billion rubles in 1941 building air bases within a half hour's flying distance of Hitler's Reich. Whatever else may be said about this, it was clearly an extraordinary and high-risk strategic investment.[16]

The most interesting aspect of the new Soviet deployment pattern lay in its lopsided emphasis on the southwestern front, facing Galicia and Romania. To be sure, Hitler had never made a secret of his interest in the economic resources of Ukraine, a theme he first sounded in *Mein Kampf* in 1925. The Führer's fixation on Ukraine would have been an argument in favor of Stalin devoting significant military resources there. But the Soviet deployment pattern in Ukraine in 1940–1941 was not defensive. There was no Maginot Line going up south of the Pripyat marshes. Unlike in the years before 1914, when the Tsarist government had disappointed Russia's French ally by refusing to invest in new rail lines in the West for fear they would be used by the Germans, this time the Russians were building as many roads and rail lines as Beria's NKVD slave conscripts could manage, along with tank parks and petrol stations. Even the last line of Russia's logistical defense—the wider rail gauge of 1,524 mm (5 feet), incompatible with the European standard of 1,435 mm (4 feet, 8½ inches)—was being eroded in the borderlands, with Soviet engineers re-gauging 7,500 kilometers of the railway network to facilitate movement westward. It is true that there were still defensive fortifications left in place from the "Stalin line" built behind the old frontier between 1926 and 1937, mostly concrete pillboxes housing machine guns. Roughly 200 to 250 kilometers (about 140 to 180 miles) west of the Stalin line, in territories occupied since 1939, construction of pillboxes had begun in June 1940, but coverage was thin; border troops referred to the half-hearted defensive system derisively as the "Molotov line." Rather than fortification to slow down an advancing army, far more Soviet resources were devoted to building infrastructure to speed an army's movement.[17]

The first hint that something new was afoot in Soviet war planning came in General Staff exercises conducted from January 2 to 6, and 8 to 11, 1941. Defense Commissar Timoshenko directed the games at General Staff headquarters in Moscow, with the participation of four Soviet field marshals and forty-nine generals, including the commanders of all of the European military districts that would be tasked with fighting the Germans. Stalin and the entire Politburo watched as a kind of board of judges. One group, led by the commander of the "Western Special Military District," General D. G. Pavlov, a career officer and World War I veteran, would direct Soviet operations, while Zhukov led a team fighting for Germany. Two plans were road tested, and they both assumed that the Soviets—after an initial attack by Germany and its allies that somehow failed to gain traction—would go on the offensive, either north of the Pripyat marshes from Bialystok and Lithuania against German Poland and East Prussia (variant one), or south of them from Western Ukraine and Moldavia SSR, against southern Poland, Hungary, and Romania (variant two).[18]

Not surprisingly, in view of the lopsided concentration of motorized and tank divisions on the southwestern front, the northern variant proved disappointing. In this version of a Red Army counterattack, Pavlov's counterthrust did reach Rastenburg and Allenstein, penetrating some two hundred kilometers northwest of Bialystok. But his armies were bogged down quickly in the marshy, heavily forested East Prussian plain. Pavlov failed to encircle any of Zhukov's German armies or reach the Vistula (Wisła), much less Danzig (Gdańsk), which was the strategic objective of the exercise. Zhukov's Germans had little trouble grinding down the invading Reds before seizing the initiative themselves in a series of counterattacks. The offensive was judged a failure.[19]

In the southern variant, Pavlov swept to a crushing victory over the Germans. Within five weeks, following a prospective launch date in the drier period of late summer—with remarkable specificity, this was declared to be August 8, 1941—the Soviet armies on the southwestern front had advanced nearly three hundred kilometers beyond the German frontier into Romania (reaching Timișoara and Craiova), marched into Hungary all the way to Budapest, conquered Slovakia, and swept into Poland from the southeast toward Lublin as far as Cracow. In this version, unlike the northern one, the Red Army even reached the Vistula (Wisła) in central Poland, the scene of its furthest advance in the Polish-Soviet War of 1920. Impressively, Pavlov was able to force a contested crossing of the Dniestr River and fight off Zhukov's German counterattacks near Kovel and Stryi, despite enjoying only 30 percent superiority in troop numbers. Most important, Pavlov succeeded, by way of his broad thrust into Poland and Hungary, in cutting Zhukov's Germans off from the Romanian oil fields.[20]

The lessons of the January war games were incorporated into the next mobilization plan drawn up by Timoshenko and Zhukov, the latter of whom Stalin promoted to chief of the General Staff on February 1, 1941. It was now clear that Stalin expected his generals to meet a German-led invasion (if and when this occurred) with a massive counterattack onto enemy territory. The northern variant was mothballed, and still more armor was concentrated on the southwestern front. In view of Hitler's well-known designs on Ukraine, it was assumed, in the new Timoshenko-Zhukov plan drawn up on March 11, that the enemy would "concentrate its main forces in the southeast—in between Sedlets [Siedlce, due east of Warsaw in German-occupied Poland] to Hungary, in order to prepare an attack on Kiev via Berdichev." Romania was expected to throw thirty divisions into Bessarabia and northern Bukovina. Diversionary German attacks were also expected in the Baltic region, accompanied by a Baltic blockade and a landward strike by Finland across the Karelian Isthmus. The enemy would not get far, however, before a Russian counterattack would begin and thrust deep into enemy territory. Perhaps overoptimistically, in view of the blitzkrieg tactics the Germans had road tested in Poland and France, Timoshenko and Zhukov assumed that they would be given a grace period of "10–15 days" to prepare their own counteroffensive on the southwestern front as the German armies concentrated for the initial assault. An idea of the heady atmosphere in which this plan was prepared can be gleaned from a note scribbled by one of Zhukov's staff officers (probably the deputy chief of staff, N. F. Vatutin) on the back of page twenty-seven of the original, discovered recently by a Russian military historian who writes under the pseudonym Mark Solonin. Stalin, this bold general proposed—confusingly, in view of the assumption of a German first strike—should "commence the attack on June 12."[21]

Still, however belligerent the mood in the Soviet General Staff might have been by March 1941, there remained considerable uncertainty about how an armed conflict might start. While Soviet procurement and war planning was now entirely focused on the scenario of a European war against Germany and its allies in the West, with only a holding pattern against Japan in the Far East, there was no reason for Timoshenko and Zhukov to assume that Stalin would have the luxury of striking first (indeed, the plan of March 11 still assumed that Hitler would). All winter, reports of alarming German military preparations near the Soviet frontier were pouring into Moscow. Then there were German forward moves in Finland, Romania, and Bulgaria, and Ribbentrop's assembling of a coalition of neighbors keen to avenge recent territorial losses at Soviet expense. However impressive Stalin's amassing of armor and airfields near the German frontier may have appeared in material terms, Soviet military planners faced an imposing multinational coalition of enemies. Between the September and December 1940 mobilization plans, Hungary had been added to Finland and Romania among Timoshenko's expected opponents. By March 1941, Italy, too, was reckoned among Stalin's likely adversaries in a European war, rounding out an enemy coalition of five.* Nor was the Japanese threat neutralized, as Zhukov and Timoshenko were forced to concede in their March mobilization plan, which still allotted "between 28 and 30 infantry divisions" to defend the Soviet Far East. Even the United States remained distinctly cool toward Stalin, with Roosevelt's "moral embargo" on strategic exports to Moscow imposed during the Finnish war still, theoretically, in force. In diplomatic terms, the USSR was nearly as isolated as it had been twelve months earlier, before the end of the Finnish war.[22]

Stalin, however, still had tricks up his sleeve. Just as it seemed that Hitler's diplomats had seized the initiative, Molotov and Stalin turned the tables, ending Soviet isolation for good.

---

* Or seven, if one counted Slovakia and Bulgaria, which had both signed on by then to the Tripartite Pact. But Soviet planners did not count them, reckoning that neither country would contribute significantly to a German-led invasion force. Slovakia did contribute some fifty-two thousand troops to Barbarossa. Bulgaria, though sympathetic, stayed formally neutral.

14

The Battle for Belgrade

As IN THE Sitzkrieg of 1939–1940, the lull in serious campaigning during the second war winter opened up possibilities for diplomatic intrigue. The attempted Italian invasion of Greece had been bogged down in a stalemate after the Italians had been repulsed from the Greek frontier in November and pushed back into Albania. Meanwhile, Mussolini's equally desultory invasion of British Egypt from Italian Libya in September 1940 had gone into reverse after Britain launched Operation Compass in December. There remained a sense of dread in Athens that the Wehrmacht would sweep down through the Balkans to bail out the blundering Italians, although Hitler had so far resisted the temptation, preferring to let the Italians do their own fighting. Of course, the creeping German military presence in Bulgaria was also a possible threat to Greece, but it remained smaller than the half million German soldiers in Romania further north—so small that Sofia kept denying all winter that the Wehrmacht was in Bulgaria at all. Only on March 2, when the first large echelon of German troops crossed the Danube heading south, was the Bulgarian government forced to admit to Moscow that, contrary to its earlier denials, it had indeed given consent to the arrival of German military personnel. Was Hitler, despite rumors of plans to invade the USSR, preparing to intervene in Greece after all?[1]

Adding to the complications of Balkan geopolitics was the neutrality of Yugoslavia. The advent of Communism in Russia had broken the bond between the Serbs and the Russians, who had fought for Serbia in 1914, leaving the new Serb-dominated state of Yugoslavia distinctly cool toward the USSR. Yugoslavia had

had no formal relations with the Soviet Union until June 25, 1940, when, after the fall of France, recognizing Moscow allowed Belgrade to escape isolation. Since 1934, Yugoslavia had adhered to a Western-oriented Balkan Entente alongside Romania, Greece, and Turkey. But France and Britain had not extended to Yugoslavia the same security guarantees they had to Poland, thus leaving it vulnerable to German pressure. In view of the country's prime strategic location, Hitler had repeatedly promised Yugoslavia's sovereign, Prince Paul, that he would respect the country's borders. (Paul had been regent, or acting head of state, since the assassination of King Alexander I in 1934, and he would remain regent until Alexander's son Peter turned eighteen in August 1941.) True to his word, Hitler had ensured that Belgrade, unlike Bucharest, forfeited no territory during the Balkan shake-up of fall 1940, although Yugoslavia had enlarged itself in the postwar treaties just as Romania had. Hitler had also respected Belgrade's neutrality by refusing to deploy troops in Yugoslavia, which had forced the Germans to take a circuitous path south toward Greece via Romania and Bulgaria. Germany's slow-motion deployment, from the arrival of the first echelon in Bucharest to the crossing of the Danube into Bulgaria, took nearly five months.[2]

The long delay gave Hitler's opponents plenty of time to prepare countermeasures. Churchill's new Special Operations Executive (SOE), established on July 19, 1940, was tasked with "co-ordinating all action by way of subversion and sabotage against the enemy overseas." Yugoslavia and the Balkans—which Hitler desperately needed to keep quiet to ensure the flow of oil, chrome, and foodstuffs into the Reich—were obvious targets for no-holds-barred, consequences-be-damned sabotage. Quietly, the SOE infiltrated Belgrade in fall 1940, cultivating ties with opposition figures, including the seventeen-year-old heir to the throne, Prince Peter.[3]

So seductive was Balkan war intrigue that winter that US president Roosevelt dove in too, belying his government's ever-less-credible professions of neutrality. In January 1941, Roosevelt dispatched to the region his trusted friend, the colorful World

War I veteran Colonel William "Wild Bill" Donovan, who had recently visited London and met with Churchill and the head of Britain's Secret Intelligence Service (MI6), Stewart Menzies. A gung-ho warrior in Churchill's mold who was fervently committed to plunging the United States deeper into the war, Donovan was an inspired choice for Roosevelt's Balkan initiative. Churchill had wired ahead to British ambassadors and commanding officers in the Mediterranean war zone that Donovan "has been taken fully into confidence." Donovan was flown around by the RAF and his expenses were paid by MI6, which attached a British liaison officer to him. In a sense, Donovan was carrying out a mission for both Roosevelt and Churchill, even if his official status was as a US envoy spreading the president's message that "Franklin Roosevelt did not intend to let Great Britain lose this war."[4]

Arriving in Athens on January 11, 1941, with this signed letter of introduction from Roosevelt, Donovan assured the Greek government that, if Hitler intervened in the Greek-Italian war, Athens could count on US support. On January 21 and 22, Donovan visited Sofia and met with King Boris III and Premier Filov, promising that, if Bulgaria resisted German encroachment, it would receive US aid. Donovan "would not talk about peace," Filov wrote in his diary, "until the Germans had been definitively crushed"—an interesting vow, given that the United States was still neutral in the war. Finally, Donovan visited Yugoslavia from January 23 to 25. His movements across the Balkans were closely followed by German intelligence—so closely that a German agent stole one of his bags from a hotel room in Sofia, unless it was on the train from Sofia to Belgrade. The "burgling" of Donovan's briefcase became a news sensation.[5]

Even discounting press exaggeration, the Donovan mission to Belgrade was a critical episode in the diplomatic history of the Second World War. At a time when American support for Britain against Hitler was widely assumed in Europe but not officially declared, Wild Bill left the Yugoslav government in no doubt about where Roosevelt really stood. "The United States," the president vowed in a letter he authorized Donovan to share with his hosts, "is looking forward not merely to the present but to the future, and any nation which tamely submits on the grounds of being quickly overrun [i.e., by German troops] would receive less sympathy from the world than the nation which resists, even if this resistance can be continued only a few weeks."[6]

What Roosevelt implied, his envoy stated openly. Donovan, a Belgrade official told an American journalist later that spring, "told the [Y]ugoslav leaders there was no halfway house in this war. . . . They must make a flat choice between the British-American combination and the Axis." Donovan struck a chord with General Dushan Simovich, the commander of the Yugoslav Air Force, who assured him that "Yugoslavia would not permit the passage of German troops through its territory." Prince Regent Paul also assured Donovan that "Yugoslavia would not permit [German] troops or war materials to pass." After receiving this encouraging news, Roosevelt promised the Yugoslav ambassador on February 14 that the lend-lease bill working its way through Congress, designed to enable the president to sidestep restrictions on sending arms to belligerent countries, would soon "give the United States government the power to help effectively those peoples who might be the victims of aggression or who are threatened with aggression."[7]

Neutral or not, under Roosevelt's leadership the United States was getting more deeply involved in the European war by the day. After winning reelection to an unprecedented third term in November 1940, the president launched his campaign to sell lend-lease to the public in a fireside chat radio broadcast on December 30, admonishing Americans that their country must become "the great arsenal of democracy." Parallel to his introduction of the lend-lease bill before Congress, Roosevelt wanted to lift his own moral embargo against strategic exports to the USSR. In January 1941, the Soviet ambassador in Washington, Konstantin Umansky, complained to Roosevelt's trusted undersecretary of state, Sumner Welles, about "anti-Soviet trade discrimination."

(The well-informed Soviets knew the president had no confidence in his secretary of state, Cordell Hull, a Tennessean appointed to appease the Democratic Party's southern conservative wing.) After Welles, a close confidant of the president, passed on Umansky's complaint, the president, seeing a chance to cultivate Stalin as a counterweight to Hitler, dispatched his Soviet-friendly White House adviser, Harry Hopkins, to meet Umansky on February 11. Over the heads of Hull and other State Department officials, Hopkins approved a backlog of import orders placed by the Soviet purchasing agency, Amtorg, including airplane engines, trucks, oil-well drilling equipment, electric furnaces, and machine tools, all to be shipped to Soviet Arctic ports. Hopkins quietly established a liaison committee to coordinate future Soviet orders between Umansky and the White House.[8]

In the congressional debates over lend-lease in February 1941, Republicans and conservative southern Democrats cried foul at the idea of military aid being sent to Soviet Russia, a country still allied with Nazi Germany. On February 7, Republican representative George Tinkham of Massachusetts, denouncing Roosevelt's "carefully planned involvement of the U.S. in war," tried to booby-trap the lend-lease bill by inserting an amendment designed to exclude Stalin. ("After the words 'any country,' insert 'other than the Union of Soviet Socialist Republics.'") Robert Reynolds of North Carolina, a Democrat, introduced a similar amendment during the Senate debate. After these amendments were voted down (185 to 94 in the House, 56 to 35 in the Senate), FDR's Democratic loyalists inserted a clause granting the president "moral discretion" to determine which countries were worthy recipients of lend-lease military aid, if "his decision" on whether their defense was "vital to the defense of the United States" was "reached . . . in good faith." It was this implicitly pro-Soviet version that was voted into law on March 11, 1941. In this way, Roosevelt assured himself a free hand to send arms not just to England, Greece, and other countries already resisting armed aggression by Nazi Germany and Fascist Italy, but also to the neutral USSR—no matter that Stalin had invaded seven sovereign countries in the past two years in quasi alliance with Hitler. The Neutrality Acts were dead, along with Roosevelt's own moral embargo on arms exports to the Soviet Union.[9]

Churchill could not have been more pleased. Even though the terms of lend-lease aid to Britain were debilitating and deliberately insulting, he acclaimed lend-lease as "the most unselfish and unsordid financial act of any country in history."[*] Aside from ensuring that Britain could fight on, lend-lease, as interpreted by Roosevelt and his supporters, represented a cautious endorsement of Churchill's vision of a grand alliance uniting Washington, London, and Moscow against Nazi Germany—Stalin's pact with Hitler notwithstanding.[10]

Reinforcing the trend toward Anglo-Saxon rapprochement with Moscow was the shake-up in the British Foreign Office after the long-serving British ambassador to Washington, Lord Lothian, died in December. The opening up of this post gave Churchill an excuse to rid himself of the last remnant of Chamberlain's influence by booting Halifax over to Washington. Replacing Halifax was former foreign secretary Anthony Eden, who, although a Tory, was preferred by Churchill and his Labour allies as a committed anti-Fascist closely aligned with Churchill on the need to cultivate Stalin. His appointment was welcomed by the Soviet ambassador, Maisky.[11]

The first road test of the grand alliance implied in Roosevelt's Lend-Lease Act came in Belgrade later in March 1941. Because Yugoslavia blocked Hitler's most direct path south to Greece, keeping the Wehrmacht out of Belgrade was now a cardinal interest of

---

[*] The Lend-Lease Act was entered into the *Congressional Record* as H.R. 1776—the year the United States had declared independence from England. The final installment of Britain's crushing World War II debt burden incurred to the United States was paid on December 29, 2006, by electronic funds transfer. In defense of the hard bargain Roosevelt drove with Churchill, Britain never paid off its World War I debts to the United States, but had defaulted on them in 1934.

Britain. Stalin and Molotov had just observed Yugoslavia's neighbor Bulgaria adhere to the Axis and were anxious that the regime in Belgrade, once so friendly to Moscow, not do the same. Why any of this concerned the ostensibly neutral United States was less obvious, but the Donovan mission to Belgrade had made clear to "every carpenter and clerk in Belgrade"—as an American correspondent in the city noted in wonderment—that it did.[12]

Yugoslavia—like Bulgaria had been three months earlier—was suddenly at the heart of geopolitics because of the belligerent powers' intensifying focus on Greece, and the country faced a wrenching strategic dilemma. Hitler had been exceedingly polite to Prince Regent Paul at Berchtesgaden, assuring him that no German troops would violate Yugoslavia, allowing Belgrade to remain neutral in the war if its leaders desired to, and promising to support the "extension of [Yugoslavia's] sovereignty to the city and harbor of Salonika" on the Adriatic coast. But the Führer had also made it clear that a refusal to adhere formally to the Tripartite Pact would be viewed as a hostile act. So effusive was Hitler that he confessed to Paul his plans to invade the USSR, perhaps hoping that this would reassure Yugoslavia he had no designs on its territory.* But Roosevelt had made it equally clear that, if the prince regent signed a deal with Hitler, he would view this as a hostile act—strange, in view of the fact that the United States was neutral, but FDR was no less emphatic for that. Neither Churchill nor Stalin had gone this far yet. Indeed, fearing that a coup in Belgrade might trigger a German forward move, Stalin was loath to authorize subversive action by the Yugoslav Communist Party, headed by Josip Broz (Communist code name Tɪᴛᴏ). So carefully was Stalin treading that the Comintern had not even authorized the resumption of pan-Slavist propaganda in the country, as Dimitrov had done in

---

* This confession was shared with the US minister in Belgrade, who forwarded it to Roosevelt. Arriving before the passage of the Lend-Lease Act, this intelligence coup helped buttress the president's commitment to support Stalin if war broke out on the eastern front.

Bulgaria. The furthest Stalin was willing to go was to let Tito stage demonstrations in favor of a "Yugoslav-Soviet friendship treaty," an implied rebuke of the Tripartite Pact, but only implied.[13]

The British were less careful. In general, London and Britain's Cairo command were focused more on Greece than Yugoslavia. A British expeditionary force was duly dispatched from Egypt to Greece on March 8, along with an RAF squadron sent to Athens. Still, Britain's minister in Belgrade, Ronald Campbell, and the SOE maintained close contacts with General Simovich and other pro-Allied Serbian Army officers. Campbell even asked Eden, on March 21, whether he should break off relations with Belgrade if Yugoslavia signed on to the Tripartite Pact. Eden urged caution but also advised that Campbell "should bear in mind that rather than allow Yugoslavia to slip by stages into the German orbit we are prepared to risk precipitating German attack" on Yugoslavia. Churchill, after learning that Prince Regent Paul had visited Hitler in Berchtesgaden on March 18, sent a warning on March 22, which reinforced the impression that Britain was coordinating its Balkan policy with the Americans. Although offering no military aid, Churchill said it would behoove Paul to choose the right side in a war in which "the British empire and the United States have more wealth and more technical resources and they make more steel than the whole of the rest of the world put together." Choose unwisely now, and Yugoslavia would face the wrath of the freedom-loving Brits and Americans after the war.[14]

Not surprisingly, the beleaguered prince regent found Hitler's implied threat of immediate consequences more credible—in view of the fact that his country was surrounded by German troops—than the vaguer danger of displeasing the distant US and British powers in the future. ("You big nations are hard," Paul told the US minister in Belgrade, Arthur Bliss Lane. "You talk of our honor, but you are far away.") On March 24, 1941, the Yugoslav ambassador in Washington informed Roosevelt that Paul had dispatched his prime minister and foreign minister to Vienna to sign a deal with Hitler. The next day, Yugoslavia formally joined the

Tripartite Pact. Hitler and Ribbentrop had won another major trick against Stalin and Molotov.[15]

They had not reckoned, however, on the curious convergence of foreign policy aims among Moscow, Washington, and London. So vehement was the reaction in the US and Soviet capitals to the news from Vienna that the Yugoslav ambassadors in each city decided, as the Washington ambassador Constantin Fotitch recalled, to "coordinate our actions with a view to forming a Committee for a Free Yugoslavia." In London, Churchill asked the secretary of state for India, Leo Amery—a Serbophile who had served on the Balkan front in World War I—to issue an appeal to Belgrade in a BBC radio broadcast. Goading the Serbs, Amery saluted their heroism in the last war, which had "won the admiration of the world," before sinking in the knife of shame. "Do you want now to be classed among the Romanians and Bulgarians," he asked, "as second-class men who followed the Germans because they dared not face them in the field?" It thus came about that a public relations campaign, loosely coordinated between the Yugoslav embassy in Moscow and the governments in Washington and London, set out to undermine the Yugoslav government within hours of the signing ceremony in Vienna.[16]

It is important to emphasize the semiofficial nature of the campaign to discredit the government of the prince regent, at least in Washington and London; Stalin and Molotov, still wary of provoking Hitler, were keeping their hands clean for now. The results were serious. At 2 a.m. on March 27, 1941, Yugoslav officers in the Royal Guard Corps in Belgrade, along with air force officers stationed nearby—nearly all Serbs—spread out across the capital, seized key strongpoints, surrounded the royal palace, and declared the government deposed. German-owned businesses and tourist bureaus were sacked, along with Italian shops. The prime minister and foreign minister, signatories of the Tripartite Pact, were arrested, and Prince Paul was sent into exile. Prince Peter, the soon-to-be-eighteen-year-old heir, was installed on the throne. The leader of the revolutionary government and its first premier

was, significantly, air force general Dushan Simovich—the man
who had promised Donovan back in January that the armed forces
would resist a German violation of Yugoslavia. As if to confirm
that the inspiration for the coup had originated in Washington,
the first public demonstration in Belgrade celebrating it was held
in front of the US legation, which was soon, as an American journalist observed,

> stormed by crowds of cheering Serbs who demanded that the
> American Minister, Arthur Bliss Lane, should bring out the Amer-
> ican flag. When he finally yielded to the clamor they tore the ban-
> ner from his hands, and men and women trampled one another
> in their efforts to touch our flag and kiss it. . . . Later that same
> day, when the American minister drove through the streets of
> the capital, he was lifted out of his automobile and carried on the
> shoulders of the Serb demonstrators.[17]

Far from disowning involvement in the coup d'état in Belgrade,
Roosevelt and Churchill immediately endorsed it. The president
cabled the new teenage king, Peter II, to celebrate "the freedom
and independence of Yugoslavia" before news of the deposition
of the prince regent had even been transmitted to the US government. By noon on March 27—just hours after the coup had
begun—Churchill declared during a scheduled public address in
London that "the Yugoslav nation has found its soul," in time for
this catchy endorsement to make the evening papers. The coup
was heralded in the New York Times on March 28 as a "lightning
flash illuminating a dark landscape." On April 3, Roosevelt called
in the Yugoslav ambassador and instructed his right-hand man
Harry Hopkins, whom he had just put in charge of the lend-lease
program approved by Congress, to "devote all his attention . . . to
the supplies for the Yugoslav army."[18]

Stalin was more circumspect in embracing the new anti-
German government in Belgrade. The news was welcome as a
blow to Hitler's ambitions in the Balkans: "German circles were

dumbfounded," Filipp Golikov, the head of Soviet military intelligence, reported to Stalin. But the strange thing was that the Yugoslav Communists—though no friends of the prince regent and his
government, which they had frequently protested—had had very
little to do with the coup. The Soviet chargé d'affaires in Belgrade,
V. Z. Lebedev, did boast to Molotov that he had been surrounded
by well-wishers, but in truth the real action was at the US legation, not the Soviet one. Tito's initial line on the revolutionary
government was cool. Party pamphlets printed up on March 31
warned Yugoslav comrades not to be drawn in "by the ferocious
British war instigators and the Greater Serbian national extrem-
ists who, with their provocative behavior, drive the country into
war," urging instead that the country sign a mutual assistance pact
with the USSR. Still, as signs emerged of the popularity of the revolution, Tito's oppositional stance began to seem like a liability to
Stalin. Was Russia, historic patron of the Serbian people, going to
abandon the cause, even as it was being championed by the hated
British and Americans?[19]

Not if Stalin had anything to say about it. Quietly, with none
of the fanfare with which London and Washington had celebrated
the anti-Axis coup in Belgrade, the Soviet government opened
back-channel negotiations with Simovich's advisers. As early as
March 30, the revolutionary government in Belgrade submitted
a request for Soviet arms exports. In a pattern soon to become
familiar across Eastern Europe, Churchill and Roosevelt had thus
helped midwife a new government that immediately fell into
Moscow's orbit. As the new Yugoslav war minister explained to
the Soviet chargé d'affaires, if Belgrade accepted military aid from
London, "it would mean war," whereas Stalin could use his friendship with Hitler to "prevent Germany from attacking us." Just past
midnight on Saturday, April 5, Molotov signed a "friendship and
non aggression pact" with Belgrade, in time for the news to be
trumpeted by the Soviet press Sunday morning. Stalin had surprised the Yugoslav ambassador to Moscow, Milan Gavrilovich,
by inviting him to the Kremlin Saturday night, offering a "hearty

welcome" and suddenly agreeing to all terms the ambassador had demanded, including massive shipments of Soviet anti-tank guns and warplanes. Helpfully, a special envoy of General Simovich, Major Sima Bozich, had just arrived in Moscow to draw up a list of Yugoslav Army needs. Stalin told Bozich he had in mind not simply a treaty but a "military alliance" between Belgrade and Moscow. Gavrilovich, a career diplomat, was cautious. "What if Germany becomes angry, and attacks you?" the ambassador asked the Vozhd, who replied—in a manner Gavrilovich found "unperturbed and serene"—"Let them come!"[20]

Unfortunately for the peoples of Yugoslavia, Hitler responded immediately to the anti-German coup d'état in Belgrade—a coup now endorsed by Churchill, Roosevelt, and Stalin—not by invading the USSR, as Gavrilovich had plaintively wished, but by invading Yugoslavia in retaliation (the operation was code-named *Strafgericht*, "punishment"). As early as March 30, the German minister to the deposed Yugoslav government left Belgrade. Over the next week, Wehrmacht commanders in German Austria, Romania, and Bulgaria prepared invasion plans with their usual thoroughness, in coordination with the Hungarian and Italian armies and with renegade Croatian leaders, who were promised independence if they broke with Belgrade. The German invasion timetable was unrelated to the Yugoslav-Soviet alliance talks in Moscow, although Hitler and Ribbentrop were informed of these negotiations. It was nonetheless striking that the Luftwaffe began bombing Belgrade just past 6:30 a.m. on Sunday April 6, 1941,* just hours after Yugoslavia had signed a mutual defense alliance treaty with the Soviet Union.[21]

Over the next two days, the Yugoslav capital was subjected to a brutal aerial bombardment that destroyed much of the inner city.

---

* After learning of the German bombing of Belgrade, Stalin ordered the treaty to be backdated from April 6 to April 5 to avoid the implication that it had been signed as a response to the German invasion, which might have given offense to Hitler.

Casualty estimates there ran as high as thirty thousand. The initial armored thrust came from Twelfth German Army in Bulgaria, which occupied Belgrade on April 13. Over the next few days, armored divisions poured into Yugoslavia from Austria, Romania, and Hungary. On April 11, Mussolini's Italy also joined in—invading Slovenia, seizing Ljubljana and Istria, and then sweeping down the Dalmatian coast—aided by tacit support from the Croatian population, most of whom had not welcomed the Serb-led coup of March 27. By April 17, it was all over, and what remained of the Yugoslav Army command signed an unconditional surrender in Belgrade. German losses were modest, about 150 killed and 400 wounded or missing, plus 60 downed aircraft—astonishingly light in view of the smashing of the Yugoslav Army and the taking of more than three hundred thousand prisoners. Considering how much trouble Serbia had given the Central powers in World War I, Yugoslavia's poor showing in April 1941 was a national humiliation. Still, a semblance of honor was saved by a band of renegade Serb officers, led by the deputy chief of staff of the Yugoslav Second Army, Colonel Draža Mihailović, who escaped into the Serbian highlands at Ravna Gora and began organizing resistance forces. Tito's Communists, though quiet for now, would soon have rich opportunities for partisan sabotage operations, if and when Stalin gave the signal. As for Stalin's promised arms shipments to Yugoslavia, those would have to wait, as the Wehrmacht had closed off all incoming roads and rail lines.[22]

However ineffectually Yugoslavia had resisted the invasion, the Belgrade coup had provided a serious distraction for the Germans. As soon as Hitler heard the news on March 27, he told the Wehrmacht high command that "operation Barbarossa [the invasion of the Soviet Union] will have to be postponed at least four weeks." Even Operation Marita—the plan to invade Greece to bail out the Italians—was delayed by the coup and then subordinated to the Yugoslav campaign. By the time the Wehrmacht crossed onto Greek soil, a British Egyptian expeditionary force of three divisions had taken up positions north of Mount Olympus. They did not stay there for long. In another stunning victory, German armies took less than two weeks to conquer Greece, pushing the British all the way to the Peloponnese in a chaotic scorched-earth retreat. On April 20, just three days after the fall of Yugoslavia, Hitler sent General Alfred Jodl to Athens to take the surrender of the Greek armies, with several Italian officers invited to the ceremony in a sop to Mussolini. The British Expeditionary Force, after losing fourteen thousand prisoners to the Germans, was evacuated by the Royal Navy from the Peloponnese to Crete, harassed by Luftwaffe dive-bombers all the way.[23]

In this way, Wild Bill Donovan and his British handlers helped Churchill and Roosevelt embroil Yugoslavia and Greece in war with Nazi Germany, with devastating consequences for the peoples of both countries. As Stalin remarked acidly to Voroshilov, "The English send forces to the Balkans as if teasing the Yugoslavs and Greeks." In strategic terms, the Allied debacle in Greece spoke poorly of Churchill's decision to pull three divisions away from the campaign against Italian Libya, where they had been doing well, in an honorable but quixotic attempt to save Greece. In that the Balkan campaign cost Hitler and the German command valuable time, the Belgrade coup can be said to have accomplished something.[24]

Still, Britain's embarrassing performance in Greece, and the rout of the revolutionary government in Belgrade that Churchill and Roosevelt had embraced with such gusto, called into question whether these Balkan maneuvers served genuine British or American interests. The reason the Germans had reacted so decisively to British moves was to safeguard Hitler's Balkan supply lines of chrome and other ferrous metals and prevent the RAF from acquiring air bases close enough to seriously threaten the Romanian oil fields and refineries. Only a truly decisive intervention, involving enough British troops to secure a real foothold in Greece or Yugoslavia, would have harmed the Wehrmacht, and the British were now holding on for dear life in Crete too. Italian and German propagandists were cackling after this new round of British humiliations. "I understand," the Italian journalist Luigi Villari wrote on May 6, 1941, "that Italy and Germany are about to send a joint petition to President Roosevelt requesting him either to send Colonel Donovan back to Europe or some other personal envoy of the same caliber. Two or three more such visits should really bring the war to an end in conformity with the aspirations of the Axis in a few weeks."[25]

Like the equally futile British-French declaration of war on Poland's behalf in September 1939, the Allied interventions in Greece and Yugoslavia in March 1941 had ultimately benefited another power far more: the USSR, even if Stalin had done little to bring them about. Of course, the Germans' Balkan campaign, like the invasion of France and the Low Countries, was much less costly to Hitler than either Churchill or Stalin would have wanted. Even so, it is undeniable that Hitler's timetable for invading the USSR was thrown back, and not the four weeks he had guessed on first hearing of the Belgrade coup, but five, from May 15 all the way to late June. Barbarossa might be held up longer still if the British could hold on in Crete, where the Blenheims of the RAF remained within bombing distance of the Romanian oil fields. The US- and Britain-backed, and Moscow-endorsed, coup in Belgrade and the British deployment in Greece had failed miserably, but they had both redirected Hitler's armies from the Soviet border, buying Stalin precious time to prepare his own armies for the clash with Hitler that nearly everyone in Eastern Europe was now expecting. It also deprived the Wehrmacht of five weeks of good campaigning weather before the autumn rains would fall on European Russia.[26]

Meanwhile, the Roosevelt administration, for reasons almost certainly related to the president's desire to cultivate Stalin as a counterweight to Hitler but never publicly explained, had abandoned its moral embargo on the USSR and was now green-lighting dual-use strategic imports for the Red Army. If and when a Soviet war with Hitler's Germany began, the Roosevelt administration had hinted in its negotiations with Congress in March 1941, Stalin could count on lend-lease aid from Washington. One did not have to trust American capitalists to realize that material support from them might offer the USSR tremendous benefits.

Even so, there remained one painful strategic thorn in Stalin's side. Before he could feel confident about entering the European war creeping ever closer to his western borders, the Vozhd needed security in the East. It was time to cut a deal with Japan.

15

Operation Snow

Stalin Secures His Eastern Flank

ON MARCH 24, 1941, Molotov and Stalin received Japan's foreign minister, Yosuke Matsuoka, in the Kremlin. Considering that the USSR and Japan had been at war over a series of Far Eastern frontier disputes on and off for the past decade, and that Molotov continued to cold-shoulder the British ambassador, this was a remarkable honor. En route to Berlin to meet with Japan's key alliance partner, Matsuoka was keen to bury the hatchet with Russia to free up Japanese forces from the Manchurian front for services elsewhere—whether in mainland China or, as hotheads in Tokyo partial to the navy's "strike south" faction desired, against US or British interests in the Pacific. While Japanese troops had already moved into French Indochina in September 1940 to block ports used to supply Chiang Kai-shek's armies in China via the Sino-Vietnamese railway, they had done so with the permission of the Vichy government and were careful not to overstep the boundaries agreed on, denying an obvious casus belli to the Allied powers.

Ironically, in view of Hitler's now imminent plans to invade the USSR, it was largely at German insistence that Matsuoka was reaching out to Stalin. Ribbentrop had encouraged Japanese-Soviet rapprochement the previous fall, in the hope of enticing Stalin to join the Tripartite Pact. Japan's motivation in signing this pact on September 27, 1940, was—according to then prime minister Fumimaro Konoe, the man who had appointed Matsuoka—to "adjust our relations with Soviet Russia through the intermediary of Germany." As an early gesture, on October 3, 1940, Japan agreed not

to attack Mao's Communists in the three northwestern provinces
in China, and in exchange Stalin agreed to cease all support for
Chiang's nationalists. Japan's ambassador in Moscow, Yoshitsugu
Tategawa, then presented a draft of a nonaggression pact to Molotov on October 30. Prior to his upcoming meeting with Hitler in
Berlin, Molotov explained to Tategawa, he was reluctant to sign
until "outstanding issues" were resolved.[1]

Oblivious to the war clouds darkening over Eastern Europe in
spring 1941, Matsuoka operated under the assumption that Hitler
and Stalin were still allies against the Western imperialist powers, as they had been in 1939 and 1940. According to Stalin's top
Tokyo journalist-spy, Richard Sorge, who was meeting regularly
with German embassy and Japanese cabinet officials, Prime Minister Konoe had asked Matsuoka prior to his trip to learn, when
he visited Berlin, whether Hitler still planned to invade Britain.
Whatever Hitler's intentions, Konoe wanted Matsuoka to agree to
a nonaggression pact with Moscow, with Stalin confirming his earlier pledge to cease supporting Chiang Kai-shek's forces in China.[2]

Granted an audience with Molotov on March 24, Matsuoka
wasted little time declaring Tokyo's interest in a nonaggression
pact with Moscow. Molotov responded coolly, retorting that Japan, in exchange for such a pact, would have to cede territory, including southern Sakhalin and the Kurile Islands to the USSR, and
relinquish oil and coal leases on northern Sakhalin too. With few
signs of agreement, the meeting concluded after only ten minutes.[3]

Stalin was warmer than Molotov. "Japan's war in China," Matsuoka told Stalin, "is really a war against Anglo-Saxon capitalism
and individualism, against England and America." In the moral
sense, Matsuoka explained, collectively minded Japan was "really
Communist." It was the right approach to take. "As for the Anglo-
Saxons," Stalin replied, "Russians have never been friendly to
them, and do not want now to befriend them." Matsuoka and Stalin agreed that Japan and the Soviet Union should work together
to "annihilate Anglo-Saxon ideology" and build a "new world order." On this note of shared hatred of Britain and America, Japan's

foreign minister departed for Berlin, although not before reporting on his audience with Stalin to the German ambassador. Matsuoka, Schulenburg reported to Ribbentrop, saw no contradiction at all between his fervent desire for "better relations between Japan and the USSR," and Tokyo's obligations to the Tripartite Pact.[4]

Unfortunately for Matsuoka's vision of an alliance uniting Tokyo, Berlin, and Moscow, Hitler had other ideas—namely, invading the Soviet Union. The Führer did not intend, however, to discuss these plans with Japan's foreign minister. On March 5, Hitler had given an order forbidding German diplomats from discussing Operation Barbarossa with their Japanese counterparts, ostensibly to prevent the news from being leaked to Stalin. That Sorge later passed on news about Barbarossa to Stalin suggests that Hitler was not wrong to be concerned with leaks in Japan. His failure to trust Matsuoka, however, was insulting and strategically counterproductive, as it ruled out cooperation between Berlin and Tokyo against Stalin. It was emblematic of Hitler's haphazard approach to governance that Ribbentrop had dispatched a special envoy to Tokyo with secret orders to "investigate to what extent Japan would be able to participate" in the forthcoming war against the USSR, even while Hitler had not allowed Ribbentrop to mention Barbarossa plans to Japan's foreign minister. Matsuoka, for his part, was aware of the chatter surrounding Barbarossa prior to his trip to Berlin. Before leaving Moscow on March 24, he told US ambassador Steinhardt that, on arriving in Berlin, he "intended to ask Hitler point blank whether he intends to attack the Soviet Union as it is of vital importance to Japan to know Germany's intentions towards the Soviets."[5]

Hitler's refusal to trust the Japanese left Ribbentrop in a difficult position when he received Matsuoka in Berlin in late March 1941. Unable to disclose information about Barbarossa, all he could do was hint that all might not be well between Berlin and Moscow, in the hope that this might subtly discourage closer cooperation between the Japanese and the Soviets. "In confidence," Ribbentrop informed Matsuoka in their first audience on March 27, "I can inform you that [our] current relations with Russia are correct, but not very friendly." After Molotov's visit to Berlin in November 1940, the German foreign minister continued, Stalin "had posed conditions which were unacceptable," from the "surrender of German interests in Finland, to the positioning of [Soviet] military bases at the Dardanelles, to the strong expansion of [Soviet] influence in the Balkans, especially in Bulgaria." For months, Ribbentrop told Matsuoka, "the Russians have displayed all manner of unfriendliness towards Germany." While he hoped that the Vozhd would moderate his hostile attitude, Ribbentrop confessed that he had no way of divining Stalin's intentions. He therefore wanted Japan's government to know that "the German armies in the East are ready. If Russia adopted a posture threatening to Germany, then the Führer will smash Russia."[6]

In his own audience with Matsuoka later that day, Hitler was cagier, speaking with more discretion than his chief diplomat. Ranging broadly over the European war and the struggle with the "Anglo-Saxon combination," the Führer avoided the delicate subject of his relations with Stalin entirely, dropping only a casual aside that Germany had "160–180 divisions available for defense against Russia," if such "defense" ever became necessary. Matsuoka, for his part, informed Hitler about his audience in the Kremlin, even sharing his remark to Stalin that "the Japanese were moral communists," though he added that this did not mean that the Japanese people believed in Soviet-style "political and economic Communism." The point was that the Japanese, like the Soviets and the Germans, were opposed to the "liberalism, individualism, and egotism prevailing in the West." In Matsuoka's formulation, "the Anglo-Saxon powers were the common enemy of Japan, Germany, and Soviet Russia," and Stalin, he informed Hitler, had assented strongly to this view, adding that "the Soviet Union and Great Britain had never gotten along well and would never get along." Hitler, though pleased to hear that Stalin viewed Britain and the United States as his mortal enemies, said nothing. Despite his vow to Steinhardt, Matsuoka did not ask Hitler directly whether he planned to invade Russia. Because of Ribbentrop's indiscretion, he may not have needed to.[7]

Ribbentrop, in two follow-up meetings with Matsuoka on March 28 and 29, was more careful than in his first audience, but still less discreet than Hitler had been. Ribbentrop assured his Japanese counterpart that "if Russia undertakes anything against Japan, Germany will come to her aid at once." "Whether or not Stalin's current policy of unfriendliness towards Germany will deepen or not," Ribbentrop allowed, "is unknown." But he did want Matsuoka to know that "a conflict with Russia . . . lies within the realm of possibility" and that he should not "report to the Emperor . . . that a conflict between Germany and Russia can be ruled out." When Matsuoka asked whether Stalin's accession to the Tripartite Pact was still possible, Ribbentrop replied that Germany would "probably not try again to bring this about," owing to the conditions Stalin had laid down, "particularly in regard to Finland and Turkey," along with "the Russian demand for a guarantee to Bulgaria requiring the landing of Russian troops there" and Stalin's insistence on the right to garrison the Turkish Straits. Without owning up to Hitler's plans to invade Russia, Ribbentrop had dropped such obvious clues that only a fool could have missed them.[8]

Matsuoka was no fool. Since Ribbentrop seemed so enthusiastic about a Japanese attack on Singapore, which would humiliate the hated British, Matsuoka did not deny that such plans were under consideration. But he was less forthcoming about his intentions vis-à-vis Stalin. Ribbentrop's indiscreet remarks had made it plain that the Germans would keep most of Stalin's armies occupied in Europe for the foreseeable future. And yet Ribbentrop had demanded nothing in return from Japan, certainly not military cooperation against Soviet Russia. Suddenly remembering his brief from Hitler, which was to discourage closer cooperation between Moscow and Tokyo (though the Führer had not explained why this was desired), Ribbentrop advised, but did not demand, that Matsuoka confine himself to signing a "strictly formal, superficial agreement" with Stalin, focused on economic matters. Matsuoka told the German blandly that he hoped to make progress, on his second visit to Moscow, in expanding the size of Japan's oil concession in north Sakhalin. Having been refused Hitler's confidence, Matsuoka saw no reason to share with Ribbentrop his own intention of betraying the Germans to sign a pact with Stalin.[9]

On April 7, 1941, Japan's foreign minister returned to Moscow. In the two weeks since his previous visit, Soviet-German relations—already tense over Finland, the Baltics, Romania, and Bulgaria—had plunged to new depths. On March 24, Schulenburg had lodged a sharp protest over the arrest of 384 German nationals in the three Soviet-occupied Baltic ex-countries. On March 26, Soviet counterintelligence intercepted a telegram from the Turkish embassy in Moscow to Ankara, passing on a report that Germany was preparing "to strike the USSR." On March 27, Beria's NKVD spies in Berlin reported to Stalin that Göring's Aviation Ministry had begun "intensive preparations for a bombing campaign of strategic targets inside the Soviet Union in the case of war." That same day had also seen the Allied-backed coup in Belgrade. On April 4, Schulenburg had confronted Molotov after hearing rumors that Stalin planned to sign a "friendship and nonaggression Pact" with Belgrade. Defiantly, Stalin had signed such a pact anyway on April 6—hours before Hitler retaliated by invading Yugoslavia and Greece. If the danger of war between Germany and the USSR was as serious as Matsuoka now suspected, strategic logic suggested that Stalin, to secure his eastern flank, would agree to terms with Tokyo.[10]

Stalin was just as accommodating as Matsuoka could have hoped. In a remarkable gesture, the Vozhd invited Japan's foreign minister to his "near dacha" outside Moscow on April 12—the first foreigner Stalin had ever received there. Matsuoka, stating that he would soon have to return home, said that he would prefer to do so after signing a neutrality pact. "Does the Tripartite Pact forbid you from doing so?" Stalin asked. "To the contrary," Matsuoka replied, our "pact with Germany was designed to improve

Soviet-German relations, and I just spoke in this sense with Ribbentrop in Berlin." Of course, Matsuoka felt no need to share with Stalin what Ribbentrop had really told him. Once more, the two men agreed heartily, as they had in March, that their common enemy was the United States and Britain, with Matsuoka accusing Chiang Kai-shek of being "an agent of Anglo-Saxon capital." Interestingly, Matsuoka did not once mention Mao, demonstrating his lack of importance in Japanese eyes as any kind of military threat.[11]

Sensing Stalin's hunger for a deal, Matsuoka proposed to put off talks over the Sakhalin and Kurile Islands disputes indefinitely, focusing on a sweeping neutrality pact. "For more than thirty years," Stalin responded warmly, "Japan and Russia have regarded each other as enemies. We have fought wars. We made peace, but never became friends. Perhaps, if we sign a neutrality pact, it will show the way from enmity to friendship." Stalin, however, was a tough negotiator. Having expressed his desire that Japan and the USSR become "friends," the Vozhd then reminded Matsuoka that, since the Russo-Japanese War, Japan had controlled Korea, the Tsushima Strait, the Kurile Islands, southern Sakhalin and its coastline, and even (via concessions) the mineral resources of northern Sakhalin. In this way, Japan had cut Soviet Russia off from the Pacific. "Do you wish," Stalin asked Matsuoka, "to strangle us? What kind of friendship is that?" Taking a page from Hitler's playbook, Matsuoka tried to reorient Stalin's attention southward, proposing that the USSR seek a warmwater outlet in the Indian Ocean. Mischievously, Japan's foreign minister offered to share with Stalin "the resources of [Dutch] Indonesia," a country Japan had not yet occupied. Having none of this, Stalin returned to northern Sakhalin, and said that without Japan renouncing its interests there, "the USSR cannot live." At last Matsuoka relented, promising to consult Tokyo and resolve the Sakhalin question "within 2–3 months." With all serious obstacles now removed, Stalin instructed Molotov to draw up terms for a deal with Matsuoka.[12]

The resulting Soviet-Japanese Neutrality Pact, signed in the Kremlin at 3 p.m. on April 13, 1941, revolutionized the strategic landscape. Both powers agreed to *uvazhat'* (respect) each other's "territorial integrity," which entailed Soviet recognition of Japan's conquest of Chinese Manchukuo and Japanese recognition of the Soviet position in Mongolia and Stalin's recent territorial gains in Finland, the Baltics, Poland, and Romania. Each signatory agreed that, if the other power found itself "at war with one or several third powers," it would "remain neutral for the entire duration of that conflict." The neutrality pact would be in force for five years, and if neither party renounced it after four years, it would renew for another five. While frontier disputes were unresolved, the strategic implications were clear. With its position in Manchuria secure, Japan was now free, if it wished—and Stalin's hint could not have been clearer—to strike into Southeast Asia and the Pacific against British and US interests. The *Japan Times and Advertiser*, a semiofficial mouthpiece of the Japanese Foreign Office, declared that "Japan can now undertake either a defensive war, or an offensive-defensive one. . . . She is confident that the pact with Soviet Russia assures her rear and right flank against military and naval action." Stalin, with his eastern flank secure against Japan, could move Soviet troops from Siberia west to reinforce his European fronts against Hitler's Reich. As *Pravda* crowed, the neutrality pact "had made it possible for the USSR and Japan to fulfill their special historical missions."[13]

So explosive were the implications of the neutrality pact for Japanese foreign policy that it precipitated a political crisis back in Tokyo. For years, Japanese Army generals had viewed Soviet Russia as their adversary, both in the literal sense that it was the Red Army they had fought against until 1939, and in the ideological sense as the source of Communist contagion in Asia. Matsuoka even admitted, in one awkward moment in Moscow, that the Japanese Army liaison officers in attendance were "always thinking of how to defeat the Soviet Union." After Matsuoka had wired ahead for approval of Molotov's terms, Prime Minister Fumimaro Konoe had gone straight to Emperor Hirohito to obtain sanction for his signature, bypassing both the cabinet and the Japanese Privy Council, which ratified the pact reluctantly and, the statement read, "with aching heart." Previous Japanese cabinets had been overthrown for much less, and Matsuoka knew that he had put his job—and possibly his life—on the line in Moscow. At the banquet held to celebrate the conclusion of the neutrality pact on April 13, Matsuoka offered Stalin a geopolitical blood oath. "The treaty has been made," he told the Vozhd. "I do not lie. If I lie, my head shall be yours. If you lie, be sure I will come for your head." "My head," Stalin pointed out, "is important to my country. So is yours to your country. Let's take care to keep both our heads on our shoulders." More warmly, Stalin reminded Japan's foreign minister, "You are an Asiatic. So am I." Seeing his cue, Matsuoka agreed that "we are all Asiatics. Let us drink to the Asiatics!"[14]

After the banquet, an extraordinary scene ensued at the train station as Matsuoka and his team boarded the Trans-Siberian for the journey home, in full view of the Moscow diplomatic corps. Never before had Stalin come to see off a foreign visitor. A British journalist was therefore astonished to see the Vozhd lumber onto the platform "in his military coat, in leather boots and overshoes, and his brown vizored cap," followed by Molotov. The Japanese diplomats, the Briton observed, "came to life with a bang when Stalin and Molotov made their appearance. They surrounded the Soviet leaders, and began shaking their heads, slapping their backs, and talking in several languages and in very raucous voices." Molotov and Stalin then

> began embracing the Japs, patting them on the shoulders and exchanging expressions of intimate friendship. Stalin went up to the aged and diminutive Japanese Ambassador-General, punched him on the shoulder rather hard, with a grin and an 'ah . . . ah,' so that the General, who has a bald and freckled pate, and is not more than four feet ten in height, staggered back three or four steps, which caused Matsuoka to laugh in glee.

Far from minding this brutal display of Georgian charm, the Japanese diplomats were delighted to be singled out (it helped the mood that everyone was still sozzled from all the toasts at the banquet). "We will organize Europe, and Asia," Stalin was heard to tell Matsuoka. "We will even organize the Americans," Stalin added, bursting into a "guffaw, which Matsuoka echoed."[15]

All this was unusual enough to excite the attention of the foreign press corps. But they were not Stalin's target audience. Stalin gave a hint of what he was up to when he looked through the crowd for Ambassador Schulenburg and embraced him ostentatiously. "We must remain friends," Stalin declared, "and you must do everything to keep this so." Stalin then accosted the German military attaché, Colonel Hans Krebs, and asked him, "Are you a German?" Then Stalin declared loudly, "We will always be friends." There was no doubt, Schulenburg reported to Ribbentrop, that Stalin sought "deliberately to create a situation which would be noticed by the many people present."[16]

Stalin's act on the train platform was likely contrived to reassure Hitler about his intentions after the blowup that had seen the Germans invade Yugoslavia right after Stalin signed a pact with Belgrade. But he was not faking the high spirits. The Soviet-Japanese Neutrality Pact was a coup nearly as momentous as the Moscow Pact, and with eerily similar consequences. Just as his agreement with Hitler had engulfed Europe in conflict, Stalin's deal with Matsuoka, by redirecting Japanese resources south and east, opened the floodgates to war in the Pacific. Stalin had pulled off, as Matsuoka himself recalled in bewilderment, an act of "diplomatic blitzkrieg." If Stalin had his way, the Americans and British would soon be embroiled in an Asian war, diverting critical capitalist resources away from the European theater. As a correspondent for the London *News Chronicle* reported from Moscow after the pact was signed, "What better guarantee against Japanese hostility than that Japan turn south and cross swords with the United States? . . . Moscow will feel secure in the Far East only when the Japanese and American navies engage."[17]

To assert that this was Stalin's intention in signing a neutrality pact with Japan on April 13, 1941, is not mere speculation.* To ensure that this pact had the desired result of spreading the world war to Asia and the Pacific, after signing it Stalin put his spies to work on Operation Snow, a plot to exacerbate US tensions with Japan by manipulating Washington into sharply restricting exports of American oil and other strategic commodities to Tokyo. The conduit for the operation would be Harry Dexter White, chief adviser to Treasury secretary Morgenthau.

White, like many Soviet assets in London and Washington who spied for Moscow out of ideological sympathy for Communism (or hostility to Fascism), had gone cold after the Molotov-Ribbentrop Pact. Whether this was because of White's moral objections to the pact or because his Soviet handlers had lost trust in him because they suspected that he felt that way is unclear. In the first months of the European war, as Stalin was helping Hitler dismember Poland, Beria had conducted a purge of the Soviet intelligence apparat, recalling hundreds of spies to Moscow and cutting their foreign sources loose. White was one of them, not so much fired as left to his own devices.[18]

In the wake of the Soviet-Japanese Neutrality Pact, Stalin's long-dormant man in the US Treasury was suddenly Beria's top intelligence priority. But there was a problem. White's previous handler, Iskhak Akhmerov—an NKVD rezident who had directed ten of the highest-level Soviet agents working in the Roosevelt White House, State Department, and Treasury—had been recalled to Moscow in 1939 after he had violated protocol by marrying the niece of CPUSA leader Earl Browder (it was apparently

---

* Aside from getting Stalin to cut off aid to Chiang Kai-shek, Matsuoka's motivation is harder to fathom. After learning of Barbarossa, he advocated tearing up the neutrality pact he had signed and joining the Germans and Italians against the USSR—and then resigned after failing to win over the cabinet. Stalin, it seems, had temporarily charmed Matsuoka into violating his own principles.

a love match). White had trusted only Akhmerov, though he knew him as Bill (short for Akhmerov's assumed American name, William Grienke). Unable to return to Washington, Akhmerov briefed a young NKVD agent, Vitaly Pavlov, about White: his phone number at the Treasury, his appearance and demeanor, his work routine and habits, and his political beliefs (White, a non-party member, was a classic anti-Fascist recruit from the Popular Front era). Akhmerov instructed Pavlov to telephone White "on any weekday other than Monday" after he had arrived in Washington, "ideally between 10 and 11am."[19]

Pavlov did as he was told. After arriving in Washington on a Monday in mid-May 1941, he patiently waited until the following morning to make the fateful phone call. At 10 a.m. on Tuesday, Pavlov entered a phone booth and dialed the number Akhmerov had given him. Introducing himself as "a friend of Bill's," Pavlov informed White, untruthfully, that Bill was tied up "in the Far East" and had asked him to pass on a message. White, pleasantly surprised to hear news of his old friend (who was in fact under house arrest in Moscow), agreed to meet; Pavlov invited him to lunch the following day at the Old Ebbitt Grill. This was the same restaurant, conveniently located across the street from the Treasury Department on Fifteenth Street NW, where White had met Akhmerov before. "How will I know who you are?" White asked. "I'm of average height," Pavlov told him, "with blond hair, and I'll carry a copy of New Yorker and leave it on table." Pavlov knew what White looked like from Akhmerov's detailed description.[20]

The historic meeting took place, as planned, in the Old Ebbitt Grill on a Wednesday in the second half of May 1941 (probably May 21). After exchanging pleasantries, Pavlov let White know that Bill, supposedly visiting China, was "trying to figure out the American and Japanese attitudes. The expansion of Japan into Asia has him constantly alert." Pavlov reached into his pocket and pulled out a note outlining the Soviet stratagem to get the US Treasury to impose draconian export controls on Japan in retaliation for its aggressive moves in Asia, accompanied by a point-blank demand that Japan withdraw its forces from Manchuria and China and a no less peremptory (and bizarre) demand that Japan sell the bulk of its arms production to the United States. So well had the NKVD agents read their man that White declared himself "amazed at the concurrence of my own ideas with what Bill thinks." According to Pavlov, White folded up this policy note and was about to slide it into his own pocket when Pavlov insisted that he memorize it and hand it back, to avoid the risk that it be captured. On the pretext that he, too, would shortly visit China (this was also a lie), Pavlov asked White to reassure "his friend Bill" that he was on the job at Treasury and that "something will be done to bridle the Asian aggressor." Carefully, White assured Pavlov that he could "tell Bill this from me: I'm very grateful for the ideas that corresponded to my own about that specific region . . . and I believe with the support of a well-informed expert, I can undertake necessary efforts in the necessary direction."[21]

White was true to his word. Within days, he had drafted a bold policy memorandum for Morgenthau that bore an uncanny resemblance to Pavlov's note, up to and including Soviet-style swipes at British imperialism (White's memo promised, without consulting Churchill, that Britain would give up its rights in China, including the cession of Hong Kong). After rhetorical preliminaries about the importance of diplomacy and the need to satisfy Japan's grievances regarding discriminatory clauses in US immigration law, White's memorandum of June 6, 1941, proposed that Japan be asked to "withdraw all military, naval, air police forces from China (boundaries as of 1931), from Indo-China and from Thailand";* withdraw all support from "any government in China other than that of the National government"; "lease at once to the U.S. government for 3 years . . . up to 50 per cent of Japan's Naval and air strength" while also selling "to the United States up

---

* This demand was bizarre in view of the fact that in June 1941 Japan had no troops in Thailand, a country it invaded only after Japan went to war with the United States.

to half current output of war material"; and to sign a ten-year non-aggression pact with the United States, China, the British Empire, the Dutch Indies, and the Philippines. White did offer Japan, as a bribe, a $3 billion loan at a low rate of 2 percent. White thought that these insulting terms—the acceptance of which would have doomed any Japanese cabinet and possibly provoked riots across Japan—should be offered to Tokyo with a firm time limit of thirty days, with failure to ratify understood "to mean only that the present Japanese Government prefers other and less peaceful ways of solving these difficulties, and is possibly awaiting the propitious moment to carry out further a plan of conquest." The "first step" of the US response to a rejection would be "a complete embargo on imports from Japan."[22]

Taken aback by its stridently anti-British tone, Morgenthau did not immediately assent to White's memorandum, nor did he forward it to President Roosevelt, but he did keep it on file as a historically significant document (it was later reproduced in Morgenthau's memoirs). In early June 1941, when this surefire recipe for provoking war with Japan was written, Roosevelt had more pressing priorities, from the series of humiliating failures that continued to bedevil Britain's war effort to the rumors swirling around Europe that Hitler was about to invade the Soviet Union. But White had laid down an unmistakable marker in US policy toward Japan.[23]

Whatever transpired between the United States and Japan in the Pacific, Stalin's eastern front was now secure for at least five years, allowing him to concentrate everything he had in the West. Whoever struck first in the titanic game of chicken being played out at the German-Soviet frontier, Stalin had ensured that the Red Army would be prepared for a European war.

16

To the Brink

BY THE END of April 1941, the prospect of a Soviet-German clash of arms was the main subject of conversation all over Europe, from London—where Churchill, facing yet another run of defeats, was hoping desperately for Hitler to blunder into it—to Istanbul, where Turkish officials were almost gleeful that the Soviet bully might be taken down a notch. Churchill, in a letter to Stalin on April 19, shared genuine intelligence on troop movements in Eastern Europe (gleaned, we now know, from Ultra decoding of the German Enigma code): namely, that the German high command (OKW), as soon as Yugoslavia was defeated, had ordered five tank divisions transferred from Romania to occupied Poland. Over the coming weeks, Churchill shared more Ultra-decrypted intelligence of a similar nature with Stalin. For now, all the Vozhd had to say in response to these friendly intelligence leaks—in a message delivered verbally by Ambassador Maisky, as Stalin was still refusing to write Churchill directly—was that "Europe was now a jungle; what was needed was not words but deeds."[1]

The Germans were busy elsewhere in April 1941, of course. Still, Hitler's decision to bail out Mussolini's blundering Italians in the Balkans was so stunningly successful that it seemed only to accelerate the momentum toward a true clash of the titans. Scarcely missing a beat despite the Balkan diversion—even as General Erwin Rommel's Afrikakorps threw the British back from Libya into Egypt and German spies pulled off an anti-British coup d'état in Iraq for good measure—the OKW was methodically reinforcing the Soviet fronts, just as Churchill had reported to Stalin. As soon as Athens fell on April 27, German troops not immediately needed for occupation duty—or for the paratroop descent to expel the British from Crete, where they had fled from Greece—were routed north. Four Wehrmacht divisions arrived on the central front against the USSR in the last week of April, raising the total to sixty. The OKW suspended all civilian rail traffic in central-eastern Europe in early May 1941 to clear the lines for troop transports. Clearing out civilian traffic allowed OKW to bring in another twelve German divisions by May 14, and another twenty-one by June 5. This still left the Wehrmacht, with perhaps 93 full-strength divisions facing the USSR, grossly outnumbered by the Red Army, which OKW estimated to have 150 divisions on Stalin's western frontier. Still, the ramp-up of German strength in the East was un-mistakable. Most alarming of all from the Soviet perspective were the overflights of Göring's Luftwaffe pilots, who violated Soviet airspace eighty times between March 27 and April 18, according to a complaint filed by Molotov on April 22, 1941. On April 15, a German surveillance plane had been forced to land in Western Ukraine, near Rovno, after being witnessed flying over from the old fortress town of Przemysl (a city jointly occupied in 1939, with the German-Soviet border crisscrossing the town along the San River). A search of the plane turned up a camera, rolls of used film, and "a torn topographical map of the districts of the USSR." Whatever the Germans were up to near the Soviet frontier, it did not appear to be tourism.[2]

Still, obvious as signs of preparations for Barbarossa seem to us in retrospect, at the time no one was sure if, when, and how the Germans would strike. By early May 1941, so many warnings were pouring into Moscow that it was easy to believe some of them were disinformation. From a spy in Berlin, Beria learned on May 22 that the attack would come on June 25. Soviet agents in Bucharest said it would come between June 15 and 20. The flood of reports about Barbarossa from Richard Sorge in Tokyo (RAMZAI initially claimed the attack was planned for June 15, later revising this to "by the end of June") annoyed Stalin so much that offi-cials stopped forwarding them to him, filing them in a thick folder marked "dubious and misleading reports." Molotov's complaint about surveillance overflights, lodged with Schulenburg, was polite. He even reassured the Germans that Soviet border authorities had been given orders not to fire on German warplanes, so long as "the overflights do not become too frequent."[3]

In view of what we now know of Stalin's colossal mobilization drive, his rationale for not objecting more vigorously to Luftwaffe violations of Soviet airspace may have been to encourage German surveillance of the buildup of armor near the frontier and discourage German aggression. To this end, the Vozhd even organized tours of Soviet aviation and tank factories for German diplomats and liaison officers. Surely, Stalin appears to have thought, Hitler would not be so foolish as to take on an enemy with such massive advantages in armor and manpower. Stalin even learned, via spies inside Germany, that OKW had not ordered the sheepskin coats experts believed to be necessary for winter campaigning in Russia, and that the fuel and lubricating oil used by the Wehrmacht's armored divisions would freeze in subzero temperatures. In retrospect, it is obvious that Hitler and OKW were simply far too sanguine about a quick campaign in Russia and failed to prepare adequately for winter conditions. But to Stalin, the lack of Wehrmacht preparations for cold-weather warfare suggested not Hitlerian hubris but German caution about attacking Russia that year. The Vozhd even intervened, at the end of April, to order that Molotov's diplomats cease haggling over frontier questions with the Germans. Soviet oil deliveries to the Reich, after being slow-walked all winter, were stepped up, with volume nearly doubling from April to May 1941. Whether out of a desire to appease Hitler or out of confidence in his own military preparations, Stalin was signaling to anyone paying attention that he had no concerns about the German arms buildup.[4]

As if annoyed by the press Hitler was getting for Germany's Balkan victories, Stalin ensured that the annual May Day parade in 1941 was a caricature of Soviet militarism. "The noise of the motors of the Army," observed the Romanian ambassador, "so thoroughly mechanized both on the ground and in the air, lasted throughout the day and the following night. It left the thought that advantage was being taken of the Festival of the Revolution to move more troops along the main roads to Minsk and Leningrad than had been in the march-past in Red Square."[5]

Four days later, Stalin announced in the Kremlin that the "the era of the peace policy is at an end" and vowed to shift the Soviet military posture "from defense to offense." This controversial part of Stalin's speech to military academy graduates was, of course, left out of the whitewashed version of his remarks published the next day in *Pravda* and *Izvestiya*. Even so, the speech had made such an impact that rumors were flying. While German ambassador Schulenburg heard (or preferred to report to Berlin) only the sanitized version, better-informed diplomats learned the gist immediately. Stalin, the Romanian ambassador reported, "exalted the heroism and fighting spirit of the Red Army, saying that the soldiers of the Soviet must not confine themselves to the defensive, but must be prepared to . . . take the offensive."[6]

It was clear to the Moscow diplomatic corps that something was brewing in Soviet foreign policy. On Tuesday, May 6, Stalin created still more buzz when he pushed Molotov aside and became president of the Council of People's Commissars, taking formal responsibility into his own hands (although Molotov remained as foreign affairs commissar). In his report to Berlin, Schulenburg put a positive spin on the news, interpreting Stalin's self-promotion as a rebuke of Molotov for the Yugoslav debacle and a sign that Stalin was devoted to "the improvement of Soviet-German relations." Lending credence to this interpretation, on May 9 Stalin threw Hitler a bone by expelling the diplomats of all the countries currently occupied by Germany: Belgium, the Netherlands, Greece, Norway, and even Yugoslavia, with whom Stalin had just signed a defense pact (the Vichy ambassador was allowed to stay). On May 12, Molotov recognized the pro-Nazi Iraqi government of Rashid Ali al-Gaylani, just installed after an anti-British coup. On the surface, Stalin appeared to be courting Hitler's favor, responding to cascading rumors of impending hostilities with a brutal diplomatic charm offensive.[7]

There is another interpretation of Stalin's appeasement of Berlin in May 1941, however. Just as Schulenburg and other German diplomats were taking considerable pains, on orders from Ribbentrop and Hitler, to scotch rumors of German invasion plans, so was Stalin keen to conceal his own military preparations against Germany. Even as the Vozhd was extending his olive branch to Berlin, Stalin's defense commissar, Marshal Timoshenko, and the chief of the Soviet General Staff, Zhukov, were updating the Red Army mobilization plan in accordance with the offensive doctrine he had proclaimed on May 5. The resulting war plan, completed on May 15, proposed a "sudden blow on the enemy, both from the air and on land." After the Red Army conducted "hidden mobilization," Zhukov and Timoshenko envisioned a massive Soviet thrust on the southwestern front from Ukraine into southeastern Poland, even while the slightly less-well-mechanized Soviet armies on the western front moved more gingerly against Warsaw. In the first thirty days, the Red Army was expected to reach Lódź, Cracow, and the Czech city of Olomouc, just one hundred miles from Vienna, thus "cutting Germany off from her southern allies." This would pave the way for a crushing offensive by eight Soviet armies from southwestern Ukraine into Hungary and Romania to seize the Ploeşti oil fields. Although preparations were far from complete, and details vague after the first month, it is significant that the Soviet war plan of May 15, 1941, spoke explicitly for the first time of the "sudden blow" of a preventive or preemptive strike. "It is necessary," Timoshenko and Zhukov advised Stalin, "to deprive the German command of all initiative, to *upredit' protivnika* [forestall the adversary] and to attack the German army when it is still in the deployment stage and has no time to organize the distribution of forces at the front."[8]

The preceding weekend, an intrigue had developed on the other side of Europe with potentially enormous consequences for the coming clash of arms in the East. Late in the afternoon

on Saturday, May 10, 1941, the pilot of a German Messerschmitt
Bf-110 bailed out over the Scottish lowlands on a farm just south
of Glasgow. Introducing himself to the farmer as German captain "Alfred Horn," the pilot was quickly revealed to be Rudolf
Hess, Hitler's deputy Führer, on a mission so mysterious that
controversy still rages over it. Hess was known to be a devoted
anti-Communist and conservative Anglophile in the Nazi camp.
For this reason, news of his disappearance from Berlin, confirmed
by an embarrassed German government after the British had arrested Hess and treated him "as a prisoner of war," was greeted
with alarm in Moscow. Although Ribbentrop disowned Hess as
a renegade, the Russians were not apt to believe this. Molotov,
after all, had met Hess in Berlin just six months before. Whatever
the real story behind the Hess mission, Stalin, a dictator par excel-
lence himself, was unlikely to believe that Hess would have flown
across the English Channel without the Führer's authorization.
Soviet spies reported that Hess was sent to Britain on a genuine
German peace mission. Was Hitler keen to come to terms with
Britain to free his hands for an attack on the Soviet Union? Or was
the Führer angling for a momentous *renversement d'alliance* that
might see Britain—possibly following a cabinet shake-up toppling
Churchill from power—join Hitler in an anti-Bolshevik crusade?
No one was more alarmed about Hess than Stafford Cripps, the
British ambassador in Moscow, whose worst fear was that "influ-
ential circles in Britain might begin to press for peace with Germany on an anti-Soviet basis."[9]

As for Britain's possible role in the Hess affair, Stalin was inclined to believe the worst. Churchill's sharing of intelligence
on German military preparations now took on a sinister aspect.
As the Vozhd told his Politburo colleagues after the Hess affair
broke, "Churchill sends us a personal message in which he warns
us about Hitler's aggressive intentions and on the other hand, the
British meet Hess, who is undoubtedly Hitler's confidant, and
conduct negotiations with Germany through him." The aim of
Britain's arch-imperialist prime minister in warning him about

hostile German troop movements, Stalin concluded, was that "he believed that we would activate our military mechanism. Then Hitler would have a direct and fair reason to launch a preventive crusade against the Soviet Union."[10]

Although this interpretation of Churchill's motives was tinged with Stalin's habitual paranoia, it contained an element of truth. With no sign that the United States was primed to enter the war, Churchill was desperate for Hitler to embroil himself in war with the Soviet Union to relieve the military pressure on Britain. The Ultra intelligence he was sharing with Stalin was genuine enough and so, too, was the premise that Hitler was preparing to invade the USSR, but this tells us little about the prime minister's motivation in sharing it. Churchill had been urging Stalin to break with Hitler ever since the fall of France, and it was not difficult to fathom why. It may have been in Britain's interest that Stalin and Hitler destroy each other, but this was all the more reason for Stalin to look askance at Churchill's intelligence gift.

Besides, Stalin had his own sources on German military preparations, and these were more detailed than Churchill's Ultra intercepts. While the closed nature of the Nazi and Communist systems posed obstacles to intelligence gathering unknown in the days of the kaiser and the tsar, when it had been possible in peacetime to wander around freely taking pictures, both sides had hundreds of spies behind enemy lines who filed regular reports on troop deployments. Beria even had sources in the Gestapo, although their reports had to be viewed with caution, owing to suspicion that they were double agents. One of these, a Latvian code-named LIT-ZEIST (STUDENT), reported from Berlin on May 19, 1941, that "Germany has between 160 and 200 divisions on the Russian border, the vast majority of which are equipped with tanks and warplanes, numbering about 6000." OKW, according to STUDENT, had excellent intelligence on Soviet deployments, particularly on the location of Soviet tank parks. The German war plan, he reported, was to conquer most of European Russia in "six weeks," forcing Stalin to evacuate the government east to the Urals, after which Hitler

would negotiate a settlement. This was accurate enough. But STU-
DENT also advised Beria that Hitler did not intend to attack until
after Britain was defeated.[11]

It was not only German war preparations attracting notice, either. British and American efforts to warn Stalin about Barbarossa,
from Churchill's sharing of Ultra intercepts to tips passed on by
the US military attaché, have entered the lore of 1941. Far less well
known is the abundant intelligence shared with the Germans by
friendly diplomats and sympathizers, who all reported masses of
Soviet troop trains heading west toward the German border in
spring 1941. In early April, a German-speaking businessman, who
had just traveled across Siberia, reported to the German embassy
in Moscow on heavy military traffic on the Trans-Siberian and
Amur Railways, with "ten trains a day heading west" from the
Far East, all "filled with soldiers." On April 7, the Swedish air attaché in the USSR shared a report that "60% of the Russian army is
mobilized on the western frontier, especially facing Romania." On
April 23, the Italians passed on intelligence from the Danube delta
of "intense Soviet military preparations on the frontier" and of
"monstrous concentration of Soviet troops in Bessarabia and Bu-
kovina, of whom many were transferred in from Finland and the
Caucasus." On May 5, Franco's government shared a report that
Stalin had "begun pulling back forces from the Far East to western
[Russia]."[12]

Crackdowns on enemy spies were frequent and ruthless. On
May 14, Beria ordered the NKVD to cleanse "anti-Soviet, criminal, and anti-social elements" in the entire Baltic region. A Politburo resolution (no. 117), passed that same day, extended the
crackdown to the entire "western border region," with special,
heavily armed NKVD battalions tasked with rounding up "counterrevolutionaries," including "Ukrainian and Polish nationalists,"
and with "seizing weapons" and "rooting out banditry." NKVD
commanders were assigned to each border region, with Ivan Serov overseeing Western Ukraine and Panteleimon Ponomarenko
Western Belorussia. Serov's instructions of June 4 stipulated that,

for security reasons, fathers would be separated from their wives and children "without notifying them of the separation confronting them."[13]

For the Germans, the most sensitive area was Romania, where Soviet agents were everywhere, and where planes with visible Russian markings were hovering over the airspace far too often for it to be a coincidence. Both the German and Romanian governments filed complaints about Soviet violations of Romanian airspace as early as October and November 1940, violations that only increased in frequency in the first six months of 1941. In March, the Romanian legation in Moscow complained of four separate violations. In April and May, Soviet warplanes started crossing the Romanian frontier with impunity, sometimes in groups of three or four, often two or three times in a single day. On several occasions, Russian tail gunners fired on Romanian fighters tracking them. On May 3, a squadron of five Soviet warplanes surveilled Romanian air defenses at leisure, conducting slow-motion flybys of seven towns at an altitude of between 1,500 and 2,000 meters before being chased back into occupied Bessarabia. On every single day between June 1 and 9, 1941, Russian warplanes violated Romanian airspace at altitudes between 1,200 and 11,000 meters. In a sign of either increasing boldness or recklessness, the Soviets even sent a four-engine TB-3 heavy bomber into East Prussia on June 12, 1941, which circled over Wehrmacht positions near Tilsit for nearly twenty minutes before returning to Soviet airspace.[14]

On June 13, 1941—Friday the thirteenth—a curious Soviet communiqué was published by the TASS news agency. "Rumors are swirling in the foreign and especially the English press," it read, "relative to an 'imminent war between the USSR and Germany.'" With a remarkable lack of tact, TASS fingered Stafford Cripps—the British ambassador who had been trying to court Molotov and Stalin for an entire year—as the likely source of these foul "rumors," as they appeared in British papers after Cripps had returned to London on June 5 for debriefing. Cripps had allegedly told Fleet Street friends that "Germany has begun to concentrate her troops on the frontier of the U.S.S.R. for the purpose of attacking the Soviet Union" and that "the Soviet Union, on its side, has begun intensive preparations for war with Germany, and to concentrate its troops along its frontier." TASS dismissed such reports as a "clumsy product of the propaganda of forces inimical to the U.S.S.R. and Germany"—Cripps, Churchill, and British imperialism. This denial has been cited as proof of Stalin's lack of warlike intent in June 1941. But this is an incurious reading of Soviet agitprop. For why, if the rumors about an impending clash of arms between the USSR and Nazi Germany were truly baseless, would Stalin need to deny them?[15]

In light of what we now know about ongoing Soviet military preparations, the TASS editorial reads like subterfuge, and maybe like a critical mistake. As Timoshenko and Zhukov pointed out to Stalin, the communiqué's dismissive attitude, and almost obsequious tone toward the Germans, could undermine Soviet morale at the front just as it should have been peaking. In May and June 1941, eight hundred thousand Red Army reservists were called up for frontline service. As early as May 22, we know that Soviet Sixteenth Army (with three tank and one motorized divisions) and Fifth Mechanized Corps were loaded on trains in the Soviet Far East to be transferred to the German fronts in Europe, with expected arrival dates between June 17 and July 10. Other Soviet General Staff orders in May concerned the concentration of the Nineteenth, Twentieth, Twenty-First, Twenty-Second, Twenty-Fourth, and Twenty-Eighth Armies on the western frontier, to be completed between July 1 and 10. As the Russian military historian writing under the pseudonym Mark Solonin discovered in the Soviet military archives, between June 12 and June 15, 1941—just as the misleading TASS communiqué was released—"the western district command received orders to move 'remote divisions' closer to the state border. The deadline for completing the regrouping was July 1. *For purposes of secrecy, the troops were to move only at night.*"[16]

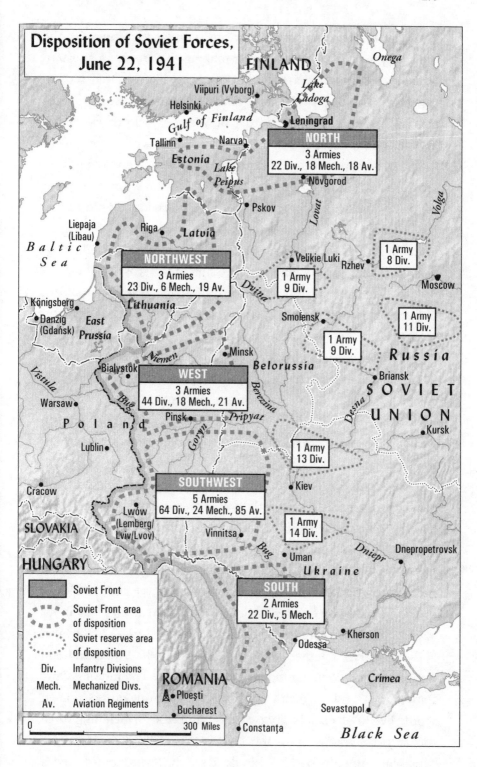

Disposition of Soviet Forces, June 22, 1941

FINLAND

Onega

Viipuri (Vyborg)

Lake Ladoga

Helsinki

Gulf of Finland

Leningrad

Tallinn

Narva

NORTH
3 Armies
22 Div., 18 Mech., 18 Av.

Estonia

Lake Peipus

Novgorod

Pskov

Lovat

Volga

Liepaja (Libau)

Riga

Latvia

Velikie Luki

Rzhev

1 Army
8 Div.

Baltic Sea

NORTHWEST
3 Armies
23 Div., 6 Mech., 19 Av.

Dvina

1 Army
9 Div.

Moscow

Königsberg

Lithuania

Smolensk

1 Army
11 Div.

Danzig (Gdańsk)

East Prussia

Niemen

Minsk

Belorussia

1 Army
9 Div.

Russia

Vistula

Bialystok

WEST
3 Armies
44 Div., 18 Mech., 21 Av.

Berezina

Briansk

SOVIET

Warsaw

Bug

Pinsk

Pripyat

Goryn

Desna

UNION

Poland

Lublin

1 Army
13 Div.

Kursk

Cracow

SOUTHWEST
5 Armies
64 Div., 24 Mech., 85 Av.

Kiev

Lwów (Lemberg/ Lviv/Lvov)

Vinnitsa

1 Army
14 Div.

SLOVAKIA

Bug

Uman

Dniepr

Dnepropetrovsk

HUNGARY

Ukraine

SOUTH
2 Armies
22 Div., 5 Mech.

Kherson

Odessa

Crimea

	Soviet Front
	Soviet Front area of disposition
	Soviet reserves area of disposition
Div.	Infantry Divisions
Mech.	Mechanized Divs.
Av.	Aviation Regiments

ROMANIA

Ploeşti

Bucharest

Sevastopol

0   300 Miles

Constanţa

Black Sea

Soviet border-cleansing operations were accelerating. On the night of June 12–13, Serov began making the arrests in Western Ukraine and Bessarabia that the Politburo had ordered him to carry out. On June 14, Ponomarenko launched his purge of suspicious elements near the border in Western Belorussia, including the Baltic district. Thousands of families were deported to the Soviet interior over the next week, with men and older boys separated out and usually executed. As a Latvian woman survivor recalled, "The vehicle began to roll. One more look at our home, the buildings, the fields, and the path we knew so well leading up to the hill where we loved to walk and play. Mother blessed everything that remained behind with the sign of the cross."[17]

The Germans were not unaware of Soviet war preparations. Between June 10 and 19, 1941, Red Army spotters recorded eighty-six Luftwaffe violations of Soviet airspace. Of those overflights, in a sign of the emerging belligerent lineup, sixty-three crossed over from German territory, twelve from Romania, nine from Finland, and two from Hungary. None of this was surprising to Soviet military planners, who for months had been reckoning on Finnish, Hungarian, and Romanian intervention alongside the German Wehrmacht.[18]

Of course, the Germans and their allies were still more advanced than the Russians in their war preparations. Mannerheim and the Finnish General Staff began coordinating invasion plans with OKW between June 3 and 5, 1941: the Finns would contribute seventeen infantry divisions and two brigades, about 475,000 men. Antonescu and the Romanians—contributing another eleven divisions, including one tank brigade; in all, two armies and about 325,685 troops—were brought on board on June 12. Slovakia and Hungary, together adding another hundred-thousand-odd not-particularly-well-equipped troops, had joined by June 15. Only Italy among Hitler's major partners was kept out of the loop (it would eventually send sixty-two thousand troops, including three motorized divisions), probably because the Führer did not trust Mussolini enough to share his dark secret. Spain contributed a "blue division" of volunteers, numbering just under eighteen thousand men. As for the main Wehrmacht forces, these were divided into three army groups. Army Group Center, based in German-occupied Poland and commanded by General Fedor von Bock, was the strongest, deploying thirty-one infantry, nine tank, and six motorized infantry divisions, including one Waffen-SS. Army Group South, facing Soviet Ukraine and commanded by General Gerd von Rundstedt, would deploy twenty-five infantry divisions, three motorized infantry divisions (including one Waffen-SS), five tank divisions, one mountain division, four light, and three security divisions. Finally, Army Group North, commanded by Wilhelm Ritter von Leeb, would throw twenty infantry, three motorized infantry, and three tank divisions into the Baltic region. When allied divisions were added, the invading force comprised 152 divisions (including 26 in reserve), in all a bit more than 3 million men, 3,300 panzers, 2,250 warplanes, and 7,146 mobile guns and artillery pieces. Although these figures paled in comparison to Stalin's resources in manpower and matériel in the theater, unlike the Soviets, the Germans were armed, primed, and ready to attack.[19]

In part, Hitler's edge in forward deployment over Stalin was the natural result of German efficiency and recent experience with wartime logistics. But the German head start also owed to the vagaries of geography. Because the plans for Barbarossa required a deep motorized thrust by Army Group Center (involving three out of Hitler's four main tank groups) across the flatlands north of the Pripyat marshes via Warsaw-Brest-Minsk-Smolensk, the best time to launch it was early in the dry season, in mid-May (May 15 was Hitler's original target date, before the Balkan complications of April) or mid-June at the latest, to allow time for German motorized divisions to reach Moscow, Leningrad, and the Volga before the fall rains came. The latest Soviet war plans, finalized on May 15, placed the main blows south of the Pripyat marshes, northwest toward Cracow and Warsaw, and southwest into Romania, with secondary thrusts toward Prague and Budapest. With shorter distances to cover and a less daunting timetable, the ideal launch date for the Soviet offensive, stipulated in Soviet war-gaming exercises conducted in January, March, and May and suggested by the deployment timetable of June–July 1941, fell in late July or August.[20]

Neither the Soviet war plan of May 15 nor the subsequent orders shifting Soviet armies to the western frontier in May and June 1941 proves that Stalin had already resolved on war, whether preemptive, defensive, or otherwise. That Stalin responded to galloping reports of an impending German-led invasion of European Russia by accelerating his own war preparations (even while denying belligerent intent in *Pravda* on June 13) should not surprise us. Since the dissident Soviet historian Vladimir Rezun (pen name Viktor Suvorov) first proposed in his best-selling *Icebreaker* (1990) that Stalin was planning an offensive war against Germany in 1941, scores of Russian historians have investigated the "Suvorov thesis" and turned up thousands of intriguing documents. In the late 1990s, two thick volumes of these documents, drawn from a half dozen Russian archives—including hypersensitive military archives that no longer grant free access to this material—were published in Moscow as *The Year 1941*. Russian historians, many of whom now write under pseudonyms to avoid government scrutiny, continue to probe the secrets of the Soviet military posture in June 1941. But considerable mystery remains surrounding Stalin's intentions on the eve of war. In the thaw of the late perestroika years, *Izvestiya* published a logbook showing that Stalin hosted his military chiefs on May 24, 1941—including Timoshenko, Zhukov, head of the Red Army operations department N. F. Vatutin, and head of the Red Army Air Force Pavel Zhigarev—in the Kremlin. In his 2000 study *Stalin's Missed Opportunity*, Mikhail Mel'tyukhov surmises that "a decision was made" at this conference "regarding the completion of [Soviet] military preparations." And yet neither Mel'tyukhov nor his scholarly heir Mark Solonin has unearthed a transcript of this meeting. None of the principals left behind an account in diaries or memoirs. The same is the case for shorter meetings between Stalin and his military chiefs held on June 3, 6, 7, and 9, 1941: we know the names of those the Vozhd met (including Timoshenko, Zhukov, Vatutin, and Voroshilov), but not what they discussed. Nor is there mention of these meetings in the Politburo Special Files declassified in the late Yeltsin years.[21]

What these Special Files do reveal, if not a smoking gun about Stalin's offensive intentions vis-à-vis Hitler, is a positively breathtaking ramp-up in Soviet military preparations from April to June 1941. Any lingering notion, which one still sometimes encounters in general histories of the Second World War, that Stalin and his generals were asleep at the wheel as Hitler's generals prepared for Barbarossa, must now be dismissed as absurd. We can glean an idea of the scale of Soviet military preparations, and their potentially offensive character, from Politburo resolution no. 171 of March 24, 1941, which assigned the construction of 251 new Soviet military aerodromes bordering the German Reich to the NKVD and assigned four hundred thousand slave laborers for the task, of which the NKVD was authorized, beginning in April, to source twenty-five thousand from NKVD road-building labor battalions in European Russia. The new NKVD aerodrome agency was also allowed to conscript 2,300 engineering students. On May 5, 1941—the day Stalin renounced defensive doctrine in his speech to the military academy graduates—the Politburo authorized the NKVD to draft another one hundred thousand laborers for its aerodrome construction battalions, from birth years 1913 to 1921, who were not already conscripted into the Red Army. Urgent Politburo resolutions were passed every day in spring 1941 related to weapons procurement, T-34 and KV tanks, anti-tank guns, Mig fighters and light bombers, weapons systems and ammunition, the construction of tank parks and petrol depots near the German frontier, and on and on.[22]

Still, the abundant archival evidence we now have of aggressive Soviet military preparations prior to June 22, 1941, does not by any means suggest that Hitler conceived of Barbarossa

as a *Präventivkrieg* (preemptive or preventive war).* As early as
March 30, the Führer told his generals that Barbarossa would be
a *Vernichtungskrieg* (war of extermination), waged as much for
racial-ideological purposes—to win Lebensraum for Germans in
Ukraine while cleansing Jews and Slavs from occupied areas, and
to stamp out the "asocial criminality of Bolshevism"—as for strategic reasons of state. In terms of timing, Hitler made the final decision to strike in December 1940, well before the really massive late
buildup of Soviet armor and air bases on the frontier, subject to
the requirements of unfolding German operations elsewhere and
the vagaries of the weather. The proximate cause for this decision,
judging from Hitler's remarks at the time and subsequently, was
Stalin's effort to blackmail him in November and December 1940,
not anything related to Soviet mobilization. In his "Speech to the
German People" on June 22, 1941, which justified the attack once
it was in progress, Hitler made only a pro forma reference to the
Soviet military buildup on the German frontier and more recent
provocations such as the coup in Yugoslavia (which he blamed on
Churchill and Stalin, carefully avoiding mention of Roosevelt and
the still-neutral United States). Hitler spent most of his energy on
old business, citing chapter and verse from his bitter encounter
with Molotov in Berlin, including all key points from Stalin's ultimatum of November 25 demanding a German withdrawal from
Romania and Finland, a Soviet guarantee to Bulgaria, and the right
to occupy the Turkish Straits. "Moscow not only broke our treaty
of friendship," Hitler concluded his rant, "but betrayed it!"[23]

By 1941, so little trust was left in the devil's bargain signed in
Moscow in August 1939 that an armed clash was almost bound to
ensue, whoever initiated hostilities. Much would be determined

---

* At least, not in the literal sense of forestalling an imminent Soviet attack. Goebbels's diary entry for June 16, 1941, has Hitler telling him,
"We must act. Moscow intends to keep out of the war until Europe is exhausted and bled white. Then Stalin will move to bolshevise Europe and
impose his own rule. We shall upset his calculations with one stroke."

by who would strike first, gaining control of enemy airspace and knocking out airfields and tank parks. Soviet commanders, no less than their German counterparts, had been drilled in the importance of *vnezapnost'* (suddenness) and the element of surprise. The Red Army had struck first in Finland in November 1939, had crushed the Baltic states in less than three days in June 1940, and had swept into Bessarabia before the Romanian Army could react. After Stalin's May 5 speech, party propagandists were ordered to step up the "Bolshevik indoctrination of the personnel of the Red Army and of the whole Soviet people in the spirit of burning patriotism, revolutionary decisiveness, and *constant readiness to go over to a crushing offensive against the enemy.*"[24]

The problem Stalin and his army chiefs faced in June 1941 was that the Germans were simply far better at offensive planning and logistics. There was a sense of creeping horror as it dawned on the Soviet high command that the Germans had the jump on them. On Tuesday, June 17, the Soviet NKVD rezident in Berlin reported to Stalin that "German military preparations are complete. We can expect an attack now at any time." The Vozhd was alarmed enough that he summoned his army and foreign intelligence chiefs to the Kremlin. A summary of all Soviet intelligence on German military preparations since fall 1940 was prepared and handed to Stalin three days later. Later on June 17, the Politburo issued resolution no. 19, appointing 3,700 new politruks (political commissars) to the Red Army by July 1941, with all commissars required to be "robust, healthy, and . . . between 22 and 30 years old." On June 18, the NKVD forwarded a report that thirty-four German embassy employees and dependents had left Moscow and others were applying for visas. A bonfire of papers was witnessed in the German embassy courtyard.[25]

Panic now descended on the Kremlin. Timoshenko and Zhukov were certain that the Germans were on the cusp of invading, certain enough to make Stalin angry, but the Vozhd was still disbelieving. On June 16, he admonished Merkulov, the head of military intelligence, "Tell the 'source' in the Staff of the German Air

Force to fuck his mother." And yet if we examine Stalin's remarks
to his generals in the Kremlin on June 18, recalled by Timoshenko,
they reveal as much about the intensity of Soviet preparations for
war against Germany as they do about Stalin's denialist streak.
Timoshenko, Stalin raged "harshly," was "preparing everyone for
war, he ought to have been shot." After relenting and agreeing to
spare this "fine man" with his "small brain," Stalin then "uttered in
a loud voice: 'If you're going to provoke the Germans on the frontier by moving troops there without our permission, then heads
will roll, mark my words,' and slammed the door."[26]

With a German attack imminent, the Red Army found itself
strung out in slow-motion, mid-mobilization limbo. It neither
had orders to attack Germany nor orders to prepare for a German attack. The roads and railroads running west to the German
border were teeming with tanks, troop transports, supply trucks,
and rail wagons carrying fuel (one hundred thousand tons of petroleum were en route to the front), plus supplies, ammunition,
and spare parts. Hundreds of aerodromes and tank parks near the
frontier were under construction, most of them still lacking roofs.
On Thursday, June 19, Timoshenko and Zhukov reported to the
Politburo that, "regarding the *maskirovka* [camouflaging] of aerodromes, bases, and other military targets . . . nothing substantial
has yet been done." Tank parks, motorized vehicle centers, and
artillery and fuel depots were all, they noted, full of "flammable
material" lying in the open, fully visible from the air.[27]

It was one thing to diagnose the problem, however, and another to fix it. In a directive soon rendered obsolete by events,
the Soviet Politburo resolved to camouflage visible surfaces in the
new aerodromes in western border regions to match the look of
"the surrounding fields" as closely as possible, with a target date of
July 1. By that day, the Politburo also mandated the *okrasku* (masking) of all "tanks, armored vehicles, transport, special, and command vehicles." July 5 was the target date for the construction of
dummy aerodromes to fool German bombers, of which at least "8
or 10" were to be built near "every air base within 500 kilometers

of the enemy border." Each dummy aerodrome would house "40 to 50 dummy airplanes." As for the remaining Red Army bases and tank parks near the German frontier, the target date for camouflaging them was July 15, 1941. In a sign of its critical importance, the "camouflaging operation" was entrusted to "Comrade Beria," Stalin's fellow Georgian, and the NKVD.[28]

Elsewhere on June 19, 1941, the NKVD arrested 19,585 suspected enemy agents in the new border zone of Moldavia SSR (occupied Romania)—that is, 5,106 suspected adult male agents plus their entire families. In Lithuania, 34,260 more unfortunate souls were rounded up and deported to the Soviet interior. In Estonia, 12,000 met the same fate. Of the 14,693 Latvians deported, we know that 3,065 were children, with half of these "under six years old." In a sign of vigilance, on the German frontier of Western Belorussia (Soviet-occupied Poland) the NKVD issued orders on Friday, June 20, for at least three men to be in each border observation post from 11 p.m. to 5 a.m., and canceled all furloughs and days off until the end of June.[29]

An exchange between Stalin and his Ukrainian party boss Nikita Khrushchev that same afternoon gives a tantalizing hint of Stalin's thinking on the eve of the German invasion. Khrushchev, who was expected to assume political direction of the all-important southwestern front, was anxious that he would be stuck in Moscow if Hitler struck. "Comrade Stalin," he recalled admonishing the Vozhd, "I really must go. War will break out at any moment, and it might find me here in Moscow or on the road," as the journey to Kiev required an overnight train ride. Stalin responded immediately, "Yes, you are right. You must go." Khrushchev promptly left for the station, arriving in Kiev by midday Saturday, June 21. Recalling these events in his memoirs twenty years later, Khrushchev concluded that Stalin's ready assent meant that he, too, knew perfectly well on June 20 that a war with Nazi Germany "was about to break out."[30]

Staring catastrophe in the face, Stalin's resistance to his commanders' advice that he take more proactive defensive measures finally wore down. On Saturday, June 21, the Vozhd ordered the Soviet embassy in Berlin to demand an explanation of German military activity on the border from the German Foreign Ministry. The answer was not reassuring: Ribbentrop, Soviet diplomats were told, was out of town and could not be reached. Soviet military intelligence reported that not only Germany but also Romania, Hungary, Slovakia, and Finland stood "at full war readiness." Reports from sympathetic deserters crossing over Soviet lines began to pour in, warning of the coming assault. Both Zhukov and Timoshenko called the Kremlin repeatedly on Saturday night to pass on reports from these frontline sources that the Germans would attack at dawn. Shortly before midnight, the Vozhd at last relented and ordered the Leningrad, Baltic, western, Kiev, and Odessa military districts to "full combat readiness." This order was accompanied, however, by a contradictory warning that commanders should avoid "provocative" action that might give the Germans cause to attack. The result left front commanders in confusion about how to respond to enemy action if it came.[31]

Despite these signs that Khrushchev, Zhukov, Timoshenko, and virtually everyone in the Soviet high command—excepting, perhaps, Stalin himself—suspected that a German invasion was imminent, in the final hours before Hitler struck the Politburo kept issuing resolutions pursuant to the offensive campaign Timoshenko and Zhukov had been instructed to plan for back in May. Undermining urgent instructions to camouflage Soviet aerodromes near the German frontier, a directive on June 18 demanded that construction of "operative" aerodromes in border districts be accelerated, with a new target date of August 1. Rather than hide the new military airfields, this jumped-up construction activity would help Luftwaffe pilots locate them simply by opening their eyes and ears. On June 19, Stalin set a new aviation production guideline of "fifty planes a day"—including eight Petlyakov Pe-2s, three Sukhoi Su-2s, and two Ilyushin Il-2s—to spearhead light bomber regiments. The final prewar Politburo resolutions set day-by-day production targets for specific warplanes at specific factories. Factory No. 1 in Tretyakov, for example, was to ramp up to three Mig-3s per day by July 10, five by July 15, eight by July 20, and an astonishing sixteen by July 25, when the Red Army would, at last, be ready to fight.[32]

Even after reports of massive violations of the border by German warplanes trickled in during the early morning hours of Sunday, June 22, 1941, production orders were being sent out as if on autopilot, as the Soviet Politburo micromanaged the inputs of Stalin's colossal war machine. But the day for plans was past. In the battle of the titans, Hitler had struck first.

17

Hitler Smashes Stalin's War Machine

JUST PAST 3 a.m. on June 22, 1941, Nazi Germany and its allies launched a devastating artillery barrage along the thousand-mile-long western Soviet border from the Baltic to the Black Sea. Beyond the frontier, German commandos and paratroopers set to work cutting telephone and telegraph lines, disabling radio transmitters, and wreaking havoc with Red Army communications. Within minutes, the Luftwaffe had seized control of Russian airspace, offering close air support for advancing infantry and incinerating hundreds of Soviet warplanes on the ground before Red Air Force (VVS) commanders could scramble their fighters and light bombers into the air. By dawn, German dive-bombers, ruling the sky, were raining lead hail down on Brest-Litovsk, Bialystok, Minsk, Lvov, Kiev, Zhitomir, and other cities hundreds of miles inside the Soviet frontier. Stukas were seen as far east and south as Sevastopol in the Crimea. Barbarossa was off and running.

The early gains for Germany and its allies were astonishing. After the initial bombardment, Wehrmacht ground forces crossed the border and began a methodical advance, seizing and holding, by some estimates, six hundred square miles of territory per hour. Just on the first day of the war, the Luftwaffe disabled or destroyed sixty-six Soviet air bases near the frontier. Between 1,200 and 1,800 Soviet warplanes were knocked out on June 22 alone, including at least 800 and possibly as many as 1,400 on the ground (Soviet and German estimates differed radically). In Belorussia, Fedor von Bock's highly mechanized Army Group Center advanced with ruthless efficiency. Brest-Litovsk, where the Germans had dictated peace terms to the Bolsheviks in 1918, was surrounded within hours (although some troops in the fortress held out for days afterward). By the end of the first day, Bock's advance echelons had covered nearly forty miles. On this western front, the Soviet air command lost nearly half of its 1,580 warplanes in the first week.[1]

German progress on the Baltic front was nearly as rapid. Wilhelm Ritter von Leeb's Army Group North quickly seized the Dvina bridgeheads intact, losing only three dead and fourteen wounded, and crossed the river in strength, including with the Sixth Panzer Division. As the most compact front geographically, with the least strategic depth behind the frontier, the Baltic area was subject to a positively devastating bombardment by the Luftwaffe's dive-bombers, with the VVS losing an astounding 920 out of 1,080 combat aircraft in three days.

Only on the heavily armored southwestern front did the Soviets muster a halfway respectable defense. German Army Group South, commanded by Field Marshal Rundstedt, advanced only about fifteen to seventeen miles the first day. Even so, the Kiev military district still lost 340 out of 1,760 warplanes in the initial days after the invasion, of which 230 were destroyed on the ground. "Surely," Stalin asked Beria plaintively on the first night of the war, "the German air force didn't manage to reach every single airfield?"[2]

Although there had been no prior declaration of war, the Germans did observe diplomatic formalities. On the eve of the attack, Schulenburg telephoned Molotov's office to request an urgent audience at 3 a.m., almost simultaneous with the attack. Ribbentrop's statement, which Schulenburg read out only "with the deepest regret," cited grievances over the recent buildup of Soviet forces on the German frontier and stated blandly that the German government found itself obliged to respond with "military measures." Molotov, after asking why Ribbentrop had presented no demands prior to breaking off relations, raged that the German-led attack was "a breach of confidence unprecedented in history. Surely we haven't deserved that." Hitler's speech justifying the attack, in which he decried Stalin's "betrayal" of the Moscow Pact, was broadcast to the Reich over the airwaves at 5:30 a.m. After declaring that he had left "the fate and future of the German Reich and our people in the hands of our soldiers," Hitler signed off. Although arrangements were made for the exchange of diplomatic personnel and their families—a complicated undertaking,* in that more than a thousand Soviet diplomats in Europe, posted everywhere from Prague to Paris, were now effectively behind enemy lines—there would otherwise be no mercy as the terrible furies of war were unleashed in the East.[3]

What was Stalin up to as these catastrophic events were unfolding? The central myth in the popular literature relates to his alleged emotional breakdown and disappearance from the Kremlin for almost two weeks, until he emerged from his dacha in early July to address the Soviet people. Blended with the plausible idea that Stalin drank himself into a stupor after learning of the invasion, this version of events reached its apogee (or nadir) with Robert Duvall's Golden Globe–winning performance in the HBO movie *Stalin* (1992). Our main source for this seductive story is Nikita

---

*By the end of June 1941, the Germans had assembled 979 Soviet diplomats from German-dominated Europe and shipped them to Svilengrad, on the border between pro-Axis, but officially neutral, Bulgaria and neutral Turkey—whose officials actually complained to Berlin about how many Russians they were being forced to process. Molotov, by contrast, dragged his feet, taking all summer to release German diplomats and rejecting Ribbentrop's demand that they be sent to Japan proper, dumping them across the border into Manchukuo instead.

In a Bolshevik insult Stalin must have relished, Germany's diplomats were robbed before being allowed to leave the USSR on September 6, 1941. This latest looting operation netted Soviet authorities, among other less valuable items, "49 watches, 74 rings, 32 brooches, 28 bracelets, 69 silver and 2 golden spoons," four German cameras, and, interestingly, a barometer.

Khrushchev, who, in his infamous secret speech of February 1956 distancing himself from the Vozhd, used it to smear his predecessor for cowardice. "After our initial severe disasters and defeats at the front," Khrushchev intoned then, "Stalin thought it was the end. . . . After this Stalin for a long time did not direct military operations and ceased to do anything whatsoever. He returned to active leadership only when a Politburo delegation visited him and told him that steps needed to be taken immediately so as to improve the position at the front."[4]

According to a version of the story that emerged in the perestroika and post-Communist years, Stalin was so despondent that, on June 25, just three days after the invasion, he authorized Beria to send out peace feelers to Hitler by way of the Bulgarian ambassador, Ivan Stamenov.* The myth of Stalin's emotional breakdown, although less than flattering to Stalin himself, fits perfectly with the Soviet pose of innocent victimhood in 1941, of an utterly unprovoked and unexpected German attack, which is an essential component of the Russian national story to this day. It is not hard to see why it endures.[5]

Almost none of the legend is true. As Khrushchev himself was later heard to say, off the record, "No one with an ounce of political sense should buy the idea that we were fooled, that we were caught flat-footed by a treacherous surprise assault." Kremlin logbooks, made available since the fall of Communism, confirm that Stalin worked all through the day of the German invasion on June 22, receiving his first visitors (Molotov, Beria, Zhukov, Timoshenko, and Mekhlis) at 5:45 a.m. At 7:15 a.m., the Vozhd

---

*The source for this story is former NKVD officer Pavel Sudoplatov, with versions appearing in Dmitri Volkogonov's *Stalin* (1988) and Sudoplatov's memoir *Special Tasks* (1994). The Beria-Stamenov peace gambit also features in Antony Beevor's best seller *Stalingrad* (1998). Sudoplatov first told the story under interrogation in 1953, as part of a then-urgent Politburo campaign to discredit Beria, which casts doubt on his credibility. To date, no evidence has been unearthed in German or Bulgarian archives about a Soviet peace parley in June or July 1941.

authorized a wire to all front commanders, styled "directive #2" to distinguish it from the equivocal order sent out the night before, ordering them to "destroy the enemy forces." It is true that Stalin declined to address the nation by radio on June 22, but he did approve the text of Molotov's address, broadcast at noon. "Our cause is just," Molotov declared in a statement he said had been "entrusted" to him by Stalin. "The enemy will be crushed. Victory will be ours." Stalin received twenty-four more visitors during the critical first day, finally dismissing Beria around 5 p.m. After retiring to rest, Stalin conducted a war cabinet in the Kremlin from 3:20 a.m. to 6:30 a.m. on June 23, rested, then returned to the Kremlin for an all-night marathon from 6:45 p.m. to 1:25 a.m., at which he established a new Red Army command headquarters, or Stavka, chaired by Defense Commissar Timoshenko. Stalin convened war cabinets again on June 24 from 4:20 p.m. to 9:30 p.m., then from midnight to 6 a.m., and then reconvened his service chiefs—along with Molotov, Beria, and Mekhlis—from 7 p.m. to 1 a.m. on June 25. Among other important matters discussed, Stalin was the sole signatory of a Politburo resolution on June 25 "on accelerating the construction of KV, T-34, T-50 tanks . . . and diesel tank engines in the third and fourth quarters of 1941." Stalin was at his desk almost around the clock, with reasonable pauses for rest, for the whole first week after the German invasion, until Sunday, June 29.[6]

It was on the second, not the first, Sunday of Barbarossa that Stalin showed the first signs of despondency. After learning of the surrender of Minsk and the breakdown of communication with the entire Soviet western army group, Stalin "exploded in anger" at his military chiefs, according to his trade commissar, Anastas Mikoyan, and returned, briefly, to his dacha outside Moscow. "Lenin left us a grand legacy," the Vozhd was overheard telling Zhukov as he left the Kremlin, "and we, his followers, flushed that whole [legacy] down the toilet (*vsyo eto prosrali*)."[7]

There was truth in Stalin's candid self-reproach, for his own mistakes had contributed greatly to the crushing early gains of

Germany and its allies. It was Stalin—along with his not-quite-equal partner Molotov—who, by signing the Moscow Pact in August 1939, had erased the series of buffer states lying between Nazi Germany and the Soviet Union, rendering useless the defensive fortifications of the Stalin line. It was Stalin who had prioritized the procurement of light bombers and medium and heavy tanks, rather than more maneuverable fighters, anti-tank and anti-aircraft guns, small arms, and defensive fortifications. It was Stalin who had overseen the massive investment in airfields, tank parks, petrol stations, and road building in newly occupied frontier districts abutting the Reich. It was Stalin who had invaded six western neighbors between 1939 and 1941, alarming the Germans and other neighbors who were afraid of being devoured next. The Soviet invasions of Finland and Romania had backfired spectacularly, as these countries were now fighting alongside the German Wehrmacht to redeem their honor and regain their lost territory. Most of all, Stalin's attempt to blackmail Hitler during and after the Berlin summit of November 1940 had boomeranged in his face. After cheaply pocketing huge gains in the slipstream of German battlefield victories like a jumped-up Mussolini, Stalin had tried to bully Hitler into submission, using his economic leverage as a battering ram. The final straw, from the German perspective, had come when Stalin had endorsed the US-British-backed coup in Belgrade and signed a defensive alliance with Yugoslavia's new anti-German government. Stalin's actions since August 1939 had removed all effective barriers to German invasion while furnishing Hitler and Germany's allies with a half dozen plausible casus belli for war. With red flags being waved everywhere from the Arctic Circle to the Bosporus, it is not surprising the Soviet bull was gored.

The first hours and days of Barbarossa pronounced a devastating verdict on the strategic deployment of the Red Army. At Stalin's insistence, Beria's NKVD-run aerodrome construction battalions had built 80 percent of the new air bases in 1941 within a few minutes' flying distance of the German Reich, Hungary, and Romania.

The last-minute orders to step up construction in June had put a bull's-eye on dozens of vulnerable air bases, with thousands of Soviet warplanes crowded into those relatively few that had already been completed, lined up like fish in a barrel for the Luftwaffe. The same was true of hundreds of half-finished, un-camouflaged tank parks and petrol stations near the frontier, all exposed to the air and filled with "flammable material," as Timoshenko and Zhukov had warned the Politburo on June 19. These juicy targets were dry kindling waiting for a spark from enemy dive-bombers.

Worst exposed of all were the two huge salients expressly created by Molotov and Stalin in their negotiations with Hitler and Ribbentrop in fall 1939: at Bialystok in ex-Polish Western Belorussia, and in eastern Galicia west of Lvov/Lemberg. Of these, Bialystok was the first to fall, encircled in less than a week by Bock's mechanized divisions, with Hermann Hoth's Third Panzer Group curling around from Grodno in the north and Heinz Guderian's Second Panzer Group advancing from Brest-Litovsk in the south. By early July, no less than thirty Red Army divisions deployed near the western frontier were trapped in the Minsk-Bialystok pocket, where Soviet losses soon totaled 340,000 troops (nearly all taken prisoner), 4,800 tanks (of which 3,300 were captured intact), and 9,400 guns and mortars. In Bialystok, Stalin paid a heavy price for his diplomatic greed.[8]

The Lvov/Lemberg salient, which contained the best-armed and most mechanized divisions in the entire Red Army, held out a bit longer. But its fate in the early days of Barbarossa exposed, even more plainly than Bialystok, the baleful consequences of Stalin's grasping at territory in 1939 and the Red Army's offensive deployment in 1941. The southwestern front, it will be recalled, was the spearhead of all offensive Soviet war plans dating back to summer 1940. The Galicia-Lvov pocket west of Kiev alone disposed of five armies, comprising sixty-four divisions, of which twenty-four were tank or motorized divisions. In terms of manpower, the Soviets had 960,000 soldiers there, nearly 300,000 more than on the Belorussian front. In firepower, the southwestern front was astonishingly well equipped, with 12,600 guns and mortars, 4,800 tanks—more than the Wehrmacht had on the entire eastern front—along with 1,750 warplanes of all types. This was not even to count the southern front (Odessa military district) facing Romania, which disposed of another twenty-two full-strength Soviet divisions. Combined, Red Army strength on the two Ukrainian fronts amounted to 1.4 million troops spread across 96 divisions, of which more than 30 were mechanized, deploying 8,069 tanks, 85 aviation regiments flying 4,696 warplanes, and 26,580 artillery pieces and mortars. In Ukraine, at least, Stalin had provided his front commanders with every resource they could have asked for—even if the deployment had not been designed for defense.[9]

The Kiev military district was under the overall command of Colonel General Mikhail Kirponos, until the afternoon of June 22, when—in a sign of the critical importance of the southwestern front for Stalin—the Vozhd sent Zhukov to replace him. Stalin gave an idea of what he had in mind with this appointment at 11 p.m. that night, when his third directive of the war was received at southwestern front headquarters in Tarnopol (Ternopil). "While maintaining a solid hold on the state boundary adjoining Hungary," Stalin ordered Zhukov and Kirponos, *"concentrate attacks by the forces of Fifth and Sixth Armies* in the general direction of Lublin. . . . Capture Lublin by the end of the day on June 24." Here was the "powerful strike in the direction of Lublin" that Stalin had ordered Timoshenko to prepare for back in October 1940, which featured in all subsequent Red Army war plans. Significantly, the Soviet offensive on the southwestern front included bombing sorties into Romania targeting the Ploeşti oil fields, Braila, Galati and Constanţa in the Danube delta, and even Bucharest, which was hit by seventeen Soviet bombs on June 25. Far from being shattered by Barbarossa, on the first night of the war Stalin was ordering his southwestern front spearhead to attack.[10]

It did not go well. Unlike in the January 1941 war games and the March 1941 Soviet war plan that drew on them, Soviet commanders on the southwestern front were not given a grace period of

ten to fifteen days to prepare their counteroffensive. Nor did they
have the advantage of preemption and control of the airspace, as
in Zhukov's May 1941 war plan. Still, despite the unfavorable circumstances, Zhukov did his best to muster a mechanized Soviet
counteroffensive toward Lublin, led by Lieutenant General D. I.
Riabyshev's Eighth Mechanized Corps, which deployed an impressive 932 tanks (although only 169 of them were new KVs and
T-34s). To rally the men, unit commanders let them paint "bellicose signs" on their tanks, such as "Long Live Communism" and
"To Berlin!" Less encouragingly, when Riabyshev's tank crews
set out west for the border, they noticed Soviet infantrymen from
the Thirteenth Rifle Corps retreating in the other direction. More
discouragingly still, many of the T-34 and KV tanks proved too
heavy for local bridges, which often collapsed under their weight;
some two hundred tanks were lost within hours. A series of confusing and contradictory orders ensued, until Riabyshev's corps
found itself retreating back toward Lvov/Lemberg—where it was
ambushed by Ukrainian nationalist guerillas. Other units involved
in the Soviet offensive on the southwestern front, such as Major General K. K. Rokossovsky's lighter, less modernized Ninth
Mechanized Corps (which had almost no T-34s or KVs), at least
encountered and engaged German invaders instead of Ukrainian
freedom fighters, but the tank crews unlucky enough to do so
were mostly slaughtered. Soviet infantry units stationed near the
frontier were strafed by German fighters and dive-bombers from
the air. "Our marching columns," the commander of the Fifteenth
Infantry Corps headquartered in Kovel, thirty miles from the border, recalled, "did not use any proper camouflage. Sometimes on
narrow roads, bottlenecks were formed by troops, artillery, motor
vehicles and field kitchens, and then the Nazi planes had the time
of their life."[11]

Intense fighting continued around Lvov/Lemberg for nearly
a week, and Soviet bombs continued raining down on Bucharest
and Ploești well into July 1941, knocking out the main Romanian

railway and wreaking havoc with oil refining and distribution. But when German panzers rolled into Lemberg on June 30, the great Soviet counteroffensive on the southwestern front—the centerpiece of all prewar plans and war-gaming—was over. After receiving authorization from Timoshenko at Stavka, on June 30 Kirponos and Zhukov ordered a withdrawal to the pre-1939 border of Soviet Ukraine, 200 kilometers (125 miles) behind the new frontier. Although they sounded the retreat in time to avoid encirclement, and Soviet losses on the southwestern front were nowhere near as heavy as in Belorussia, the collapse of the Lvov/ Lemberg salient, into which so many Soviet strategic resources had been invested, was a humiliation of the first order.[12]

It was these catastrophic errors of prewar diplomacy and strategy compounded by Stalin's insistence on counterattacking according to reigning Red Army offensive doctrine, and not Stalin's alleged emotional collapse after the German invasion, that produced the debacle. Still, there is no doubt that the impact of Hitler's early victories was psychologically jarring. Had Stalin not directed the vast hydraulic forces of Communism to military production and planning ever since 1928? Were the Germans not massively outnumbered in troops, motorized units, artillery, shells, ammunition—in everything that supposedly mattered? In tanks, the Soviet advantage on the European front was, in theory at least, five to one (more than 15,000 out of a total Red Army tank park of nearly 25,000, to 3,300 German). So poorly motorized was Barbarossa that the Wehrmacht relied mostly on horses (625,000 in all), not trucks, to carry guns and supplies. In warplanes, Stalin's advantage was nearly seven to one, with 15,000 (out of a Soviet reserve of 23,245) against the mere 2,250 of the whittled-down Luftwaffe, which had sustained serious losses in the Battle of Britain and more recently in Crete. In artillery, the Soviet advantage was just as lopsided, with 7,146 German artillery pieces facing 37,000 Soviet guns at the front, with another 110,000 Soviet cannons and mortars in reserve. This was not to mention Soviet qualitative

advantages, such as the superior armor of the KV tanks over anything the Germans had, or the armor, flexibility, and tactical advantages of the T-34 tank.[13]

Of course, the stock of the Soviet tank park was still largely
filled with older light BT and T-26 tanks; there were only about
1,800 of the sturdier T-34s and KVs at the front. And many of these
older tanks were in poor repair, lacked ammunition or shells, or
had little to no fuel; it will be recalled that one hundred thousand
tons of petroleum was en route to the front at the time the Germans attacked. The real number of operational tanks in the Soviet
arsenal in the European theater was likely far less than the official
number of fifteen thousand. Soviet pilots, who had rarely been
given adequate training time, were still learning how to use the
new Mig-3 fighters and the Il-2, Pe-2, Su-2 light bombers. Older
Soviet fighters like the Polikarpov I-16, a workhorse of campaigning in Spain and Manchuria, were completely outclassed by the
German Messerschmitts. For all these reasons, specialist historians
of the eastern front, such as David Glantz, are right to emphasize how poorly prepared for war the Red Army was in reality, as
against how things looked in the order of battle. Even so, sheer
mass of matériel and manpower should have counted for *something*. With the Red Army's crushing material superiority in mind,
it is hardly surprising that Stalin ordered his commanders to attack, until finally learning, on Saturday, June 28, that the Soviet
Fourth Army had been annihilated, and another four armies had
been encircled by the Germans.[14]

The shocking part, for Stalin, was not that Hitler attacked—that
was what Hitler did. The shocking part was that his vaunted war
machine, which he had spent the past thirteen years assembling
and arming with all the latest foreign and domestic technology,
proved so brittle when it was finally put to the test against a first-
rate military opponent. The terrible truth, which dawned on Stalin
in that first week of war, was that his soldiers either did not know
how to or did not want to fight. No matter how well equipped
his army was with machine guns and artillery, medium and heavy

tanks, light bombers and pursuit planes, it was all to no avail if the men would not hold their ground and fire their weapons, if the tank crews failed to work together, if the pilots never flew.

By striking first, it is true, the Germans seized control of the air as they had done in Poland, France, and Norway, which allowed them to knock out thousands of Soviet warplanes on the ground and blow up hundreds of un-camouflaged tank parks and fuel depots before Red commanders could react. The experience of those earlier campaigns gave German pilots a priceless advantage against their VVS counterparts, who had little practice in real dogfighting. Still, there were thousands more Soviet warplanes and tanks that survived the initial assault, and it should not have been difficult to get them moving once the initial shock had worn off and officers had had time to recover. But the Red Army of 1941 was not designed for defensive operations, nor did it have any practice in carrying them out. As Zhukov later recalled, "At that time our military-theoretical science generally did not consider the profound problems of strategic defense, mistakenly considering it not so important." Nor was the Red Army built for unit commanders to take on-the-spot initiative, whether in attack or defense. The men were bullied by their officers, who were cowed by their superior officers, who were themselves terrorized by politruks answering to the party.[15]

Making these Soviet military weaknesses nearly fatal was the fact that they were well known to the Germans, who exploited them mercilessly. Hitler's notorious Commissar Order of June 6, 1941—which is today seen to have prefigured the Holocaust by giving license to Wehrmacht commanders to shoot Soviet commissars, many of whom were indeed Jewish—actually had an operational purpose. The idea was to undermine enemy morale by driving a wedge between Red Army troops, including officers, and their political commissars, who were viewed by the Germans, and executed, as "illegal combatants." German pamphlets dropped behind Soviet lines encouraged Russians to mutiny or desert. "Drive away your commissars and come over to the Germans," read one

leaflet addressed to "commanders and soldiers of the Red Army!"
Others assailed Stalin as a "Brazen Cheat," reminding Russians
that the "Great Stalin Constitution" had promised free speech and
freedom of conscience, only for these to prove "swindles." Lenin
had promised peasants "the land they tilled," only for Stalin to
"enslave them on collective farms." Instead of "freedom of labor
and [the] raising of living standards," Communism had brought
them merely "slavery." Another leaflet, touching a sensitive nerve
as rumors were swirling about Stalin's post-invasion disappearance, called the Vozhd a "Pitiful Coward" who was hiding in the
Kremlin, "terrified of his own colleagues, thirsting to avenge their
slaughtered comrades." A more sinister pamphlet encouraged
Soviet troops to get rid of their *zhida-politruka* (Jewish politruks),
helpfully providing an illustration of a mutiny. Huge numbers of
Soviet soldiers got the hint and deserted to German lines as soon
as the battle was joined.[16]

In view of what we know today about the draconian penalties Stalin imposed on soldiers for deserting, or for merely being
taken alive by the enemy, the fact that so many Soviet soldiers
deserted anyway speaks eloquently. Whether owing to German
propaganda or, more likely, to their desperation to escape Stalin's
murderous tyranny, thousands, and soon millions, of his troops
either deserted to, or allowed themselves to be captured by, the
enemy. By July 9, Soviet losses stood at 589,000 officially and probably as high as a million, against German losses of 23,000 killed and
44,000 wounded. The vast majority of Red Army losses were not
battlefield deaths but soldiers captured or surrendering with their
arms. By December 1941, according to German sources, more
than 3.5 million Red Army troops, including 15,179 officers, had
been taken prisoner. These devastating losses were compounded
by lost tanks and artillery pieces captured intact—as many as 3,300
and 1,800, respectively, on the Belorussian front alone.[17]

Millions more Soviet enlistees and volunteers served honor-
ably and courageously in horrendous conditions. And yet there is
no getting around the fact that even those Red Army grunts who

fought in summer 1941 did not fight very well. One Russian military historian has recently compared "irretrievable losses" (that is, soldiers either killed, grievously wounded, or captured with their arms) on the two sides for the "border battles" of the war's first twenty days and concluded that the German advantage, man for man, was thirty-five to one. Such a ratio bode poorly for Soviet chances, even if the Red Army survived the early defeats in the border regions. Stalin still had massive reserves of manpower and weapons to draw on, if and when his officers and politruks figured out how to get the men to fight. But every week brought new defeats, eating into those reserves. No army, no country, could endure such catastrophic losses indefinitely.[18]

By the time Stalin steeled himself to address the nation on July 3, the strategic picture was bleak. The Germans, having already terrified the world with lightning victories in Poland, Norway, the Low Countries, and France, had outdone themselves. In the first three weeks of Operation Barbarossa, the Wehrmacht, advancing along a front nearly a thousand miles long, was able to cross, in strength and with most bridges intact, six major rivers: the Bug, the Niemen, the west Dvina, the Berezina (made famous in Napoleon's retreat), the Goryn, and the Sluch. "The objective of shattering the bulk of the Russian army in front of the Dvina and Dniepr," the German Army chief of staff, General Franz Halder, wrote in his diary on July 3, 1941, "has been accomplished." All of Stalin's now-Pyrrhic gains of 1939 to 1941 were lost within days, as history delivered a merciless verdict on Stalin's decision to wipe out the buffer states guarding his western flank against Hitler and deploy his best troops and armor in this vulnerable frontier territory. All Stalin could say in defense of the Moscow Pact in his radio address of July 3 was that by signing it, he had "secured our country peace for a year and a half and the opportunity of preparing its forces."[19]

More plausibly, Stalin argued that Nazi Germany, by "treacherously tearing up the Pact," had gained "certain advantageous positions for its troops for a short period," but had "lost politically by exposing itself in the eyes of the entire world as a bloodthirsty aggressor." Indeed, Winston Churchill, in an evening radio broadcast on June 22, said that the evils of Communism he had criticized over the years "fade away before the spectacle which is now unfolding. The past with its crimes, follies, and its tragedies flashes away." The prime minister promised that Britain would "give whatever help we can to Russia and the Russian people." On June 24, President Roosevelt announced that American lend-lease aid would be extended to the Soviet Union. In his own radio address on July 3, Stalin warmly lauded Churchill's "historic speech" and Roosevelt's promise "to render aid to our country" as signs of the "tremendous political gain of the USSR" wrought by Hitler's betrayal, which was "a serious and lasting factor that is bound to form the basis for the development of decisive military successes of the Red Army."[20]

Even so, it would take weeks, if not months, for US and British military aid to reach the eastern front, and there was no guarantee the Red Army would use it effectively or that it could hold out that long. Whatever Stalin might have said in public about "military successes" to come, in private he had already authorized contingency measures in case of defeat. As early as June 23, 1941, the Politburo created an "evacuation committee" for Moscow. On June 27, secret orders were drawn up to ship crucial war factories eastward from Moscow and Leningrad to Kuibyshev (formerly Samara) and Kazan, in the Ural region, along with their managers, engineers, and "critical employees." The same resolution also ordered the evacuation of the state diamond fund and "Kremlin treasures" of "precious stones," including the old Romanov regalia, to Chelyabinsk and Sverdlovsk (formerly Yekaterinburg, to which Lenin's Bolsheviks had exiled the Romanovs prior to their execution in 1918). With dramatic flourish, the historic Politburo resolution of June 27, consigned by Timoshenko for Stavka, ordered a scorched-earth campaign across European Russia. "All valuable property, raw materials or food stocks, all 'bread on the vine,' which cannot be exported intact," the order stipulated, "anything which might be used by the enemy, must be reduced to total disrepair, that is, destroyed, annihilated, and burned." Among these valuables were the 9.3 billion rubles in the state bank, removed and shipped east on June 28. Just as precious to the regime was the carefully embalmed body of Lenin, which, per a resolution signed by NKVD chief Beria on July 2, was evacuated east to Tyumen'. The leading Soviet forensic expert, Professor B. I. Zbarskii, took the body there in a "first class railway wagon" set aside by the NKVD, accompanied by five bodyguards answering to Beria. Another Politburo resolution on July 3 laid down protocols for "the evacuation from frontline areas" of "family members of [Communist] Party leaders" and "the families of the command staff of the Red Army and fleet, and of NKVD officials." On July 7, the Politburo ordered the eastward evacuation of more than five hundred thousand skilled military-industrial employees and their families from Moscow and Leningrad, in all more than a million people.* Less than two weeks into the war, Stalin and his generals were preparing to abandon European Russia and fall back to the Urals. For obvious political reasons, these evacuation orders were not shared with the US or British ambassadors in Moscow.[21]

In view of the rapid advance of the Wehrmacht, these were not idle precautions. By July, Germany and its allies were no longer merely rolling back Stalin's gains from the Moscow Pact but moving into Russia proper. On July 10, German Army Group North took Pskov, just 180 miles from Leningrad. By July 9–10, the mopping up of the Minsk pocket was complete, netting Bock's Army Group Center 287,704 prisoners and 2,585 tanks. The Germans had performed an extraordinary feat of military logistics,

---

*After issuing this and several more evacuation orders, the Politburo was effectively shelved for the course of the war, abdicating authority to the streamlined State Defense Committee (GKO) formed on June 30, 1941, on which sat Stalin, Molotov, Beria, former defense commissar Voroshilov, and Georgy Malenkov, who oversaw military aircraft production; to the military command (Stavka); and, in practice, to whichever general happened to have Stalin's favor at the moment.

re-gauging the railway from Brest-Litovsk to Minsk to the European standard at a rate of twenty kilometers per day, extending the supply railhead hundreds of miles into Belorussia, sufficient to carry twenty supply trains daily. On July 16, German panzers rolled into Smolensk, less than 250 miles from Moscow. Eighty miles northwest, the Fourteenth Soviet Armored Division was encircled near Vitebsk on July 16, netting among the prisoners Stalin's son Yakov Djugashvili. On the Baltic and Belorussian fronts, the Germans were two-thirds of the way from the Reich frontier to the two Russian capitals. Even in Ukraine, where Stalin had concentrated his best armor, the Germans were approaching the Dniepr, rolling up factories and farmland as they went. In less than four weeks, the Germans had conquered 450,000 square kilometers of European Russia—more than twice the area they had conquered in Poland, and three times more land than they had taken in France and the Low Countries in May 1940.[22]

The ledger of war matériel captured or destroyed by the Germans was nearly as impressive. By July 9, the Red Army had lost 11,700 tanks (mercifully, most were outmoded BTs and T-26s) and 19,000 cannons and mortars. The annihilation of the Red Air Force was even more dramatic. By the end of July 1941, Soviet losses of warplanes reached ten thousand, more than four times the total number of aircraft the Luftwaffe had on the eastern front. In most Soviet aviation regiments, losses in June and July 1941 ran to 80 to 85 percent. To say that the Luftwaffe now controlled Soviet airspace was an understatement. On a five-day tour of ex-Soviet Galicia and Western Ukraine in mid-July 1941, German journalists did not see a single Soviet airplane in the sky.[23]

The files of the NKVD's "Main Soviet Administration of Aerodrome Construction" tell a sad but gripping tale. Every available economic and human resource in the USSR had been shifted west toward the German frontier during the first six months of 1941, until a switch was flipped and the vast operation swung into reverse as everything remaining was mounted on trains and shipped east. On June 28, an NKVD directive was sent to aerodrome

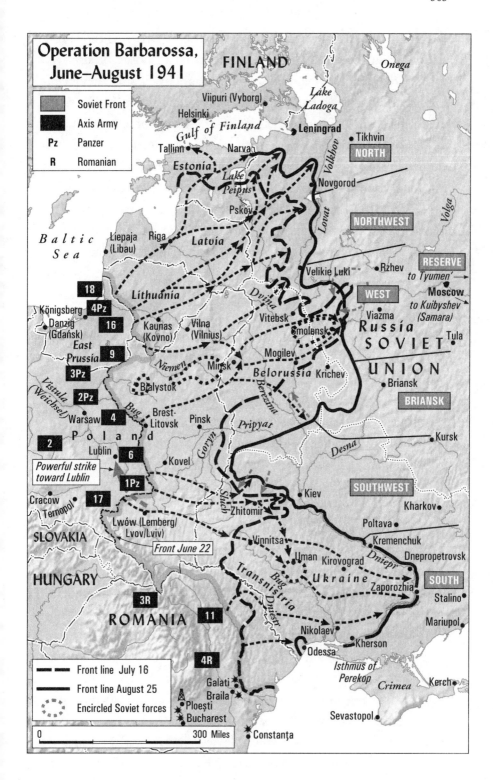

Operation Barbarossa, June–August 1941

Legend:
- Soviet Front
- Axis Army
- Pz — Panzer
- R — Romanian

FINLAND

Onega

Lake Ladoga

Viipuri (Vyborg)

Helsinki

Leningrad

Tikhvin

NORTH

Gulf of Finland

Tallinn

Narva

Estonia

Lake Peipus

Pskov

Novgorod

NORTHWEST

Volga

Baltic Sea

Liepaja (Libau)

Riga

Latvia

Dvina

Velikie Luki

Rzhev

RESERVE

to Tyumen'

Lithuania

WEST

Moscow

to Kuibyshev (Samara)

18

Königsberg

4Pz

16

Danzig (Gdańsk)

Kaunas (Kovno)

Vilna (Vilnius)

Vitebsk

Viazma

Russia

East Prussia

9

Niemen

Minsk

Smolensk

SOVIET

Tula

3Pz

Mogilev

Vistula (Weichsel)

2Pz

Białystok

Belorussia

Krichev

UNION

Warsaw

4

Bug

Brest-Litovsk

Pinsk

Pripyat

Berezina

Briansk

BRIANSK

2

Poland

Lublin

6

Kovel

Goryn

Desna

Kursk

Powerful strike toward Lublin

1Pz

Cracow

17

Ternopol

Sluch

Zhitomir

Kiev

SOUTHWEST

Kharkov

SLOVAKIA

Lwów (Lemberg/ Lvov/Lviv)

Front June 22

Vinnitsa

Poltava

Kremenchuk

Dnepropetrovsk

HUNGARY

Transnistria

Uman

Kirovograd

Bug

Ukraine

Dniepr

Zaporozhia

SOUTH

Stalino

3R

Dniestr

Nikolaev

Kherson

Mariupol

ROMANIA

11

Odessa

Isthmus of Perekop

4R

Galati

Braila

Ploeşti

Crimea

Kerch

Bucharest

Sevastopol

Constanţa

Legend (bottom):
- Front line July 16
- Front line August 25
- Encircled Soviet forces

0 _____ 300 Miles

construction battalions across European Russia, ordering the evacuation of fifty-seven aerodromes in Belorussia (those not already incinerated, that is), seven in Lithuania, eight in Estonia, eleven in Latvia, and five in Sovietized Moldavia on the Romanian frontier. The immediate fallback position for the fifty-seven Belorussian aerodromes was Smolensk, which fell to the invader on July 16. Perhaps realizing that evacuating intact air bases was impossible, the June 28 order authorized aerodrome crews, in case they ran out of time, to destroy documents and "annihilate" spare parts and construction materials instead.[24]

Still, Stalin's war was not over yet. Despite their crushing early gains, battle-hardened Wehrmacht generals were unpleasantly surprised to learn that, no matter how many tanks and warplanes they destroyed, the Red Army still had thousands more. German aerial surveillance had fixed Soviet targets for bombing sorties, but it had not given an idea of the scale of Stalin's armor in the rear. The Germans were awed by the quantity of Soviet motorized vehicles, planes, and heavy guns—and often by their quality too, after they had captured them and tried them out.

It was not that Soviet war matériel was superior to German, but that it was all brand new—so new that few Red Army grunts and officers knew how to use it. "Most of the heavy guns, tanks, and construction vehicles we have captured," a German journalist was told by Wehrmacht handlers while touring occupied Galicia in mid-July 1941, "were absolutely new" and had never been used. Although impressive at first sight, Soviet tanks were shown "on closer inspection of their parts and design to be amateurish, crudely 'thrown together' in a manner unknown to our engineers." The T-34s and KVs were better than the older tanks, but even so they had drawbacks, as their armor was "so heavy that they often sunk into the soft ground." The T-34, despite its impressive armor, was slow to fire because of an inefficient two-man turret, which meant that the driver-commander had to double as a gunner in battle. Owing to the lack of good vision devices and the hatch design— which did not allow the driver to stick his head out to get a better view—inexperienced T-34 drivers struggled to maneuver. The up-shot was that the Wehrmacht captured many T-34s fully intact, as their own tank projectiles and anti-tank guns had been unable to damage them, and Soviet tank gunners, new to their tanks and to combat, had been unable to get rounds off before they were cut off and surrounded. Once German mechanics had fixed up cap-tured T-34s and other Soviet tanks, they ran beautifully and, as German drivers reported, "reached truly impressive speeds."[25]

Despite the stunning early gains by Germany and its allies, to-ward the end of July there were signs that Russians had begun to dig in and fight, now that they were defending their own soil instead of Stalin's recent conquests. German officers acquired a grudging respect for the fighting qualities of "Ivan," the ordinary Russian soldier, who endured horrendous mistreatment by offi-cers and politruks but fought on regardless. The Soviet infantry-man, German tank commander Heinz Guderian observed, was "nearly always stubborn in defense." While masses of Red Army prisoners were taken in huge encirclements, individual units often fought tenaciously. In the citadel complex at Brest-Litovsk, iso-lated pockets of Soviet soldiers continued resisting well into July. East of Smolensk, meanwhile, Soviet reinforcements were gather-ing to stem the German advance before it reached Moscow. The war of attrition had begun.[26]

18

Terror at the Front— and in the Rear

In Hitler's mind, Barbarossa was never meant be a conventional military operation. The German need for (as he saw it) Lebensraum in the East meant that any campaign undertaken there would be merciless, designed not only to conquer land for the Reich but also to cleanse it of unwanted residents. As early as March 3, 1941, Hitler informed the chief of OKW's operations staff, Alfred Jodl, that the object of the Russian campaign was "not simply to destroy the enemy armed forces," but to wipe out the "Jewish-Bolshevik intelligentsia" and "dissolve the entire [Soviet] regime and replace it with governments, with which we can make peace." In conference with his generals on March 30, Hitler denounced Bolshevism as "asocial criminality," demanded that his officers "forget the concept of comradeship between soldiers," and wage in Soviet Russia a "war of extermination." What this might look like in practice was sketched out in the now notorious guidelines of the Hunger Plan on May 23, 1941, which established absolute priority for Germany and Europe in any food supplies obtained in the black earth belt of Ukraine and south European Russia, predicting ominously that "many tens of millions of people in this territory will become superfluous and will die or must emigrate to Siberia." A special Hitler *Führererlass* (Führer edict), transmitted to Wehrmacht front commanders the next day, authorized military executions of civilians who "attacked German soldiers," with "attack" defined loosely. Statutory immunity from prosecution was extended to German soldiers who committed crimes on Soviet territory, if these were "ideologically motivated." Politruks and Communist officials were obvious targets, and they were expressly named in the Commissar Order of June 6, 1941, which stipulated that "political commissars," as the "originators of the Asiatic-barbaric methods of fighting," were to be "dealt with promptly and with the utmost severity."[1]

While not all German officers (or enlisted men) approved of such extrajudicial killings, enough did that mass executions of Soviet commissars began as early as July 1941. Both the Third and Fourth Panzer Groups reported more than 170 such summary shootings, and Second German Army another 177. German military records show that 2,252 commissars were shot in 1941, and that was merely by the regular army. Arriving in the wake of its eastward march were Waffen-SS divisions and the Einsatzgruppen, the latter three thousand strong, tasked with rounding up commissars. If any commissars survived this first wave, they still had to face twenty-one battalions of *Ordnungspolizei*, numbering eleven thousand in all, who were not executioners but could be just as deadly in tracking down victims to hand over to the Einsatzgruppen and Waffen-SS. The Germans were often helped by local collaborators and anti-Semites, keen to avenge Soviet crimes blamed (however unfairly) on Jews. While it was true that Jewish officials were well represented in the NKVD, the Lithuanian and Latvian Communist Parties, and Soviet governing organs, this hardly justified collective vengeance against Jews as a people, of the kind that now became tragically common behind the front lines. The dynamic was brutally illustrated in a pogrom in Kaunas (Kovno), Lithuania—site of an NKVD mass execution in summer 1940—where nearly a thousand Jews were murdered in late June 1941, the first of 114,000 Lithuanian Jews killed by year's end. The early German focus on targeting commissars and saboteurs broadened, in a terrible escalation, to include "male Jews of military age" and finally all male Jews, full stop, identified by doctors examining their penises for circumcision. At least five hundred thousand Jews were shot in occupied Soviet territory in 1941 alone. Jewish women and children were not expressly targeted yet, although this was small consolation for those who lost brothers, husbands, and fathers in Kaunas-style pogroms or mass shootings in the Baltic zone, Belorussia, eastern Poland, and Ukraine, particularly in Galicia. The peoples of Russia and Eastern Europe, primarily though not exclusively Jews, would pay a terrible price for Hitler's ambition.[2]

In view of the brutality of Barbarossa, one might expect to have seen a rise in patriotic spirit as Russians rallied to defend their homeland, whatever their reservations about Stalin's regime. While this did happen eventually, it is important to remember that, in the first few weeks after June 22, 1941, the invaders were entering not Russian or even original Soviet territory, but the lands occupied since 1939. Millions of residents in Soviet-occupied Romania, Finland, Estonia, Latvia, Lithuania, ex-Polish Belorussia, and Ukraine welcomed the invaders as liberators—literally, in the case of ethnic and class enemies arrested by the NKVD since 1939, thousands of whom were sprung from prison in the early days of the invasion.

Many German generals, intelligence officers, diplomats, and occupation officials took the idea of a war of liberation seriously in 1941, even if they were undermined by Luftwaffe dive-bombers, bloodthirsty SS officers, and the killers of the Einsatzgruppen. In Sovietized Finland and Romania, the invaders were reconquering their own land, in some cases their own homes. In western, ex-Polish, and previously ex-Habsburg Ukraine, banners were unfurled in most towns reading, "Long Live Hitler, Liberator of the Ukraine," "Long Live Free Ukraine," or "Honor to the German Führer, Our Liberator." Humble villagers often welcomed the Germans with bread and salt. After Odessa fell to the invader in October, popular jubilation at deliverance took a violent turn as locals hunted down everyone associated with the now-defunct Soviet government. A local newspaper, the *Odesskaia gazeta*, was flooded with so many letters "expounding satisfaction with the collapse of Bolshevik rule" that the editorial board begged everyone to stop sending them in. The anti-Communist cause seemed just enough that hundreds of thousands of European soldiers marched willingly with the Wehrmacht into Russia, some arriving from Axis-aligned Hungary, Italy, Slovakia, Romania, and Finland, with other volunteers coming from neutral Denmark, Norway, Sweden, Vichy France, and Franco's Spain. In the initial flush of victory, morale was high on the German-allied side, buoyed by the mass surrender of enemy troops. Captured Soviet officers railed against the tyranny of Stalin's political commissars, suggesting that the Commissar Order was doing real damage. Many of them confessed that they had no faith in the fighting morale of the Red Army. Rather, they said that the men "fight only so long as the Politruk remains alive. If he is dead, then they give themselves up. Sometimes, the soldiers will kill their Politruk, so that they can surrender."[3]

In view of Stalin's capacity for vengeance, the consequences of the humiliating Soviet retreat of June and July 1941 were not likely to be pleasant for Soviet civilians trapped near or behind the front lines, particularly those suspected (or preemptively arrested) as enemy sympathizers. As early as June 24, just two days after the invasion, Beria ordered NKVD commanders in frontline districts to shoot political prisoners who had been arrested for "counter-revolutionary activities," "industrial sabotage," "diversions," or "anti-Soviet activity"—in other words, nearly all of them. In a kind of mirroring of the Nazi Commissar Order of June 6, which targeted those loyal to Stalin's regime, Beria's June 24 directive gave his NKVD men license to execute anyone behind the front lines suspected of disloyalty to Stalin or possible sympathy with the invader.[4]

The results were horrific. In the formerly Polish city of Łuck (today's Ukrainian Lutsk), where 2,055 Poles and Ukrainians had been imprisoned by the NKVD for security reasons as recently as June 10, 1941, the NKVD ordered these detainees to gather for a forced evacuation on the day after the invasion, lest they be freed by the Germans. The NKVD lined up the Ukrainians first, but instead of being loading onto trucks, the prisoners were machine-gunned en masse, with NKVD executioners then "tossing some hand grenades onto the bodies" for good measure, according to a survivor. Poles were then lined up and mowed down as well. As the survivor later recalled, "The blood ran in streams, and body parts flew through the air." So sloppy and rushed was this mass execution that survivors were told to return to prison, where all but a small handful were then finished off with pistol shots in the head. The very few prisoners left alive (probably around fifty, judging from an NKVD report stipulating that two thousand had been shot) were ordered to dispose of the bodies, after which they, too, would have been murdered—if they hadn't been rescued by the invading Wehrmacht.* The story was similar in other ex-Polish, now Soviet Belorussian, towns like Dubno, Sambor, Dobromil, and Oszmiana, which all saw mass NKVD executions of hundreds of political prisoners conducted in the chaotic first days of the war, shortly before the Germans arrived.[5]

Horrible as the atrocities in Belorussia were, they paled in comparison to the massacre in ex-Polish Lvov/Lemberg, where the imposition of Soviet rule in 1939 had been even more unpopular than elsewhere. Because Soviet military deployments were stronger on this front, the Red Army had drawn out the fighting for nearly a week. The city was bombed by the Luftwaffe, which contributed to civilian suffering and ratcheted up paranoia on the part of the NKVD guards, who oversaw three detention centers housing more than five thousand political prisoners, mostly Ukrainians, Poles, and Jews. The slaughter began on June 27 and continued all day on June 28 before the NKVD gave up and fled on June 29. As the Germans marched in on June 30, they found crude mass graves both indoors and in the streets, into which bodies had been hastily dumped with no effort to cover or bury them. "The treacly

---

* The Polish survivor on whose recollection this account is based, Mieczyslaw Ogrodowcyk, later fought against the Germans in the Warsaw uprising of August 1944. He cannot have been surprised when the Red Army failed to aid his fellow Poles.

smell of decomposing corpses," wrote a forensic doctor accompanying the Wehrmacht, "suffused the city, blending together with
the acrid smoke from burning piles of debris to form a powerful
impression on both the lungs and the stomach." Inside the prisons,
the stench was worse. Everywhere lay "fresh corpses subjected to
recent traumas, from gunshot wounds in the back of the neck to
axe blows across the body. Girls and boys as young as sixteen lay
between the elderly and old women, next to robust men of age." A
Polish woman who visited one Lemberg prison on June 30, 1941,
noted that the corpses

> [g]ave the impression that the person on and by the table had
> been beaten to a pulp. One dead man was seated in a chair, with
> a Russian bayonet sticking out of his mouth. . . . Hands and arms
> hung down in queer positions, as if they had been broken several
> times. I saw the dead body of a small girl, aged about eight years,
> hanging from the ceiling lamp. The body was unclothed, and the
> child had been hanged by a towel. The view was so terrible that
> I nearly fainted.

The scenes in the basements of Lemberg's Soviet political prisons
were almost as horrific. The "ceilings," noted a German forensic
specialist, "were splashed with blood" and the bodies were stacked
"four or five deep on the cellar floor." In one prison basement,
the layer of now-dried blood was twenty centimeters, about eight
inches, deep. In another cellar, where the killing must have begun
the earliest and putrefaction was therefore most advanced, there
was now "a layer, composed of a viscous mass, into which the
corpses had congealed." According to the official German Army
report, 3,500 political prisoners had been butchered in cold blood
by the NKVD in Lvov/Lemberg alone. Even Soviet sources admit
to 2,464 "executions." Small wonder the Germans were welcomed
into Lemberg as liberators from Stalin's murderous regime.[6]

On it went behind Soviet front lines during the German invasion of Belorussia and Ukraine. In Tarnopol (today's Ukrainian

Ternopil), the city eighty miles east of Lemberg that had served
as the southwestern front headquarters before falling to the invader, the Germans found two hundred corpses in a Soviet prison
cellar and another three hundred dead bodies shoved into a shal-
low, makeshift grave dug by the NKVD in, of all places, a Jewish
cemetery (three German Luftwaffe pilots were buried alongside
Polish and Ukrainian victims, the Jewish burial ground likely seen
by Beria's men as a way of dishonoring them). This was not the
only Soviet crime committed in the town. A grave with five hundred corpses was discovered in Tarnopol in 1990, a mass execution that can be traced to the NKVD (and thus late June 1941) via
Russian-language death sentences discovered on some of the bodies. Another 890 prisoners were murdered in Czortków, south of
Tarnopol. In another forty ex-Polish towns of Soviet Belorussia
and Ukraine, Polish historian Bogdan Musial writes, the NKVD
committed acts of preemptive mass murder, "with the number of
victims ranging from about a dozen to several hundred." While no
accurate count was kept, the number of unarmed Polish, Ukrainian,
and Jewish political prisoners executed by the NKVD in June 1941,
which Musial estimates at "20,000 to 24,000," is comparable to the
21,892 murdered in the Katyn Massacre of spring 1940.[7]

If Stalin and Beria had suspicions about the loyalty of Poles
and Ukrainians, they had still more cause to doubt the loyalty of
German nationals resident in the USSR, such as the 130,000-odd
Schwarzmeerdeutschen (Black Sea Germans) who farmed the lands
east of the Dniester River (Transnistria) above Odessa in what
had become, after the Soviet occupation of Bessarabia in 1940, a
sensitive Ukrainian borderland. These Soviet Germans lived close
enough to the frontier that only about twenty-two thousand, or
17 percent, of them were deported before the area was conquered
in July 1941. Further east, the so-called Volga Germans, invited
to settle in Russia in the days of Catherine the Great, were numerous enough that they had been allotted minority status as the
"Volga German Autonomous Soviet Socialist Republic." Because

they lived in the Volga basin, deep in the Russian interior, Volga Germans were not the first priority for the NKVD in the early days after the invasion. Once the Wehrmacht began to threaten the Russian heartland in August 1941, however, their loyalty became a more pressing concern. On August 26, the Politburo ordered the deportation of "all Germans residing in Saratov and Stalingrad provinces and in the [Volga] German [Autonomous] Republic," counting these at 479,481. In a sign of Soviet fear that the German Army might indeed reach the Volga in 1941, these Volga Germans were deported far beyond the Volga and the Ural Mountains into Siberia (75,000 to Krasnoyarsk, 85,000 to Omsk, 100,000 to Novosibirsk, 95,000 to the Altai, and 125,000 into Kazakhstan). Five days later, another Politburo resolution stipulated that all remaining German nationals in Ukraine be arrested, with males between the ages of sixteen and sixty put to work on construction battalions.[8]

It was not only Ukrainians, Germans, Poles, and Jews behind Soviet lines who would pay in 1941 for Stalin's paranoia and hubris. The terrible truth that dawned on millions of Red Army enlistees, even loyal Russian grunts, was that they had as much to fear from their own leaders as from the merciless invader. The USSR under Stalin is the only state in recorded history to have declared the captivity of its soldiers a capital crime. This was stipulated in everything from the basic *voennaia prisyaga* (military oath) taken by soldiers to Article 58 of the Soviet *ugolovnyi kodeks* (criminal code). Surrendering on the battlefield (*sdache v plen*) for an enlistee in the Red Army, amounted to the treasonous offense of "flight to a foreign country" or "desertion to the enemy." According to the "Infantry Combat Provisions of the Red Army" in force in 1941, "captivity is treason to the homeland. There is no more reprehensible and more treacherous act. . . . The highest penalty— shooting—awaits the traitor to the homeland."[9]

The legal concept of prisoner of war was unknown under Soviet Communism. The Bolsheviks, after seizing power in 1917, had withdrawn from the Hague Conventions of 1899 and 1907 on the treatment of prisoners of war. In 1929, Stalin expressly refused to sign the updated Geneva Convention on war prisoners.* With an eye on public opinion in Britain and neutral countries (above all the United States), Molotov did authorize a vague public "Decree on Prisoners of War" on July 1, 1941. In reality, however, he and Stalin refused to concede anything. On July 9, the International Committee of the Red Cross informed the Soviet Foreign Ministry of the readiness of Germany, Finland, Hungary, and Romania to exchange lists of prisoners of war on the basis of reciprocity of treatment, as per the Hague Convention. Italy and Slovakia made the same pledge on July 22. At various points in July, the German government shared war prisoner lists with Molotov via Bulgarian, Turkish, and Swedish intermediaries, but received no response. On July 13, Molotov issued a reply, of sorts, via the Bulgarian legation in Moscow. "The Soviet government refuses to believe," he wrote, in view of "German violations of international norms . . . that the German government will observe the Hague Convention." In reply, Ribbentrop informed Molotov on July 14 that the Hague Convention on the treatment of prisoners of war had been updated at Geneva in 1929, an agreement the Soviet government had not ratified. The "German government," Ribbentrop continued, was ready to grant Geneva and Hague protections to Soviet prisoners taken on the eastern front, and he even offered to let Molotov use the consulates of neutral Sweden "to defend the interests of the Soviet government" and its citizens held prisoner in the Reich. Molotov's answer was still no, though dressed up in a clever political formula. "The Soviet government," the Russian informed Ribbentrop via the Bulgarian legation on August 8, "is prepared to observe all the conventions insofar as they will be observed by Germany herself."[10]

---

*Nor did Stalin authorize the ratification of the updated Geneva Convention on the treatment of prisoners of war in 1949. Only on August 4, 1989—as the Soviet empire in Eastern Europe was beginning to crumble and Soviet financial desperation for Western loans was becoming acute—did the USSR finally ratify the Geneva Convention.

It is true that Molotov, replying to an inquiry from the International Red Cross on June 27, 1941, declared himself willing to entertain proposals regarding the treatment of war prisoners on the eastern front—a pledge he would be periodically reminded about over the coming months and years. But Molotov never actually agreed to any such proposals, nor to mediation from third powers. Even when an important neutral country like the United States, whose material aid the Red Army so desperately needed on the eastern front, made inquiries—as Secretary of State Cordell Hull did on August 27, 1941—they were brushed off, though more politely than when the Germans asked via Bulgaria, Turkey, or Sweden. The International Red Cross had not been allowed to inspect Soviet prisoner of war camps during Stalin's wars against Poland in 1939 or Finland in 1939–1940, and it would not be allowed to inspect prisoner camps during the war of 1941 either.[11]

In view of the barbarous treatment of Soviet commissars and Jews by the invaders, Molotov's cynical line on the treatment of war prisoners—"We'll observe conventions if the Germans do"—had an obvious political bite, helping to dampen foreign criticism of the Soviet refusal to honor prisoner conventions. In London and Washington, few leaders were willing to credit the Germans with any kind of legal, much less moral, integrity, and Germany's allies in arms were seen as mere Hitlerian puppets, rendering their own complaints about Soviet mistreatment of prisoners just as moot as German ones. Even at a distance of three-quarters of a century today, when far more is known about Stalin's crimes (especially during the war) than at the time, it is tempting to dismiss the Geneva/Hague issue raised by Ribbentrop in 1941 as irrelevant, in view of the grotesque violations of human rights by both sides. Obviously, neither Hitler nor Stalin had qualms about mistreating, deporting, and killing helpless civilians.

We should not let Molotov and Stalin off the hook, however. It is not mere hairsplitting to observe that Moscow, unlike Berlin, refused to accept mediation regarding the treatment of war prisoners. The contrast reflected something important about the two strains

of totalitarianism. From the Hunger Plan to the mass shooting of
Jews that some historians now refer to as the "Shoah by bullets,"
it was already unmistakably clear in 1941 that Hitler and his officials were willing to treat conquered peoples with unfathomable
cruelty. But they were just as emphatic about protecting their own
soldiers and allies if they were taken prisoner. Indeed, the uncomfortable truth of the matter is that Nazi Germany—even if only
to protect Hitler's beloved Aryans, and other peoples joining his
anti-Bolshevik crusade, captured by the enemy—was and at least
sometimes behaved like a signatory to the Geneva Convention of
1929 on war prisoners, and the USSR was not and did not. In August 1941, the governments of Germany and its allies transmitted
extensive lists of the burgeoning ranks of captured Soviet prisoners
of war to the Soviet embassy in Ankara. Molotov never replied.
Requests for information on the numbers and treatment of war
prisoners held in the USSR—lodged by the International Red Cross
all through 1941, 1942, and 1943—were likewise ignored. During
Molotov's first visit to Washington, in late May 1942, Secretary of
State Hull politely requested that the USSR "sign or adhere to the
Geneva Convention of 1929 relative to the care and treatment of
prisoners of war." Molotov refused, objecting that even raising the
issue in public would "give the Germans the diplomatic advantage
of pretending to adhere to international law"—because they, unlike the USSR, had ratified the Geneva Convention.[12]

The fact was that Stalin simply did not care about the welfare
of his soldiers taken prisoner by the enemy, viewing them not as
merely expendable but as traitors who deserved to die. This was
evident not only in Stalin's refusal to agree to mutual pledges on
the treatment of war prisoners, but also in a cascading series of
ever more draconian disciplinary measures he imposed on the Red
Army in summer 1941. A critical escalation occurred on July 16,
in the wake of the German conquest of Smolensk and the humiliating surrender of Stalin's son Yakov to the enemy. Enraged that
his son had let himself be captured alive, Stalin had Yakov's wife
arrested—a punitive measure soon applied, in theory if not always

in practice, to all Soviet prisoners of war, pursuant to NKVD order no. 246 (under Article 58-1 V of the Soviet criminal code covering the "collective guilt" of blood relations), which "stipulated the destruction of the families of men who were captured." In a secret order of July 16, the State Defense Committee (GKO) vowed to impose "the strictest measures against cowards, *panikery* [panic mongers], and deserters." Nine uncaptured senior officers from the western front, including front commander D. G. Pavlov, were court-martialed and executed. Politruks were now assigned to every unit of the Red Army, down to regimental level.[13]

To carry out the July 16 directive, on the following day the GKO authorized the formation of punitive battalions in the rear of each Red Army unit, along the lines of the control detachments created in January 1940 during the Finnish war. The latest iteration of this grotesque Stalinist institution was styled, somewhat blandly, the Osobyi Otdel' (Special Section) of the NKVD, whose operatives were ordered to "carry out a decisive struggle against espionage and betrayal in Red Army units and to liquidate desertion from directly behind the front line." To this end, the men of Beria's Special Section were authorized to "arrest deserters, and in cases where necessary to shoot them on the spot." Soviet frontline troops were now trapped between the advancing Wehrmacht and NKVD executioners behind them, who were primed and ready to mow them down if they so much as hesitated before rushing into enemy gunfire.[14]

It was not only cowardice or desertion on the part of Red Army soldiers that merited the ultimate punishment, but simply being part of a unit encircled by the enemy (or being related to someone who was). Stalin's order no. 270 of August 16, 1941, cosigned by Molotov, Voroshilov, and Zhukov, ordered that "anyone who removes his insignia . . . and surrenders should be regarded as a malicious deserter whose family is to be arrested as a family of a breaker of the oath and betrayer of the Motherland." Further, "those falling into encirclement are to fight to the last. . . . Those who prefer to surrender are to be destroyed by any available means while their families are to be deprived of all existence." This last phrase meant that families of Soviet soldiers taken prisoner would have their property confiscated and then be deported to labor camps. Whether or not this order for collective punishment of families was carried out in all cases—for logistical reasons, it is unlikely that it could have been—the message for serving men was clear: fight to the death, or see your family expropriated and worked to death.[15]

If Stalin had no mercy for his own men cast out by the hazards of war, still less did he care what happened to the capitalist dogs his own army took prisoner, as had been made abundantly clear in the mass deportations and mass executions of Poles he captured in 1939. By the end of June 1941, just days into the eastern war, advancing German units had already witnessed the results of summary executions of German prisoners (many of them pilots who had been shot down or crash-landed behind Russian lines). Some had been nailed to trees, some castrated; others had their eyes gouged out, their tongues cut out, or were burned alive. Almost invariably, captured German soldiers were stripped of their clothing and valuables, whether before or after they were slaughtered. Near Minsk on June 28, Soviet soldiers came across a German medical column, the 127th Motor Ambulance Platoon, carrying wounded men to the rear for treatment. According to an eyewitness, the Red Army not only "butchered a great many of the wounded" but shot and killed German doctors and nurses too. Dozens of gruesome mass graves like this one were uncovered by advancing German medical and forensic teams over the coming months, who painstakingly documented Soviet atrocities against captive war prisoners—and against Stalin's own subjects in places such as Łuck (Lutsk) and Lemberg—only for these reports to be ignored by British and American journalists and diplomats, who preferred not to know.[16]

The impact of the different policies of the two warring sides regarding enemy prisoners was not hard to foresee. Knowing how barbarically they would be treated if they were captured, German and allied troops displayed manic energy during the invasion,* fighting to the bitter end. Vanishingly few were captured alive in the field, aside from Luftwaffe pilots who crash-landed behind enemy lines. So few prisoners were taken by the Red Army in the initial days of Barbarossa that no one seems to have counted them until the figure reached four, and then five, digits in early 1942. The first official estimate we have is that Stalin's armies took seventeen thousand prisoners in the war's first twelve months (mostly after December 1941), a figure less than the number of Soviet troops taken prisoner over that period by two or three orders of magnitude. The relentless forward march of the Wehrmacht slowed down after the fall of Smolensk on July 16 as Soviet reinforcements arrived. This allowed a certain rebalancing of the war's lopsided loss ratios. The German advantage, in terms of irretrievable losses, thereby fell from thirty-five to one in the first weeks of the war to merely twenty-eight to one by the end of 1941. While some of these losses were deaths, the vast bulk of the difference arose in the category of war prisoners.[17]

The differential rates of prisoners taken by each side on the eastern front in 1941 is well known to military historians, but its implications have seldom been addressed. We know that, just as in Finland, Red Army grunts were told they would be subjected to horrible tortures and summary executions if they were captured by the enemy—basically, to the same treatment Stalin and Beria's NKVD meted out to the relatively few German prisoners they got their hands on. Judging from the colossal numbers of Red Army men who surrendered anyway in 1941, few of them seem to have believed these dire warnings. Some Soviet soldiers may well have fought harder out of fear of Beria's Special Section machine gunners, but the huge number of soldiers captured by Germany and its allies—three or four million by the end of 1941—suggests that

---

* Fueled in part, we now know, by a mass-produced stimulant pill called Pervitin, a low-dose methamphetamine akin to the crystal meth widely used and abused today.

even more chose to take their chances on the mercy of the invaders, despite Hitler's regime not being known for mercy. This is in spite of the dangers soldiers knew they might be subjecting their own families to if they "surrendered." That millions of Stalin's subjects chose to throw themselves into Hitler's arms anyway, despite the risk that they might thereby ruin their families back home, suggests, at the very least, that their devotion to Soviet Communism was less than robust.

It is true that Red Army soldiers taken prisoner by the Wehrmacht were neither well fed nor well taken care of. More than half of Red Army prisoners taken on the eastern front, something like 57.5 percent, would die in captivity before the end of the war, some from summary shooting but most from starvation and disease, along with complications from battlefield injuries (or from beatings by camp guards) that were inadequately treated. The attrition rate was especially high in the early months after the invasion, partly because the German high command had not made preparations for the mass surrender of three or four million soldiers, most of whom had to be frog-marched on foot and then warehoused in crude barbed-wire encampments out in the open. Not until 1942 were facilities sufficient to house war prisoners on this scale. Scenes in German prison camps in the East were terrible, as emaciated Russians stumbled around looking like, in the words of a fellow French prisoner, "walking skeletons." Whether out of neglect or deliberate intent to starve Slavic prisoners as part of the Hunger Plan, there was nowhere near enough food on hand to feed such huge numbers of people. Thousands more Soviet prisoners perished from frostbite, typhus, or related illnesses in these crude open-air prison camps once winter set in.[18]

Not all German Army officers approved of this callous treatment. Each casualty deprived interrogators of the chance to probe captured soldiers for intelligence on the Red Army. Many Wehrmacht officers wanted to recruit new troops among war prisoners, especially among Ukrainians, who tended to despise Stalin's regime and had less reason for opposing the Germans than did another anti-Stalin minority, Poles. About seventy-five thousand captured Ukrainian Red Army soldiers were simply released and allowed to return home to occupied areas behind the front lines, such as Transnistria. Although the attrition rates in prison camps worked against recruiters, it is remarkable that nearly 1.5 million Soviet war prisoners had enlisted in the Wehrmacht by war's end, of which 800,000 were Russian, 250,000 Ukrainian, 280,000 Caucasian in origin, 180,000 from the occupied Baltic countries, 47,000 Belorussians, and the rest Cossacks. The very existence of these *Osttruppen* was an eloquent indictment of Stalin's regime,* leavened by the fact that many may have agreed to fight for Hitler only to receive better food rations and improve their meager odds for survival.[19]

There was a self-reinforcing logic to this war of attrition on the eastern front. With Stalin and Molotov refusing to let the Red Cross inspect Soviet prisoner of war camps, encouraging the barbaric treatment of Germans taken captive, and declaring murderous contempt for their own prisoners taken by the enemy, there was little incentive for German camp commandants to treat Soviet prisoners decently, even had they wished to do so. In recent historical literature, the high death rate of Soviet prisoners in German captivity has begun to be taken seriously as a war crime. It is welcome that the plight of these unfortunate millions of men is now meriting some belated attention. We should not forget, however, that at least part of the reason Soviet war prisoners suffered so terribly is that they were forsaken by their own government.[20]

Meanwhile, the brutal treatment Stalin was meting out to his own soldiers via his politruks and the machine gunners of the

---

*Later in the war, when news of General Andrey Vlasov's Russian Liberation Army of Osttruppen had filtered across to Soviet lines, the Germans made this favoritism explicit, promising better food rations and a special identification card to Red Army troops who deserted voluntarily for political reasons or who surrendered while shouting, "Down with Stalin!"

Special Section, along with Beria's mass murder of political prisoners in areas soon overrun by the invaders, helped to reinforce the
genocidal logic of Hitler's Commissar Order. In late September,
after the Germans occupied Kiev, more than thirty-three thousand
Jews were slaughtered at Babi Yar outside the city, in a grim fore-
shadowing of still greater horrors to come. Other ethnic groups in
the war zone—Ukrainians, Belorussians, and Russians—were not
treated as murderously, but because these gentiles were seen as
cleaner than Jews in Nazi racial ideology, it was often their women
who suffered instead, forced to serve as sex slaves in army broth-
els. It was turning into a macabre competition on the eastern front
to see which dictator could commit the most horrible crimes.[21]

Like all conflicts, only on a much larger scale, the Soviet-
German clash provided a smokescreen for atrocities against both
soldiers and civilians, so long as it raged on. While no one knew
for sure how much fight was left in the Red Army, there were
signs that the Germans were preparing for a longer war, in which
control of economic resources would be critical.

19

War for Aluminum

By July and August 1941, the Soviet-German war was shaping up to be a conflict of unprecedented ferocity. The cascading brutality clearly reflected the ideological nature of the clash, as the cooked-up enmity between Fascists and Communists acted as accelerant to existing ethnic animus between Teutons and Slavs, Russians and Ukrainians, gentiles and Jews.

The eastern war was not only about ideology and metastasizing ethnic hatreds, however. At least some of the white-hot intensity of the fighting can be attributed to the widespread conviction among soldiers in each camp that they were fighting for survival. On the Soviet side, this was obvious enough, in view of the rapidity of the enemy advance into European Russia and the mass executions of commissars and Jews. But the Germans, too, believed they were fighting to secure land and resources without which they would be unable to withstand another crippling British blockade. It was not simply Russian oil, Finnish nickel, and Ukrainian grain that Germany needed desperately to secure, but also cotton, coal, iron, chrome, manganese, and phosphate—all of which Soviet Russia possessed in great abundance. So long as the resource-rich industrial powerhouse the United States stood behind Britain, Germany had no chance in a long conflict, unless it could secure the vast resources of Russia and Ukraine for the Wehrmacht.

It seems clear, with the benefit of hindsight, that German military planners wholly underestimated the scale of Stalin's armor behind the frontline areas and of Soviet troop reserves more generally.* But the Germans were much better informed about the Soviet economy, owing to the experience so many German engineers and industrialists had in the USSR dating back to the Treaty of Rapallo in 1922. Economic exchange in the Molotov-Ribbentrop period had provided a raw baseline of what resources Hitler hoped to secure with his eastern war—though with the expectation that German agronomists, miners, and engineers would be able to improve yields beyond what the Russians had provided. Between September 1939 and June 22, 1941, the USSR had shipped to the Reich 1.75 million tons of wheat, a million tons of petroleum products, 23,000 tons of chrome, and 214,000 tons of phosphate, in addition to materials transshipped from Asia and the Pacific region: 440,000 tons of rubber, wolfram, copper, tin, soybeans, and whale oil.[1]

In the short run, the invasion meant these huge inputs, essential to Germany's military industries, would no longer be sent voluntarily by Mikoyan's trade commissariat. In view of the likelihood of disruption to both production and transport caused by the invasion, the early economic returns would be overwhelmingly negative. But the Reich had not been receiving Soviet raw materials for free. Barbarossa also cut off German exports of finished steel products, diesel engines, locomotives, turbines, compressors, excavators, machine tools, electrical and telegraph cables and related supplies, laboratory and optical equipment, and other sophisticated manufactures. The Germans owed more of these goods to the USSR (750 million Reichsmarks) than Stalin owed Hitler (520 million Reichsmarks). The Moscow Pact had been bilateral, after all. By breaking it, Hitler forfeited immediate access to imported Soviet raw materials grown, mined, and assembled in areas behind the front, but he was also stanching the export of critical finished products to Stalin. Barbarossa was, in the economic sense, a bid

---

*Though not all of them. Generals Jodl and Keitel at OKW were less sanguine than Halder at army headquarters. Hitler sided with Halder's less pessimistic estimates when he made the final decision to attack.

for permanent Eurasian autarky, on the not-unreasonable premise that the United States and Britain would continue to seal off
Hitlerian Europe from world markets.[2]

The Wehrmacht arrived in Belorussia, the Baltic area, and
Ukraine with clear instructions to seize farms, factories, and mines
intact. The Germans knew where to look: for the machine and
tractor factories of Mogilev, on the upper Dniepr east of Minsk; for
the manganese mines of Nikopol, on the lower Dniepr in southern
Ukraine; for the gargantuan nearby iron deposits of Krivoi Rog,
totaling 1.5 billion tons; for the rich coal seams of Kirovograd and
the Donets basin; for the shipyards and steel plants of Nikolaev
on the Black Sea; and for the aluminum combines of Zaporozhia
in south Ukraine. Then there was the Caucasus. If the Germans
reached the Volga, they could cut the Soviets off from Baku's oil
and the petrol refineries of Maikop and Grozny. Perhaps the greatest prize was the high-quality manganese deposits in Georgia,
nearly 60 percent of Soviet reserves. There were also the thousands of factories in European Russia, with the heaviest concentrations around Leningrad and Moscow, and in the great industrial
cities of southern and eastern Ukraine.[3]

For a prospective German industrialist, Barbarossa presented
an embarrassment of riches. But for Hitler and his generals, the
plenitude of important economic targets posed an acute series of
strategic dilemmas. With the fall of Smolensk on July 16 to Bock's
Army Group Center, Moscow was only two hundred miles away.
The Soviet capital was the seat of the Kremlin, the communications center of European Russia, and the hub of the Soviet rail
network, and also a major industrial center in its own right, which
produced warplanes, trucks, and tanks. Moscow's capture would
be not only of political importance, but a devastating blow to Soviet war industry.

Hitler has often been faulted by strategists for postponing
Bock's thrust toward Moscow until he issued directive no. 35 on
September 6, 1941, seven weeks after the fall of Smolensk. His gen-
erals argued strongly against him, though to no avail. On July 30,

Hitler ordered Bock to assume a defensive posture around the Smolensk pocket while shifting some of Bock's best panzer divisions
to the flanks, reinforcing Leeb's Army Group North in its push toward Leningrad and Rundstedt's Army Group South in Ukraine.
Hitler overruled Bock's request to continue his offensive, largely
on the grounds that it was more vital to secure the farmland, factories, and mineral resources of Ukraine. In so doing, the Führer
lost critical time on the central Belorussian front where the main
assault was to have taken place, allowing Stalin and Zhukov to re-
group and prepare a counterthrust once reserve divisions from the
East had arrived. By dissipating instead of concentrating his forces,
Hitler showed himself to be, in the words of one military historian,
"strategically bold but devoid of operational nerve."[4]

Although postmortems must always be taken with a grain of
salt, there is something to this critique of the Führer as warlord,
the claim that Hitler allowed his feverish strategic (or racial) ob-
sessions to override battlefield priorities. We could say the same
about the Commissar Order of June 1941 and its murderous application, which motivated partisan resistance behind the lines that
grew in seriousness as the war dragged on. By unleashing a war
of extermination in order to win living space for German settlers
in the East, Hitler made the operational task of his own and allied
armies' generals and soldiers far more difficult. What might have
been a lower-friction war of liberation, eased along by local collaborators keen to avenge Stalinist crimes, turned into an increasingly
bloody and bitter war of attrition.

All this is true enough, but Hitler's shift to the flanks after Smolensk may not have been the critical blunder it is sometimes made
out to be. There were sound strategic reasons to secure Ukraine
and the hinterland of Leningrad before Bock made the final thrust
toward Moscow, lest German Army Group Center expose itself to
powerful counterattacks on its flanks. Bock himself, though firm
in his conviction that he should have pushed on toward Moscow,
admitted in his diary on July 20 that he was "doubtful that the
enemy will allow the fighting here to cease when it suits us, even

following the destruction of the forces almost encircled around Smolensk." If Army Group Center was already facing pressure from the flank at Smolensk by mid to late July, then surely it would have been still more exposed if it had raced on to Moscow in August.[5]

Securing Ukraine would also provide strategic depth for Germany and its allies in arms, especially Romania. The further east Army Group South penetrated, the safer the oil fields and refineries, on which Hitler's panzers and dive-bombers depended, were. This was the same logic that had animated the German push into Greece and Crete earlier that spring, and it had basically worked: British bombers could no longer reach the Romanian oil fields. The last major Soviet air raid on Ploeşti in 1941, likewise, took place on the night of July 10–11. Russian pilots would not be able to return to Romanian airspace in similar strength for nearly three years.[6]

In economic terms, the shifting of German armor southward in August 1941 was an obvious move. In a literal sense, the invasion of Ukraine could pay for itself, as the advancing Wehrmacht (helped by Germany's Romanian and Hungarian allies) seized rich farmland, mineral deposits, and factories. Because of Soviet scorched-earth tactics, much had been destroyed or dismantled before the invader arrived, but not everything. In terms of the grain harvest, Stalin's collectivization drive of the early 1930s might have driven down overall yields, but it had the welcome benefit, from the invader's perspective, of centralizing production and storage in the huge new collective farms. For this reason, the German wheat yield in 1941 turned out to be much better than in the occupation of 1918, when most Ukrainian farmers had destroyed crops or hidden their surplus underground.* According to a field report filed on August 28, Germany and its allies had already secured "the

---

*Welcome as this grain yield from the kolkhozi was to the invader, it was politically counterproductive. By leaving the hated collective farms of Ukraine largely intact, the Germans undermined the claim that they were fighting a war of liberation.

harvest of 85% of the collective farms" of central Ukraine. Future
production, too, seemed secure, as the Wehrmacht also seized intact ten "machine tractor stations," the industrial component of
the kolkhozi, placing Ukrainian engineers in charge.[7]

The yield with Soviet mines and factories was not as high in
percentage terms, but it was still often considerable. At Krivoi Rog,
when the Germans marched in on August 15, 1941, they found
two million tons of iron just waiting to be exploited. The steel and
rolling mill, which had employed four thousand workers, had not
been destroyed—although substantial repairs were needed, beginning with the power station that furnished its electricity, running
at only half of its eighty-thousand-kilowatt capacity. This was a
straightforward fix though. The manganese mines of Nikopol had
been more thoroughly sabotaged and would require time to be restored to capacity, but they were now in German hands, along with
the shipyards of Nikolaev nearby, which depended on the Nikopol
manganese. Those shipyards had sustained serious damage, but
at least three nearby power plants remained in operation, along
with a nearby brewery, which did wonders for German morale.
So, too, did the capture of a thirty-five-thousand-ton battleship
under construction, which Soviet sappers had failed to sabotage
in port. The showpiece American-designed hydroelectric plant on
the Dniepr, with an astonishing capacity of five hundred thousand
kilowatts, was captured fully intact. So, too, had the coal mines of
Kirovograd survived the invasion without substantial damage. At
Kremenchuk on the banks of the Dniepr, captured in September
1941, German engineers noted with dismay that the "huge iron
foundry" and tractor factory had been sabotaged, but the boilers
were still intact. The town also had three smaller iron foundries in
good shape, along with two functioning tobacco plants, a furniture
factory, a chemical plant producing oils and soaps, and a distillery
for producing spirits—which, like the brewery in Nikolaev, the
departing Russians may have despaired of destroying. In Poltava,
scene of the pivotal Russian victory over the Swedes in 1709, the
Germans took over the Soviet Union's only thermometer factory,

damaged but still functioning: there were more than twenty thousand finished thermometers lying around. So far, the economic war was going Hitler's way.[8]

Hitler's decision to reinforce the Baltic front after the fall of Smolensk was not as foolish as it might appear. Leningrad was of symbolic importance as the birthplace of the revolution, but like Moscow it was also a major industrial center, accounting for a tenth of Soviet industrial output, including heavy KV and T-50 tanks and their diesel engines produced at the Kirov Works and the L-11 gun mounted on the T-34. Leningrad's tank factories alone may not have been a significant enough economic target to justify Hitler's decision to pull motorized divisions off the main Belorussian front, but Leeb's Army Group North, after surrounding Leningrad by the second week of September 1941, was also assigned a target 120 miles east of the city: Tikhvin, on the canal network linking the Baltic to the Volga and home to the last remaining railway link to Leningrad. Leeb did not understand why he was asked to take Tikhvin, an order he vehemently disagreed with, but he carried it out. The operation he conducted in October 1941, on what the Russians referred to (after a local river) as the Volkhov front, remains mysterious, with many military historians dismissing it as a sideshow and scratching their heads to make sense of it.[9]

In fact, Hitler had solid grounds for focusing on Tikhvin, which housed the USSR's largest deposits of bauxite, the base metal for aluminum. Because of its light weight (three times lighter than steel), tensile strength, and resistance to corrosion, aluminum was the critical input for airplanes in the Soviet Union, as it was everywhere warplanes were manufactured. But aluminum was also critical in Soviet tank production, in a way it was not elsewhere. The Germans did not use aluminum in panzer production, finding it too expensive. But Soviet T-34, KV, and T-50 tanks were so heavy, they needed aluminum-encased diesel engines to power them so as to keep the weight ratios in order. Most of the bauxite mined in the Tikhvin area was smelted in a giant combine in Zaporozhia on the lower Dniepr in Ukraine—but this combine, too, fell to the Germans in early October 1941. Because Red Army sappers had blown up the nearby dam that fueled the plant before retreating, it would be hard for the Germans to replicate prewar production levels. But the hit to Soviet production was irreparable, and aluminum was even more important in the Soviet war economy than in the German. By taking Tikhvin and Zaporozhia out of Stalin's hands, Hitler knocked out fifty thousand tons of the annual aluminum capacity of the USSR, more than 40 percent.[10]

We are told, by Stalin's defenders, that the evacuation of industry east of Moscow to form a "second line of industrial defense" was a "stupendous organizational and human achievement," which helped the Soviets win the war. As early as July 2, an armored-plate mill was shipped east from Mariupol, in southern Ukraine, to Magnitogorsk in the southern Ural Mountains. Twenty-six factories were shipped east by rail from Leningrad, Moscow, and Tula in July. According to official Soviet records, no less than 283 "major industrial enterprises" in Ukraine were moved east between June and October, along with 136 "smaller factories." The story was similar in Belorussia, with some one hundred major industrial sites evacuated east of Moscow. If we count smaller plants, as many as 1,523 enterprises were wholly or partially moved in 1941, accounting for 8 to 10 percent of prewar industrial production capacity. Even if the figures are inflated, the evacuation of Soviet industry eastward to the Volga, the Urals, western Siberia, and Kazakhstan required 1.6 million railway cars ferrying 870,000 tons of industrial equipment. This herculean effort allowed the resurrection of a tenth or more of lost Soviet war production capacity, and the denial of this industrial capacity to the invader.[11]

Special care was also taken to shift as much modern tank production eastward as possible. As early as July 1, 1941, the GKO ordered the urgent construction of a new factory, named Krasnoe Sormovo, to produce the T-34 tank in Gorky (formerly and currently Nizhny Novgorod), 260 miles east of Moscow on the Volga. GKO resolution no. 2 ordered the construction of a new facility in

Chelyabinsk to build KV tanks. Related GKO resolutions between July 1 and 5 shifted the production of aluminum-encased diesel engines for the T-34 and KV tanks to Gorky and Sverdlovsk—the KV tank facilities, significantly, were evacuated from the famous Kirov Works in Leningrad, which was vulnerable to the German advance on the northern front. In view of the critical role tanks would play on the eastern front, these resolutions, many passed in the first two weeks of the war, displayed impressive foresight on behalf of Stalin and his advisers.[12]

We must be cautious with the evacuation story, however, as it is so central to the Great Patriotic War myth. German military records make clear that huge numbers of Soviet factories were captured undamaged. In addition to the Ukrainian facilities mentioned earlier, the Germans captured factories all over Belorussia and the Baltic region. In Mogilev, the Germans, according to Wehrmacht files, took "a whole range of facilities fully intact," including a chemical plant, two furniture factories, and a textile plant. In Krichev, in eastern Belorussia, the Germans discovered a huge combine producing fertilizer and phosphate, with significant military-industrial applications. The factory was fully intact, needing only its power plant to be repaired. Vilna (Vilnius) was captured with almost no damage done to its numerous sawmills, wood processing plants, and furniture, paper, and cardboard factories. In the other Baltic capitals, the Germans seized intact twenty-eight textile plants, seven leather tanneries, five fur processing facilities, and four major rubber plants, thus knocking out the entire production complex for Red Army uniform and boot supply.[13]

Even if we were to grant the higher estimates of restored production capacity of Soviet facilities evacuated to the east in 1941, we must also factor in the loss of critical material inputs. The German conquest of Zaporozhia and Tikhvin gravely undermined Soviet aluminum production, and through it the capacity to produce modern T-34 and KV tanks—even in the evacuated factories at Gorky and Chelyabinsk—not to mention Soviet warplanes and aeroengines. It is not mere speculation that the loss of aluminum-smelting capacity posed a mortal threat to Soviet war industry. Stalin himself said as much repeatedly in 1941, demanding that Washington and London ship him refined aluminum (his baseline demand was 5,000 tons up front and 2,500 tons per month thereafter), or the war was lost. "Give us the aluminum," Stalin informed Roosevelt's special envoy, Harry Hopkins, on July 30, 1941—before Zaporozhia and Tikhvin were lost—"and we can fight for three or four years."* Without foreign aluminum to replace warplanes and tanks lost in summer 1941 and to equip motorized divisions with new T-34 and KV tanks, fighters, and bombers, the Red Army would not be able to fight that long.[14]

Soviet losses in coal and steel output were even greater. The Germans' seizure of Krivoi Rog alone deprived Soviet industry of fifty-two thousand tons of iron ore deposits that had been mined every day. Sabotage by Red sappers had plunged capacity to only two thousand tons per day when the Germans arrived, although German engineers tripled this figure within ten days and expected to reach prewar production levels in four to twelve months. But the loss to Stalin was two hundred million tons of iron ore per year. Manganese mines at Nikopol, likewise, were damaged when the Germans seized them, but this was poor consolation to Stalin's industrial commissars, who lost eighty thousand tons of manganese inputs per month (a million tons per year). Without manganese, the USSR would be unable to smelt iron into the steel that gave Stalin his name, but then Stalin was losing iron ore too. Nor would it be easy to fuel Soviet blast furnaces without Ukrainian coal. At Kirovograd, coal production dropped by two-thirds after Russian sabotage to only one hundred thousand tons daily. In that town alone, Soviet war industry lost three hundred thousand tons of coal daily, or 110 million tons per year.[15]

---

* Significantly, aluminum had been banned from being exported to the USSR in the moral embargo President Roosevelt had declared after Stalin invaded Finland. Roosevelt's decision to reverse that embargo earlier in 1941 had enormous strategic consequences.

All of these figures, meanwhile, dated to August 1941, before the Wehrmacht had reached the highest-value economic areas: the gargantuan coal and iron deposits of the Donets basin in eastern Ukraine and the Tula war factories southwest of Moscow, not to mention Moscow itself. Despite Rundstedt's Army Group South having gotten off to a slow start because of the heavy concentration of Soviet armor on the southwestern front, by late summer the Ukrainian rout was on. On September 15, Rundstedt's Sixteenth and Third Panzer Divisions, after surrounding Kiev from north and south, met up at Lokhvitsa, 125 miles east of the Ukrainian capital, completing a devastating encirclement of four entire Soviet armies. The soon-legendary Kiev pocket netted 665,000 prisoners for Germany and its allies, bringing the prisoner total to date to more than two million. The path was now open south, to the Black Sea and the Crimean Peninsula, and in left-bank Ukraine, eastward to Kharkov and the Donets basin.[16]

The capture of Crimea—effected, but for pockets of resistance at Kerch and Sevastopol, by the Germans and Romanians in the second half of October 1941 after General Erich von Manstein's Eleventh Army broke Soviet resistance at the isthmus of Perekop—was devastating for Soviet war industry. Although the peninsula was known more for its naval bases, summer resorts, and palaces than for industry, Crimea contained the largest iron deposits in the entire Soviet Union: estimated at 2.7 billion tons, nearly 50 percent more than the more famous seam at Krivoi Rog. A single Soviet ironworks in Kerch employed twenty thousand people who churned out sixty thousand tons of pig iron a month and twenty-four thousand tons of finished steel. Kerch also housed war factories producing everything from battleships and naval warplanes to anti-tank guns, field artillery, light howitzers, and mine throwers. Further west on the peninsula, Sevastopol, a heavily armed fortress town that was the main Soviet naval base on the Black Sea, housed 10 percent of Soviet naval production capacity. Crimean farms also produced large shares of Soviet cotton, fruit, tobacco, and other foodstuffs.[17]

Almost simultaneous to Manstein's conquest of Soviet Crimea, the German Sixth Army, commanded by Field Marshal Walther von Reichenau, pushed on eastward into left-bank Ukraine, rolling up Sumy on October 10, Stalino (today's Donetsk, a town of a half million residents) on October 20, and finally the great industrial center of Kharkov, a city of 840,000 (prewar) inhabitants, on October 25, 1941. While the departing Soviet authorities tried to sabotage factories and critical infrastructure, they had mixed success. In Stalino and Kharkov, locals helped Wehrmacht sappers and engineers safely remove mines and explosives before they detonated. The coking plants of Stalino were mostly destroyed, but the benzene refinery was undamaged. Electrical capacity was down to two thousand kilowatts, but this was enough to power several surviving factories, including a machine-tool factory and the Kirov ironworks, with annual capacity of 1.2 million tons, captured largely intact. Many other local factories—including leather, textile, and soap plants along the rail connection to Kharkov—had been damaged beyond immediate repair.[18]

The story in Kharkov was similar. Some of the town's industrial base had been evacuated eastward before the Wehrmacht arrived, including equipment from the deceptively named "Kharkov Locomotive Plant," or Factory No. 183, which housed the design bureau and finished assembly plant for the T-34 tank, of which more were produced here than anywhere else in the USSR (the local production target for 1941 had been 300). After the last T-34 rolled off the assembly line in Kharkov in October 1941, the design bureau of Factory No. 183, along with critical machines and equipment, trained engineers, and staff workers, were evacuated to Nizhni Tagil in the Ural Mountains, where a new Factory No. 183 was assembled to produce T-34s safely behind the front line. The new Kharkov-esque T-34 factory in the Urals was in operation by mid-December 1941 and reached full capacity in March 1942.[19]

Most factories in Kharkov had been sabotaged. The departing Soviet authorities, sensing which way local sympathies were tending, had looted the food stores, leaving empty shelves as residents

hunkered down for winter. Local Ukrainians had then exacted revenge on the departing Stalinist officials, who had ordered them to
evacuate, by staying behind to disarm mines and explosives. Some
facilities, including an electrical plant and a locomotive-engine factory, had survived. Many locals also turned over Soviet commissars
and partisans to the Germans. The result was that the inhabitants
of Kharkov won the Germans' sympathy, although the Germans
did not have enough food supplies on hand to feed them. It would
be a tough winter in Kharkov—although no tougher than the
prospect facing the Soviet high command, which had just seen yet
another major industrial center, housing the most critical single
war factory in the entire USSR, fall to the enemy.[20]

It is worth pausing here to examine the ledger in the economic
war on the eastern front in the second half of 1941, as it was so
critical to the fortunes of each side. With the foresighted evacuation of tank and diesel-engine production from areas conquered by
the Wehrmacht, Stalin had spared himself the worst-case scenario.
Nonetheless, the fact remained that production of both T-34s and
KVs—the two highest-priority items in Stalin's arsenal—although
ramping up for the first eight months of 1941, actually declined
over the coming months, bottoming out in October and November 1941 at levels 57 percent and 25 percent below their August
peak, just as the battle outside Moscow was being joined. In those
critical two months, only 430 T-34s and 333 KVs were produced,
an average of less than 400 modern tanks monthly at a time when
the Red Army was losing more than 3,500 tanks per month to enemy action, capture, or simple breakdowns. By year's end, the Red
Army had lost 22,340 tanks. Far from increasing in size because of
ramped-up production, Stalin's tank park was being stripped bare.
If Soviet industry won the war, it certainly did not win it in 1941.[21]

Already a war of human attrition at the front, Operation Barbarossa was rapidly turning into a war to the economic death. It
was anyone's guess who would prevail.

20

On the Ropes

On September 6, 1941, Hitler issued directive no. 35, which declared that rapid German progress on the "flanks" had now "provided the basis for a decisive operation against the Timoshenko Army Group," which "must be beaten to destruction in the limited time before the onset of winter weather." It took another four weeks to reinforce Bock's Army Group Center in sufficient strength to carry out this offensive targeting Moscow. In addition to manpower and armor being stretched thin across three major fronts, the Germans were woefully short of trucks. When Bock's attack began on October 2, however, the impact was devastating. By October 7, two panzer groups had closed in from opposite directions on Viazma, a railway junction where the main east-west Smolensk-Moscow line crossed over a north-south line from Rzhev to Briansk. Briansk was an important rail hub and also a significant industrial center, housing twenty-five metalworking and machine factories. Almost simultaneously, Guderian's Second Panzer Group, on the southern flank of Bock's army group, raced around Briansk and took it from behind. The twin encirclements at Viazma and Briansk, which the Germans dubbed the *Doppelschlacht* (double battle), netted Bock 660,000 prisoners, almost as many as Rundstedt had taken at Kiev. Of the 1.25 million troops deployed in Timoshenko's army groups defending Moscow at the start of October, nearly a million were lost by month's end. The fate of Soviet armed formations was grim: Timoshenko and Stalin lost sixty-four rifle divisions, eleven tank brigades, and fifty artillery regiments.[1]

In strategic terms, the Viazma/Briansk encirclement was a far more devastating loss for Stalin than Kiev was. The collapse of

Timoshenko's army group opened the road (and railroad) to Tula, the beating heart of Russian war industry since the eighteenth century. Tula's factories produced everything from artillery and shells to machine guns, pistols, rifles, ammunition, and gunpowder to bombs, hand grenades, and, above all, explosives. The city accounted for 12 percent of total Soviet war-industrial production. Tula's Factory No. 7 alone, which produced handheld weapons, employed twenty thousand people. Whether or not German engineers would be able to seize all this intact, depriving Stalin's armies of the output of Tula would basically disarm them.[2]

Just north of Tula lay Moscow itself. As early as October 5, a Soviet pilot observed a "massive armored and motorized [German] column some twelve miles long" southeast of Viazma, moving into essentially undefended territory. So alarming was the news that the VVS commander who passed on this report to Stalin and Beria, Colonel N. A. Sbytov, was hauled before an NKVD interrogation team as a "panic monger." Although told to keep his mouth shut, Sbytov survived.[3]

On Stalin's orders, a new Soviet defensive perimeter was established seventy-five miles west of Moscow, running from Volokolamsk in the north, through Mozhaisk to Kaluga to the south. But with Timoshenko's armies all but destroyed in the Viazma/Briansk encirclements, this was a mere Band-Aid. As Zhukov told Stalin on the telephone on October 8, "Nearly all routes to Moscow are now open, and the weak covering forces on the Mozhaisk Line cannot be a guarantee against the sudden appearance of enemy tank forces in front of Moscow."[4]

Whatever they may have said later, at the time Soviet leaders were terrified. On October 7, the chairman of the Moscow city soviet signed a decree evacuating women and children from the capital. On October 8, Stalin ordered the GKO to draw up a list of industrial enterprises in and around Moscow to be sabotaged or blown up in case the Germans broke through the final Soviet defensive lines, including "bakeries, refrigerated stores, meat-processing

338

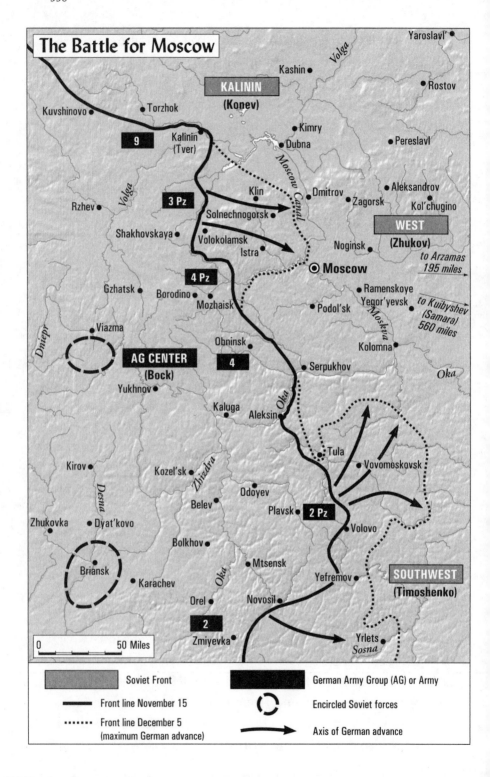

The Battle for Moscow

Yaroslavl'

Kashin

Rostov

KALININ
(Konev)

Kuvshinovo

Torzhok

Kimry

Pereslavl

9

Kalinin
(Tver)

Dubna

Rzhev

Volga

3 Pz

Klin

Dmitrov

Aleksandrov

Zagorsk

Kol'chugino

Solnechnogorsk

WEST
(Zhukov)

Shakhovskaya

Volokolamsk

Istra

Noginsk

to Arzamas
195 miles

Moscow

4 Pz

Ramenskoye

Gzhatsk

Borodino

Mozhaisk

Podol'sk

Yegor'yevsk

to Kuibyshev
(Samara)
560 miles

Viazma

Obninsk

4

Kolomna

Oka

AG CENTER
(Bock)

Serpukhov

Yukhnov

Kaluga

Aleksin

Kirov

Kozel'sk

Tula

Vovomoskovsk

Desna

Odoyev

Zhukovka

Dyat'kovo

Belev

Plavsk

2 Pz

Volovo

Bolkhov

Mtsensk

Briansk

Yefremov

SOUTHWEST
(Timoshenko)

Karachev

Orel

Novosil

2

Zmiyevka

Yrlets
Sosna

0   50 Miles

Soviet Front

German Army Group (AG) or Army

Front line November 15

Encircled Soviet forces

Front line December 5
(maximum German advance)

Axis of German advance

plants, stations and other railway buildings, tram and trolleybus parks . . . power stations, bridges," the TASS news bureau, and even the Bolshoi Theater. While *Pravda* continued churning out implausible stories about heroic Red Army resistance at Viazma, these were belied by visible signs of an impending mass evacuation from Moscow, such as the assembly of thirty-nine thousand railway wagons in the city's rail stations that faced north and east. Members of the foreign press corps began to leave on October 8 and 9.[5]

Preparations for a last-ditch defense of Moscow continued. On October 9, Stavka merged with the Moscow district command to coordinate emergency measures, from the digging of trenches and ditches outside the city to the mobilization of 450,000 civilians into makeshift militia units. On October 10, when the first German panzer group reached the Mozhaisk line, the "Moscow reserve front" was subsumed into the western front, and a new defensive line was established just forty miles west of Moscow. Zhukov, who had been overseeing the defense of Leningrad, was flown to Moscow and placed in overall command of what was left of the Red armies at the front—a skeletal force of ninety thousand—even while a GKO decree of October 11 placed the Moscow region under the control of Beria's NKVD, at least in theory.[6]

These measures did little to slow down the relentless German advance. On October 12, in a giant pincer movement, the imposing twelve-mile column of German armor observed by the alarmed Soviet pilot back on October 5 rolled into Kaluga, between Yukhnov and Tula on Moscow's southern flank, even while motorized divisions on Bock's left wing rolled north and west through Rzhev toward Kalinin (Tver) on the Volga, which fell on October 14. By seizing Kalinin, Bock had cut off the main rail connection between Leningrad and Moscow, even while his right wing had the vast arms complex of Tula in sight. Meanwhile, in Bock's center, the Germans fought their way onto the heights of Borodino, where Napoleon had defeated Mikhail Kutuzov in 1812 prior to marching into Moscow.[7]

The situation in the Soviet capital was dire. With the Wehr-macht close enough for Muscovites to hear the booms of artillery fire, there was an exodus from the factories and offices and a rush to the train stations. Toward evening on October 15, a GKO decree, signed by Stalin, was posted, making the evacuation of Moscow official. All foreign missions and embassies were ordered to relocate 650 miles east to Kuibyshev (Samara) on the Volga, along with main offices of the Soviet government (under Molotov's supervision) and the political administration of the Red Army. Stavka—the Red Army's operational command—was evacuated too, although not quite as far east; it was relocated 260 miles east of Moscow, to Arzamas, so as to enable communication with the frontline commanders defending the capital. With tantalizing ambiguity, the evacuation decree of October 15 stipulated that "comrade Stalin will evacuate either tomorrow or later, *smotrya po obstanovke* [depending on circumstances]." According to Zhukov's later recollection, Stalin asked Beria to "use his 'Organ' to sound out the possibilities of making a separate peace with Germany, given the critical situation." Beria moaned, "We shall be shot down like partridges" and argued that Moscow should be abandoned. According to Anastas Mikoyan, Stalin agreed that the Politburo could leave but insisted on staying one more day himself. "Why should we leave today," Mikoyan asked, "if you are leaving tomorrow?" "I will stay and leave with you tomorrow," replied Stalin. A special train was prepared for Stalin and top Politburo members, and four American Douglas DC-3 airplanes were fueled and ready, in case an even quicker departure was required. But the Vozhd decided to stay in Moscow and fight,* sleeping and working underground in the Kirov metro station (today's Chistye Prudy).[8]

---

*The Moscow Metro was built deep underground to double as a bomb shelter. The precaution proved wise. Even while Stalin ruled what was left of the USSR from the Kirov underground station, Zhukov set up a makeshift military headquarters in Belorusski station.

Unlike in 1812, Moscow was not declared an open city. Zhukov prepared a final line of defense, mustering as many anti-tank guns as he could and terrorizing everyone into mounting a suicidal last stand in the capital. In a typical directive, Zhukov demanded that "cowards and deserters on the field of battle should be shot on the spot." With similar ruthlessness, he ordered Soviet sappers to mine fifty-six bridges in and around Moscow and ordered demolition crews to ignite their charges "at the first sight of the enemy," without regard for the fate of civilians. Beria's NKVD was rounding up and forcibly impressing civilians to dig ditches and man trenches. On the foothills between Borodino and Mozhaisk, Siberian riflemen were fighting a ferocious rearguard battle against elite German SS units. Stalin's own suburban dachas were dynamited by Beria's NKVD men, in case the Germans discovered secret papers or seized personal artifacts as war trophies. At dawn on October 16, Zhukov authorized a broadcast on Moscow radio in which it was finally admitted that, although the heroic Red defenders had "inflicted heavy losses on the enemy," the "fascist German forces" had "overwhelmed our defenses" on the Viazma front.[9]

Panic engulfed Moscow. On October 16, the metro stopped running. "All the street cars and buses," one Muscovite recalled, "were mobbed by people and their suitcases." The "roads running east to Gorky and Kuibyshev," he continued, "were swarming with cars and pedestrians." In the western rail stations, the backwash of the defeated Soviet armies began to pour in, with wounded soldiers laid out on stretchers. Even the Kremlin was camouflaged on the side facing the Moscow River, where a canvas painted to mimic a row of ordinary houses had been erected, although it was unclear how this would fool Luftwaffe bombers.[10]

Although Stalin and his generals were still in the city, they were underground and out of sight. The ubiquitous secret policemen who had terrorized Moscow for more than two decades were nowhere to be seen. "Everyone is boiling with indignation," a Russian journalist observed, "shouting that they have been betrayed, that 'the captains were the first to abandon ship' and took their valuables with them in the bargain." He continued, "People are saying things out loud" that "three days ago would have brought them before a military tribunal." Muscovites and other Russians, he observed, were beginning

> to count up all the humiliations, the oppression, the injustices, the clampdowns, the bureaucratic arrogance of the officials, the conceit and the self-confidence of the party bureaucrats, the draconian decrees, the shortages, the systematic deception of the masses, the lying and flattery of the toadies in the newspapers. . . . People are speaking from their hearts. Will it be possible to defend a city where such moods prevail?[11]

One of the few NKVD agents still working observed a factory protest at which a metalworker who had previously spied for him began "haranguing his fellow workers on the iniquities of the Soviet regime." Rioters looted food stores, pharmacies, museums, government buildings, and deserted foreign compounds, including the British embassy. At a nearby kolkhoz, liberated collective farmers looted the NKVD barracks. "In the crowds," the historian Peter Mill wrote in his diary, "people are saying that the Germans will arrive tonight."[12]

At NKVD headquarters in the Lubyanka building, smoke poured out from the chimneys and windows, in scenes reminiscent of the burning of the Tsarist Okhrana (secret police) headquarters in Petrograd during the February Revolution of 1917. For three exhilarating days, anarchy reigned on the streets of Moscow. Communist slogans were defaced, Soviet hammer-and-sickle flags torn down. A rumor went around that "Lenin's tomb had been boarded over and the coffin removed."* Muscovites scrubbed their houses and storefronts of Stalinist paraphernalia and burned

---

*Lenin's embalmed body had long since been removed from Moscow, but this had never been publicly announced.

their party membership cards. In an ominous sign for the city's Jewish population, anti-Semitic demonstrations broke out in several of Moscow's industrial suburbs. Outside one police station, a drunken laborer was overheard shouting, "The Jews have sold Russia, there is nothing with which to defend Moscow, there are no rifles, no cartridges, no shells. The Jews have stolen everything!" As one foreign military attaché recalled of the heady time, "If the Germans had cared to drop 500 parachutists over Moscow and take over the radio stations, they could have had it for the asking."[13]

With his dreams of forward European conquest shattered, and his vast mechanized war machine crippled by Hitler's audacious three-pronged attack, Stalin's war had devolved into a bitter battle for survival. The future of Communism appeared bleak.

IV.

CAPITALIST LIFELINE

21

Lifting the Moral Embargo

FAR FROM CONQUERING Europe and the world, Communism was, by October 1941, contracting to its original core between Moscow and the Urals. On every front and by every metric, the Germans were winning the battles. But there was one thing Hitler had not reckoned on, which might still lose him the war. By a kind of public-relations miracle, Hitler's sudden attack of June 22, 1941, had turned his fellow mass murderer and swallower of small nations, Stalin, into a victim in the view of much of the Western public and Stalin's people into heroes. As Stalin himself had presciently noted in his July 3 radio address, the mere fact that Germany had invaded Russia, rather than the other way around, had brought "tremendous political gain to the USSR." The newfound enthusiasm for his bloodstained regime in London and Washington was, the Vozhd rightly noted, "a serious and lasting factor that is bound to form the basis for the development of decisive military successes of the Red Army." In a twist Lenin could scarcely have dreamed of, the fate of Communism now depended on the generosity of Stalin's sworn and oft-declared archenemy: Anglo-Saxon capitalism.[1]

In December 1939, as noted earlier, the Roosevelt administration had declared a moral embargo on strategic exports to Russia, including aluminum, because of Stalin's brutal invasion of tiny Finland. So long as the Soviet Union was allied with Nazi Germany, and was able to draw on German industrial resources and expertise, Roosevelt's embargo had been little more than an annoyance. After Hitler's invasion, however, the Soviet war economy was cut off from German strategic imports and, more importantly, from the economic resources of Belorussia and Ukraine. Even as the Red Army's need for war matériel ratcheted up with every passing day, Soviet production of virtually everything plummeted in the second half of 1941, from T-34 tanks to warplanes to anti-tank guns to machine guns, rifles, and ammunition. In the first six months of the eastern war, the Red Army lost 22,340 tanks, or nearly 91 percent of Stalin's original tank park, while only 5,400 new tanks were produced—not even a fourth of Soviet losses. The ratio was still worse with anti-tank guns, with 12,100, or nearly 81 percent of the original stock, lost by December 1941 and only 2,500, or scarcely more than 20 percent, being replenished. Of 8,400 Soviet bombers on hand at the time of the invasion, 7,200 were lost by December 1941, against only 2,500 produced. With fighters, production did not lag losses quite so severely. Still, of the 9,600 out of 11,500 lost from prewar stocks, only two-thirds could be replaced from new production, about 6,000. As for primary inputs, Soviet production of iron plunged by two-thirds from 1941 to 1942, steel and aluminum by 50 to 60 percent, and coal by more than half. Absent material inputs (especially aluminum) imported from Britain and the United States, there was no way Soviet war industry could equip the Red Army with what it needed to fight. Before the new factories of Kuibyshev (Samara), Kazan, and the Urals cranked up to full capacity, losses would have to be made up in finished war matériel.[2]

It was therefore salutary, from Stalin's perspective, that President Roosevelt had lifted his moral embargo in January 1941, despite no evidence of improved Soviet behavior. In February, Roosevelt's aide, Harry Hopkins, had established a liaison committee with the Soviet embassy to coordinate strategic exports. Catching wind of what Roosevelt and Hopkins were up to, many congressmen during the lend-lease debate had objected to sending military aid to the Soviet Union. Although amendments excluding the USSR were defeated, Roosevelt's opponents had laid down a marker, and many congressional Republicans, along with conservative southern Democrats (thirteen Democratic senators had voted against the Lend-Lease Act), remained staunchly opposed to arming Stalin. As late as June 13, 1941, the Soviet Foreign Ministry prepared a dark assessment of the state of US public opinion, warning Molotov and Stalin that "the entire American press is waging a furious campaign against the USSR," blaming a recent wave of industrial strikes on "agents of Moscow." The report predicted that the Roosevelt administration would shortly be forced by the growing public outcry to hold up strategic exports to Russia and detain or seize Soviet ships in US ports. The mood in Washington by June 1941 was so anti-Soviet that two high-ranking Russian aviation officers, Colonel P. F. Berezin and Major K. I. Ovchinnikov, both working under diplomatic cover at the Soviet embassy as "aides of the Soviet military aviation attaché," were declared "persona non grata" by the US secretary of war, Henry Stimson, for suspected spying on June 10, and they were scheduled for deportation on June 21—the day before Barbarossa was launched.*[3]

After the German invasion, the debate over American aid policy toward Stalin took on world-historical importance, as it had the potential to decide the outcome of the war on the eastern front. While Roosevelt himself, like Churchill, expressed strong support for the Soviet cause in public after learning of the German invasion, his partiality was not universally shared in Washington. Senator Hiram Johnson of California, one of the "irreconcilables" who had opposed joining the League of Nations back in 1919, surprised no one when he inveighed that "I would leave these two scoundrels Hitler and Stalin to fight it out." But Johnson was not alone. Hamilton Fish III, a congressman from western New York whose grandfather had been secretary of state, thundered on a nationally syndicated radio broadcast that, opposed though he was to "Nazism," he was certain that "American mothers will not willingly sacrifice their sons to make the world safe for Communism."

---

* On July 2, after President Roosevelt had declared full-throated support for Stalin against Hitler, the deportation order was rescinded.

It was "preposterous," Fish continued, "to think of America being aligned with Joe Stalin as our pal and comrade, with his hands
dripping with blood of murdered priests and nuns and the same
dagger in his hand which he plunged into the backs of Poland, Latvia, Estonia, Lithuania and our friend the little honest Republic of
Finland." Congressman Frank C. Osmers Jr. of New Jersey vowed
in the House that the United States must "make no ill-considered
promise to send nonexistent war material on nonexistent ships to
a nation whose whole concept of life is repugnant to us." More
colorfully, Representative Robert F. Rich of Pennsylvania argued
that "those who want us to get into war on the side of Russia want
us to get in bed with a rattlesnake and a skunk."[4]

Midwestern senators expressed similar views, not surprisingly
in light of the war wariness of the American heartland. Senator Arthur Capper of Kansas said that, while he was "against Hitler," he
also had "no sympathy for Stalin. The latest developments confirm
me in the conviction I long have held that these European wars are
not our wars. We should stay out of them." Senator Bennett C.
Clark of Missouri, although a Democrat, did not agree with Roosevelt that Stalin was worthy of US support, proclaiming the war
"a case of dog eat dog. Stalin is as bloody-handed as Hitler. I don't
think we should help either one. We should tend to our own business." Senator Robert M. La Follette Jr. of Wisconsin warned that

> in the next few weeks the American people will witness the great-
> est whitewash act in all history. They will be told to forget the
> purges in Russia by the OGPU [secret police], the persecution of
> religion, the confiscation of property, the invasion of Finland and
> the vulture role Stalin played in seizing half of prostrate Poland,
> all of Latvia, Estonia and Lithuania. These will be made to seem
> the acts of a "democracy" preparing to fight Nazism.

Thinking strategically, Senator Robert Taft of Ohio warned
that, however menacing Hitler appeared at the moment, "the victory of communism in the world would be far more dangerous to

the United States than the victory of fascism." Along these lines, Harry Truman, a rising star in the Democratic Party, proposed on the Senate floor on June 23, 1941, that US policy should be conditional on the progress of the fighting: "If we see that Germany is winning we ought to help Russia and if Russia is winning we ought to help Germany."[5]

Skepticism about aiding Stalin was not confined to Congress. General Robert E. Wood, on behalf of the huge America First movement, issued a public statement declaring that "the entry of Communist Russia into the war certainly should settle once and for all the intervention issue." With "the ruthless forces of dictatorship and aggression now clearly aligned on both sides" of the European war, he continued, "the war party can hardly ask the people of America to take up arms behind the red flag of Stalin" or "undertake a program of all-out aid to Russia." In a national radio broadcast, former president Herbert Hoover reminded Americans that Stalin's regime was "one of the bloodiest tyrannies and terrors ever erected in history," which had "violated every international covenant" and had "carried on a world conspiracy against all democracies, including the United States." That the two "hideous ideologists," Hitler and Stalin, were locked "in deadly combat," should be regarded as positive news, for their "fratricidal war" must weaken them both. "Statesmanship," Hoover argued, "demands that the United States stand aside in watchful waiting, armed to the teeth, while these men exhaust themselves." Colonel Robert McCormick, editor of the *Chicago Tribune*, asked, "Are we to send an army to reestablish atheism in Russia and the slaughter of the priests?" The *Tribune* thundered all summer against lend-lease aid to Stalin.[6]

The American Communist Party, for its part, had flatly reversed its position on the European war after Hitler turned on Stalin, from full-throated opposition to intervention (and frequent denunciations of President Roosevelt as a "warmonger") to a new line of "full support and cooperation with the Soviet Union in its struggle against Hitlerism." But this position of enthusiastic support for Stalin was not widely shared. While nearly three-fourths of the country sympathized with the Soviet Union after the German invasion, nowhere near this many Americans wanted to support Stalin's armies. According to a Gallup poll in July 1941, a clear majority (54 percent) opposed extending military aid to the USSR. As late as October 1941, another poll showed that only 8.5 percent of Americans expressed a strong preference for Stalin's government over Hitler's.[7]

Public opinion, of course, did not determine policy. Because of the "good faith" clause in the Lend-Lease Act, the only argument that mattered was the one in Roosevelt's head, and there it was not much of a debate. Asked, at the June 24 press conference where he pledged to "give all possible aid to Russia," whether he had determined that the defense of the USSR was vital to "the defense of the United States" as required in the lend-lease statute, the president played dumb: "Oh, ask me a different type of question—such as 'how old is Ann?'" (referring to his daughter, Anna). The only clue Roosevelt offered to his thinking was that "until this government obtained a list of what Russia needed . . . no moves could be made toward supplying her wants."[8]

Even before this bizarre press conference, powerful figures in the Roosevelt administration had determined that, regardless of congressional and public opinion, the USSR was eligible for, and would receive, lend-lease aid. On June 23, the president's closest adviser, Harry Hopkins, commissioned a study of the legal issues involved, from amendments proposed to limit White House authority to determine countries eligible for aid (all defeated) to objections raised before the Senate Foreign Relations Committee (all subsumed, it was determined, in the "good faith" clause). Secretary of War Stimson, whose approval would be necessary to free up war matériel needed by the US Army for shipment to Russia, agreed that the president had the legal authority to send aid to Stalin "if he reached that conclusion in good faith."[9]

Stimson was so moved by Hitler's invasion of the USSR that he composed his own memorandum for President Roosevelt on

June 23, which all but declared American neutrality a dead letter. Had congressional skeptics received copies, they would have been floored to learn that the secretary of war, a Republican, was advising the president that

> by getting into this war with Russia Germany has relieved our anxiety, provided we act promptly and get the initial dangers over before Germany gets her legs disentangled from the Russian mire. . . . Germany's action seems like an almost providential occurrence. By this final demonstration of Nazi ambition and perfidy, the door is opened wide for you to lead directly towards the winning of the battle of the North Atlantic and the protection of our hemisphere in the South Atlantic.[10]

There remained staunch opposition in the American heartland to aiding Stalin, but Hopkins was confident that Roosevelt could use the bully pulpit of the presidency to bulldoze his way through. "We are facing an articulate minority," Hopkins wrote on June 23, "which will yowl about Communism. It will be led by questionably motivated members of the R[oman] C[atholic] Church." Curiously, Hopkins seemed less concerned about the likely opposition of mostly Protestant German Americans, so numerous in the upper Midwest, to a policy of aiding Stalin, than about Polish and Irish Catholics. With remarkable chutzpah—in view of Stalin's being the first explicitly atheist regime in human history, and the Red Army the only one in which soldiers were subjected daily to atheistic agitprop—Hopkins proposed that "the anti-religious part of the Nazi policy ought to be emphasized to prevent too many Catholics from getting confused into a policy of no support for the Russian fight." Rather than abetting Communism, Roosevelt was to explain, Americans, by sending aid to Stalin, could help Russian Christians, in spite of their hitherto brutal persecution by Stalin's regime. "Our policy is clear," Hopkins wrote in a draft speech for Roosevelt to deliver to Congress. "We will take every action which will stall the Nazi machine in the fields of Russia or on the channel guarding the British Isles. We shall aid the Russians fighting for their homeland. We shall aid them, not by words of encouragement alone, but by all the materials we can practicably give them."[11]

Hopkins had little trouble convincing the president that the policy of aiding Stalin was the right one. On June 24, Roosevelt freed up $39 million in frozen Soviet funds to lubricate Russian arms orders. On June 25, he announced that he would not invoke the Neutrality Act regarding the Soviet-German war, which meant that US ships could legally carry goods to Soviet ports, so long as they were distant from the war zone. Remarkably, this was more than Roosevelt had been able to do yet for England. (Although Roosevelt had extended US naval patrols into the mid-Atlantic as far as twenty-five degrees west longitude in April, the British Isles remained off-limits because of the U-boat campaign raging around the long British coastline.)* On June 30, the Soviet embassy placed its first request, for $1.8 billion worth of American warplanes, anti-aircraft guns, toluol (the critical input in TNT), aviation gasoline, and lubricants. On July 8, Roosevelt approved the Soviet request in principle, and gave Stalin's ambassador, Konstantin Umansky, his personal assurance that "all possible aid will be given by the United States Government in obtaining munitions, armaments, and other supplies needed to meet [Stalin's] most urgent requirements." A special office in the War Department, answering to Hopkins, was established to process military supplies destined for Russia. A Soviet military mission, headed by the head of Soviet military intelligence, Lieutenant General Filipp Golikov, was invited to Washington, arriving on July 26.[12]

The American public was far less warmly disposed toward Stalin than Roosevelt's advisers. Knowing this, Roosevelt was careful with his language. "I couldn't say," he later recalled, "we needed Russia on our side to win the war because Russia is not our kind of

---

* The 1939 Neutrality Act gave the president authority to "find" where war zones existed.

country and I couldn't be pictured as a communist sympathizer." Instead, the president deputized his fellow Groton/Harvard man, Undersecretary of State Sumner Welles, to inform the *New York Times* on June 24 that, whatever objections Americans had to "principles and doctrines of Communist dictatorship," it was "Hitlerism and its threat of world conquest" that was now "the main issue before the world. Hitler's armies are today the chief dangers to the Americas." With impressive guile, Roosevelt asked Welles to inform the readers of the *Times* that the issue of aiding Russia remained "hanging in the air"—his decision to unfreeze Soviet funds earlier that very day and Hopkins's White House memorandum on lend-lease notwithstanding.[13]

Politically speaking, the president was right to be reticent. Aside from Gallup's July poll, public-opinion surveys conducted by Hopkins's own lend-lease staff in July and August 1941 determined that "majority opinion" in only "eleven states [out of forty-eight] now supports our present program of aid." Not even Roosevelt's home-state New Yorkers supported his policy of extending lend-lease aid to Stalin's Russia. And even in those eleven states, people were ambivalent. In Michigan, home to the automotive factories that would be expected to churn out trucks for Stalin, the prevailing view was that it was acceptable to arm Russia so long as it fought Germany, but most people "preferred both to lose." In New York and California, from whose ports the vast majority of lend-lease stores would be shipped to the USSR, public opinion was guarded at best. The "promise of aid to Russia," a lend-lease administrator reported from the Golden State, "has led to some confusion of thought. Thinking public also accepts logic of move, but for many, logic and sentiment are in conflict. . . . Average person because of meager reports of happenings on eastern front, believes Germans and Russians are destroying each other, and consequently feels danger to United States is growing less." In midwestern states such as Indiana and Oklahoma, opposition to aiding Stalin's Communist regime was well-nigh universal. The Soviet embassy in Washington, concerned that media hostility would upend Roosevelt's

policy of supporting Stalin's war, prepared press summaries for
Molotov on "isolationist" newspapers (such as the *Chicago Tribune*
and the New York *Post, Daily News, Herald Tribune,* and *World-
Telegram*) and compiled enemies lists of "pro-fascist elements,"
such as former president Hoover, newspaper mogul William Ran-
dolph Hearst, Charles Lindbergh of America First, and Senator
Taft.* To dampen Soviet fears, Harry Hopkins gave Stalin's ambassador to the United States, Konstantin Umansky, his personal
assurance that he would keep "incorrigible anti-Soviet types" in
Washington away from President Roosevelt.[14]

It is worth pausing to examine the character and views of Harry
Hopkins, who would play such a critical role in unleashing the flood
of American largesse to Stalin in the teeth of widespread public opposition. Unlike Roosevelt's other favorite, Sumner Welles, Hopkins came from a humble, midwestern, middle-class background,
growing up and going to college in Iowa. A veteran of social welfare agencies in New York City, Hopkins was initially a protégé of
the president's wife, Eleanor, who ushered him into Roosevelt's
inner circle. An able administrator, Hopkins made himself indis-
pensable, running powerful New Deal agencies such as the Federal
Emergency Relief Administration and the Works Progress Administration. By 1940, Hopkins had become so much a part of the furniture of the Roosevelt White House that he literally moved in,
sleeping in the Lincoln bedroom until 1944. In this way, Hopkins
was able, as *Life* magazine gushed, to "see the President early, late,
and frequently in between." Hopkins had, as one of Roosevelt's
biographers noted, "an almost extrasensory perception of the President's moods."[15]

Hopkins's lend-lease brief was a natural progression for this
born administrator, a global scale-up of his role overseeing domestic New Deal agencies. It helped that he had the president's

---

*Despite his speech in the Senate dumping cold water on Soviet lend-
lease, Harry Truman was not yet on Stalin's radar and was not mentioned in press summaries in 1941.

personal confidence. Despite being in very poor health—Hopkins had been diagnosed with stomach cancer in 1939 and had had almost 75 percent of his stomach removed—he agreed to travel to Moscow on Roosevelt's behalf in July 1941 to give Stalin the president's reassurance that American material aid was forthcoming. "I ask you to treat Mr. Hopkins," Roosevelt wrote in his letter of introduction, "with the identical confidence you would feel if you were talking directly to me. He will communicate directly to me the views that you express to him and will tell me what you consider are the most pressing individual problems on which we could be of aid."[16]

After stopping briefly in London to confer with Churchill, Hopkins was flown by the Royal Air Force to Archangel, on Russia's Arctic coast. It was a tense and arduous flight, lasting nearly twenty-four hours—far from an idle undertaking for a man in Hopkins's condition. Nor was the ordeal over after Hopkins landed at Archangel, where yet another plane—appropriately, in the spirit of lend-lease, an American Douglas transport—was waiting to fly him on to Moscow (another four-hour flight). On Tuesday, July 29, 1941, Harry Hopkins touched down in Moscow, where he was greeted by the US ambassador, Laurence Steinhardt, and a delegation of Soviet officials.[17]

The timing of Hopkins's Moscow visit was favorable, or as favorable as it could have been during that terrible first summer of Barbarossa. He arrived during the welcome pause on the central Belorussian front, between the fall of Smolensk and the resumption of the German drive for Moscow in September. The situation in the capital was calm enough that Steinhardt was able to take Hopkins on a sightseeing tour on Wednesday. Steinhardt briefed Roosevelt's envoy on views in the embassy on the Soviet war effort and the chances the regime would survive the German onslaught. While Steinhardt himself did not think the conquest of the Soviet Union would be "easy," he noted that the US military attaché, Colonel Ivan Yeaton, was more pessimistic. Hopkins was thus put on his guard about Yeaton as a skeptic of Soviet fighting capacity.[18]

Hopkins was not wrong to view Yeaton as an obstacle to his plans. Not unlike the former US ambassador, William Bullitt, whose increasingly critical view of Stalin led to his replacement by the reliable yes-man Joseph Davies, Yeaton had been in Moscow long enough to shed whatever illusions he might once have had about Soviet Communism. While being escorted with other attachés by his NKVD overseers on a tour of Moscow aviation factories in 1940, Yeaton had been horrified when his driver blithely mowed down a pedestrian at sixty miles an hour. (Asked why he had not slowed down, the NKVD driver replied, "I didn't feel like it.") Yeaton was told by his well-connected German counterpart about Soviet accounting tricks—this was in the days of Moscow Pact cooperation—and that production was usually only 40 to 60 percent of reported capacity: "Pay little attention to the line count. The Soviets always pad the line in preparation for foreign inspectors." More perceptive than his controversial predecessor, Colonel Raymond Faymonville, who is now known to have been an NKVD asset,* Yeaton learned and reported accurately to Washington that the NKVD was "in the construction business as well as controlled uniform and secret police." Having observed in June 1941 that "troop trains from the Far East had been passing through to the White Russian front for weeks," Yeaton did not buy the official Soviet line on the "unexpected German invasion" either. Stalin, Yeaton believed, "not only knew he was going to be attacked, but he was warned of the date. The reason that he wanted

---

*Faymonville's partiality for Stalin was so suspicious that army intelligence recalled him in 1939 and the FBI opened an investigation. Roosevelt, viewing the affair as a conservative-army-brass witch hunt, invited Faymonville to the White House and on a fishing trip. Reassured by this treatment, Faymonville handed Colonel Yeaton "two books published by the French Ordinance on Field Artillery Construction and marked secret" and "requested that [he] turn them over to a Red Army captain in Moscow." The Venona decrypts declassified and published in the 1990s confirmed the suspicions of army intelligence that Faymonville was reporting regularly to the NKVD.

the world to believe it was a surprise, was, in my opinion, because it was the only way he could avoid admitting his inability to check the initial thrust of Germany's panzer divisions." With views like this, Colonel Yeaton was a marked man in Moscow. Stafford Cripps had asked Churchill to demand that Roosevelt recall him, and a Reuters correspondent had laid down a $100 bet that Yeaton would not last the summer. This was not a man likely to fall in line with the Roosevelt-Hopkins policy of sending unconditional military aid to Stalin.[19]

Predictably, Hopkins and Yeaton did not hit it off at their first meeting, over breakfast in the mess hall of the US embassy on July 30. "The Soviets had the manpower," Hopkins argued, "and we had the money and tools to accomplish the destruction of Hitler's armies." What he wanted Yeaton to know was that, first, "we would furnish the Russians all possible military and economic assistance" and, second, that "lend-lease would never be used as a bargaining agency." The watchwords were unconditional aid, dispensed with no questions asked, no quid pro quo demanded. Nor would the United States expect to be paid back for loans or military aid extended to Stalin. Hopkins's "enthusiasm to get us involved in this war," Yeaton recalled, "and his readiness to negotiate with Stalin on an 'I trust you' basis gave me reasons to question whether or not his illness had affected his mind." When Yeaton "impugned the integrity and methods of Stalin, [Hopkins] could stand it no longer and shut me up with an intense, 'I don't care to discuss the subject further.'"[20]

Not surprisingly, Hopkins did not invite Yeaton to his first meeting that evening with Stalin, despite the fact that the military attaché was the best-informed American in Moscow about Soviet war industry. Setting a personal tone, Hopkins informed Stalin that he had come to Moscow "not in any official diplomatic capacity," but "as a personal friend of Roosevelt, with whom he lived and worked." The president, Hopkins informed Stalin, "is confident in Soviet victory and is prepared to do whatever is required to get the necessary aid to the Soviet Union."[21]

Encouraged by the guilelessness of Roosevelt's envoy, Stalin took advantage. Asked what the Red Army "most desperately required," the Vozhd told Hopkins: "We need anti-aircraft guns of calibers between 20 and 37 mm, capable of being fired from 120 to 180 rounds per minute, large-caliber machine guns of 12.7 mm caliber, 7.72 mm caliber rifles, and aluminum." "Give us anti-aircraft guns and the aluminum," Stalin said, "and we can fight for three or four years." The Red Army also needed "20,000 pieces of anti-aircraft artillery, large and small," and as many "large size machine guns for the defense of his cities" as Hopkins could provide. Stalin added that he "had heard there were many rifles available in the United States" and that "he believed their calibre corresponded to the caliber used in his army. He stated that he needed one million or more such rifles." Ammunition was less important, so long as the caliber matched.[22]

After Hopkins assented to these requests, Stalin proceeded to second-tier requirements. These included "fighters, pursuit planes, and medium-range bombers capable of flying from 600 to 1,100 kilometers." Pursuit planes were the most important: Stalin needed two thousand of these as soon as possible. Hopkins noted that 200 American-built Curtiss P-40 Tomahawks were already en route to Russia, including 140 sent from England (that is, reassigned from the lend-lease consignment for Churchill) and another 60 directly from the United States. Informed by the Vozhd that his preferred delivery route was the northern seaway to Murmansk and Archangel, Hopkins replied that the United States would be happy to "arrange convoys" to the Soviet Arctic—at a time when convoys to England were not allowed because the British Isles were considered a war zone. Amazed, Stalin informed Hopkins that he would send military experts to meet with him later that evening, and that he would place himself "at [Hopkins's] disposal from 6pm to 7pm" for each subsequent day of the American's visit to Moscow.[23]

Later that night, Hopkins sat down with Stalin's artillery expert, General V. F. Yakovlev, to discuss technical issues. The discussion was less amicable than the one with Stalin, in part because

Hopkins had to let the US military attaché, Colonel Yeaton, sit in. The Vozhd had been wrong about rifle calibers: although close, Soviet 7.62 mm rounds would not fit American rifles. Nor would 37 mm Soviet anti-aircraft shells fit American medium-size guns, and the heavy machine guns would not necessarily match up either, owing to the discrepancy between metric and US measures (the Soviet 12.7 mm version, at 0.499999 inches, was just off the American 0.50). The upshot, Yeaton and Yakovlev concluded, was that "to do the Russians any good it would be necessary to send both guns and ammunition." Yakovlev said the Red Army needed at least ten thousand medium-size anti-aircraft guns and at least one million rifles "to replace lost or broken rifles and to equip new divisions until the population was exhausted." Further, Yakovlev insisted that, rather than American experts coming to Russia to study Soviet equipment, Russians should be allowed to travel freely in the United States to study American weapons. Hopkins put up no objection. Yeaton, realizing it was pointless to resist, remained silent.[24]

In the mess hall the next morning, Yeaton apologized to Hopkins for his bluntness the day before but was rebuffed. The second Hopkins-Yeaton encounter was significant because it paved the way for Yeaton's sacking and replacement by his predecessor, the American NKVD asset Colonel Faymonville, but also in that Hopkins made official the forfeiting of American leverage over lend-lease deliveries to Stalin. Having realized that Roosevelt and Hopkins meant to send war matériel to Stalin essentially free of charge, Yeaton hoped, at least, to secure a local quid pro quo. Could Stalin, Yeaton asked Hopkins, allow him permission to visit the front and Soviet war factories? "If the United States and Soviet Union were to be allies," he argued, "I was certainly entitled to some freedom of movement and communications. [Hopkins] rewarded me with a cold, emphatic 'no.'"[25]

That afternoon, Hopkins, accompanied by Ambassador Steinhardt, called on Molotov at the Soviet Foreign Ministry. The main topic of conversation was Japan. While Molotov was confident the neutrality pact signed in April would endure, he let Hopkins and Steinhardt know that Stalin would appreciate extra insurance against the possibility of Japanese intervention in the Soviet Far East. Molotov requested that President Roosevelt "find some appropriate means of giving Japan . . . a 'warning,'" which would "include a statement that the United States would come to the assistance of the Soviet Union in the event of its being attacked by Japan." Hopkins assured Molotov that he would "give the President his message regarding [Stalin's] anxiety about Siberia and his desire to have the President indicate to Japan that further encroachments would not be tolerated." It did not occur to Hopkins to demand a reciprocal promise from Molotov that the USSR would "come to the assistance" of the United States if it was attacked by Japan. As with lend-lease aid, Hopkins preferred a one-way relationship, with the United States going along with any and all Soviet requests and making none of its own.[26]

As if to confirm that he was running the show alone, that night Hopkins invited neither Colonel Yeaton nor Ambassador Steinhardt to his meeting with Stalin, nor even an American interpreter. In a self-abnegating violation of diplomatic protocol, Hopkins requested that Maxim Litvinov, the former foreign affairs commissar, translate Stalin's remarks into English for him. Further, Hopkins assured Stalin that he would pass on his words (as translated by Litvinov) directly to the president, for Roosevelt's eyes only, with no comments by sniping intermediaries such as Steinhardt or Yeaton.* Sensing opportunity, Stalin gave Hopkins three whole hours of his time.[27]

Questionable as Hopkins's jettisoning of advisers and translators was in diplomatic terms, historians can be grateful for this clearing of the decks. The transcript gives us an extraordinary snapshot of Stalin's thinking in the sixth week of the war. Knowing

---

* Steinhardt's days, too, were numbered. The ambassador soon fell afoul of Hopkins because he expressed mild doubts about Soviet war-fighting capacity.

Hopkins was convinced Soviet morale would hold, Stalin felt no need to sugarcoat the truth, confessing that he did not think Britain and the USSR could defeat Germany alone. Stalin wanted Hopkins to plead with Roosevelt to get the United States to enter the war, which was "the one thing that could defeat Hitler." While confident the Red Army had enough troop reserves to survive the winter, the Vozhd did not hide how desperate the Soviet material situation now was, owing to the German advance into the Soviet industrial heartland. Stalin told Hopkins that "about 75% of the sum total of his munitions plants . . . were in the general areas of which Leningrad, Moscow, and Kiev were the centers." While noting that the evacuation of industrial equipment to the east had already begun, the Vozhd admitted that if the Germans occupied these areas, "they would destroy almost 75% of Russia's industrial capacity." Stalin was concerned enough that he

> stated that they would be short of steel for tank manufacture and wished that orders for [American] steel be placed at once. He later said it would be much better if his tanks could be manufactured in the U.S. He also wished to purchase as many of our tanks as possible to be ready for the spring campaign. Stalin said the all important thing was the production of tanks during the winter—the tank losses on both sides were very great but that Germany could produce more tanks per month this winter than Russia. *Hence the aid of the U.S. in supplying steel and tanks is essential.* He would like to send a tank expert to the U.S. He stated that he would give the U.S. his tank designs.

Stalin also lamented the ongoing destruction of aircraft factories, including two near Moscow. He requested that Soviet pilots be allowed to train in the United States with American warplanes, in view of an impending "shortage of pilots" and the difficulty of training more so close to the war zone. Stalin also desired long-range American bombers "in order to bomb the Romanian oil-fields." "The outcome of the war in Russia," Stalin told Hopkins, "would largely depend on the ability to enter the Spring [1942] campaign with adequate equipment, particularly in tanks and anti-aircraft guns." Just as vital was American aluminum, which the Soviets needed to build their own tanks and warplanes. When Hopkins asked him to list immediate priorities, Stalin scribbled, on a small pad, "1) light anti-aircraft guns; 2) aluminum; 3) 50 calibre machine guns; and 4) 30 calibre rifles."[28]

Hopkins delivered Stalin's material requests to the president as promised, along with his plea that the United States enter the war. Despite constraints related to the needs of his own army and promises already made to Britain, Roosevelt agreed to deliver massive volumes of war matériel to the USSR over the coming months, setting aside one hundred large transport vessels exclusively for Stalin's needs. On August 31, 1941, the president ordered Secretary of War Stimson to allocate for the USSR, directly out of US Army stocks, 1,200 warplanes "of all types" (to be "diverted from Lend-Lease contracts for the British"), 20,000 submachine guns, 2,194 transport trucks, 729 light and 795 medium tanks, 991 anti-tank guns (37 mm), 1,135 mortars, 152 heavy 90 mm guns, and 155,341 miles of field telegraph wire, along with locomotive and steam engines, electric furnaces, machine tools, searchlights, sound locators, and surgical and hospital supplies. There was also toluol for TNT explosives (527,153 pounds), rubber tires, leather for Red Army boots (3 million pounds worth for immediate delivery), motor fuel and aviation gasoline (2.1 million barrels in the first shipment), aluminum (2,188 tons), 3 million pounds of copper wire and cable, 9.7 million pounds of barbed wire, tungsten, and molybdenum.[29]

The terms Roosevelt was offering Stalin for this aid were, as Yeaton had objected to Hopkins, absurdly generous. At Churchill's time of dire need in summer 1940, during the desperate juncture after the fall of France when a German invasion of the British Isles seemed imminent, Roosevelt had offered England fifty decrepit World War I–vintage destroyers, in exchange for which Churchill had basically mortgaged the British Empire to Washington. For

Stalin, by contrast, Roosevelt had opened a virtually unlimited credit line (initially $1 billion) to order whatever he desired, in exchange for nothing whatsoever. In the Soviet case, there was not a whiff of pretense that dispensing lend-lease aid was akin to, as Roosevelt had told Congress, a "garden hose" loaned to a "neighbor whose house [was] on fire" with the hope that it might be returned "after the fire is over." With the exception of the Siberian-Alaskan link—which Stalin had explicitly rejected in favor of the dangerous northern sea route to Murmansk and Archangel—the USSR was about the most distant neighbor the United States had on the planet. Sending war matériel from America to the east European front by way of the North Atlantic, patrolled by German U-boats, and the frigid Arctic would cost a fortune. Then there were the perils to life and limb along the way.* And the odds of Washington recouping the weapons, vehicles, mineral inputs, and foodstuffs loaned to the USSR were infinitesimal.[30]

Of course, Congress and broad swaths of the American public would likely have objected if, in the summer of 1940, Roosevelt had offered Churchill more generous terms of aid than the decrepit-destroyers-for-British-bases deal. But it is equally true that, had Congress and the public known what the president had agreed to give Stalin in summer 1941, there would have been an even more massive outcry. In one of his last acts before being recalled for insufficient enthusiasm, Ambassador Steinhardt begged Molotov's deputy at the Soviet Foreign Ministry, the former prosecutor at the Moscow show trials A. Y. Vishinsky, not to mention to Western reporters that President Roosevelt had approved $1 billion worth of strategic exports to Stalin "without reference to Congress, and without the knowledge of the [US] public."[31]

Making the slanted disbursement of American military aid in Stalin's favor, as compared to Churchill's, still more striking was

---

* So precarious was the northern route in winter that US insurers refused to post bonds on ships berthing at Soviet Arctic ports after November 15 at any price, even in peacetime.

the fact that Churchill himself was going all out to arm Stalin too, at the expense of Britain's own desperate wartime needs. In an impulsive decision as selfless as it was strategically foolish, the prime minister decided as soon as he heard news of Barbarossa to send Stalin two hundred brand-new Hawker Hurricane fighters that had been pledged to defend Singapore against Japanese attack. The Hurricane was the workhorse of the RAF, having inflicted nearly 60 percent of the losses sustained by the Luftwaffe in the Battle of Britain. Churchill further agreed to send Stalin, as a gift, two hundred US-made Tomahawk fighters already delivered to Britain via lend-lease. In September 1941, Churchill instructed his personal envoy to Stalin, Lord Beaverbrook, to offer regular monthly deliveries of two hundred pursuit planes, both Hurricanes and Spitfires, beginning in October 1941. Churchill also promised to supply Stalin 259 Canadian-made Valentine and 145 British Matilda tanks—so desperately needed by Stalin's generals in the defense of Moscow—despite Britain's entire tank park numbering only 1,770, a mere fraction of the size of Stalin's gargantuan arsenal in June 1941. Even after the crushing losses of summer, the Soviet tank park was ten times the size of the British. As a lend-lease scholar has noted, Stalin's demand for gifted Matildas was like "a bankrupt millionaire turning to a pauper for salvation." Churchill further promised to send Stalin three hundred American-made Douglas A-20 Havoc light bombers, supplied to him via lend-lease, for immediate delivery, with the loss to RAF stocks to be replenished at a later date by the Americans. Churchill also agreed to ship to Stalin two thousand tons of processed aluminum, even though it was just as desperately needed in British warplane production as in Soviet factories, along with "1.5 tons of cocoa beans, $150,000 worth of industrial diamonds, 10 tons of cobalt, 300 tons of shellac, 1,500 tons of tin, 800 tons of nickel, 4,000 tons of jute, 6,000 tons of rubber, 7,000 tons of lead, and large amounts of wool."[32]

In fairness to Churchill, he was under heavy pressure from Washington to agree to all this. Air Marshal Archie Sinclair, head of the British Air Ministry, wrote to Harry Hopkins on September 21, 1941:

> The proposals which your people brought us *and which we felt bound to accept* mean a long postponement of our hopes of building up an Air Force of overwhelming strength. In fighters, it will mean that we shall have to run risks at home and shall have no margin for such additional calls upon us for fighter squadrons as are certain to be made during 1942. Nevertheless we realise that sacrifices and risks must be accepted in order to keep Russia in the war.[33]

However generous Churchill was, British shipments paled in comparison to American ones. In the first protocol—approved on September 19, 1941, and covering the period from October 1, 1941, to June 1942—Roosevelt agreed to supply the Red Army with 500 tanks per month (using British lend-lease stocks until American supplies were forthcoming) of the 1,100 per month Stalin claimed he needed to replenish losses in the field and in domestic production caused by damage to factories and losses in aluminum and steel inputs. Despite the vaunted evacuation of Soviet tank factories east of Moscow, the German conquest of industrial areas had already caused Soviet output to drop from 2,000 to 1,400 tanks per month, with a further decline expected when Kharkov, home to the flagship T-34 factory, fell to the Germans (as it would in October). To keep Soviet tank production going at even reduced levels, Stalin said he needed 2,000 tons of armor plate per month. Additionally, Roosevelt agreed to supply Stalin with four hundred warplanes per month, a mixture of Tomahawk and Kittyhawk fighters, to be replaced as soon as possible with more-advanced models, along with Douglas A-20 Havoc light bombers, later to be replaced with B-25s and B-26s when they became available. The protocol envisioned monthly shipments to the USSR of 10,000 American trucks and 5,000 jeeps, 200,000 Red Army boots, 400,000 yards of khaki for uniforms, 1,500 tons of leather hides and boot-sole leather, 200,000 tons of wheat, and 70,000 tons of sugar.[34]

Still more generous were allotments of American chemical, mineral, and metallic inputs for Stalin's war factories. These included monthly deliveries of armor plate (1,000 tons), sheet steel (8,000 tons), steel wire (7,000 tons), steel wire rope (1,200 tons), tool steel (500 tons), aluminum ingots (1,000 tons), duralumin (250 tons), tin (4,000 tons), toluol (2,000 tons), ferro chrome (200 tons), ferro silicon (300 tons), rolled brass (5,000 tons), and copper tubes (300 tons). The first protocol stipulated that five hundred thousand tons of American goods would be shipped monthly until June 1942. No payments of any kind were expected until after the war was over.[35]

It is important to emphasize here that, whatever Stalin and his defenders later claimed about the triumph of Communist production, in 1941 they were perfectly clear that—in addition to desperately needing finished matériel—the Soviet war industry under the German onslaught would not be able to function at all without massive American aid. Stalin's requests for "ferro-alloys, steel, and aluminum" were justified to the Americans expressly because of lost production. As W. Averell Harriman, US envoy at the Moscow lend-lease conference in late September 1941, wrote Hopkins and Roosevelt on October 10, Soviet "production of aluminum has been badly damaged and . . . this material is badly wanted in aircraft production." Likewise, Harriman reported that "Russian production of trucks has decreased greatly because of damage to steel factories and at the same time there has been an increase both in the Army's demand for trucks and in the transport of imported products." Even the vaunted war factories of the eastern Volga and Ural region, supposedly all ready to go when the war broke out, were in dire need of "miscellaneous factory equipment, electric furnaces, forging equipment, and various other factory items," along with monthly deliveries of American aluminum, steel, and ferroalloys.[36]

Later in October 1941, after much of the Soviet government had evacuated Moscow, Molotov was still more explicit in his first audience in Kuibyshev (Samara) with the US ambassador. The Red Army, Molotov informed Steinhardt on October 22, was "short of tanks" and "did not have enough warplanes," with the shortage made still more acute by the "evacuation of Moscow's factories." In a tacit admission that the VVS was already reliant on lend-lease deliveries, Molotov complained that Soviet aviators were disappointed in the performance of the 141 P-40 Tomahawks diverted from Britain and wanted Kittyhawks instead. Steinhardt promised that future fighter deliveries would be either Kittyhawks or more-advanced Bell P-39 Airacobras and offered to send American aviation experts to help Soviet pilots master these warplanes.[37]

To ensure that there would be no more obstacles placed in the way of prompt delivery of war matériel to Stalin's Communist empire, Hopkins convinced Roosevelt to cashier Colonel Yeaton as US military attaché and send in Colonel Faymonville, a man we now know to have met regularly with the Soviet secret police. Owing to his checkered reputation in the US Army, where his personnel file described him as "irrefutably a captive of the NKVD," Faymonville was not appointed military attaché but instead named the president's "representative in Russia on all matters pertaining to the supply of war materials from America to the U.S.S.R." This ersatz appointment ensured that Faymonville answered directly to Hopkins, instead of to the US Army.* He also got his funds from Hopkins, who set him up nicely in Moscow. Faymonville's first lend-lease requisition was for "three six-passenger Buick sedans" for himself and his personal staff, each equipped with "heaters,

---

*Hopkins also ensured that Yeaton was delayed leaving Russia. When he reached San Francisco, Yeaton tried to proceed on to Washington to plead his case against Faymonville, but his passport was seized. Yeaton was demoted to a field artillery unit in Fort Ord, California.

defrosters and all accessories [and] spare parts necessary for extended winter conditions."[38]

Back in Washington, Hopkins appointed his friend Edward R. Stettinius Jr.—a businessman who had worked for both General Motors and US Steel, with excellent contacts in American industry—to handle the US side of the lend-lease pipeline to Russia. While Stettinius, unlike Faymonville, was no Soviet agent, he was a political naïf of limited Washington experience who, like Faymonville, answered directly to Harry Hopkins. ("Does the President want to talk it over with me first?" Stettinius asked Hopkins on being named lend-lease administrator. Hopkins replied, "Not unless you have something you particularly want to talk over with him.") As Roosevelt's speechwriter Robert Sherwood, a close friend of Hopkins's, described the appointment, "Stettinius was [Hopkins's] friend and they could work together—and that was that."[39]

It was strange enough that the Roosevelt administration—or at least Harry Hopkins, who seemed to have taken over personal direction of its foreign policy—had gone all in on the Soviet side, despite the United States still being officially neutral in the European war. But what on earth was Winston Churchill, supposedly an arch imperialist devoted to shoring up the British Empire at all costs, thinking when he agreed to deprive Egypt, Singapore, and other vulnerable imperial strongholds like Malaysia and Hong Kong of desperately needed tanks and pursuit planes?

The usual explanation for the sudden enthusiasm for the Soviet cause that overwhelmed the capitalist powers in 1941 is that Roosevelt and Churchill saw a way of weakening the Wehrmacht without risking American or British lives. In Roosevelt's case, this may well be true, even if the intention of saving American lives at a time when the United States was neutral was illogical on its face. Had this been Roosevelt's primary goal, it would have been served more obviously by staying out of the European war, rather than letting lend-lease suck the United States further into it. As with so many of Roosevelt's other policies, his decision to mobilize the arsenal of democracy behind Stalin's war effort in summer 1941 was premised on his view that the United States was bound to enter the war against Nazi Germany at some point, whether or not most Americans supported Roosevelt's interventionist policy just yet. The president was not saving American lives now, but trying to husband them for a future war against Hitler he hoped his country would soon fight, so as to avoid another repeat of the western front meat grinder his countrymen had experienced the last time around (even if only in the last blood-soaked months of 1918).

Britain, on the other hand, was already two years into the war with Hitlerian Germany in summer 1941, and had been fighting alone for the last twelve months, so the "saving lives" justification behind the decision to go all out in aiding Stalin makes more sense. No one in Britain, not even the gung-ho Churchill in full warrior cry, wanted to repeat the horrors of the western front in 1914–1918, which had killed off nearly an entire generation of young men. Although short-lived, the Battle of France of May–June 1940 had seen casualty rates, on a week-by-week basis, surpass even the worst periods of the First World War. Churchill jumped at the opportunity to help equip the Red Army—at a time when Britain's armies had been expelled from the main battlefields on the Continent—without risking incurring massive casualties by assaulting Nazi Europe directly. As Stalin and his apologists began to claim then, and have claimed ever since, the Russian people "paid in blood" for these shipments of capitalist war matériel, doing the lion's share of the actual fighting against Nazi Germany at a time when the Americans were still neutral and Britain was fighting only in peripheral theaters such as Libya. There is a painful element of truth here: the Russians were indeed fighting, bleeding, and dying in great numbers in 1941, at a time when very few Britons and no Americans were engaging Germans in combat. A cynical interpretation of lend-lease, from the Soviet perspective, is that it amounted to capitalists paying off impoverished, cannon-fodder Russians like mercenaries.

This line of thinking would make more sense, however, if there was the faintest whiff of reciprocity from the Soviet side. Stalin had not helped Churchill during the Battle of Britain, after all, nor even maintained a benevolent neutrality. During the first two years of the European war, Stalin had not simply collaborated with Hitler in carving up Eastern Europe, but had supplied and fueled Hitler's armies as they invaded Poland, France, and the Low Countries. Stalin had likewise literally fueled the Luftwaffe when it bombed London. Stalin had rebuffed every one of Churchill's advances and refused even to reply to his letters until Hitler turned the tables on him and invaded the USSR. Churchill owed Stalin precisely nothing. Nevertheless, the prime minister was diverting to the USSR warplanes and tanks desperately needed to shore up British imperial defenses. Certainly there was a strategic argument for doing this in the context of the war against Germany, an argument Churchill made at the time and that his defenders maintain to this day. It remains inarguably true, however, that whatever short-term gains these two hundred Hurricanes might have helped Stalin's air force achieve came at a steep price for the long-term interests of the British Empire.

Nor was there any sign that Stalin cared about British or American interests in Asia. In April 1941, the Vozhd had signed a neutrality pact with Tokyo with the express goal of encouraging Japan to attack US and British positions in the Pacific. At a minimum, Roosevelt and Churchill could have requested, in exchange for sending Stalin vast stores of war matériel, a commitment to fight Japan if war broke out in the Pacific, or at least to maintain enough troops in the Far East to keep Japanese divisions tied down in Manchuria. At the lend-lease conference in September 1941, Stalin made it clear that he had no intention of helping his allies against Japan. "Russia," Harriman was informed by Stalin, "might be neutral if hostilities developed between Japan and the United States. I asked him whether he thought such neutrality was likely. His answer was a smile."[40]

Whatever else may be said about him, the Vozhd had an acute sense of raw strategic self-interest, especially in moments of imminent danger. Just as he had staved off catastrophe in Finland with a mixture of guile and ruthlessness in March 1940, Stalin's exploitation of Anglo-American generosity and naiveté, along with his unashamed hypocrisy toward his so-called allies vis-à-vis imperial Japan, produced a Moscow miracle that would turn the tide of the entire war.

22

The Hinge of Fate

December 1941

THE DRAMATIC AMERICAN about-face on sending strategic exports to the USSR, amounting to a 180-degree turn from moral embargo to moral imperative, was not the only fruit born of Stalin's cunning diplomacy in 1941. Although his nonaggression treaty with Japan did not win enough time for the Vozhd to complete Soviet military preparations in Europe, it did ensure that, after Hitler invaded, Stalin did not have to worry about his eastern flank. True, Japan's final decision to go to war with the United States and Britain did not come until November 1941, by which time the Battle of Moscow had already been joined. But US-Japanese tensions had been building for months. The critical escalation came on July 26 when, in response to the Japanese incursion into Indochina authorized by Vichy France, Roosevelt froze Japanese assets in the United States and clamped down on oil exports to Tokyo. Although not an outright ban, it was a de facto oil embargo, as Japan was forced to apply for export licenses via the US State Department, which were then denied on the basis that Japanese assets were frozen. Although Roosevelt had given himself some wiggle room, the cutting off of US oil exports to Japan, a country at war and burning through 450,000 metric tons of oil monthly, was a ticking time bomb that could lead to war at any time.[1]

From the Soviet perspective, it was not imperative to know exactly when a war between Japan and the United States would begin, but simply that relations between Tokyo and Washington had declined to a point where Stalin could rule out the threat of a

Japanese attack in the Far East. While some armored units were transferred west from Siberia in late June in the immediate aftermath of Barbarossa, it was not until mid-September 1941 that Stalin learned for certain that his eastern flank was safe. Until then, a Pacific war between Japan and the United States was far from a done deal. All through August 1941, while the Wehrmacht was rolling up Ukraine, Tokyo had extended feelers to Washington, requesting a summit between Prime Minister Fumimaro Konoe and President Roosevelt to clear the air and hopefully get the oil embargo lifted. Because this was the month Roosevelt met Churchill at Placentia Bay off the coast of Newfoundland to issue the Atlantic Charter of August 14, 1941, laying out principles for a postwar world free of "Nazi tyranny," the augurs for an American modus vivendi with Tokyo were not favorable (even if Japan was not mentioned in the charter). On August 17, the president warned the Japanese ambassador to Washington that, "if the Japanese Government takes any further steps in pursuance of a policy or program of military domination by force or threat of force of neighboring countries, [the US government] will be compelled to take immediately any and all steps which it may deem necessary toward . . . insuring the safety and security of the United States."[2]

Nonetheless, things were still undecided when, on September 6, Ambassador Kichisaburo Nomura handed to Secretary of State Cordell Hull a proposal from Tokyo. The idea was that Japan, in order to have the US sanctions and the de facto oil embargo lifted, would promise to "withdraw its armed forces from China as soon as possible" (although not from Manchukuo), and refrain from making any "military advancement from French Indochina" into adjoining areas or "resort to any military action against any regions lying south of Japan," meaning British Malaya, Dutch Indonesia, or the American colony in the Philippines. Nomura's draft offer also included the stipulation that "in case the United States should participate in the European War, the interpretation and execution of the Tripartite Pact by Japan shall be independently decided"—a hint that Japan felt itself under no binding military obligation to Nazi Germany. Believing that Roosevelt would not likely humor such terms, Hull rejected Nomura's proposal on September 9 without even making a counteroffer. The failure of the Japanese peace gambit ultimately led to the fall of Konoe's cabinet and his replacement by Hideki Tojo. As early as September 14, Stalin's spy in Tokyo, Richard Sorge, reported to Moscow that, according to his source in the Konoe cabinet, "negotiations with the United States had reached a terminal stage" and that "if these negotiations do not result in success, then Japan will strike south." Sorge reported confidently that "Japan has decided not to attack the Soviet Union this year."[3]

Stalin had discounted intelligence from Sorge before, but this time he had multiple channels of information that all pointed in the same direction. By late September 1941, Soviet signals intercepts confirmed that Japan was moving troops, including aviation divisions, away from the Soviet-Manchurian frontier. On October 3, Sorge reported that Japan was preparing a ground offensive toward Burma via Thailand, along with amphibious strikes against Malaya, Dutch Indonesia, and Manila in the US-occupied Philippines. "As soon as negotiations between Japan and the United States are exhausted," Sorge reported, "Japan will launch her offensive."[4]

We know that Stalin found Sorge's reports about Japanese war preparations in Asia credible, because he authorized the withdrawal of eleven Soviet divisions from the Manchurian frontier to the Moscow front in late September and early October 1941 (added to four rifle divisions already transferred over the summer), along with 1,800 warplanes and 1,000 tanks (added to 700 tanks already transferred). Although it would take weeks for them all to arrive, newly transferred Siberian rifle divisions saw action, near Borodino, as early as October 14 and 15, just as morale in Moscow was at the breaking point. It helped that, after a surprise snowfall in early October, the weather stayed temperate but rainy during the second half of October—with the resulting muds of the famous Russian *rasputitsa* slowing down the German panzers just when they were on the cusp of victory—until the ground finally froze in mid-November. The monthlong respite was more than enough for the bulk of the Siberian reinforcements to arrive in Moscow, including five crack divisions from the Soviet Far Eastern army group shipped west on October 12. While these units formed only a fraction of the overall reinforcement of the Moscow sector, where Red Army commanders were frantically forming units out of whatever human material they could find, as "well-trained forces in being" the Siberian soldiers punched well above their weight in fighting quality. They had been victorious against Japan at Khalkin-Gol in 1939, under Zhukov's command. Zhukov knew he could count on them.[5]

Still, Stalin was not satisfied. Confirming that the Soviet-Manchurian front would be inactive for the rest of 1941 allowed the Vozhd to strip his Far Eastern defenses to reinforce Moscow. But would it not be still better to push Japan over the edge into war with the United States, to ensure the safety of Siberia for the following year and years to come? As Ambassador Bullitt had tried to warn Roosevelt in 1935, "It was the heartiest hope of the Soviet Government that the United States will become involved in a war with Japan." Had provoking such a conflict not been Stalin's intention after all—had the Vozhd cared a whit for collective security or the welfare of his accidental allies—he could have shared Sorge's intelligence coups about Japanese troop movements in the Pacific with Churchill or Roosevelt. He did no such thing. Stalin could also have requested that Sorge use his contacts in the Japanese government to advise Konoe to back down.* Instead, Sorge had these contacts tell the prime minister that Japan was much better

---

*Sorge's main contact in the Japanese Communist Party, Hotsumi Ozaki, belonged to Prime Minister Konoe's "breakfast club," a kind of unofficial advisory board. After his connections with Sorge were discovered, Ozaki was executed for treason.

off going to war with the United States and Britain than doing anything that might disturb the Soviet Union.[6]

With the Battle of Moscow raging, the last thing Stalin wanted was for Tokyo and Washington to bury the hatchet. It was therefore with trepidation that Soviet agents learned that a high-level envoy from Tokyo, Saburo Kurusu, had arrived in Washington on November 15, with instructions to make one final push for a truce. Tojo had provided Kurusu with two genuine offers, known as "proposal A" and "proposal B." Under proposal A, Japan would subtly distance itself from Mussolini's Italy and Hitler's Germany, acting "in accordance with Japan's own interpretation of the meaning of the [Tripartite] Pact—not that of Germany and Italy," and would promise, on the conclusion of a peace treaty with Chiang Kai-shek, to withdraw from Indochina and to remove "all Japanese troops in China" within two years, "except for garrisons in North China, on the Mongolian border regions [that is, facing the USSR] and on the Island of Hainan." If this failed to entice Roosevelt to the negotiating table, Kurusu was authorized to present proposal B, a temporary truce under which Japan would propose an immediate withdrawal from Indochina, pursuant to negotiations envisaging "the restoration of general peace between Japan and China."[7]

Of course, these proposals—especially after they were intercepted by US cryptographers, which gave a negotiating advantage to Washington—were unlikely to be accepted as worded. But there were unwelcome signs (from Stalin's perspective) that Roosevelt, whose strategic goal was to focus on defeating Nazi Germany in Europe, was angling for rapprochement with Japan. On November 6, the president had informed Secretary of War Stimson that "he might propose a truce in which there would be no movement or armament for six months." In the cabinet on November 7, Roosevelt declared that he intended to "strain every nerve to satisfy and keep on good relations" with Japanese diplomats. "Let us make no move of ill will," the president instructed Secretary of State Cordell Hull. "Let us do nothing to precipitate a crisis."[8]

When he got wind that a modus vivendi between Tokyo and Washington might be in sight, Stalin's man at the Treasury, Harry Dexter White, was apoplectic. White promptly wrote up a memorandum to Roosevelt in Morgenthau's name, warning him that acceding to a "Far Eastern Munich" would "sell China to her enemies for . . . thirty blood-stained coins of gold."* To ensure that no "Munich" would be possible, White composed a list of ten demands to be presented to Japan, which bore an uncanny resemblance to those his NKVD handler Pavlov had asked him to memorize back in May 1941. Typed up by White on June 6, 1941, the Soviet-Pavlov version had demanded that Japan "withdraw all military, Naval, air police forces from China (boundaries as of 1931) from Indo-China and from Thailand." In White's November draft, which was handed over by the secretary of state to Kurusu and the Japanese ambassador on November 26 (known to history as the "Hull note"), the wording was almost identical, excepting that Thailand was dropped, ostensibly because Japan had still not occupied that country: "Japan will withdraw all military, naval, air and police forces from China and from Indo-China."[9]

Whether or not White's November 26 draft was intended as an ultimatum, this is certainly how the "Hull note" was interpreted in Tokyo. On December 1, Emperor Hirohito met with Tojo's cabinet. "It is now clear," Tojo stated, "that Japan's claims cannot be attained through diplomatic means." The cabinet agreed, voting unanimously for war. One week later, Japanese dive-bombers launched a furious assault on the US fleet anchored at Pearl Harbor on Oahu, Hawaii, along with nearby airfields. Although the Pearl Harbor attack garnered the most headlines, Japanese raids were carried out simultaneously in Hong Kong, Singapore, and Malaysia, plunging the British Empire into the Pacific war, along with attacks on Thailand, the US territories of the Philippines and

---

* A biblical reference, although a sloppy one: it was thirty pieces of silver, not thirty gold coins, for which Christ was allegedly betrayed by Judas Iscariot.

Guam, and even the international settlement in Shanghai. In this way, Stalin's goal in negotiating his neutrality pact with Tokyo in April—to embroil Britain and the United States in war with Japan—was achieved. Siberia was safe; the reinforcement of Moscow could continue. Of course, Stalin was supposedly now allied to the very powers he had encouraged Japan to "annihilate"— powers now supplying his armies with vast quantities of war matériel. But so long as they did not make reciprocal demands of Moscow—such as asking for help against Japan—this was not Stalin's problem.[10]

The timely reinforcement of Zhukov's western army group with fresh Siberian divisions was the most important factor enabling the Soviet recovery on the Moscow front after the near collapse in mid-October 1941, heralded by a stunning counterattack launched on December 5–6. In terms of morale, Stalin's decision to stay in Moscow was also critical, as was his decision to go ahead with the annual revolution anniversary parade on November 7, with the Germans just forty miles away and Moscow under siege. On the evening before the parade, Stalin addressed the Politburo inside the Mayakovsky metro station and denounced Hitler for seeking "the extermination of the great Russian nation." "If they want a war of extermination," Stalin vowed, "they shall have it. Our task will be to destroy every German, to the very last man, who had come to occupy our country. No mercy for the German invaders! Death to the German invaders!" In his public address on Red Square before the parade on November 7, Stalin struck a similarly defiant but more patriotic tone, saluting "the heroic figures of our great ancestors." Steeled by Stalin's courageous example in staying on in Moscow, his revival of patriotic themes, and the timely arrival of fresh troops from Siberia, Soviet morale on the Moscow front held strong.[11]

Important as these factors were in enabling Soviet recovery, we should not discount the significance of lend-lease aid, which began arriving on the Moscow front simultaneously with the Siberian divisions. In his Mayakovsky station address, Stalin had reminded his Politburo colleagues that Britain and the United States had agreed "to supply the USSR systematically with planes and tanks," along with "aluminum, tin, lead, nickel and rubber." Stalin even referenced the billion-dollar loan Roosevelt had approved for Soviet lend-lease orders, soon to be doubled to $2 billion. "The coalition between the three countries," the Vozhd declared, "is a very real thing which will go on growing in the common cause of liberation." To seal the improbable new alliance between Anglo-American capitalism and Soviet Communism, on November 7, day of the Red Square parade, President Roosevelt published his administration's finding that the "defense of the Soviet Union" was "vital to the defense of the United States," making public and official the heretofore secret extension of American lend-lease aid to Stalin.[12]

While the bulk of the supplies promised to Stalin so far, because of the logistical hurdles involved, would arrive only later, the amount of war matériel already delivered to the USSR by December 1941 was substantial. As noted earlier, the Red Army had lost 20,500 tanks between June and November 1941, amounting to 80 percent of Stalin's armored strength. Because of Britain's geographical proximity, the shipment of British (and regifted American) tanks and warplanes made up the largest share to date. These included 466 British medium Matilda (MK-2) and Canadian-built Valentine (MK-3) tanks, and 31 American-made M-3 Stuarts—in all, nearly 500 tanks. Not all of these had reached the front by December 1941, but we know that 216 Valentines and 145 Matildas had already been registered for service by the Red Army, of which the first 20 arrived at the Red Army tank-training school in Kazan as early as October. On November 14, 1941, a team of British tank instructors arrived on the Moscow front to provide instruction in the use of the Matilda and Valentine. By the end of November, the Red Army had formed six new tank battalions out of twenty Matildas and ninety-seven Valentines. Then there were the 230 American Tomahawk P-40 fighter planes, sent to Britain via lend-lease, which Churchill had shifted over to Stalin in September 1941, along with the forty British-built Hurricanes (model MkIIB), which arrived in Vaenga in the Soviet Arctic, just north of Murmansk, that same month. These British tanks and warplanes helped replenish Soviet supplies just when they were most needed.[13]

Lend-lease supplies shipped from the United States, though slower to arrive, were not negligible either. By the first week of December 1941, 57 ships, carrying 342,680 tons of supplies, had left US ports destined for Russia. Two vessels were lost at sea, but the rest got through. As of November 15, 1941, the Red Army had received 2,186 American trucks—more than a quarter of the 8,000 Zhukov had available on the Moscow front—with 20,000 more promised by March 1942 to replenish stocks lost in the battle. The United States had also shipped ninety-four light and four medium tanks directly to the USSR (distinct, that is, from tanks forwarded from British lend-lease consignments), rounding out a US-British contribution of nearly 600 tanks to the rapidly dwindling Soviet tank park as of December 1941, with 725 more promised by March 1942. The United States had shipped 114 warplanes to date, mostly Tomahawks, adding up to a lend-lease contribution of 354 fighter planes to the Moscow counteroffensive, with 630 more promised by March 1942. Then there were the 2.4 million barrels of American fuel and aviation gasoline shipped by November 1941, without which many Red Army tanks and planes would have been grounded. Rounding out lend-lease war supplies delivered by December 1941 were 5,000 field telephones and 20,000 kilometers of telephone wire, 11 million pounds of barbed wire, a half ton of toluol for TNT, machine guns and ordnance, shells, cartridges, detonating fuses, and 1,500 tons of boot leather—not counting the aluminum, steel, nickel, and other critical inputs needed for Soviet war industry, all arriving in quantities measured in thousands of tons at Murmansk and Archangel.[14]

Owing to Soviet caginess and the renewed clampdown in Russian archives in recent years, we may never know exactly how many Matilda, Valentine, and Stuart tanks, or how many British Hurricanes and Curtiss P-40 Tomahawks, were deployed by

Zhukov in the great Moscow counteroffensive of December 1941. The files of the Red Army's "Command of Tank and Mechanized Divisions" do record how many British tanks were on hand at various stages of the battle. Thus, on November 25, there were forty-nine Matildas and Valentines in Zhukov's tank park on the western front; on December 10–11, as the fighting was at its most intense, there were sixty-nine on hand, of which seventeen were undergoing repairs; and on December 25, as the lines began to stabilize again, there were sixty-two British tanks in active service. The most thorough research suggests that 182 British tanks saw action at some point during the Battle of Moscow, of which 77 were knocked out of action.[15]

Churchill's Hurricanes, it is true, were used mostly in the Arctic region, helping to secure the vital lend-lease lifeline to Archangel and Murmansk against Luftwaffe raids, rather than on the Belorussian front. In so doing, these British fighters unquestionably freed up Soviet pursuit planes to be deployed in defense of Moscow. And we know that some of the American Tomahawks transferred over to Stalin by Churchill were used on the Moscow front in 1941. The celebrated VVS regiment 126 IAP, commanded by Soviet flying ace Viktor Naidenko, began switching from Soviet I-16s and Mig-3s to American P-40Bs on September 15, 1941. Naidenko's men began the first combat missions with Curtiss Tomahawks as early as October 12 and had registered 985 sorties by early 1942. Because Soviet troops were still learning how to fly Tomahawks and Hurricanes, it is likely that these lend-lease fighters—like the Matilda, Valentine, and Stuart tanks—were used in only a limited capacity in the ambitious flanking operation that began on December 5 and 6 along the 560-mile-long front outside Moscow. If there was a genuine material contribution from lend-lease in 1941, it probably came at the margins.[16]

The margins, however, matter. General I. S. Konev, who commanded the Kalinin army group on Zhukov's right flank, had repeatedly complained of "his lack of tanks" in the weeks prior to the counteroffensive. The Soviet 108th Tank Division had only

15 tanks left out of its original stock of 217. Zhukov himself told Stalin on the telephone, sometime in the third week of November 1941, that he expected to "hold Moscow," but only if he was given "two more armies and 200 tanks." The armies, because of Stalin's intelligence coups from Tokyo, came from Siberia, and at least two hundred tanks promptly arrived from Britain and the United States. Official Soviet sources claim Zhukov had 670 tanks on the Moscow front in late November 1941 and 774 tanks when the Moscow offensive was launched on December 5 (of which 205 were the new T-34s or KV models). This was fewer than the 1,170 panzers in theater the Germans had (though many of these were grounded because of lack of fuel and lubricants able to avoid freezing in low temperatures). Of these 774 Soviet tanks, at least 182, we now know, were British Matildas and Valentines.* At the least, we may infer that lend-lease aid, including American trucks, made a substantial contribution to Soviet mobility during the Moscow counteroffensive of 1941, and was more critical still as a material reserve to make good any of Zhukov's losses sustained during the battle.[17]

Zhukov's resulting offensive, known as Typhoon, was far from elegant, amounting to little more than a frontal assault on German positions in four different sectors of the Moscow front. The casualty ratio was predictably lopsided, if nowhere near so as that from summer campaigning, with the Russians losing perhaps 140,000 dead and 230,000 wounded, against German losses of 30,000 to 35,000 dead and comparable numbers of wounded. On the positive side, the Red Army hemorrhaged far fewer prisoners outside Moscow than in the earlier engagements of 1941, losing

---

* To downplay the significance of lend-lease tanks in the Battle of Moscow, some Russian historians have retorted that Matildas and Valentines were actually light, not medium, tanks. In terms of weight, the Matilda MK-2 was roughly equal to the T-34, and its armor equal to the heavy KV, though it was slower than both. The Valentine MK-3 fell in between the T-26 series and the T-34 in both weight and armor; it is best described as a "light medium" tank.

only 75,440 for the whole month of December 1941—a mere fraction of the losses from summer and early fall. The butcher's bill, indeed, does not support the Soviet narrative, pushed by Stalin and his admirers, of a historic, crushing Soviet victory in the Battle of Moscow, but rather a kind of winding down after six months of much more intense combat. As David Glantz writes, the Wehrmacht and Red Army resembled "two punch-drunk boxers" with "swollen eyes . . . unable to see with sufficient clarity to judge their relative endurance." There was no great follow-up after Zhukov's initial advances, no sustained Soviet effort to punch forward and cut off exposed Wehrmacht flanks, no huge envelopments netting large numbers of German prisoners. It was a victory for Zhukov and Stalin, but hardly a decisive one.[18]

What mattered was not so much the execution of the Soviet offensive, or the modest scale of the battle, but the very fact that Stalin and Zhukov, because of Siberian reinforcements and the cascading influx of lend-lease supplies, were able to mount an offensive at all. For the first time, the Germans were thrown back, puncturing the Wehrmacht's reputation for invincibility. Hitler's directive no. 39, issued on December 8, 1941, ordered his armies to assume a defensive position across the entire eastern front. Although later countermanded by Hitler's notorious "stand fast" order of December 20, directive no. 39 still crossed a historic watershed, marking the moment when Nazi Germany began to lose the war by virtue of not winning it.[19]

Still, however welcome the dramatic turnabout on the Moscow front was, the very success of Stalin's Far Eastern policy in 1941 nearly came back to haunt him. The entry of the United States into the war in the wake of Pearl Harbor introduced potentially crushing demands on US naval tonnage, which might upend lend-lease shipments to the USSR. By enraging the American people against the Japanese, Pearl Harbor threatened to drown out Europe entirely in terms of US strategic priorities. For how could President Roosevelt possibly justify spending American blood and treasure on the USSR, not to mention devote scarce shipping-container space and convoy destroyer escorts, at a time when the United States had to fight its way across the Pacific Ocean to Japan?

Fortunately for Stalin, Hitler, his former partner and now deadly enemy, came to the rescue of Russia's lend-lease lifeline by unilaterally declaring war on the United States on December 11, 1941, a move so self-sabotaging as to defy explanation to this day.* Compounded by his foolish refusal to coordinate his assault on Soviet Russia with his Japanese ally, the strategic upshot of Hitler's declaration of war was that Germany had pledged to help Japan defeat the United States and Britain even while Japan would do nothing to help Hitler in his own life-and-death struggle against the Soviet Union. For these strategic own goals, Hitler has been ridiculed ever since.[20]

If there is any explanation for Hitler's illogical Japan policy, it lies in the question of American economic resources and where they would most likely be deployed. In the months prior to Barbarossa, Hitler and Stalin had agreed that convincing Japan to abandon its "strike north" posture against the Soviet Far East and to attack US and British possessions instead was in the interest of both Germany and the USSR. Both dictators viewed "Anglo-Saxon capitalism" as their ultimate adversary and wanted to bleed its strength in Asia. The Pearl Harbor attack was the logical result of this curious mirroring between the two dictators, who sought to clear the decks for their own war to the death in Europe.

Had Roosevelt reacted in a straightforward manner to what he famously called the "infamy" of the Japanese attack, Hitler's gamble might even have worked. Declaration of war or no, by December 1941 the Germans already viewed the United States as a

---

*Hitler may have been provoked by a cover story on "F.D.R.'s War Plans!" in the *Chicago Tribune* on December 4. An exposé of the genuine "Rainbow Five" war plan to create a ten-million-man army to invade Hitlerian Europe by 1943, the story was not denied by the White House, despite a manhunt for the "leaker." Some have suggested that Rainbow Five was leaked by the president himself to goad Hitler into declaring war. If true, this was a brilliant political coup.

belligerent ally of Britain, and for good reason. The passage of the Lend-Lease Act, sold to Congress as a means to help Britain, had merely confirmed what everyone already knew: that Roosevelt supported Churchill's war unequivocally (though while charging a steep price for the war supplies Britain was now sending to Stalin effectively free of charge). To Hitler, declaring war on the United States was a formality that would allow his U-boats to loosen their rules of engagement, possibly enough to tip the balance in the Battle of the Atlantic. The idea that Roosevelt would react to Pearl Harbor by giving priority to Europe and the war against Germany, up to and including underwriting Stalin's war, did not cross Hitler's mind until weeks later, after a military treaty was signed by the Axis powers on January 18, 1942, when the Führer finally remembered to ask Japan to cut off American arms shipments to Russia via Vladivostok and to try to tie down Soviet forces in Siberia—and even then he did not get these pledges in writing. It may be that Hitler was too provincially European in his outlook, too ignorant of Asian and Pacific affairs, to perceive the importance of coordinating a global strategy with Tokyo.[21]

And yet this is exactly what Roosevelt did. Far from walk back his promises to Stalin after the onset of war with Japan, Roosevelt reaffirmed them wholeheartedly—subject only to the availability of shipping tonnage overseen by the US Maritime Commission and the capacity of the US Navy to arrange and arm convoys. In this, he was backed to the hilt by Great Britain, after Churchill arrived in Washington on December 22, 1941, for a series of meetings code-named ARCADIA to plan US-British strategy in the new global war. On the view that Japan posed no direct threat to either the United States or Britain, whereas Hitler's regime threatened Britain at least (if not also the American homeland), the resulting policy memorandum established the cardinal principle of "Germany first." In the memo, Roosevelt and Churchill declared, to reassure Stalin that they would not be distracted by the Japanese war, that "in 1942 the main methods of wearing down Germany's resistance will be . . . *assistance to Russia's offensive by all available*

means." Despite the need for a large US-British convoy of reinforcements for the southwest Pacific, code-named POPPY, both
Roosevelt and Churchill adamantly rejected the requests of their
service chiefs to reduce Soviet aid shipments by 30 percent. Pearl
Harbor or no Pearl Harbor, Stalin would get his American tanks,
warplanes, trucks, foodstuffs, steel, and aluminum.[22]

23

Capitalist Rope

ROOSEVELT'S DECISION TO devote scarce tonnage and naval resources to Soviet lend-lease supplies was a priceless gift to Stalin.
In exchange for opening up this vital lifeline for the beleaguered
Soviet war effort, the US government could have asked any price:
payment in cash, by loan, or in kind; political concessions inside
Russia; or promises from Stalin of better behavior abroad, such as
abandoning his spying operations in Washington or offering token
support for the US-British war against Japan. Instead, the Americans simply gave and demanded nothing in return aside from
a vague, nonbinding promise of loan repayment beginning five
years after the war was over, at no interest.[1]

There was little Soviet gratitude. Everything the Americans
gave turned out to be less than what Stalin wanted. As early as
October 1941, Andrei Gromyko, sent to Washington as Stalin's
personal lend-lease envoy, complained to Averell Harriman that
the US Maritime Commission had devoted exclusively to Russia
"only" thirty-one merchant vessels with six million cubic feet of capacity, whereas Stalin needed forty ships at a minimum. "It should
be borne in mind," Gromyko lectured poor Harriman, "that tanks
and airplanes occupy much space on ships."[2]

Nor was Stalin any more polite at the Moscow lend-lease conference. As a bewildered Harriman reported to Roosevelt after a
grueling session on September 29, 1941:

> The evening was very hard sledding. Stalin seemed discourteous
> and at times not interested, and rode us pretty hard. . . . He turned
> to me once and said, "Why is it that the United States can only

give me 1,000 tons of armor steel plate for tanks—a country with
a production of over 50,000,000 tons." When I tried to explain the
length of time required in increasing capacity of this type of steel
he brushed it aside by saying "One only has to add alloys."[3]

Despite the Pearl Harbor attack, the vulnerable 150,000-strong
American garrison under ferocious Japanese assault in the Philippines,* and the need to devote American tonnage and naval
strength to the Pacific war—not to mention prior lend-lease commitments to Britain and China and huge commercial demand in
Latin America—the US Maritime Commission promised on December 31, 1941, after the ARCADIA resolution reaffirming the
US-British strategy of "Germany first," to more than double cargo-
ship carrying capacity for Stalin, from six to fourteen million cubic
feet. Monthly shipments of American lend-lease aid to the USSR,
it was determined, would include 50,000 tons of "metals, chemicals, and other heavy materials," 20,000 tons of "petroleum products," 10,000 trucks, 550 tanks (mostly M-3s), 144 pursuit planes,
and 133 bombers, along with ten cargo ships full of American
"wheat, flour, and sugar." Still this was not enough, the Russians
told lend-lease officials, even as the Red Army was launching a
counteroffensive outside Moscow enabled by British and American tanks, trucks, and warplanes; Stalin wanted thirty-four million
cubic feet of American goods per month.[4]

Part of the reason the Russians were perennially disappointed
in the volume of American lend-lease aid being received in Soviet ports was that so much of it ended up at the bottom of the
northern Atlantic Ocean or Arctic Sea. Convoys faced not only the

---

* As General Douglas MacArthur, the doomed American commander
in the Philippines, would later ruefully recall, "A top-level decision had
been reached" at the Washington conference in December 1941 "to concentrate first on the defeat of Germany . . . no matter what the cost in
the Far East. . . . I was not informed . . . and believed that a brave effort
at relief was in the making."

ever-present threat of German U-boats and destroyers but the perils of heaving Arctic waves, freezing cold, ice and icebergs, snow, and fog. Once they reached the Barents Sea, they also had to run the gauntlet of Luftwaffe air raids launched from nearby Petsamo, including a squadron of twenty-four German torpedo-carrying seaplanes and converted Ju-88 and He-111 bombers. Just in the first month after Pearl Harbor, three American cargo ships sank en route to Archangel, and another was sabotaged on board for unknown reasons.[5]

Compounding the already colossal costs of these lend-lease operations in winter was the inadequacy of Russian defenses and off-loading capacity on the other end. Some of the Soviet deficiencies had been made up for by the British Admiralty, which delivered shells and explosives for shore batteries to Archangel at its own expense and had spent much of summer and fall 1941 laying magnetic mines to guard the approaches to the port. Luftwaffe bombing sorties against Murmansk from Petsamo, just a few minutes' flying time across the Barents Sea, had rendered this closest Soviet port to Britain and the United States (close being a relative term, as Murmansk was still 4,500 nautical miles from New York) inoperable for now. Murmansk, built almost entirely out of wood, presented an easy target for incendiary bombs. Its acute vulnerability forced lend-lease convoys to steam for Archangel, five hundred miles further and more rigidly icebound in winter, instead. Because the Soviets had no real naval air force in the Arctic, British naval aviators, taking off from the aircraft carrier HMS *Victorious*, sustained heavy losses dogfighting with the Luftwaffe over the Barents Sea, losing sixteen warplanes and their crews in summer 1941.[6]

Just as the British Admiralty had provided Archangel with some strategic defense by fall 1941, the Arctic winter intervened. To their chagrin, American ship captains discovered that Soviet icebreakers were unarmed, and were thus sitting ducks for German destroyers and U-boats. Nor were the dozen-odd Russian merchant vessels Stalin was able to provide for the Arctic route armed. Never shy,

Gromyko submitted a "requisition form" in Washington on January 18, 1942, for "degaussing, repairs, and installation of guns and gun mounts on . . . Russian merchant vessels." And so, the US Navy, as assistant naval secretary Ralph Bard informed Roosevelt on February 14, "undertook to arm three Russian icebreakers and thirteen merchant ships. Subsequent to this agreement the Russians asked us to arm a fourth icebreaker, the KRASSIN, and this vessel has been armed."[7]

If the behavior of Soviet officials in Washington was presumptuous, inside the USSR it was positively rude. The abusive nature of the partnership was brought home at a meeting in Kuibyshev (Samara) between Ambassador Steinhardt and Molotov's deputy A. Y. Vishinsky on November 4, 1941. With Moscow nearly overrun and its government evacuated, the Soviets enjoyed, at this desperate time, no leverage over the Americans promising to bail them out. But Vishinsky still complained about an American request to send sixty-six shipping experts to Archangel to inspect its port facilities. Among other issues, the port lacked sufficient ballast, which was a huge problem, as American vessels were returning home empty; the Soviets had almost nothing to give them. Stalin, Vishinsky explained, wanted Roosevelt to send him everything his armies required, with the United States taking on all the risk and expense, without Americans being allowed to set foot on Soviet soil. As Vishinsky lectured Steinhardt, "We don't need American experts. We need tanks, warplanes, and guns."[8]

Roosevelt was trying. In view of the terrors of the Arctic route, lend-lease officials had first requested that Stalin consider receiving shipments via Iran and the Persian Gulf or at Vladivostok. But Stalin insisted on Archangel, which was closer to the front, whatever the risk to American life and limb. The hazards of this route were severe enough that the US Maritime Commission could not formally authorize missions to this port; American vessels had to leave Archangel by November 15 in order not to forfeit insurance coverage. There were further legal risks involved in shipping war matériel to Soviet Arctic ports, located as they were in a war zone blanketed with Luftwaffe fighters, German destroyers, and U-boats (thus falling plainly in the legal purview of the Neutrality Act, whatever Roosevelt's advisers claimed). It was in view of such risks that Gromyko was demanding that the US Navy arm Soviet icebreakers and merchant vessels, illustrating that the pretext Hopkins had proposed to exempt Soviet Arctic ports from Neutrality Act restrictions before Pearl Harbor—that they were not war zones—was implausible.[9]

Hopkins himself recognized as much. On October 15, 1941, he submitted a tortured legal finding to President Roosevelt, noting that "Section 3a of the Neutrality Act provides that no American ship shall proceed through a combat area, except under such rules and regulations as may be prescribed" by the executive branch. With circular reasoning, Hopkins concluded that "the President, or the Secretary of State, may therefore at any time make rules or regulations authorizing American ships to proceed with war supplies to Archangel." The Neutrality Act passed by Congress and signed into law by the president applied only when Hopkins and Roosevelt wished it to. In the case of Stalin's war-fighting needs, they preferred that it did not apply.[10]

To avoid headaches with Congress, which the Roosevelt administration was deceiving every day about Russian aid, Hopkins's lend-lease officials pleaded with Gromyko and Soviet ambassador Umansky to allow shipments via Vladivostok instead (a port far enough from the war zone to raise no legal hassles), only to come up empty. With Moscow still in danger, the Soviets insisted that the Americans stick to the Arctic route that winter while also agreeing to supply Murmansk and Archangel and "provide foodstuffs, clothing, and technical supplies for military, naval, and meteorological and scientific posts" throughout the Russian Arctic.[11]

In view of the primitive conditions in the USSR's Arctic ports, it was not a bad idea to ask the Americans to provision them. As Edward Lewis, a British coxswain, recalled of his first visit to Murmansk in winter 1941–1942, "We disembarked and were taken to some barracks, which were virtually windowless. Inside were rows of bunks . . . on which were palliasses filled with straw and a rough blanket." There was no food in the barracks, necessitating a two-mile walk to a Russian labor camp where he could obtain "a form of very thin soup with a few pieces of fat yak meat and a small piece of black rye bread." There were no bathrooms, certainly none with toilets or sinks. Instead, Lewis was shown a "trench over which a plank had been placed," in the open air. "In sub-zero conditions," he recalled, "this wasn't very pleasant. And no [toilet] paper was supplied."[12]

Another group of British naval officers in convoy PQ 13, who came ashore at Murmansk at the end of March 1942 after running a deadly gauntlet of German Luftwaffe and U-boat attacks, found the city "a drab, depressing place, inhabited by drab, grey people who showed no inclination to fraternize with them." Although offended at first by this cold reception, the Britons realized that Russians, "cowed by their rulers," had very good reason to be wary of "these strangers who came from the capitalist world which was to communism, like daylight to Count Dracula."[13]

Shipping tanks, warplanes, trucks, and guns to Stalin via Vladivostok, after the Vozhd relented and authorized this in January 1942, was no picnic either. There was a rich irony in Stalin's reversal on the Pacific route. Before Pearl Harbor, when the Neutrality Act was in force, the waters around Vladivostok were not a war zone. Lend-lease shipments could have proceeded there without legal complications or danger of engagement by hostile navies. But Stalin ruled this route out, demanding that Roosevelt sidestep the Neutrality Act and ship war supplies via the U-boat-infested waters of the North Atlantic and Arctic instead. Now that the United States was at war with Japan—a country scarcely five hundred miles from the Soviet Far East, with its home islands sitting squarely astride the principal sea lanes—the route to Vladivostok was as perilous as could possibly be imagined, an obvious war zone. That Stalin gave his blessing for this route now, after insisting on the more dangerous and legally dubious Arctic option when the Pacific had been safer and legal, suggests either that he actually wanted American capitalists to die at sea while supplying his armies, or that he was playing a wicked joke at Roosevelt's expense.[14]

On the other hand, Stalin may have known something about Japan that Roosevelt did not, owing to his April 1941 neutrality pact with Tokyo. It turned out that Japan's Pacific fleet commanders—keen to keep Stalin content, and not unhappy that the Americans were undermining their own war effort—took an indulgent attitude toward convoys heading for Vladivostok in 1942. Nor did anyone in the Japanese Admiralty bother to humor Hitler's request that Japanese vessels block shipments of American war matériel to Stalin. When the Japanese Navy later stopped a few US merchant vessels in Japanese territorial waters, Hopkins's lend-lease officials conceived a solution emblematic of Roosevelt's self-effacing relations with Stalin: they transferred title to fifty-seven American merchant vessels used in the Pacific Ocean to Soviet Russia, so that the Japanese fleet would not bother them.[15]

By spring and summer 1942, Soviet purchasing agents had such influence in the Roosevelt administration that they functioned, for all intents and purposes, like members of the US government. Until Hopkins and Roosevelt had green-lit lend-lease aid for Stalin, the USSR had routed import orders via Amtorg, a front corporation chartered to contract for the Soviet government with private American firms—firms it actually paid for the products they delivered. Reflecting its need to deal with major US corporations, Amtorg was located in Manhattan. After the shift to a lend-lease model, the director of Amtorg, K. I. Lukashev, was given a new title as head of the "Government Purchasing Commission of the Soviet Union in the USA," with its headquarters on Sixteenth Street NW in Washington, DC—down the street from the White House (and the Soviet embassy, also located on Sixteenth Street). The vocabulary of the transactions changed too, from "purchases" in Amtorg days, to "aid" in the early days of lend-lease, to simply "requisitions" by 1942. The Lend-Lease Administration provided requisition forms to Soviet purchasing agents, identical to those

used by the US armed forces, which sped up processing time of
Russian requests from an average of 33.2 days in 1941 to forty-
eight hours by January 1942. Stalin's agents now had legal writ in
the United States over essential war supplies.[16]

Remarkably, Lukashev's Soviet purchasing agents were also
allowed to inspect whatever American factories they wished to—
invited, in effect, to commit industrial espionage. It was not an
accident that his two most important aviation experts were Stanislav Shumovsky (code name BLÉRIOT) and Pyotr Belyaev (code
name MIKHAILOV), sleeper agents Stalin had placed in the United
States back in 1931. Spying was superfluous in the lend-lease era,
as Shumovsky and Belyaev no longer had to copy files and recruit
informants. They could now tell Stalin what to order directly from
the best US aviation factories: Bell, Douglas, and Curtiss-Wright.
Indeed, the Soviet cause "enjoyed such huge popularity" in Washington by the end of 1941, as Gromyko informed Molotov, that
Soviet assets in the US government, like Harry Dexter White, no
longer felt the need to lay low and wait for instructions from their
handlers. White could walk over to the Soviet embassy and casually suggest reorienting the US machine-tool industry to meet
Stalin's needs, as White promised Gromyko he would do on December 24, 1941. Nor did Soviet purchasing agents have to pay
in cash for planes, specialized machine tools, or prototypes, as
they had done in the 1930s. Everything would be delivered to the
USSR, essentially free of charge.[17]

That Soviet industrial espionage in the United States during the
war took place on a massive scale is confirmed in the files of the
Lend-Lease Administration and the State Department. Lukashev's
men did this dozens of times in 1942 alone, touring, for example,
the Homestead Steel plant in Marshall, Pennsylvania; the National
Tube Works in McKeesport, Pennsylvania; and the Gary steelworks in Indiana. Lukashev's agents were regular visitors at the
main US tank-testing facility in Aberdeen, Maryland, where Soviet
officers were allowed to inspect M-3 series Stuart tanks as they
were put through their paces. Reciprocity was nonexistent. The

former US military attaché in Moscow, Yeaton, had frequently requested access to Soviet facilities, only to be denied.[18]

That this industrial espionage was conducted at the behest of Soviet authorities at the highest level is confirmed in the Molotov papers at the Communist Party archives. On December 1, 1941, Vyacheslav Malyshev—vice chairman of the Council of People's Commissars, and also (from October 1940) commissar of heavy machine building and (from September 1941) commissar of the Soviet tank industry—wrote Molotov that it would be "extremely desirable to become acquainted with and to study in greater detail the processes and phenomena currently used in industrial factories in America." Malyshev instructed Molotov to send to Washington "a team of 15-20" experts, with representatives from the commissariats of tank, ship, heavy machine building, armaments, aviation, metallurgy, and electricity, to study "the technology and organization of mass production of tanks, warplanes and ammunition, in particular learning what is new and different in American methods, compared to the principles known to us of auto-tractor technology." With these words, the man in charge of all Soviet tank production from 1941 to 1945 gave the lie to the Soviet claim of disinterest in American tank technology because of the T-34 breakthrough (and even the T-34 used the suspension design of the American engineer J. Walter Christie). As to aviation, Stalin's keen interest in American technology, never well hidden, was now an openly acknowledged secret, registered with every new requisition his spies made.[19]

Thanks to Hopkins, viewed by Gromyko as a reliable yes-man, industrial espionage was easy for Soviet agents to conduct in the United States. It was not simply that Soviet buying agents and engineers were given free rein inspecting factories and tank-testing facilities. Hopkins's lend-lease team approved the transfer of entire American factories to the USSR, including their in-house intellectual property. The process began in July and August 1941, when the United States was still neutral and Roosevelt personally approved contracts to have built in the USSR a $4 million tire plant, a $3 million catalytic cracking plant to process high-octane gasoline, a $2.75 million hydrogen plant, a $2.2 million cracking and crude distillation plant, a $1.75 million dehydrocyclization plant for producing TNT, a $1.5 million aviation lubricating oil plant, a $4 million aluminum rolling mill, and a $400,000 high-octane gasoline plant.[20]

Far from slowing down after Pearl Harbor, Soviet orders only grew more ambitious. On December 30 and 31, 1941, Lukashev placed two orders, the first for 8.5 million "high chrome" stainless-steel ball bearings to be delivered in 1942, and the second for monthly shipments of 6 million pounds of "solventless" nitroglycerine powder, for use in Red Army flamethrowers. As Lukashev knew perfectly well, the US Army, in the wake of Pearl Harbor, was trying to ramp up production of military vehicles, which placed huge strain on chrome supplies. "Current demands for bearings resulting from our own expanding aircraft and tank programs," Stettinius was informed by US Army engineers, "have critically affected our supply. I am sure you understand the difficulties." Because "stainless steel balls have been denied our own military forces," W. L. Batt wrote to Stettinius on behalf of the army, "we therefore ask that the USSR give consideration to accepting corrosion-resistant plating rather than high chrome steel balls." Hopkins was having none of this. Instead of disappointing Stalin, he would disappoint the US Army brass, approving, on March 19, 1942, a shipment of 2.5 million high-chrome stainless-steel balls to the Red Army, a volume large enough to produce serious shortages in the first year the United States fought in the war.[21]

The Soviet order for solventless nitroglycerine powder was even more brazen. The production method Lukashev's engineers requested was unknown to the US explosives firms contacted by the Lend-Lease Administration, which raised the interesting question of why the Russians did not simply make the stuff themselves, rather than demanding that Americans mix and then ship this volatile explosive blend halfway across the world. The basic ingredients—ammonia, colloxylin, and a few acid compounds—

were neither rare nor expensive. The key to making dynamite, cordite, or other nitroglycerine-based explosives lay in the chemical formula and proprietary blending technique, not in the materials as such. For the United States to be able to produce the solventless nitroglycerine powder the Red Army liked to use in its flamethrowers, US Army engineers estimated in February 1942, would require the investment of $50 million to build a new plant from scratch and the technical assistance of Soviet experts, who were invited to share the proprietary formula they used in their flamethrowers with American chemists if they wished to secure the supplies Stalin wanted. This was the last the Lend-Lease Administration heard about Stalin's nitroglycerine order.[22]

Once in possession of US Army requisition forms, Lukashev's purchasing commission could place exotic orders for things like "pontoon boats and 1500 tons monthly of any type of powder . . . suitable for use in artillery shells" (March 13, 1942). Lukashev demanded monthly deliveries of eight hundred tons of rubber, tin, and nickel (March 18, 1942), Stalin having lost his supplies of the latter from Petsamo after Finland declared war. Soviet factories were also in desperate need of "boilers and steam generating equipment" (June 1942); 1.8 million tons of black tea purchased from India (August 1942); pneumatic hammers and chain hoists (September 1942); and electric furnaces, motors, and locomotives (October 1942). That month, Lukashev requisitioned the "processes and information" pertaining to a state-of-the-art American oil refinery (October 16, 1942) and an American vitamin factory. Until this technology arrived in the USSR, Lukashev requisitioned five tons of vitamin B1 per month (October 22, 1942).[23]

One of the most remarkable Soviet requisitions was for three Westinghouse one-thousand-kilowatt steam turbine power plants, placed in October 1942. This order is worth examining in detail, as it was authorized by the US Treasury—that is, by Henry Morgenthau, meaning his right-hand man, the Soviet asset Harry Dexter White. The Treasury Department literally ordered the Westinghouse corporation "to divert to Russian use three 1000 KW Steam

Turbine Power Plants originally ordered by the Universal Trading Corporation." Of course, the deal would still be profitable for
Westinghouse, as US taxpayers would pay. The amount billed,
Westinghouse's executives were told, would include "storage and
handling charges, reboxing, revision of engineering details and
manual covering the installation, operation and service necessitated by changes in grouping from 3 boilers with 2 turbines in one
location to 2 boilers with 2 turbines in one location and 1 boiler
with 1 turbine in another location . . . [and] possibly the differential
in the cost of the equipment."[24]

The most ambitious Soviet order placed in 1942 was for an
eighteen-inch "Merchant" or steel-rolling mill, to be built over
twelve to eighteen months in the United States, then shipped to
Archangel and transshipped by river and rail to the Urals. The
reason this was necessary, Lukashev's agent confessed, was to
mass-produce the "square and strip steel required in the production of armaments," because the only steel-rolling mill of sufficient
capacity in the USSR had been lost to the Germans. The desired
capacity to meet Stalin's war-industrial needs was a mill capable of
churning out "180,000 metric tons of finished rolled steel (annual
capacity), figuring on 300 working days a year by three shifts."
The material to be rolled would consist of "carbon structural and
tool steel as well as alloy steel, having a tensile strength of 120 kg
per square mm." American and Soviet engineers were duly set to
work inspecting mills in Pittsburgh, Pennsylvania, and Gary, Indiana, taking on bids to build a giant steel-rolling mill for Stalin. In
theory, the idea was to help the Red Army fight and kill Germans,
but the technology and production capacity being transferred
would have civilian applications too, and for years if not decades
after the war.[25]

Lend-lease sharing with Stalin extended even to top-secret military intelligence. In September 1941, a Soviet inspection team
was given a tour of a US air base in Riverside, California. A concerned US Air Force intelligence officer, Captain Newman White,
reported in a complaint filed with the Lend-Lease Administration:

All members of the party gave the impression of being highly trained technical engineers who knew exactly what to look for. . . . [They] seemed particularly interested in the method and means of supply, ordnance and ordnance repair, types of oils and gasoline, engineer and repair equipment, high-altitude oxygen masks and regulating valves, gun mountings, ammunition supplies, field shop equipment, field gasoline supplies, tankers, all types of special tools for aircraft repair, and the means of determining necessary amounts of such tools.

The Soviet observers, White continued, "did not hesitate to pull out rulers and measure sizes of gun mountings and any equipment that caught their eye. It was necessary to request that one member of the party not measure the gun ports on a B-17." One Russian was even observed "pull[ing] the zipper on the covering which concealed Confidential AUTOMATIC FLIGHT CONTROL ENGINEER (AFCE) equipment installed in the plane." In this way, Stalin's purchasing agents obtained intelligence on the state-of-the-art US Norden bombsight targeting system, the most closely guarded secret in the American arsenal, by invitation, in broad daylight.[26]

The case of the Norden bombsight provides a fascinating illustration of the double standard of the Roosevelt administration. For all the vaunted partnership between Roosevelt and Churchill, the United States shared this sensitive technology with the RAF only after being granted reciprocal access to the secret of British sonar tracking of submarines. In the same fashion, every single lend-lease item Britain imported from the United States had to be paid for in full—and it was all paid. By contrast, Stalin paid nothing for lend-lease goods, aside from a few token shipments of gold bullion sent to the United States as a goodwill gesture in early 1942—shipments that were cut off after the HMS *Edinburgh*, carrying 465 gold bars, was sunk by the Germans in the Arctic on May 2, 1942.[27]

Lenin had once prophesied that, after the revolution, capitalists would be happy to sell Communists the rope they would use to hang them. And yet not even Lenin could have imagined that American capitalists would hand over the rope free of charge—and not just any rope either. In October 1941, the Roosevelt administration agreed to supply Stalin with "453 tons of Manila hemp rope" of the kind desperately needed by the US Pacific fleet, along with 2,250 tons of raw Manila hemp—all diverted from the Philippines, already a strategic hot spot and about to become a war zone. Because of the controversial nature of the request, Harry Hopkins intervened personally to expedite it. "I understand that there is going to be a great shortage of Manila hemp," he wrote to his friend Stettinius, "and there is a great objection to sending any hemp to the Russians. Would you have someone explore this?" Stettinius leaned on the US Navy to assure compliance. In October 1942, Hopkins and Stettinius went further, authorizing shipments of "315 long tons of British East African sisal rope" to the USSR from the supplies ordinarily used by the US fleet. There were also regular monthly shipments of 1,200 tons of American "steel wire rope" to the USSR for the needs of Soviet war industry in the first protocol covering 1941–1942.[28]

The most shameless Soviet requisition was for decadent, bourgeois rope: silver braid. As Major General C. M. Wesson reported to Stettinius in February 1943, Stalin "has recently introduced epaulets in the Red Army. The War Department has just received a requisition calling for 2,961,900 yards of braid, costing approximately $7,000,000." This braid was "in part 1/2 % gold content on a sterling silver base and in part in silver braid on a sterling silver base." As this was "the type of item which might receive considerable attention in the public press," Wesson suggested that Stettinius and Hopkins "consider the [political] problems involved." Wesson need not have worried. To protect the lend-lease program, Harry Hopkins was careful to make sure the American public never learned about sensitive requisitions like this one.[29]

24

Just-in-Time Delivery

Lend-Lease and Stalingrad

HOWEVER STUPENDOUS THE variety of goods Stalin's agents were able to requisition from American capitalists, it remained frustrating to Soviet officials that not all of this largesse arrived as soon as they would have liked it to. The inadequacies of Russia's Arctic ports—until these were remedied at British and American expense—posed logistical hurdles. Murmansk, vulnerable to Luftwaffe raids, did not have enough anti-aircraft guns, and Archangel did not have enough icebreakers. It was for these prosaic reasons that only twenty lend-lease ships sailed from US ports for the Soviet Arctic in January 1942, and just fifteen in February.[1]

The winter slowdown in deliveries certainly reflected no conscious intent on Roosevelt's part. "Although we are having our immediate troubles in the Far East," the president wired Stalin on February 11, 1942, "Every effort is being made to get shipments off." Despite post–Pearl Harbor demands on merchant tonnage and US military needs, Roosevelt was happy to report that, "for January and February [1942] our shipments have included and will include 449 light tanks, 408 medium tanks, 244 fighter planes, 24 B-25s, and 233 A-20s." Roosevelt wired again two days later to promise that, as the Russians had blown through the first $1 billion already, he had opened for Stalin a second billion-dollar credit line, no questions asked. The president had also appointed a new ambassador to the USSR, Admiral William H. Standley, after Stalin complained that Steinhardt had "spread defeatist rumors." Standley, who had accompanied Averell Harriman to the lend-lease conference back in September 1941, was a devoted lend-leaser who submitted meekly to Soviet bullying, such as the assigning of a three-man NKVD detail to shadow him wherever he went in Russia. ("I tried to look upon the services of these NKVD men," Standley recalled, "in the way I was told they were offered—for my protection and safety.") In this way, Roosevelt conceded veto power over his diplomatic appointments to the Soviet dictator.[2]

While Stalin was polite enough to extend "sincere gratitude" to Roosevelt for firing Steinhardt, and for extending him another $1 billion loan unconditionally, the Vozhd was not shy in complaining about the pace of lend-lease supplies arriving in Russia. The president must understand, he wired Roosevelt on February 18, "the extremely strained state of the resources of the USSR." Carefully, Stalin wrote that "Soviet organizations when realizing the loan granted to the USSR are at present experiencing great difficulties with regard to the transport of armaments and materials purchased in the USA to USSR ports."* What Stalin wanted was for the US Navy to convoy every shipment of war matériel from the East Coast all the way to the Soviet Arctic, rather than simply from England to Murmansk and Archangel, as had been done previously.[3]

Roosevelt promptly agreed to Stalin's terms. In March 1942, the president issued his strongest directive yet prioritizing Stalin's needs. Pearl Harbor notwithstanding, Roosevelt ordered Admiral Emory S. Land, formerly of the US Maritime Commission and now head of the brand-new War Shipping Administration, to "give Russia first priority in shipping" and take merchant vessels off Latin American and Caribbean routes "regardless of other

---

*On several occasions, Stalin referred to lend-lease aid shipments as "sales," only to be corrected. As Churchill informed him on September 4, 1941, "You used the word 'sell.' We had not viewed the matter in such terms and have never thought of payment." As Roosevelt put it during negotiations for the second protocol, his goal was to "eliminate the silly, foolish, old dollar sign"—that is, give Stalin whatever he needed for the war against Hitler at no charge.

considerations." Roosevelt ordered Donald Nelson, the lend-lease administrator in charge of procurement, to prioritize Russian shipments "regardless of the effect . . . on any other part of our war program." To Hopkins, the president simply said, "Get enough ships." The goal was fifty for March 1942.[4]

These were not idle words. While Hopkins and Land did not produce the fifty ships Roosevelt wanted for Stalin's needs in March, they did send forty-three. In April 1942, seventy-nine US merchantmen set off for Soviet ports, nearly all for Murmansk and Archangel. Stalin's exorbitant military and war-industrial needs had produced a bottleneck of ships off the coast of Iceland, which presented fat targets for German destroyers and U-boats. Sinkings numbered fourteen by the end of March and then ramped up severely in April, when nineteen Allied merchant ships went down.[5]

Emblematic of the pluck of the Allied ship captains and the horror of the passage was the fate of the armed British transport *Empire Starlight*, with seventy-six men aboard. The *Empire Starlight* discharged its precious cargo at Murmansk under constant Luftwaffe raids between April 3 and 7, was moved to a safer anchorage for repairs on April 9, was bombed again on April 13, was towed to safe anchorage for more repairs on April 16, returned to sea on April 23 only to be bombed three days in a row, and returned to Murmansk again for repairs, where it was bombed fifty-six more times before finally sinking to the bottom of the Arctic on June 1, 1942.[6]

Stalin remained unimpressed. Despite the ARCADIA declarations by Roosevelt and Churchill that the Japanese war would not slow down lend-lease shipments to Russia, Stalin used Pearl Harbor as an excuse to slight one of their key allies: the Poles. As a sop to Churchill, the Vozhd had consented to release Polish prisoners with military experience from Soviet labor camps to form their own military units: three infantry divisions in all, under the command of General Wladyslaw Anders, who had survived a brutal interrogation in the Lubyanka NKVD headquarters. Delicately, Stalin had Molotov ask Beria how many Poles captured in 1939 were still alive in Gulag camps. The answer, as of August 12,

1941, was 391,575 in various states of declining health and vigor, of whom 16,647 still-able-bodied Poles had volunteered to serve under Anders in Soviet-subordinate military units, including 527 Polish women. Not trusting the Poles' loyalty, Stalin had insisted that Anders's divisions be transported to Iran to join the British, who had occupied the country's southern ports. Churchill agreed. The one thing Churchill, backed by Roosevelt, had insisted on was that Stalin feed and supply these divisions until they reached Iranian territory.[7]

Now that the United States and Britain were at war with Japan, Stalin informed General Anders that he would no longer be feeding his Polish divisions, not even until they left the USSR. Although unsurprising in view of Stalin's murderous hostility toward Polish military officers, the reasoning behind Stalin's decision is revealing. "The Americans promised us more than a million tons of grain," Stalin informed Anders on March 8, 1942, "but have given us only a hundred thousand tons . . . because of the Japanese war." Inside the USSR, Stalin confessed, there was no grain to be had "because we lost Ukraine" to the Germans.[8]

Stalin was not wrong, therefore, to emphasize the USSR's acute economic vulnerability when he lodged complaints with Roosevelt about inadequate lend-lease deliveries. The Americans and Britons had been generous and courageous, too, in sustaining such heavy losses on the perilous North Atlantic route. Nonetheless, deliveries remained disappointing to the Russians, and lend-lease shipments were increasingly seen, by Soviet leaders, as a cheap Anglo-American substitute for engaging German armies more directly. Stalin had first broached the idea of a "second front somewhere in the Balkans or France" with Churchill on September 3, 1941, even before the United States was in the war. It was to deflect this request that Churchill had declined payment for British arms sent to Stalin and that he had put so much effort into arranging convoys, deploying the Royal Navy to arm and defend Soviet ports. All these herculean British efforts availed Churchill was for Stalin's demands for a second front to grow louder and shriller in the course of 1942, even as Allied shipping losses mounted. It was expressly in order to pressure the Allies into opening a new front in Europe that Stalin dispatched Molotov to Washington in May 1942 to lobby the US president.[9]

In fairness to Stalin, Roosevelt had invited this pressure on himself. The president had written Churchill on March 18, "I know you will not mind my being brutally frank when I tell you that I think I can personally handle Stalin better than either your Foreign Office or my State Department. Stalin hates the guts of all your top people. He thinks he likes me better, and I hope he will continue to do so." In this vain state of mind, Roosevelt then wrote to Stalin on April 11, without consulting his generals or Churchill, that "I have in mind a very important military proposal involving the utilization of our armed forces in a manner to relieve your critical Western Front." The Vozhd could be forgiven for taking the president at his word when Roosevelt told Molotov on May 29 that "it is necessary to make sacrifices to help the USSR in 1942." "It is possible," the president added, "that we shall have to live through another Dunkirk and lose 100,000–120,000 men," all but confessing that he did not expect an amphibious landing on the Channel coastline of Europe to succeed. Roosevelt authorized Molotov to inform Stalin "that we expect the formation of a second front this year." The only condition the president attached to this promise was that Stalin reduce his demand for lend-lease supplies, to allow the United States to convoy more supplies to Britain to prepare for his hoped-for Allied invasion of Europe.[10]

Roosevelt's reckless promise of a second front during Molotov's first Washington visit has become notorious, and for good reason. In the coming months and years, Stalin would repeat the president's second front vow to shame his allies for not doing what they had promised. Because Roosevelt had not cleared the idea with Churchill, his promise also placed a strain on US-British relations. When Molotov, passing through London on June 10 on his return voyage to Russia, informed the prime minister of Roosevelt's bizarre pledge of a "second Dunkirk," Churchill told him that "we shall not win the war by doing stupid things." Realizing that a blanket refusal to open a European front would not please Stalin, Churchill outbid Roosevelt and promised the Vozhd that the Allies would "mount a large scale invasion of the Continent of Europe by British and American forces in 1943," once they had assembled an invasion force of "over a million men, British and American, with air forces of appropriate strength." In this way, Roosevelt's effort to please Stalin loosened Churchill's tongue too, as the two statesmen wrote checks to Stalin that they likely knew to be un-cashable, whether in 1942 or 1943.[11]

The timing of these second front pledges is significant. The Soviet lend-lease convoy PQ 16, which left Iceland on May 21, was pummeled by the Luftwaffe and German U-boats as it passed through the Denmark Strait, with seven of the thirty-five merchantmen in the convoy going down, a loss ratio of 20 percent. Losses in the even more heavily armed PQ 17, which left Iceland on June 27, were worse still, with twenty-five out of thirty-six merchant vessels sunk by enemy attack and one hundred thousand tons of American war matériel sinking en route, including 430 tanks (out of 594 sent), 210 warplanes (of 297), and 3,150 trucks (out of 4,246). With loss ratios approaching three-quarters of war matériel shipped, including 131,716 tons lost at sea in the last two convoys alone, Roosevelt and Churchill would temporarily abandon the northern route to Russia after July 1942. With deliveries to the Soviet fronts taking a major hit because of these losses, Roosevelt and Churchill felt the need to reassure Stalin they were fully committed to defeating Hitler.[12]

This is not to say, however, that lend-lease aid to Stalin was abandoned; it was simply shifted to other routes. Although Vladivostok was further from the European war theater than Archangel, the Pacific route was much safer, owing to Japan's decision not to molest ships carrying American war matériel to the USSR. By the end of June 1942, seventy-six ships had arrived safely in Vladivostok, carrying 412,160 tons of lend-lease supplies.[13]

The Atlantic–Persian Gulf route, which required avoiding German U-boats in the Mediterranean (unless the much longer route around the Cape of Good Hope was chosen) was not as safe as the Pacific, but Iran was closer to the Russian fronts. Back on September 1, 1941, at a time when the United States was still neutral, Britain and the USSR had invaded Iran from the south and north, respectively, with the Red Army and NKVD seizing Teheran and the Royal Navy taking Bushehr and the country's other ports along the Gulf. Although the purpose of this strange joint invasion, at the time, was to secure Iran's oil supplies for Stalin in case the Wehrmacht seized Baku,* by 1942 Allied-occupied Iran had become an increasingly vital part of the lend-lease pipeline to Russia, especially after losses mounted on the northern route. In May and June 1942, twenty-one US merchant vessels carrying Soviet lend-lease aid set off for Iran.[14]

The Persian Gulf route, however, posed its own problems. Stalin had initially objected to it because of what he accurately called "the limited capacity of the Iranian railways and highways." All winter 1941–1942, American and British engineers were put to work building wharves, piers, and jetties, dredging channels to open them up to deeper draft vessels, installing cranes, finishing roads, and leveling airfields. On an inspection tour of the Gulf in April 1942, en route to his new post as US ambassador to Soviet Russia, Admiral Standley observed that many ships had to idle offshore at anchor for "two to three weeks to be unloaded" and that some were diverted to Karachi, in the far west of British India. Many Tomahawk and Bell Airacobra fighters, Standley noted, were just "sitting there in the shifting winds" for long periods in port, "sanding up." Longer-ranged bombers, such as the American

* Britain also offered in August 1941 to send a demolition team to blow up the oil wells and refineries of the Transcaucasus, a gift Stalin did not look kindly on after the Massigli affair of 1940, when the then-hostile British had war-gamed bombing them from the air.

A-20s and a few B-25s, were flown across the Atlantic to North Africa to save cargo space on ships, but many of these arrived showing wear and tear from the journey. Small wonder Russian inspectors rejected many American warplanes on arrival at the Soviet border when they reported finding "sand in the engines."[15]

It was in the nature of a planetary-scale shipping operation such as the Soviet lend-lease program that not everything Stalin's men ordered would arrive on time or in perfect condition. Even so, enough did arrive in Russia in 1942 to make a difference, just in time to help Stalin's reeling armies recover. In the rush of confidence following the repulsion of the Germans outside Moscow in December 1941, Stalin had ordered a broad array of counteroffensives on the central and northern fronts, only for these to stall quickly. While some territory was recaptured and some Wehrmacht units were isolated in pockets near Demiansk and Kholm, the Germans fought tenaciously in defense and inflicted fearsome casualties on the Red Army, which suffered losses of 272,000 dead or captured in the Rzhev-Viazma sector west of Moscow alone, and another 210,000 in subsidiary offensives by April 1942, when the rasputitsa floods grounded Zhukov's offensives. While winter conditions explain some of the Soviet failures in the second round of Moscow battles, Zhukov lamented his lack of mobile armor. "We simply did not have enough mechanized and tank units at the disposal of the front commanders to conduct offensive operations on a scale sufficient to achieve decisive goals," he explained in his postmortem on the winter campaign. Stalin's enormous prewar tank park had been whittled down to almost nothing by the crushing German offensives of 1941, and, as of February and March 1942, lend-lease shipments had not yet remedied this critical deficit.[16]

Lending credence to Zhukov's complaint about the lack of armor hindering offensive operations—more so than the heavy snows of central Russia in winter—his counterparts further south in Crimea fared little better. Although the Soviet fortress at Sevastopol held out, after the fall of Kerch in mid-November 1941

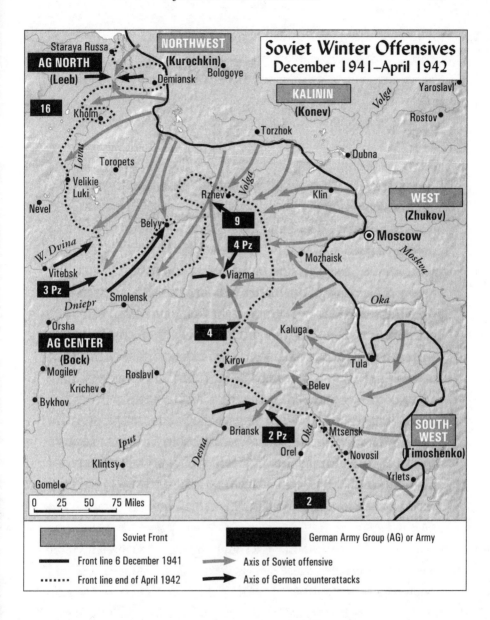

Soviet Winter Offensives
December 1941–April 1942

Staraya Russa
AG NORTH
(Leeb)
NORTHWEST
(Kurochkin)
Demiansk
Bologoye
16
Kholm
KALININ
(Konev)
Yaroslavl'
Rostov
Torzhok
Dubna
Volga
Toropets
Velikie
Luki
Nevel
Rzhev
Klin
WEST
(Zhukov)
Lovat
Belyy
9
Moscow
W. Dvina
4 Pz
Mozhaisk
Moskva
Vitebsk
Viazma
3 Pz
Smolensk
Dniepr
Oka
Orsha
4
Kaluga
AG CENTER
(Bock)
Kirov
Tula
Mogilev
Roslavl
Krichev
Belev
Bykhov
Iput
Briansk
2 Pz
Mtsensk
SOUTH-WEST
(Timoshenko)
Desna
Orel
Novosil
Klintsy
Yrlets
Gomel
0 25 50 75 Miles
2

Soviet Front	German Army Group (AG) or Army
Front line 6 December 1941	Axis of Soviet offensive
Front line end of April 1942	Axis of German counterattacks

most of the peninsula had fallen into German hands. After the Soviet commander in Kerch, Marshal G. I. Kulik, was sacked, Stalin called in General D. T. Kozlov of the Transcaucasian Army. Boldly, Kozlov sent an amphibious force of forty thousand westward across the Kerch Strait in late December 1941 to land on the eastern edge of the Crimean Peninsula at Kerch and Feodosiia, catching the Germans by surprise. After the straits froze in January,

Kozlov was able to reinforce his amphibious echelon over the ice, creating a new Crimean army group nearly 260,000 strong. But Kozlov had only 350 tanks and few trucks. Nor did he have any real air support, which allowed the Luftwaffe to rain bombs onto his men when they pushed forward in futile offensives in March and April 1942. By May, Kozlov's invading force had been virtually wiped out, losing 240,000 men (including 170,000 prisoners), 1,100 guns, and 250 of his 350 tanks, nearly all captured intact by the Germans.[17]

Timoshenko launched his own offensive against Kharkov in the relatively favorable conditions of southern Ukraine on May 12, 1942, only to make no more headway than Zhukov or Kozlov had done. As if to illustrate the devastating consequences of the loss of Kharkov, birthplace of the T-34 and beating heart of the Soviet tank industry, Timoshenko's southwestern army group was infantry heavy, with only General A. M. Gorodiansky's Sixth Army, attacking on the southern flank, possessing much armor. Within days, the Germans had launched a devastating counterattack, cut off the exposed Sixth Army, and trapped most of Gorodiansky's tanks in the resulting pocket. The battle of Kharkov was yet another catastrophe for the Red Army, which lost 171,000 men according to Soviet sources—or as many as 214,000 prisoners, according to the Germans, along with 1,200 armored vehicles and tanks and 2,600 guns.[18]

Compounding the damage wrought by the failed Soviet winter and spring offensives, these defeats were followed, once the spring flooding eased, by a massive German thrust from eastern Ukraine toward the Volga. Overruling his generals, who would have preferred to revive the drive for Moscow on the central front—this is what Zhukov and Stalin were expecting and preparing for—Hitler threw everything into Operation Blau (blue), a two-pronged southern offensive to bring what the Führer predicted would be "final victory in the East." Blau was a streamlined version of Barbarossa, stripped to essentials: it was Hitler's bid for autarky, an attempt to seize the coal of the Donets River basin (which accounted for 60 percent of Soviet production), Caucasian oil, and Georgian manganese. By crossing the Volga, ideally at the great industrial port of Stalingrad, Hitler's armies would cut the Soviet Union off from the vast economic resources of the Caucasus and Caspian basin, after the Germans had already taken Ukraine. Stalingrad itself was a huge prize, accounting for, according to German estimates, 20 percent of Soviet tank production (including Factory No. 264, which produced the T-34 tank), 27 percent of tractors, 4 percent of steel, and 7 percent of munitions.[19]

On June 28, 1942, German Army Group South, commanded by Field Marshal Fedor von Bock, launched Operation Blau along the entire Don front between Kursk and the Sea of Azov. This was ideal panzer terrain. "As far as the eye could see," a journalist observed, "armoured vehicles and half-tracks are rolling forward into the steppe." With every day's advance, the Germans deprived Stalin of critical economic resources. By July 22, an advance echelon of German Sixth Army, commanded by General Friedrich Paulus, was within fifty miles of Stalingrad on the Volga.[20]

Stalin was apoplectic when he heard the news from the Don front. In his soon-notorious "no-retreat" order no. 227, issued to Red Army commanders on July 28, 1942, the Vozhd lamented the loss of "Ukraine, Belorussia, the Baltic region, the Donbass" to the enemy—losses not only of territory but of "people, wheat, metals, plants, factories."* The USSR, Stalin reminded his generals, had been deprived of "70 million people, more than 800 million pounds of grain per year, and more than 10 million tons of metals produced annually." Even before seizing the bounty of the Caucasus and Caspian, the Germans had achieved rough economic parity with the USSR. Belying the claim of many historians that superior Russian resources and reserves would inevitably turn the

---

* Order no. 227 also stepped up disciplinary measures against officers who fell back. In practice, Stalin took the ongoing Don and Caucasus battles seriously enough that he allowed tactical retreats, refusing, unlike in 1941, to cashier commanders who fell back.

tide of the war, Stalin confessed that "we no longer have an advantage over the Germans, not in human reserves, not in grain." Only 58 percent of the agricultural land cultivated prewar was still in Soviet hands, with forty-five million hectares lost already. "Every new strip of land gained by the enemy," the Vozhd warned, "will appreciably strengthen the enemy and appreciably weaken our defense." Every commander, Stalin emphasized, "must realize that our resources are not limitless." The watchword must therefore be "Ni shagu nazad": not a single step back![21]

Despite, or perhaps because of, Stalin's no-retreat order, the German drive east picked up speed in August 1942.* On July 23, List's Army Group A secured Rostov-on-Don and launched Hitler's push to Baku and the Caspian. German progress was swift. Stavropol fell on August 3. List's Edelweiss Division pushed southeast into the Kuban River basin. Maikop, just north of the Caucasus Mountains and home to critical oil refineries, fell on August 10. By mid-August, German panzers were approaching Grozny, an oil-refining city on the Terek River. Just beyond lay Ordzhonikidze (formerly Vladikavkaz), gateway to Georgia and the Transcaucasus. If this pace continued, the Germans would reach the Caspian in September, seizing control of three-quarters of Soviet oil production. Meanwhile, German Sixth Army, under General Paulus, was fighting its way into Stalingrad, with Paulus's panzers rolling into the city's western suburbs in the first days of September.[22]

Some of this depressing ledger of failure reflected superior German tactics and operational élan, honed over the first several years of the European war. The British, after all, were faring little better against Rommel's armored divisions in the North African desert

---

* After copies of Stalin's July 28 order were captured by the Wehrmacht, his laments about lost economic resources did wonders for German morale. "The Russians have lost provinces with 70 million and 45 million hectares of grain!" wrote one officer gleefully to his wife on August 7, 1942. "And soon [they] will lose one petroleum producing area in the Caucasus after another. First Maikop, then Grozny, then the great Baku!"

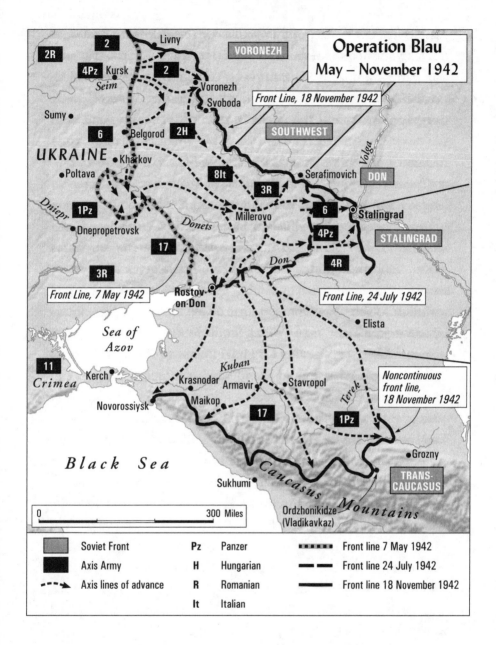

Operation Blau
May – November 1942

than were the Russians in Eastern Europe. Through years of practice, German officers and men had mastered the art of mobile warfare. Their opponents were clambering up an imposing learning curve.

But the Germans were not invincible, nor were their enemies in arms without resources to draw on. The critical X factor on the eastern front in 1942 was the relative order of battle, and this was not static. Whereas, in the first seven or eight months of 1942, the Luftwaffe dominated Soviet airspace and German armored divisions enjoyed parity at worst and often considerable local superiority over the Red Army's depleted tank park, once lend-lease supplies began arriving at the front in appreciable quantities, the material equation began to shift in Stalin's favor.

The date of June 30, 1942, marking the end of the first Soviet lend-lease protocol period, was a significant milestone. To meet protocol targets, Roosevelt had ordered his men to go all out over the final weeks. He had leaned on Churchill to strip Britain's Middle Eastern command of its tanks, sending them directly to Russia via the Persian Gulf, with American ones later shipped across the Atlantic to replace them. From March 1942 on, virtually all gasoline-powered light tanks in the US and British supply pipeline were requisitioned for Stalin, helping to meet the protocol demand for 2,250 tanks. Lend-lease officials also gave Stalin priority in the shipment of trucks (36,865 delivered by June 30, 1942), jeeps (6,823), scout cars (400), and rubber floats (2,421). Foodstuffs—including grain, corn, dehydrated milk, butter, meat, and the soon-infamous canned meat product Spam (known to the Russian soldiers as *tusonka* pork)—were also sent in vast quantities: 167,995 tons by June 30, 1942. Fully 100 percent of telephone wire produced in the United States in January 1942, and 90 percent of that produced in the next few months, was requisitioned and sent to Stalin. By summer 1942, 56,445 US-manufactured field telephones and 381,431 miles of field telephone wire had arrived in the USSR. Then there were the 1,285 lend-lease warplanes delivered as of June 30, 1942, including not only Kittyhawks and Bell Airacobras but Douglas A-20 Havoc attack bombers. Most critical was the delivery of three hundred thousand tons of refined American petroleum by June 1942, of which half was refined aviation gasoline. While not all of this bounty of war matériel could be used immediately on arrival, the target date of June 30 helped ensure that it could reach the front in time to make a difference in the critical battles of late summer and autumn 1942.[23]

A snapshot of Red Army mobile and mechanized units in formation at Gorky in early July 1942, while the Germans were launching Blau, gives an idea of the role of lend-lease aid in restoring mobility to Stalin's armies. Gorky, 260 miles east of Moscow, was an important center of war production (some T-34 production was shifted there after July 1941), as well as a training ground for new mobile units. On July 1, 1942, the new 119th Tank Brigade was created in Gorky. It consisted of forty-four Canadian MK-3 Valentine tanks, fifteen Ford trucks, and four Studebakers. The 153rd Tank Brigade, formed the same day, comprised twenty-four medium American Stuart M-3 tanks and twenty-seven light Stuart M-3s, along with forty-one Dodge, seventeen Ford, and four Studebaker trucks. The 190th Red Army Tank Brigade had ninety Stuart medium M-3 and sixty-one light M-3 tanks, along with seven Ford trucks. The 194th and 196th Red Army Tank Brigades were more British, deploying eleven and forty-four British Matilda MK-2 medium tanks, respectively (the 194th also had nine MK-3 Valentines). These brigades still relied on American trucks: fifteen Dodges, ten Fords, and four Studebakers each.[24]

Showing that this was no one-off, the following week saw a similarly vigorous rollout, with a heavier tilt toward American tanks. On July 8, the 134th, 154th, and 193rd Red Army Tank Brigades were formed with twenty-one American M-3 Stuart medium tanks and thirty-two light Stuart M-3s each. While many of these Stuarts were short of spare parts (and a few still needed filters), it was clear that the M-3 Stuart, whatever Soviet propagandists later claimed, was becoming an important part of the Red Army's arsenal in mobile warfare.[25]

Lend-lease warplanes were also reinforcing the Soviet Air Force. On June 22, 1942, the Soviet State Defense Committee informed VVS commanders on the Moscow front—where the big German summer attack was still expected—that all Soviet pilots and trainers must prepare for "the arrival of American Boston-3 and B-25 bombers," which "have entered and will continue to enter into service in the Soviet air force." In July 1942, VVS commanders on the western front received directives regarding the incorporation of hundreds of British fighters, with twenty-four Hurricanes assigned to each aviation regiment. August 1942 saw the incorporation of American Kittyhawks, Mustangs, and above all Airacobras into "the 8th [Soviet] Air Army on the Stalingrad front."[26]

Even if they forgot this (or pretended not to remember) later, Soviet leaders were perfectly aware at the time of how important lend-lease imports were on the battlefield as the fighting grew more intense around Stalingrad and Grozny in summer 1942. On July 18, Stalin thanked Roosevelt for the 115 American tanks the Red Army had just received, with the caveat that he would have preferred diesels. Gasoline tanks, Stalin explained, "caught fire too easily when hit by enemy gunfire." Five days later, Roosevelt replied that American engineers were working on the problem. By August 18, Roosevelt was able to promise Stalin that "over 1000 tanks will leave the United States in August for Russia"—tanks now retrofitted to Soviet needs.[27]

While much was made by Soviet propagandists (and the Western journalists and historians who continue to cite them) about the superiority of Russian tanks such as the T-34 to comparable American and British models, in private Russian experts conceded that US and British tanks had many positive attributes. American M-3 Stuart light and medium tanks, according to a Red Army study conducted in August 1942, were found to produce a "high density of fire." The medium Stuart M-3 had "excellent visibility from the perspective of the commander," and the light M-3 was distinguished by its "superior mobility." Both light and medium Stuarts were well designed ergonomically, with "convenient crew placement," and were quieter than many Soviet models, giving them a greater chance of creeping up on the enemy. Of course, no tank is perfect, and Soviet crews complained that the medium M-3s had a "large turning radius," and that both light and medium

Stuarts had difficulty in rough terrain and when encountering "obstructions." Interestingly, this weakness was a strength of the British Valentine tank, which was tested against the T-34 in crossing wet, marshy ground and in "overcoming roadside ditches." The MK-3 Valentine proved the equal of the T-34 in handling and maneuverability in both tests.[28]

General Belyaev, the sleeper Soviet spy turned requisitioning agent, had invested so much time studying American armor that he actually grew annoyed with the negative reporting in the *Chicago Daily News* and *New York Post* by a prominent American correspondent, Leland Stowe, concerning American tanks. Stowe had been taken in by the arch-Bolshevik propagandist Ilya Ehrenburg, who fed him a steady diet of agitprop about the superiority of Soviet tank technology. Despite certain disadvantages inherent to American tanks' lighter weight and gasoline engines, which rendered them vulnerable in rough conditions, Stuart M-3s had favorable features too, Belyaev noted, including "considerable firing power," "good performance of transmission and engine assembly," "sufficient cruising range," "great mobility and good maneuverability . . . and visibility." The "armored protection of the turret and front part of the bow," Belyaev observed in a letter to an American brigadier general named John Christmas, although not as strong as that of Soviet T-34s or KVs, was "satisfactory." Belyaev concluded that "it would not be right to come to a conclusion that American made tanks are not effective in our country." Belyaev's letter to Christmas remained unpublished, which allowed Ehrenburg and Stowe to crystallize the now-ubiquitous narrative that the mighty Soviet T-34 (itself riding on an American "Christie suspension") was superior to anything American or British capitalism could produce.[29]

Still, whatever their underrated merits, American tanks were not the Red Army's most pressing need at the front. "I would like to emphasize our special interest at present time," Stalin wired the president on August 22, 1942, "in receiving from U.S. aircraft and types of armaments and also trucks, in the greatest possible quantity . . . [and by the] most expeditious delivery . . . by northern sea route." Churchill and Roosevelt promptly reopened the northern route at Stalin's request, sending off PQ 18 on September 2 with forty-four merchant vessels, accompanied by a strike force of destroyers and thirty-two torpedo-carrying aircraft. Despite this powerful escort, PQ 18 sustained heavy losses—with ten ships knocked out by Luftwaffe bombs and three sunk by German U-boats, in all losing thirteen of forty-four—but it did arrive in Murmansk between September 17 and 21, 1942.[30]

Of more lasting significance than the dangerous voyage of PQ 18 was the long-awaited opening of the Alaskan air route to Siberia (soon referred to in shorthand as ALSIB) the same week it sailed. After initially objecting to this route on grounds of its distance from the German fronts, Stalin consented in early July 1942—in the desperate days after Hitler launched Operation Blau—on the condition that no Americans would be allowed to touch down in the Soviet Far East. Roosevelt had offered to have US pilots ferry the planes as far as Lake Baikal, only for Stalin to reply, on July 1, that his own pilots would "take delivery" in Fairbanks, Alaska, instead. Just as Stalin requested, Roosevelt agreed that US pilots would fly Douglas A-20 Havoc bombers, P-40 Kittyhawks, and Douglas C-47 transport planes as far as Alaska, where Soviet pilots, after being introduced to the planes, would fly them home. The first 143 warplanes arrived in Alaska in September 1942, with another 272 flown into Fairbanks in October. Larger planes, such as the Douglas transports,* also carried cargo to the USSR, including, as a US Army Air Force manual observed, "airplane parts and accessories, books, magazines, drills, nails and bolts, newspapers, drawings and blueprints, drugs, and diplomatic mail." ALSIB was off and running.[31]

The opening of ALSIB came at a critical time for the Soviet war effort, as the VVS was now engaged in a furious struggle with the

---

*In December 1941, the Soviet high command had begun requesting Douglas C-47 transports, initially for the purpose of launching paratroopers behind German lines.

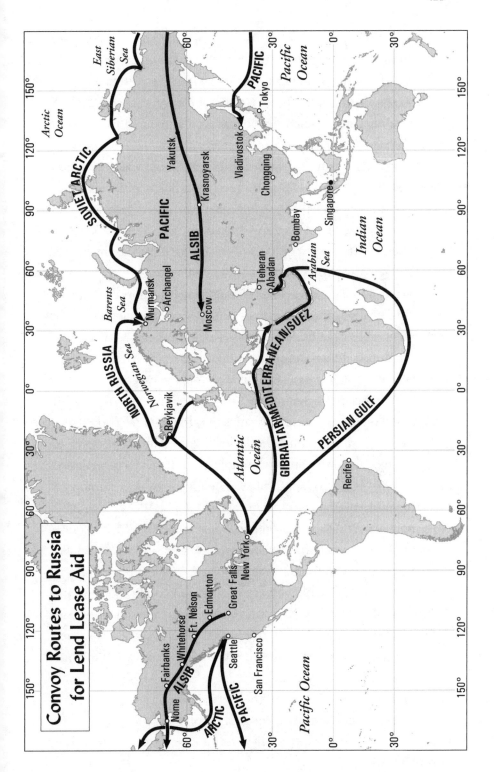

Convoy Routes to Russia for Lend Lease Aid

Luftwaffe for control of the airspace over the North Caucasus and Stalingrad. Ratcheting up the urgency of Alaskan deliveries was the British War Office's message to Stalin's ambassador in London, Ivan Maisky, on September 15 that Operation Torch—the US-British landings in French northwest Africa planned for November, which had been hashed out between Churchill and Roosevelt in July as a substitute for the second front in Europe they would be unable to open in 1942—required Churchill to pull back delivery of 154 American lend-lease fighters Britain had promised Stalin in the next Arctic convoy, replacing them with 280 trucks. Painfully, these fighters were Bell P-39 Airacobras. This was the pursuit plane, nicknamed the Kobrushka, that most Russian fighter aces now wanted to fly, owing to its efficiency in low-altitude dogfighting and "ground-strafing" enemy infantry. Learning this, Stalin exploded, cabling Ambassador Maisky on September 20 that "I consider English conduct on the question of Airacobras tremendously insolent. The English had no right to divert the cargo without our consent." In his mind, Stalin now had the right to every Kobrushka that rolled off the Bell assembly lines in Buffalo, New York.[32]

"I have to inform you," the Vozhd wrote Churchill on October 3, "that the situation in the Stalingrad area has deteriorated since the beginning of September. The Germans [have] managed to secure superiority in the air of ratio 2:1." The VVS did not have "enough fighters for the protection of our forces," Stalin continued, alluding to Churchill's diversion of 154 Kobrushkas, and, Stalin conceded, "even the bravest troops are helpless if they lack air preparation." If Airacobras were not available, he requested that Churchill ship him British Spitfires as soon as possible. In a sign of how critical a priority US and British pursuit planes now were at Stalingrad, Stalin requested that the Allies reduce the quantity of "tanks and artillery equipment" on lend-lease ships to make room for fighters. To beat off the German offensives at Stalingrad and in the North Caucasus, the Vozhd demanded eight hundred pursuit planes per month—five hundred American and three hundred British.[33]

Stalin was no less demanding with Roosevelt, although he was more polite than with Churchill. "We are willing to discard for the time being," Stalin wired the president on October 7, 1942, "all of the deliveries of tanks, artillery, munitions, pistols, etc. . . . But at the same time we are extremely in need of an increase in the delivery of pursuit planes of modern type (such as the 'Airacobra'). . . . It should be born in mind that the 'Kittyhawk' planes do not stand the fight against present German pursuits." "The experience of the war," the Vozhd concluded his plea, "has shown that the bravest armies become helpless if they are not protected from the blows from the air."[34]

Stalin was no less forthright about Soviet desperation for American foodstuffs. In order to make up for lost agricultural production owing to the German occupation of the Ukraine and southern Russia's black earth region, Stalin informed Roosevelt on October 7 that "it is essential to secure the delivery within 12 months of 2 million tons of grain (wheat) as well as such quantity as possible of fats, concentrated food and canned meat." Roosevelt complied with alacrity, having Hopkins and the Lend-Lease Administration commandeer almost the entire rolling stock of the western United States for Stalin, shipping an astonishing 112,000 tons of foodstuffs from Seattle, Portland, and San Francisco to Soviet Far Eastern ports in November 1942 alone. During the second protocol, in force through June 30, 1943, the United States delivered to Stalin's armies 997,783 tons of foodstuffs, including grains, canned and smoked meats, sausages, fats, vegetable oil and shortening, canned and dried milk, dehydrated cheese, eggs, vegetables, fruits, salt, sugar, coffee, tea, and vitamins.[35]

Stalin did not conceal his desperate need for trucks either, informing Roosevelt in his October 7 plea that the Red Army needed monthly supplies of "8,000 to 10,000." The soon-famous Willys MB and Ford GPW all-wheel-drive off-road jeeps and Studebaker trucks, which had begun arriving in Russia in 1942, were outfitted with 76 mm Red Army guns and placed into immediate use, playing a critical role supplying mobile forces deployed beyond railheads. Jeeps, because of their maneuverability and versatility, proved immensely popular with Russian drivers—and with Wehrmacht commanders lucky enough to capture them, who found the Willys to be much better than the German equivalent, the Volkswagen-made *Kübelwagen*. In addition to the 36,865 trucks and 6,823 jeeps delivered by June 30, 1942, between 25,000 and 30,000 had arrived by mid-November 1942, when the Soviets were preparing their counteroffensive to cut off Stalingrad—a mobile flanking maneuver which, according to Soviet sources, required the use of 27,000 trucks. By this point, more than seventy thousand Studebakers, Fords, Dodges, and Willys jeeps had already arrived in Soviet ports. While not all were in active service yet, this figure dwarfed the number deployed at Stalingrad by two and a half to one. Small wonder that, as a German General Staff officer observed in a letter to his wife airmailed home from Stalingrad on December 1, 1942, "50% of the motor vehicles in the new brigades being thrown against us are American manufactured."[36]

Lend-lease tanks began to play a role on the southwestern fronts too. American M-3 Stuarts saw action in an attack by the Soviet Sixty-Sixth Army against the vaunted German Sixteenth Panzer Division north of Stalingrad in early September 1942, helping draw German panzer units in from the southern flank of Stalingrad. Several dozen British and American lend-lease tanks also contributed to an attack on September 30 near Kotluban, on the southern side of Stalingrad, generally faring less well than the Soviet T-34s (many Canadian Valentines were knocked out), but once again drawing in German armor reinforcements needed elsewhere. By December 1942, at least one armored Soviet unit at Stalingrad, the new Fifth Mechanized Corps of the Fifth Tank Army, was dominated by lend-lease tanks: 191 out of its 200.[37]

Lend-lease tanks were still more significant on the north Caucasian front. The Soviet Ninth Army, guarding Grozny and the Terek River, was given top priority in receiving tanks forwarded from Britain's Middle Eastern command via Iran, mostly British Valentines and American light and medium M-3 Stuarts. At least

15 percent of the tanks in action on this front in 1942 were of British or American origin. Data from the Soviet military archives confirms that these lend-lease tanks saw action in the North Caucasus, with the Red Army reporting battlefield losses of eighty-six light M-3 Stuarts, twenty-nine medium M-3s, and fifty-nine MK-3 Valentine tanks in November and December 1942.[38]

Both Soviet and traditional Western accounts tend to stress the importance of the T-34 at Stalingrad, a tank that was indeed produced in great numbers in 1942. Soviet factories relocated east of Moscow allegedly turned out 2,200 per month (in reality 1,043) and 26,400 in all (in reality 12,527) during this critical year. Impressive as even the less inflated numbers are, these Soviet tanks could not have been forged at all without American aluminum. Stalin admitted as much in his October 7 plea to Roosevelt, when he asked that the Americans slow down deliveries of "tanks, artillery, munitions, pistols, etc." in order to make room for "5,000 tons of aluminum" per month to replace lost Soviet annual production of 60,000 tons, more than half of the prewar capacity of 110,000 tons. Soviet shortages of other nonferrous metals critical in tank, airplane, and weapons production—including nickel, ferrochrome, and ferrosilicon—would be filled by the Americans, who were supplying Stalin with eight hundred tons a month of each of these scarce industrial inputs.[39]

Soviet losses in steel production were even steeper, from over 20 million tons forged in the last pre-Barbarossa year, 1940, to a mere 8.8 million tons in 1942. While, owing to limited shipping space, a steel deficit of this volume could never be made up via lend-lease, American shipments were still critical in 1942, because they were concentrated in specialty steels for military use—including railroad rails and accessories—at a time when Soviet engineers were desperately reinforcing the rail lines of south Russia in preparation for the great flanking maneuver outside Stalingrad.[40]

Another American arms category for which there was a desperate Soviet need at Stalingrad was TNT and other high explosives—four thousand to five thousand tons per month, according to

Stalin's demand lodged with Roosevelt on October 7, 1942. Then there was the weather-resistant vulcanized rubber compound called Vistanex, used in the separation plates in Soviet tank and airplane batteries, which Stalin's agents in Washington demanded that same week. Remarkably, Hopkins's lend-lease administrator, Stettinius, agreed to expedite deliveries to Stalin of twenty-five tons of Vistanex, the first ten by November 1942, despite US reserves of the material being "exceedingly low" at the time. These were the first of three hundred tons of Vistanex sent to Stalin during the second protocol. Hopkins also promised to share with Soviet experts a design, being developed by US Army engineers, for "a new form of impregnated fabric for protection against gas, which will stand up in low temperatures." German soldiers at Stalingrad had nothing like this.[41]

Roosevelt was happy to oblige. With impressive alacrity, he replied to Stalin's urgent plea of October 7 almost immediately after he received it, wiring the Vozhd on October 8:

> I am now trying to find additional planes for you immediately and will advise you soon. I am also trying to arrange to have some of our merchant ships transferred to your flag to increase your flow of materials in the Pacific. I have just ordered an automobile tire plant to be made available to you. We are sending very substantial reinforcements to the Persian Gulf to increase the flow of supplies over that route and are confident that this can be done. We are sending a large number of engines and other equipment as well as personnel.[42]

This was only a preliminary response, delivered before Roosevelt had been able to lean on Hopkins and Stettinius to bring the Lend-Lease Administration in line. By October 12, Roosevelt was able to report to Stalin that he had ordered the US Army Air Force to reshape its procurement priorities to meet Soviet needs at Stalingrad, increasing production of Airacobras "at the expense of other types *in order to give you more planes*." During the remainder of

October, the president promised the Vozhd, "we will ship to you 276 combat planes and everything possible is being done to expedite these deliveries." As for Stalin's other urgent requirements—for aluminum, nickel, trucks, explosives, Vistanex, and foodstuffs— Roosevelt promised to set aside another twenty merchant ships exclusively for Stalin's use in the Pacific, to step up deliveries through Iran, and to inform the Vozhd of the exact date of each shipment of American aluminum. "I have given orders," the president continued, "that no effort be spared to keep our routes fully supplied with ships and cargo in conformity with your desires." In order to front-load second-protocol targets in time to make a difference for the Soviet armies fighting in Stalingrad and the North Caucasus, Roosevelt promised Stalin, in a third urgent wire sent on October 16, to make available for immediate shipment:

> Wheat: two million short tons during the remainder
>   of the protocol year
> Trucks: 8000 to 10000 per month
> Explosives: 4000 short tons in November
>   And 5000 tons per month thereafter
> Meat: 15000 tons per month
> Canned meat: 10000 tons per month;
> Lard: 12000 tons per month
> Soap stock: 5000 tons per month
> Vegetable oil: 10000 tons per month.[43]

It was this lend-lease aid, delivered prior to or during the battle for Stalingrad, that restored mobility and morale to Stalin's armies when they most needed it. While it was the brutal close-order fighting in the streets, factories, and rubble of Stalingrad that captured the world's attention, along with the heroism of snipers like the legendary proletarian shepherd Vasily Zaitsev,* what decided

---

* Zaitsev has now been immortalized in film, played by Jude Law in *Enemy at the Gates* (2001). Some of the now-familiar legend, like Zaitsev's

the outcome of the battle was the lend-lease-lubricated ramp-up in Red Army armor and mobility, which made possible the gigantic Soviet flanking operation, Uranus, launched on November 19, 1942. It was not that the heroic struggle inside the city did not matter—it did. But in strategic terms, the intensifying urban fighting between September and November was a Soviet feint, designed to lure the Germans in with the prospect of capturing "Stalin's city," even while the decisive blow, a double envelopment deep in the city's rear designed to cut off German Sixth Army, was prepared elsewhere. It was this ambitious plan, conceived by Zhukov, that Stalin had approved on September 13, 1942.[44]

Zhukov's plan, buttressed by great discipline in guarding against leaks, worked brilliantly. Letters home from German officers confirm that, although local Romanian commanders on the upper Don noticed a Soviet buildup across the river beginning in late October, the staff of German Sixth Army commander General Paulus had no real idea what was in store. It may have helped Zhukov that there was so much chatter about Soviet troop movements prior to the intended launch date of November 9. A final ten-day postponement—owing to a shortage of lend-lease trucks and fuel, supplies that were still en route to the front—likely led the Germans to put down their guard.

When the attack was launched on November 19, surprise was almost total. General N. F. Vatutin's southwestern army group, spearheaded by the Fifth Tank Army, smashed through the weakly held Romanian sector and raced south along a line some one hundred miles west of Stalingrad. Next day, General Andrei Yeremenko's Stalingrad army group attacked from the southern flank, pushing north and west until his motorized divisions (the Fourth Mechanized Corps) met up with Vatutin's on the middle

---

duel with the head of the German sniper school, is myth. Zaitsev, who notched 149 kills, was not even the most prolific Soviet marksman— others topped 200. Still, his influence was not fictional either. Zaitsev trained dozens of snipers in Stalingrad, and he was clearly an inspiration to Russians and other Soviet patriots.

Don, near Kalach, on November 24. Just five days into Operation Uranus, Zhukov had trapped Paulus's Sixth Army in a giant *kotel* (pocket). Hitler ordered Paulus to stand his ground, adopt a "hedgehog defense" supplied from the air, and make no attempt to break out of the pocket. While it took another two months of increasingly bitter fighting in the ruins of Stalingrad, in reality the fate of the German Sixth Army was sealed.[45]

Generals K. K. Rokossovsky and Vatutin and their men deserve great credit for mounting this bold double envelopment entrapping Paulus's Sixth Army. Stalin, too, did his part by sticking patiently with Zhukov's plan, despite the obvious violation of his no-retreat order of July 28 inherent in retreating into Stalingrad. Uranus was a triumph of strategic thinking, patience, and thorough execution, well worthy of the praise lavished upon Zhukov for giving the Germans a taste of their own medicine and thereby turning the tide of the war on the eastern front.

It remains no less true that mounting a mobile-flanking operation as ambitious as Uranus would not have been possible without lend-lease supplies—from seventy thousand trucks and jeeps to half a million tons of American aviation and motor fuel and lubricants—all of which was so crucial that shortages of these very items forced Zhukov to postpone his launch by ten days. Nor should we underestimate the role played by lend-lease tanks, despite Stalin's protestations that they were less important than pursuit planes. To date, according to a top-secret Soviet intelligence report on the "income and distribution of foreign tanks" on November 15, 1942—four days before Uranus was launched—the Red Army had incorporated into its mobile divisions 1,063 Canadian MK-3 light-medium Valentine tanks, 715 British MK-2 medium Matildas, 681 American Stuart light M-3 tanks, 676 American Stuart medium M-3s, 90 American Sherman M2A1 tanks, 41 American Sherman M-2s, 84 new Churchill tanks, 20 older MK-7s, and fully 1,099 Bren Gun Carriers (the mobile workhorse of the British Army), adding up to 4,469 tanks and gun carriers delivered to Stalin. On the eve of the most critical battle in Soviet military history, there were 446 more US and British tanks and 93 Bren Gun Carriers sitting in Soviet ports awaiting delivery to the front, including Sherman M4A2 medium tanks with diesel engines, designed exclusively for the Red Army. And none of these totals included the thousands of tanks shipped to Russia but lost to enemy action on the perilous Arctic route.[46]

This was not to reckon with the US-British contribution that helped the VVS contest the skies with the Luftwaffe—from Hurricanes, Kittyhawks, and Kobrushkas to Douglas A-20 Havoc (Boston) and B-25 bombers and transports. This lend-lease bounty of 1,663 warplanes, delivered to Stalin by the time Uranus was launched, was larger than the entire number of warplanes the VVS deployed at Stalingrad (1,115).[47]

That lend-lease warplanes saw action in dogfights with the Luftwaffe is amply confirmed in the VVS files at the Soviet military archive in Podolsk, now available to researchers. In June 1942, the VVS "lost in action at the front" thirty-six Hurricanes (of which fourteen fell on the southwestern fronts over Stalingrad and the North Caucasus), eleven Tomahawks, four Airacobras, and three Boston 3s. In July, lend-lease fighter losses rose to fifty-seven Hurricanes (thirteen on the southwestern front), twelve Airacobras, four Tomahawks, and thirty-three Boston bombers. By September 1942, the influx of American P-40 Kittyhawks and P-39 Airacobras began to show, with losses of these new American fighters edging out Hurricanes for the first time (thirty-six, compared to twenty-three). It was clear the Kittyhawks and Airacobras were being rushed to the highest priority areas too, as losses of these American fighters in September were heaviest on the Stalingrad front (nine and five, respectively). Part of the reason is that, in fall 1942, these planes were arriving via Iran instead of Murmansk and Archangel—hence closer to the Don and Caucasus fronts. By November 1942, when Uranus was launched, Baku was the prime training area for Soviet pilots learning to fly US and British planes. Soviet ace Stepan Novichkov of the 436th Aviation Regiment—who flew British Hurricanes from May until October 1942 and Airacobras thereafter—achieved six kills over the skies of Stalingrad in his Hurricane and thirteen more in his Kobrushka. Pilots like him were the living embodiment of the lend-lease spirit.[48]

Nor should we forget the impact on Stalingrad of the British offensive launched at El-Alamein in western Egypt in late October 1942, or the US-British Operation Torch landings carried out in Vichy France–controlled Morocco and Algeria between November 8 and 16. These dual blows forced Göring to withdraw four hundred Luftwaffe fighters from the Soviet fronts to the Mediterranean and North African theater just days before the launch of Operation Uranus. The brief Allied amphibious raid on the northern French Channel port of Dieppe in August 1942, likewise, had spooked Hitler enough that he pulled his most elite striking force, the Leibstandarte armored SS division, from the eastern front. There is no way of knowing for sure whether this armored Wehrmacht unit, or the four hundred Luftwaffe fighters, would have made a difference to Paulus at Stalingrad, but their redeployment west gave the lie to Stalin's complaint that his allies were not engaging the Germans directly and helping the Red Army. This Allied help—combined with the cascading influx of lend-lease supplies, particularly fuel, trucks, jeeps, and pursuit planes—was critical to the success of Operation Uranus.[49]

Of course, it was the bravery of Soviet aces like Stepan Novichkov, and the grit and determination of the largely nameless Red Army tank drivers, gunners, and infantry grunts fighting in the streets, that ultimately won the battle. It is hard to imagine them being able to do so, however, without the supplies sent by their gallant and unappreciated allies. Whatever the exact proportion of the share, and however impolite it may seem to some Russians to mention it, it is an imperishable historical fact that Anglo-American capitalism helped win the battle of Stalingrad.

An MK-3 Valentine tank produced in England for Stalin, presented to Soviet ambassador Ivan Maisky before being shipped to the USSR, c. 1942 (Library of Congress.)

The ruins of Stalingrad after the Red Army recaptured the city from the Germans, February 2, 1943. Visible, on left, is a destroyed apartment building; on right, ruins of what had been the Railwaymen's House. (RIA Novosti archive, image #602161 / Zelma / CC-BY-SA 3.0.)

Excavation of graves of murdered Polish
military officers at Katyn, April 1943
(Polish Red Cross.)

Corpses of Polish officers and officials
murdered in 1940 and later discovered at
Katyn, April 1943 (Polish Red Cross.)

American-made Stuart M-3 tanks in action during the battle of Kursk, July 1943 (Ministry of Defense of the Russian Federation, mil.ru.)

A convoy of American lend-lease trucks, covered in snow, passes through the mountains in Iran en route to the USSR, March 1943. (Library of Congress, photo id 8d29573a.)

A truck assembly plant in Iran processes trucks shipped CKD from the United States en route to the USSR, 1943. (US government.)

A US Army truck carries supplies across a sandy desert road in Iran to the USSR, March 1943. (US government.)

An American airplane mechanic puts the finishing touches on a Douglas A-20 Havoc Boston before delivery to Russia, somewhere in Iran, March 1943. (Photographed by Nick Parrino. Office of War Information Photograph.)

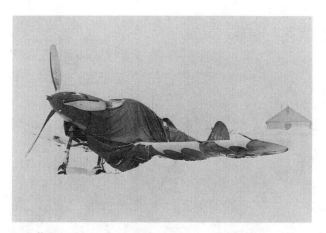

A Bell P-39 Airacobra on the runway in Nome, Alaska, during a winter storm in 1943–1944 (Library of Congress.)

The Bell P-39 Airacobra, nicknamed the Kobrushka by Stalin and Soviet pilots, fires its weapons in nighttime action. (Taken by a US Air Force pilot while on public duty, property of US government.)

An American P-39 Airacobra Kobrushka, being flown to Siberia to join the Soviet Air Force, crashes in Nome, Alaska, c. 1943–1944. (Library of Congress.)

A diesel-powered American Sherman M4A2 tank, fitted with a 75 mm M3 L/40 gun, built exclusively for the Red Army. This one was restored by the Russian government in the 1990s. (Alan Wilson of Hawkeye UK.)

Lend-lease supplies bound for Soviet Russia are off-loaded in the Persian Gulf, March 1943. (US government.)

An American Douglas A-20 Havoc Boston bomber, flown to Soviet Russia via Alaska, was discovered at an airfield north of Vladivostok, restored after the fall of the USSR, and put on display at the Air Force Museum in Moscow. (Alan Wilson of Hawkeye UK.)

Standing outside the Soviet embassy in Teheran in December 1943, from left to right: an unidentified British officer; General George Marshall, US Army chief of staff, shaking hands with Sir Archibald Clark Kerr, British ambassador to the USSR; Harry Hopkins; Stalin's interpreter; Stalin; Molotov; and General Voroshilov. (Library of Congress.)

Red Army soldiers ride into occupied Bucharest on an American lend-lease Studebaker, August 30, 1944. (Romanian Communism Online Photo Collection [Fototeca online a comunismului românesc], cota 57/1944. Accessed February 10, 2020.)

Winston Churchill shakes the hand of Josip Broz Tito at Queen Victoria's summer villa in Naples, Italy, August 1944. (Photograph number NAM 144 of the Imperial War Museums in London.)

Soldiers from Berling's Polish People's Army, occupying Warsaw after it was conquered by the Soviet Red Army, stand in front of an American lend-lease Willys jeep, regifted by Stalin to Berling, in late January 1945. (Polish government.)

Churchill, Roosevelt, and Stalin pose for an official photograph at the Yalta conference in the Crimea, February 1945. (Library of Congress.)

On board the USS *Quincy* after the Yalta conference, February 14, 1945. From left to right: John G. Winant, US ambassador to Great Britain; President Roosevelt; Secretary of State Edward R. Stettinius Jr.; and Harry Hopkins. (US Army Signal Corps Photograph. Office of War Information Collection. [2016/08/30].)

Soldiers in Berling's Polish People's Army ride American lend-lease Harley-Davidson motorcycles, April 1945. (Polish government.)

A Red Army soldier drives a lend-lease Studebaker in occupied Berlin, May 1945. (Bundesarchiv, Bild 204-018.)

The famous staged photograph of two Red Army soldiers, Meliton Kantaria and Mikhail Yegorov, raising the flag over the Reichstag, taken by Yevgeny Khaldei on May 2, 1945. It was originally published in *Ogonyok* magazine on May 13, 1945, with at least one (presumably looted) wristwatch erased from one of the Soviet soldiers' hands in the background.

Soviet marshals Georgii Zhukov and K. K. Rokossovsky in front of the Brandenburg Gate in Berlin, circa May 1945 (Library and Archives Canada.)

V.

SECOND FRONT

25

Keeping Stalin Happy
Unconditional Surrender and Katyn

THE HUMILIATING SURRENDER of the German Sixth Army at Stalingrad on February 2, 1943, was a huge propaganda triumph
for Stalin and a debacle of the first order for Hitler and German
morale. Compounded by the news from North Africa, where
the Americans and their British allies established a beachhead in
Vichy-controlled Morocco and Algeria after the Torch landings
of mid-November 1942—hard on the heels of the British rout of
Erwin Rommel's Afrikakorps at El-Alamein—Stalingrad marked
an obvious strategic milestone. The combination of Russian grit,
Soviet generalship, and Anglo-American material generosity had
ended a nearly unbroken run of German victories and stopped
Nazi expansion at the Volga. From now on, the Allies would press
in on Hitler's "Fortress Europe" from all sides.

The strategic revolution in this fourth winter of the European
war presented great opportunities to the Allied coalition. But considerable friction remained below the surface. Stalin had been
polite enough in congratulating Roosevelt and Churchill on the
success of Operation Torch, but in reality he saw North Africa as
a cheap substitute for a genuine second front in Europe. In view
of the reinforcements Hitler had stripped from the Russian front
in the wake of the Dieppe raid, Operation Torch, and El-Alamein,
this was unfair. But Stalin was not known for his generosity of
spirit. It also did not sit well with the Vozhd that his allies had
sustained relatively light casualties during Torch, owing to a controversial agreement General Dwight Eisenhower, commander of

American forces in North Africa, had struck with Admiral François Darlan, commander in chief of Vichy France's armed forces, under which Darlan ordered French troops in the theater not to resist. In exchange, Darlan would be recognized by the Allies as high commissioner of French North Africa. Stalin did not object to the Darlan deal on moral terms—in wartime, he wrote Churchill, one must be prepared to "use the devil and his grandma." But he remained unconvinced that the Britons and Americans were serious about fighting Germans. "I hope," Stalin wrote Churchill after Torch and El-Alamein on November 27, "that you change your mind with regard to your promise given in Moscow to open a second front in Western Europe in the spring of 1943."[1]

This Darlan "deal with the devil," as it was christened in the American press, undoubtedly saved American lives. But it also became a cudgel with which Roosevelt's domestic critics could beat him. This was shortly after his party had fared badly in the midterm elections of November 3, 1942, in something of a repudiation of the president's wartime leadership. (Although the Democrats retained control of Congress, they lost forty-seven seats in the House and nine in the Senate, along with three governorships.) The Darlan deal was denounced as a "sordid nullification of the principles for which the United Nations were supposed to be fighting." Other critics hinted that the deal set a dangerous precedent and that Roosevelt might soon "make one with a Goering in Germany or with a Matsuoka in Japan." Morgenthau, Roosevelt's trusted Treasury secretary, was incensed about the Darlan deal, giving the president an earful about his appeasement of "fascism."[2]

Much of this criticism was unfair. The decision to work with Darlan was really made by Eisenhower in the field, in conjunction with his British counterparts in the Mediterranean, not by the president in Washington. Churchill was fully on board, even if, in public, he was reticent about this. But the insults rankled Roosevelt, especially the implication that he was keen to cut deals with "Darlans" in Germany or Japan. As Samuel Rosenman, one of the president's aides, recalled, Roosevelt "strongly resented this criticism. . . . Indeed I do not remember his ever being more deeply affected by a political attack, especially since it came from those who usually supported him."[3]

Roosevelt's embarrassment was partially alleviated when, on December 24, 1942, a young French royalist patriot assassinated Darlan in Algiers. But the abuse the president had endured was not easily forgotten, and it contributed to his discomfiture over America's so-far dilatory contribution to the war against Nazi Germany as compared to that of the USSR. "I am very anxious to have a talk with you," the president wrote Stalin on December 2, inviting the Vozhd to meet with him and Churchill at Casablanca, Morocco's port on the North Atlantic, in January 1943—only to be put off. Roosevelt declared himself "deeply disappointed." Intuiting the president's anxieties, Stalin wrote back, downplaying "rumors about the attitude of the U[SSR] toward the use made of Darlan and of other men like him" and reassuring Roosevelt that he, personally, thought Eisenhower's policy was "correct." But the Vozhd—protesting, plausibly enough, that he could not afford to leave Russia while serious fighting continued at Stalingrad— refused to travel to Casablanca.[4]

There was just enough truth in the idea that the Americans and British were fighting Nazi Germany only at the margins, rather than head-on like the Russians, to get on Roosevelt's nerves. Did Stalin think he was soft? In the president's correspondence with Stalin from this period, there is a plaintive quality, as he tries to convince the Vozhd that he really does want to fight the Germans. The "menace of Japan," Roosevelt took pains to reassure Stalin, "can be most effectively met by destroying the Nazis first." The president offered repeatedly, in November and December 1942, to send US-British air units to the USSR via Iran (Operation Velvet) to engage the Luftwaffe in the skies over the North Caucasus and Stalingrad—a contribution of as many as twenty-two thousand Allied personnel to the Soviet theater. But Stalin rejected this idea no less firmly than he had Roosevelt's earlier offer for American pilots to fly warplanes into Siberia: he wanted the planes, but not foreign pilots, not on Soviet soil. Perhaps American and British pilots, Roosevelt asked on December 17, could operate in the Stalingrad theater "under overall Russian command"? Still the answer was no.[5]

Stalin's brusque dismissal of the president's pleas and proposals shows that the Vozhd did not much care what Roosevelt thought of him personally. But the reverse was far from true. Projecting his own emotional complexes onto the Soviet dictator, Roosevelt surmised, in a meeting with his Joint Chiefs of Staff (JCS) on January 7, 1943, that Stalin "probably felt out of the picture as far as Great Britain and the United States were concerned" and "that he has a feeling of loneliness." The idea that Stalin did not place a high priority on meeting him did not occur to Roosevelt.[6]

Nowhere was the imbalance of this relationship more obvious than in the question of Japan. Over and over in 1942, Roosevelt had offered to send US Army Air Force squadrons to the Soviet Far East to help defend the Russian position there and—he implied more delicately—to engage the Japanese if and when Moscow joined the war against Tokyo. Loyal to a fault to his neutrality pact of April 1941 and loath to risk inciting armed hostilities with Japan, Stalin coldly rejected every one of these proposals, along with Roosevelt's request that American pilots fly lend-lease warplanes to Siberia, even just to train VVS pilots in their use. So little did Stalin care for Roosevelt's sensitivities that, to reassure the Japanese, the Vozhd had all five US crew members of a B-25 bomber that had participated in the famous Doolittle Raid over Tokyo on April 18, 1942, arrested and interned for an entire year. (Running low on fuel and unable to reach China, the plane had crash-landed on Soviet soil outside Vladivostok.) Several of the American prisoners, deprived of vitamins by Soviet camp guards, contracted scurvy and pellagra.* Far from being released—it was Stalin's

---

* In order not to offend Stalin, this entire story, despite being rich with drama, was left out of *Thirty Seconds over Tokyo*, the 1944 Hollywood film made to glorify the Doolittle Raid.

position that, having violated Soviet territory, the American airmen were prisoners of war—in April 1943 the suffering American prisoners escaped confinement and bribed their way across the Soviet border into Iran.[7]

Scratching this painful Japanese itch one more time, Roosevelt pleaded with Stalin, in a message sent on New Year's Eve 1942–1943, to allow twenty American officers to fly "from Alaska along the ferry route into Siberia, thence under Russian direction to the headquarters of the Soviet armies in the Far East," to discuss the possibility of "combined Russo-American operations in the Far Eastern theater." As a sweetener, the Americans would supply one hundred heavy bombers. In his reply on January 5, 1943, Stalin rejected this proposal even more bluntly than usual, objecting both to the sending of American officers—as a violation of his neutrality pact with Japan—and to the dispatch of heavy bombers to the Soviet Far East. "We do not need warplanes in the Far East," the Vozhd lectured Roosevelt, "where we are not at war, but on the front where the cruel war with the Germans is being fought, that is, on the Soviet-German front." Moreover, even for that front, Stalin insisted for what must have seemed like the hundredth time, he wanted the Americans to send him "planes but not pilots." No matter how hard Roosevelt tried, he could not make Stalin happy.[8]

It is important to grasp the pressure Roosevelt felt himself to be under prior to the Casablanca summit in January 1943. The stench of the Darlan deal had not dissipated, nor had the aspersions on Roosevelt's honor. Oddly enough, Stalin had defended Roosevelt on the Darlan matter more vigorously than some of the president's own people had done—and yet the Vozhd had needled him every other way over the past two months about his lack of commitment to his own stated doctrine of "Germany first." Since Stalin was not coming to Casablanca, Roosevelt would have no chance to charm the Soviet dictator, as he complained to Churchill after the conference started without the Vozhd. Trying to reassure the president, Churchill told him that all Stalin would have asked him, if he had come, was "How many Germans did you kill in

1942? And how many do you intend to kill in 1943?" How, then, could Roosevelt convince Stalin that he was serious about killing Germans, while also putting domestic critics of the Darlan deal in their place?[9]

The answer was unconditional surrender. On January 7, 1943, Roosevelt outlined his ideas about the "postwar disarmament of the Axis" to his military advisers and informed them that he "was going to speak to Mr. Churchill about the advisability of informing Mr. Stalin that the United Nations were to continue on until they reach Berlin, and that their only terms would be unconditional surrender." Significantly, Roosevelt proposed at this January 7 meeting that General George Marshall, the army chief of staff, travel to Moscow to inform Stalin personally about unconditional surrender, in order to give "impetus to the Russian morale."[10]

When Roosevelt wired Moscow on January 8 to propose Marshall's visit—without mentioning unconditional surrender, which was meant to be a kind of diplomatic gift Marshall would bear—Stalin responded coldly. The point of Marshall's visit, the Vozhd replied, "is not quite clear to me," although he might approve it if the "purpose and aims" of Marshall's mission "were explained to me." To do that, of course, would ruin the surprise.[11]

With Marshall unable to deliver Roosevelt's message in person, the best way to get Stalin's attention was through blaring newspaper headlines. And so the president unveiled his signature doctrine at a raucous press conference in Casablanca on January 24, 1943, declaring that "peace can come to the world only by the total elimination of German and Japanese war power," which required "the unconditional surrender by Germany, Italy, and Japan." To make sure his message was loud enough to reach Stalin's ears, Roosevelt added that Casablanca should be known henceforth as the "unconditional surrender meeting." Although taken aback, Churchill was game enough to chime in that Britain, too, would pursue victory until the Allies had obtained "the unconditional surrender of the criminal forces who have plunged the world into storm and ruin."[12]

Roosevelt's unconditional surrender doctrine did not arrive out of nowhere, of course. Like Churchill—and like the Frenchmen who had felt betrayed by US-British appeasers in the 1930s—the president believed that the Entente powers had let Germany off too easily in 1918, thus midwifing another terrible war that could have been avoided. Roosevelt's view that the Versailles Treaty had been too soft on Germany was shared by few of his countrymen, however. Outside of a few pockets of elite opinion on the East Coast, most Americans had come to see Versailles as an unjust peace, marked by British and French imperial greed. A Gallup poll taken in 1937 found that 70 percent of Americans thought US intervention in World War I had been a mistake. In propagating his unconditional surrender doctrine in January 1943, Roosevelt was thus doing what he had done with Russian lend-lease in 1941: deciding a hugely consequential US foreign policy question almost entirely on his own, with no congressional input or public discussion, on the basis of views far out of the American mainstream. Roosevelt's unspoken motivation in propagating this doctrine when he did—based on the evidence of the Joint Chiefs meeting of January 7 and his proposal to send Marshall to Moscow to inform Stalin—was to reassure the Soviet dictator that the United States would not go easy on the Germans at a time when the Russians were doing almost all of the fighting (against Germany, that is; certainly not against Japan). As Roosevelt himself later confessed, he unveiled unconditional surrender when he did as a "political and psychological substitute for a second front." That these two history-altering decisions by Roosevelt both aimed to please Stalin and serve the needs of his armies may only have been a coincidence.[13]

Far from pleasing its intended audience, however, Roosevelt's pledge of an unconditional surrender, of war to the death, fell flat with Stalin, who saw it as yet another irrelevant distraction from the urgent business of opening a second front in Europe. All the Vozhd said, by way of response after Casablanca, was that he would be "very obliged" to receive "information on the concrete operations planned in respect [to a second front] and on the scheduled times of their realization." Like the president's premature promise of a second front back in May 1942, unconditional surrender was a futile gesture to please Stalin. It served no American, or British, strategic interest. Churchill was nearly as annoyed as Stalin after Roosevelt blindsided him at Casablanca. "The Prime Minister was dumbfounded," a British official told Secretary of State Cordell Hull after the January 24 press conference. Nor did Churchill, despite assenting publicly to unconditional surrender, necessarily agree that it was in Britain's interest to fight Germany, Japan, and Italy to the bitter end, which would inevitably bankrupt the British Empire and leave much of Europe and Asia in ruins.[14]

Whatever Roosevelt wanted to believe about the grand alliance against Hitler, the fact was that American interests and war aims were not necessarily aligned with British ones and bore even less resemblance to Soviet ones. There was, for example, the ticking diplomatic time bomb of Stalin's territorial conquests from the Molotov-Ribbentrop era. Soviet officials had repeatedly demanded that the USSR's "1941 frontiers" be recognized in any postwar settlement, a demand that sat uneasily with the denunciation of "territorial gains" in the Atlantic Charter. While the fact that Romania and Finland had jointly invaded the USSR alongside Germany in 1941 gave plausible cause for Soviet border adjustments vis-à-vis those countries, for the Western Allies to endorse Stalin's annihilation of the Baltic countries in 1940 was entirely problematic. And what about the Soviet carve up of Poland in 1939—the country for which Britain had gone to war in the first place? Thus far, there had seemed no need for formal agreement on such matters, but they could not be put off forever, as Churchill warned Roosevelt on February 2, 1943 (signing off again as "former naval person" to ensure confidentiality). In a bilateral treaty signed by Anthony Eden and Molotov on the latter's visit to London in May 1942, the prime minister noted, the USSR had "renounce[d] all idea of territorial gains," but Stalin and his diplomats "no doubt interpret this as giving them the right to claim, subject to their agreement with Poland, their frontier of June 1941 before they were attacked by Germany."[15]

Whatever the United States and Britain chose to do about Stalin's Baltic conquests, Poland was the issue that could blow up the entire wartime alliance. As early as May 1942, when Molotov stopped over in London for talks en route to Washington, the Polish question had almost ruined his visit. While Churchill had agreed to concede Soviet claims in the Baltic region if Stalin would allow the right of emigration for the Baltic peoples—an interesting demand that showed Churchill had no illusions about the benevolence of the Soviet dictatorship he was signing off on—the prime minister had not budged on Poland. Molotov was so flummoxed by Churchill's stand that he wired Stalin that it would be "pointless to return to Britain after my visit to the USA, because I see no prospect for improvement" (that is, for Britain to endorse Stalin's Polish gains from 1939).[16]

Tensions over the Polish question were thus already running high when, in early 1943, the first fragmentary evidence of Stalin's mass murder of Polish officers and elites at Katyn was uncovered. In late February 1943, a group of Soviet prisoners of war who worked for Colonel Friedrich Ahrens of Signal Regiment 537 discovered bones in a forest not far from Smolensk, unearthed by a wolf. Wiring Army Group Center command, Ahrens requested that its forensic expert, Dr. Gerhard Buhtz, be sent in to investigate. But the ground had refrozen before Buhtz arrived, which forced him to wait until the end of March to investigate more thoroughly.[17]

The grisly site was worth the wait. By early April 1943, Buhtz and his workers had uncovered eleven mass graves. The largest pit contained twelve layers of neatly stacked corpses, each layer containing some 250 bodies. This ghastly grave thus contained nearly three thousand corpses. So far, only a hundred or so identities had been confirmed, but markings clearly established the victims as Polish Army officers. What locals had suspected, and the Polish government-in-exile in London had feared, was now confirmed: the thousands of Polish Army officers and officials missing since fall 1939 had been executed. Since the terrible war winter of 1939–1940, Poland's exile government, along with Poland's still-extant foreign consulates in the United States and elsewhere, had been fielding queries from relatives of these missing officers and officials about their whereabouts. In March 1942, after Barbarossa had turned Poland and Soviet Russia into allies of sorts, both General Wladyslaw Sikorski, premier of the London exile government, and General Wladyslaw Anders, commander of the Polish divisions made up of former war prisoners on Soviet soil, had requested information about the fate of 8,700 Polish officers "previously imprisoned in the camps of Starobel'sk, Kozelsk and Ostashkov," among 15,000 missing officers in total. Stalin, Molotov, and Beria, despite knowing perfectly well what had been done to the missing Polish officers, did not deign to reply. Now many of the missing Poles had been found by the Germans—in a mass grave.[18]

Sensing a brilliant coup, Hitler's propaganda chief, Goebbels, invited Polish leaders to the gravesite to verify the discovery. On April 13, 1943, Radio Berlin announced its bombshell: the Germans had discovered mass graves containing the bodies of "thousands of officers of the former Polish army, interned in the U.S.S.R. in 1939 and bestially murdered by the Bolsheviks" during the Soviet occupation in 1940. Two days later, Radio Moscow issued a rebuttal, claiming that the Polish officers had been murdered by "German-Fascist hangmen in the summer of 1941." At 4:30 p.m. on April 17, representatives of the Polish exile government in London filed a request in Geneva for an investigation by the International Red Cross, only to discover that the Germans had just filed a similar motion. Red Cross executives, not wishing to appear partial, agreed only on the condition that all three interested parties (Germany, Poland, and the Soviet Union) approved. Tellingly, Moscow denounced requests for a Red Cross investigation as "villainous tricks." To any impartial observer, this suggested strongly that, however horrendous the war crimes committed so far by the Germans might have been, in this case it was Stalin who was guilty.[19]

For Stalin's Western allies to conclude this, however, would be awkward. To entertain the possibility that Stalin was guilty of the Katyn Massacre would remind everyone that he had been Hitler's partner in invading Poland and call into question the purpose of the war of 1939—a war ostensibly launched by Britain and France to liberate Poland from foreign subjugation. It would make a mockery of the Atlantic Charter and every speech Roosevelt and Churchill had given about the values they were fighting for. Moreover, it might raise awkward questions about the decisions Roosevelt and Churchill had made to lavish Stalin with lend-lease aid and arms—questions their domestic critics had sensibly raised back in 1941, only to be silenced.

To make sure no such questions were asked, Stalin went on the offensive immediately, smearing Sikorski and the Polish exile government, along with the International Red Cross, as "Hitlerite lackeys" and (in a brutal headline in *Pravda* on April 19, 1943) "the helpmates of Cannibal Hitler." "The fact that this campaign hostile to the Union of Soviet Socialist Republics," Stalin wrote to Churchill and Roosevelt on April 21,

> broke out simultaneously in the German and Polish press, and is being conducted in the same direction, cannot leave any doubt that between the enemy of the Allies—Hitler—and the Government of General Sikorski there exist contact and understanding with regard to this hostile campaign. At a time when the peoples of the Soviet Union are shedding their blood in the most difficult struggle against Hitler[ian] Germany . . . the Government of General Sikorski delivers a treacherous blow to the Soviet Union to serve the cause of Hitler's tyranny.[20]

In retaliation for Sikorski demanding an impartial Red Cross investigation of the mass murder he and Beria had perpetrated, Stalin declared that he was breaking off all relations with the Polish exile government in London. Adding to its unpleasant effect, Stalin's poison-pill letter was hand delivered to Churchill at his country house, Chartwell, where the overworked prime minister was enjoying a rare day of rest on Good Friday.[21]

It was a moment of truth for Churchill and Roosevelt. Would these signatories of the Atlantic Charter swallow Stalin's slanders against the International Red Cross and the Polish government, on whose behalf the war had been fought in the first place?

The answer was yes. Churchill, who replied first, reassured Stalin on April 24 that Britain would "oppose vigorously any 'investigation' by the International Red Cross or any other body in any territory under German authority," and promised to send his foreign minister to meet with Sikorski and "press him as strongly as possible to withdraw all countenance from any investigation under Nazi auspices." In a follow-up telegram sent on April 25, Churchill did remind Stalin, delicately, that Sikorski had "several times raised this question of the missing officers with the Soviet government, and once with you personally," suggesting that he suspected Stalin knew more than he was letting on. But Churchill then forfeited any possible leverage on the matter when he promised Stalin that he would lean on Sikorski to "restrain Polish press from polemics."[22]

Roosevelt, in his reply to Stalin, declared that Sikorski had "made a mistake" in asking for a Red Cross investigation, and that he was confident Churchill would find a way to set the London Poles straight, so they would "act in the future with more common sense." Roosevelt did express hope that Stalin would order a mere "suspension of conversations with the Polish Government-in-Exile rather than a complete severance of relations," but this was only a suggestion. The president even promised Stalin that he would try to "help [him] in any way" with his Polish problem—for example, by "looking after any Poles which you may desire to send out of the Soviet Union." Stalin politely declined the president's bizarre offer to cleanse the USSR of unwanted Poles, assuring Roosevelt, with a wink, that he viewed any and all Poles residing on Soviet soil as his close personal "friends and comrades," of whom there was no "question of their being deported from the Soviet Union."[23]

Encouraged by the obsequious response from his allies, the Vozhd broke off relations with Sikorski's government. In a letter to Sikorski's liaison diplomat in Moscow on April 25, nearly as brutal as the ultimatum he had served the Polish ambassador prior to the Soviet invasion in September 1939, Molotov faulted Sikorski for "fail[ing] to offer a rebuff to the vile fascist calumny" that the Soviet government had murdered the Polish officers. "The Soviet government are aware," Molotov continued, "that this hostile campaign against the Soviet Union has been undertaken by the Polish government in order to exert pressure . . . for the purpose of wresting from them territorial concessions at the expense of the interests of Soviet Ukraine, Soviet Belorussia and Soviet Lithuania." In this way, Stalin and Molotov misdirected their own guilt by slander, and ascribed to the Polish exile government the very imperialistic motives they had used to dismember Poland. Here was Soviet diplomatic cynicism raised to an art form.[24]

Far from objecting to this bullying, Stalin's Western allies fell quickly into line. In his telegram to Stalin on April 25, Churchill reassured the Soviet dictator that he was "examining the possibility of silencing those Polish papers in this country which attack the Soviet government." As early as April 23, the head of the US Office of War Information, Elmer Davis, based on no evidence whatsoever, broadcast a report about Katyn endorsing Stalin's claim that the mass graves represented a Nazi and not a Soviet crime—a position that would remain the official line of the US government until 1951. As Churchill's ambassador to Sikorski's government, career diplomat Sir Owen O'Malley, wrote to Foreign Secretary Anthony Eden in May 1943 after investigating the Katyn matter, in order to maintain "cordial relations with the Soviet government" Americans and Britons had been

> obliged to appear to distort the normal and healthy operation of our intellectual and moral judgments . . . [and] to restrain the Poles from putting their case clearly before the public, to discourage an attempt by the public and the press to probe the ugly story

to the bottom. In general we have been obliged to deflect attention from possibilities which in the ordinary affairs of life would
cry to high heaven for elucidation. . . . We have in fact perforce
used the good name of England like the murderers used the little
conifers to cover up a massacre.[25]

In supporting the Soviet line on Katyn and suppressing further
investigation or discussion, Churchill and Roosevelt had adopted
an attitude of willful blindness toward Stalin's crimes.* Of course,
neither statesman had distinguished himself, either, in responding proactively to news of Hitler's greatest crime: the ongoing
mass murder of European Jewry, which had begun on the eastern front in 1941 and then picked up terrible momentum with the
construction of death camps in German-occupied Poland in 1942.
To this day, controversy rages about what might have been done
to slow down the Holocaust, whether via Allied bombing runs
on the train lines running to the death camps of Belzec, Sobibor,
Treblinka, and Auschwitz or, in one gruesome what-if scenario,
by aerial bombing of the camps themselves—the idea being that
even death by friendly fire was preferable to the terrible fate that
awaited Jews, Roma, and others gassed by the Germans.[26]

In fairness to Roosevelt and Churchill, there were no easy answers to the horrors engulfing the bloodlands of Eastern Europe by
1943. Although rumors had begun to seep out of occupied Europe
by late 1942, the reality was that even the best-informed leaders
knew far less at the time than we know today about the Nazi death
camps, and even had more been known, there was no surefire,
low-risk way of putting them out of commission. In the war so far,
no belligerent's bombing raids had been especially precise. Even if

---

* Churchill suspected the truth after reading O'Malley's report. He even
told Sikorski that he thought "the German revelations are probably
true." But in public, he kept his mouth shut. When Harold Nicolson
later asked Churchill about Katyn, the prime minister "grin[ned] grimly"
and remarked under his breath, "The less said about that the better."

Allied bombers had succeeded in damaging the rail lines running
to Treblinka or Auschwitz, in view of the horrifying priority Hitler
placed on the death camps, German sappers would surely have
just fixed them, and German anti-aircraft gunners taken countermeasures against future raids. For us to judge statesmen today for
failing to mitigate the Holocaust, at a time when they were responding to myriad operational and strategic problems, is redolent
of hindsight. The only certain way they could have helped was to
bring Hitler's evil regime to an end, a goal trumpeted to the heav-
ens by Roosevelt's unconditional surrender doctrine.

By failing to distance themselves from the brutal methods of
their accidental Soviet ally exposed in the Katyn Massacre story,
however, Roosevelt and Churchill missed a genuine chance in
1943 to redefine the coalition's still-nebulous war aims in a more
civilized direction. Stalin, after all, had helped Hitler plunge Europe into war in 1939 and invaded six neighboring countries
while allied to Nazi Germany. In destroying Europe alongside
Hitler, Stalin had also, it now seemed clear, conducted a premed-
itated massacre of thousands of Polish war prisoners, alongside
the millions of deportations, thefts, and crimes that had accompanied the Soviet conquests. Despite receiving—in the months
after Barbarossa had turned him from Hitler's partner in crime
into an ally—vast stores of American and British war matériel,
Stalin was still refusing to cooperate on anything of substance,
such as humoring Roosevelt's many requests for help in the war
against Japan. At the least, Roosevelt and Churchill could have
responded to Stalin's bullying over Katyn by placing conditions
on future military aid, or demanding that Stalin finally join the
war against Japan, or insisting, at a bare minimum, that he cease
arresting American pilots who landed on Soviet territory and
treating them as prisoners (the Doolittle airmen were the first of
hundreds so treated). Any or all of these conditions could also
have been insisted on in exchange for the British and Americans
opening a second front in Europe. Instead, it was business as usual
in this strange alliance between the liberal Western powers and

the murderous Communist dictatorship with whom they happened to share one enemy, but not two. By endorsing Stalin's line on Katyn and demanding nothing in return, Roosevelt and Churchill missed a golden opportunity to seize control of the war and shape the postwar peace.[27]

They may even have missed a chance to end the European war in 1943, saving millions of lives—beginning with the Jews already or soon to be sent to Nazi death camps—and Europe's cities from burning. Unconditional surrender gave German soldiers white-hot motivation to fight harder, as American officers grumbled. Major General Ira C. Eaker, commander of the US Eighth Air Force, recalled, "Everybody I knew at the time when they heard [of unconditional surrender] said: 'How stupid can you be?' All the soldiers and airmen who were fighting this war wanted the Germans to quit tomorrow." General Albert Wedemeyer, who accompanied General Marshall to Casablanca, informed Marshall that "my 'off the cuff' reaction to unconditional surrender [is] that we, the Allies, would be playing right into the hands of Hitler and his henchmen. We would be compelling the German People to remain with Hitler supporting him and go right down with him to the very end." Wedemeyer, who had served as liaison officer in Germany before the war, told Marshall that "there were many people in Germany—more than we were permitted to realize because of anti-German as distinct from anti-Nazi propaganda—who wanted to get rid of Hitler. Our demand for unconditional surrender would weld all of the Germans together."[28]

Just as Wedemeyer's dissent suggested, Roosevelt's unconditional surrender doctrine cut the legs off a burgeoning anti-Hitler conspiracy, which nearly succeeded in assassinating the Führer in March 1943, after Hitler visited the eastern front's Army Group Center headquarters near Smolensk to discuss the upcoming German summer offensive against the Red Army. A bomb was smuggled onto Hitler's plane, scheduled to detonate after the Führer boarded for the return flight. Five coup d'état squadrons of 220 men each—organized by high-ranking eastern front commanders led by Field Marshal Günther von Kluge and the chief of staff of Army Group Center, General Henning von Tresckow—had been ordered to surround the airfield, in case Hitler's SS bodyguards sniffed out the plot. Meanwhile, Wilhelm Canaris, head of the German Abwehr (intelligence services), had recruited police commanders in Berlin and about a half dozen ranking army officers who were tasked with ordering the troops under their command to neutralize local SS garrisons and seize strongpoints in the capital once the "flash" signal, confirming Hitler's assassination, was received from Smolensk.[29]

President Roosevelt, of course, was not privy to the details of this Hitler-assassination plot when he announced his new strategic doctrine to the world. Nor did unconditional surrender factor into its failure, which was caused by prosaic physical problems. Although Hitler boarded the aircraft with a bomb on board and a coded signal was sent to Berlin indicating that "flash" was imminent, the bomb failed to go off, likely because the explosive froze from the frigid temperatures at altitude, saving Hitler's life and dooming the plot before it got off the ground.[30]

Still, the propagation of Roosevelt's unconditional surrender doctrine in late January 1943, apparently in an utterly futile effort to appease Stalin, did not help. It was a slap in the face to Canaris, the mastermind of anti-Hitler plotting in Germany. So stunned was Canaris by Roosevelt's announcement that he traveled to Istanbul at the end of January to meet with the US naval attaché in Turkey, the former governor of Pennsylvania George H. Earle, at the time Roosevelt's all-purpose emissary on Balkan affairs. If Roosevelt would recant on unconditional surrender, Canaris promised Earle, a post-Hitler German government would seek an armistice with the Western Allies to allow the Wehrmacht to concentrate on the Soviet war. Earle, hopeful of getting Roosevelt to at least reconsider unconditional surrender, if not actively pursue a separate peace with a post-Hitler Germany, duly reported Canaris's proposals to the president. Roosevelt was not interested. He ordered Earle to cut off all further contact with Canaris.[31]

Despite the firm rebuff from Roosevelt, Canaris did not give up. All through spring 1943, the head of German intelligence dispatched emissaries to neutral capitals in Spain, Switzerland, and Sweden to open talks with British and American diplomats. Both the head of the British Secret Intelligence Service (MI6), Stewart Menzies, and the head of the American Office of Strategic Services (OSS, forerunner of the CIA), Roosevelt's trusted troubleshooter Wild Bill Donovan, sent word to Canaris that they were willing to meet with him in Spain. In June, Canaris sent Count Helmuth von Moltke, scion of the legendary clan of Prussian generals, to Istanbul to meet with Donovan and Earle. Canaris and Moltke prepared a memorandum for Donovan, bearing the letterhead of the German embassy in Turkey, that included a promise that German military commanders would not resist an Allied invasion of France, and German acceptance of a US British occupation of Germany "on the largest possible scale . . . eastward to an unbroken line from Tilsit to Lemberg"—that is, including German-occupied Poland—to counter the "overpowering threat from the East." To establish his bona fides with Washington and London, Canaris leaked genuine German war plans to the OSS chief in Switzerland, future CIA director Allen Dulles. That these plans were authentic was confirmed by British and American intelligence officers who, having broken many Nazi codes, were themselves reading similar traffic.* Dulles reported breathlessly to Washington that "whole streets in Germany were being plastered at night with signs reading 'Down with Hitler and Stop This War!'"[32]

Roosevelt was having none of it. In a terse wire to Istanbul, the president ruled out any deal with "these East German Junkers." So angry was Roosevelt that he interrupted urgent business at the TRIDENT conference in Washington, DC, in the last week

---

* While this confirmed Canaris's credibility, it also harmed his negotiating position. Since the Allies were already reading German codes, they did not need his intelligence scoops.

of May 1943—the conference where US-British plans for invading Europe were hashed out—to ask Churchill whether they might issue a statement affirming that, as Roosevelt's speechwriter Robert Sherwood recalled, "the unconditional surrender formula meant that the United Nations would never negotiate an armistice with the Nazi Government, the German high command, or any other organization or group or individual in Germany." Although Churchill persuaded the president that such an addendum to unconditional surrender was superfluous, Roosevelt issued a standing presidential order to the US Office of War Information's censors "forbidding all mention of any German resistance," an order in force until the end of the war.[33]

There is no way of knowing for sure why Roosevelt felt so strongly about unconditional surrender that he ruled out negotiation with Canaris and the Abwehr, the German high command, or "any other organization or group or individual in Germany." Not even Stalin, the man Roosevelt seemed so desperate to impress with his toughness, would go anywhere near this far. In fact, in April 1943, even as the US president was loudly advertising his intransigence against negotiating with Germans and courting Stalin by endorsing his Katyn line, Soviet diplomats, including Stalin's trusted NKVD troubleshooter Boris Yartsev—the man sent to Helsinki in 1938 to demand Soviet basing rights in Finland—were discussing a separate peace with German negotiators in Stockholm. These talks were serious enough that they were resumed on June 17, just days before the Germans planned to launch their summer offensive. According to Edgar Klaus, the Abwehr agent who met Yartsev, the initiative came from the Soviet side, not the German. "I guarantee you," Klaus reported to Canaris, "that if Germany agrees to the 1939 frontiers [i.e., the Molotov-Ribbentrop borders] you can have peace in a week." Even as Roosevelt was ruling out discussions with the anti-Hitler resistance in Germany, Stalin was approaching Hitler for an armistice, however tenuously. Significantly, it was Hitler who intervened with Canaris to cut off peace talks in Sweden—not Stalin.[34]

Should we be surprised? Judging by his record faithfully delivering supplies to the Wehrmacht between 1939 and 1941, and his
refusal to humor even the mildest request from Washington or
London regarding help against Japan or allowing British or American pilots to touch foot on Soviet soil, Stalin felt more comfortable
partnering with Hitler, his fellow totalitarian dictator, than with
these strange, democratically elected leaders who were so anxious
to please him, even—perhaps especially—when he treated them
with contempt. So obsequious was the White House posture
toward Stalin that, when rumors reached Washington in March
and April 1943 for the first time that Ribbentrop and Molotov—
signatories of the Europe-swallowing pact of 1939—were "reported to be working for a separate Russo-German compromise
peace," Roosevelt sent the deeply compromised Stalin apologist
Joseph Davies—the former ambassador who had whitewashed
reports on the Great Terror show trials in order to facilitate his
heiress wife's Russian art purchases—on a goodwill mission to
Moscow to reassure Stalin that the United States still had his best
interests at heart. This was appeasement of the most abject kind.[35]

Stalin had never asked for the friendship of "the Anglo-Saxons,"
as he had unsentimentally informed Japan's visiting foreign minister in April 1941. When Churchill had come to Moscow in
mid-August 1942 to inform Stalin in person that there would be
no second front in France that year, he received a cold welcome,
later recalling the atmosphere as "bleak and sombre." This was
the meeting later remembered for Churchill's drawing of a croc-
odile to illustrate his idea of attacking Europe's "soft underbelly"
via the Mediterranean, prior to striking the animal's "hard snout"
in northern France. But at the time, all Churchill's theatrics availed
him was a lecture from Stalin about Britain's failure to open a second front in 1942, culminating in Stalin's rather serious accusation
that Red Army commanders had planned operations for the second half of the year with the expectation of an Allied landing in
France. At this, Churchill had "exploded" in a tirade lasting about
five minutes, a rant so impassioned and long-winded that neither

the British nor Soviet interpreter was able to record what he said. "Did he not realize who he was speaking to?" Churchill later asked the British ambassador to the USSR, Sir Archibald Clark Kerr, after recovering his composure. Stalin reported to his ambassador in London, Maisky, after this unpleasant first meeting, that he had "the impression that Churchill is holding a course heading for the defeat of the USSR, in order thereafter to reach agreement with the Germany of Hitler . . . at [the] expense of our country."[36]

Stalin also felt no need to reciprocate Roosevelt's ever more extravagant gestures of unilateral courtship, or the ridiculous hero worship he was receiving in the American press. In January 1943, a chiseled, demigod portrait of Stalin had graced the cover of *Time* magazine as "Man of the Year" for 1942. Were it not for Stalin's indifference, still more flattering profiles would have appeared in 1943. The Vozhd turned down dozens of exclusives with reporters who came begging at the Kremlin, including a pitch from Simon & Schuster for an autobiography that would allow Stalin to "give the world a far more comprehensive statement of Soviet war and peace aims" than he could do in mere interviews. Whether declining Roosevelt's requests for help against Japan, arresting American pilots who landed on Soviet air bases without permission, breaking off relations with the Polish exile government in London, smearing Polish leaders as collaborators and demanding that Roosevelt and Churchill embrace his slanders, or trying to guilt-trip his accidental allies into launching a bloody second front on Fortress Europe even while he was quietly angling for a separate peace with Hitler, Stalin had one goal and one goal only: serving the interests of the Soviet Union.[37]

26

Stopping Citadel

The Second Front?

COLD AS STALIN'S treatment of his allies was in early 1943, it was not only out of contempt that he had declined the invitation by Roosevelt and Churchill to join them at Casablanca. In view of Stalin's paranoia about security and his need for a direct phone connection to Moscow and military headquarters, the very location of the January 1943 summit more or less ruled out Stalin's participation, although, as the Vozhd had not spelled out these conditions explicitly, neither Roosevelt nor Churchill would likely have known this yet.

The rollout of unconditional surrender in late January also coincided with the final drama in Stalingrad, even as Stalin and Zhukov were launching a series of major offensives elsewhere. Uranus, the encirclement operation outside Stalingrad, was only one of the "planetary" offensives planned that winter by Stalin's generals. There was also Zhukov's Operation Mars, which aimed to trap the exposed salient of German Army Group Center west of Moscow in between Rzhev and Viazma and Briansk, an operation launched six days after Uranus on November 24, 1942. Uranus was supposed to be followed by Saturn, whereby mobile Soviet units on the southern flank of Stalingrad would wheel southwest to Rostov-on-Don to cut off Germany Army Group A from the North Caucasus. Mars would then be followed by Jupiter and Neptune, which would see Zhukov's forces envelop German Army Group Center from behind. Stalin devoted more resources overall to Mars, Jupiter, and Neptune—amounting to six entire armies,

including six tank corps and nearly two thousand tanks—than to
Uranus and Saturn. Far from the isolated, heroic last-ditch defense
of legend, Stalingrad was supposed to be the first step in the annihilation of the Wehrmacht up and down the entire eastern front.[1]

Things did not turn out as Stalin had hoped. While Uranus came
off well enough at Stalingrad, the redoubtable General Manstein,
commanding Army Group A in the North Caucasus, staged a disciplined retreat to Rostov-on-Don, rendering Saturn moot. Operation Mars was a bloody debacle for the Red Army, which lost
100,000 dead and 235,000 wounded in the first several weeks, along
with 1,655 tanks. It is a reflection of the enduring influence of Soviet propaganda themes on the historiography of World War II
that Operation Mars remained almost unknown in the West until
David Glantz published *Zhukov's Greatest Defeat* in 1999.[2]

In spite of Zhukov's failure to break through west of Moscow,
neither he nor Stalin were willing to forfeit the initiative. There
were positive signs in the south. Even as Paulus was surrendering
what remained of the German Sixth Army in Stalingrad, the Soviet
southern army group, under General Rodion Malinovsky, pursued
the German Don army group toward Rostov-on-Don and Voro-
shilovgrad, which both fell in mid-February 1943. Rokossovsky's
Soviet Don army group, after receiving Paulus's surrender in Stalingrad, wheeled west to smash through weakly held Hungarian
and Italian lines on the upper Don to seize Voronezh and the critical railway junction of Kastornoe, opening the road northwest to
Kursk, which fell on February 6. On February 16, Filipp Golikov's
Voronezh army group rolled into Kharkov, prompting Stalin to
give the go-ahead for an ambitious strike across the Dniepr, deep
into Ukraine (Operation Gallop). On the northern front, operations were underway to cut off the German Sixteenth and Eighteenth Armies (Operation Polar Star) and open up a land supply
route to Leningrad, a city suffering under a crippling German siege
since September 1941 that had already cost the lives of hundreds
of thousands of Russians by 1943, mostly to malnutrition, disease,

and starvation. In the heady days after Stalingrad, it appeared that
Stalin's armies were still poised to strike a series of deadly blows to
the Wehrmacht.[3]

It was not to be. While the February 1943 offensives did not
fail as spectacularly as Mars, none came close to succeeding because of the German ability to adapt. In the wake of the Stalingrad
debacle, even the usually stubborn Hitler showed strategic con-
trition, giving Manstein permission to withdraw Army Group A
all the way into the Donbass region to reassemble a consolidated
Don army group. Likewise, in the north, the Germans withdrew
and consolidated defensive lines around Leningrad, rendering Polar Star moot. Most critically, on March 1, 1943, Hitler ordered a
strategic withdrawal from the Rzhev-Viazma salient on the central
front, which offered relief to the exhausted units that had parried
Zhukov's Operation Mars, shortened defensive lines, and freed
up reserves for redeployment north and south. Meanwhile, Hitler
was reinforcing his eastern armies with first-line units, including
Waffen-SS and SS armored divisions such as the Adolf Hitler Leibstandarte and the fearsome *Totenkopf* (death's head), comprising
an entire SS panzer corps. Spearheaded by these reinforcements,
Manstein ordered a bruising counteroffensive on March 7, which
smashed into Golikov's Voronezh army group at Kharkov, which
fell back into German hands on March 14–15. What remained of
Golikov's group retreated northeast to his headquarters at Belgorod on the upper Donets, only for that city to fall to Manstein's
revamped Don army group on March 18. In all, the Red Army suffered another three hundred thousand losses in the failed February
offensives following Stalingrad. The most exposed salient now was
a Soviet one, some 90 miles deep and 120 miles wide, bulging westward from Kursk, north of once-more-German-held Kharkov.[4]

When the rasputitsa flooding came later that March, a lull descended on the eastern front as both armies licked their wounds
from the intense winter battles, formed new armored divisions,
and called up reserves. It was in this period, from April to June
1943, that peace initiatives were floated either to or by the Ger-

man Abwehr, including the Soviet approach to Canaris's men in Stockholm and the German feelers to the Western Allies in neutral Spain, Switzerland, and Turkey. That the broadsides between Goebbels and Soviet propagandists over Katyn coincided with these peace probes, and with the TRIDENT talks in Washington about ways of assaulting Fortress Europe, added to the sense of intrigue, as statesmen on all sides thought through scenarios that might end the terrible war.

The upshot of TRIDENT was deeply disappointing to Stalin. On June 2, 1943, Roosevelt informed the Vozhd that, while the Allies were stepping up their strategic bombing campaign in Germany "for the purpose of smashing German industry, destroying German fighter aircraft and breaking the morale of the German people," they would not be launching a cross-Channel invasion in 1943 after all, but "in the spring of 1944." Contrary to Soviet complaints that the Allies were refusing to open a second front, they had just crushed the last German and Italian resistance in North Africa, taking the surrender of nearly 275,000 Axis troops in Tunisia on May 13, including seven full-strength Wehrmacht divisions, bringing total Axis losses in the theater to date to 950,000 killed or captured, 6,200 guns, 2,550 tanks, and 70,000 trucks, not to mention 2.4 million gross tons of Axis war matériel lost at sea in the Mediterranean. Hitler had responded to the fall of Tunis by dispatching ten Wehrmacht divisions to Yugoslavia and seven more to Greece. The Allies were now preparing to invade Sicily and Italy, which would inevitably draw in still more German reinforcements. "Eisenhower," Roosevelt informed Stalin, "has been directed to prepare to launch offensive immediately following successful completion of HUSKY (viz the assault on Sicily), for the purpose of precipitating the collapse of Italy and thus facilitating our air offensive against Eastern and Southern Germany as well as continuing the attrition of German fighter aircraft and developing a heavy threat against German control of the Balkans."[5]

These were all worthy strategic objectives, and they promised to tie down the bulk of Göring's Luftwaffe and draw reinforcements from the Soviet front. But Stalin would not budge from his view that the Allies had promised him a second front in France. The "decisions postponing the British-American invasion of Western Europe until the spring of 1944," the Vozhd responded coolly to Roosevelt on June 11, create "exceptional difficulties for the Soviet Union, which has already been fighting for two years, with the utmost strain of its strength, against the main forces of Germany and her satellites." Stalin asked Roosevelt whether it was "necessary to say what painful and negative impressions will be made in the Soviet Union, upon its people and its Army, by the new postponement of the Second Front and by leaving our Army, which has made so many sacrifices, without expected serious support from the British-American armies?" Having thus threatened to salt Soviet propaganda with smears against the Allies for this second-front betrayal, Stalin resumed secret peace talks with the Germans outside Stockholm on June 17.[6]

To be sure, subterfuge was involved in the Swedish peace probes. Both sides were intensively upgrading their armaments. The Germans were about to unveil a new generation of tanks, designed for tactical combat in the slower, more evenly matched conditions of 1943 instead of the more fluid mobile offensive operations of 1941. The Panzerkampfwagen Panther 5 was the German answer to the Soviet T-34—a bit heavier than the latter at forty-four tons but with impressive speed and mobility, owing to its advanced V12 Maybach 230 engine. The Panther's 75 mm gun was just as powerful, but more accurate, than the T-34's 76 mm. The Henschel-designed Tiger 1, weighing in at nearly sixty tons, was slower than the Panther but was so heavily armored as to be nearly invulnerable, described by one driver as "all muscle, a slab-sided beast." The Tiger's 88 mm gun had such impressive range that its gunners could sit back and knock out Soviet T-34s and KVs at leisure, before their crews could fire back. Ferdinand Porsche's sixty-seven-ton Ferdinand tank, mounting an 88 mm L70 cannon, was still more massive. Functioning more like a tank-destroying artillery piece, the Ferdinand was quickly nicknamed the Elephant, which was not a compliment. Even so, from long range, these two 88-mm-gun monsters packed a lethal punch.[7]

Stalin and Zhukov, for their part, used the strategic pause of the rasputitsa to fortify the Kursk salient, which presented an obvious target for a German flanking offensive. Soviet sappers thoroughly blanketed the Kursk salient with minefields (640,000 mines were laid in all), laid five hundred miles of barbed wire (of which one-tenth was electrified), dug trenches (seventy kilometers per division), and erected fortifications designed to negate the advantages of the new German tanks. Cleverly, minefields were left with narrow gaps to lure German tanks into prepared tank-killing zones, where Red Army artillerists were waiting with anti-tank guns, including camouflaged T-34 and KV tanks, ranged into fixed positions. Meanwhile, hundreds of Soviet tanks were held in reserve near the rear of the Kursk salient, ready to move in once the widely expected German armored assault had bogged down.[8]

While plans for a Red armored offensive thrust, to be undertaken in case the Germans did not attack, were in the works too, the preparations undertaken at Stavka for a strategic defense at Kursk showed that Stalin had learned from the failed winter offensives. Despite the triumph at Stalingrad, the bloody winter battles of 1942–1943 had seen the Red Army lose thousands of tanks and self-propelled guns (6,368 between the launching of Uranus on November 19 and the end of fighting around Kharkov on March 25, an average of 1,500 per month) and warplanes (1,520, or 370 per month). The loss rates were not quite as catastrophic as in the war's first six months, when the Red Army had lost 3,723 tanks per month; in 1942, the monthly tank loss average dipped to 1,403. The key point is that, despite the miracle enabled by the Soviet industrial evacuation of 1941, even in the highest priority sector of the Russian war economy, tanks, production was barely keeping pace with battlefield losses. In the second half of 1941, Soviet tank production had amounted to barely a quarter of losses (6,750 against 22,340), a ratio that depleted Stalin's prewar tank pool and left Zhukov dependent on lend-lease motors in the Battle of

Moscow. In both 1942 and 1943, Soviet tank production averaged about 2,000 per month, enough to stay ahead in 1942 but only to tread water in 1943, with 24,006 tanks produced that year against 23,500 lost in action or mechanical breakdown. Just as in December 1941, it was the margins that mattered: a margin provided, in late June 1943, by the 625 lend-lease tanks per month Stalin was receiving in the second protocol, adding up to 5,000 tanks since Uranus and Mars in November 1942 had depleted his tank park again.[9]

Rather than draw down his motor pool with more costly offensives, the logic of lend-lease meant that if Stalin simply bided his time, the surpluses of American capitalism would allow his armored divisions to sprout like mushrooms. In accordance with the second protocol, in force from July 1, 1942, to June 30, 1943, the United States shipped more than 3.4 million tons of goods to Stalin, including war matériel critical in the Kursk salient, such as barbed wire (4,000 tons shipped each month), machine guns (120,000), Thompson submachine guns (another 120,000), anti-tank mines (60,000 per month), anti-aircraft guns (5,117 during the second protocol), tarpaulin (24 million square yards), oil pipe and tubing (75,000 tons), TNT (181,366 tons), field telephones (173,000 shipped by July 1943), telephone wire (580,000 miles), and petroleum products (220,000 tons in second protocol, most of it refined aviation gasoline). Stalin's generals had also laid in 144 American cranes and hoists over the winter, along with vast quantities of "shovels and compressors," which all came in handy for erecting defensive fortifications at Kursk. Then there was leather (19.34 million tons so far) and lend-lease boots (3.14 million pairs shipped by July 1943 and 400,000 now arriving in Russia every month), American trucks and jeeps (120,330), and warplanes (2,403, including 1,107 flown to Siberia via Alaska). Five thousand tons of armor plate were now arriving monthly for Soviet tanks, and a steady five thousand tons of aluminum since March 1943, after Stalin had complained that British shipments were slowing down and that shortages "would have a very serious effect on [Soviet] aircraft production." Roosevelt had complied, prioritizing the Soviets over the US Army Air Force.* There was also copper (12,500 tons arriving monthly), nickel (3,000 tons so far in 1943), ferrochrome and ferrosilicon (800 tons each), and refined steel products—over a million tons of these metals had arrived by July 1943, with 406,983 tons sitting in US warehouses awaiting shipment. These figures did not account for $400 million worth of American industrial equipment, including tire factories and oil refineries dismantled for shipment to and reassembly in the USSR, by 1943. The Germans may have had superior tanks, but they had nothing to match the sheer volume of supplies Stalin's armies were receiving every month. The only things Stalin's armies were not receiving from their allies were mine detectors, which were declined on the grounds that, as the head of the Soviet military mission in Britain, General Ivan Ratov, explained to his hosts, "in the Soviet Union we use people" to clear mines.[10]

By 1943, the lend-lease contribution to the Red Army's motor pool was so enormous that it could scarcely be hidden, much as Soviet propagandists would have liked to. It wasn't only jeeps, trucks, and tanks either. By early 1943, Soviet fighter pilots had come to rely on the P-39 Bell Airacobra, also known as the Kobrushka, in dogfights with German Messerschmitts, and Soviet bombing crews had adopted the Douglas A-20 Boston bomber as their own. So important were these two warplanes to the Soviet war effort that Stalin quietly allowed engineers from the Bell plant in Buffalo, New York, and the Douglas factory in Southern California, to visit the front and observe the planes in action. This was at a time when American and British officers were not allowed

---

* The reason Churchill had scaled down aluminum shipments to Stalin was to allow Britain's own aircraft industry to supply the Royal Air Force, owing to his creeping realization of Britain's declining power compared to the United States and the USSR. Roosevelt, despite being warned that scaling up aluminum shipments to Stalin would limit US airplane production, did not have to care.

to do so, nor were American pilots allowed to fly the P-39s or A-20s onto Soviet territory—they were not even allowed to land at Nome, the last Alaskan refueling outpost before they crossed the Bering Strait. Based on real-time input from American engineers, the VVS was able to repair or retrofit 774 grounded Boston bombers in 1943. Unusually in the VVS, only a tenth of Boston losses (ninety in the first half of 1943) came from mechanical failure. Expert advice from American Douglas engineers improved the Boston bomber's performance to the point where it could fly, on average, forty-nine sorties before breaking down—and, in the "best Soviet aviation regiment," as many as eighty. By 1943, the VVS had more Douglas A-20 Havoc bombers in service than the US Army Air Force did.[11]

All this was unknown at the time—it remains largely unknown to this day—which was revealing. In March 1943, long-simmering American frustrations boiled over when the US ambassador in Moscow, Admiral Standley, complained at a press conference that the Soviet government was concealing the US contribution to the Russian war effort. Back in January, Standley had received a request from Washington to obtain statements from Stalin, Molotov, or other Soviet officials acknowledging the material contribution of lend-lease aid to the Red Army's campaigns. But all he got, Standley complained to Washington, was "the usual Russian runaround." Stalin, still enraged by the Allies' refusal to open a second front in Western Europe, was in no mood to humor American requests. On March 16, the Vozhd pointedly complained to Roosevelt that even the planned invasion of Sicily had been delayed by Allied dithering in North Africa, which had allowed Hitler to transfer thirty-six divisions to the eastern front. This was a wild exaggeration of German reinforcements prior to Operation Citadel, but Stalin's complaint was indicative of the mood in the Soviet camp at the time of Standley's press conference. No high Soviet official would go on record that winter thanking the United States for lend-lease aid.[12]

Nor was anyone in the Soviet government willing to share information about how American equipment was being used at the front, much less allow American observers to go see for themselves (other than the Bell and Douglas engineers, who were sworn by Stalin to secrecy). In a speech to the Red Army on February 23, Stalin neglected to mention lend-lease and complained that, because his allies refused to open a second front, the USSR was "bearing the whole brunt of the war." Although there was truth in Stalin's complaint about the unequal fighting burden, Soviet ingratitude for lend-lease aid was becoming so brazen that Standley let down his guard, declaring in his March 8 press conference, "It's not fair—the American people are giving millions to help the Russian people and yet the Russian people do not know where the supplies are coming from." Standley's rant raised a ruckus back home. The *Chicago Tribune*, under the headline, "REDS HIDE OUR AID," demanded an investigation.[13]

Although Standley's outburst annoyed Soviet leaders, it also forced Molotov and Stalin to publicly acknowledge, for the first time, the scale of American aid to the Soviet war effort. On March 15, *Pravda* devoted half of its foreign section to describing lend-lease aid, and Soviet officials were suddenly forthcoming when asked about it by Western reporters. To dampen the political fallout in Washington, Litvinov, the Soviet ambassador, issued a public statement of gratitude, which was picked up by all the main radio broadcast networks. Catching the hint, many Western reporters, who had previously soft-pedaled lend-lease stories so as not to offend Stalin, began to report the truth. The Associated Press correspondent, Henry Cassidy, though not allowed near the front, filed an effusive dispatch in June 1943, noting that he saw "Airacobra, Kittyhawk and Tomahawk fighters in service at an airport outside Moscow. I saw American medium and light M-3 tanks, Mathildas and Valentines, being turned over to Red Army brigades behind the front. I rode in jeeps at an artillery camp. I saw a Cossack unit using American field telephones in maneuvers."[14]

Were it not for this cascading influx of American armor on the eastern front, the order of battle in summer 1943 would have looked very different. Hitler, keen to exploit a decisive new advantage in tank technology, seems to have had no inkling of what Stalin was receiving every month from the Americans. If he had, he would scarcely have ordered Manstein to delay the planned German offensive—initially scheduled for the first week of May 1943, as soon as the muds had dried out—to wait for his new tanks to arrive. The delay did allow the Germans to assemble an impressive 8,170 guns and artillery pieces and augment their motor pool with 150 Tiger 1s and a few dozen Panthers and Ferdinands, although the vast majority of the 2,451 panzers available for Citadel were older, far less deadly Panzerkampfwagen 3 and 4 models. But the delay also ensured that the Red Army was flush with mobile armor, as Stalin had been sensible enough to sit on his hands and allow lend-lease to work its magic. By the time the Germans finally struck in early July, the Soviet force pool at Kursk counted 8,200 tanks, armored combat vehicles, and self-propelled guns, and 47,416 guns and artillery pieces. Owing to the US-British strategic bombing campaign, Göring's Luftwaffe could spare only 1,372 warplanes for Citadel, against a lend-lease-inflated Soviet count of 5,965. Ratios in manpower, tanks, and self-propelled guns thus favored the Soviets by more than three to one, in warplanes by more than four to one, and in guns and artillery pieces by five or six to one, with these advantages compounded by the fact that the Russians could choose and fortify their ground for defense. The order of battle was a bald inversion of normal operational doctrine, which held that attackers needed superiority of at least three to one; in this case it was one against three at best. In trucks and jeeps, the Soviet advantage, owing to the influx of more than one hundred thousand American trucks in the second protocol, was so extreme as to defy comparison.[15]

Much of this Soviet material advantage was because of American generosity. But there is another sense in which Stalin owed even his edge in manpower to his allies. While it is true that the

Soviet population remained larger than the German, the huge Soviet advantage in 1941 had declined precipitously due to both the loss of populated territory and the lopsided casualty ratios on the eastern front. By the end of June 1943, the Red Army had suffered more than 14 million casualties, according to new research, including 6,768,914 dead, taken prisoner, or missing and 7,294,420 sick or wounded, against German losses of 1.15 million (mostly deaths). Although some of the Soviet sick and wounded casualties later returned to battle, the casualty ratio up to July 1943 was still between ten to one and fourteen to one, sharply eroding the initial Soviet edge in manpower. With both sides drafting as many men as possible, the size of the German armed forces was increasing faster than the Red Army, reaching near parity by 1943 with 9.48 million Germans under arms, spread out across about 275 active divisions, against 10.5 million Soviets. Were it not for the fact that Hitler, unlike Stalin, was fighting a war on more than one front— on many fronts, in fact—the Germans might have been able to muster superior numbers on the eastern front. At least twenty-five German divisions were deployed in northern France, Belgium, and Holland—guarding the Channel against possible US-British attacks—a number that would double over the next year. There were twenty German divisions in Norway and Finland, guarding Hitler's Scandinavian iron ore and nickel supplies against US-British encroachment, and thirty stationed in Germany and Central Europe, mostly Luftwaffe divisions defending the homeland against US-British bombing raids. Another twenty-one German divisions guarded the Balkans after Hitler had reinforced Yugoslavia and Greece after the Axis debacle at Tunis. The Wehrmacht's non-eastern-front European deployment comprised nearly a hundred divisions, still less than the 185-plus deployed on the Soviet fronts, but amounting to more than 30 percent of the total by June 1943 (a share soon augmented dramatically by the German redeployment after the Allies invaded Sicily and Italy). Because Stalin only had to keep masking forces in the Far East, owing to his neutrality pact with Japan and his refusal to aid China, three million Germans

faced nearly seven million Russians on the eastern front, where
Stalin could deploy nearly all of his available manpower. For all his
complaints about his allies' failure to open a second front in France
to draw off "forty German divisions" (on top of the one hundred
or so already deployed defending Europe), Stalin's refusal to aid
the Americans against Japan ensured that he could enjoy comfortable superiority in manpower on the eastern front.[16]

Soviet commanders also knew—from defectors, signals intercepts, and Allied warnings—almost exactly when the attack was
coming: in the early morning hours of July 5, 1943. So well tele-
graphed was Citadel that, at 10:30 p.m. the night before, Soviet
gunners launched a barrage of *kontrpodgotovka* (disruptive fire)
at German frontline troops even as the massively superior Red
Army force staged preemptive sorties against German airfields,
only to find most of them empty. Operation Citadel, like Barbarossa in 1941, pitted meticulous German planning and operational élan against overwhelming Soviet superiority in manpower
and matériel, only this time against an even greater disparity in
armor and with no element of surprise allowing the Wehrmacht
to capitalize on Soviet complacency. It was a test of quality against
quantity.[17]

In the early stages, it appeared that quality was winning. Although the vast array of mines and defensive fortifications, and
the preemptive Soviet artillery counter barrage, prevented early
breakthroughs on the morning of July 5, German progress was
thereafter swift and unrelenting. The six panzer divisions of General Walter Model's Ninth Army, attacking the Soviet Thirteenth
and Seventieth Armies on the central front at the northern hinge of
the Kursk salient, advanced nine miles (more than fifteen kilometers) in the first forty-eight hours. Elite formations from Manstein's
formidable Army Group South—including the panzer corps of
Hoth's Fourth Panzer Army, spearheaded by the *Grossdeutsch-
land* armored infantry division, which had received fifteen Tiger 1
tanks and forty-four Panthers—attacked the vulnerable hinge of
the Soviet defense between the Voronezh and steppe fronts and

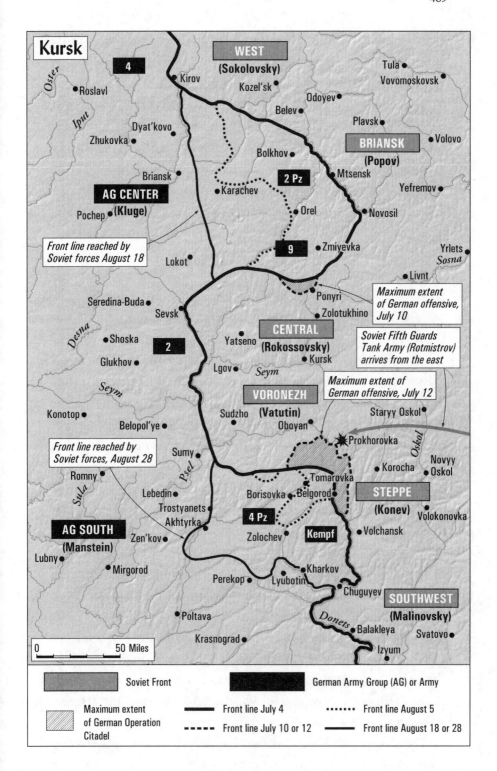

swiftly broke through to a depth of nearly eighteen miles (thirty kilometers) in the first four days. By July 11, Hoth's panzers were approaching Prokhorovka and Oboyan, south of Kursk. Owing to the need to navigate minefields and the blistering counterfire from Soviet gunners firing from fixed tank positions, progress was much slower than in the mobile campaigning of 1941 and 1942. Nonetheless, it was clear that the Germans had recovered from Stalingrad and regained the upper hand on the eastern front. "If the Russians had any success against us before," the commander of 332nd German Infantry Division exhorted his men marching into battle with Hoth's Fourth Panzer Army, "it was in the main owing to their tanks. But now we have a better tank than the enemy!" A sergeant in a German flak battalion captured the surging morale of the attackers when he wrote: "I believe that this time the Russians are going to get a very heavy beating."[18]

By July 11, the Red Army was in serious trouble. Because of the early crisis on the northern side of the salient, Zhukov had peeled armor off from the south, which left little standing in the way of Hoth's Fourth Panzer Army other than the Thirty-Third Guards Rifle Corps outside Prokhorovka. While German casualties were heavy, Soviet losses in the southern sector were far greater, already more than 1,000 tanks, 1,200 anti-tank and field guns, and more than 20,000 casualties. Stalin called in Rokossovsky, commander of the central front, to warn that, if the Germans broke through at Prokhorovka, "they could reach the rear of your army." General Paul Hausser's Second SS Panzer Corps, the battering ram of Hoth's Fourth Panzer Army, was preparing for a final assault on Prokhorovka. The Soviet position was dire enough that Zhukov ordered Pavel Rotmistrov's Fifth Guards Tank Army to reinforce Prokhorovka from deep in the rear, almost two hundred miles to the east. On July 11, Zhukov and another Marshal from Stavka, A. M. Vasilevsky, arrived in Prokhorovka to supervise the defense. The danger of the Soviet position was acute.[19]

Then, something remarkable happened. Just as the centerpiece clash of the campaign was unfolding at Prokhorovka on

July 12–13, 1943, Hitler summoned his two senior commanders from the Kursk sector, Manstein of Army Group South and Kluge of Army Group Center (the same who had been involved in the Canaris plot back in March), to his "Wolf's Lair" headquarters in the Masurian forest east of Rastenburg and ordered them to call off the offensive. In view of the then-exploding second-front controversy between Stalin and his allies and the enduring hold of Stalinist spin on this subject in the historical literature on World War II, Manstein's account deserves a close reading. "Hitler opened the conference," we are told,

> by announcing that the western Allies had landed in Sicily that day [actually three days previously] and that the situation there had taken an extremely serious turn. The Italians were not even attempting to fight, and the island was likely to be lost. Since the next step might well be a landing in the Balkans or lower Italy, it was necessary to form new [German] armies in Italy and the western Balkans. These forces must be found from the Eastern Front, so "Citadel" would have to be discontinued.

True to his word, Hitler ordered Manstein to cough up several of his best armored divisions, including the Adolf Hitler Leibstandarte, which was sent to Italy, the first of a dozen first-line German divisions transferred from the Soviet to the Italian fronts over the next four months. Any further German offensives in the Kursk sector were ruled out.[20]

Hitler's halting of Operation Citadel to counter the Allied move into Sicily was the greatest possible gift to Stalin. It allowed the Soviets to claim a decisive victory in a battle they had been losing, and to enshroud that battle in layers of myth that have been only recently unpeeled. Prokhorovka was turned into a new Stalingrad, where, Soviet propagandists claimed, 1,500 tanks had "grappled tread to tread" in an enclosed space three miles wide, which by nightfall was strewn with "over four hundred disabled or burning [German] panzers, seventy of them Tigers." Prokhorovka became the kernel of the legend of Kursk as the "greatest tank battle of all time," in which, Soviet accounts claimed, the vaunted Wehrmacht lost 2,900 tanks including 700 Tigers—a claim embraced by a popular Western historian in the 1974 study *The Tigers Are Burning*.[21]

The real story was nothing like this. By the time Hausser's Second SS Panzer Corps engaged the Russians at Prokhorovka, his three armored divisions contained all of 211 operational tanks, of which only 15 were Tigers and none were Panthers. German losses at Prokhorovka between July 11 and 13, during the most intense fighting, amounted to 48 panzers, against Soviet losses of between 400 (Rotmistrov's own estimate) and 650 tanks—a ratio favoring the Germans by nearly ten to one. Even the low-end Soviet estimate is now 1,614 tanks lost in the Kursk sector up to July 23, while some specialists believe the correct figure is 1,956. This compares to German panzer losses of 252 (low end) and 278 (the high estimate). The armor-loss ratio in this supposedly crushing Soviet victory thus favored the Germans by at least eight to one. The story was similarly lopsided in the air: the VVS saw somewhere between 459 and 1,961 warplanes knocked out of action, against Luftwaffe losses of 159. In manpower, there were Soviet losses between 177,847 (low) and 319,000 (high), compared to German losses of 54,181. Citadel had failed, owing to Soviet grit and Hitler's intervention. But if Kursk was a Soviet victory, it was a costly one.[22]

This depressing ledger was registered only when the Germans were on the offensive, which gave advantages to Soviet commanders who had spent all spring fortifying defensive positions. Once the Red Army resumed the offensive on July 23, the slaughter was sickening. During the two campaigns of the Soviet counteroffensive—Kutuzov, launched in mid-July on the northern sector targeting Orel, and Rumiantsev, on the southern side, aiming to recapture Belgorod and Kharkov—Soviet losses in armor mounted to epidemic proportions. By the time Kharkov was retaken on August 28, these two forgotten Kursk campaigns had cost the Red Army another 785,466 casualties, with 4,450 more tanks knocked out of action. The butcher's bill for Kursk as a whole included Soviet casualties of between 863,303 (low end) and 1,677,000 (high end), 5,244 guns, between 1,626 and 4,108 warplanes, and 6,064 tanks, according to the lowest official estimates. The Germans had lost heavily too, suffering 170,000 casualties in the Kursk sector by the end of August and losing 760 panzers and 524 warplanes. And the Russians were now in Kharkov to stay, having regained the strategic initiative, even if they were still more than one thousand kilometers from the old Soviet border.[23]

By abandoning the offensive on the eastern front to shore up vulnerable German positions in Italy and the Balkans, Hitler had allowed Stalin to claim a legendary victory. Kursk was a decisive battle, to be sure, marking the failure of the last major German offensive on the eastern front in the war. But the victory was, even more than Stalingrad, an Allied one, won as much by the material contribution of lend-lease aid and the complementary US-British landings in Sicily as by Soviet generalship and Russian blood and grit. For neither the first nor the last time, Stalin's faltering fortunes had turned around because of a timely intervention by his Western allies.

27

Operation Tito

STALIN SHOWED LITTLE gratitude for the way the Allied landing at Sicily had bailed him out at Kursk. He was even less disposed to thank the British government for Churchill's bizarre decision to abandon Britain's client in Yugoslavia, the minister of the army of the royal Yugoslav exile government in London, Draža Mihailović, in September 1943, throwing all of the Western Allies' support instead to Stalin's man, the Communist Josip Broz Tito.

Colonel Mihailović, a Serbian-born officer in the Yugoslav Army, had taken to the hills after the Nazi takeover in April 1941, rallying hundreds of patriotic officers to his opposition band of "Chetniks." Significantly, the Croatian-born Yugoslav Communist leader Broz-Tito was at the time still cautiously pro-German, owing both to Stalin's then alliance with Hitler and to the fact that, at the time of the invasion of Yugoslavia by Germany and its allies, Tito had found himself in Zagreb, Croatia—a city not so much invaded as occupied by invitation because of the deal the Germans had struck with Croatian leaders. It was only after Hitler invaded the USSR on June 22, 1941, that Tito's Communists rose up against the occupiers.

Occupied Yugoslavia was a mosaic of competing factions in which the Germans, although in nominal control of the whole, were not always the most influential piece. Until 1943, Italy had the most troops on the ground and the most weapons on hand. An uneasy demarcation line between the Italian and German zones bisected Croatia, from Slovenia in the northwest to Montenegro in the southeast. Even Serbia, despite being occupied by Germany and (after 1942) by Bulgaria, had its own puppet government and

police forces, although these were not trusted enough to be supplied with substantial amounts of guns, let alone artillery. The Bulgarian First Occupation Corps would gradually ramp up its own
commitment until, by 1943, it was the largest armed faction in
occupied Yugoslavia.[1]

In this maelstrom of divided loyalties, Mihailović's mostly Serbian Chetniks and Tito's Communist partisans, answering to Stalin, were only two players at first. Mihailović was loath to engage
Wehrmacht forces directly in the early months of the occupation,
preferring to husband his forces and build up his strength gradually. He picked his spots carefully. Even so, the Chetniks gave the
Germans fits when they did engage them. A Wehrmacht situation
report from occupied Croatia on September 23, 1941, observed
that "unfortunately the [Croatian Ustashe] government has not
succeeded in rendering the Chetniks harmless, rather the bands
have gained strength in the last weeks and have penetrated further
[into Croatian territory]. In fact, German occupying forces *had
to deploy tanks against the Chetniks*. It will not be easy to come to
grips with these mobile bands, who are so familiar with the mountainous terrain." German military records prove baseless the later
canard of Stalinist propaganda that Mihailović was a collaborator
who was unwilling to risk casualties by engaging the enemy.[2]

Tito, later lionized as one the great guerrilla leaders of the
twentieth century, was in reality a career politician. It is true that
he had fought in the Habsburg armies during the First World War
and later in the Russian Civil War. But he had spent the next two
decades working his way up the ranks of the Yugoslav Communist
Party before being promoted to the top spot by Stalin and Dimitrov,
the Bulgarian secretary of the Communist International, in 1937. It
was only after Stalin, under the onslaught of the German invasion,
gave permission, that Tito stirred a finger to resist. The partisans
fought with guerrilla-style slash-and-burn tactics. Whereas the
Chetniks, a German intelligence officer reported from Belgrade
on August 28, 1941, "tend to target German soldiers, or Serbian

government collaborators, while avoiding especially cruel atrocities . . . [it is] entirely different with the Communists. These are
pronouncedly asocial elements, who will kill anyone, even harmless Serbian peasants or merchants in the towns, whom they rob.
These Communist bands also commit grotesque acts of cruelty."
Because of such tactics, the German officer observed, the Communist partisans had virtually no support in Serbia, where "Broz"
(that is, Tito) was viewed as a bandit and a butcher.[3]

As the highest-ranking officer in the country, Mihailović was
the legatee of the pro-Allied Simovich government that repudiated
the Tripartite Pact during the March 1941 coup. Once Mihailović
opened a line of communication with British Cairo (via Malta) in
fall 1941, he was recognized by the London exile government and
given the rank of chief of staff of the supreme command. In effect,
this set up a kind of proxy war between the royalist Chetniks, ostensibly sponsored by Britain, and Tito's Communists, answering
to Stalin and the USSR.[4]

Relations between Mihailović and his British handlers got off
to a poor start, however, after the first liaison mission from Cairo,
headed by Captain "Marko" Hudson, arrived in Yugoslavia on
October 25, 1941. Mihailović, not wanting to burnish Communist
pretensions to equal status, did not let Hudson attend a meeting
he had set up with Tito on October 27 to discuss the best ways of
organizing resistance to the Germans without provoking civilian
reprisals. Mihailović told Hudson haughtily that he was "the legitimate representative of his government," and that his relations
with the Communist partisans were "entirely a Yugoslav affair"
and therefore none of his business. In his first telegram to Cairo
headquarters, an annoyed Hudson wired, "Suggest you tell MI-
HAILOVIĆ full British help not forthcoming unless attempt made
to incorporate all anti Fascist elements under his command."[5]

In a pattern soon familiar in enemy-occupied countries where
the claim to leadership of the resistance was contested between
pro-Western and pro-Soviet factions, Britain made aid to its own

client conditional on collaborating with Stalin's. While a trickle of British supplies was airlifted into Yugoslavia in 1942, it was not enough to support an active military campaign. In the entire eighteen-month period when they were sponsored by Britain, Mihailović's Chetniks received only 242 tons of war matériel—scarcely enough to supply a company. And even those few tons that arrived came with strings attached, as each British liaison officer insisted that Mihailović collaborate with the pro-Soviet partisans. In July 1942, the Special Operations Executive's Cairo office (known in British intelligence shorthand as MO4) appointed a Yugoslav Communist, known under the alias "Charles Robertson," to Mihailović's headquarters. Robertson took charge of the radio link with Cairo and launched a smear campaign against Mihailović. Receiving his slanted reports in Cairo was a highly placed Soviet asset: one of the Cambridge five, James Klugmann, who worked for MO4. After the war, Klugmann was recorded by MI5 boasting about how he ruined Mihailović's reputation in Cairo by doctoring maps to attribute to Tito partisans victories actually won by the Chetniks and blasting around Tito's charges that Mihailović was collaborating with the Nazis—charges originating in Moscow with Dimitrov at Comintern headquarters and spread by Soviet propaganda organs in the West.[6]

Equally damaging to Mihailović's reputation with the British was the activity of another Cambridge spy recruited by Stalin's agents in the 1930s, Guy Burgess, who promoted the cult of "Marshal Tito" in BBC radio broadcasts to Yugoslavia. Burgess's slanted, increasingly pro-Tito broadcasts were devastating to Chetnik morale. As Mihailović complained to Colonel Bill Bailey—the head of the Eighth British Expeditionary Mission, sent to him in December 1942—"the B.B.C. with revolting cynicism dropped its support of the sacred Serbian cause, and functions now publicizing a band of terrorists because [the] latter provide cheap sensational and apparently false news." When Bailey forwarded Mihailović's complaints to BBC headquarters, the justification offered was that

English values required "even-handedness." Yet as one of the few BBC employees clued in to totalitarian agitprop, a certain "Miss Baker," wrote the Foreign Office,

> The Soviets have no such scruples. Not only do they ignore Mihailović (the Yugoslav Government's representative with whom they are supposed to be in alliance and whom they know we support), but in their endeavor to build up the Partisans they openly attack him, call him a traitor and demand his extermination. We, on the other hand, have not only refrained from attacking Mihailović's opponents, but in the last few months we have actually boosted them. The impression it has made on Mihailović has been disastrous.[7]

It is true that, as British liaison officers complained in their dispatches to Cairo, Mihailović often preferred to fight Tito's partisans instead of the Germans, and on several occasions met with German or pro-German Serbian officials to negotiate cease-fires and arms-sharing agreements. The reverse was equally true, however, of Stalin's man Tito and the partisans, who also obtained arms where they could, usually from the Italians, and who negotiated tactical cease-fire or prisoner-exchange agreements with the Germans on at least two occasions, in November 1942 and March 1943. On March 29, 1943, Tito instructed the partisans that "our most important task now is to destroy the Chetniks of Draža Mihailović and to break up his administrative apparatus, because they represent the greatest danger for the further course of the national liberation struggle."[8]

What Stalin understood better than Churchill in 1943 was that Mihailović and Tito were fighting for different versions of Yugoslavia's future, a struggle in which propaganda was hugely important. Mihailović was fighting on behalf of the royal government-in-exile. Tito wanted to impose Soviet Communism on the country. As such, it was natural that Stalin would back Tito. Because there was no overland contact between the Red Army and Yugoslavia, sending arms was, for now, impossible. As Comintern secretary Dimitrov wired Tito from Moscow on February 11, 1943, "You should not doubt for a minute that, if there were the smallest chance of our getting arms to [you], we would have done so long ago." All Stalin could offer, for now, was propaganda smearing Tito's enemies, and political advice. The international agitprop campaign against Mihailović-as-collaborator was coordinated between Tito—wiring Moscow under his Comintern code name, VALTER—and Dimitrov, who passed on Tito's slanders to be broadcast to Yugoslavia in Serbo-Croat by Russian radio operators and by Soviet agents like Burgess at the BBC. The British *Daily Worker* also published Tito's smears, as did Communist newspapers published in Serbo-Croat in North America. By spring 1943, VALTER began accusing even British officers attached to Mihailović of being collaborators, including Captain Hudson, despite Hudson having gone out of his way to cultivate Tito. Hudson, outmuscled by the Communist spy Robertson at Mihailović's headquarters—who prevented him from using the radio—was unable to respond to these charges until Robertson, growing bored of agitprop, stole arms and equipment in July 1943 and fled to fight with the partisans.[9]

It should have been equally natural for Britain, the country hosting Yugoslavia's royal government-in-exile, to support Mihailović, that government's recognized supreme commander in the field. There was no reason why any British leader needed to take seriously the Stalinist smear campaign against Mihailović, the Chetniks, and British liaison officers. Such agitprop was the stock-in-trade of international Communism, taken at best with a grain of salt, at worst as pathological lying. Instead, in the course of 1943, British leaders, parroting Tito's slanders against Mihailović ever more abjectly, shifted dramatically against their own client to favor Stalin's. Making the British failure to support Mihailović still more damaging was the fact that, in June 1943, Cairo command sent a military mission to Tito and began airlifting war matériel to the partisans, in volumes soon dwarfing that given Mihailović. To

Mihailović and his men, it seemed that Britain had taken sides in Yugoslavia's civil war—the side of Stalin's Communists.[10]

Worse was to come. In the wake of the Allied landing in Sicily in July and devastating US-British bombing raids on Italy's cities, the Fascist Grand Council in Rome deposed Mussolini and appointed in his place a retired field marshal, Pietro Badoglio. After an armistice between the Allies and the Badoglio government was made public on September 8, 1943, and US-British troops landed at Salerno the next day, the British liaison officer to Mihailović, Colonel Bailey, received orders from Cairo that he must force the Chetniks to stand down and negotiate with the Italians in Croatia, notwithstanding the fact that British officers, repeating Communist smears, had been accusing Mihailović all year of collaborating with the Italians. Tito, too, entered into negotiations with the departing Italian authorities in Croatia to "obtain arms," as he reported to Dimitrov and Stalin on September 13. The Italians had never seen eye to eye with their arrogant Teutonic allies, and they bartered or sold arms to the partisans and Chetniks largely to spite the Germans.[11]

Making these new British instructions telling Mihailović to stand down still stranger, they were given just as the Chetniks were fighting for their lives against German troops in western Serbia—and winning. August and September 1943 saw Chetnik military activity ramp up to its highest level yet, with 216 attacks registered by the Bulgarian occupation forces in Serbia, 14 killings of German or Bulgarian soldiers, and 30 killings of Serbian officials working for the puppet government in Belgrade. It is true that the number of attacks claimed by Tito's partisans in this period was higher overall, but as always it was the disciplined Chetniks doing more damage, defeating a German battalion in open battle on September 13. The Chetniks also blew up an important bridge near Visegrad, in the greatest sabotage feat to date in the wartime Balkans, personally witnessed by a British officer, Brigadier Charles Armstrong, who had just been sent to help Bailey evaluate the Chetnik forces. Instead of congratulating Mihailović's Chetniks for their valor, Cairo command ordered Bailey and Armstrong to force them to withdraw from the area they had just won with their own blood and let Tito's partisans occupy it. The BBC then gave credit for the Chetniks' demolition of the Visegrad bridge to Marshal Tito. Another Chetnik triumph, the detonation on September 30, 1943, of a critical junction on the Belgrade-Salonica railway used by the Wehrmacht, which put the line out of action for nearly ten days, was falsely credited to the partisans on a BBC broadcast beamed into Yugoslavia.[12]

Making this British betrayal still more painful, the highest-level British military mission to Yugoslavia to date now arrived—at Tito's headquarters in Jajce in central Bosnia. Fitzroy Maclean— the ex-diplomat, Soviet expert, and member of the House of Commons—answered directly to Churchill, who gave him the rank of brigadier. Whereas the Hudson and Bailey missions to Mihailović had been set up to fail, Maclean's mission was designed to succeed. "What we want," Churchill told Maclean in London before the latter returned to Cairo to take flight for Bosnia, "is a daring Ambassador-leader to these hardy and hunted guerillas."[13]

If the timing of the Maclean mission to Tito was unfortunate for Mihailović, its political composition was positively insulting. Maclean, like the man who appointed him, was a conservative and ostensibly a principled anti-Communist. And yet here the two conservatives were, conspiring to sell out Mihailović and the Chetniks fighting for the royal government of Yugoslavia and support the Communists answering to Stalin instead. "Information reaching the British Government from a variety of sources," Churchill told Maclean—with no indication that these sources were all Soviet or Soviet influenced—"had caused them to doubt whether the resistance of General Mihailović and his Chetniks to the enemy was all that it was made out to be." So the Chetniks were out, and the partisans were in. When Maclean wondered aloud whether Britain might be playing into Stalin's hands by throwing its support behind Tito, Churchill remarked cryptically that "we were as loyal to our Soviet Allies as we hoped they were to us."[14]

These exchanges between two British conservatives provide a window into the naiveté and wishful thinking that led to the Anglo-American betrayal of Yugoslavia to Stalin's clients—and, ultimately, the selling out of the Balkans and Eastern Europe writ large, followed in short order by China. Spurred by Soviet agit-prop that had caused him to doubt Mihailović—and likely by the psychological appeal of selfless, politically disinterested generosity (the kind animating lend-lease aid)—Churchill decided to throw in his lot with the Communists in Yugoslavia in their civil war with the Chetniks for leadership of the resistance and Yugoslavia's political future, without realizing that this decision helped ensure that they would win. The credentials and instructions Maclean received from Churchill made it clear the prime minister wanted a positive report on the partisans, and his envoy gave him what he wanted. Maclean's evaluation was based only on fireside chats with Tito and his adjutants; he did not observe a single battle or sabotage operation during the three weeks he traveled with the partisans in Bosnia and Herzegovina before returning to Cairo. Nor did Maclean visit Serbia, where the most serious fighting was happening during the period of his visit, from September 17 to October 5. That fighting was being done by Chetniks, not the partisans Maclean claimed were the only ones fighting Germans in Yugoslavia, a claim buttressed by two erroneous BBC broadcasts. The report Maclean submitted in October 1943 was based on what Tito had told him about partisan exploits, not anything Maclean had witnessed. The same was true of Maclean's claims disparaging the Chetniks, in which he simply repeated slanders Tito fed to him.[15]

Only if we understand the gullible way it was put together can we make sense of Maclean's "blockbuster report" (as it was soon styled). The brigadier claimed that Tito's partisans lost only "one man killed for five of the enemy against Germans and ten against Ustash[e] or Chetniks." In view of the casualty ratios on the eastern front, where the Germans had bested the Russians by as much as thirty-five to one and never less than three to one, this was preposterous. When combined with Maclean's estimate of partisan fighting strength at 220,000 men spread across twenty-six divisions, these numbers prompted the question of why this huge force had not crushed the mere four lightly equipped German divisions deployed against them in Bosnia and Croatia earlier that year in Operation Weiss. In reality, the Germans had easily defeated the partisans there, inflicting casualties of 8,500 and taking more than 2,000 prisoners, against losses of 335 dead and 101 missing. Maclean's figure for partisan actives was at least three times too high, the real number being somewhere between sixty thousand and eighty thousand. Maclean's estimate of Chetnik forces at just "10,000 to 20,000" in all of Yugoslavia was just as distorted in the opposite direction. If the partisans really outnumbered the Chetniks by ten to one, then why had they not already swept them from the field? Maclean's numbers did not add up.[16]

In politics as in history, it does not always matter who is right, but who gets their story in first. Maclean's wildly inaccurate report on Tito's partisans was bound and circulated in Cairo and forwarded to London on November 6, 1943—one day before Armstrong and Bailey wired their own report on the Chetniks from the field. (Having devoted themselves, unlike Maclean, to witnessing and participating in actual operations, Armstrong and Bailey took longer to finish their more careful evaluation.) Significantly, the Armstrong-Bailey report was not circulated right away either. Almost certainly owing to the Soviet agent Klugmann's interference at MO4—it was an easy trick to slow-walk deciphering—the Armstrong-Bailey report was not typed up until November 18. It was submitted to London only on November 23, and even then by the slowest, safest transmission method, so that it arrived on November 27, three weeks after Maclean had rigged the deck against Mihailović. By that time, Churchill was no longer in town, having left England for his upcoming summit with Stalin and Roosevelt at Teheran.[17]

Judging by material commitment, Churchill had already made up his mind on Yugoslavia long before Maclean killed off

Mihailović's chances for good. There was a brutal irony in Maclean's claim that Mihailović was "not doing enough" to kill Germans with arms Britain was not sending him. In the three months after Churchill sent in Maclean in mid-September 1943, the partisans received 4,222 tons of war matériel, almost twenty times as much as Mihailović had received in the eighteen months when Britain had supported him—and Mihailović was now cut off for good. In the first nine months of 1944, the partisans would receive 22,584 tons of war supplies from the British—one hundred times more than the Chetniks had been given.[18]

Tito and Stalin could hardly believe their luck. At a time when the Red Army, still lumbering its bloody way forward a thousand kilometers from the old Soviet border, was unable to get arms to the partisans in Yugoslavia, Churchill had decided to do Stalin's work for him, and at precisely the moment when the Americans and British had opened an air base on the Adriatic coast at Bari, just three hundred flying miles from Tito's headquarters in Bosnia. Maclean's team of officers assigned to Tito, which soon included Americans, would not attach any conditions on the aid they were sending—not even quid pro quos on intelligence sharing. Maclean's men learned only what Tito allowed them to see. As Tito informed Dimitrov and Stalin, "The English want to know too much about our forces. We are sharing only information that we feel like giving them."[19]

Far from the "independent" spirit Maclean made him out to be in his best-selling memoir *Eastern Approaches*, Tito, we know now that the Soviet archives are open, discussed Maclean's every move with Dimitrov and Stalin, provided detailed reports on everything the British airlifted to him, and demanded instruction from Moscow on even the smallest matters of protocol. While Maclean answered to Churchill on arms deliveries, he answered to Stalin on all political questions, albeit unwittingly. Maclean's efforts to open negotiations with the Hungarian occupation authorities were shot down by Tito after he referred this to Molotov, and Maclean's proposal to have Polish expeditionary forces airlifted into Yugoslavia was vetoed by Stalin—with the helpful suggestion that Tito accuse the Poles of being Chetnik sympathizers. The bizarre British relationship with the partisans was nicely captured in Tito's complaint, wired to Stalin in early 1944, that Maclean had told him that there were second thoughts at Cairo command about abandoning Mihailović. Tito wanted the Vozhd to write Churchill personally to set him straight on the political line emphasizing Chetnik treachery.[20]

The timing of Churchill's embrace of the partisans could not have been better for Tito. Nor could it have come at a worse time for Mihailović and the Chetniks, who now found themselves isolated, their prestige and ability to arm and equip their men so shattered by the British about-face that finding new recruits would be next to impossible. The Communist smear of the Chetniks for "collaboration," long asserted in Soviet radio broadcasts from the Caucasus and implied in slanted BBC broadcasts, had now been endorsed by Maclean in his "blockbuster report," receiving the imprimatur of the British government. "The B[ritish] L[iaison] O[fficer] now with the Partisan forces," Colonel Bailey reported from Mihailović's headquarters, "for reasons best known to himself, has accepted these imputations at their face value, and passed them on to his superiors. I refrain from commenting on the professional propriety of [Maclean's] behavior . . . with the Partisans." It would be a miracle if the Chetniks could survive the coming winter.[21]

Rubbing still more salt in Mihailović's wounds, *Time* magazine, having already lionized Stalin as man of the year, put Marshal Tito on its cover as a "Hero of the Week."[22] The stage was set for the Allies' official embrace of Stalin's Yugoslav client at Teheran.

28

Teheran and Cairo

By fall 1943, it should have been clear to any objective British or American observer—had Stalin allowed any such observers near the front*—that the Red Army was hopelessly outclassed in open battle against the Wehrmacht, unless the Germans made an obvious error such as the overextension of the Sixth Army in Stalingrad, for which Paulus had paid dearly. What Soviet Communism may have lacked in fighting morale and competence, however, was made up for by Stalin's political cunning. To be sure, the miracle of the American lend-lease largesse that was doing so much to keep the Red Army in the field owed as much to Roosevelt's personal predilections as it did to the activity of Stalin's agents of influence in Washington.[1]

No one had forced Churchill to abandon Mihailović and embrace Stalin's Communist client Tito. So hard did Churchill fall for Soviet propaganda about Yugoslavia that Soviet leaders were taken aback, scarcely believing how gullible the British were. When Anthony Eden proposed to Molotov in November 1943, after Churchill had abandoned Mihailović, that the Soviets send a military mission to Tito—offering Stalin the exclusive use of a British air base in Cairo for the purpose—it was Molotov who

---

* As a reward for the loyalty he had displayed since his appointment as Hopkins's lend-lease liaison to Russia in October 1941, Colonel Faymonville (the NKVD asset) was allowed to visit the front for the first time in May 1943, accompanied by another lend-leaser, Major General J. H. Burns. The men answered not to the army but to Harry Hopkins (who had appointed them both). They refused to share their findings with Ambassador Standley.

suggested that the Chetniks might be worth a second look. "From reports he had received from British officers," Eden informed Molotov, to the latter's amazement, "M[ihailović] would not be good to deal with." Nonetheless Eden agreed that Stalin was perfectly free to send a liaison mission to Mihailović and the Chetniks, if he insisted on doing so.[2]

In the case of Churchill, Maclean, and Eden on Yugoslavia, as with Roosevelt's constant efforts to please and reassure Stalin, it seems to have been naiveté and sentimentality, rather than ideological sympathy with Communism as such, that aligned policy with Soviet interests. In the case of Roosevelt's right-hand man Harry Hopkins, sentiment and ideological sympathy were joined. At a revealingly titled "Russia Aid Rally" in New York City on June 22, 1942, Hopkins had declared, "We are determined that nothing shall stop us from sharing with [Soviet Russia] everything we have." Whereas more-cautious Roosevelt advisers had rationalized arming the USSR on the grounds that, unlike Nazi Germany, it posed no long-term threat to the Western democracies, Hopkins argued, in an August 1943 memorandum, that the United States must give Stalin all the weapons and industrial equipment he wanted precisely because the Red Army would soon be allpowerful. "Russia's postwar position in Europe," Hopkins wrote, "will be a dominant one. With Germany crushed, there [will be] no power in Europe to oppose her tremendous military forces. . . . The conclusions from the foregoing are obvious. . . . [Soviet] Russia must be given every assistance and every effort must be made to obtain her friendship." Far from keeping these controversial views secret, Hopkins openly boasted about his devotion to the Soviet cause. In a *New Yorker* profile in August 1943, the author observed that everyone in Washington knew that Hopkins had been "an articulate propagandist for all-out aid to Russia since the summer of 1941." Chief of Staff George Marshall, in charge of procurement for the US Army, later recalled matter-of-factly that Hopkins's "job with the President was to represent the Russian interests. My job was to represent the American interests." Hopkins himself told journalists unapologetically that he carried the Soviet "banner around town," adding that "Marshall is fine with it."[3]

Hopkins was not alone in his admiration for the Soviet Union, which became increasingly mainstream during the war as the compliant US media turned Stalin into "Uncle Joe." Two Hollywood feature films glorified the Vozhd in 1943, including *Mission to Moscow*, based on the memoir of Joseph Davies, the US ambassador who had whitewashed the Great Terror. On his goodwill mission to Moscow in May 1943, Davies proudly presented Stalin a copy of the film.[4]

Nonetheless, there was something different about the fervor with which Hopkins promoted Soviet interests. Beginning with his Kremlin summit with Stalin in July 1941, Hopkins had come genuinely to prefer the Soviet way of doing things to that of American liberals and socialists. In a remarkable exchange with Molotov in the White House in May 1942, Hopkins disparaged even American Communists as inferior to their Russian counterparts. Not unlike Hitler after Stalin had sacked his Jewish foreign affairs commissar Litvinov in May 1939, Hopkins thought Stalin had improved Communism by purging it of Jewish influence. According to the transcript typed up by a Russian literature professor at Harvard, Samuel H. Cross, serving as President Roosevelt's White House translator,

> Mr. Hopkins remarked that, while the American Communist Party had played ball one-hundred percent since December 7 [Pearl Harbor] the fact was that its composition of largely disgruntled, frustrated, ineffectual, and vociferous people—including a comparatively high proportion of distinctly unsympathetic Jews—misled the average American as to the aspect and character of the Communists in the Soviet Union itself.[5]

Roosevelt was too adroit a politician to be caught saying anything like this with a stenographer present. Even so, the president's obsequiousness toward Stalin could, at times, rival Hopkins's own. As Roosevelt once told William Bullitt, the former ambassador to the USSR sacked for being too critical of the Vozhd, "I just have a hunch that Stalin isn't that kind of man. Harry [Hopkins] said he's not and that he doesn't want anything but security for his country, and I think that if I give him everything I can and ask for nothing in return, *noblesse oblige*, he won't try to annex anything and will work with me for a world of democracy and peace."[6]

Contrary to usual practice in relations between a democratic republic of impeccable legitimacy commanding near-universal respect (the United States), and an outlaw regime set up in opposition to all existing capitalist governments—which had been expelled from the League of Nations for blatant acts of armed aggression and, unlike Nazi Germany, had refused to ratify the Hague or Geneva Conventions—(the USSR), it was not Stalin who was pleading for a summit at which he might be respected as an equal. Instead, it was Roosevelt who was desperate for the Vozhd to meet him. The record shows that Roosevelt first began pleading for an audience with Stalin in December 1941; that these pleas grew more insistent in April and May 1942, culminating in the president's premature pledge of a second front during Molotov's visit to Washington; and that Roosevelt courted Stalin with undiminished energy all through 1943.[7]

In May 1943, in the wake of the Katyn Massacre affair, Roosevelt tried a new tack, proposing "an informal and completely simple visit for a few days between you and me," without Churchill present. The president proposed that this intimate summit would take place "either on your side or my side of the Bering Straits," in Alaska or the Soviet Far East. To sweeten his offer, Roosevelt promised not to bring any pesky staffers from the army or the State Department, inviting only Hopkins, a man Stalin knew was committed to the Soviet cause.[8]

It was an enticing offer. Stalin still said no, although he did offer the president one gesture. On May 22, 1943, TASS declared that Stalin had abolished the Communist International, which would allow Roosevelt to reassure domestic critics that the USSR no longer sought to overthrow the US government. Of course, as Stalin privately explained to Molotov and the Politburo, this was a purely tactical move in view of the now overweening devotion of the US and British governments to serving Soviet interests, which made overthrowing those governments counterproductive. But it fit in beautifully with Soviet agitprop in Western capitals, offering a ready-made counterargument to anyone skeptical of the wisdom of supplying Stalin's armies.[9]

As summer wore on, Roosevelt's courtship of the Vozhd grew more plaintive. With Stalin playing hard to get, the locations proposed by the president for his longed-for tête-à-tête kept shifting closer to Stalin's lair in the Kremlin. After the Vozhd rejected Alaska, the Bering Strait, Iceland, Tunisia, Sicily, formerly Italian Eritrea, and—once Roosevelt had given up on excluding Churchill—Cairo, the president declared himself willing to go as far as Ankara, then Basra in the Persian Gulf. Having been informed of Stalin's penchant for security, Roosevelt offered to have "a special telephone, controlled by you, laid from Basra to Teheran where it would connect with your own line into Russia." When Stalin balked, Roosevelt declared himself willing to go as far as Baghdad—but no farther, as the final leg over the mountains into northern Iran, where "planes in either direction are often held up for three or four days" by weather delays, would make it impossible for him to return to Washington in time to sign congressional bills and resolutions within the constitutionally mandated ten-day limit. As we, unlike the American public at the time, know (and it is impossible that Stalin, with his spies in Washington, did not know), the president was an invalid, owing to the adult onset of polio, which posed serious logistical hurdles to overseas travel, on top of the physical exhaustion that attended any long voyage. Asking him to travel all the way to Russia, or even northern Iran, was an enormous imposition.[10]

Nonetheless, Stalin insisted. The furthest the Vozhd was willing to go was Teheran. The Iranian capital was under Soviet occupation, with the NKVD controlling the streets. Still, the last leg of this grueling journey was a step too far for the invalid president. On October 21, 1943, Roosevelt informed Stalin that he was "deeply disappointed" that the Vozhd was not willing to accommodate his physical and constitutional needs. "With much regret," the president informed Stalin "that I cannot go to Teheran." Responding on November 6 with deadpan wit, Stalin informed Roosevelt that he was very sorry that he would have to meet with Churchill without him. Reeled in by a master fisherman, the president agreed to go to Teheran after all.[11]

As Roosevelt left the White House on November 11, 1943, he was accompanied by his most trusted adviser, Harry Hopkins. Considering the critical stakes of the trip, it is noteworthy that the president did not bring along his secretary of state, Cordell Hull, or any other senior career diplomats. Roosevelt frequently disparaged his own State Department in his letters to Stalin. Roosevelt had sacked Ambassador Bullitt in 1936 because of his critical reports on the Moscow show trials, abolished the Eastern European division in 1937 to improve relations with Stalin, sacked Ambassador Steinhardt in 1941 on Stalin's request, and cashiered the experienced liaison officer Major Yeaton after Hopkins asked him to. In March 1943, the Soviet ambassador to Washington, Litvinov, handed Hopkins a list of "objectionable" diplomats Stalin wanted to purge from the State Department, including Loy Henderson and Ray Atherton from the old Eastern European division. Teaming up with Undersecretary of State Sumner Welles, the Roosevelt confidant who frequently undermined Hull, Hopkins exiled Atherton to Canada and Henderson to Iraq, ensuring that neither man could influence Soviet policy.[12]

When Hull learned of the purge conducted under his nose and complained to the president, Roosevelt decided, at last, to part ways with his friend Welles to stave off Hull's resignation. But Hull was still savaged in the press. In his Washington Merry-Go-Round column published in the *Washington Post* on August 21, 1943, Drew Pearson wrote that the secretary of state "has long been anti-Russian." On NBC radio, Pearson claimed that Hull and his staffers "would really like to see Russia bled white—and the Russians know it." Hull contacted the Soviet embassy to deny this, but the damage to his reputation was done, in all likelihood by one of the two American Communist Party members who worked on Pearson's staff, David Karr (whose ties to Soviet intelligence were later confirmed by the Venona decrypts) and Andrew Older. In this way, Soviet influence operations purged the State Department of its last anti-Communist Russia experts and put the dagger into Cordell Hull, ensuring the secretary of state would not be invited to Teheran,* an obvious slight as both Molotov and Eden would be there.[13]

Without Hull or any other anti-Communists on board to annoy Roosevelt and Hopkins, it was a mostly uneventful crossing. After putting in at the Algerian port of Oran, where he met with Eisenhower and other Mediterranean-front commanders, Roosevelt flew on to Cairo on November 22. In British Egypt, unlike in Teheran, Churchill would be his host, and the two statesmen met with Chiang Kai-shek and his wife Soong May-ling. The reason the Chinese generalissimo came to Cairo is that Roosevelt and Churchill had been informed by Stalin that he could not meet Chiang—or even be in the same country as him simultaneously—lest he violate his neutrality pact with Japan. Stalin's adherence to the letter of this agreement was strict. Not only had the Vozhd interned the Doolittle Raid pilots in 1942, but the NKVD had arrested dozens more Americans who had bailed out over the Soviet Far East. At the time of the Cairo and Teheran meetings in November 1943, there were sixty American pilots interned in a Soviet prison camp near Tashkent in Central Asia, including one

---

* To avoid a breach with his party's southern wing, Roosevelt did allow Hull to attend the pre-Teheran Moscow conference in October alongside Molotov and Eden, where diplomatic preliminaries were negotiated. But he was not invited to Teheran.

seriously ill and urgently in need of surgery.* In view of Stalin's callous treatment of American pilots from the Pacific war, it is perhaps not surprising that he refused to humor his Allies by shaking Chiang's hand. To placate Stalin's foreign policy needs, Chiang Kai-shek, commander of an army of four million then tying down thirty-five Japanese divisions, was demoted to a sideshow, uninvited to the main summit.[14]

The one thing working in Chiang's favor was that Roosevelt genuinely liked China. Over dinner, the president assured the generalissimo that China, after its provinces lost to Japan (including Manchuria and Taiwan) were restored, would be accepted as one of the "Big Four" powers after the war. Chiang was pleased by the flattery, but he wanted reassurance that he would be allowed to participate in Allied planning conferences, such as the one at Teheran. This reassurance, because of Stalin's opposition, Roosevelt could not give, although the president did promise, verbally, that the United States would stage an amphibious operation via the Andaman Islands in the Bay of Bengal (Operation Buccaneer), in coordination with a Chinese offensive from the north and a hoped-for British push overland, to reopen the Burma Road for supplying China. The United States would then, Roosevelt suggested—again verbally—commit itself to sending enough war matériel along the Burma Road to equip ninety Chinese divisions indefinitely, helping Chiang defeat the Japanese and, Chiang hoped, Mao's Communists too, once the invaders were expelled from China. Everything in China's future depended on this Burma operation.[15]

So long as Chiang and Soong May-ling were in Cairo, they were able to charm Roosevelt into these ambitious but nonbinding

---

* As a diplomatic gift to Roosevelt, this pilot was airlifted from Tashkent to Teheran, in time for the "Big Three" summit. The rest of the sixty pilots were later smuggled into Iran by the NKVD, released, and, according to General John R. Deane, head of the US military mission sent to Moscow after Teheran, "pledged to secrecy until the end of the war as to what had occurred."

promises—promises never put in writing. The Cairo Declaration of November 27, 1943, pledged the US and British Allies to restoring "all the territories Japan has stolen from the Chinese," including "Manchuria, Formosa [today's Taiwan], and the Pescadores." But Chiang was not able to win a firm commitment from Allied military planners, or a target date, on Operation Buccaneer. Still, Chiang left Cairo in good spirits, believing Roosevelt was on his side in his struggle against Japan, and against Mao's Communists.[16]

Unbeknownst to the generalissimo, the deck had been stacked against him by Roosevelt's own advisers. Just as remarkable as the exclusion of the secretary of state from the Cairo-Teheran trip was the number of obscure American officials who did show up in Cairo. Among these was Harry Dexter White, the Soviet asset who had authored the final ultimatum to Japan before Pearl Harbor. Before leaving Washington, White told another Treasury official to come meet him in Cairo: Solomon Adler, the US Treasury liaison to Chiang Kai-shek's government, head of the "currency stabilization board" that controlled the money pipeline from Washington to Chungking. Like White, Adler is now known to have been a Stalin asset who reported to the NKVD. Somehow White and Adler contrived to travel roughly five thousand miles each, in opposite directions, in wartime, to sabotage Roosevelt's summit with Chiang. After leaving Cairo, White, in Washington, and Adler, in Chungking, would write nearly identical reports accusing Chiang of "collaboration" with the Japanese and of embezzling funds, recommending that $200 million in aid promised to China be cut off unless Chiang brought Mao's Communists into his government.[17]

Just past dawn on Saturday, November 27, 1943, the president's Douglas VC-54C Skymaster, known as *Sacred Cow*, took flight from Cairo for Teheran. In addition to Hopkins, Averell Harriman, a Democratic party donor whom Roosevelt had just appointed ambassador to the USSR, Roosevelt's son Elliott, and his son-in-law John Boettiger, who had been recently commissioned as an army captain, were aboard *Sacred Cow*. There were also military advisers, including General Marshall, the army chief of staff; Admiral Ernest King, chief naval officer; and Admiral William D. Leahy, chief of staff to the president. The only career diplomat on the plane was Charles "Chip" Bohlen, an experienced Soviet hand brought along as an interpreter (though emphatically not, Bohlen would learn, as a diplomatic adviser).[18]

Although Iran was theoretically neutral in the war, northern Iran had been invaded by the Red Army in August 1941 and occupied, while the British were occupying the southern half. The summit in Teheran would have been inconceivable otherwise, in view of Stalin's paranoia. An advance guard of the NKVD had been on the ground for two weeks, preparing the Soviet embassy compound. Stalin had never flown before, which compounded his ordinary paranoia about security. After touching down in Teheran, Stalin was whisked quickly to the Soviet compound, accompanied by Molotov, his secret police chief Lavrenty Beria, his ever-loyal military adviser Marshal Klim Voroshilov, and a heavily armed personal bodyguard of twelve Georgians.[19]

Scarcely had the Americans unpacked than they were informed that NKVD spies had uncovered a plot by German agents in Teheran to assassinate the "Big Three." Would the president's entourage, Molotov asked Harriman, care to join Stalin in the Soviet compound, which was more secure? Molotov did not explain why, if German agents were really underfoot, the British had not likewise been invited into the secure Soviet compound. Roosevelt's choice of advisers now loomed large. If any Soviet experts from the State Department had been there, Roosevelt would have been warned that Stalin wanted to listen in on his conversations. Chip Bohlen knew this, but he was treated as a mere "interpreter and note-taker" in Teheran, and no one asked his opinion. Living in terror of another State Department purge of "Russia hands," Bohlen was wary that Hopkins might overhear him saying anything critical of Stalin, so he kept his mouth shut. Roosevelt, for his part, told

Harriman that he was "delighted at the prospect" of moving into the Soviet compound, as it would make it easier for him to cultivate Stalin. Although the evidence is inconclusive, some historians have surmised that Roosevelt knew that his rooms in the Soviet compound would be bugged and therefore welcomed the chance to make a positive impression by allowing Stalin to overhear him saying flattering things about him.[20]

Late on the Sunday morning of November 28, 1943, President Roosevelt and his entourage drove up to the gate of the Soviet compound in Teheran, manned by Beria himself. Escorted by a special NKVD detachment to the main embassy building, the Americans installed themselves in their new quarters, in which even Hopkins noticed that "the servants who made their beds and cleaned their rooms were all members of the . . . NKVD."[21]

Roosevelt soon had a visitor. It was Stalin himself, who strolled across the embassy grounds at around 3 p.m. on Sunday afternoon with the star of the Order of Lenin on his chest, accompanied by his Georgian bodyguards and his interpreter, V. N. Pavlov. Bohlen was quickly called in to translate for the president. Roosevelt and Stalin were left alone with their interpreters.[22]

"Hello Marshal Stalin," the president greeted his guest, "I am glad to see you." With laconic understatement, Roosevelt noted that he "had tried for a long time to bring this about." Stalin got straight to the point, stressing the need to open a second front in Europe as soon as possible. Roosevelt did not object, as he might have, by pointing out that there were already a half million American, British, Canadian, and Commonwealth troops in Italy, whose invasion of Sicily had bailed out the Red Army at Kursk in July. Nor did he remind Stalin that his countrymen were fighting a bloody and expensive war against Japanese aggression in Asia, which the USSR had failed to aid in any way. Far from indulging Roosevelt's request for help in Asia, Stalin actually insulted the American client Chiang, remarking that "the Chinese have fought very badly but, in his opinion, it was the fault of the

Chinese leaders." Stalin then made similarly rude remarks about General Charles de Gaulle and the largely American-equipped Free French forces he commanded, which were better received; disparaging de Gaulle and the French was one thing all of the Big Three could agree on. Roosevelt seconded Stalin's proposal that Indochina should not be returned to France after the war.[23]

Then came a stunner. Unprompted by Stalin, though evidently angling for his favor, Roosevelt volunteered that India, too, should be detached from Britain. Explaining that he thought it was "better not to discuss the question of India with Mr. Churchill," Roosevelt proposed that the United States and USSR work together to reform British India "from the bottom, somewhat on the Soviet line." Amazed to hear the president proposing to subject the crown jewel of the British Empire to a Soviet-style revolution, Stalin objected that "the India question was a complicated one, with different levels of culture and the absence of relationship in the castes." Like Molotov reminding Eden that not only Tito's partisans but also Mihailović's Chetniks were fighting the Germans, Stalin was reading what should have been the president's lines for him. Before meeting Roosevelt, the habitually paranoid Stalin had expected the two capitalist statesmen to gang up on him. Hearing Roosevelt disparage Churchill before the summit began, Stalin could scarcely believe his luck.[24]

Nor could Molotov quite believe it when he was informed, in his own meeting with Averell Harriman that evening, that Roosevelt's team had not prepared a written agenda for the conference. Was not the idea of a summit with Stalin the president's idea in the first place? Surely, Molotov said, Roosevelt had some idea what he wanted to talk about in this meeting he had been requesting for two years. Not really, Harriman informed the Russian. What Roosevelt had in mind was not a formal conference but "an informal get-together" of a "personal" nature between "him, Marshal Stalin and Churchill with their respective advisers." The president had come to Teheran with hardly any agenda at all, aside from a memorandum requesting that Stalin let US experts inspect Soviet air bases in the Far East for possible use in bombing raids against Japan.*[25]

Stalin, by contrast, knew exactly what he wanted: a firm pledge from his allies to abandon their Italian offensive, a promise that they would rule out further operations in the Adriatic or Balkans beyond supplying Tito's partisans in Yugoslavia, and a commitment on the second front—that is, a frontal US-British-led amphibious invasion of France as soon as possible. For longer-term goals, Stalin wanted to keep American and British troops out of Eastern Europe, to secure a "friendly"—that is, Communist—Poland and sideline Poland's exile government in London, and to get Roosevelt and Churchill to sign off on the USSR's Molotov-Ribbentrop borders of 1939–1941, including gains won at the expense of Finland, the Baltic states, Poland, and Romania. The collapse of Italy in summer 1943 had added one more item to Stalin's list: he wanted his share of the Italian fleet and merchant marine, despite the USSR having played no role in the war against Italy. All these positions had been unambiguously stated by Molotov at the pre-Teheran planning conference in Moscow in October.[26]

It was not hard to predict who would prevail between a statesman knowing his precise negotiating aims (Stalin), and one wanting mostly to make a nice personal impression (Roosevelt). Had Roosevelt coordinated strategic aims with Churchill, he might have found some common ground in moderating Stalin's demands on Eastern Europe, Poland, and Italy—or even a positive goal, such as demanding Soviet help against Japan (at least the use of Russian air bases in the Far East) or, failing that, a pledge to

---

*A second Roosevelt memorandum proposed something similar in Europe, with Allied pilots being allowed to refuel at Soviet air bases after bombing runs in Germany. This one had already been accepted "in principle"—although it took until summer 1944 for the Red Army to grant landing permission, and even then conditions were imposed strictly limiting access.

stop arresting American pilots who landed on Soviet territory. But Roosevelt had already had two summits with Churchill in 1943. Teheran would be the president's chance to charm Stalin, and the last thing he wanted was for the Vozhd to think he and the prime minister were teaming up against him. As Hopkins confided to Churchill's doctor and confidant, Lord Moran, the president "has come to Teheran determined . . . to come to terms with Stalin, and he is not going to allow anything to interfere with that purpose." In a sign of things to come, Roosevelt declined Churchill's invitation to meet before the first plenary session on Sunday, receiving Stalin instead.[27]

At 4 p.m., the first plenary session opened in the great hall of the Soviet compound, where the Americans were now staying. Churchill declaimed with his usual flair that "in our hands we have the future of mankind." The Big Three, along with their interpreters and advisers, sat around a large circular oak table specially constructed by local carpenters, the idea being that no one must take precedence. Even so, Stalin and Churchill agreed that Roosevelt would chair the meeting.[28]

After describing the latest developments in the Pacific war and introducing the idea of a Burma offensive (Buccaneer), Roosevelt promptly dropped the subject of Japan, which had been his only real priority at Teheran, and pivoted to Stalin's priority, the cross-Channel invasion of Fortress Europe, known as Operation Overlord. Given the cue he needed, Stalin argued for the earliest possible date for Overlord, insisting that the Italian front should be abandoned by the British and Americans because the Alps presented "an almost insuperable barrier" to the north. Although a legitimate point, the impassibility of the Alps was not absolute. Nor was it true that, as Stalin baldly asserted to scotch British hopes of an Adriatic landing, "the Balkans are far from Germany." Certainly they were no farther than France's Channel coast, where Stalin insisted the Allies land instead. Likely landing spots on the Adriatic, such as Trieste, were about 400 kilometers from Munich, nearly twice as close as Normandy or Calais were to the Rhine (750 kilometers). German defenses were also much thinner in Austria and Hungary than in northern France, Belgium, and on the Rhine. The roads and railway infrastructure were better in northern France than in the Balkans, for which reason most of Roosevelt's military advisers, and some of Churchill's, had come to see the merits of Overlord. There was also the difficulty of advancing from Italy into the Balkans through the narrow "Ljubljana gap" along the Adriatic, a dauntingly mountainous region where so much of the fighting on the Austro-Italian front had bogged down in the First World War. A frontal assault on Fortress Europe also fit in better with reigning military doctrine about the concentration of force for decisive battle. Even so, the Allies already had boots on the ground and air bases in Italy, which would be foolish to waste. If Rome were taken and US-British forces reached the Pisa-Rimini line, the German industrial heartland would be in easy flying range of Allied bombers taking off from air bases north of Rome, a point emphasized in preconference military staff talks by Churchill's air chief, General Sir Alan Brooke. Ground troops could also be transported from Italy by sea or air into the Balkans, an "Adriatic strategy" Marshall had discussed with Roosevelt before the plenary session. As Churchill knew better than anyone at the table, it was the Allied breakthrough in Macedonia in September 1918—breaking out from the Salonica beachhead at the northern littoral of the Aegean—that had convinced Erich Ludendorff and the Germans to sue for peace, ending the last war. Surely it was worth considering alternatives to a frontal assault on the fortified Channel beaches of northern France, or thinking about diversionary operations in the Mediterranean area to draw in more German divisions to Italy, Greece, and the Balkans.[29]

Churchill was hoping Roosevelt would do so. Before traveling to Teheran, Churchill had been forced, under heavy American pressure, to agree to pursue Overlord in 1944, although he had insisted that, because of weather conditions, such an amphibious operation could not be undertaken before May, more realistically in June. In the intervening six months, he argued now, the Allies

could accomplish great things in the Mediterranean: capturing
Rome, aiding Yugoslavia, seizing Rhodes and the Dodecanese Islands, enticing Turkey to abandon its costly neutrality (Ankara was
selling chrome to Hitler), and opening the Dardanelles for arms
shipments to Russia. To Churchill's surprise, Roosevelt chimed in
here, saying that "he had thought of a possible operation at the
head of the Adriatic, to make a junction with the Partisans under Tito and then operate north-east into Romania in conjunction
with the Soviet advance from Odessa." Here was the "Adriatic
strategy" Marshall had outlined as a kind of "middle option," short
of a ground invasion of the Balkans from Italy through the Ljubljana gap. So far as we can ascertain, the president's thinking was
that Stalin might welcome a coordinated Allied assault in Eastern
Europe, which would draw German reinforcements off his back
further north.[30]

If this was Roosevelt's hope, he was gravely mistaken. Stalin
rejected the president's offer and soundly rebuked Churchill, dismissing Rome as a useless strategic objective. Rather than anywhere in the Adriatic or the Balkans, he urged that the Allies land
their troops from Italy in southern France to support Overlord: a
subsidiary operation soon named Anvil. Roosevelt withdrew his
Adriatic trial balloon as soon as he had offered it, whether because
of Stalin's dismissal or because he was quietly warned off by Hopkins, who passed a note to Admiral King under the table demanding to know "who's promoting the Adriatic business the President
continually returns to"—possibly fishing for the name of another
anti-Communist adviser to purge. King, to his credit, refused to
give Marshall's name, whispering to Hopkins that he thought the
"Adriatic business" was Roosevelt's own idea. Marshall might have
spoken up here in support of a modified version of Churchill's Balkan stratagem, except that he was not in the room. Despite being
the president's highest-ranking and best-informed military adviser,
Marshall had been dismissed on a hiking tour of the Teheran foothills. Deprived of Marshall's expert commentary on the feasibility
of an Adriatic operation, Roosevelt quietly dropped the matter.

At one point during this critical exchange about Allied military strategy, the president actually winked at Stalin—and Churchill saw it. The prime minister now knew that, on Overlord, he was outvoted.[31]

On another critical issue, it was Roosevelt who was the outlier. For all his courting of Stalin, the president received no reciprocal support from the Vozhd on his own pet issue of unconditional surrender. Stalin told him, in his typically blunt way, that the policy was a terrible idea, as it would only "unite the German people" against the Allies—a similar objection to that of Roosevelt's military advisers, who thought it would make the Germans fight harder. Instead, Stalin proposed that the Allies draw up explicit, and harsh, peace terms and tell the Germans "that this was what they would have to accept," in order to "hasten the day of German capitulation." Curiously, it was on this one subject, on which he disagreed with his own military advisers, that Roosevelt was unbendable, as inflexible as iron. On every other strategic question pitting Soviet against American or British interests, he put up little fight at all.[32]

After an inconclusive first session, the Big Three adjourned. Because they were already inside the American residence in the Soviet compound, Roosevelt invited the British and Russian delegations over for dinner. As everyone loosened up over drinks, Stalin said that Germany must be "dismembered." Roosevelt, thinking he was agreeing, proposed that the German Baltic coastal area near the Kiel Canal be put under "some form of international trusteeship." Because of a mistranslation, the Vozhd thought Roosevelt had proposed restoring the independence of the conquered Baltic nations of Latvia, Lithuania, and Estonia. This subject was, Stalin growled, "not one for discussion": these countries had all voted "by an extension of the will of the people" to join the USSR in 1940. Exhausted by his futile efforts to please Stalin, Roosevelt asked to be wheeled to his room.[33]

Churchill was now face-to-face with Stalin, the man of whom he had once said that to make an alliance with him would be like "shaking hands with murder." Churchill proposed a toast: "God was on the side of the Allies." Chuckling, the Communist dictator fired back, "And the Devil's on my side. The Devil's a Communist and God's a good Conservative!" Churchill was in a black mood as he returned to the British legation. "Stupendous issues are unfolding before our eyes," he told an aide, and yet "the President was inept. He was asked a lot of questions and gave the wrong answers."[34]

Matters did not improve for Churchill on Monday. For the second day in a row, the prime minister requested a private audience with the president. Again Roosevelt declined, in order not to displease Stalin. The second plenary session was defined by Stalin's mounting impatience with Churchill about Overlord. No longer ceding the agenda to Roosevelt, Stalin opened debate by brusquely asking, "Who will command Overlord?" When Roosevelt confessed that this had not yet been decided, Stalin remarked brusquely, "Then nothing will come out of these operations." Gamely, Churchill tried to sell everyone on the Mediterranean--Balkan stratagem one last time. Pressing on to Rome and landing troops in northern Italy, Yugoslavia, or Rhodes to bloody the forty-odd German divisions engaged in Italy and southeastern Europe, he argued, would provide critical insurance for the success of Overlord. Moreover, "Balkan operations would be a great factor in stretching the Germans and giving relief to the Russian front." Churchill admitted that, by tying up landing craft, an amphibious landing in northern Italy, Yugoslavia, or Rhodes might delay Overlord to early June. But this was a small price to pay, Churchill argued, for the chance to "nail down the 21 German divisions in [the Balkans] and destroy them," which would also give the half million Allied soldiers and pilots in Italy something to do. At the least, the prime minister said, "the whole Mediterranean situation should be carefully examined to see what could be done to take the weight off the Soviet front." Here was Churchill's last stand, his final gambit to retain initiative in the war and preserve what was left of Britain's waning influence.[35]

It failed. Sensing that this was the moment to seize the baton from a fading Britain, Roosevelt threw in his lot with Stalin. The president pressed Churchill on Overlord: if not May 1, could the British agree it would "take place . . . not later than 15 or 20 May"? When Churchill refused to commit to this timetable, for fear of ruling out operations in the Balkans, Roosevelt proposed that an "ad hoc committee" select the date. Stalin was having none of this. "Do the British really believe in Overlord," he asked, "or are they saying so only to reassure the Soviet Union?" When Churchill refused to agree to a date, Stalin stood up, turned to Molotov and Voroshilov, and said, "Let's not waste our time here. We've got plenty to do at the front." Sensing that Churchill was about to boil over, Roosevelt suggested that the session be adjourned as "a very good dinner" would be waiting within the hour; a final decision could be reached tomorrow. Under his breath, Roosevelt told his son Elliott, as they left the room, "Winston knows he is beaten."[36]

After dinner, Stalin, with his tongue loosened by vodka, lit into the prime minister. Russians "were not blind," he said. They could see that "Mr. Churchill nursed a secret affection for Germany and desired to see a soft peace." Sensing from the prime minister's pained expression that his jibes were working, Stalin proposed that the Allies should agree, at the end of the war, to execute "50,000 or perhaps 100,000 German officers." By now Churchill, who knew what the Soviets had done at Katyn, was in a rage. Knocking over his brandy glass, Churchill fumed that "the British parliament and people would never support the cold blooded execution of soldiers who had fought for their country." At this, Stalin repeated his line about "Mr. Churchill's secret liking for the Germans." Churchill roared in response that he would rather "be taken out into the garden here and now and be shot myself than sully my own and my country's honor by such infamy."[37]

To calm Churchill down, Roosevelt quipped that perhaps a compromise could be reached and only forty-nine thousand German officers shot. His son Elliott, who had been invited by Stalin personally to the dinner, then chimed in: What difference did it make, as fifty thousand German officers would surely die in battle anyway? At this, Stalin toasted Roosevelt's son: "To your health, Elliott!" Churchill cast a withering glare at Elliott Roosevelt, mouthed "How dare you?" and headed for the door—only to be grabbed from behind by Stalin, who claimed that he was only teasing. Somehow this worked, and Churchill sat down again. Now in a ribald mood, the Vozhd taunted his foreign minister, "Come here, Molotov, and tell us about your pact with Hitler." Stalin, Churchill had to admit, had a sense of humor: warped, homicidal, and sinister, but oddly disarming. As for Roosevelt, Churchill's sense of betrayal was palpable. Churchill's doctor recorded in his diary that night that "until he came here, the P[rime] M[inister] could not bring himself to believe that, face to face with Stalin, the democracies would take different courses. Now he sees he cannot rely on the President's support. What matters more, he realizes that the Russians see this too. It would be useless to take a firm line with Stalin. He will be able to do what he pleases."[38]

The third plenary session on Tuesday, owing to Churchill's creeping resignation to his powerlessness, was less fractious. Significantly, Hopkins had visited the prime minister in the British legation late the previous night to inform him that Roosevelt's mind was made up on an early date for Overlord, adding that "the Soviet view was equally adamant"—an interesting aside coming from someone who worked for the US government. Stalin did seek out Churchill to apologize for needling him so rudely at dinner, but also to put the squeeze on regarding Overlord. If the Allies failed to invade France in May, he warned, it would cause a "feeling of isolation" at Red Army command—a subtly veiled threat Churchill took to mean that Stalin might seek a separate peace with Hitler. Once Roosevelt joined the two for lunch (with only interpreters present), the Big Three agreed on "Overlord in May," with Stalin pledging to launch a diversionary attack simultaneous with the Allied amphibious offensive.[39]

Having won the day, Stalin toned down his threats and barbs, spending most of the afternoon smoking and doodling with his pencil (he liked to draw wolf heads). Churchill, puffing away at his cigar, began to work out a fallback position, whereby the pull-back of Allied forces in Italy to France would be compensated by abandoning the Andaman Islands campaign (Buccaneer) desired by Roosevelt and Chiang Kai-shek, so as to shift over landing craft from the Asian theater to support an Aegean or Adriatic landing. Because of the pressing needs of the US fleet in its Pacific island-hopping campaign and the upcoming plans for Overlord and Anvil, landing craft were, by now, in such demand in the US-British camp that they had begun to dictate strategy into these kinds of zero-sum equations. The president, still focusing mostly on Stalin, did not consent to Churchill's Aegean idea, but he did not object either.[40]

As it was Churchill's birthday, the British legation hosted the others for dinner. The toasts came fast. Roosevelt, despite his anti-monarchical streak, toasted King George VI. Churchill saluted the president as "Defender of Democracy" and Stalin as "Stalin the Great," the equal of Russia's greatest tsars. Stalin saluted the Russian people and American industry, acknowledging that "without the United States as a source of motors, this war would have been lost"—a small hint of appreciation for lend-lease. The only note of discord came when the Vozhd singled out General Sir Alan Brooke, the British air chief reputed to be less than enamored with all the kowtowing to Stalin at the conference. Drinking to Brooke's health, Stalin expressed the hope that Sir Alan "would come to know us better and find we are not so bad after all." Brooke took time to compose himself before coming up with a toast related to the need for a "cover plan" to camouflage Overlord. Possibly, Brooke said, he may have misjudged the Russians because of the "Soviet cover plan" in the early part of the war in "associating with Germany." Stalin, Chip Bohlen recalled, "dryly interjected 'that is possible'" and laughed, to everyone's immense relief.[41]

Although Overlord and Anvil had been settled, there remained many critical issues to discuss, from China, Japan, and the Pacific war; to Allied policy on Yugoslavia and the Balkan area more generally; to Aegean operations, Rhodes, and the entry of Turkey into the war. Stalin also had his own agenda, related to his desire to dismember Germany and his territorial ambitions in the Baltics, Finland, and Romania. And of course, there was Poland.

Considering the gravity of these questions, one might have expected a dignified and sober mood as the Big Three reconvened, with less mirth and fewer wisecracks. But Roosevelt had other ideas. Hopkins had been pressuring him all week to get closer to Stalin, saying that Churchill was not to be trusted. By the final day, Chip Bohlen recalled, "Roosevelt was relying more and more on Hopkins, virtually to the exclusion of others." Stalin, clued into this dynamic from his morning briefings on Roosevelt's (bugged) private remarks, had begun flattering Hopkins more and more openly, at one point walking all the way across the conference room to embrace him. "Stalin showed Hopkins a degree of personal consideration," Harriman recalled, "which I have never seen him show anyone else." Hopkins had been the first Western leader to visit Stalin in Moscow after Barbarossa, arriving in July 1941, when the outcome of the eastern war was very much in doubt. Indeed, Hopkins seemed to have broken through to the Vozhd emotionally in a way even Roosevelt, with his legendary charm, had not yet been able to do.[42]

Roosevelt now made a play for Stalin's affections. It was a calculated effort, as we know from the president's own recollection. He warned Churchill beforehand, whispering, "Winston, I hope you won't be sore at me for what I'm about to do." As the final plenary session began, the president stage-whispered to the Russian side of the room, loud enough to be heard, that "Winston is cranky this morning, he got up on the wrong side of the bed." Roosevelt then proceeded to (in his own recollection) "tease Churchill about his Britishness, about John Bull, about his cigars, about his habits." Churchill, turning red, was not amused. Stalin, for his part, did not know at first what to think, but gradually he realized that Roosevelt was trying to make him laugh. To humor his strange new friend, the dictator finally "broke into a deep, heavy guffaw" (so Roosevelt later claimed, at any rate). "It was then," the president recalled with curious pride, "that I called him 'Uncle Joe.' He would have thought me fresh the day before, but that day he laughed and came over to shake my hand."[43]

Stalin may not have been genuinely charmed by Roosevelt's awkward flirtations, but he sensed that it offered him an opening. During the break before the evening session, Roosevelt invited the Vozhd into his chambers for another one-on-one. If we did not have a stenographic transcript of the conversation that followed—witnessed by both Harriman and Bohlen—it could scarcely be believed. But the president really did tell Stalin that he would go along with Soviet plans to annex eastern Poland, so long as Stalin understood that "there were six or seven million Americans of Polish extraction" and that, "as a practical man, he did not wish to lose their vote[s]." For this reason, "he could not take any part publicly in any such arrangement at the present time," but Roosevelt promised that would have a free hand after the 1944 elections.*

As for Latvia, Lithuania, and Estonia, Roosevelt "jokingly" assured Stalin that "when the Soviet armies re-occupied these areas, he did not intend to go to war with the Soviet Union" as long as the principle of self-determination was vaguely respected, in order to appease American voters "of Lithuanian, Latvian, and Estonian origin." The president added that he was confident the Baltic peoples, if asked, "would vote to join the Soviet Union." Even this obsequious comment was not enough for Stalin, who objected that the Baltic states had belonged to Tsarist Russia: "No one had raised the question of public opinion" then, and "he did not quite see why it was being raised now." Nevertheless, the Vozhd agreed to arrange an "expression of the will of the people in accordance with the Soviet constitution" in the Baltic states—that is, without

---

* In this way, the president casually revealed to Stalin that he intended to run for an unprecedented fourth term, before even informing his own advisers (other than Harriman and Bohlen, who overheard simply because they were in the room).

international observers present—if it would make the president happy. Roosevelt agreed.⁴⁴

The affairs of Europe were thus settled according to Stalin's wishes at Teheran. In the official communiqué of the conference now referred to as EUREKA, the United States and Britain committed themselves to attack the heavily fortified German positions on France's Channel coast (Overlord) and land "at least two divisions" in southern France (Anvil), rather than advancing through Italy with the army already encamped there or landing troops in the Balkans. Either of the latter options might have allowed the British and Americans to reach Germany—not to mention, along the way, Yugoslavia, Romania, Hungary, and Poland—long before the Red Army. But this was now ruled out, beyond logistical support airlifted to the partisans in Yugoslavia and "commando operations" there. (EUREKA thus made official Britain's abandonment of Mihailović, although Churchill had decided this beforehand.) Although US and British troops were "permitted" to advance north as far as the "Pisa-Rimini" line, the commander of Allied forces in Italy, General Mark Clark, was informed that he would have to surrender his sixty-eight landing craft by January 15, 1944, to ensure a long enough lead time for Overlord. Stalin would also be given his share of the Italian Navy and merchant marine. The money line was this: "Overlord and Anvil are the supreme operations for 1944. They must be carried out during May, 1944. Nothing must be undertaken in any other part of the world which hazards the success of these two operations." Stalin had thus assured himself a free hand as the Red Army crashed into Eastern Europe and the Balkans, with no US or British troops nearby to contest him.⁴⁵

The only really critical European matters left unsettled at Teheran were the final borders of postwar Poland and the fate of Germany after Hitler's defeat, and here, too, the discussion had moved decisively in Stalin's direction. During the final plenary session on December 1, there was a moment of tension when Stalin, to forestall any effort by Churchill to pull back Roosevelt's promises regarding Poland, slandered the Polish government-in-exile, which, he claimed, was "closely connected with the Germans and their agents in Poland were killing [Soviet] partisans." Rejecting this libel, Churchill reminded Stalin that "England declared war because of Poland," at a time—he could have added, but did not—when Stalin was collaborating with Hitler. Knowing he had Roosevelt in his pocket, Stalin felt no need to humor Churchill, demanding that the United States and Britain give him a "guarantee that the Polish government in exile would cease the killing of partisans in Poland" and agree to sign off on the "1939 line" between Poland and the Soviet Union. Backing up the prime minister, Anthony Eden demanded clarification: Was it "the Molotov-Ribbentrop line" that Stalin meant? "Call it what you will," Stalin replied. "We still consider it just and right." When Molotov repeated his canard that Soviets were only asking for the Curzon Line of 1919–1920 to be restored, Eden whipped out a map to show everyone the differences. Here, at a critical moment in negotiations over the postwar borders of Eastern Europe, when a combined US-British stand might have salvaged something for Poland, Roosevelt intervened again on Stalin's side, asking "whether an involuntary transfer of peoples from the mixed areas was possible," to help rearrange Poland's borders to Stalin's liking. Of course, Stalin replied drily, "such a transfer was entirely possible."[46]

Having encouraged Stalin to cleanse eastern Poland of Poles before annexing it, Roosevelt then changed the subject before Churchill and Eden could object to his astonishing sellout. "The question," the president proposed, "was whether or not to split up Germany" to enable Poland to be compensated for its territorial losses to the USSR. Stalin spurned Roosevelt's suggestion as inadequate, replying that he "preferred the dismemberment of Germany." To show that he was no softer than Stalin, Roosevelt proposed instead what a stenographer described as "a complicated partition of Germany into five or more areas" (as Churchill remarked, "The President had said a mouthful"). Still Stalin was unsatisfied, repeating that "if Germany was to be dismembered, it should really be dismembered, and it was neither a question of the division of Germany in five or six states and two areas as the President suggested." When Churchill tried gamely to revisit the question of Poland's borders, Stalin proposed that, in exchange for settling for only the Curzon instead of the Molotov-Ribbentrop borders, he would annex Tilsit, Königsberg, and the adjoining Baltic littoral section of Lithuania and East Prussia, along with the entire left bank of the Niemen River. Stalin also demanded German industrial reparations to replace factories and equipment destroyed in the war. Browbeaten into submission, neither Roosevelt nor Churchill agreed formally to all of this, but they did not object either.[47]

Europe aside, two critical issues were on the table as Churchill and Roosevelt, after taking leave from Stalin, regrouped in Cairo on December 4. The first was what to do about Turkey and its semi-benevolent, semi-hostile neutrality. Turkey's president Ismet Inönü, invited to attend, listened politely to Churchill's pitch for intervention. But the Allies' hands had been tied by the commitment to Overlord in May: they could not promise Inönü the scale of military aid he felt was required to make the risk of entering the war against Nazi Germany worthwhile for Turkey. Roosevelt, sympathizing with Inönü's dilemma, agreed that "the Turks did not want to be caught with their pants down." Churchill—still clinging to his last hopes for a Mediterranean strategy to contest the Balkans and hoping (as it turned out, forlornly) that Inönü would let Britain use Turkish air bases to seize control of the skies over the Aegean, which might enable Allied landings on Rhodes or the Dodecanese Islands—was less obliging. But, in the absence of Roosevelt's backing, he was forced to give in.[48]

After this latest setback, Churchill resolved not to give any further ground to the president. Unfortunately for Chiang and China, the one area where Churchill still had leverage was in the Pacific theater, where he wanted to pull the plug on Buccaneer to recall transports for his hoped-for Mediterranean operations. As Churchill reminded Roosevelt, Stalin had quietly promised them at Teheran, unofficially and off the record, that the USSR would go to war with Japan within three months of the end of the European war in exchange for Soviet territorial gains in Mongolia, Sakhalin, and the Kurile Islands.* Siberia and Manchuria, Churchill pointed out, offered a better staging ground for invading Japan than south China, and most of Japan's ground troops were in northern China and Manchukuo (Manchuria). "In the face of Marshal Stalin's promise that Russia would come into the war [against Japan]," Churchill concluded his pitch to call off Buccaneer, "operations in the South East Asia Command had lost a good deal of their value." It was a plausible argument, if a callous one from Chiang's perspective. It was also perfectly in tune—as were the EUREKA decisions on Europe—with Stalin's interests, this time in northern Asia.[49]

The president was not ready to give up on his beloved China, in particular his plans to include it in the Big Four powers of what he now referred to as the United Nations (occupied France being then excluded from the club). The Allies, Roosevelt told Churchill, had a "moral obligation" to do something for China. No one knew when the Soviets would join the war against Japan. "Suppose Marshal Stalin," the president told Churchill in a rare moment of clear thinking about the Soviet dictator, "was unable to be as good as his word, we might find that we had forfeited Chinese support without obtaining commensurate help from the Russians." If Chiang did not get the promised Andaman operation to open up the Burma Road, the president warned, China might drop out of the war, freeing up thirty-five Japanese divisions—nearly 80 percent of the Japanese Imperial Army—for operations elsewhere. Admiral King, who shared Roosevelt's view on China, promised that he

---

*This agreement had been left out of the conference memoranda for the same reason Stalin had refused to shake Chiang's hand: his neutrality pact with Tokyo. Stalin was so loyal to Tokyo that, although 60 American pilots were allowed to escape NKVD camps as a goodwill gesture during the Teheran conference, in the course of December 1943 another 110 American pilots were arrested in the Soviet Far East after conducting bombing raids on Japan.

could find landing craft elsewhere for Europe, enabling Buccaneer to go forward.[50]

For four days, Roosevelt remained "stubborn as a mule" on the Bay of Bengal operation. Then, he gave in. In part, this owed to the president's feeling that he needed to agree with Churchill on something after leaving him out to dry in Teheran and cruelly mocking him in Stalin's presence. "The British just won't do the operation," he told the commander of American forces in China, General Joseph Warren "Vinegar Joe" Stilwell, who had just arrived in Cairo, referring to Buccaneer, "and I can't get them to agree to it." To maintain appearances, Roosevelt thought that "it won't do for a conference to end that way." Having agreed to cede Eastern Europe to Soviet domination at Teheran, Roosevelt now agreed to sell out China at Cairo.[51]

The president sent off a "terse wire" to Chiang Kai-shek in Chungking, informing the generalissimo that "Buccaneer is off." (Churchill had suggested fudging the rejection by claiming that Buccaneer was postponed until "after the monsoon." Roosevelt, to his credit, thought Chiang deserved the truth.) Chiang accepted the news gracefully, asking in return that the Americans ship him more warplanes and the financial aid he had requested, in gold.[52]

It was the last gasp of a dying cause. Lend-lease deliveries to China, already a tiny fraction of those allotted to Britain and Russia—only $126 million worth was sent to Chungking during all of 1941 and 1942, or 1.5 percent of the global total—were reduced in 1943 and 1944 to a mere 0.4 percent of lend-lease spending. Although Churchill's opposition to Buccaneer had pressured Roosevelt into withdrawing his commitment to China, Stalin's spies in the US camp, in particular Solomon Adler, the Treasury man in Chungking, had been poisoning the well against Chiang for months. Like Churchill on the Chetniks in Yugoslavia, Roosevelt began to doubt whether Chiang was really the right man to back in China. "Chiang would have us believe," he told his son Elliott after speaking with Stilwell in Cairo, "that the Chinese Communists are doing nothing against the Japanese—we know

differently." This was manifestly untrue: in October 1940 Stalin
had brokered a secret deal in which Japan promised not to attack
Mao's forces and vice versa. Ominously, Roosevelt began to talk
after Cairo about withdrawing military aid from China unless
Chiang "democratized" his regime by forming a "unity government with the Communists at Yenan." After returning to Washington from Cairo, Harry Dexter White slow-walked, diminished,
and ultimately curtailed deliveries of the $200 million promised
to China. When Secretary Morgenthau enquired why Chiang was
not receiving the gold Roosevelt had promised him, Morgenthau
was set straight by three Treasury advisers now known to have
been Soviet agents: White, Adler, and Frank Coe, who told him
Chiang's cronies would "steal or squander" the gold. This Communist talking point about the irredeemably corrupt Chiang Kai-
shek, crafted by three Soviet agents in the Treasury Department,
was Washington conventional wisdom by the end of the war—
and it remains a standard trope of the historical literature on China
to this day.*[53]

Lending a noxious bite to these Communist slanders was that
they flattered—and likely helped shape—the racial prejudices of
General Stilwell. Stilwell was no Communist, but he despised
Chiang, calling him "peanut" or sometimes "rattlesnake." "The
cure for China's trouble," Stilwell often told his aides, "is the
elimination of Chiang Kai-Shek." According to the memoirs of

---

* The author once unthinkingly parroted the "corrupt Chiang Kai-shek"
line in a freshman history seminar at Stanford University, only to be rebuked by Chiang's grandniece. That corruption was present in wartime
Chungking was obviously true, but then this was true of every belligerent. Stalin's government, which was receiving fifty to one hundred times
more lend-lease aid than Chiang's, even resold American wheat in Iran
for profit in spring 1943. That corruption became the go-to charge in the
Washington whisper campaign that ultimately led to the cutting off of
aid to, and the final defeat of, the Kuomintang says little about Chiang
Kai-shek's style of governance and a great deal about Communist message discipline.

Stilwell's assistant, Lieutenant Colonel Frank Dorn, Stilwell told Dorn in Chungking after returning from Cairo that "I have been directed to prepare a plan for the assassination of Chiang Kai-Shek." As for who ordered this, Stilwell said it "came from the very top"—meaning the president—although Dorn thought it "could have come from Hopkins." "The Big Boy," Stilwell told Dorn, "is fed up with Chiang and his tantrums. In fact, he told me in that Olympian manner of his: If you can't get along with Chiang and can't replace him, get rid of him once and for all. You know what I mean. Put in someone you can manage." Dorn, a loyal soldier, duly set to work studying possible assassination plans, although, to his immense relief, the order to strike was never given. Even so, Roosevelt's sharp turn against Chiang after Cairo meant that the generalissimo had lost his diplomatic Waterloo.[54]

So, too, had Churchill. With the death of the Mediterranean stratagem, Britain had forfeited its last chance to win the war on its own terms and shape the postwar world—and to salvage some degree of US-British influence in Eastern Europe and the Balkans. Cornered by Roosevelt, who had lined up with Stalin on all important policy questions, Churchill could only fume at his creeping irrelevance. In reality, it was Britain that had missed the chance in 1940 to strike at the hydra-headed alliance of dictators by bombing the Baku oil fields fueling their brutal conquests and thus turn the war of 1939 into a principled fight against totalitarian aggression. By supporting Stalin unconditionally after Hitler's attack, and demanding nothing in return, Churchill and Roosevelt had stacked the decks against themselves. The fight against Hitler, Britain's "finest hour" when England stood alone, was Stalin's war now.

29

Second Front

STALIN'S ACROSS-THE-BOARD VICTORIES at Teheran, ensuring his armies a free hand in Europe from Scandinavia to the Black Sea, left US and British policymakers in a curious position. Now that even Churchill had agreed to "Overlord in May," the perennial Soviet complaint about the unequal fighting burden borne by the Red Army would soon be put to rest. There was no longer any real doubt that the Allies would win, even if it was far from clear how long this would take and what it would cost. Nor was there a fear that any of the Allied countries might go under—certainly not the United States, which had never been under much genuine danger from the Germans anyway, beyond the threat of U-boat attacks on its ports and shipping lanes. Britain, in 1940, and the Soviet Union, in 1941 and 1942, had endured a great trial by fire, but they had emerged from the danger point and were now bringing the fight toward enemy territory.

These facts sat uneasily with the lend-lease program on which the Soviet armies had become so dependent. Open-ended as the Lend-Lease Act was in granting the president powers to tap the vast hydraulic forces of the US economy for the benefit of any country he chose "in the interest of national defense," it was not entirely unlimited. Congress was supposed to review the program regularly and renew funding on an annual basis. There was even a sunset clause in section 5C, which set an automatic expiration date, absent new congressional authorization, on June 30, 1943—by coincidence, the date the second Soviet protocol was completed—although contracts entered into before then could be brought to fruition. In view of the colossal volumes of war matériel sent to Russia during that second protocol—and the crucial role these deliveries had played at Stalingrad and Kursk, thereby ending the danger of a Soviet collapse on the eastern front—the sunset clause could easily have been applied, with lend-lease shipments to Russia curtailed or slowed down after June 30, 1943, if not shut down entirely.[1]

By 1943, however, logic and restraint had been vanquished by war fever in Washington. Congress had previously served as a brake on President Roosevelt's authoritarian instincts, but this had become harder in wartime. The lend-lease bill (H.R. 1776) had rolled together all countries into one congressional resolution, to be passed or rejected as a whole. If anyone wished to vote against continuing to supply Stalin's no-longer-as-desperate armies at US taxpayer expense, they would have to vote against military aid for Britain and China too, along with Free France, Belgium, Greece, Yugoslavia, and other Nazi-occupied nations in Europe. Even neutral countries like Turkey, Iran, and Saudi Arabia were receiving lend-lease aid. Whether or not it had made sense to give the president unilateral authority to use taxpayer funds to arm and supply (by the end of the war) thirty-six different sovereign nations, few congressmen wanted to go on record opposing aid to all of these countries. And so, despite the March 1943 scandal when Admiral Standley had complained about Soviet ingratitude, the vote extending the Lend-Lease Act beyond June 30, 1943, had passed by 406 to 7 in the House and 82 to 0 in the Senate.[2]

One can hardly blame Hopkins and Roosevelt for taking this vote as a ringing endorsement of their Soviet aid policy, however indirect the connection to Russia in the vote to reauthorize lend-lease may have been. The Soviet aid program had anyhow long been run independently of congressional oversight. In the first months after Barbarossa, President Roosevelt had approved two successive billion-dollar appropriations for Stalin, interest-free, with "repayment of principal to commence five years after the war's end." This deferred repayment framework was loosened still further in the "Master Lend-Lease Agreement" signed on June 11, 1942, covering the second and future protocols, which superseded all earlier Russian appropriations. Under the master agreement, Soviet payment to the US government was deferred "until the extent of the defense aid is known and until the progress of events makes clearer the final terms and conditions and benefits which will be in the mutual interest of the United States of America and the Union of Soviet Socialist Republics and will promote the establishment and maintenance of world peace." The master agreement thus made Soviet repayment of lend-lease loans conditional on the "establishment of world peace." Legally and financially speaking, there were no obstacles to Hopkins's policy of "sharing everything we have" with the USSR. The only thing that might have stayed Hopkins's hand was intervention from Roosevelt, and in view of the president's growing enthusiasm for Stalin and the Soviet war effort, this was unlikely to happen.[3]

And so the Roosevelt administration ratcheted up aid shipments to Stalin to almost unfathomable levels in the second half of 1943 and early 1944, just as the Red Army, after decisively repulsing Hitler's last offensive on the eastern front, began its long march to Berlin. While the ambitious targets of the second protocol had, despite heroic efforts, not quite been met, after June 1943 Hopkins's men went full throttle and began to exceed monthly targets in their Soviet deliveries. By now, shipping lanes and ports on the Persian Gulf and Pacific routes were running at full capacity, with these routes together handling over 500,000 tons of supplies per month for Stalin's armies between July and October 1943, hitting 569,000 tons in November—the month of Teheran—and an astonishing 600,000 tons per month in December and January, despite the hazards of cold and ice on the route to Vladivostok. During the third protocol period from July 1, 1943, to June 30, 1944, the United States shipped more than six million tons of warplanes, tanks, trucks, weapons, ammunition, industrial equipment, metals, and foodstuffs to Stalin, nearly twice as much as had been shipped in the second protocol when such aid was far more desperately needed, and 30 percent more than had been promised to Stalin by the protocol committee.[4]

There was precious little strategic rationale for this sharp up-tick in already gargantuan aid deliveries to the Red Army in the second half of 1943. Whereas in the first two protocols, Hopkins and his men could argue that it was necessary to support the Red Army because American soldiers were not yet fighting Germans in strength, July 1943—the first month of the ramped-up third protocol—brought the massive Allied invasion of Sicily, followed by the invasion of the Italian mainland, where there were now a half million American and British troops. By the second half of 1943, when the third protocol entered into force, the percentage of Wehrmacht divisions defending Europe against the Americans and British (as opposed to those fighting the Red Army) crossed 40 percent. At Teheran, Roosevelt and Churchill had agreed on Overlord and Anvil, even while continuing the hard slog against first-line German troops in Italy. By the time of the D-Day landings in early June 1944, the Germans had sixty-six divisions defending France and Western Europe against the Americans and British, twenty in Scandinavia, another twenty-seven in Italy engaged in active operations, and twenty-four more in the Balkans defending against Adriatic or Aegean landings. US-British bombing raids on the German Reich were, by 1944, tying down nearly a dozen Luftwaffe divisions and anti-aircraft crews. Even before the D-Day landings, German force strength engaged against (or guarding against landings by) the Americans and British had reached near parity with those fighting on the eastern front, roughly 144 divisions compared to 150 (in percentage terms, 49 percent versus 51 percent). Then there were the mounting demands on production capacity and shipping tonnage of the war against Japan. It would have been natural for the United States to shift war-industrial resources and shipping capacity to meet galloping requirements in Europe and Asia in 1943–1944, concomitantly reducing those allotted to Russian lend-lease, now that the Americans and British were doing more of the fighting.[5]

Nothing of the kind was going to happen on Hopkins's watch. The declassified Lend-Lease Administration files make clear that Soviet requisitions all received "A-1" priority ratings, putting them in front of the queue. In one extraordinary episode in June 1942, the Soviet air attaché in the United States, Colonel A. N. Kotikov, demanded that American Airlines be banned from using Newark Airport after one of its planes accidentally brushed against a Russian A-20 Havoc bomber (one consigned to Stalin, that is). Kotikov's request that the offending American pilot be executed was, mercifully, denied. But after the Soviet attaché complained to Hopkins, American Airlines was banned from using Newark Airport, as were all the other major US carriers: United, TWA, and Eastern. Although described as a temporary "suspension," the order remained in force until the end of the war. On Hopkins's say-so, Newark Airport had been turned over to the Soviet Union.[6]

This was not the only American airfield given to the exclusive use of the Russian lend-lease program. By the end of 1942, Gore airfield in Great Falls, Montana, the main jumping-off point for warplanes flown to Siberia via Canada and Alaska, had become, for all intents and purposes, a Soviet air base. On January 1, 1943, Major General George Racey Jordan, the US liaison officer to Kotikov's Soviet aircraft procurement operation in Great Falls, received an order from air force headquarters that "the President has directed that . . . the modification, equipment and movement of Russian planes have been given first priority, even over planes for U.S. Army Air Forces." When he showed this presidential order to a "flying Colonel" passing through Great Falls to explain why he had to wait for a Soviet lend-lease aircraft to be serviced before his plane could be winterized, Jordan recalled, the US Army Air Force colonel was "positively speechless. . . . He went around with a puzzled look, muttering 'First priority! I'll be damned.'"[7]

The ALSIB route across Alaska to Siberia also required American pilots to risk their skins flying thousands of miles across north country. Because of Stalin's paranoia, US pilots usually flew these planes only as far as Ladd Airfield in Fairbanks, Alaska, where

Soviet pilots "took delivery" of them. From Great Falls to Fairbanks was two thousand miles, via Edmonton and Whitehorse,
Canada, across the subarctic wilderness of the Yukon. It was no
picnic flying the planes to Great Falls either, as it was 2,000 miles
from Buffalo, New York, where Bell aircraft were manufactured,
and 1,200 miles from the Douglas plant in Southern California.
Simply landing and taking off in Great Falls was a chore. Perched
at 3,665 feet above sea level above a broad plain, Gore Field had
exceptional visibility, but it was also one of the coldest places in
the continental United States, where a temperature of seventy below zero had been recorded; it was fifty below for most of the winter of 1942–1943. ALSIB pilots then flew in unheated cockpits over
the tundra-like wastes of the Yukon, punctuated by frozen lakes or
black spruce trees that might, as surviving pilots recalled, "cushion
your crash if the wings iced over, or your engine seized up when its
oil gelled in the extreme cold." Even in the mild summer months
from June to September 1943, 61 planes went down flying from
Montana to Alaska (out of 1,769). Pilots sometimes survived these
crashes only to succumb to frostbite (one was found dead wrapped
in his parachute). Soviet pilots traversing the Bering Strait, too,
lost eighteen planes per month that summer on the leg to Siberia.[8]

The ALSIB story displays the unsung heroism of the Americans who satisfied Stalin's gargantuan lend-lease orders, but also
the political illogic of the program. No matter how many Americans risked their lives flying into the Arctic Circle to turn over
the finest products of the US aviation industry to the Soviet Air
Force, none of them were allowed to visit Russian territory. If any
of them flew on to Uelkal, the first Soviet air base on the far side
of the Bering Strait, they would have been interned as prisoners
of war. In the other direction, things were different. Soviet pilots were not only permitted to fly in via Nome to Fairbanks, but
were invited to take over Ladd air base, and soon the rest of the
town too. Bill Schoeppe, one of the American mechanics who serviced lend-lease warplanes in Fairbanks before they were turned
over to the Russians—no easy job in temperatures often reaching

forty and fifty degrees below zero—recalled that even Alaskans proud of holding their drink were put to shame by the "Red Army men," who "could put away much more liquor than Americans." Schoeppe was struck by the voracious appetite of Soviet pilots for American consumer goods:

> Whenever there was a gang of [Soviet] pilots in town waiting for airplanes, they roamed the streets of Fairbanks, some buying women's silk stockings and underwear. Most unusual was their use of perfume! Some rough-bearded guys in britches and fine leather boots . . . all men, only lots of drinks and smoking, and all these guys loaded with perfume! Some said it was because they had no antiperspirant.

Soviet pilots were demanding when it came to their planes, especially the beloved Airacobras. Constantly suspecting "sabotage," the Russians objected violently when they learned that Schoeppe was merely "sand-blasting and checking" the engine's twenty-four spark plugs after the long flight in from Montana. Instead, they "demanded all replacement plugs be factory new."[9]

Stalin was given first priority on more than just warplanes. American civilians were forced to tighten their belts to provide Russians with foodstuffs at a time of strict wartime rationing back home. There were eight thousand rationing boards in the United States during the war, restricting consumption of everything from grain, milk, butter, bacon, and sugar to fuel, rubber, tires, fabrics, and shoes. Every American family that lived through the war remembers the wartime ration books and exhortations to scale back, from "Meatless Mondays" to "Wheatless Wednesdays." What only a few of them suspected was that the things they missed were being rerouted to the other side of the world to nourish Russian soldiers who were never told (even if many of them suspected) that they were being fed on the commodity surpluses of American capitalism.

So colossal were shipments of lend-lease foodstuffs to Stalin by 1943—the volume in the third protocol would surpass 1.7 million tons—that American store shelves emptied of essentials. Butter shortages were reported in 1943 in the following states: California in January, Colorado in March, Ohio in February, New Hampshire in May, Oregon in August, Pennsylvania and Massachusetts in October, and New Jersey in November. A frustrated Boston grocer asked his congressman in October 1943 why his country was sending the USSR "ninety million pounds of our butter" while "many millions of our own people haven't had an ounce of butter in many weeks." Making shortages bite, Americans were barraged with ads touting "oleomargarine" while the Russians refused to accept margarine in lieu of butter. So enormous were butter shipments bound for Vladivostok that rumors coursed through Pacific port towns "that the Russians are using our butter to grease their boots."[10]

More poignant were the complaints of poor Americans who had just begun to enjoy butter after the lean Depression years, only to now be forced to give it up again, this time to Stalin. These were Roosevelt's constituents, the children of the New Deal, and they felt betrayed. "I am only a cog in the wheels," Marie Zgone of Wickliffe, Ohio, wrote Washington in February 1943,

> a poor working girl. In Depression times, I was on WPA, and I couldn't afford to buy butter on $15.00 a week and support my mother and pay rent, light, gas, etc. Now, I make a little more money, I still can't buy butter because its [sic] all gone before I can go to the store. If I am fortunate, I can get some oleo, but many times I haven't even had that. If oleo is good enough, for me, an American, I'm sure it ought to be good enough for Russia as I am now paying an income tax for the first time in my life.

Miss Zgone would have been still more flummoxed had she learned that her taxes also paid for $181 million worth of women's apparel, all sent to the USSR.[11]

In the April 1943 issue of *The American Magazine*, the Hopkins loyalist who ran the lend-lease program, Edward Stettinius, admitted that Russians were given priority with butter. "Why such a luxury for the Russian Army?" he asked. Shipping ninety million pounds of butter to the USSR (forty-five thousand tons), as allotted in the third protocol, Stettinius admonished Americans, "permits the Russian soldier fighting the bloodiest battles in history to have American butter on his black bread once a week. Would you be willing to cut down your own butter supply so that the Russian soldier could have butter on his bread almost every day?"[12]

Judging from the volume of angry correspondence it produced, Stettinius's lecture did not go over well in the American heartland. Churchgoing Americans have always been charitable by nature; their generosity had helped feed Soviet Russia during the Volga famine of 1921–1922, and many thousands would certainly have donated foodstuffs to the suffering soldiers of the Red Army if local charities had asked them to. But lend-lease was not asking for voluntary donations; it was coercing food by government fiat. To dampen growing public skepticism, Stettinius and Hopkins—after consulting their Soviet contacts—came up with a reason Russians needed butter, while Americans could make do with margarine. The Red Army, Americans were told beginning in October 1943, had specially requested butter "for use in military hospitals for the consumption of recuperating wounded soldiers." How, exactly, eating butter helped wounded Russians convalesce, aside from lifting their spirits, was not explained. This was not a rational but an emotional argument.[13]

This was not the first time Hopkins had used the same argument. In spring 1943, the population of crab began to dip in the waters of the Pacific Northwest, in particular king crab, a lucrative catch that was a staple of the regional diet. Secretly, the Lend-Lease Administration had granted a Soviet request to allow Russian fishing vessels to haul for crab, including king crab, from Northern California all the way up to the Alaskan coast, while also requisitioning—at US taxpayer expense—"crab nets, tin plate for the canning of crab meat, and the repair of some floating [Soviet] crab canneries." Before long, Oregon and Washington fishermen

were complaining that their waters were being fished out by Communists and their livelihoods destroyed, loudly enough that their
complaints were taken up in Congress. No matter: on Hopkins's
orders, Lend-Lease Administration officials ruled that, because
"crab meat has been found to be particularly helpful in the care
of convalescent wounded soldiers," allowing Soviet vessels to fish
for crab from Oregon to Alaska was "a program of military necessity." The Russians could haul as much American crab as they
wished to.[14]

Shortages of butter and crab were not unique. The most
famous lend-lease foodstuff given to Russians during the war—
Spam, or tusonka pork—was so highly prized by the Red Army
that the American pork and meat-canning industry was reshaped
in 1943 to meet Soviet demand. Taste tests were conducted to find
a recipe of "cooked pork, lard, onions, salt and spices" to the Russians' liking. The US Department of Agriculture then placed an
order for twenty-three million pounds of pork. Extra-large, thirty-
four-ounce tin cans were designed, stackable for shipping. By the
second quarter of 1943, the US pork industry was sending 13 percent of its total production to the USSR, up from 9.7 percent in
1942—and the Soviet share would soon ramp up even higher.[15]

The impact on domestic consumption was predictable. As a
grocer in Baltimore, E. C. Newman, complained on March 18,
1943, meat canneries working for Stalin had stopped supplying local stores. "When my grocer customers tell me," Newman wrote
Senator Millard Tydings of Maryland, "that workmen are being offered a dollar an hour overtime to work on packing this shipment
so that it will get out and be shipped to Russia; surely this is not
playing fair with the American people to put us on a short ration
when such a company can pay such terrible overtime wages in
order to get a shipment out under [Soviet] Lend-Lease." Although
denying that they had imposed wage controls, Hopkins and Stettinius informed Senator Tydings that it was true they expected
suppliers to "meet their demanding delivery schedules" and that
lend-lease imposed "penalties for non-delivery." If contractors did

not want to lose Stalin's business (paid for by the US taxpayer), it
was up to them to figure out how to satisfy the needs of the Red
Army, whether with the carrot of overtime pay or the stick of firing tardy workers.[16]

Spam was the showcase product of the American aid effort
to the USSR, but it was far from unique. The percentage of US
pork production devoted to Stalin's needs in 1943, 12.8 percent,
was spot-on average for foodstuffs in the third protocol. Stalin's
allotment of canned and frozen fish was almost identical, at 12.9
percent, not counting the crab hauled out by Soviet fishermen in
the Pacific Northwest. With some vitamin- and protein-rich items,
Stalin's share would be even higher: 15.3 percent of US production of eggs (dried and dehydrated for shipment to Russia), 15.7
percent of dried fruit, and 16.8 percent of beans. The Soviet take
of American production of carbohydrates such as wheat and sugar
was smaller, but the two hundred thousand tons of wheat and seventy thousand tons of sugar shipped to the USSR made up a huge
percentage of Soviet consumption of each item. By 1943, American wheat was furnishing nearly a third of Soviet consumption
and even subsidizing Soviet purchases of Persian pilaf, after this
grain was sold in Iran. The US contribution to the Soviet sweet
tooth was near exclusive, providing 70 percent of Russian sugar
consumption by 1944.[17]

So important were American foodstuffs to the diet of Red Army
soldiers by 1943 and 1944 that a special manual was prepared and
distributed to each unit, explaining what was in the cans and pack-
ets they gleefully opened and providing metric conversions for
pounds and ounces. With a characteristic lack of gratitude, the
manual described the American lend-lease bounty blandly as "New
Kinds of Products Arriving in the Stores of the Red Army." Citing what was supposed to have been the logic of lend-lease, the
manual's authors reported that these foodstuffs had been sent to
Russia "on loan or rental," without explaining how one rented cans
of Spam, beans, fish conserves, or dehydrated butter. (In the Russians' defense, no one in Washington had explained this either.)[18]

Just as Soviet pilots marveled at the perfume and silk stockings on sale even in an Arctic backwater like Fairbanks, Alaska, it must have been bewildering for hitherto starving Red Army grunts to learn the varieties of processed pork Americans had sent them: nine different brands of *rublenaia svinina* (chopped pork), seven brands of "luncheon meat," five kinds of "chopped ham," five more of pork sausage, "pork sausage links in their own juice," corned canned pork, canned pork tongue, dehydrated pork, bacon, "Vienna sausage," and, finally, tusonka. There were also a dozen-odd varieties of "corned beef" and of pork, soy, beef, potato, and vegetable soups and stews. American canneries even conjured up a dried-powder version of borscht, sent in millions of tiny boxes with the ingredients listed in numbing detail for suspicious Russians (32 percent dried beets, 30 percent dried potatoes, 10 percent dried cabbage, 10 percent fat, 10 percent wheat flour, 8 percent salt, 3 percent dried onions, 2 percent dried carrots, 4 percent tomato powder, 0.4–0.7 percent citric acid, 0.2 percent ground pepper, 0.1 percent bay leaves). In a literal sense, American capitalism was feeding the Red Army.[19]

Yankee capitalists were just as creative in satisfying the special requirements of Soviet war industry. Here, too, the dramatic ramp-up began in the second half of 1943, by which time the strategic rationale of sharing critical military technology with a Red Army now advancing (however slowly) on all fronts was questionable at best. Even before the third protocol period began in July 1943, Stalin's procurement agents had already requisitioned $500 million worth of "industrial equipment"—an amount comparable to $50 billion today—consisting of everything from machine tools, electric furnaces, motors, cranes, and hoists to oil refineries, tire manufacturing plants, and aluminum and steel-rolling mills.[20]

Reading through the minutes of Harry Hopkins's Soviet protocol committee from 1943, it is hard to escape the impression that Soviet agents of influence had taken over the White House. On January 5, 1943, the "Treasury Procurement Division" reported matter-of-factly to Hopkins's committee that "the Ford Tire Plant is being dismantled and shipped. The Douglas [oil] refinery will be dismantled by February 23. 50,000 tons of power plants will be shipped in January. Although the steel rail mill requisition is in, certain essential parts have not yet been requisitioned." On February 23, the Soviet protocol committee was informed that "the refinery program is progressing satisfactorily. The Douglas Plant will be dismantled by March 15th." By July 1, there were 569,000 tons of industrial and refinery equipment in US Treasury warehouses awaiting expedited shipment to the USSR. On July 23, Treasury reported to Hopkins that eleven hydroelectric plants had just been requisitioned for Stalin, "having an aggregate capacity of 54,500 KW hours." By August 1943, 110,000 tons of petroleum products had been warehoused for delivery to Stalin, including the refinery already ordered and $22 million worth of oil field equipment. The justification was that Hopkins was not certain the United States, already shipping 5 percent of its domestic oil output to Stalin, could satisfy the Vozhd's third-protocol petroleum requisition of 514,000 long tons of petroleum products unless technology transfer allowed the Soviets to ramp up their own drilling and refining capacity. The volume of US industrial equipment shipped in the third protocol was 739,000 tons, with a dollar value of $401 million, the equivalent of $40 billion today. To guard against the risk that Congress might object, Hopkins front-loaded the orders, with 90 percent of these requisitions for the protocol period (July 1, 1943, to June 30, 1944) placed by September 1, 1943.[21]

However enthusiastic Hopkins was about transferring US industrial secrets and know-how to the Soviet Union, not all American industrialists were as sanguine. The money was good: the US government paid top dollar to Stalin's suppliers. Even so, many businessmen wondered if they should take Hopkins's easy money with no questions asked. Walter Harnischfeger, of the P&H crane company of Milwaukee, Wisconsin, was offered a lucrative $8.38 million contract to build electric hoists, cranes, and girders for the Soviet Union in March 1943, including state-of-the-art "electric traveling cranes" prized in war industry. Speaking to his industry contacts, Harnischfeger learned that Soviet requisitioners had placed similar orders worth more than $15 million over the winter. What the lend-lease people did not realize was that to build this many cranes and hoists required an investment "in machine tools and other fabricating equipment" costing ten times this much. Delicately, Harnischfeger warned Stettinius that many of these machines would take two years to build and six months to ship to the USSR, and that "an overhead crane is a type of machine which, with reasonable care, can render useful service for as long as fifty years." Hopkins, Harnischfeger explained, was asking the US taxpayer to pay for "the installation of industrial capital goods" in the Soviet Union "representing a value of about $150,000,000"—the equivalent of $15 billion today—"and of a useful life of up to fifty years."[22]

Harnischfeger was not the only one to notice this danger. E. J. Sadler, chairman of Standard Oil, refused a lucrative lend-lease requisition to transfer an oil refinery to the USSR on the grounds that "the Russians may use our equipment as a pattern and later on compete with our oil industry." With Standard Oil opting out, the Lend-Lease Administration spread the order around to a half dozen smaller energy firms. Just as Soviet tank experts were allowed free access to the US Army training facility in Aberdeen, Maryland, and Russian aviation experts got to poke around the US Army Air Force base in Riverside, California, so were Soviet petroleum engineers given free rein inspecting Texas oil refineries. In the end, Stalin's agents requisitioned $6,689,742.25 worth of intellectual property from firms including the Petrolite Corporation, Ltd., the International Catalytic Oil Processes Corporation, the Houdry Process Corporation, Universal Oil Products Corp., Texaco Development Corporation, and the Max B. Miller Company. The hit to the US taxpayer was not quite this high. With astonishing naiveté, Hopkins's men informed contractors that, because Stalin's people had promised that they would cease using the refining processes "after the termination of the present emergency," they demanded a discount on the royalties they were paying the six firms revolutionizing the Soviet oil industry. These firms were thus forced to take a haircut, accepting only about 20 percent of what these processes were worth ($1,347,840.32).[23]

Soviet requisitions of American technology were no less brazen in the rubber industry. During the third protocol—but front-loaded, as with all the other industrial orders, to arrive "by early 1944"—US firms were required to supply Stalin with "complete equipment for plants, including all auxiliaries and accessories," capable of producing thirty-eight thousand tons of synthetic rubber annually, along with tens of thousands of tons of natural rubber, oil, and other byproducts. US firms would also be asked to provide "complete technical information (technological drawings regarding organization of production, technical calculations, information regarding various apparatus, the method of preparation of catalyzers, material balance of production, and other information requested regarding installation and operation of plants)."[24]

The Soviet government also requisitioned a Ford tire factory, along with patents owned by the Firestone company and five smaller firms for the following products and processes:

Truck Tire Building Machine
Tire Building Compensator
Air Bag Extractor
Peeling Machines
Inserting and Shaping Machines
Tire Molds
Rotary Bias Cutter
Bias Cutter
Mill Mixing Knife (Demattia)
Penetrometer
Plastrometer
Stock Shells—Tray skids
Tread Cutting Machines
Tire Building Drums
Tread Tubing Machines

This requisition also included "a power station . . . for this plant, the power station to have a capacity of about 12,000 KW and 60 tons of steam under pressure of not less than 8 atmospheres per hour, and to include all the essential boilers, turbines and other equipment," and "equipment for the production of pelletized carbon black and dustless carbon black (20 tons per day)."[25]

It was not hard to see why Stalin's men were eager to requisition vast troves of American technology and intellectual property. But how did Hopkins and Stettinius justify this bizarre policy, which went well beyond any reasonable interpretation of the Lend-Lease Act—allowing the president to share finished defense articles with US allies—to include sensitive industrial and military technology too? When industrialists and concerned citizens wrote in to complain, Hopkins responded,

> The President has the power as Commander in Chief . . . to exchange with our Allies secret information concerning processes and patents which he deems essential for the joint war effort. Likewise he can furnish such information to our allies to be used in furtherance of the war effort even though we receive none in exchange. . . . [This] power is granted by the Lend-Lease Act to transfer such information to countries the defense of which is deemed by the President to be vital to the defense of the United States.[26]

In case resistance was offered by "private owners" unwilling to share with Stalin "additional secret processes, or other information or data or blueprints, flow charts, or other records, papers or documents in connection with patents and processes," Stettinius and Hopkins determined, by legal whim, that they could invoke the "requisitioning powers of the President or the powers of eminent domain of the United States Government."[27]

Hopkins certainly behaved as if eminent domain—the legal principle used to acquire private land for public development—gave him the right to seize whatever he liked and share it with

Stalin. Perhaps the most shocking lend-lease requisition of all was
the one placed on February 1, 1943, for enriched uranium, which
helped kick-start the Soviet atomic bomb program. By war's end,
the United States had shipped to Stalin, in at least three known
installments, three-quarters of a ton of uranium 235, 1,100 grams
of deuterium oxide (heavy water), 835,000 pounds of cadmium
metal (used to control the intensity of an atomic pile), 25,000
pounds of thorium, and 13.8 million pounds of refined aluminum
tubes of the kind used to cook uranium into plutonium. According
to the lend-lease air liaison officer stationed in Great Falls, Major
George Racey Jordan, Harry Hopkins phoned him personally in
April 1943, as the first of these sensitive packages were being prepared for Stalin, to request that he expedite "a certain shipment
of chemicals" to the Soviet Union—something "very special." "It
is not to go on the records," Hopkins told Jordan. "Don't make a
big production of it, but just send it through quietly, in a hurry."[28]

When Jordan called attention to these shipments in postwar
testimony before Congress, he was informed that the US government had authorized the sharing of uranium and even deuterium
oxide (heavy water) on the interesting logic that the men running
the Manhattan Project to produce the world's first atomic bomb
"did not wish to call attention to this material." A "refusal to ship"
uranium or heavy water, this legal finding continued, "might have
been more informative to the Russians than any help they could
derive from the small quantities of materials requested."[29]

There was nothing illegal, then, in Hopkins's request that Major Jordan expedite his "very special" shipments to Stalin. One
can nonetheless appreciate Jordan's mounting concern when he
began opening some of the boxes and suitcases stowed away on
airplanes bound for Siberia and found things like the "complete
plans for a General Electric Plant at East Lynn, Massachusetts,"
where airplane turbochargers were manufactured, and "blueprints
of the Electric Boat Corp., of Groton, Conn[ecticut], where [by
the late 1940s] our new atomic submarines are being built." One
load of "diplomatic suitcases" Jordan opened in summer 1943

contained nothing but "reprints of the patents in the U.S. Patent Office." When he asked the Soviet liaison officer, Colonel Kotikov, about this, Kotikov replied that such patent records "would be coming through continuously."* Patent reprints shipped to the USSR included designs for "bomb-sights, military tanks, airplanes, ship controls, bomb-dropping devices, helicopters, mine sweepers, ammunition, bullet-resisting armor." On one occasion, Jordan climbed aboard a loaded C-47 bound for Fairbanks, opened some of the boxes and bags and discovered "scientific papers by the thousands, road and railway maps detailing every point in the U.S. and American military papers by the score marked 'secret,'" some of which bore the letterhead of the "Manhattan Engineering District." Other strange packages were found to include rolls of film taken from inside US war factories, accompanied by a letter on US government letterhead authorizing a Soviet colonel "to visit any restricted plant, and to make motion pictures of intricate machinery and manufacturing processes."[30]

Major Jordan saw only a small fraction of the items passing through Great Falls, and usually of the small-volume kind that could fit onto airplanes. It was enough, though, to give him a taste of what he later called "the greatest mail-order catalogue in history." Just in the category of "atomic materials," Jordan observed or saw files recording the shipment of beryllium metals (9,681 pounds), cadmium alloys (72,535 pounds), aluminum tubes (13,766,472 pounds), cadmium metals (834,989 pounds), cobalt ore and concentrate (33,600 pounds), cobalt metal and cobalt-bearing scrap (806,941 pounds), and beryllium and cadmium compounds. Jordan's list of "Metals and Metal Manufactures" shipped to Stalin

---

*When Congress looked into these charges in 1949, it was discovered that Soviet agents had acquired hundreds of thousands of patents simply by walking into the US Patent Office and making copies. They did pay the copying fees, contributing, at least in this case, *something* to the US taxpayer in exchange for the priceless intellectual property Stalin was acquiring.

goes on for seven pages, before moving into nonatomic chemicals of industrial use (ten pages), "iron, steel, & Allied products" (four pages), "machines, machine tools & parts" (three pages), "electrical equipment" (three pages), "rubber commodities" (two pages), "generating equipment" (two pages), "photographic supplies" (two pages), and then "miscellaneous items" like electrical batteries, firefighting equipment, radios and radio equipment, railway signals and switches, "diamonds for industrial use," graphite, ink, and typewriters, portable sinks and bathtubs, optical lenses, office supplies, musical instruments, aluminum foil, liquor, cigarettes, and on and on in a giant "etc."[31]

Because Major Jordan's postwar testimony, delivered to Congress in 1949, was rapidly subsumed in Cold War polemics, it has generally been dismissed as a relic of Red Scare hysteria. But numerous other American pilots who flew in and out of Great Falls—such as James N. Daniel, Joseph A. Berger, and Ben L. Brown—reported similar stories of suspicious cargo smuggled onto C-47s bound for Siberia, accompanied by two plainclothes Soviet agents armed with submachine guns who took turns guarding the cargo while the other agent slept. Many US lend-lease records, including the correspondence of Hopkins and Stettinius and the minutes of the Soviet protocol committee, were only declassified in the 1970s, long after opinions about Soviet espionage had hardened into dogma. These files are now open, and they confirm the veracity of nearly all of Jordan's claims, except for his allegation that Hopkins's actions were illegal. Whether or not it was wise, shipping Stalin everything that his agents and spies asked for was perfectly legal at the time—it was Roosevelt administration policy.[32]

Although the most sensitive items were flown to Siberia, the greatest volume of lend-lease material was still being sent to Soviet Russia by sea. By summer 1943, many of the logistical problems of the Iran route had been worked out, owing to heavy US-British investment in dredging harbors, building new docks and modern port-loading equipment, maintaining roads, extending and double-tracking rail lines, and constructing truck assembly plants at Umm Qasr, Iran, and at Andimeshk, Iran, north of Bandar-Shahpur. These assembly plants allowed trucks to be shipped from US East Coast ports to the Persian Gulf "completely knocked down" (CKD), which increased the number loaded onto each merchant ship from 670 to 1,640 trucks in the standard C-2 cargo vessel. It was because of the ingenious CKD and reassembly on-site method, and the bravery and pluck of American and British engineers and drivers in Iran, that the United States was able, during the third protocol period, to surpass Stalin's demand for ten thousand trucks per month, allowing the aggregate total of American lorries arriving in the USSR in 1943 and 1944 to reach an astonishing three hundred thousand.* After being assembled in Iran, lend-lease trucks were driven to the Soviet Caucasus, itself not an easy job in a region where temperatures sometimes topped 120 degrees Fahrenheit, over unfinished roads so dust choked that drivers "had to be equipped with respirators." As a *New York Times* correspondent marveled in spring 1943, US-British ingenuity had transformed "Persian plains and plateaus into a vast conveyor belt."[33]

Deliveries on the Pacific route, too, were reaching unheard-of volumes by 1943 and 1944, in an increasingly bizarre coda to the American war against Japan. It was 5,815 nautical miles from San Francisco to Vladivostok, the last stretch of which passed through the heavily guarded waters around Japan. This perilous journey took as many as 140 days round trip during the winter months, when the northern seas would ice up, in merchant vessels flying the Soviet flag to deny a pretext for Japanese submarines or destroyers

---

* Stalin's monthly target of 10,000 trucks would have been reached even sooner, except for his habitual paranoia about capitalists. Hopkins offered to have an even larger reassembly plant constructed on Soviet soil, which would allow 5,000 CKD trucks to be reassembled there every month. But Stalin did not want this many American engineers and construction workers prowling around Russia.

to sink them. By July 22, 1943, the Roosevelt administration had transferred title to—that is, given to Stalin—63 merchant vessels with a carrying capacity of 613,000 deadweight tons, of which 28 were new Liberty ships. Although now owned and captained by Soviet crews, the vessels were still serviced in US ports, which performed expensive repairs after every round-trip voyage. Soviet seamen had the unfortunate habit of pilfering anything on board not nailed down—compasses, hoses, and rope were especially prized—and even expensive equipment such as deck lashings and turnbuckles. During the twelve months between July 1, 1943, and June 30, 1944, these "Russian" ships carried 2,589,424 metric tons of lend-lease supplies across the Pacific Ocean, including 305,166 tons of industrial equipment; 312,430 tons of ferrous and nonferrous metals; 100,000 tons of trucks, tanks, and warplanes; and most of the motor fuel and aviation gasoline allotted to Stalin in the third protocol (401,434 metric tons). No less remarkable than this logistical achievement was the fact that none of these ships was molested by Japan. Clearly, the Japanese did not mind that their US enemy was wasting precious military and shipping resources on the neutral USSR, instead of deploying these resources against Japan or sending arms to Chiang's forces in China.[34]

Not all Americans felt the same way when they learned this was happening. It was difficult to conceal the shipment of four hundred thousand metric tons of refined gasoline from San Francisco, Portland, and Seattle to the Soviet Union, right through a war zone. In September 1943, a sensational and basically accurate story was published in the usually pro-Roosevelt *Chicago Sun*: "Ships built in America are manned with Russian crews and started across the Pacific for Russia, loaded with lend-lease goods, mostly gasoline. Japanese pilots guide these ships through Japan's mine fields, for Japan is not at war with Russia. Japan takes off as much gasoline as it wants and fills the emptied cargo space with rubber [that] goes on to Russia."[35]

Fueled by this and other stories of waste and corruption, a bipartisan group of five senators—led by Georgia's Richard Russell of the Democratic Party's southern wing, who had just returned from a tour of the war fronts—launched a probe of the lend-lease program. The president, the senators charged, had displayed a "prodigal hand," with the United States becoming a "global sucker," paying for every country's interest but its own. Although Roosevelt dismissed the group as a bunch of "Cook's Tourists from the Senate," the criticism stung. This Democratic criticism, salted by a senator's threat to expose a sex scandal involving Sumner Welles, helped convince Roosevelt to sack the liberal Welles to appease the party's conservative southerners. To camouflage Hopkins's influence over Soviet aid programs, Roosevelt created a new umbrella agency called the Foreign Economic Administration (FEA)—headed by a businessman named Leo Crowley acceptable to southern Democrats—under which lend-lease was now subsumed, at least on paper. Testifying before the House foreign affairs committee, Crowley affirmed the original conception, dating to March 1941, that lend-lease was a "wartime emergency measure," not intended to be an open-ended foreign aid program.[36]

The president was nothing, however, if not a political survivor. By replacing Welles at the State Department with Edward Stettinius, Roosevelt neutralized Secretary Cordell Hull's influence still further. Although Stettinius was viewed in Congress as a steady hand, a straight shooter with business experience, the truth was that he was fully loyal to Hopkins. With Soviet skeptics from Litvinov's list of objectionables purged earlier that year, Hopkins was now more influential than ever in the State Department. Meanwhile, under Crowley's energetic though politically naive direction at the FEA, the demand for greater congressional oversight of lend-lease aid was somehow funneled, in the now-familiar pattern of wartime Washington, into the curtailment of arms shipments to Britain instead of to Russia. Despite the fact that the United States was gearing up for an all-out assault on Fortress Europe across the English Channel, the Lend-Lease Administration reduced shipments to Britain by $300 million in early 1944—a reduction equivalent to some $30 billion in current terms—even while continuing to exceed shipments promised to the USSR in the third protocol. The United States even curtailed deliveries of marine diesel engines to England, of the exact kind used in the amphibious landing craft needed for Operation Overlord, to meet Soviet requirements of fifty in the third protocol, and the Russians were not even using the ones the Americans were sending them. As the newly appointed US ambassador in Moscow, Averell Harriman, learned in January 1944, of the ninety marine diesel engines sent to the USSR, only three had been installed.[37]

Like Standley before him, Harriman had arrived in Russia full of enthusiasm for lend-lease and the heroic Soviet war effort, only to be disillusioned. Harriman even conducted a housecleaning, with the NKVD asset Faymonville recalled and replaced by the more independent General John R. Deane, who headed a US military mission sent to the USSR after the Teheran conference. Harriman and Deane began talking about a "firm but friendly *quid pro quo* approach," hoping to get access to genuine military information, at least, in exchange for the lend-lease aid being lavished on the Red Army. In April 1944, Harriman cabled Hopkins that, "in view of our estimates of the reduced German air strength on the Russian front, the fact that the Soviets are at present nowhere subjected to strategic bombing by the Germans, and the fact that the Soviets do not engage in strategic bombing requiring fighter support, there is . . . an element of doubt as to the Soviet need for additional fighters."

Delicately, Harriman pointed out that Molotov had made it clear to him that, while viewing lend-lease allocations as their birthright, the Russians "do not consider themselves called upon to do anything that would be helpful to our forces in return." Unless Hopkins allowed the embassy to apply some pressure on Molotov and Stalin, Harriman warned, he and General Deane did "not find them at all impressed by any obligation on their part to reciprocate."[38]

The ambassador should have known better than to ask Harry Hopkins. While Harriman, a Democratic Party donor close to the president, was too well-connected to be disposed of as easily as Yeaton had been cashiered back in 1941, Hopkins slammed the door shut on any talk of quid pro quos. As Harriman informed his Moscow embassy staff on May 4, 1944, "The [Soviet] Protocol Committee had resisted our intention to ask the Soviets to allow us to analyze the use they make of our supplies. We thought we could break it down (i.e. the Soviet resistance to giving us any information); but the Protocol Committee has the idea that the way to get along with the Russians is to do everything they ask."[39]

Hopkins was consistent in his policy of "sharing with Stalin" everything the United States had, with no questions asked or conditions applied. What Hopkins was objecting to here was not a demand that serious quid pro quos be applied to Soviet lend-lease aid—such as Stalin doing anything to help the Allies against Japan, or making concessions regarding the postwar settlement of Eastern Europe—but Harriman's polite suggestion that Stalin be asked to provide a few scraps of information about how his country was using American supplies being sent to the USSR.

One way the Soviets could have done something "helpful to [US-British] forces," had Harriman's policy of a "firm but friendly quid pro quo approach" been tried by the Roosevelt administration, was by fulfilling Stalin's promise at Teheran that Soviet forces launch an offensive "at about the same time" as Overlord to hinder German efforts to bring reinforcements into France. What, after all, was the purpose of supplying the Red Army with thousands of trucks, tanks, and warplanes, with millions of boots and cloth uniforms, with the food its men ate, with all the metals and industrial inputs, factories, "special chemicals," and intellectual property, if not to help the US-British war effort? As Roosevelt and Churchill reminded Stalin in a joint message on April 19, 1944, as final preparations for Overlord were underway, "[We] trust that your armies and ours, *operating in unison in accordance with our Teheran agreement*, will crush the Hitlerites."[40]

Stalin pretended to go along. "As agreed in Teheran," he replied on April 22, "the Red Army will undertake at the same time" as

Overlord, now planned for May 31 or early June, "its new offensive in order to give maximum support to the Anglo-American operations." But the Vozhd, having needled Roosevelt and Churchill for two years about the second front, did not wish to make things easier for them. As D-Day grew closer in May, Stalin ceased mentioning his reciprocal obligation to his allies in correspondence with Churchill and Roosevelt, and he was relieved that neither of them called him out on it. Of course, Stalin and his generals were busy in May 1944 planning the great Belorussian offensive—code-named, after a wounded hero of Borodino from 1812, Operation Bagration— just as Roosevelt, Churchill, and Eisenhower were busy planning Overlord. It was not Stalin's fault if his allies were too distracted to remember his promise of a simultaneous offensive at Teheran, and he was not about to remind them.[41]

On June 6, 1944, the greatest amphibious armada ever assembled ferried 160,000 American, British, Canadian, Australian, and Polish troops across the Channel to the beaches of Normandy, where they waded ashore in the teeth of German artillery and machine-gun fire and a deadly array of coastal defenses.* The Allied disinformation campaign suggesting that the landing was coming at Calais instead helped ensure that the Germans did not have enough troops and armor in Normandy to repel the invasion, which, however costly—the Allies lost 10,000 casualties in the first twenty-four hours alone, including 4,414 confirmed deaths— could have been still bloodier. With the eastern front quiet, Hitler transferred the Second SS Panzer Corps from there to Normandy, which by mid-June 1944 saw an imposing concentration of German armor, including six armored SS divisions. No longer could

---

* This was just two days after the US Fifth Army, commanded by General Mark Clark, entered Rome—the first Axis capital to fall. Clark had disobeyed orders to ensure that he could conquer Rome before D-Day. Although usually excoriated for vainglory, Clark's action could be interpreted as a protest against the Stalin-pleasing decision at Teheran to shortchange Italy of troops, landing craft, and warplanes and throw everything into Overlord instead.

the Russians complain—at least not with justification—that they were facing the enemy's best and their allies mere skeletal forces. A Red Army liaison officer who visited the headquarters of the British Seventh Armored Division was dismissive of its progress, until he learned that this army group was facing ten German divisions, of which six were panzer divisions, along a front just sixty-two miles long. Only on June 23, seventeen days after Overlord, did the Red Army finally launch Operation Bagration, long after the Second Panzer Corps had left for France and at least two weeks too late to make any appreciable difference for the Australian, British, Canadian, American, and Polish troops now fighting for their lives in Normandy.[42]

By neglecting his Teheran promise to launch a simultaneous offensive alongside Overlord, Stalin ensured that his allies would be badly bloodied as they fought their way into France, giving them a taste of the bitter medicine Russians had been taking since 1941. In Normandy alone, the Western Allies would incur more than 200,000 casualties by August 1944, including 125,847 Americans and 83,045 combined among Australians, Britons, Canadians, and Poles, not counting another 16,714 killed or missing Allied airmen. The peeling back of the German Second Panzer Corps from the northern Ukrainian-Galician sector of the eastern front to Normandy, meanwhile, allowed Stalin and his generals to expand the scope of the Bagration offensive to include southern thrusts from the Ukraine toward Lemberg/Lvov and Lublin—basically, the "powerful strike in the direction of Lublin" that had been integral to Red Army planning and war-gaming prior to Barbarossa. After the D-Day landings and the German scramble to reinforce France, the balance of Wehrmacht forces deployed on the Soviet fronts dropped below half for the first time since Barbarossa was launched, to just 124 divisions out of 271 (46 percent) by July 1944, when Bagration was in motion.[43]

It is true that 19 of the 147 non-Soviet-front Wehrmacht divisions were deployed on the relatively quiet Scandinavian fronts and 50 in Italy and the Balkans; they were not all in Western

Europe guarding against an Allied breakthrough to the Rhine. Nonetheless, the order of battle, from July 1944 onward, no longer supported the always-exaggerated Soviet complaint that the Red Army alone was fighting and tying down serious enemy strength. That the German response to D-Day marked the moment when the ratio of German divisions facing Stalin's armies dropped to less than half was yet more proof, from Stalin's perspective, that opening a second front in France (instead of reinforcing Italy or the Balkans) was the best way of aiding the Red Army. But the fact remained that even before D-Day, US-British operations in the Atlantic and North Sea, in North Africa, Italy, and the Balkans, along with the ever-present buildup of force in southern England, had tied down an ever-growing share of Hitler's available manpower and airpower—from a third in the first half of 1943, to 40 percent after the Italian campaign, to nearly 50 percent before D-Day. The Normandy campaign, however dilatory from Stalin's perspective, was the culmination of years of careful planning and campaigning by Stalin's allies, who had now provided him with an opportunity to take advantage of a depleted German force pool in the East.[44]

The Red Army, after gorging on the surpluses of the third protocol, was primed and ready. Stalin's armies enjoyed on the central Belorussian front, as of the launch of Bagration on June 22–23, 1944, superiority of nearly four to one in manpower (1.254 million to 336,573), more than eight to one in tanks and self-propelled guns, thirteen to one in artillery (34,016 to 2,589), and eight to one in warplanes (4,853 to 602). Despite the ever-louder Soviet boasts that the T-34 had rendered lend-lease tanks superfluous, data from the Soviet military archives shows that British and American tanks made up more than 18 percent of the Red Army's operational tank park as of July 1 (1,556 out of 8,574) and more than 28 percent—nearly a third—of operational tanks on the main Belorussian fronts from which Bagration was launched (844 out of 2,994, of which fully half of the lend-lease models were American Sherman diesel M4A2s). In terms of trucks and jeeps, once again the Soviet advantage over the Wehrmacht was so extreme as to defy comparison.

Red Army files show that at least 143,395 American Ford, Stude-baker, Dodge, Chevrolet, and Willys jeeps were in active service on the German fronts in June and July 1944, when Bagration was launched.[45]

Small wonder that some mobile Soviet units advanced as far as three hundred miles in the five weeks after the launching of Bagration, as the Red Army swept up all of Belorussia, including Minsk, and crossed the Berezina and Niemen Rivers. On the left Galician flank, vacated by the departure of the Second Panzer Corps for Normandy, Konev's First Ukrainian Front Army smashed into Lemberg/Lvov even as Rokossovsky's First Belorussian Front Army raced toward Lublin and Marshal Vasilevsky's Third Belorussian and First Baltic Army groups marched into Latvia and Lithuania. The Red Army reached Vilna (Vilnius) on July 13, Grodno on July 16, the Bug River on July 21, the Vistula (Wisła) on July 25, Bialystok on July 27, and Kaunas on August 1. By early August, advanced motorized Red Army columns from Vasilevsky's armies reached the Gulf of Riga.[46]

In terms of territory and targets gained per unit of time, Bagration was the greatest Soviet victory of the war, even if its strategic importance was less than that of Stalingrad, which had ensured Soviet survival, and Kursk, which had marked the turning point that shifted the Wehrmacht squarely onto the defensive on the eastern front. Although the deep Soviet thrust into Belorussia and the Baltic area owed much to Hitler's shifting of armor and manpower to France to meet the long-awaited Normandy landings and to the material aid of lend-lease, Bagration also displayed the increasing competence of Red Army commanders such as Rokossovsky and Konev, as Stalin's generals applied lessons in mobile warfare learned painfully from the Germans between 1941 and 1944. Soviet losses were still heavy, amounting to 770,888 casualties including 180,000 killed or missing, 2,957 tanks and self-propelled guns, 2,447 artillery pieces, and 822 warplanes. But for the first time in the eastern war, Wehrmacht losses were nearly as severe, at 589,000 casualties including almost 200,000 prisoners taken by

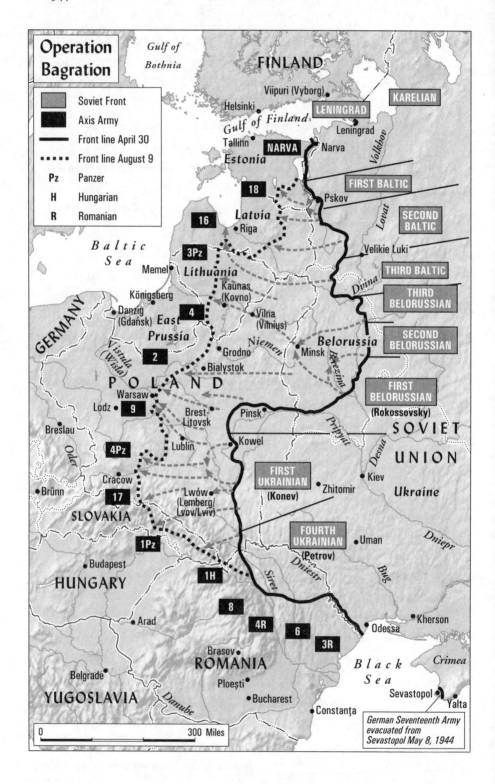

Operation Bagration

▨	Soviet Front
▓	Axis Army
——	Front line April 30
····	Front line August 9
Pz	Panzer
H	Hungarian
R	Romanian

Gulf of Bothnia

FINLAND

Viipuri (Vyborg)

KARELIAN

Helsinki

LENINGRAD

Gulf of Finland

Leningrad

Tallinn

Narva

NARVA

Estonia

Volkhov

18

FIRST BALTIC

Pskov

Lovat

16

Latvia

Riga

SECOND BALTIC

Velikie Luki

Baltic Sea

3Pz

Lithuania

Dvina

THIRD BALTIC

Memel

Kaunas (Kovno)

THIRD BELORUSSIAN

Königsberg

4

Vilna (Vilnius)

Danzig (Gdańsk)

East Prussia

Niemen

Belorussia

SECOND BELORUSSIAN

Vistula (Wisła)

2

Grodno

Minsk

Berezina

GERMANY

POLAND

Białystok

FIRST BELORUSSIAN

(Rokossovsky)

Warsaw

Łódź

9

Brest-Litovsk

Pinsk

Pripyat

SOVIET

Breslau

Oder

Lublin

Kowel

Desna

UNION

4Pz

Kiev

Cracow

FIRST UKRAINIAN

Zhitomir

Ukraine

Brünn

17

Lwów (Lemberg/ Lvov/Lviv)

(Konev)

SLOVAKIA

FOURTH UKRAINIAN

Uman

Dniepr

1Pz

(Petrov)

Bug

Budapest

1H

Siret

Dnestr

HUNGARY

8

Kherson

Arad

4R

6

3R

Odessa

Brasov

Black Sea

Crimea

ROMANIA

Belgrade

Ploeşti

Sevastopol

Yalta

YUGOSLAVIA

Danube

Bucharest

Constanţa

German Seventeenth Army evacuated from Sevastopol May 8, 1944

0 ——————— 300 Miles

the Red Army—a sign of faltering German morale. This was more losses than the Wehrmacht sustained in France and Italy in the same period (157,000), showing that, while the Normandy landings had balanced out the fighting burden, it was still the Red Army doing the most damage against the Germans, even if its share of Wehrmacht casualties produced dropped from 80 to 90 percent in the two years before D-Day to 62 percent from June to November 1944. More importantly from Stalin's perspective, the combination of cascading lend-lease aid, improved generalship, and the opening of the second (or third) front in France had fully restored the strategic initiative in Eastern Europe that he had lost after the German invasion.[47]

It would not be long before the Red Army would roll into central Poland in American Studebakers and jeeps mounting Ford and Firestone tires, guided by ground-strafing Airacobras, while hundreds of Boston bombers rained down lead hail on German positions in Poland and East Prussia. Warsaw looked ripe to fall. The war was going Stalin's way now.

VI.

PLUNDER

30

Warsaw

IF THERE WERE any lingering doubts in London and Washington about Stalin's intentions for the soon-to-be-conquered peoples of Europe, these should have been dispelled by his behavior as the Red Army, riding on the trucks and rubber tires of lend-lease, powered into formerly (and soon again) occupied Poland in the second half of July 1944.

Stalin's intentions for the Poles should have been clear long before the Red Army reached the outskirts of Warsaw. The Vozhd was as ruthlessly consistent on the Polish question as he was on not breaking his neutrality pact with Japan. In a revealing exchange in February 1944, Roosevelt had reassured Stalin that he was willing to accept his proposed borders for postwar Poland, and that he fully understood the "impossibility from the Soviet point of view of having any dealings with the Polish Government-in-Exile in its present form." All the president wanted in exchange was that Stalin consider working with that Polish government if some of Stalin's people (that is, Communists) were added to it, while carefully avoiding, in order to keep American Poles quiescent, the impression of "pressure or dictation from a foreign country." If the Soviet government showed him this "consideration," Roosevelt suggested, it would help reinforce the "cooperation so splendidly established at [Teheran]," while also helping ensure that, as the Red Army entered Poland, "Polish guerrillas should work with and not against your advancing troops." Stalin replied, on February 16, that Poland's borders were nonnegotiable. As for the Polish exile government, Stalin refused to entertain the possibility of "neighborly relations with a pro-fascist, imperialist government, in which there are practically no democratic [i.e., Communist] elements." As for working together with "Polish guerrillas"—the Polish Home Army, recognized as an auxiliary arm of the London exile government—the Vozhd promised Roosevelt nothing.[1]

Stalin delivered what he promised: nothing. On July 24, 1944, after the Red Army occupied Lublin, the Vozhd bluntly informed Roosevelt that he was setting up a Soviet puppet government in Lublin called the "Polish Committee of National Liberation," and that neither the Red Army nor the Lublin Polish Committee would have any dealings with the Polish government-in-exile or with what Stalin called the "so-called underground organizations working for the Polish government," which he dismissed as "farmers without influence." Stalin had begun assembling a Polish puppet government in spring 1943, after the Katyn story broke, styled, with grim irony, as the "Union of Polish Patriots" and headed by a loyal Communist called Boleslaw Bierut, who had spent the war in Moscow. All Stalin needed to install Bierut's committee was a foothold on Polish territory—the part of Poland he did not plan to annex, that is. Lemberg/Lvov in Galicia did not qualify, having been part of the Soviet zone from 1939 to 1941. Lublin, though, a city with a rich Polish history dating to medieval times, was subject to a ferocious German occupation from 1939 to 1944. Because the city was nearly 40 percent Jewish, it suffered terribly in the Holocaust. Most of its twenty-six thousand Jews had been sent to the death camps at Belzec and Majdanek in 1942, leaving the city barren and ripe for an easy occupation. Majdanek, on the outskirts of Lublin, was the first Nazi death camp seized by the Red Army. Although much smaller than Treblinka and Auschwitz, its capture was a propaganda triumph and lent prestige to the liberation of Lublin, a city that had also been one of the prize objectives in Red Army war-gaming in 1940 and 1941. Lublin thus served Stalin's purposes admirably.[2]

Stalin had given a hint of things to come on July 12, 1944, when, after Rokossovsky's Ukrainian front army crossed the Bug River, he sent a special command to all Red Army front commanders converging on Poland. "Soviet troops in Lithuanian, Belorussian, and Ukrainian territory," the Vozhd instructed his generals, "have encountered Polish military detachments run by the Polish émigré government. These detachments have behaved suspiciously and have everywhere acted against the interests of the Red Army. Contact with them is therefore forbidden. When these formations are found, they must be immediately disarmed and sent to specially organized collection points for investigation." Stalin and Beria had already begun training their own Polish army of occupation (the First Polish Army, later restyled as the "People's Army"), commanded by the Polish general Zygmunt Berling, and they did not want rival militias or armies on Polish soil. Unlike the Polish Army of General Anders, which had been allowed to leave the USSR via Iran and later fought heroically with the British and Americans in Italy at Monte Cassino, Berling's army, 104,000 strong by summer 1944, was fully Sovietized, trained by Soviet superiors and subject to surveillance by Red Army political commissars. To make certain of Berling's loyalty, Beria even forced him to visit the mass graves at Katyn in person and publicly endorse the Soviet lie that the fifteen thousand Polish officers (and nearly eight thousand civilian Poles) murdered in 1940 were victims of a Nazi, not an NKVD, mass execution.[3]

Stalin thus already had a puppet regime ready when the Red Army crashed into Poland in July 1944. For Bierut and Berling to be able to take charge, however, would require not only defeating the Germans but crushing local rivals too. In the winter of 1939–1940, those few Polish officers who had escaped the Gestapo and NKVD had taken the Polish Army underground, just as Mihailović had done with Serbian officers in Yugoslavia. Initially called the Union of Armed Struggle (Zwiazek Walki Zbrojnej) and renamed the Home Army (Armia Krajowa, or AK) in 1942, the army took its orders, like Mihailović did in Yugoslavia, from the country's exile government. Although the AK was certainly hostile to the

Soviets, who had (until Barbarossa) occupied their country no less brutally than the Germans had done, for Stalin to call the AK and the London exile government to which it answered "fascists" was a grotesque slander. Not only did the AK frequently attack German strongholds, but its leaders were instrumental in getting the story of the Holocaust out to the world. Jan Kozielewski (alias Karski), an AK courier, visited the Warsaw Ghetto in summer 1942 and brought one of the first authentic reports of German death camps (including those at Chelmno and Treblinka) to the world via General Sikorski, premier of the Polish exile government in London. Sikorski then issued an appeal to Poles to "give all help and shelter to those being murdered" and the AK took action, issuing orders to shoot Polish collaborators who turned Jews over to the Nazis and taking thousands of Jews into protective custody. This took astonishing bravery. Even as the AK decreed capital punishment for Poles who betrayed Jews to the occupier, the German occupation authorities issued ever-more-draconian decrees mandating the death penalty for Poles who helped Jews escape ghettos (August 22, 1942) or just "offered them shelter, food or a hiding place" (October 28, 1942).[4]

Contrary to the later Soviet smear that the AK was a "collaborationist" organization, which allegedly helped the Germans suppress the Warsaw Ghetto Uprising of April 1943, the AK smuggled weapons to the groups that fought to free the ghetto, including the Jewish Military Union and the Jewish Combat Organization. The AK also conducted seven (albeit limited) armed operations in support of the Warsaw Ghetto Uprising, losing several fighters in the process. Although not primarily a Jewish organization, the AK had thousands of fighters of Jewish origin, who saw themselves as Polish patriots.[5]

What the AK was fighting for was very similar to what Mihailović and the Chetniks sought to achieve in Yugoslavia, or what Chiang Kai-shek's Kuomintang wanted in China: to free their country of foreign domination and be sovereign again. The AK, which could draw on nearly four hundred thousand fighters in the Polish underground by summer 1944, including twenty-five thousand in Warsaw—all loyal to the Polish exile government in London headed (after Sikorski's death in a plane crash in July 1943) by Stanislaw Mikolajczyk—posed a mortal threat to Stalin's aim to create a Soviet satellite state in Poland. The AK commander on the ground in Warsaw, General Tadeusz Bór-Komorowski, and Mikolajczyk in London did not trust the Russians, and for that reason they did not want to miss their chance to shape Poland's future before the Red Army did it for them. Moreover, if the AK did not take up arms prior to (or in coordination with) the Red Army's entry into Warsaw, it would give ammunition to Stalinist agitprop accusing it of collaborating with the Germans. There was even a risk that the four-hundred-odd Polish Communists in Warsaw answering to Bierut's Lublin committee, although massively outnumbered by the AK, would raise the red flag, welcome in the Red Army, and steal the AK's thunder. By the last week of July 1944, when an advance echelon of Rokossovsky's Second Guards Tank Army was approaching Praga, the Warsaw suburb on the eastern side of the Vistula (Wisła), the boom of guns could already be heard in the city. Rokossovsky's orders, received from Stavka on July 27, were to occupy Praga with his right flank by August 5–8, while his left flank crossed the Vistula further south. With the Reds about to surround Warsaw, and the Germans preparing for a scorched-earth defense, the stage was set for a brutal showdown.[6]

Because the Warsaw Uprising became embroiled in controversy almost from the start, it is important to get the dates right. On July 21, Bór-Komorowski informed Mikolajczyk that the AK would declare a "state of alert" on July 25. On July 22, Radio Moscow announced the creation of the Polish Committee of National Liberation and declared it the only sovereign authority in Poland. Although Bierut's puppet government, still en route from Moscow, was not installed in Lublin until August 1, this was a clear shot across the bow of the AK and the exile government in

London. On July 25, the day the AK went on alert, Mikolajczyk wired authorization from London for the AK to take up arms in Warsaw, although without specifying the date. On July 26, Mikolajczyk, after Churchill had first obtained Stalin's permission, left London for Moscow in order to discuss Poland's political future and to negotiate Soviet support for the imminent AK uprising in Warsaw. On July 27, the German governor of occupied Warsaw ordered one hundred thousand males to report the following day for forced labor. On July 29, two Polish-language radio broadcasts from Moscow appealed for Poles in Warsaw to begin "active struggle" against the occupiers and to "fight against the Germans." Later that day, General Berling's pro-Soviet Polish force, although it had still not reached Lublin, yet alone Warsaw, was renamed the People's Army. On July 30, Communist posters were placarded around Warsaw denouncing the London exile government as "usurpers." On July 31, Mikolajczyk informed Molotov in Moscow that "the Polish government was considering a general uprising in Warsaw and would like to ask the Soviet government to bomb the airfields near Warsaw." That afternoon in Warsaw, the AK issued orders for an armed uprising to begin in the city at 5 p.m. on August 1.[7]

This much is now known about the sequence of events. But a good deal remains mysterious about the motivations of Mikolajczyk, Bór-Komorowski, and the Poles they ordered to take up arms at 5 p.m. that fateful August 1—an anniversary now sacred in Poland. Did Polish leaders believe that the Moscow radio broadcasts on July 29 implied Stalin would order the Red Army to aid the Polish Home Army if it took up arms against the Germans? Mikolajczyk did ask for such aid in Moscow, but he realized from Molotov's cool reaction that it would not likely be forthcoming. He and Bór-Komorowski knew what Stalin had done at Katyn. It seems more plausible that Bór-Komorowski saw the Soviet moves announcing the creation of Bierut's puppet government and Berling's People's Army as preemptive maneuvers to sideline the AK and the London government, and wanted to act before it was too late. The Nazi occupation of Warsaw had lasted for nearly five years, and most Varsovians had had enough. The prospect of waiting for the Russians to arrive and liberate the city in a bloody firefight with the Wehrmacht, SS, and Gestapo had little appeal to patriotic Poles. In this sense, it is not so much surprising that the AK leadership chose to act on August 1, 1944, as that they did not do so earlier.[8]

For all the recriminations that would come later, the mood in Warsaw during the early hours and days of the uprising was euphoric. Finally, Poles—after helping the Allies in Finland, in the skies of England, in Italy, and on the beaches of Normandy—were fighting for their own country again. The AK was clearly in the lead, but within hours nearly every organized group in Warsaw had joined in, from a far-right militia called the National Armed Forces to the few hundred local Communist adherents of Berling's new People's Army. So, too, did Jewish survivors of the Warsaw Ghetto Uprising of 1943 emerge from hiding to join the fight, some with the AK and some with the People's Army. As one Jewish volunteer recalled, "Poles had taken up arms against the mortal enemy. Our obligation as victims and as fellow citizens was to help them." In his influential study *Bloodlands*, Timothy Snyder claims that "more Jews fought in the Warsaw Uprising of August 1944 than in the Warsaw Ghetto Uprising of April 1943." One of the AK's early successes was to seize control of the Jewish ghetto from the ninety-odd SS officers guarding it on August 5, liberating in the process 348 Jewish prisoners.[9]

Unfortunately for everyone else in Warsaw, this was an isolated victory. German occupation troops, well-informed about AK preparations, succeeded in holding on to most of the strongholds in the city. While morale was sky-high in the AK, and some units had machine guns, the rebels had no artillery and very few fighters even had rifles. Only if the Red Army could keep the Germans pinned down in Praga or south of the city, or if Soviet or US-British

pilots could air-drop weapons and supplies into Warsaw, would
the rising have a real chance. But in the early days, there were
few signs of support coming from outside. On August 4, Churchill authorized a dangerous mission to send pilots from Italy over
the Alps to airlift sixty tons of equipment and ammunition "into
the southwest quarter of Warsaw," but this would require Soviet
cooperation, both to assure the pilots would not be fired on by
Russian anti-aircraft gunners and to use nearby Red Army airfields to land in case of trouble. Stalin responded coolly, informing
Churchill that "the information which has been communicated to
you by the Poles is greatly exaggerated and does not inspire confidence." Denied access to Red Army airfields near Warsaw for refueling, those courageous RAF pilots—most of them, predictably,
were Polish volunteers—had to contend not only with German
anti-aircraft guns but also with the prospect of being forced to land
on enemy territory if they ran out of fuel returning to Italy. By the
end of August, only one out of the original five RAF crews had
survived. In all, thirty-one RAF planes went down on the perilous
Italy-Warsaw route. The British air marshal overseeing these missions estimated that the RAF lost one bomber crew for each ton
of war supplies delivered to the AK fighters in Warsaw. The vast
majority of these lost pilots were Poles, falling victim to Stalin's
refusal to help them.[10]

From the eastern bank of the Vistula, the signs were ominous.
At 4:10 a.m. Moscow time on August 1, about twelve hours before the uprising began, Rokossovsky was ordered to stand down
his offensive into Praga, "assume a defensive posture," and await
developments. The pretext for this order was a counteroffensive
that had just been launched by four panzer divisions of Walter
Model's Army Group Center from the northeast. After consulting with Zhukov at Stavka, Rokossovsky informed Stalin that his
army would be ready to resume his Warsaw offensive only on August 25. It is unknown whether this long postponement reflected
concern over Rokossovsky's flanks because of Model's armored

counterthrust or a cynical calculation by Molotov and Stalin that it was better to let Polish patriots bleed themselves to death in Warsaw than aid them. Both Stavka's strategic caution and Stalin's calculating cruelty could have factored into the decision to postpone Rokossovsky's advance, thus ruling out any genuine cooperation on the ground between the AK and the nearby Red Army for at least four weeks.[11]

Four weeks was more than enough time for the Germans to bring reinforcements into Warsaw and adopt even more brutal countermeasures than Poles had seen in 1939 or 1943. Lending a particular savagery to the counterinsurgency operations was the use of foreign SS units. Atrocities were particularly gruesome in the westernmost districts of Wola and Ochota, where the AK had established a kind of rear firewall. Heinrich Himmler, who came to Warsaw to personally oversee the crushing of the uprising, ordered SS commanders to shoot all Polish combatants and the women and children supporting them and to burn down any buildings housing rebels. By August 9, approximately forty thousand Poles had been executed in Wola and Ochota alone. Some relief came on August 13, when Himmler's orders were countermanded by the commanding SS general, Erich von dem Bach, who wished to transform the crackdown into more of a proper military operation, while also easing up on the civilian atrocities that were playing into the AK's anti-German propaganda. But this was small mercy, as it also cleared the path for the use of artillery and Luftwaffe dive-bombers, which by the second half of August were strafing Warsaw's Old Town from the air. By the time Rokossovsky finally resumed his offensive on August 26, Polish casualties in Warsaw were approaching one hundred thousand, including thirty thousand in the Old Town.[12]

Churchill followed these events with incomprehension. Could not Stalin do something to help these courageous Polish patriots in Warsaw, with the Red Army perched just on the other side of the Vistula River? If Stalin would not allow RAF pilots to land on

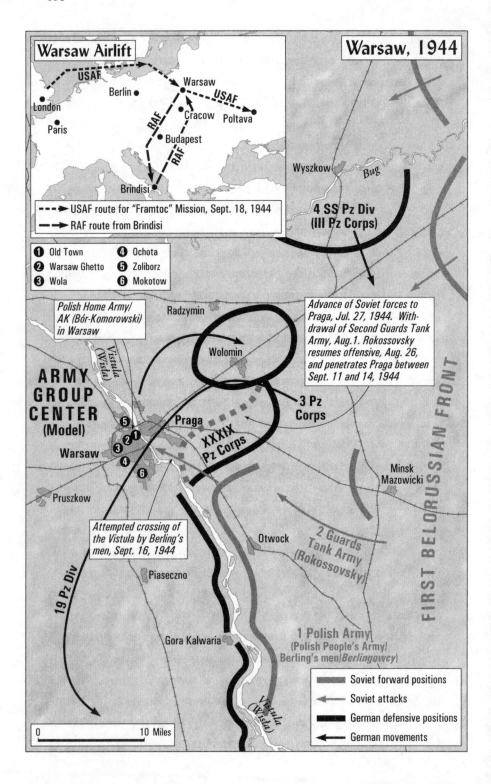

Warsaw Airlift

London
Paris
Berlin
USAF
Warsaw
USAF
Cracow   Poltava
RAF
Budapest
RAF
Brindisi

- - - ▶ USAF route for "Framtoc" Mission, Sept. 18, 1944
—— ▶ RAF route from Brindisi

❶ Old Town   ❹ Ochota
❷ Warsaw Ghetto   ❺ Zoliborz
❸ Wola   ❻ Mokotow

Warsaw, 1944

Wyszkow   Bug

**4 SS Pz Div
(III Pz Corps)**

Polish Home Army/
AK (Bór-Komorowski)
in Warsaw

Radzymin

Wolomin

*Advance of Soviet forces to
Praga, Jul. 27, 1944. Withdrawal of Second Guards Tank
Army, Aug.1. Rokossovsky
resumes offensive, Aug. 26,
and penetrates Praga between
Sept. 11 and 14, 1944*

**ARMY
GROUP
CENTER
(Model)**

Vistula
(Wisła)

❺
❷❶
❸
❹
❻

Praga

XXXIX
Pz Corps

**3 Pz
Corps**

Warsaw

Pruszkow

Minsk
Mazowicki

*Attempted crossing of
the Vistula by Berling's
men, Sept. 16, 1944*

Otwock

2 Guards
Tank Army
(Rokossovsky)

Piaseczno

19 Pz Div

Gora Kalwaria

1 Polish Army
(Polish People's Army/
Berling's men/*Berlingowcy*)

Vistula
(Wisła)

FIRST BELORUSSIAN FRONT

Soviet forward positions
Soviet attacks
German defensive positions
German movements

0   10 Miles

Red Army airfields near Warsaw, then maybe Soviet pilots, taking off from Russian air bases less than one hundred miles away, could airlift supplies to AK fighters themselves. On August 13, Stafford Cripps's successor as British ambassador in Moscow, Sir Archibald Clark Kerr, handed Stalin a wire from Churchill that included the text of a plea for help from the AK command in Warsaw, sent to Mikolajczyk via London. "The soldiers and population of the capital," the message read, "look hopelessly at the sky expecting help from the Allies. On the background of smoke they see only German aircraft. Have you discussed in Moscow help for Warsaw? I repeat emphatically that without immediate repeat immediate support consisting of drops of arms and ammunition, bombing of objectives held by the enemy, and air landing, our fight will collapse in a few days." Stalin did not reply. Smelling a rat, on August 14 Churchill wrote Foreign Secretary Eden that "it certainly is very curious that the Russian armies should have ceased their attack on Warsaw and withdrawn some distance at the moment when the underground army had revolted."[13]

Curious or not, when it came to the decision to stand down Rokossovsky's offensive on August 1, Stalin could at least defer to the judgment of his commanders. But there was no military rationale behind the Soviet refusal to supply the AK with airdrops or to let the RAF land and refuel on Russian airfields after flying supplies in from Italy. This was eminently political. When the Vozhd finally responded to Churchill's pleas, he scarcely hid his hostility. "After having familiarized myself more closely with the Warsaw affair," Stalin wrote Churchill on August 16, "I am convinced that the Warsaw [uprising] is a reckless and terrible adventure." The huge civilian losses, he continued, "would not have transpired if the Soviet command had been informed before it began and if the Poles had maintained contact with them." While it was true that the uprising was costing Warsaw's people dearly, Stalin's assertion that the AK had not informed the Soviets beforehand was a bald lie. Mikolajczyk had told Stalin in person on July 31 and requested

Soviet cooperation. It was pure cynicism that lay behind Stalin's assertion to Churchill that "the Soviet command has come to the decision that it must dissociate itself from the Warsaw adventure as it cannot take either direct or indirect responsibility for the Warsaw action."[14]

Stalin meant what he said. On August 16, Molotov handed the British and US ambassadors a policy memorandum stating that he and Stalin did not "object to English or American aircraft dropping arms in the region of Warsaw, as this is a British and American affair." But the "Soviet Government decidedly objects to British or American aircraft, after dropping arms in the region of Warsaw, landing on Soviet territory, since the Soviet government do not wish to associate themselves either directly or indirectly with the adventure in Warsaw."[15]

Stalin's disavowal of support for the Warsaw uprising was so brutal that even Roosevelt, normally so solicitous of the dictator's favor, was taken aback. His ambassador in Moscow, Averell Harriman, was sending bad tidings. After being subject to a "savage" dressing down by Molotov's deputy Vishinsky on the night of August 15–16, Harriman reported to Roosevelt that "I am for the first time since coming to Moscow gravely concerned by the attitude of the Soviet Government. If the position of the Soviet Government is correctly reflected by Vishinsky," Harriman continued, "its refusal [to help] is not based on operational difficulties, nor on a denial that resistance exists [in Warsaw] but on ruthless political calculations." Although not convinced Stalin's motives were really this cynical, President Roosevelt did sign a joint letter with Churchill, wired to Moscow on August 20, 1944. Appealing to "world opinion," the British and American statesmen pled that "we hope that you will drop immediate supplies and munitions to the people of Warsaw, or you will agree to help our planes in doing it very quickly."[16]

Stalin was unmoved. In his response, wired to London and Washington on August 22, the Vozhd reiterated his view of the Warsaw uprising as an "adventure" and even blamed the AK fighters for undermining the Soviet position in Poland by "increasingly drawing the attention of the Germans to Warsaw." Claiming that the best help he could offer was for the Red Army to "break the Germans around Warsaw and free Warsaw for the Poles," Stalin made no promise to airlift supplies to the AK nor to allow American or RAF pilots doing so to land on Soviet air bases. We now know that the Vozhd issued orders the same day—this part was left out of his message to Churchill and Roosevelt—for the NKVD to "arrest and disarm" all captured Polish insurgents who fell into Soviet hands. Bierut's puppet government in Lublin also received orders to "arrest all [AK] bands operating in the vicinity of Tomaszow-Lubelski and Hrubieszów," towns located about 120 kilometers southeast of Lublin, near the present-day border of Ukraine. Further, the Vozhd ordered Rokossovsky to postpone his Warsaw offensive yet again and transfer armored units to the north. Although neither of these moves was publicly advertised, Stalin's actions reveal that he wanted the Polish AK disarmed at best and bled to death at worst.[17]

By now Churchill was livid, and he was not the only one in the Allied camp. In a draft letter to Roosevelt on August 25, Ambassador Harriman accused Stalin of encouraging "uprisings in Warsaw . . . during the latter days of July," an allusion to the Soviet radio broadcasts of July 29. (Realizing that this was a serious accusation, Harriman decided not to send this letter.) The US chargé d'affaires in Moscow, George Kennan, saw Harriman after his meeting with Vishinsky and found him "shattered by the experience." As Kennan later recalled of this historic moment:

This was a gauntlet thrown down, in a spirit of malicious glee, before the Western powers. What it meant to imply was: "We intend to have Poland lock, stock, and barrel. We don't care a fig for those Polish underground fighters who have not accepted Communist authority. To us, they are no better than the Germans; and if they and the Germans slaughter each other off, so much the better. It is a matter of indifference to us what you Americans think of all this."[18]

After receiving Stalin's brusque dismissal of August 22, Churchill wired Roosevelt and proposed, "unless you directly forbid it," that the United States and Britain start landing their Warsaw supply planes at Soviet bases near Poltava in once-again-Soviet Ukraine, whether or not Stalin authorized this. At Teheran, Stalin had promised to allow the use of these Poltava bases to the US Army Air Force for refueling after bombing raids on Germany, although even this permission had been withheld until June 1944. On August 17, Molotov had threatened, in a meeting with Harriman, to withdraw landing permission again, even for American bombers raiding Germany that came nowhere near Warsaw.[19]

Roosevelt, although frustrated by Stalin's behavior, was not willing to go along with either Harriman's advice to be firmer or with Churchill's proposal of handing Stalin a fait accompli and landing supply planes at Poltava. A terse telegram from Washington warned Harriman not to press the Soviets about landing rights for Warsaw sorties, lest he jeopardize the "smooth functioning of the shuttle bombing arrangements" for Germany, which Roosevelt did not wish to be "imperiled by this [Warsaw] question." "There is a tendency on the part of the British," the message continued, "to go considerably farther than the President is prepared to go." Roosevelt swallowed Stalin's insulting August 22 telegram whole, telling an aide, "I do not think this needs an answer."[20]

With Roosevelt refusing to pressure Stalin, the Soviets continued denying landing rights to British and American planes supplying the AK rebels. Only on September 9 did Stalin relent and allow Allied supply planes to land on Ukrainian airfields near Poltava— because, by then, the AK had been decisively defeated. On September 2, the last resistance in Warsaw's Old Town crumbled and the Germans marched into what was now a bombed-out, depopulated ruin, with the last few thousand AK fighters and civilians left alive in the Old Town escaping into the sewers. While sporadic fighting continued in the northern district of Zoliborz and the southern district of Mokotow, the last stand of the Polish Home Army in central Warsaw had come and gone.[21]

The sense of betrayal in the Polish camp was palpable, especially in London, where it seemed that years of support for the Allied cause had gone for naught. Churchill and RAF pilots were trying their best to supply the AK forces in Warsaw—the RAF flew the vast majority of the sorties from Italy, with the US Army Air Force not really joining in until landing rights in Ukraine were granted on September 9—only to be undermined, just as at Teheran, by Roosevelt's desire to stay on Stalin's good side, so it was not really fair for Poles to blame the British. Still, it was the British who had gone to war for Poland in 1939, and who had enlisted exiled Poles in their own armies and the RAF ever since. On September 1, General Kazimierz Sosnkowski, the inspector general of the armed forces of the Polish exile government in London, to whom Bór-Komorowski and the AK answered, published a copy of his order no. 19 to the Polish Home Army in the *Times of London*:

Five years have passed since the day when, encouraged by the British government and its guarantee, Poland stood up to its lonely struggle with German might. For the last month, the soldiers of the Home Army and the people of Warsaw have again been abandoned in another bloody and lonely fight. This is a tragic and repeated puzzle which we Poles cannot decipher. . . . We hear arguments about gains and losses. But we remember that in the Battle of Britain Polish pilots suffered over 40 per cent casualties, while the loss of planes and aircrews in the flights to Poland [from Italy] is 15 per cent. If the population of our capital is to be condemned to perish in mass slaughter under the rubble of their homes through [Britain's] calculated passivity and indifference, the conscience of the world will be burdened by this terrible and unparalleled sin.[22]

The Germans observed the discomfiture of their enemies with schadenfreude, making great propaganda hay out of the Warsaw debacle. Polish-language leaflets were dropped into Warsaw blaming the Russians for the uprising, arguing, plausibly enough, that "the bloodshed serves only Moscow's purposes." Wehrmacht communiqués instructed Poles to wave white flags and surrender, promising that "anyone voluntarily leaving the city will not be harmed," that "those able to work will be provided with work and bread," that "whoever is not able to work will be supplied with food," and that "anyone who is sick will receive health care and accommodation." Polish nationalists were assured that "the German army is fighting only against Bolshevism. The uprising was the means the Bolsheviks used against the Germans."[23]

While the ferocious resistance in Warsaw suggests that few Poles believed German promises, which were belied by the brutal treatment accorded to civilians and AK fighters captured by the SS, by September Soviet inaction and Western betrayal had seriously damaged Home Army morale. After the fall of Old Town, AK leaders opened back-channel negotiations with the German command, which agreed to recognize AK fighters as "combatants," meaning that captured soldiers would be treated as prisoners of war instead of being summarily executed as rebels. Some twenty thousand Polish civilians were evacuated from the city by agreement. Bór-Komorowski was considering a negotiated surrender when, between September 11 and 14, Rokossovsky resumed the offensive on the Praga front and swiftly approached the Vistula. The VVS then began airlifting supplies into Warsaw. Stalin's motives in this unexpected 180-degree policy shift can only be guessed at. It may be that Rokossovsky, after pausing for over a month, had received enough reinforcements to feel secure on his flanks. Or the Soviet shift "may have been," as Evan Mawdsley has recently suggested, "Stalin's cynical way of prolonging the agony of the Home Army and causing it maximum casualties."[24]

There is another explanation, however. If we look closely at the timing, it becomes clear that both the renewal of Rokossovsky's offensive and Stalin's reversal on supply airdrops into Warsaw coincided with the arrival at the front of General Berling and his First Polish Army, or Polish People's Army—referred to by non-Communist Poles as *berlingowcy* (Berling's men). On September 16, after Rokossovsky's Forty-Seventh Army had secured Praga and reached the Vistula—forcing the Germans to blow the bridges—Berling ordered his men to be the first to wade across the river into Warsaw. It was not a phantom operation. The People's Army company that made the crossing into the teeth of German gunfire from the opposite bank incurred 120 casualties (out of 150). Still more casualties were sustained by Berling's men in less successful crossings attempted over the next week, as German resistance stiffened. Berling's attempted forcing of the Vistula was plainly intended as a symbolic act of liberation by Polish Communists, to secure the claim of Bierut's Lublin committee to rule Warsaw—and Poland.[25]

What Stalin did not want to do was to help the Polish Home Army liberate Warsaw. We know this because, just as the Red Army and Berling reached the city, Bór-Komorowski contacted Rokossovsky, informing the Soviet commander on September 17 of the precise location of the underwater cable linking Warsaw to Praga so that the AK and Red Army could set up a secure line. Between September 15 and 18, an envoy of the Polish exile government delivered this and two other critical messages to the Soviet embassy in London, only to be told on September 18, in a cold rebuff, that "the Polish Government are no doubt aware that between [the Soviet] Government and them no diplomatic relations exist." Back in Warsaw, Bór-Komorowski was horrified to learn that, just as contact was finally possible with the Red Army at the gates of the city, his men were being arrested by the NKVD in Praga, ostensibly on the charge of collaboration (the pretext being a captured Polish-language German propaganda leaflet, similar to those cited above, urging Varsovians to fight against "Bolshevism"). One AK soldier reported that "the NKVD put a gun to prisoners' heads to extract the names of officers and the location of

arms" and that two new detention camps had been opened in eastern Poland for captured AK fighters. There would be no friendly
cooperation from the Red Army. The Soviet supplies airlifted into
the city, it was now clear, were intended for Berling's men, not
Bór-Komorowski's.[26]

Exploiting the disunity of their opponents, the Germans resumed the offensive. Even though Warsaw was now enveloped
by Soviet troops, the Wehrmacht went back on the attack, rooting
out the last AK strongholds in Mokotow (on September 27) and
Zoliborz (September 30). Villages near Warsaw that offered ref-
uge to AK fighters were burned down.[27]

On September 30, Mikolajczyk sent one final appeal for help
to "Marshal Stalin." "After sixty days of relentless fighting," the
Polish prime minister in London informed the Vozhd, "the defenders of Warsaw have reached the limits of human endurance. . . . At this extreme hour of need, I appeal to you, Marshal, to
issue orders for immediate operations that would relieve the garrison of Warsaw and result in the liberation of the capital. [Gen-
eral Bór-Komorowski] has addressed the same appeal to Marshal
Rokossovsky." Neither Stalin nor Rokossovsky replied to these
appeals. The Polish Home Army was on its own.[28]

By the time the AK leadership finally capitulated on October 2,
1944, the Polish Home Army in Warsaw had lost between 16,000
and 18,000 fighters, while another 120,000 or 130,000 Polish civilians had been killed in the fighting or dispatched by Himmler's
executioners. Of the five hundred thousand or so civilian survivors
hiding in the rubble, ninety thousand were sent to forced labor
camps in the Reich, sixty thousand sent to even harsher concentration camps, and the remainder evacuated to other German-
controlled areas of western Poland, out of the path of the Soviet
advance. Some fifteen thousand captured AK fighters were sent to
German prisoner-of-war camps.[29]

Although about five thousand surviving AK troops went underground, they would now be pursued not only by the Germans but
also, if they ventured east of the Vistula, by the NKVD, Berling's

men, and Bierut's Lublin prison guards. To help Bierut and Berling with the hunt, Stalin authorized the regifting of 485 Dodge trucks, 300 Willys jeeps, and 350 Harley-Davidson motorcycles from the Red Army's overflowing lend-lease stocks to Bierut and Berling in November 1944, with another 850 American trucks promised to the puppet Lublin government by January 1. With Bierut, Berling, and their Soviet handlers finishing the work begun by the NKVD at Katyn and continued by the SS in Warsaw, Poland would soon be purged of potential opposition to the installation of a friendly Communist government, fulfilling one of Stalin's key war aims.[30]

31

Soviet High Tide in Washington
The Morgenthau Plan

At Teheran, Stalin and Roosevelt had aligned on the basic approach they would take to Germany after Hitler's defeat. All of the main belligerents had agreed on the need to disarm the Reich, impose controls to prevent German rearmament, and ban the Nazi party. While the Vozhd had not fully embraced unconditional surrender, and Roosevelt had not signed off on Stalin's proposal to "dismember" Germany and on Soviet claims on East Prussian territory, the two statesmen had agreed that Germany must be severely punished, setting themselves against what Stalin scoffed at as Churchill's "desire for a soft peace." The most dramatic moment came when Stalin had proposed the summary shooting of "50,000 or perhaps 100,000 German officers" after the war to intimidate the German people, prompting Churchill's objection and Roosevelt's compromise solution that the Allies might shoot only forty-nine thousand German officers instead. As we saw, Stalin prevented a breach by embracing Churchill and telling him that he was only teasing.[1]

Stalin was not joking, however, about his desire to dismember Germany—or to conduct mass shootings of German officers. We know this because US Treasury secretary Henry Morgenthau and his assistant, the Soviet asset Harry Dexter White, specifically referenced "Marshal Stalin's list of 50,000" from Teheran when they discussed preparing a list of Germans who "ought to be shot" on September 4, 1944, in a planning session for the upcoming inter-Allied conference in Quebec—a proposal that had evidently been taken seriously in the Treasury Department.[2]

Why shooting Germans was US Treasury business was not obvious. Nonetheless, that this *was* considered Treasury business by summer 1944 is clear in the historical record. Somehow, in the aftermath of the Allied landings at Normandy, which brought the prospect of Germany's final defeat in sight, a long-running policy discussion in the Treasury on how to administer the German economy after the war morphed into an open-ended revenge fantasy. During the same meeting at which he and White spoke of death quotas for captured Germans, Morgenthau also proposed "the complete shut-down of the Ruhr [industrial area]" in terms clearly designed to inflict maximum human suffering: "Just strip it. I don't care what happens to the population. . . . I would take every mine, every mill and factory and wreck it . . . steel, coal, everything. Just close it down. I am for destroying it first and we will worry about the population second. . . . Why should I worry about what happens to [the German] people?"[3]

Morgenthau's talk of deindustrializing the Ruhr was not mere rhetoric, either. The Treasury secretary had been stirred to action when White warned him about softer plans for postwar Germany being prepared by the State Department and the US Army. The State Department plan for Germany, drafted on July 31, 1944, recommended the "rapid reconstruction and rehabilitation of war-torn areas," including German industrial areas (which must not be "permanently impaired") and the "eventual reintegration of Germany into the world economy," in order to aid postwar European recovery, trade, and growth. Although reparations would understandably be demanded by countries invaded by Nazi Germany, the authors recommended that payments be limited to ten years, so as not to "prejudice the establishment of democratic government in Germany" as the notorious Versailles reparations imposed in 1919 had done.[4]

Significantly, the State Department memorandum was brought to Morgenthau's attention by two Treasury officials now known to have been Soviet agents answering to Stalin. The first, Frank

Coe, obtained a copy and passed it on to White, who shared the news with his NKVD handler, code-named Koltsov, on August 5, 1944. White then waited until he and Morgenthau had boarded a flight in Maine the next day, en route to the British Isles, and pulled a copy of the soft State Department policy memorandum out of his briefcase. "As we were swinging out over the Atlantic," Morgenthau recalled, "I settled back to read it, first with interest, then with misgivings, finally with sharp disagreement." White had arranged things perfectly—so perfectly that even he was taken aback by "the shattering violence of the secretary's reaction."[5]

After landing in Scotland, Morgenthau was handed a copy of the draft plan of the "Handbook for Military Government in Germany" being prepared at the Supreme Headquarters of the Allied Expeditionary Force (SHAEF). Like the State Department memorandum, the army handbook emphasized the need for humane treatment of the population and expressed the hope that Germany would recover its footing enough to prevent the Allied armies from becoming "bogged down in a morass of economic wreckage." Reading this reinforced Morgenthau's view that action was necessary to ensure that postwar Germany was not given the soft-glove treatment, an opinion reinforced after SHAEF officers showed him damage caused both from the fighting in Normandy and from the German bombing of London. Striking an emotional tone, Morgenthau told a British radio interviewer that "it is not enough to say, 'we will disarm Germany . . . and *hope* that [Germans] will learn to behave themselves as decent people.' Hoping is not enough."[6]

Shortly before he left England on August 13, Morgenthau met with Anthony Eden, who showed him the minutes of the Teheran conference. The Treasury secretary was encouraged to learn that "Stalin, determined that Germany should never again disturb the peace of Europe, strongly favored its dismemberment" and that "Roosevelt backed him wholeheartedly." Though noting that Churchill had not agreed, Morgenthau decided that "German dismemberment," endorsed by Stalin and Roosevelt, was the true policy of the Allies, and that anyone advocating policies tending toward German recovery or unity was doing so improperly. On August 19, after returning to Washington, Morgenthau met with the president and denounced the too-soft State Department memorandum. According to Morgenthau, Roosevelt replied, "Give me thirty minutes with Churchill and I can correct this." As for what the president planned to tell Churchill, it was akin to what Morgenthau claims he told him now: "We have got to be tough with Germany and I mean the German people not just the Nazis. We either have to castrate the German people or you have got to treat them in such manner so they can't go on reproducing people who want to continue the way they have in the past." In this way, Morgenthau—stirred to action by a Soviet agent and citing Stalin as the Allied authority on "German dismemberment," a Stalin policy, he reminded the president, that Roosevelt had endorsed at Teheran—helped goad Roosevelt into endorsing the castration of the German people as a capstone to unconditional surrender.[7]

It was in this spirit of outdoing Stalin in vindictive bloodlust that Morgenthau and his Treasury aides formulated one of the most significant policy doctrines of the Second World War. Morgenthau's own blood was clearly up, at least in part out of genuine conviction. The secretary was Jewish, which gave him a personal stake in holding Hitler and the Germans responsible for the ongoing mass murder of European Jewry. Like Roosevelt with unconditional surrender in 1943, Morgenthau had sincere personal reasons for advocating the policy line that he did, even if it did dovetail neatly with Soviet foreign policy objectives.

The genesis of the Morgenthau Plan was not entirely innocent, however. The Venona decrypts have revealed that as many as seven Soviet agents answering to Moscow had a hand in drafting this document, including White, Solomon Adler (who had gone to Cairo in 1943 to sabotage Chiang Kai-shek and who would move to Communist China after Mao was in power), Frank Coe (the man who handed White the soft-glove State Department plan for occupied Germany and who would, like Adler, end his career working for Mao), and four others. Of these agents, White was the most important. It is now known that he was the principal author of the Morgenthau Plan, even if some of its vengeful tone regarding the harsh treatment of the Ruhr area and the people living there was contributed by Morgenthau himself. White actually objected at one point to the planned destruction of the Ruhr coal mines, proposing that the industrial area be put "under international control which will produce reparations for twenty years," thus enabling Stalin to claim a share of the proceeds. Morgenthau insisted that the Ruhr be "stripped of its machinery, the mines flooded—dynamited—wrecked" to "make [the Germans] impotent to wage future wars." If this brought starvation or depopulation, Morgenthau thought, all the better. Citing as precedent the Greece-Turkey population exchange of 1923, the secretary proposed cheerfully, "If you can move a million, you can move 20 million [people]."[8]

The final draft of the US Treasury's "Suggested Post-Surrender Plan for Germany" reflected both Morgenthau's nihilistic vision of a deindustrialized Germany and White's Stalinist case for industrial asset-stripping. Clause 3 proposed that the entire Ruhr area "should not only be stripped of all . . . existing industries but so weakened and controlled that it cannot in the foreseeable future become an industrial area." All "industrial plants and equipment not destroyed by military action," a White-influenced passage proposed, "shall be completely dismantled and *transported to Allied nations as restitution.*" Clause 3 also advocated the depopulation of the Ruhr: "All people and their families having special skills or technical training should be encouraged to migrate permanently from the area and should be as widely dispersed from the area."[9]

White's hand, and Soviet influence, was most clearly visible in clause 4, on "restitution and reparation." Rather than regular annual payments, what this clause demanded was that "restitution and reparation be effected by the transfer of existing German resources and territories," including "property looted by Germans in territory occupied by them," an allusion to the contested borderlands of Eastern Europe into which the Red armies were now advancing. White added here that the occupying powers had the right to the "confiscation of *all* German assets of any character whatsoever outside of Germany." More broadly, this clause envisioned the "removal and distribution among devastated countries"—such as the USSR—of "industrial plants and equipment situated within the International Zone [of occupied Germany] and the North and South German states delimited in the section on partition." White's clause 4 also authorized the use of "forced labor outside Germany" for restitution or reparation of war damages, inviting Stalin to take in as many slave-labor prisoners as the Red Army and NKVD could capture.[10]

This policy memorandum was met with bewilderment when it was first circulated around Washington. Philip Mosely, a State Department adviser who worked closely with the US ambassador in London on postwar planning, thought the Morgenthau Plan "fantastic, childish, and imbecilic." When Francis Penrose, another American diplomat long resident in London, asked Morgenthau what he proposed to do with people uprooted from the Ruhr, the secretary responded that Germany's "surplus population should be dumped in North Africa." Henry Stimson, the secretary of war, expressed "grave reservations" about Morgenthau's desire for "mass vengeance" against "the entire German people without regard to individual guilt."[11]

Stimson requested an audience with the president on August 26, 1944, to state his case against Morgenthau's plans for Germany, although he discovered when he arrived at the White House that the Treasury secretary had beaten him to it. Not only had Morgenthau turned Roosevelt against the State Department blueprint, but the day before, Morgenthau had visited the White House to poison the president's mind against the SHAEF "Handbook for Military Government in Germany" too. "This so-called Handbook," Roosevelt chided Stimson, "is pretty bad. It gives me the impression that Germany is to be restored just as much as the Netherlands or Belgium." Despite recent news from Germany, where Hitler had nearly been assassinated on July 20 in Operation Valkyrie, a conspiracy involving thousands of Germans who would pay with their lives, Roosevelt would still brook no discussion of any German resistance, of any Germans untainted by collective guilt in the crimes of Nazism. Roosevelt told Stimson that "it is of the utmost importance that everyone in Germany should realize that this time Germany is a defeated nation. I do not want them to starve to death, but . . . the German people as a whole must have it driven home to them that the whole nation has been engaged in a lawless conspiracy against the decencies of modern civilization."[12]

Knowing that Stimson, with cabinet rank, enjoyed access to the president and could thus derail his plan, Morgenthau invited him over to dinner with White on September 4. Stimson was aghast after White informed Stimson that he and Morgenthau favored mass shootings of captured Germans without trial. While the secretary of war shared Morgenthau's desire for a "rigorous prosecution of war criminals" and some adjustment of Germany's eastern borders to reassure Russia and Poland about their security, he was adamantly opposed to extrajudicial shootings and to deindustrializing the Ruhr and Rhineland. "To destroy much of German industry," he told Morgenthau and White, "would be to force thirty million people into starvation." (Asked to explain where he got the number from, Stimson explained that thirty million was the difference between the agrarian population of Germany in the mid-nineteenth century and that of the early twentieth, after industrialization allowed the country to import foodstuffs.) Revealingly, although White and Morgenthau disputed Stimson's estimate of Germans who would starve to death in their plan to wreck the German economy, neither man objected to his accusation that they did want to starve millions of Germans. "Stimson," Morgenthau told his Treasury advisers the next day, "is opposed to making Germany a barren farm country" out of misplaced "kindness and Christianity." The Treasury secretary then called Hopkins on the phone to dish on Stimson, a man they both agreed came from "that school" that believed "that property [was] sacred"; he was "one of those fellows that are afraid of [Communist] Russia." Hopkins chimed in that he thought postwar Germany should be allowed "no steel mills at all." The battle lines were drawn: Hopkins, White, and Morgenthau for deindustrializing and depopulating Germany and allowing Stalin to pillage Germany's property and people for "restitution," and Stimson for an approach drawing on what he called "kindness and Christianity," which would harness German productivity for European recovery.[13]

It was not a fair fight. Morgenthau, a prominent Democratic Party donor whose own Hudson Valley estate was only twenty miles from the Roosevelt compound in Hyde Park, New York, had worked Roosevelt over thoroughly on the weekend of September 2 and 3. The president made a few suggestions of his own to Morgenthau, such as that "no [German] should be allowed to wear a uniform, and . . . no marching [will be allowed]," and that "Germany should be allowed no aircraft of any kind, not even a glider." These provisions were duly added to the Morgenthau Plan, in clauses 10 through 12. To pin his boss down, Morgenthau insisted that Roosevelt agree "to see the Ruhr dismantled, and the machinery given to those countries that might need it"—meaning, presumably, to Stalin's USSR, although Morgenthau was careful not to state this openly. Morgenthau shared a Treasury Department estimate that doing this "would put eighteen to twenty million people out of work," and Roosevelt approved of this too. The president invited Morgenthau to Quebec to make his case. Stimson was not invited, nor was Hull. Significantly, Morgenthau brought along Harry Dexter White.[14]

Still, Roosevelt knew that it would not be easy to win over the British prime minister. Churchill had expressed private reservations about the president's unconditional surrender doctrine, and he had violently objected at Teheran when Stalin and Roosevelt proposed the mass shooting of German officers. He had also refused to go along with Stalin's Teheran line on "dismembering Germany." Judging by the fact that Roosevelt invited Morgenthau to Quebec at the last minute, the president would have preferred not to have to convince Churchill at all. Instead, he let Morgenthau do the talking.[15]

It did not go well. Morgenthau, who had not been invited to any of the earlier Big Two or Big Three summits, found himself face-to-face with an on-form Churchill at a formal dinner banquet. "After I finished my piece," Morgenthau later recalled, "he turned loose on me the full flood of his rhetoric, sarcasm and violence. [Churchill] looked on the Treasury Plan, he said, as he would on chaining himself to a dead German." The Morgenthau Plan, Churchill objected, was "unnatural, unchristian and unnecessary. . . . I'm all for disarming Germany, but we ought not to prevent her living decently. There are bonds between the working classes of all countries, and the English people will not stand for the policy you are advocating." Roosevelt remained silent as Morgenthau was abused, allowing Churchill to "wear himself out attacking [Morgenthau]," using Roosevelt's Treasury secretary, as the latter complained, "to draw the venom."[16]

Roosevelt's gambit worked. On the day after the prime minister had declared his full-throated opposition, Morgenthau threatened to withhold lend-lease funds for Britain—basically the entire amount allotted for Britain's postwar recovery (referred to as "Phase II Lend-Lease")—unless Churchill signed on to his plan. This was not a small sum, either, but $6.5 billion, the equivalent of two-thirds of a trillion dollars today. "What do you want me to do," Churchill asked, according to White's recollection, "beg like Fala?" (Fala was Roosevelt's dog.) With the British Empire dependent on the flow of dollars and supplies from America to keep fighting, there was little the prime minister could do but agree. To assuage his pride, Churchill did insist on dictating a version of the Morgenthau Plan in his own words, subject to the president's approval, in order to make it sound more elegant and less cruel.[17]

The Churchill version of the Morgenthau Plan, initialed by both prime minister and president on September 15, 1944, is a remarkable historical document. At financial gunpoint, Churchill signed off not only on Morgenthau's plan of "eliminating the war-making industries in the Ruhr and in the Saar," but also eradicating "the metallurgical, chemical and electrical industries in Germany"— that is, in Germany as a whole, not just in the greater Ruhr area. The reason for this addition became clear in a passage, likely put in at White's insistence, recalling that "the Germans have devastated a large portion *of the industries of Russia* and of other neighboring Allies, and it is only in accordance with justice that these injured countries should be entitled to remove the machinery they require in order to repair the losses they have suffered."[18]

Anthony Eden, who may not have known how much financial leverage the Americans had brought to bear against the prime minister, objected violently to Churchill's about-face. "You can't do this," Eden blurted out. "After all, you and I publicly have said quite the opposite." Lamely, Churchill tried to justify signing off on Morgenthau's plan to wreck German industry as a way to aid British manufacturing, but his heart was not in it. At last the prime minister quieted Eden's objection by insisting, in a veiled allusion to Morgenthau's financial blackmail, that "when I have to choose between my people and the German people, I am going to choose my people."[19]

As interesting as what was decided by Churchill and Roosevelt at Quebec about postwar Germany is what was not decided there about the future of non-German Europe. The conference, held from September 13 to 16, 1944, coincided with the decisive phase of the Warsaw Uprising, when the Red Army resumed its offensive into Praga, aimed at installing Berling's men in Warsaw. In theory, Stalin had consented, by this point, to allow US and British supply planes to land in Ukraine, which offered the chance of a final push to save Warsaw. Because of the fireworks over the Morgenthau Plan, there was no real discussion of Poland at Quebec.

Another critical issue neglected was Yugoslavia, where the decision to back Tito in 1943 had raised the prospect of a Communist takeover of the entire region. Waking up belatedly to his mistake, Churchill warned Roosevelt at Quebec about what he called "the

rapid encroachment of the Russians into the Balkans and the con-
sequent dangerous spread of Russian influence in the area." He
requested that the US Navy provide landing craft to ferry troops
from Italy to the Istrian Peninsula to stake a claim in Yugoslavia
and ideally race north and beat the Red Army to Vienna. A Soviet
military mission—airlifted in by the Royal Air Force—had arrived
at Tito's headquarters, handing him $2 million in cash and station-
ing at least two Soviet officers in every partisan corps. By late June
1944, the Red Army had acquired bases close enough to Yugoslavia to airlift supplies. Although Stalin, Molotov, and Tito took
loud public credit, Soviet supplies were delivered in a fleet of ten
Douglas C-47 transport planes, provided to Stalin via lend-lease
and now delivering print runs of *Izvestiya*, *Pravda*, and *Krasnaia
Zvezda* (red star). As a British liaison officer reported from Tito's
headquarters in bewilderment, "The 'Soviet' goods were largely
American packed in American containers dropped by American
parachutes"—except for the agitprop, which was standard Soviet
issue, translated into Serbo-Croat.[20]

The coup de grâce came on September 19, just three days after
the Quebec conference ended, when Tito slipped his British handlers and flew to Moscow in a regifted American plane. Indignant
that Tito had "levanted" without warning, Churchill ordered Fitzroy Maclean to find him. Maclean—unaware that Tito had been
denouncing him behind his back for months, at one point thanking Stalin for "saving him from the English"—was unable to track
him down. So taken in were Maclean and Churchill by the man
they were showering with supplies that it did not occur to them
that Tito, a loyal Communist, was simply reporting to Moscow for
instructions. Churchill solved the mystery of Tito's whereabouts
only in October, after he had flown to Russia himself and asked
Stalin, who replied drily, "Tito came to Moscow."[21]

Roosevelt refused to consider at Quebec the idea of landing
troops in Yugoslavia or applying pressure on Stalin over Poland.
Instead, the president went all in on Morgenthau's Soviet-inspired
plan to wreck the German economy and establish the Stalin-friendly

legal principle that the war's victors could loot German industrial assets for restitution or reparation. Churchill, for his part, would have loved to talk about Poland and Yugoslavia in Quebec, but he was under evident duress. Morgenthau observed somewhat ruefully, even while getting his way, that "Churchill was quite emotional and at one time had tears in his eyes."[22]

Churchill was not wrong to be emotional. The humanitarian consequences of the Morgenthau Plan, if taken literally and seriously applied, would have been horrifying. Cordell Hull told Roosevelt to his face that the Treasury program "to wipe out everything in Germany except land" meant that, as "only 60 per cent of the German people could support themselves on German land," "the other 40 percent would die"—as many as thirty million people. There were strategic implications, too, that posed grave risks for Allied soldiers. "If the Morgenthau plan leaked out, as it inevitably would," Hull warned Roosevelt after the latter returned from Quebec, "it might well mean a bitter-end German resistance that could cause the loss of thousands of American lives." Hull was so upset that he lost his appetite and stopped sleeping. On October 2, 1944, his seventy-third birthday, the ailing secretary of state left his office, never to return; Hopkins's lend-lease loyalist, Edward Stettinius, took over as acting secretary of state. In November, an ailing Hull resigned, ostensibly because of failing health, but really because of the "Morgenthau business," as he told *New York Times* columnist Arthur Krock.[23]

Stimson was no less disturbed. The Morgenthau Plan, he pointed out to Hull before the latter stepped down, explicitly violated the Atlantic Charter, in which the United States and Britain had promised to "endeavor . . . to further the enjoyment of all states, victor and vanquished, great and small, of access, on equal terms, to the trade and raw materials of the world which are needed for their economic prosperity." Stimson predicted that the destruction of the "metallurgical, chemical and electrical industries in Germany" would throw forty million Germans out of work, including twenty million in the Ruhr area alone. Stimson also objected to a clause

under which "so-called archcriminals shall be put to death by the
military without provision for any trial and upon mere identification after apprehension." Stimson showed the offending passage
to the usually docile army chief of staff, General Marshall, who
told the president he was aghast at "the notion that we should not
give these men a fair trial."[24]

President Roosevelt was not prepared for the firestorm of criticism that greeted him on his return to Washington. Although the
Morgenthau Plan was not released to the public, it did not take
long for a version to leak to the press. As early as September 21,
Drew Pearson picked up the thread in his Washington Merry-Go-
Round column, in a story planted by Morgenthau and White, who
told Pearson they had read over the army handbook for occupied
Germany in August and, "in disgust," had taken "the proofs over
to the White House [and] tossed them on the President's desk."
"This is a very bad job," Roosevelt was said to have admonished
Stimson. White and Morgenthau thus smeared Stimson, only for
Stimson to retaliate by leaking news of cabinet dissent over the
Morgenthau Plan to the *New York Times* and the *Wall Street Journal*.[25]

Livid over the leaks, Roosevelt issued a misleading statement to
the press on September 29, insisting that postwar occupation policy on Germany had not yet been settled. Calling in the secretary
of war on October 3, the president, Stimson recalled, "grinned and
looked naughty and said 'Henry Morgenthau pulled a boner,'" denying that he had himself expressed the "intention of turning Germany into an agrarian state." Stimson showed Roosevelt the text
of what he and Churchill had signed at Quebec. Unable to deny
that his signature was indeed there, the president played dumb.
Roosevelt told Stimson that he "was frankly staggered," adding
that "he had no idea how he could have initialed this." It seems
clear that the president disavowed the Morgenthau Plan—to Stimson, at least—once he realized that he would pay a political price
for it in the final weeks of an election campaign. Roosevelt's wife,
Eleanor, later disavowed her husband's disavowal, recalling that "I
never heard my husband say that he had changed his attitude on

the [Morgenthau] plan. I think the repercussions brought about by the press stories made him feel it was wise to abandon it at that time." A harsher version of the army handbook, drafted by the Soviet agent White, was adopted in September 1944 as Joint Chiefs of Staff directive 1067. Like the Morgenthau Plan, JCS 1067 stipulated that "no steps will be taken leading toward the economic rehabilitation of Germany." This would be the US Army's policy as it entered Germany in 1945.[26]

Goebbels wasted little time making propaganda hay out of the news from Washington, thundering on Berlin radio about "the plan proposed by that Jew Morgenthau which would rob 80 million Germans of their industry and turn Germany into a simple potato field." Allied hopes of a triumphal march to Berlin that fall, ignited after the relatively rapid liberation of Paris on August 25, proved premature. The senior American commander on the ground in Western Europe, General Omar Bradley, noted that in the first half of September 1944 "most men in the Allied high command believed that victory over Germany was imminent. The near-miraculous revitalization of the German Army in October [came] as a shock." General Marshall was angry enough that he complained to Morgenthau. "Just as the army placed loudspeakers on the front urging Germans to surrender," he railed, the news of the Morgenthau Plan "stiffened the will of the Germans to resist." Lieutenant Colonel Marshall Knappen, chief of the US Army's religious affairs section, wrote after interviewing American soldiers that "weary men returning from the field reported the Germans fought with twice their previous determination after the announcement of the Morgenthau policy." Roosevelt's intelligence chief, Wild Bill Donovan, informed the Joint Chiefs of Staff in November 1944 that "the German spirit of resistance has been bolstered greatly by fear of the consequences of unconditional surrender."[27]

Just as Roosevelt had feared, the Morgenthau Plan became a campaign issue. "Almost overnight," his Republican opponent, New York governor Thomas Dewey, thundered on October 18, 1944, "the morale of the German people seems wholly changed.

Now they are fighting with a frenzy of despair. We are paying in blood for our failure to have ready an intelligent program for dealing with invaded Germany." This might be dismissed as campaign rhetoric, except that Dewey's views of the Morgenthau Plan were shared by most of the American officer corps, the head of the OSS, the army chief of staff, the secretary of war, and the secretary of state. Once confident of receiving better treatment if they surrendered to the civilized Western Allies, many Germans now saw Roosevelt as no better than Stalin. It was no coincidence that, just as Berlin radio was warning German troops that the Americans wanted to "destroy German industry" and turn their country into a "potato field," German-language Soviet radio transmissions were telling them that "Hitlers come and go, but the German people [and] the German state remain"—suggesting, disingenuously, that Stalin did not plan to punish the German people collectively for Hitler's crimes or to break up Germany into pieces. In private, the Soviets were pleased with White's work in muscling through the Morgenthau Plan, a draft version of which was shared with the NKVD by one of White's Soviet subagents, Nathan Silvermaster, in October 1944. The Soviet ambassador to Washington, Andrei Gromyko, met with White to thank him in person. The Soviet government's own position on the treatment of occupied Germany, Gromyko told White, was "very close or closer to what is spoken of as 'the Morgenthau Plan.'" Soviet diplomatic cynicism over plans for defeated Germany, as on the Warsaw uprising, was breathtaking.[28]

The ultimate price in blood for the Morgenthau Plan was paid by those Americans and Britons who would soon face a devastating, and almost wholly unexpected, German counterattack in the Ardennes Forest. Although this offensive, known to history as the Battle of the Bulge, was not launched until mid-December 1944, we now know that Hitler revealed the plan to his generals in late September, shortly after learning about the Morgenthau Plan. This gave the battle a political rationale to match the strategic objective of reaching Antwerp, splitting Allied lines, and prodding the Western Allies to negotiate before they reached German territory. In his New Year's message to the German people, issued as that battle was being bloodily joined, Hitler railed against Morgenthau's plan of "completely ripping apart the German Reich, [the] uprooting of 15 or 20 million Germans and transport abroad, the enslavement of the rest of our people, the ruination of our German youth, but above all, the starvation of our masses." Small wonder one American writer described the Morgenthau Plan as "psychological warfare in reverse."[29]

Just as with Roosevelt's unveiling of the unconditional surrender doctrine, the real beneficiary of the Morgenthau Plan was Josef Stalin, as Gromyko had revealed when he congratulated White in October. Soviet strategic interests were served by the stiffening of German resistance to the American-British-Polish forces who were repulsed at the Rhine in fall 1944, thus ensuring that the Western Allies would not reach Berlin before the Red Army grew near. That Goebbels and Hitler reacted so violently to the Morgenthau Plan was an added bonus for the Russians, as the upshot was that the German high command threw all available resources into the Ardennes operation in fall 1944, weakening defenses on the eastern front. In the months before December 1944, the Wehrmacht committed nearly three times as many newly produced tanks to the Ardennes sector (about 2,300) as to the entire eastern front (920), after having already tilted the balance of forces deployed on the non-Soviet European fronts to well over half during that summer after D-Day. Losses in Allied (mostly American) blood in the Bulge—more than 100,000 casualties, including 19,246 dead, 62,849 wounded or crippled, and 26,612 captured or missing, the costliest battle of the entire war for US troops—were Stalin's gain.[30]

Setting aside the battlefield ledger, by signing on to the Morgenthau Plan at Quebec, Roosevelt had endorsed Stalin's policy of industrial looting and the trafficking in slave labor as "restitution and reparation," as he planned to do after the Red Army occupied Eastern Europe and Germany. On pain of forcing Britain into bankruptcy, the president had bullied Churchill into approving this too. Having missed their last chance to secure a peace settlement consistent with the Atlantic Charter and with longstanding Anglo-Saxon principles of law and jurisprudence, to rescue the Polish Home Army, or to advance across the Rhine or into Yugoslavia and the Balkans before the Red Army, the Allies were losing the war even while winning it. The stage was set for the final surrender of US-British interests to Stalin at Yalta.

32

Moscow and Yalta

Unfinest Hour of the Anglo-Americans

IF THERE WAS anyone in a position to head off the impending disasters born of Soviet influence operations and Roosevelt's blindness to them, it was Winston Churchill. And yet Churchill seems to have given up on Roosevelt after Quebec. Churchill's buckling on the Morgenthau Plan under financial pressure was a sad reflection of Britain's waning power and influence. The prime minister did what he could to conceal his frustrations with furious activity. Unlike Stalin, who remained anchored to Moscow for almost the entire war, and Roosevelt, a paraplegic who traveled abroad only when absolutely necessary, Churchill spent much of the conflict carrying out a desperate shuttle diplomacy—now flying to Canada or the United States to wheedle what he could out of Roosevelt, now flying counterclockwise around southern Europe to Stalin's lair in the Kremlin—always in uncomfortable, unheated military cargo planes.

After the debacle in Quebec, Churchill flew to Moscow yet again to salvage what he could out of Roosevelt's refusal to stand up to Stalin on Poland and the Balkans. Making Balkan matters still more pressing was the fact that, in the wake of D-Day and the great Soviet Belorussian offensive (Bagration), many of Hitler's allies had given up on the Germans. Even the staunch Finns gave up the fight after winning one last face-saving victory in a battle fought at Tali-Ihantala on the Karelian Isthmus northeast of Viipuri (Vyborg) in July 1944, suing Stalin for peace on terms similar to those he had offered in March 1940. (Finland was forced, in the final treaty

signed on September 19, to cough up Petsamo, expel any remaining German soldiers, pay reparations, and agree to a Red Army
base stationed outside Helsinki.) In the Balkans, first Romania (on
August 23) and then Bulgaria (in early September), broke with the
Germans and switched sides in the war after opportunistic coups
d'état, allowing Stalin to conquer these countries almost by invitation. Ploești, home to the oil fields fueling the German armies
(although by 1944, Allied bombing runs had rendered production
nugatory), fell to the Red Army on August 30 and Bucharest the
next day. Soviet mobile troops were soon wheeling northwest into
the Transylvanian Alps, threatening to burst into the Hungarian
plain. The Red Army sustained only sixty-nine thousand casualties
subduing Romania, far fewer than losses being incurred that summer in Belorussia, Poland, and the Baltic area. Bulgaria fell into
Stalin's lap basically as spillover from Romania, as the arrival of the
Red Army on the lower Danube in late August 1944 made plain
that the Germans were finished in the Balkans, throwing Sofia
into political chaos. Stalin did declare war on Bulgaria on September 5—although Bulgarian troops had been helping the Germans
garrison the Balkans, Bulgaria had declined to join Barbarossa in
1941—but the Soviet invasion that followed was little more than
a formality; Red Army losses were less than one thousand casualties. Four days later, the pro-German regime was toppled and
a Communist-friendly government, supplied with $50,000 in cash
smuggled into Sofia by Soviet agents, invited in the Red Army. By
September 15, the country was firmly under Stalin's control, occupied by the Fifty-Seventh and Thirty-Seventh Soviet Armies, with
VVS planes landing troops and supplies at Sofia's air bases.[1]

Yugoslavia, too, was falling rapidly into Moscow's orbit. Churchill's folly in backing Tito had ruined the Chetniks. The prime
minister's bizarre hostility toward Mihailović, who commanded
the armed forces of the Yugoslav exile government Britain was
hosting in London, was so extreme by summer 1944 that SHAEF
had, on Churchill's instructions, issued a ban on any American or
British officer working with him, even as an observer. By October

1944, when the Russians arrived in force, the Chetniks were reduced to begging Cairo command to help evacuate them from
the country, warning the British that "the Russians are treating
our people as enemy prisoners. Concentration camps have been
formed." Even if Churchill had wanted to help, it was now impossible, as Tito was no longer allowing English troops in; on October 24 he even forced two British detachments that had landed on
the Montenegrin coastline to re-embark and leave. Adding an element of the absurd to the US-British betrayal of Yugoslavia was the
arrival of the Red Army in American lend-lease trucks and jeeps,
adorned with "red stars, hammers and sickles," as Churchill's envoy to Tito, Fitzroy Maclean, observed. "You can't produce this
sort of thing in capitalist countries," one Russian ammunition
driver taunted Maclean—from inside a Chevrolet truck.[2]

Churchill may not yet have appreciated how badly he had let
down his own side in Yugoslavia. Only months later, in the pained
aftermath of Yalta, did the prime minister express his first regret
about backing the partisans, when he wrote privately to Eden ("for
your eyes alone") that "Tito can be left to himself in his mountains
to stew in Balkan juice which is bitter." But as he touched down in
Moscow on October 9, 1944, Churchill had few illusions about Stalin's intentions for Eastern Europe. Romania, Bulgaria, and Hungary were as good as gone, under Soviet occupation, or soon to be
in Hungary's case, and fated to be Communist satellites. The question of Poland was more contentious, although Churchill thought
that the Polish expeditionary forces fighting under the flag of the
London exile government in Italy and France gave him some
leverage. A bit more hopeful was the situation in Greece, where
Cairo command had quietly begun landing troops in late September 1944 (Operation Manna), first in the Peloponnese and then at
Megara, outside Athens, on October 4. In a sign of intent, British
airborne troops landed in Athens on October 14, while Churchill
was in Moscow bargaining for Greece's future with Stalin.[3]

That Fourth Moscow Conference, code-named TOLSTOY and
conducted from October 9 to 19, 1944, was the longest of Stalin's

bilateral encounters with Churchill and the most consequential. Tolstoy is best remembered for an informal exchange the very first night, when Churchill "produced," in the version of the story told by his interpreter, Major Arthur Birse, "what he called a 'naughty document' showing a list of Balkan countries and the proportion of interest in all of them." Turning the tables on Roosevelt, who had left him isolated at Teheran, Churchill explained that, while he was sure "that the Americans would be shocked" by "how crudely he had put it," he knew that "Marshal Stalin was a realist." The prime minister then scribbled out, on a notepad, a scheme to assign to the Soviet Union 90 percent of Romania (giving "the others"—that is, Britain and the United States—the remaining 10 percent), while reversing the share in Greece, where the British and Americans got 90 percent and the Soviets 10 percent. Stalin was also allotted 75 percent of Bulgaria. Optimistically, Churchill proposed a fifty-fifty split in Yugoslavia and Hungary. The blue check mark now visible next to Romania was, according to Churchill, inked by Stalin to indicate agreement with the whole proposal (although we know that Stalin later objected to 75 percent of Bulgaria as inadequate). Somewhat embarrassed to have inked a territorial carve up of Eastern Europe that bore some resemblance to the Molotov-Ribbentrop Pact of 1939, Churchill asked Stalin whether it would be best if they burned it. "No, you keep it," Stalin replied, and Churchill did: the original, in the British Archives in Kew, is now available for public view.[4]

This so-called percentages agreement was a gross violation of international norms, but it has also been defended as the height of Churchillian realpolitik, a brave effort to save Greece (90 percent British) and half of Yugoslavia and Hungary from the burning. There is something to this, in that by October 1944, with the Red Army on the scene, there were few good options left to uphold Britain's faltering regional position. Because of his own decision to back Tito and because of Roosevelt's refusal to land troops in Yugoslavia, Churchill was forced to play Stalin's game in the Balkans. Judging by his behavior after giving his blue check mark, Stalin did not really assent to Churchill's percentages—certainly not 50 percent for Hungary and Yugoslavia—so much as accept that Britain meant to play hardball in Greece, which was clear enough in its recent landing of troops there. It was British armed intervention, not a naughty napkin, that saved Greece from a Communist takeover in the civil war that erupted in Athens in December 1944—not least because the Soviet cause was popular in Greece, owing both to the galloping prestige of the Red Army and to traditional Russophilia in an Orthodox country created largely under Russian auspices after the Greek War of Independence fought against the Ottoman Empire in the 1820s. Britain's interests in Greece had been accepted in principle in talks between Eden and the Soviet ambassador in May 1944, as Churchill had reminded Stalin on July 11. All Churchill's naughty napkin did was make explicit what Roosevelt had agreed at Teheran: that Eastern Europe (except Greece) was Stalin's sphere of influence.[5]

During the entire war, Churchill had conceded far more to Stalin than Stalin expected to receive. As early as October 1939, Churchill had proposed to the British war cabinet that the Baltic Sea—and its littoral states—lay in the Soviet sphere of influence, including Finland. In May 1942, Churchill had agreed to Soviet claims on the three ex-Baltic countries, insisting in return only on a vague agreement on the "right of emigration" for Estonians, Latvians, and Lithuanians anxious to escape Stalin's clutches. At Teheran, the prime minister had surprised Stalin by promising, apropos of nothing, to revise the Montreux Convention to ensure that the Soviet fleet would have the "access to warm waters" it deserved, based on little more than Churchill's nostalgia for the British-Russian brotherhood of arms in World War I. All these concessions, which dovetailed closely with the spheres of influence demanded by Stalin in the Moscow Pact, and (in the case of the Turkish Straits) by Molotov at his Berlin summit with Hitler in November 1940, were made long before the Red Army had arrived in the Baltics or Balkans, before it had even reconquered Ukraine. The real novelty of the naughty napkin is that Churchill, bowing to the advancing Red Army and anxious to salvage a share of Greece, signed off on Soviet domination of Romania and Bulgaria: the two countries Hitler had refused to assign to Stalin in 1940. Churchill's percentages agreement offered Stalin more than Hitler had done at the height of Soviet-German collaboration in the Molotov-Ribbentrop era.[6]

Of course, Stalin wanted still more than this, and he would soon get it. In view of the arrival in Yugoslavia of the Red Army, which was now financing and collaborating with Tito and had Soviet officers in every partisan unit, Churchill's suggestion of an even split there was a fantasy based on his erroneous reading of Tito. Stalin—who received Tito's reports on Maclean and English activities in Yugoslavia, and who had just received Tito in the Kremlin for a weeklong political instruction session—knew this perfectly well, although he was diplomatic enough not to rub it in Churchill's face. British press reports, as Stalin informed Tito on October 7, 1944, had taken note of his recent disappearing act, and so it was best that the two men be discreet about their relationship. Still, if anyone asked—as Churchill did during the TOLSTOY meetings—then there was no reason for Stalin or Tito to deny that the visit had taken place. Rather, the cover story these men agreed on was that "Tito came to Moscow to ask for arms."[7]

Nor was it likely that the United States and Britain would be able to seriously contest Soviet influence in Budapest after the Red Army entered Hungarian territory on October 6, 1944, three days before Churchill presented Stalin with his proposal. Because the Germans had reinforced Hungary much more strongly than Yugoslavia, Romania, Bulgaria, or Greece, owing to its proximity to the Reich and its economic importance, the fight for Budapest would be far bloodier than for Belgrade, Bucharest, Sofia, or Athens, lasting into December 1944 and costing the Red Army more than 100,000 casualties, 1,760 tanks, and 290 warplanes. But this fight was exclusively a Soviet affair. After shedding this much blood in the battle for Budapest, Stalin was hardly going to let the British and Americans have an even share of influence over Hungary's political future.[8]

Poland was conspicuously left out of the percentages agreement. Churchill had enough spirit to invite the Polish premier in London, Mikolajczyk, to join him in Moscow during the TOLSTOY conference, and Stalin was game enough to receive him. Mikolajczyk flew into Moscow on the evening of October 12, 1944, just two weeks after Stalin had rebuffed his last request for aid for the AK in Warsaw. Churchill's goal in arranging the meeting was to negotiate a deal whereby Mikolajczyk would become prime minister of postwar Poland, with other cabinet posts split fifty-fifty between the London Polish exile government and the Lublin committee, in exchange for which the Polish premier would agree to Stalin's preferred borders for Poland, tracking the Curzon Line the British had favored since 1919. To make things easier for Churchill, Molotov had agreed to pull back the Moscow Pact claims in the Bialystok bulge and west of Lvov/Lemberg, although retaining Soviet title to the Galician oil fields. But, not wishing to give up Poland's claim on Galicia, Mikolajczyk would not accept the Curzon Line, even though the contested territories were already under Soviet occupation. "I know that our fate was sealed at Teheran," the Polish premier informed Churchill. Nonetheless "I am not a person," Mikolajczyk admonished him on October 14, "completely devoid of patriotic feeling, to give away half of Poland." To this, Churchill retorted that "twenty-five years ago we [i.e., Britain] reconstituted Poland although in the last war more Poles fought against us than for us. Now again we are preserving you from disappearance, but you will not play ball. You are absolutely crazy. . . . Unless you accept the frontier you are out of business forever. The Russians will sweep through your country and your people will be liquidated. You are on the verge of annihilation." Still, Mikolajczyk said no. After receiving a final refusal later that afternoon, Churchill exploded at the proud Polish premier, accusing him and his fellow ministers in London of being "callous people who want to wreck Europe." If the Poles "want to conquer Russia we shall leave you to do it. I feel as if I were in a lunatic asylum. I don't know whether the British government will continue to recognize you." In this way Winston Churchill, after abandoning Mihailović's Chetniks and thus rendering impotent the royal Yugoslav government in London, threatened to do the same thing to Mikolajczyk and the London Poles.[9]

To be fair to Churchill, the Polish premier was indeed being stubborn about Poland's eastern borders, despite the fact that Poles made up a minority in much of this contested region absorbed by Poland after its war with the USSR in 1920. Mikolajczyk may have been worried about his political flank back in London, where he was seen as something of a moderate vis-à-vis the grasping Russians. He was also counting, erroneously, on Roosevelt's support, owing to the US president's warm talk about Poland in the election campaign, and the fact that he had been told, on a visit to Washington in June 1944, that the US government had not, unlike Britain and the USSR, agreed to the Curzon Line. Mikolajczyk was disabused of this notion by Molotov in the Kremlin on October 13, when Molotov read back to him the minutes from Teheran where Roosevelt had sold out Poland. According to Ambassador Harriman, who sat in on this meeting, "Mikolajczyk showed shock and surprise at this statement," compounded by Harriman's failure to refute it. The idea that his country had been betrayed by both the United States and Britain, and that Roosevelt had lied to his face in order not to alienate American Poles in an election year, was too much for this proud Polish patriot to bear. In any case, Mikolajczyk wanted to go down swinging. After begging the US president one last time after returning to London, in a wire to Washington on October 27, to "throw the weight of your decisive influence and authority" behind Poland's territorial claims, only to be denied yet again, Mikolajczyk resigned his office.[10]

We should not let Churchill off so easily, however. What made Churchill's bullying of Mikolajczyk in Moscow especially unfortunate was that, even as he was using the specter of the Russians "sweeping through" Poland and "liquidating" Polish patriots to threaten the Polish premier into accepting the Curzon Line, Soviet and pro-Soviet Polish forces were being harried by devastating AK and partisan attacks all over Poland. Despite being lavished with regifted American lend-lease weapons and supplies to lord it over the country they claimed to rule, neither Bierut's puppet Lublin government nor Berling's Communist army had popular support. On October 15, the day after Churchill's brutal outbursts against Mikolajczyk, no less than two thousand of Berling's men deserted to the Polish Home Army with their weapons. This was the climax of a long-burgeoning trend, which had seen, according to NKVD files, "an average of between 40 and 60 soldiers and officers desert with their arms every day for the past two months," making a total, since the Warsaw Uprising began, of more than five thousand desertions. The situation was most serious in Lublin itself, where Bierut's government was harassed by a powerful AK underground network numbering more than one thousand fighters. Even as Churchill, in Moscow, was trying to sell out Mikolajczyk's London government to cut a deal with Stalin, the AK fighting on behalf of that government, according to an NKVD report submitted to Beria and Stalin, was placarding signs all over Lublin announcing that "The Home Army Lives!" and "Long Live General Bór!"[11]

Far from a hopeless cause, the battle for Poland was just beginning—and it was hottest in the contested eastern regions abutting Galicia and Ukraine, where Mikolajczyk wanted Churchill and Roosevelt to back Poland's claim. In Krasnystaw, forty miles southeast of Lublin, two AK regiments seized control of the prison, liberating five captured fighters. In Chelm, still closer to Stalin's proposed Curzon frontier, the AK had three hundred men under arms who had carried out ten armed attacks in September and early October 1944. These operations had taken the lives of fifteen Bierut officials, including four armed guards escorting a political prison convoy, and liberated four AK fighters from Communist custody. In Zamosc, sixty miles southeast of Lublin, an AK ambush freed twelve fighters in a daring raid that cost the lives of

six Bierut security guards and five Red Army troops accompanying them. Another five Soviet soldiers had already been killed in
AK attacks in Lublin itself. Yet another AK ambush—in Krasnik,
forty miles southwest of Lublin—had freed ten Home Army men,
with five more Bierut security officers killed. Making these attacks
especially disheartening from the Soviet perspective, they were all
carried out in the vicinity of the capital of Stalin's puppet regime.
If Bierut and Berling could not subdue opposition in the sixty-mile
radius around Lublin, they could hardly be expected to rule Poland as a whole—absent massive help from the Red Army, which
was itself losing casualties in the fight.[12]

In response to the burgeoning security crisis in eastern Poland,
Stalin issued an extraordinary order at the end of October 1944
to the Soviet Sixth Air Force, based in the Lublin area. "From
tomorrow," its men were instructed "to fight under the flag of
Poland." Soviet warplanes, many of them American lend-lease,
were repainted and labeled Polish; Soviet pilots were told to learn
Polish; and within weeks, a VVS officer named Georgii Dranunov
recalled, "the majority of our pilots were wearing Polish uniforms,
and all our documents were in Polish." Soviet occupying forces
were now playacting the part of Polish soldiers in order to give the
Lublin Poles a fig leaf of legitimacy.[13]

To quell the burgeoning AK rebellion in the Lublin area, Stalin
and Beria regifted more lend-lease vehicles to their Polish puppets.
Not trusting Bierut and Berling to know what to do with them,
the Soviets instructed the Poles to form "armed automotive battalions" sporting fifty trucks each, subdivided into three or four com-
panies of twelve to fifteen vehicles, and assigned two Red Army
officers to oversee mobile operations. Just as in Yugoslavia, both
the Red Army and the local Communist forces supporting it moved
about the country subduing rebels in lend-lease jeeps, trucks, and
Harley-Davidson motorcycles, riding on American rubber.[14]

Churchill did not have a way of knowing what was really going
on in Poland in October 1944, any more than earlier historians—
who have written little on the civil war that spread across Poland

after resistance in Warsaw collapsed—did. But even if he had known more, it is unclear that Churchill, whose main goal in Moscow was to get Stalin to sign off on British predominance in Greece, would have acted much differently. The uncomfortable fact is that the prime minister, though ostensibly upholding the cause of the London Poles vis-à-vis Stalin, did not really like them very much on a personal level. In spring 1943, Churchill had forced the Polish exile government to clam up about Katyn, despite learning, from his own queries, that the Polish allegation that the mass murders of 1940 were committed by Stalin was likely true. It was Churchill's frustration with Mikolajczyk, not some compelling strategic rationale, that prompted his bullying of the premier in Moscow. Even had Mikolajczyk been less stubborn over Poland's eastern frontier, there is no reason to believe, as Churchill had implied with his threats, that Stalin would have agreed to make Mikolajczyk Poland's prime minister. Whatever Stalin may have told Churchill in Moscow about having "no plans to Sovietize Poland," the Red Army and the NKVD were shedding Polish blood in October 1944 to do just that. What would decide the fate of Poland was not Churchill's inept stab at realpolitik over the country's borders, but the outcome of the increasingly savage war in the countryside between the AK and the NKVD and Red Army troops (some wearing Polish uniforms) propping up the Berling-Bierut regime in Lublin.[15]

Even this ineffectual Churchillian negotiating performance with Stalin was, by fall 1944, more than Roosevelt was capable of. The president's health had become a key campaign issue in the final months of the 1944 election, with rumors rampant that Roosevelt, who was seen being accompanied everywhere by his doctor, naval cardiologist Howard Bruenn, had been diagnosed with heart disease. We now know those rumors were true: the president had been subjected to a battery of tests in March and May 1944 and found to be suffering from "severe hypertension and the early stages of congestive heart failure." The president did agree to reduce his intake of fat, limit his smoking, take digitalis, and rest as much as he could, but he insisted on running for a fourth presidential term. Summoning all his strength, Roosevelt had put in impressive performances on the hustings in September and October, but the effort had left him spent. After celebrating his reelection on November 7, 1944, the president took time off to convalesce in Warm Springs, Georgia, under constant observation by Dr. Bruenn. His blood pressure had climbed to a frightening 260/150, suggesting a stroke was imminent. When his cousin Daisy Suckley saw him, she observed that the president "looks ten years older than last year." After recuperating in Georgia, Roosevelt gathered his strength for his inauguration on January 20, 1945, which he wrapped up, mercifully, in under five minutes, the shortest inauguration speech in US history. Edward Stettinius, now secretary of state, wrote in his diary that night that the president "seemed to tremble all over. It was not just his hands that shook but his whole body as well."[16]

This was the enfeebled condition of the man representing the richest and best-armed country in the world as 1945 dawned, with the affairs of Europe and Asia hanging in the balance. Although Roosevelt's advisers dreaded the prospect, they knew that the president was insisting on another Big Three summit with Churchill and Stalin to negotiate the architecture of the postwar world. In an almost parodic replay of the negotiations preceding Teheran in 1943, Stalin had rejected every one of the ailing Roosevelt's suggestions for a venue: from Quebec (where he and Churchill had met alone in September), to Iceland, to England, to warmer climes in Malta, Athens, nearby Piraeus, or British Cyprus. Knowing his health was frail, Roosevelt had the happy inspiration to convene the summit in a Mediterranean port city. "I prefer traveling and living on a ship," the president informed Stalin confidentially on October 25, 1944, just days before the elections, all but confessing how close he was to invalid status. In November, Churchill had chimed in too, proposing to host the Big Three in British-controlled Alexandria, Athens, or Jerusalem, or in another warmwater city on the Mediterranean coastline—a diplomatic way of reassuring

Roosevelt that the prime minister understood his health concerns. If the Germans withdrew from northern Italy, Roosevelt proposed that the Big Three might even meet in style "on the Riviera." "Almost any place in the Mediterranean is accessible to me," Roosevelt explained delicately, not wishing to confess to Stalin that he would not be able to leave his ship for long.[17]

Stalin, unlike Churchill, did not care to indulge Roosevelt. He insisted that the others come to him. On October 29, Stalin informed the president that he was unable to leave the USSR: a Black Sea resort in Crimea was the best he could do. Roosevelt replied that "my naval authorities strongly recommend against the Black Sea" because "they do not want to risk a capital ship through the Dardanelles or the Aegean as this would involve a very large escort which is much needed elsewhere." Still Stalin refused to budge, informing Roosevelt on November 25, with irony either bitter or intentionally malicious, that "I have to take under advice the warnings of Soviet doctors about the dangers of distant travel." It was the Crimea or nothing.[18]

And so it was that, to make things as easy as possible for the Soviet dictator, Roosevelt, a sick and dying man, agreed to undergo a 14,000-mile round trip to the Crimea in high winter, the last 1,400 miles of which involved a perilous flight from Malta over the Adriatic and Aegean Seas, accompanied by a large fighter escort to fend off possible Luftwaffe attacks. Although the Germans had by now mostly withdrawn from Greece and the Balkans, they still had anti-aircraft batteries on Crete and other islands in the Aegean. The danger was heightened by the fact that Roosevelt's doctors, owing to his elevated blood pressure, forbade the pilot from going above six thousand feet, lest the decreased air pressure in the cabin kill the president. There was also the risk that Soviet Black Sea port batteries, on high alert, might fire on the American presidential squadron by accident; in fact, in late January 1945, they had opened fire on a British plane flying to the Crimea on a preconference scouting trip. To avoid being shot out of the sky, British and American pilots were ordered to undertake precise "identification maneuvers" before landing at Saki airfield. Once all this was navigated safely, the president and his entourage still had to endure an eighty-mile ride, lasting five hours, over the bumpy Soviet roads in the recently devastated Crimea. "If we had spent ten years in our research," Churchill remarked acidly, "we could not have found a worse place in the world than Yalta" to meet. It was a wonder that Roosevelt was alive when he arrived in Crimea, although he did not look better for the trip. Churchill's doctor, Lord Moran, who accompanied the president and prime minister on the drive to Yalta from Saki airstrip—in lend-lease jeeps and trucks, of course—noted that "the President looked old and thin and drawn. He sat looking straight ahead with his mouth open, as if he were not taking things in."[19]

Debilitating as the journey was for Roosevelt, it was not cruelty per se that lay behind Stalin's insistence on the Crimea. In a sense, Stalin had accommodated the president's wishes in choosing a seaside resort town to host him, albeit not on the Mediterranean but on the more distant and less inviting Black Sea. The effort required to whip the ex-Tsarist palaces in and around Yalta into shape for a summit was colossal. Reconquered for good by the Red Army only in April 1944, the Crimean resort was something of a ghost town, looted by the retreating Germans and then cleansed of many of its survivors by the NKVD in ruthless sweeps for collaborators. In May 1944, more than 225,000 people were deported from the Crimea to Soviet labor camps—the vast majority of whom were Crimean Tatar Muslims, although thousands of Greeks, Armenians, Bulgarians, and Germans were expelled too. A final round of NKVD sweeps carried out in late January 1945 netted another 835 arrests. The roads over which convoys traveled en route from Saki airstrip were cleared of vehicles and pedestrians, with heavily armed soldiers placed fifty feet apart the entire way. The Livadia Palace, where the Americans would stay (and the plenary sessions would be held), and the Vorontsov Palace, hosting Churchill, had been renovated by thousands of NKVD-directed construction crews of workers who—in a hint of Stalin's intent for

Eastern Europe—were mostly prisoners of war conscripted into forced labor, including, as Roosevelt's daughter, Anna, noticed, "a small army of Romanian POWs." While the material results were sometimes impressive—special care was devoted to preparing a wheelchair-accessible bathroom for President Roosevelt—Stalin's men could not extinguish traces of the poverty of the wartime Soviet Union. Because of the lack of housing outside the palaces, most visitors would sleep, as a British conference manual noted, "two and four, some six to nine in room," with "bathrooms few and far between."[20]

Still more Soviet was the security atmosphere. American officials were issued stern instructions that, when an armed Soviet policeman "asks for your 'documente,' 'propusk,' 'passport' or 'bumagi,' show him your identification card without hesitation. . . . Do not try to bulldoze the guards—they have strict orders." Roosevelt's daughter, Anna, noticed that "we have to carry our identification cards everywhere," whipping them out "every 25 feet." Despite staying in a palace overlooking the Black Sea, the Americans were not permitted to visit the beach. Sailors aboard the few American and British ships allowed to dock at Sevastopol harbor to provide logistical and communications support were allowed to visit shore only under NKVD escort. Allied airmen were shadowed everywhere they went by Soviet minders. The NKVD commander of the Crimean special zone surrounding the conference, General Sergei Kruglov, had orders from Beria to ferret out Allied spies and to forestall "provocations and other anti-Soviet manifestations on the part of hostile elements"—that is, unauthorized contact between Westerners and Soviet subjects. It was like visiting, Churchill later recalled, "the Riviera of Hades."[21]

In view of the paranoia and scarcely concealed hostility with which—elaborate dining spreads and Roosevelt's personal toilet aside—the Vozhd treated his distinguished guests, Stalin's bullying of the British and Americans at Yalta should not surprise us. By the time the Big Three reunion opened in the Livadia Palace at 4 p.m. on February 4, 1945, the strategic equation had shifted dramatically in Stalin's favor. The Morgenthau Plan had inspired the Germans to fight much harder in the West, helping goad Hitler into the Ardennes-Bulge offensive that had so badly bloodied the Americans. Belgrade had fallen to the Red Army, in coordination with Tito's partisans, in October. The Germans were holding out longer in Prague and Budapest, although both of these cities were now isolated after the Soviet Eighteenth Army had swept into Transylvania. Throwing his last reserves of armor and manpower into the Ardennes offensive of December–January, Hitler had left Poland and East Prussia wide open for the major new Soviet offensive that began on January 12, 1945: the Vistula-Oder operation. By month's end, Rokossovsky's Second Belorussian Army Group had swept up central and northern Poland and East Prussia, reaching the Oder River just forty miles short of Berlin, cutting off the German garrisons at Königsberg and reaching Danzig (Gdańsk), over which the European war had ostensibly broken out in 1939. In a cruel afterthought, the Red Army had also conquered Warsaw in January, five months too late for its battered inhabitants (the population was down from a prewar figure of 1.3 million to about 150,000), marching into a depopulated pile of rubble. By month's end, Soviet troops had also liberated Auschwitz-Birkenau, saving about 7,500 emaciated Jewish survivors of this soon-notorious Nazi death camp. While Eastern Europe was not all under Soviet control yet, Stalin held all the cards east of the Oder, and he was not going to yield any of them.[22]

Certainly the Vozhd had no intention of making concessions on Poland. At Teheran, Roosevelt had agreed to what Stalin euphemistically called the "1939 borders" with Poland (meaning the post–Moscow Pact ones), which, despite the stubborn refusal of the London Poles to accept them, were now the diplomatic status quo. The new Soviet provinces of what used to be Poland, although not all Polish majority, were still home to some eleven million Poles who were not consulted about their political fate. Poland would be compensated with German territory in East Prussia, from which Poland would be invited to expel, by Churchill's count, six million Germans in order to make room for Poles fleeing westward to escape Stalin's clutches. On the contentious matter of Polish elections, Churchill put up some fight—more, certainly, than Roosevelt, who muttered on February 9 that all he wanted was "some kind of gesture to appease six million Polish Americans." Churchill insisted that the London Poles be allowed to participate in any future elections. Although not promising this, Stalin did agree, at Churchill's insistence, to stop calling former premier Mikolajczyk and the Polish Peasant Party and government-in-exile he had headed "fascist." When Churchill insisted on holding "free elections," Stalin retorted: "You mean free like your elections in Egypt?" Roosevelt chimed in that the Polish elections should appear "like Caesar's wife"—the head of Rome's vestal virgins. It was the wrong analogy. Stalin replied, "Caesar's wife was no virgin." It was all too much for the exhausted Roosevelt, who proposed that the meeting adjourn so he could rest.[23]

The following night, Stalin and Churchill parsed Polish elections further in a private session after Roosevelt had retired to bed. Churchill proposed that Stalin could send his own Soviet electoral observers to France, Italy, Greece, or anywhere else, so long as he would allow one single British observer in Poland. Grudgingly, Stalin agreed. And yet even this concession was rather hollow, because both Roosevelt and Churchill had already recognized, in the lead-up to Yalta, the right of Stalin's puppet government in Lublin to represent Poland at Allied conferences. The president and prime minister had insisted only that the Lublin delegation be reinforced by a few non-Communists they hoped to get Stalin to sign off on. Here was the rub: Stalin insisted on the right to veto any representatives the Allies might suggest for the Lublin proto-government—representation he whittled down from two-thirds (as Churchill first demanded) to half and, finally, to a mere token three people. Moreover, Stalin was also given the right to vet these non-Communist Poles in Moscow, out of sight of the Western Allies. As Fleet Admiral William D. Leahy, Roosevelt's chief of staff, noted after reading the agreement on Poland drawn up between Churchill and Stalin, "This is so elastic the Russians can stretch it all the way from Yalta to Washington without even technically breaking it."[24]

After the bruising he had received from Roosevelt at Quebec and Stalin in Moscow, at Yalta Churchill was exhibiting signs of battered-statesman syndrome. Whereas at Teheran, Churchill had tried to leave the room when Roosevelt and Stalin spoke of mass executing German officers, this time he did not blink when Stalin boasted that "there were no Germans left alive" in areas of the Reich that the Red Army had already conquered, and that he hoped "to kill another 2 million Germans" by summer to obviate the need to cleanse them from newly Soviet territory.* "I do not wish to put an end to the extermination of Germans," Churchill assured Stalin, before gently suggesting that any Germans left alive at war's end would have to live *somewhere*. But he did not press the point. On the treatment of Germans, Churchill was now singing Stalin's tune.[25]

In Churchill's defense, he got no help from Roosevelt on anything of substance at Yalta. The only issue that seemed to engage the president was his idea for a new "United Nations," with a Security Council composed of the major powers to remedy the flaws of the toothless League of Nations. To the bewilderment of Churchill and Stalin, Roosevelt seemed indifferent at Yalta about the fate of Poland, of Allied war prisoners, and other contentious matters; he wanted only his UN, with the USSR lending it weight by participating. It was an apposite homage to Woodrow Wilson, who at Versailles in 1919 had neglected the nitty-gritty of geopolitics

---

* It is a sign of Roosevelt's near-catatonic condition at Yalta that he did not chime in here, on a theme—exacting violent retribution against the Germans—usually so dear to him. The president did privately tell Stalin, before the conference began, that viewing the war damages in the Crimea had made him even more "bloodthirsty" than at Teheran. "I hope," he told the Vozhd, "you make another toast proposing the execution of 50,000 German officers."

in his white-whale obsession with the League of Nations. Stalin did agree that the USSR would join the new body, though he still made trouble by demanding a full Security Council veto and that constituent Soviet Republics—or at least Russia, Ukraine, and Belorussia—receive votes in the General Assembly. Even on his pet issue, the president gave way, giving Stalin a secret assurance that he would support three votes for the USSR's main constituent republics, a clear violation of the "one nation, one vote" policy agreed on at the UN planning conference held in the Dumbarton Oaks mansion in Washington, DC, the previous fall. That Roosevelt surrendered on this cardinal principle contradicts the claims of his defenders that he won some kind of victory at Yalta by cajoling Stalin into joining the United Nations, a decision that cost Moscow nothing, lent prestige to Soviet Communism, and offered Stalin rich opportunities for mischief.[26]

Stalin gained still more ground from Roosevelt at Yalta on the one real American strategic concern in 1945: Japan. At Teheran, the president had already agreed to Soviet territorial gains in the Far East in exchange for Stalin's pledge to go to war with Japan within "three months" of the end of the European war. Roosevelt had not consulted Chiang Kai-shek, whose forces had been at war with Japan since 1931, about any of this, nor was Chiang invited to Yalta. In view of the progress the United States had made in the Pacific war since Teheran—the Burma Road to China had finally been opened in late January 1945 and the United States had taken the Gilbert, Marshall, and especially the Mariana Islands, getting close enough to Japan to rain down firebombs on Tokyo and the country's other largely wood-built cities—it was by no means clear that the United States needed Soviet help against Japan at all. True, the Japanese were still resisting savagely, launching the first kamikaze suicide plane attacks at Leyte Gulf in the Philippines in October 1944, suggesting that an invasion of Japan's home islands would meet stout resistance. But signals intercepts suggested that morale was faltering in the Japanese armed forces and sinking still more rapidly on the home front. As Fleet Admiral Leahy recalled, "I was of the firm opinion that our war against Japan had progressed to the point where her defeat was only a matter of time and attrition. Therefore we did not need Stalin's help to defeat our enemy in the Pacific." According to Colonel Truman Smith of the US Army's G-2 intelligence branch, in the days before Yalta "there were few, if any, [G-2] Specialists who felt that Russia's help was needed to finish off an already groggy Japan. Indeed, I am sure there was no Specialist in G-2 at this time who would have paid Russia a penny of our own money or Chiang's to enter the war."[27]

Not everyone in the American camp agreed that Soviet entry into the Pacific war would be superfluous. What seems to have preoccupied the president at Yalta was a Joint Chiefs of Staff memorandum, submitted on January 23, 1945, and put into his briefing book for the conference, that estimated that the United States would incur 350,000 casualties in an amphibious assault on Japan's home islands. It advocated that the USSR therefore enter the war with Japan at "as early a date as possible" to reduce American losses in this invasion. The memorandum was the work of General Marshall and his Pentagon war-planning staff, who had become understandably concerned about casualties in the wake of the Battle of the Bulge. It cleverly mimicked the supposedly realpolitik logic of the Soviet lend-lease program in proposing to arm and fund the casualty-prone Red Army, mercenary-style, to save American lives. Marshall's position was not unequivocal, however. We now know that this memorandum advocating for Soviet entry into the Pacific war was one of two prepared for the Yalta conference, with the other arguing the opposite position, reflecting the more optimistic view of the army's G-2 branch that Japan would soon be defeated without the need for Soviet help. Somehow it came about that, according to disgruntled naval intelligence officer Admiral Ellis Zacharias, the second briefing book "was pigeonholed by a special intelligence outfit in the assistant secretary's office, which allowed only the pessimistic report to go up to the Joint Chiefs and through them to Roosevelt."[28]

On the basis of this manipulated intelligence briefing, Roosevelt went even further at Yalta than at Teheran in bribing Stalin to promise to intervene later against Japan. Having already won Roosevelt's pledge to give him the Kurile Islands, southern Sakhalin, and Outer Mongolia at Teheran, Stalin now demanded that Port Arthur—won by Tokyo in the Russo-Japanese War of 1904–1905 and now called Dairen (today's Chinese Dalian)—be turned over to the USSR, along with control of the railway lines of Manchuria connecting to Dairen and Vladivostok through Harbin. While Roosevelt remembered himself enough to say that it might, perhaps, be a good idea for him to talk with Chiang Kaishek about this, he did not object to Stalin's demand for a "Soviet sphere of influence in northeastern China." This included not just Outer Mongolia but all of Manchuria—the area the Chinese nationalists had been seeking to liberate from Japan since 1931—and Roosevelt's acquiescence to this demand sat oddly with the president's supposed devotion to China. In theory, details were still to be negotiated with Chiang, but the principle of Soviet domination of Mongolia and Manchuria was now agreed. Stalin demanded a share in "the custody of Korea" as well and asked Roosevelt whether he "planned to station [American] troops in Korea?" The president assured the Vozhd that he had no plans to do so, thus extending a green light to Stalin for an invasion of northern Korea whenever the USSR entered the war with Japan.[29]

American bribes for belated Soviet intervention against Japan were not only territorial. At the TOLSTOY conference, the US military attaché, General Deane, was given a list of the supplies the Red Army would require to enter the Pacific war. Even though the United States was already sending Stalin five million tons of foodstuffs, fuel, and war matériel in the fourth protocol, including 9,183 American trucks shipped to Vladivostok in January 1945 alone; even though the US Army Air Force had sent to Siberia, via ALSIB, nearly 8,000 warplanes prior to Yalta; even though lendlease had supplied Stalin's Far Eastern armies with enough weapons and supplies to overmatch the Kwantung Army many times over, Stalin demanded the special delivery, by June 30, 1945, of "a two months' supply of food, fuel transport equipment, and other supplies, calculated on the requirements of a force of 1,500,000 men, 3,000 tanks, 75,000 motor vehicles, and 5,000 airplanes," requiring extra Pacific tonnage of 860,140 tons of dry cargo and 206,000 tons of liquid. If the president delivered all of this, Stalin would be happy to conquer northern Asia for Communism. Roosevelt agreed.[30]

In view of the president's inept performance at Yalta vis-à-vis Stalin, there has been much speculation about the role of Soviet agents of influence in the proceedings. We do know that Alger Hiss, a Soviet agent fingered in the Venona decrypts, played a role at Yalta in discussions of the United Nations and of China, intervening on one notable occasion to "stress the importance which the United States attaches to" forging unity between Chiang Kai-shek's nationalists and Mao's Communists. Harry Hopkins also played his by-now-familiar role as pro-Soviet whisperer in Roosevelt's ear at Yalta, passing the president a note at one point, during a discussion of reparations to be demanded of the defeated Germans, in which he wrote that "the Russians have given in so much at this conference that I don't think we should let them down." Hopkins also told Stalin, speaking for the president on another occasion at Yalta, that "the United States would desire a Poland friendly to the Soviet Union"—that is, a Sovietized Poland. In general, though, Hopkins was fairly quiet at Yalta, his own health being scarcely better than Roosevelt's.[31]

Interesting as these questions are, the painful truth about Yalta is that the concessions made to Stalin there were consistent with policies Roosevelt and Churchill had been adopting ever since Barbarossa was launched in 1941. The fates of Yugoslavia, Poland, and China were largely settled at Teheran, with Churchill's abandonment of Mihailović, Roosevelt's promise to let Stalin control Poland and redraw its borders as long as this was not publicized until after the 1944 presidential election, and the president's decision to abandon Buccaneer and curtail financial aid to Chiang. The only real addendums at Yalta concerned the final betrayal of the London Poles, when Churchill agreed to let Stalin veto appointments to the Lublin puppet government and gave in on election observers, and Stalin expanding his Asian sphere of influence to include Manchuria and Korea.

Even the most controversial agreements made at Yalta, relating to Stalin's desire to claim human and economic reparations from Germany, were consistent with earlier US-British policy. The seizure of German industrial property both inside Germany and in German-occupied countries, along with the exploitation of "the forced labor of German workers outside Germany," had been written into the Morgenthau Plan adopted at Quebec. The only change at Yalta was the codification of the principle that German reparations could be taken "in kind" as well as in cash, and that "the use of German labor" and the "removal of property" were acceptable substitutes. At Yalta, the Allies also put a dollar sign on Soviet reparations claims from Germany, set at $10 billion (about $1 trillion in current value), howsoever Stalin chose to collect his debt.[32]

So, too, had the involuntary repatriation of Soviet war prisoners—known today via the Yalta Memorial in London—been raised before, at the TOLSTOY conference in Moscow in October, when Molotov had delicately informed Anthony Eden that "some Soviet citizens might not wish to come back because they had been helping the Germans"—an allusion to the million-plus Soviet Osttruppen serving in the Wehrmacht. When Churchill reassured Stalin at Yalta that the British and Americans had already repatriated eleven thousand Red Army prisoners from camps liberated in Western Europe and would shortly return seven thousand more, Stalin explained that this was not his main concern. "There are Soviet citizens," the Vozhd explained, "who have taken up arms against the Allies." "These people," Stalin told Churchill, "must, of course, be held responsible for their actions." While Churchill did not wish to go on the record, he agreed privately that, in view of Britain's desire to repatriate its own captured soldiers imprisoned by the Germans in Eastern Europe, he would "strive to meet the demand of the Soviet government."[33]

In this way, Stalin roped Roosevelt and Churchill in to his plans to seize and transport industry and moveable property from Germany and its wartime allies for restitution, exploit enemy soldier-prisoners as slave laborers for reparation, and exact vengeance against his own former subjects unlucky enough to be captured by the Germans during the war. With a license to loot from London and Washington, and a massive mechanized army rolling west on lend-lease trucks and tires, Stalin was ready to claim the spoils of Hitler's short-lived Reich for Communism.

33

Booty

STALIN HAD NEVER made a secret of his philosophy of war. Before 1939, the Vozhd had often spoken about "pushing forward" the boundaries of Communism. Molotov had boasted regularly about the thousands of square miles and millions of subjects Stalin's "peace" policy allowed the USSR to conquer, from eastern Poland to Finland to the Baltic countries, Bessarabia, and Bukovina. When it came to territorial claims in Eastern Europe, there was no real difference between Molotov's ever-mounting demands vis-à-vis Hitler, circa 1939–1941, and Stalin's demands vis-à-vis Churchill and Roosevelt, circa 1943–1945, except that, unlike Hitler, Churchill and Roosevelt were willing to concede him the entirety of the Balkans, excluding only Greece.

Nor was there any secret as to what Sovietization meant in practice, as American officials had learned after Stalin had nationalized the banks of the three Baltic countries in 1940 and demanded that the United States turn over their foreign gold deposits—though many of the Americans seem to have later forgotten. The Bolsheviks had thoroughly Sovietized Russia in 1917–1918, but the property nationalizations of 1940 represented a significant escalation: Stalin was now stealing private property in foreign countries too. The files of the Soviet economic planning committee, Gosplan, contain numbingly detailed lists of factories and moveable goods seized in 1940 in eastern Poland, Latvia, Lithuania, Estonia, and Romania. The essence of Sovietization was embodied in Gosplan decrees like this one, dated August 15, 1940: "In accordance with laws of the USSR now in force in Bessarabia, the Supreme Soviet decrees that all banks, credit institutions, private concerns, railways and waterborne transit facilities located on the territory of Bessarabia are hereby nationalized." Rinsed and repeated, this principle applied in every territory the Red Army occupied for Stalin.[1]

Stalin was not finished with Romania either. When the Russians returned to the country in August 1944, Stalin and Molotov insisted, as a price for Romania having joined Barbarossa, on wresting still more territory from Bucharest than they had in 1940—including a number of strategic towns and passes in the high Carpathians and all the islands and waterways in the Danube delta Hitler had denied Stalin in 1940, which were affixed to Moldavia SSR. The Soviets also received basing (and ship-docking) rights at Constanța and uncontested control of Romanian airspace twenty-five kilometers inside the new frontier. Less officially, the occupiers claimed forced-labor booty. In addition to the 190,000 Romanian troops taken prisoner by the Red Army in the field since 1941, another 130,000 Romanian soldiers were deported into the USSR after the armistice, along with 100,000 Romanian nationals who had been serving in the Hungarian Army. In all, some 420,000 Romanian prisoners were inducted into Gulag camps, fewer than half of whom would ever return home. In 1945, Stalin also imposed reparations of 300 billion lei on Romania (roughly $125 million at the time, or about $12.5 billion today), in effect for the crime of fighting back after being invaded by Russia in 1940.[2]

Hungary, another of Hitler's cobelligerents, fared still worse after the Russians arrived. More than six hundred thousand Hungarian nationals were deported to Soviet labor camps, including many Hungarian Jews liberated from the death camps of Auschwitz and Buchenwald. In part to appease Stalin's new puppet government in Bucharest, which was smarting from its loss of territory, Stalin reassigned most of Transylvania to Romania, reversing Ribbentrop's Vienna Award of 1940, and imposed $300 million in reparations on Budapest—almost three times more than Romania was forced to pay. The Vozhd also commandeered all coal available in Hungary in winter 1944–1945 and sent some of it to Tito so the Soviets wouldn't have to spare their coal for Yugoslavia. (Stalin had angered Tito by requisitioning the Yugoslav harvest of fall 1944 for Soviet consumption.) Tito was encouraged to levy his own reparations demands on Hungary and Germany. But when Tito's representatives in Moscow asked Stalin, on January 9, 1945, to share some of the loot the Red Army had taken in Hungary and from Yugoslavia itself, Stalin swatted him down brutally. "Trophies," the Vozhd explained, "belong to the army that captures them."[3]

This was certainly how the Red Army conquerors were behaving in Poland in their guerrilla war against the AK's underground network of Polish patriots. This conflict was heating up in the weeks after Yalta, with dozens of Home Army fighters (and Poles who harbored them) executed, including forty landowners and farmers in one brutal mass execution in Miechow district. A British intelligence summary forwarded to Churchill reported that, in the district of Sandomierz, "more Poles have been arrested during the few months of Soviet occupation than during the whole five years of German occupation." The fate of those arrested was grim. The NKVD, no longer trusting Berling's men to do the job of rounding up political enemies, had commandeered cellars and air-raid shelters to house prisoners before they were sent to Gulag camps. In February 1945, 367 cattle trucks filled with Polish prisoners from the frontier provinces of Grodno and Bialystok set off east for Soviet labor camps, the first of ninety-one thousand Poles deported by the end of March. On Marshal Zhukov's orders, a special "war trophy commission" was established in March 1945 to adjudicate property disputes between the Red Army and the Lublin committee. When it came to war booty, the Russians shared nothing of value. Although agreeing to help furnish Bierut's new presidential palace, the Red Army commandant would part only with cheap modern tables and chairs, reserving "valuable antiques taken as trophies" for the occupiers.[4]

The most valuable trophies the Red Army seized in Poland were the few surviving AK leaders who had launched the Warsaw Uprising in August 1944. When the Red Army marched into a ruined Warsaw on January 17, 1945, Moscow Radio broadcast the "Manifesto of the Lublin Provisional Government," which included a terrifying message to the Polish people. While "the Polish Army"—that is, Berling's men—"was fighting for the liberation of Warsaw," Soviet propagandists claimed, "members of the Home Army . . . were murdering and assisting the Germans in the forcible evacuation of entire towns and villages. Brothers! We wish to assure you we shall deal with those traitors of the Nation as they deserve!" Giving teeth to this deadly slander, the NKVD commander of occupied Poland, General Ivan Serov, reported to Beria that "Chekist groups have been organized for the filtration of all inhabitants wishing to cross into Praga," and that "operational groups are at work, consisting of our own Chekists and of employees of the Polish Ministry of Security, and aiming to expose and capture the leadership of the AK." In March, Serov claimed his prize for Stalin, capturing sixteen AK leaders through the ruse of offering them a safe-conduct pass to London, then shipping them to Moscow instead to face trial. The NKVD's prisoner haul included the last commander of the Home Army, General Leopold Okulicki, Minister Stanislaw Jaslukowski, Vice Premier Jan St. Jankowski, and nine leaders of Polish democratic political parties. When Churchill wrote Stalin on April 28, 1945, to protest these "fifteen arrests" and the mass deportations of AK fighters and sympathizers from eastern Poland, the Vozhd replied on May 4, dismissing "complaints of deportations and so on." With blithe contempt, Stalin corrected Churchill and informed him he had arrested "not fifteen, but sixteen Poles."[5]

Churchill's and Roosevelt's protests over Stalin's treatment of their own war prisoners were just as hapless as over his treatment of Poles. In theory, the British and Americans had agreed to repatriate the Soviet POWs who were falling into their hands as they swept through France and the Low Countries in 1944 and into Germany in 1945, in order to guarantee that their own men held in German POW camps liberated by the Red Army would be sent home. Agreeing to this came at a great cost—namely, the repatriation of 2,272,000 Soviet subjects to summary punishment back home for the crime of being taken prisoner. We now know that tens of thousands of non-Soviet subjects, including White Russian and Cossack veterans who had fled after fighting against the Reds in the Russian Civil War—many of whom had joined the Osttruppen—were also sent east by the British authorities to almost certain death. More than thirty thousand Cossacks, including women and children, were rounded up in Austria amid heart-wrenching scenes marked by beatings, deaths, and suicide attempts, a story first chronicled by Nikolai Tolstoy in *Victims of Yalta* (1976).[6]

The Americans were not innocent either. The post–Morgenthau Plan army occupation handbook stipulated that Soviet prisoners falling into American hands would be "released expeditiously to the control of the USSR without regard to their individual wishes." The involuntary repatriation of Soviet subjects was given the code name Operational Keelhaul, an allusion to a brutal form of naval punishment wherein victims were dragged under the keel of a ship, suggesting that the US high command had few illusions about the fate awaiting those repatriated to Stalin's mercies. US Army bases in Italy, Germany, and New Jersey witnessed mass suicide attempts by Soviet war prisoners told they were being sent back home, an indictment of Stalin's regime even more dramatic than the existence of the Osttruppen.[7]

Most of the American and British officers and officials knew it was a moral disaster to send these men back to certain imprisonment and likely death, and many of them protested courageously at the time. If any excuse is offered for the decision Churchill and Roosevelt made at Yalta to pawn Soviet prisoners off to Stalin, it was to save the lives of their own men captured by the Red Army. This excuse, however, is belied by the transcript of the Yalta conference, which shows that, even after Stalin explicitly told Churchill, in their bilateral late-night session on February 10, that he wanted all of the "Osttruppen" back—whether or not they were Soviet citizens—to "make them answer for their actions," Churchill promised to send to Stalin "all categories" of Soviet prisoners "as soon as possible." In exchange, all the prime minister asked for was "an estimate of the number of British war prisoners liberated by the Red Army."[8]

Nor did Roosevelt extract solid guarantees from Stalin on the repatriation of American prisoners. The "Agreement Relating to Prisoners of War and Civilians Liberated by Forces Operating Under Soviet Command and Forces Operating Under [US] Command," signed by the president at Yalta on February 11, 1945, did stipulate that both Soviet and US authorities would "have the right of immediate access into the camps and points of concentration where their citizens are located," but there was no timeline on repatriation from Soviet camps. Stalin's camp commandants found it easy to slow-walk the processing of American and British war prisoners after Yalta, as both Churchill and Roosevelt would soon complain. Nor did the NKVD or Red Army command allow American or British warplanes to land repatriation crews near camps where Americans and Britons were being held. Even the docile Roosevelt grew alarmed, writing an urgent plea on March 4 that Stalin grant authorization for "ten American aircraft with American crews to operate between Poltava and places in Poland where American ex-prisoners of war and stranded airmen may be located," in order to "transfer the injured and sick to the American hospital at Poltava." On March 6, Stalin replied brutally that "the Red Army liberated no American prisoners between Poltava and Poland" and revoked permission from the US military attaché, General Deane, to visit Poland to check on them. All American prisoners captured in Eastern Europe, the Vozhd insisted, were being held in Odessa. Roosevelt was perturbed by these denials, but he confined himself to a polite expression of dissatisfaction over Stalin's "reluctance to permit American officers and means to assist their own people." Stalin did admit, on March 22, after realizing he had offended Roosevelt with his brazen lying, that there had been "17 sick Americans" in Poland, but he insisted that these men would soon be airlifted to Odessa. The Vozhd would still not allow Deane, or any American repatriation officials, to visit Poland. Stalin even claimed that Soviet officials were "giving better treatment to American war prisoners" than "Soviet citizens were receiving in [American camps]"—an amazing complaint in view of Stalin's plan to imprison or murder those very prisoners as soon as the Americans handed them back to him.[9]

On the prisoners of war issue, there were signs the president was finally awakening to the true nature of the dictator he had been courting for three years. It was increasingly clear that Stalin did not want any Britons or Americans prowling around Poland, whether doctors tending to Allied war prisoners or election observers—as was made plain when Bierut's puppet government began arresting pro-Western politicians and barred US and British observers from Lublin, a decision publicly confirmed by Molotov on March 17, 1945. In Romania, too, although King Michael—who had expelled the pro-Axis Ion Antonescu and promised to cooperate with the Soviets—was allowed to remain on his throne for now, Molotov's deputy Vishinsky had flown into Bucharest in late February to direct a purge of the new government. So, too, was Roosevelt alarmed when Stalin announced that he would not send Molotov to the inaugural United Nations conference in San Francisco, to be held in April, but a lower-level diplomat instead. For all these reasons, the president was becoming concerned that, as he wrote Churchill on March 29, if Stalin continued behaving like this, it "would cause our people to regard the Yalta agreement as having failed."[10]

What really got Roosevelt's goat, however, was an accusation Stalin and Molotov levied against him about going soft on the Germans. On March 8, the Waffen-SS commander in northern Italy, General Karl Wolff, sent a message to the head of the American OSS office in Bern, Switzerland, requesting a cease-fire and the possible surrender of German forces in Italy. Knowing how explosive such negotiations might be, both the British and US ambassadors in Moscow, Sir Archibald Clark Kerr and Averell Harriman, informed Molotov about the German approach on March 12 and were told the Soviets were fine with it, so long as

Soviet representatives were present. The British agreed, but the Americans, for once, said no. Harriman and General Deane, still smarting from Stalin's refusal to let Deane visit wounded American soldiers in Poland, objected that waiting for the Soviets to send representatives to Bern would cost time and soldiers' lives in Italy, a theater of the war where the Soviets had contributed nothing (while still being promised the Italian merchant marine). On March 16, Stalin retaliated by demanding that the Bern talks be suspended. On March 22, Molotov accused Roosevelt and Churchill of "carrying on negotiations" with the Germans "behind the back of the Soviet government." That this was a sincere accusation, not a negotiating tactic, is confirmed in private remarks Stalin made to Czech Communists that same week, saying the British and Americans "will try to save the Germans and come to terms with them. We will be merciless with the Germans, but the allies will try to settle things in a gentler way."[11]

On April 3, Stalin accused Roosevelt of signing a separate peace deal with the German high command at Bern that "permitted the Anglo-American troops to advance to the East and the Anglo-Americans promised in return to ease for the Germans the peace terms." The advisers who had apprised him of this, the Vozhd continued, must be "close to the truth," in view of the "fact that the Anglo-Americans have refused to admit at Bern representatives of the Soviet government." "As a result of this," Stalin concluded, "the Germans on the western front have in fact ceased the war against England and the United States," while Germany "continues the war with Russia."[12]

In that the Germans had begun transferring troops and armor back east after the Battle of the Bulge, tipping the share of Wehrmacht divisions facing the Red Army back over 50 percent by February 1945, there was substance to Stalin's complaint about an unequal fighting burden, even if it was manifestly untrue that the Germans had "ceased the war" on the western front. In Italy, so often derided by Stalin as a useless theater, the Wehrmacht had suffered 536,000 casualties to date. In any case, the accusation of double-dealing enraged Roosevelt. Chip Bohlen, who was with him when the message was read out, said he had never seen the president this angry. On April 5, Roosevelt steeled himself to reply from his sickbed in Warm Springs. "Frankly I cannot avoid," the president wrote to Stalin, "a feeling of bitter resentment toward your informers, whoever they are, for such vile misrepresentations of my actions or those of my trusted subordinates." Even so, Roosevelt assured Stalin that he would subordinate his frustration "for the advantage of our common war effort against Germany" and "continue to assume that you have the same high confidence in my truthfulness and reliability that I have always had in yours." Off the record, Roosevelt had complained to Anne O'Hare McCormick of the *New York Times*, on March 29, 1945, that "Stalin was not a man of his word; either that or he was no longer in charge of the Soviet government."[13]

It is testimony to Roosevelt's questionable political judgment that what finally convinced him of Stalin's unreliability was not the Vozhd's aggressive moves in Poland or his lies about American war prisoners, but his accusation that the president had gone soft on Germany. On the matter of punishing Germans, Roosevelt and Stalin had always seen eye to eye. One of the last advisers to visit the president in Warm Springs, on the night before Roosevelt died of a cerebral hemorrhage on April 12, 1945, was Henry Morgenthau, anxious to ensure that General Eisenhower followed the harsh army handbook guidelines drawn up for occupied Germany. Roosevelt, Morgenthau recalled, "looked very haggard." His hands shook so badly that Morgenthau had to hold the glasses as the president poured cocktails. Even in this condition, Roosevelt lit up when the Treasury secretary told him that he was "going to fight hard" to cripple the postwar German economy so that "she won't be able to make another war," and Morgenthau repeated this "two or three times" to make sure the president heard him correctly. "Henry," Roosevelt said in what turned out to be his last-ever statement on foreign policy, "I am with you 100 per cent." The Morgenthau Plan provided a fitting epitaph for a

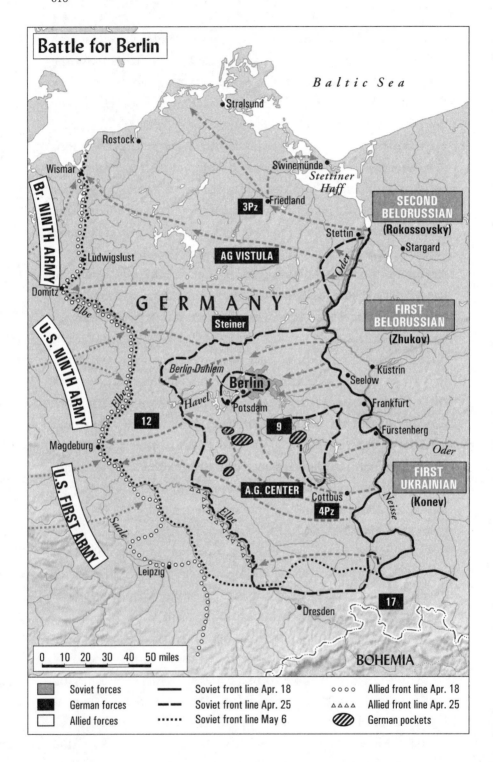

Battle for Berlin
Baltic Sea
Stralsund
Rostock
Wismar
Swinemünde
Stettiner Haff
Friedland
3Pz
SECOND BELORUSSIAN
(Rokossovsky)
Stettin
Stargard
Br. NINTH ARMY
Ludwigslust
AG VISTULA
Oder
Domitz
Elbe
GERMANY
Steiner
FIRST BELORUSSIAN
(Zhukov)
U.S. NINTH ARMY
Berlin-Dahlem
Berlin
Küstrin
Seelow
Havel
Potsdam
Frankfurt
Elbe
12
9
Fürstenberg
Oder
Magdeburg
FIRST UKRAINIAN
(Konev)
U.S. FIRST ARMY
A.G. CENTER
Cottbus
4Pz
Neisse
Elbe
Saale
Leipzig
17
Dresden
0 10 20 30 40 50 miles
BOHEMIA
Soviet forces
German forces
Allied forces
Soviet front line Apr. 18
Soviet front line Apr. 25
Soviet front line May 6
○○○○ Allied front line Apr. 18
△△△△ Allied front line Apr. 25
German pockets

president who had been trying, since 1941, to convince Stalin he was as tough on the Germans as the Soviets were, if not more so.[14]

Now that the Red Army was crashing into East Prussia, the Germans would learn just what Stalin had in store for them. To the chagrin of Churchill and the British high command, General Eisenhower had agreed to let the Russians take Berlin, even after US-British troops had crossed the Rhine in force during the second week of March 1945, and Roosevelt did not overrule him. Not trusting Eisenhower and taking no chances—Soviet intelligence suggested that the Germans had a nuclear research facility in Berlin-Dahlem, including uranium reserves—on April 1 Stalin called in Marshals Zhukov and I. S. Konev—commanding the armies on the First Belorussian and First Ukrainian fronts, respectively—and goaded them to race the Americans, and each other, to Berlin. On April 16, 1945, the final two-pronged Soviet assault on the German capital was launched with a furious artillery barrage by Zhukov's armies along the Oder, even while Konev's men pounded the opposite bank of the Neisse River. The last four of Hitler's elite Waffen-SS divisions—about forty-five thousand strong in total, many of them composed of foreigners who knew execution awaited them if they ever returned home—along with German volunteer units known as *Volkssturm*, fought a furious scorched-earth defense. Before German resistance crumbled and the Soviet flag was raised over the Reichstag on May 2, the Red Army, including elements of Rokossovsky's second Belorussian front along with those of Zhukov and Konev, lost 361,367 casualties in the Battle of Berlin—nearly four times as many as the US Army lost in the Ardennes, in the worst battle the Americans fought—including nearly 100,000 Soviet dead, along with 2,000 tanks, 2,108 guns, and 917 warplanes.[15]

Because of Eisenhower's decision not to contest Berlin, the booty would belong, as Stalin had told Tito, to the Red Army. But the take from Berlin was disappointing, as so much of the city lay in ruins. All that was left of the once-overflowing coffers of the Berlin Reichsbank were 2,389 kilograms of gold, 12 tons of silver

coins, and paper money confiscated from occupied Europe. Red
Army grunts, restricted officially to five kilos of loot, helped themselves to watches (which were especially prized), drank whatever
booze they found, and engaged in a great wave of rape and random violence, but in general there was little left for the taking. Stalin's biggest priority was to secure material from German factories
and laboratories, such as the German nuclear research facilities in
Dahlem, but here, too, the yield was disappointing. Dahlem did
net Stalin, according to an NKVD report, "250 kgs of metallic uranium, three tons of uranium oxide," and "twenty liters of heavy
water," along with two scientists who were flown to Moscow,
but Germany's top chemists and nuclear scientists from Dahlem
had already fled to the British and Americans. Most disappointing, Hitler's bunker was empty of Hitler, Goebbels, and any other
top Nazi officials, although Stalin did get the most important prize
when a team of operatives, members of the elite Soviet counterintelligence organization known as SMERSH,* discovered Hitler's
remains in a shell hole near the bunker on May 5 (his identity was
confirmed based on a five-hour deposition with the dentist who
had done Hitler's most recent cavity fillings).[16]

With the capture of Berlin epitomized by the soon-famous photograph of the raising of the hammer and sickle over the Reichstag,
the Red Army finished off the last serious German armed resistance and forced what remained of the German high command in
Berlin, namely Field Marshal Wilhelm Keitel, to sign a surrender
document at 10:43 p.m. on May 8, 1945, with Zhukov taking the
honors for Stalin. (Field Marshal Alfred Jodl had already signed an
"Act of Military Surrender" to General Eisenhower on May 7 at

---

* Created in April 1943, SMERSH was tasked with hunting down sensitive targets such as deserters and spies; "counterrevolutionaries" such
as White Russians, Cossacks, and leading officers in the anti-Soviet Osttruppen, among the prisoners of war being repatriated to the USSR; and
high-profile enemy targets such as Hitler. Although in theory part of the
NKVD headed by Beria, SMERSH answered directly to Stalin.

the latter's command center in Reims, northeast of Paris, a document that was initialed by the Soviet general I. A. Susloparov. Nevertheless, Stalin did not recognize the May 7 surrender as official.) Although there was a mad dash by German troops to cross the Elbe to surrender to the Americans and British instead of to the Soviets, the Red Army still captured more than two million Wehrmacht prisoners, including a million in occupied Czechoslovakia alone. Still, satisfying as the victory and the take in German prisoners was, to get the material compensation he felt was his due, Stalin would have to look elsewhere.[17]

Two weeks after the final German surrender on May 8, subsequently known as VE Day, the new US president, Harry Truman, sent Harry Hopkins to Moscow to meet with Stalin to demonstrate his "desire to continue President Roosevelt's policy of working with the Soviet Union." More delicately, the president wanted Hopkins to see if Stalin could do something to ameliorate the "deterioration of public opinion" in the United States caused by Stalin's recent behavior in Eastern Europe. Truman also wanted Hopkins to discuss Soviet cooperation in the war against Japan. But Stalin, as always, had his own agenda, using the amenable Hopkins—whom he greeted "like an old friend," according to Harriman—to whitewash the Polish issue. Blaming Western criticism of Soviet actions in Poland on Churchill and "British conservatives"—who supposedly had returned to their prewar policy of seeking a cordon sanitaire to contain Soviet expansion—Stalin found a receptive audience in Hopkins, who assured the Vozhd that "neither the American people, nor the American government, want anything of the kind." It was not Stalin's mass deportations of Poles, or his banning of Allied observers and even doctors from the country, that bothered Hopkins, but rather the darkening "mood of public opinion in America" about Soviet actions in Poland, which he, personally, did not understand. The "United States," Hopkins assured Stalin, "desires that the Soviet Union is surrounded with friendly governments." If that is "true," Stalin said with evident satisfaction, "then we are in agreement."[18]

Stalin also used Hopkins to ratchet up Soviet demands for German war booty. Stalin wanted one third of the German fleet now controlled by British and American crews—whose navies had done the work of defeating and commandeering it, even as the Red Army had done the vast bulk of the damage against Germany's land forces. To justify his claim, Stalin informed Hopkins, on May 27, 1945, that Soviet Russia deserved this compensation, along with other myriad reparation claims, because it had "lost five million men in the war."* Hopkins assured the Vozhd that the US Navy was fully willing "to turn over the German ships" and that, despite questions being raised in Congress over why military aid to the USSR was continuing after the European war was over, US lend-lease commitments in Asia "would be fulfilled to the end."[19]

Relieved that Truman—despite rumors that he would be tougher than Roosevelt, owing to a soon-infamous dressing down the president had given Molotov in the White House on April 23†—was still trusting Hopkins to handle sensitive foreign policy matters, Stalin loosened up. He even had a little fun when

---

* By 1947, the figure of "Soviet losses" was up to 8 million; then it jumped to 20 million in the Khrushchev era, 27 million under Gorbachev, and, in an influential publication in 1996, 42 million, of which 26.4 million were counted as military deaths. There is no reason to credit Stalin with greater accuracy than later demographers and historians. Nonetheless, the fact that the Soviet leader, in the immediate flush of anger after the war and with no motivation to minimize losses—he was trying to justify reparations claims—came up with a figure of military deaths five times lower than recent estimates (and nearly ten times lower if civilian deaths are included) suggests that we should approach all of these numbers with caution.

† According to legend, Truman told Molotov, who complained about his rough tone in a discussion of Poland, "Carry out your agreements and you won't get talked to like that." "I let him have it," Truman later boasted. "A straight one-two to the jaw." Still, whatever toughness Truman showed in conversation with Molotov in April 1945 was belied by the faith he put in Harry Hopkins to negotiate critical matters with Stalin in May, including Poland's future.

Hopkins asked him whether the Soviets had any news about Hitler's whereabouts, speculating that the Führer had "escaped in a submarine to Japan." (By now, a SMERSH team had confirmed Hitler's identity from dental records.) On May 28, the Vozhd spoke cheerfully with Hopkins about his use of "slave labor" in lieu of reparations, as agreed by the Allies at Yalta. Stalin openly boasted that the Soviets now had 1.7 million German war prisoners working in Soviet forced-labor camps, along with 800,000 Hungarians and Romanians and Italians. Italians, Stalin told Hopkins in an interesting confidence, were more productive than the other groups, because Soviet camp guards actually fed them halfway decently.[20]

Still, exploiting slave labor was old hat to Stalin. What he really wanted from Germany was its industrial wealth: factories, patents, engineers, and their manufacturing know-how. At Yalta, Roosevelt and Churchill had agreed to a Soviet reparations bill of $10 billion to be levied on Germany in cash, kind, and labor. Having already looted the Reichsbank of cash and acquired nearly two million German slave laborers, Stalin would now claim his share of German commercial and industrial property. A crude monetary estimate of the industrial equipment stripped from German factories and shipped to the USSR in the first eighteen months after VE Day was 10.369 billion Reichsmarks ($4.12 billion, nearly half a trillion dollars in current equivalent).[21]

Overseeing this, the greatest organized looting operation in history, was a kind of "war booty" army inside the Red Army, which had begun operating as early as January 1943, when Stalin created the first fifteen "looting battalions," each 500 strong, and 2,500-strong "looting brigades" composed of five battalions each. In April 1943, these had been subordinated to the State Ministry of Defense, which oversaw six "looting battalions," with a total strength of 15,000, and thirty-nine "independent looting battalions," numbering 19,500 actives. By 1945, these Red Army looting units were assigned five entire trains devoted exclusively to carrying loot back home, along with several dozen heavy tractors, tugboats, and an array of cranes (many of them given by American lend-lease). They were also assigned, beginning in February 1945, eighty thousand men, divided into forced "labor battalions" of five hundred men, along with (lend-lease) cars and trucks. To help with more delicate extractions of specialized equipment, chemicals and sensitive material, and blueprints and intellectual property, after VE Day the looting battalions were reinforced with 432 Soviet engineers, 184 technicians, 206 master builders, and 1,092 skilled workers. Small wonder Stalin's looting battalions were able to cart off from Germany alone, by the end of 1946, 4.15 million tons of industrial, commercial, artistic, and intellectual property, in 519,000 railway wagons—an operation that would ultimately net Stalin 9.991 million tons of industrial goods. Taking no chances, Stalin ordered his looters to front-load shipments as much as humanly possible in case the Western Allies cried foul. By August 2, 1945, less than two months after VE Day, nearly half of the total volume of loot, 4.68 million tons, had already crossed the Soviet border.[22]

A list of the items shipped by rail and road from Germany to Russia after 1945 bears a curious resemblance to the lend-lease goods shipped to Russia between 1941 and 1945, except that, for the German goods, the Russians had to pay for the shipping the Americans had provided free of charge. Stalin laid claim to many of the same industrial inputs: for example, finished steel products, especially rails and rolling stock (260,024 tons), and nonferrous metals (49,600 tons, including aluminum and zinc). German property looted by Stalin included, by November 1946, 3,024 entire factories; 1,323 locomotive engines; 20,432 types of "lifting equipment," including 5,500 industrial cranes; 394,754 machine tools; 4,667 foundries; telephone switchboards, cables, and wire; steel-smelting Bessemer plants (Siemens-Martin design); coking plants; diesel engines and generators; electric motors and generators; furnaces and hydroturbines; chemical and textile factories; printing works; and passenger cars.[23]

The Germans were not the only ones being looted. Stalin's men also carted off 211,500 railway wagons' worth of booty from Poland (that is, not counting the parts of Poland annexed by the

USSR), 31,200 from Austria, 2,800 from Hungary, and 6,500 from Czechoslovakia. Just as in Germany, this loot included everything from iron and steel (610,000 tons) to nonferrous metals (200,000 tons) to cranes, motors, pumps, engines, generators, turbines and locomotive engines, telephone equipment (354 telephone switching stations with 456,300 "telephone connections"), woodworking facilities, and even paper (10,100 tons). If we include non-German countries, the Soviet intake of war booty totaled, by the end of 1947, the equipment, inventory, intellectual property, and records of 1.2 million separate factories or enterprises, including Siemens, BMW, and Allianz insurance. In this way, Bogdan Musial argues in a brilliant 2011 book, it was the "plundering of Germany" and the other countries Stalin conquered in 1945 that helped turn the impoverished and inconsistently industrialized USSR into a superpower.[24]

In a pattern familiar to beleaguered residents of Russia in 1917–1918 and all the countries Stalin had occupied and looted in 1939–1941, the plundering of Eastern Europe brought not only property theft but cultural destruction and desecration on a massive scale. In addition to the Red Army war booty detachments, in February 1945 Stalin created a special committee to oversee the "Selection of Trophies for [Soviet] Cultural Organizations and Their Transport to Moscow." At least some of his motivation was patriotic, if not scholarly: Stalin made a specific demand that "valuable materials" related to Russian literature, poetry, and history be seized from German libraries and "repatriated." While not much effort was put into selecting materials for scholarly significance, the haul was impressive by volume, with Moscow University being enriched by 13 railway wagons full of books, the Soviet Health Ministry getting 24 wagons, and the Lenin Library (which still exists today) receiving 760,000 volumes. By 1948, more than 2.5 million "trophy books" were claimed, or put on display, at 279 separate Moscow cultural institutions.[25]

Still, most Red Army soldiers had little interest in such cultural priorities. Hundreds of museums and libraries in Poland and East

Prussia were put to the torch before Stalin's looting commissions could do their job. Ironically, it was in Dresden—the East German Saxon town firebombed by the RAF and US Army Air Force between February 13 and 15, 1945, producing an inferno that destroyed the old city and killed twenty-five thousand civilians—that Stalin's cultural looting commission had its best haul of artwork, carting off seventy paintings by European Old Masters to Moscow, including fourteen Rembrandts.* Bombed-out Berlin, too, netted a good artistic haul once the NKVD brought in heavy equipment to cart off some of the larger Greek sculptures from the world-renowned collections housed on the city's Museum Island. But in occupied East Germany as a whole, Musial notes, Soviet troops destroyed far more cultural artifacts and artistic objects than Stalin's looting battalions succeeded in carting off to Russia.[26]

Looting and theft on this massive scale was accompanied, predictably, by horrific acts of violence. In Yugoslavia alone, by 1945 local authorities had reported 1,204 cases of looting with assault and 121 cases of rape by Red Army soldiers, of which 111 were rape-murders. As one of Tito's partisans observed, "We are witnessing a return to the administrative methods of Attila and Genghis Khan." And this "Genghis Khan" treatment was accorded to Yugoslavia, a friendly country that supposedly had been jointly liberated by the partisans of Stalin's client Tito.[27]

The horrors awaiting occupied Germany were not hard to foresee. Ilya Ehrenburg, the Soviet Goebbels—anointed "Stalin's favorite rabble-rouser" by Goebbels himself—whose bloodthirsty column in the Red Army newspaper *Krasnaia Zvezda* was widely read by frontline troops, topped himself in one memorable passage: "We shall not speak any more. We shall not get excited. We

---

*It has sometimes been asserted that Churchill and Roosevelt bombed Dresden, a city in the path of the Red Army advance into eastern Germany, at Stalin's insistence. This is untrue. What did happen is that the Allies agreed at Yalta on a narrow "zone of limitation" on the eastern front for bombing raids by either side, in which zone Dresden fell.

shall kill. If you have not killed at least one German today, you have wasted that day. If you kill one German, kill another—there is nothing funnier for us than a pile of German corpses." In another celebrated line, Ehrenburg exhorted Soviet soldiers to "hang them and watch them struggle in their nooses. Burn their homes to the ground and enjoy the flames."[28]

Red Army Ivans got the message. Aleksandr Solzhenitsyn, then a Soviet artillery captain, recalled with a shudder how his fellow "soldiers have turned into avid beasts. In the fields lie hundreds of shot cattle, on the roads pigs and chickens with their heads chopped off. Houses have been looted and are on fire. What cannot be taken away is being broken and destroyed." Near Nemmersdorf in East Prussia, a Soviet military doctor observed

> a column of refugees . . . rolled over by Russian tanks; not only the wagons and teams, but also a goodly number of civilians, mostly women and children, had been squashed flat by the tanks. . . . On the edge of a street an old woman sat hunched up, killed by a bullet in the back of the neck. Not far away lay a baby of only a few months, killed by a shot at close range through the forehead. . . . A number of men . . . had been killed by blows with shovels or gun butts; their faces were completely smashed.

When told of a similar atrocity, which had seen Red Army tank gunners mercilessly shell a refugee column filled with women and children, Stalin was said to have replied: "We lecture our soldiers too much; let them have some initiative!"[29]

What most Germans remember about the Russian conquest of 1945, however, were the rapes, fueled not merely by pent-up rage and lust for revenge among soldiers who had seen their country invaded and brutalized, but by galloping drunkenness. In almost every village from the Baltic to the Alps, daughters and mothers and grandmothers were sexually assaulted and then beaten, stabbed, killed, or left for dead. Younger German women may have suffered the worst, as many of them were raped by dozens of soldiers

before finally being discarded; one Soviet officer met a girl who
had been raped as many as 250 times. But as a Soviet Army major
confessed to a British journalist, Red Army men were by 1945 "so
sex-starved that they often raped women of sixty, seventy, or even
eighty—much to these grandmothers' surprise." Numerous eyewitness reports backed up this claim, with the Vatican representative in Germany, Monsignor G. B. Montini, adding that elderly
nuns were raped in the middle of Berlin "wearing their religious
habits." As another Berliner recalled, "Almost no evening went
by, no night, in which we did not hear the pitiful cries for help
from women who were attacked on the streets or in the always
open houses." One Red tank gunner boasted, citing a figure close
to current historians' estimates on the number of Germans raped
by Soviet troops after the war, that "2 million of our children were
born in Germany." As Solzhenitsyn later recalled, "All of us knew
very well that if the girls were German they could be raped and
then shot. This was almost a combat distinction."[30]

To this day, there are those who say that the Germans, because
of the Holocaust and the horrific atrocities of all kinds committed
on the eastern front, had it coming. As Stalin, who knew all about
the rapes, told Tito's partisan commander, Milovan Djilas, after
the war, "Imagine a man who has fought from Stalingrad to Belgrade—over thousands of kilometers of his own devastated land,
across the dead bodies of his comrades and dearest ones? How can
such a man react normally? And what is so awful about his having
fun with a woman after such horrors?"[31]

The problem with this apologia is that it was not only German
women who were raped as the Red Army crashed into Europe in
1945, but Polish, Hungarian, Romanian, and Czech women too.
In Berlin, in the belly of the Nazi beast, Red Army soldiers raped
even Jewish women, including girls interned at a Holocaust "transit camp" on Schulstrasse. Fed on Ehrenburg's agitprop diet of indiscriminate bloodthirstiness, for most Red Army soldiers it was a
matter of "Frau ist Frau": a woman is a woman. This kind of thinking was consistent with the indiscriminate logic of retribution, of

atrocity and counter-atrocity, that had defined the bloodlands ever since Stalin's pact with Hitler had erased the borders of Eastern Europe in September 1939. It reached its culmination in the expulsion of over six million ethnic Germans—most of them women, children, and elderly men—from their homes in areas of Prussia absorbed into western Poland to accommodate Stalin's annexation of eastern Poland, followed by another more than six million German speakers expelled from Czechoslovakia, Hungary, Romania, and Yugoslavia. At least 500,000, and possibly as many as 1.5 million, civilians perished in this forgotten mass deportation.[32]

The Soviet mass rapes, civilian murders, and deportations of 1945 were significant not because they were unique, but because they were a harbinger of what lay in store for anyone liberated by the Red Army. Eastern Europe had been Sovietized. Next it would be Asia's turn.

34

Red Star over Asia

The Final Wages of Lend-Lease

OF ALL THE diplomatic coups Stalin pulled off during the Second World War, those involving Japan were the most consistently astounding. Somehow, with an assist from Hitler's self-defeating refusal to trust the Japanese and coordinate strategy against the USSR with Tokyo, the Vozhd had managed to turn hostile Japan into a friendly power in April 1941—even while preparing for war with Japan's German ally—and to remain steadfastly loyal to Tokyo even after his later allies in arms against Hitler, Britain and the United States, fought a bitter and costly war against Japanese aggression in Asia and the Pacific Ocean. More remarkable still, the Soviet dictator had cajoled Roosevelt at Teheran—despite Stalin's repeated, blunt refusals to help the United States in any way against Japan—into agreeing that Soviet Russia would get its share of Japanese war booty once he finally got around to helping, "three months" after the European war was over—and not a moment sooner.* As a US Joint Chiefs of Staff memorandum had noted ruefully in November 1944, "While the maximum advantage to us results from Russian entry prior to our invasion of Japan, the reverse

---

* Of course, from Stalin's point of view a similar dynamic had been at play in Europe, with the Americans and British waiting until the Wehrmacht had been weakened by eastern front attrition before D-Day. But then the Western Allies were hardly neutral vis-à-vis Nazi Germany, as Stalin was against Japan. Nor did the United States and Britain demand vast territorial concessions in exchange for carrying out the D-Day landings, as Stalin was now doing prior to entering the war with Japan.

is true from the Russian viewpoint. The maximum military advantage for them will obtain if they attack after . . . Japanese forces in Manchuria have begun to move to reinforce Japan."[1]

In exchange for Stalin's deliberately unhelpful promises on Japan, FDR had agreed at Yalta to sign off on Soviet control of the entire island of Sakhalin, the Kurile island chain between Japan and the Soviet Far East, and Outer Mongolia, along with a sphere of influence including de facto control of all seaports and railways in Manchuria, the main industrial zone and richest region in all of China. Those last two promises were especially striking in view of Roosevelt's sentimental attachment to China. What the president had done, in effect, was reassign Chinese territories the Japanese had invaded and fought for since 1931—an act of aggression against which all US policy on Japan had been premised for fourteen years—to the Russians, who weren't even helping the United States and China fight Japan. Of course, by failing to open the Burma Road and reducing lend-lease aid to China down to infinitesimal levels in 1943 and 1944, Roosevelt and the Americans had not offered Chiang much help, either, preferring to fight a largely peripheral (though still bloody) island-hopping campaign in the Pacific, which left China alone to fight the main Japanese armies in Manchukuo and China and opened the door to a Soviet invasion from the north once the Red Army was ready. One can hardly fault Stalin for agreeing to devour the thousands of square miles of Asian real estate Roosevelt was offering him in exchange for a promissory note to intervene only when it suited Soviet, not American, interests to do so—an intervention that would be carried out, moreover, largely with lend-lease war matériel sent to Siberia.

Not everyone in Washington was happy with these arrangements. The exclusion of the optimistic G-2 analysis of prospects for ending the Japanese war without Soviet help from Roosevelt's briefing book at Yalta was the final straw for many army intelligence officers. To salvage something from the Yalta debacle, G-2 prepared a thoroughgoing rebuttal in early April 1945. Among the key authors was Colonel Ivan Yeaton, the former military attaché in Moscow whom Hopkins had cashiered in 1941. "It may be expected," Yeaton et al. began, "that Soviet Russia will enter the Asiatic war, but at her own good time and probably only when the hard fighting stage is over." While the authors conceded that Stalin's belated entry into the war might conceivably "shorten hostilities [a] little" and effect "a slight saving in American lives," they insisted that the United States and Britain were "strong enough to crush Japan by ourselves" and that "under no circumstances should we *pay the Soviet Union* to destroy China. This would . . . injure the material and moral position of the United States in Asia." While the "military significance" of Soviet intervention "at this stage of the war would be relatively unimportant," the authors warned,

> The entry of Soviet Russia into the Asiatic war would be a political event of world-shaking importance, the ill effect of which would be felt for decades to come. . . . [It] would destroy America's position in Asia quite as effectively as our position is now destroyed in Europe East of the Elbe and beyond the Adriatic. . . . China will certainly lose her position to become the Poland of Asia. . . . To encourage Soviet intervention for such little gain, at an unpredictable cost in lives, treasure, and honor in the future—and simultaneously destroy our ally China, would be an act of treachery that would make the Atlantic Charter and our hopes for world peace a tragic farce.[2]

Completed on April 12, 1945, the day before Roosevelt died in Warm Springs, this analysis was written too late to have an impact at Yalta, and too soon to find a possibly more receptive audience after Truman became president. Like earlier G-2 estimates, this one was shelved and rediscovered only in 1951, after Mao's victory in the Chinese Civil War and the Communist invasion of South Korea had stunned official Washington into a belated search for scapegoats. In April 1945, the sober views of G-2 branch on Soviet intentions were still out of fashion.

By May, though, there were signs of a shift in the White House. While not ready to jettison Roosevelt's Stalin-friendly advisers such as Harry Hopkins just yet, the new president was willing to listen to alternative opinions. On May 15, Truman received the undersecretary of state, former ambassador to Japan Joseph Grew, who presented a strong case for revising the unconditional surrender doctrine vis-à-vis Japan to shorten the war and for revisiting the pledges Roosevelt had made to Stalin at Yalta without consulting Chiang. Assigning Manchuria to Stalin as a sphere of influence, as Grew noted, violated pledges Roosevelt had made to Chiang at Cairo in 1943 to restore China's sovereignty there. A G-2 memorandum submitted that same day recommended that a "revised demand for unconditional surrender" be issued to Japan as soon as possible to obviate the need for Soviet intervention. Truman listened politely to Grew's arguments, along with his recommendation that the president meet with Stalin soon to iron out an Asia deal. On May 28, Truman even received Roosevelt's predecessor Herbert Hoover, a close friend of Grew's, who fully endorsed Grew's advice to "waste no time in offering the Japanese peace upon specified terms" before Stalin was able to conquer Manchuria and Korea. For now, though, the president decided to stay in Washington to focus on domestic affairs and postpone discussion of Asian matters until he was ready to meet Stalin and Churchill in July.[3]

Truman's procrastination played into Stalin's hands, especially after the president chose to send Hopkins to Moscow in late May 1945. Aside from paying homage to the late Roosevelt, the choice of Hopkins as envoy was meant as a kind of peace offering after Truman's showdown with Molotov over Poland on April 23, and after members of the Soviet purchasing commission complained to Molotov on May 12 that lend-lease aid to Soviet Russia had been cut off. What had happened was that on May 10—two days after VE Day—Truman had signed a presidential directive curtailing

Soviet aid shipments sent to Europe, on the impeccable logic that the war in Europe was over. Two days later, the directive was adopted by the Lend-Lease Administration, with orders sent out to officials in Atlantic and Gulf of Mexico ports to cease loading supplies for the USSR and recall ships at sea heading for Russia. After furious Soviet protests, lend-lease officials sent a note of apology to the Soviet embassy and new orders were issued allowing ships already loaded, or at sea, to resume their prior course for Russia. No matter: when Hopkins arrived in Moscow, Stalin lit into him over the "scornful and abrupt," "unfortunate and brutal" way Truman had cut off the spigot of supplies he had been receiving. "If [US] refusal to continue Lend-Lease was designed as pressure on the Russians in order to soften them up," Stalin told Hopkins on May 27, "then it was a fundamental mistake" that might result in "reprisals."[4]

Had a principled and patriotic American statesman listened to this threat, he would have put Stalin in his place regarding the Soviet Union's apparently abject dependence on gifted American war matériel to equip its armies. Instead, Hopkins apologized and refused to back up Truman's decision to curtail lend-lease shipments to Europe after Nazi Germany had ceased to exist—a decision, Hopkins said sheepishly (and inaccurately), that resulted from a "technical misunderstanding." Lend-lease shipments to Vladivostok, to enable Stalin's armed conquest of the northern Asian mainland, would, Hopkins reassured the Vozhd, "be carried out to the end."[5]

This was no exaggeration. In hearings before the House Appropriations Committee on June 13, the man Hopkins had appointed to oversee the Soviet program, General C. M. Wesson, informed Congress that, "although the Soviet Union has not declared war against Japan, lend-lease aid is being continued to the Soviet Union . . . [on] the principle of furnishing supplies and services necessary to support programs of essential Soviet military requirements in the Far East." This included the completion of the fourth protocol commitment through June 30, 1945, along with the special list submitted to General Deane in Moscow in October 1944 specifying material requirements for equipping a Soviet "force of 1.5 million men" with supplies, food, fuel, and "transport equipment" sufficient for two months, along with two million pairs of boots. In the end, only 80 percent of these special requirements had been fulfilled by June 30, 1945, although one expects that Soviet disappointment might have been leavened by the arrival, by that same date, of 2.7 million tons of war matériel that had come to Vladivostok during the fourth protocol period before May 12, 1945, and the 1.35 million more tons that reached the Soviet Far East between that date and September 2. If we aggregate "regular" protocol and "special" lend-lease allotments for the Asian theater, over the last fourteen months of the Pacific war the Soviets received more than four million long (metric) tons of war matériel for Stalin's Far Eastern armies, including 870,000 long tons of petroleum. So voluminous were American lend-lease shipments across the Pacific to the Soviet Far East in this period—during the climactic phase of the war against Japan—that they equaled the volume shipped across the North Atlantic during the entire war to support the Red Army against the Wehrmacht, rounding out a total shipped across the Pacific of 8.244 million tons, which did not even include the warplanes flown into Siberia via ALSIB along with the sensitive and often strategic cargo they contained.[6]

In light of these material facts, it is worth revisiting the inconclusive White House debates over Stalin and Asian strategy in May 1945. Whereas Grew, Hoover, and G-2 analysts advocated flexibility over unconditional surrender to bring the Japanese war to an end sooner and not treating Roosevelt's territorial bribes to lure Stalin into the Pacific war as holy writ, George Marshall's war plans division and Henry Stimson's War Department argued against revising unconditional surrender on the grounds that doing so "might jeopardize [Stalin's] desired participation in the [Japanese] war," which would "have a profound military effect in that almost certainly it will materially shorten the war and thus save American lives." Like Roosevelt when he first unveiled unconditional surrender at Casablanca, the Marshall-Stimson position was that keeping Stalin content was worth a heavy political price—in both cases, based on the plausible premise that keeping the Russians in (or bribing them into) the fight would save American lives. Stimson further argued that Roosevelt's concessions to Stalin "on Far Eastern matters which were made at Yalta are generally matters which are within the military power of Russia to obtain," and that even if the United States contested them, the Russians would get there first. By August 8, 1945, when Stalin informed Hopkins that the USSR would be ready as agreed, three months after VE Day, to fight Japan, it may have been the case that the Soviets could conquer Sakhalin, the Kurile Islands, Manchuria, and northern Korea before American troops could get there, but if so this was true only because of the four million tons of war matériel the United States was sending Stalin that year, at the material and logistical expense of its own Pacific fleet, merchant marine, and army.[7]

Nor was it necessarily the case that showing flexibility on unconditional surrender would have ruled out Soviet participation in the Japanese war. In view of Stalin's almost total dependence on lend-lease fuel, food, and basic supplies for his Far Eastern armies, the fact that he was not even at war yet with Japan, and the fact that his claims on Manchuria depended on an agreement with Chiang Kai-shek that had not yet been reached, a decent negotiator could have gotten the Vozhd to accept a conditional peace with Japan while bartering him down on his territorial claims in Asia. Hopkins was not such a negotiator, and neither was Harriman, the ambassador to Moscow, who, by May 1945, was in battered-statesman mode. When the discussion got around to Asian questions on May 28, Harriman assured Stalin that Truman intended to "carry out the commitments undertaken by President Roosevelt at [Yalta]," adding, in a self-defeating touch reminiscent of Churchill's endorsement of Stalin's revanchist territorial moves in Eastern Europe in 1939, that "it was obvious that the Soviet Union would re-assume Russia's historic position in the Far East." Stalin replied that he "understood and appreciated" these promises, although noting, in what should have been Harriman's line, that Soviet claims in Asia "also depended on the Chinese," a hint that he wanted the Americans to whip Chiang into line. Hopkins then offered to give Stalin a share in the "trusteeship of Korea," and the latter "fully agreed." When Hopkins raised unconditional surrender, he did so in his usual deferential manner, asking "whether Marshal Stalin had any doubts as to the desirability of applying the unconditional surrender principle to Japan." The Vozhd was game enough to admit that a "conditional surrender" might offer "immediate advantages" to Britain and the United States, but added that "he personally favored unconditional surrender." Hopkins then threw him another softball, asking whether the Vozhd "thought the Japanese would surrender unconditionally before they were utterly destroyed," to which Stalin "replied in the negative." And so Hopkins reported to Truman on May 30, 1945, that "the Soviet Union prefers to go through with unconditional surrender and destroy once and for all the military might and forces of Japan," adding, with no editorial comment, that "the Marshal expects that Russia will *share in the actual occupation of Japan*." Rather than exert leverage over lend-lease deliveries to water down Stalin's claims for Asian war booty or soften up the Soviets on a negotiated peace with Japan that might end the war before Stalin claimed all of his prizes, Hopkins refused to press on unconditional surrender and allowed Stalin to ratchet up his claims further to include a share in the occupation of Japan's home islands.[8]

That American pressure on Stalin regarding Asian concessions, whether at Yalta or afterward, might have made a difference is confirmed by the transcript of Politburo discussions of the Soviet war plan for Japan on June 27 and 28, 1945—the first serious Politburo debate since the summer of 1941, after a long hiatus during the war with Germany, when Stalin and his generals had run the country and Molotov had conducted foreign policy. When Marshal Kirill Meretskov advocated an amphibious landing on Hokkaido, the northernmost of Japan's home islands, Molotov objected that seizing Hokkaido would be a violation of the Yalta agreement on spheres of influence and thus likely to occasion an American objection. With American forces, naval strength, and amphibious capacity in the Pacific theater still vastly superior to that of the Soviets, Stalin and his advisers were wary of overstepping the boundaries laid down at Yalta and not entirely confident they would reach them, unless they fought all the way there.[9]

If there was a reason President Truman gave Hopkins such leeway in making concessions in Moscow, it may have been that he thought he had an ace to play in the Pacific war. Manhattan Project engineers in Los Alamos, New Mexico, were nearing completion of the world's first atomic bomb, which was expected to be ready for testing in early July, Truman was informed on April 25, and operational by "about 1 August 1945." "Within four months," the president was then informed by Stimson and the War Department, "we shall in all probability have completed the most terrible weapon ever known in human history, one bomb of which could destroy a whole city." By June 1945 there was already a "target committee" in the White House choosing cities on which to unload this wonder weapon. At least part of the reason Truman, a noted poker player, did not press Hopkins harder to limit the Soviet role in the Pacific war is that the president hoped to have a winning hand when the Big Three convened at Potsdam, outside Berlin, in mid-July 1945.[10]

By ruling out the Grew-Hoover-G-2 idea of being flexible on peace terms and doubling down on unconditional surrender, Truman seems to have calculated that the United States could win the Pacific war decisively with the new atomic bomb, or he planned to have Soviet intervention give Tokyo the final decisive shove alongside the atomic bomb—in either case avoiding the ruinous bloodshed sure to follow an amphibious invasion of Japan's home islands. The Battle of Okinawa, concluded on June 21, had taken nearly three months and cost the US Army and Marine Corps more than 60,000 casualties, including 7,613 dead, and had killed nearly 150,000 Japanese and Okinawans, including more than 40,000 civilians. Not unlike Stalin setting Zhukov and Konev against each other to ensure they would beat the Americans to Berlin, by refusing to entertain any compromise on Japanese surrender terms, Truman had, in effect, launched a race between the Manhattan Project and Stalin's Far Eastern armies to crush Japan's will to resist. Neither side was willing to yield, which helps explain why peace feelers extended by Japan's Emperor Hirohito in June and July 1945 to Soviet diplomats in Tokyo all came to nothing. The catch was that the US government was funding both sides in this macabre contest, but it would not gain equal benefit from a Soviet victory, which would undermine American prestige in China when it should have been peaking.[11]

Stalin was well-informed about the Manhattan Project, as would later be confirmed in postwar trials of spies who passed on atomic secrets to the NKVD (two, Klaus Fuchs and David Greenglass, were tried; a third, Theodore Hall, was uncovered by the Venona decrypts in 1995; and a fourth, Oscar Seborer, was recently discovered), thus helping accelerate the Soviet atomic bomb program by a year or more. At the time, the reason Soviet knowledge mattered was that it convinced Stalin to speed up his own timetable for entering the war against Japan. The first Soviet war plan, approved by the Politburo on June 27, 1945, and wired by Stalin to front commanders on June 28, had the Red Army launching its Manchurian offensive (Operation August Storm) between August 20 and 25. But Stalin moved up his timetable even before he learned that the Americans had successfully tested an atomic bomb. In his very first conversation with Truman at the Potsdam summit, on the morning of July 17, Stalin told the president that he was planning to enter the war by the middle of August, one week earlier than in the original Politburo plan.[12]

Stalin found dealing with Truman tougher sledding than his encounters with Roosevelt had been. The president, after touring the ruins of Berlin upon his arrival on July 16, postponed his first meeting with the Vozhd, which was supposed to have taken place that night at 9 p.m., until he had gotten some sleep. Although their first and subsequent conversations at Potsdam were polite enough, the two statesmen talked at cross-purposes about Japan, as revealed in subtle discrepancies in the transcript between the US and Soviet versions. Stalin, according to Chip Bohlen's notes, told Truman straightaway on July 17 that the Soviets would soon be ready to enter the Pacific war ("we ready mid of Aug") and asked for help in obtaining Chinese approval on the Soviet sphere of influence in Manchuria promised at Yalta. Truman downplayed the American need for Soviet assistance against Japan, insisting (in Bohlen's notes) that "we are—not in dire straits as Eng[land] was in re Germany" and changed the subject. In the Soviet version, it was Truman who asked for "assistance from the Soviet Union" against Japan. As the Japanese American historian Tsuyoshi Hasegawa observes in a 2005 study, after failing to receive the invitation he desired from Truman, Stalin's stenographers "falsified the minutes of the meeting to give the impression that it was Truman who requested Soviet entry into the war and that Stalin complied with this request."[13]

There was a good reason Truman declined to invite Stalin to enter the Pacific war on July 17. The previous evening, the president had received a top secret cable from Washington confirming the successful detonation of an atomic bomb in New Mexico that morning ("Diagnosis not yet complete but results seem satisfactory and already exceeds expectations"). Truman guarded his secret for an entire week, refusing to share the news with Stalin and failing to give way on any requests important to the Vozhd at Potsdam, such as permission for a Soviet military base at the Bosporus or Dardanelles or a leading Soviet role in administering the Turkish Straits; both were shot down. On July 23, Truman met privately with Stimson, the US secretary of war, and asked him to consult with Chief of Staff Marshall to ascertain whether the Americans "[needed] the Russians in the war or whether we could get along without them." Although Marshall was more ambivalent, Stimson reported back to Truman on the morning of July 24 that (as paraphrased in Stimson's diary entry) "now with [the] new [atomic] weapon we would not need the assistance of the Russians to conquer Japan." It was only after receiving this assessment from Stimson that Truman finally approached Stalin later that evening at around 7:30 p.m. and confided in him, as if casually—he spoke without his interpreter—that the United States had tested "a new weapon of unusual destructive force." Having thus learned that the Americans had an operational atomic bomb—and having been informed in a vague manner that implied Truman was concealing something—Stalin bumped up his timetable for the Soviet invasion of Manchuria another week again, ordering front commander Marshal A. M. Vasilevsky to be ready to move by the second week in August. By the time Stalin left Potsdam on August 2, the date for August Storm had been moved all the way up to 1 a.m. on August 11. The race was on.[14]

Stalin had good reasons for haste. Truman's actions in Potsdam had made it clear that the president wanted to keep the USSR out of the war with Japan, or at least to minimize the Soviet role in its conclusion and Stalin's claims in the postwar settlement. Encouraged by Stimson's assessment that the United States no longer required Soviet intervention to defeat Japan, Truman had snubbed Stalin by refusing to let him sign the Potsdam Declaration wired to Tokyo on July 26. US diplomats had excised a moderating passage in the original draft, which had conceded that "the Japanese people will be free to choose their own form of government"— an allusion to Emperor Hirohito and the monarchy. Instead, the Potsdam Declaration, issued on behalf of Truman for the United States, Churchill for Britain, and Chiang Kai-shek for China (whose approval was "obtained by radio"), demanded the "unconditional surrender of all the Japanese armed forces," failing which Japan would be subject to "prompt and utter destruction." Significantly, the declaration was released to the press before Molotov had read the text and without Stalin's signature. Of course, the Soviets were not in the war yet, which gave this exclusion legal justification. But the fact that the Russians had not been consulted suggested, to

Stalin, that Truman was trying to undermine his negotiating position in any final peace, if not keep the Soviets out of the Japanese war altogether. In an added insult, Truman and the new US secretary of state, James Byrnes, declined Molotov's invitation to issue a face-saving "formal request to the Soviet government for its entry into the [Japanese] war," leaving it up to Stalin to find his own casus belli to justify ripping up his neutrality pact with Tokyo. By showing toughness with Stalin in a way Roosevelt never had, Truman seemed to have won a major trick, muscling the Soviets out of a war the British and Americans now hoped to end within days, as soon as the atomic weapon was unleashed.[15]

What Truman did not realize was that lend-lease aid had negated his own time advantage. On July 25, the day before Truman released the Stalin-less Potsdam Declaration to Tokyo, 60,000 tons of American petroleum arrived in Vladivostok, accompanied by 480 kilometers of six-inch oil pipe and 120 kilometers of four-inch pipe to help distribute 45,000 tons of motor fuel to the "Transbaikal front" and 15,000 tons to the "first Far Eastern front" along the Pacific coast. This was enough to fuel the American warplanes the Soviets had been stockpiling in Asia (7,995 flown in from Alaska to date, including 315 planes per month so far in 1945; 3,721 used in August Storm) and the tens of thousands of American trucks and jeeps, the last of which would arrive on September 20, 1945 (147,709 sent to the USSR in the fourth protocol; 85,819 used in August Storm). Most of the five thousand tanks used in the upcoming offensive were Soviet built, including 1,794 T-34s. Even so, Stalin's Far Eastern armies had laid in 250 Sherman M4A2 diesel tanks too. The Soviet armies in the Far East, 1.577 million men strong on the eve of August Storm, rode on lend-lease vehicles, wore American boots and shoes, and were fed, fueled, provisioned, and munitioned by the Americans.[16]

Meanwhile, the exclusion of the Soviets from the Potsdam Declaration had ignited hopes in Tokyo, however unrealistic, that Moscow might still mediate between Japan and its adversaries. Even if the United States deployed its new atomic weapon, the fact that the USSR was still neutral could be used by hard-liners in Tokyo to justify holding out for better peace terms.* Japan's response, stated at a press conference on July 28 by the new Japanese premier, Suzuki Kantaro, was to *mokasatsu* (ignore) the Potsdam Declaration (this was conveniently mistranslated in some US media reports as "reject") and to launch one final peace feeler in Moscow. Truman's decision not to let Stalin sign the Potsdam ultimatum thus sabotaged any chance that unconditional surrender might be accepted by Tokyo out of sheer Big Three intimidation, while giving Stalin motivation to hasten toward Soviet intervention. It was now a race to the finish.[17]

Because of rapid progress with the A-bomb, the United States had a head start. We now know that Little Boy, code name for the first bomb, was actually ready to go on August 1, 1945, only to be held up by a typhoon over Japan. The five-day delay allowed Stalin's generals to speed up preparations for August Storm. Stalin, returning from Potsdam, arrived in Moscow the night of August 5, just as the US Army Air Force received a favorable forecast and launched the B-29 bomber *Enola Gay*, which delivered its fateful payload on Hiroshima at 8:15 a.m. Japanese time on August 6, incinerating virtually the entire city and killing more than 20,000 soldiers and 110,000 civilians. President Truman then issued a statement confirming the attack and warned that, if Japan's leaders did not now accept the terms of the Potsdam Declaration, "they may expect a rain of ruin from the air, the like of which has never been seen on this earth." With Stalin's Far Eastern armies still needing more time to complete preparations for August Storm, it appeared that the Vozhd might have missed his chance to seize his Asian bounty.[18]

---

*On April 13, 1945, on the fourth anniversary of the Soviet-Japanese Neutrality Pact, Stalin had already declared some distance from Tokyo by refusing to prolong it for another five years. Still, as of August 1945 the neutrality pact between the USSR and Japan remained in force.

By sidelining Stalin from his ultimatum showdown with Tokyo, however, President Truman had outsmarted himself. With the USSR still neutral, the response of the Japanese cabinet to the catastrophic news from Hiroshima was to appeal to Stalin for mediation to end the war. On August 7, Japan's foreign minister, Shigenori Togo, wired an urgent telegram to his ambassador in Moscow, Naotake Sato, demanding that he meet Molotov to ascertain "the Soviets' attitude immediately." Pursuant to the Soviet-Japanese Neutrality Pact of April 1941, still in force, and perhaps fishing for sympathy after the terrible Hiroshima attack, Togo hoped that Stalin would negotiate a compromise peace. Molotov would receive him, Ambassador Sato was informed, at 5 p.m. Moscow time on August 8, which was midnight Tokyo time on August 8–9.[19]

Peace in the Far East was, of course, the last thing Stalin wanted. No sooner had the Vozhd been informed of Togo's last-minute plea for his mediation on August 7 than he decided to move up his military timetable by another forty-eight hours, as he wired Marshal Vasilevsky at Far Eastern command at 4:30 p.m. on August 7. Vasilevsky, in turn, issued urgent orders to the first Far Eastern command at 10:35 p.m., the Soviet Pacific fleet at 10:40 p.m., the Transbaikal front command at 11 p.m., and the second Far Eastern command at 11:10 p.m. to launch August Storm "at 1am on August 9, instead of at 1am Khabarovsk time on August 11," or at "6pm Moscow time on August 8"—one hour after Molotov was scheduled to receive the Japanese ambassador.[20]

Arriving at the Soviet Foreign Ministry at 5 p.m. on August 8, Ambassador Sato received the "Molotov treatment" meted out to the ambassadors of Poland, Finland, the Baltic states, and Romania in 1939–1940. Ignoring Truman's slight, Molotov informed a bewildered Sato that Japan's refusal to accept the Potsdam Declaration of July 26—a refusal premised largely on the fact that the Soviets had not signed it—meant that Japan's request "concerning [Soviet] mediation in the Far East thereby loses all basis." Stalin, Molotov lied, had been "approached" by Truman and Churchill "with a proposal" to adhere to the Potsdam Declaration and "join in the war against Japanese aggression" and thereby "save the Japanese people from the same destruction as Germany had suffered." Sato was informed that, "as of tomorrow, that is, as of August 9, the Soviet Union will consider itself in a state of war with Japan." How Stalin's declaration of war would "save the Japanese people from destruction," Molotov did not explain. Nor did Molotov explain that, by "tomorrow" he meant Khabarovsk or Tokyo time, where it was already August 9. By the time Ambassador Sato left Molotov's office to send a telegram informing Togo about the Soviet declaration of war, Soviet troops on the Transbaikal front had already crossed the Manchurian frontier, at ten minutes past midnight on August 9, 1945.[21]

The Soviet Far Eastern armies were now in a race against the clock, trying to seize as much territory and booty as they could before Japan surrendered and before American, Chinese, or British troops beat them to it. So rapidly had Stalin rushed into the war that he had not signed any kind of agreement with Chiang Kai-shek on Manchuria. Although this violated his pledges to Roosevelt and Truman, it also conveniently allowed Stalin's armies to create a fait accompli on the ground. By midday on August 9, armored divisions on the Transbaikal front had already advanced between 50 and 150 kilometers into Japanese Manchukuo, on a broad front. In central Manchuria, Marshal M. A. Purkaev's Second Far Eastern Front Armies advanced on a broad front nearly three hundred kilometers wide, although more slowly, as his men would have to cross the Amur River and the Lesser Khingan Mountains, all in a driving rainstorm. Japanese resistance was fiercest on the eastern flank, where Marshal Kirill Meretskov's First Far Eastern Front Armies fought their way from Vladivostok northwest toward Harbin and south into Korea. Even so, by day's end, Meretskov's armored corps had torn a hole thirty-five kilometers wide in Japanese lines and penetrated forward to a depth of between fifteen and twenty-two kilometers. August Storm was up and running.[22]

As if to tell Stalin to butt out of the war, President Truman authorized the use of a second atomic bomb on August 9, dropped on the secondary target of Nagasaki just past 11 a.m., less than twelve hours after the Soviet invasion of Manchuria began. By now, nearly all of the bumptious factions of Japan's ruling elite had decided to throw in the towel, although Togo and Suzuki wanted, with an eye on possible resistance in the army command, to insist on the preservation of Hirohito's ruling imperial house. It was this "one-condition" acceptance of the Potsdam ultimatum that reached Washington, DC, around 7:30 a.m. and Moscow in mid-afternoon on August 10. President Truman's refusal to accept this condition is well known, as are the harsh terms of the instrument of surrender drawn up on August 11, which were not accepted formally until Emperor Hirohito broadcast his acceptance of the Potsdam Declaration on August 15. Less familiar, though equally revealing, was Stalin's response to the Japanese offer, which was to call in Chiang Kai-shek's envoy in Moscow, T. V. Soong, and rush through an agreement recognizing Chiang's as the sole government of China and agreeing to Chinese control of Sinkiang (Xinjiang), a border region in northwest China, in exchange for Chiang's recognition of Soviet control of Outer Mongolia and a Soviet sphere of influence in Manchuria. After hammering through a compromise allowing Chinese political control of Dairen, with the Soviets controlling the port itself, and a secret protocol exempting Soviet troops from Chinese jurisdiction in Manchuria, the Sino-Soviet Treaty of Friendship and Alliance was signed on August 14, 1945, the day before Hirohito's broadcast.[23]

Truman's refusal to humor Japan's one-condition acceptance of the Potsdam Declaration on August 10 had thus given Stalin another five days to muscle Chiang Kai-shek into agreeing to his sphere of influence and to expand his Asian empire. A logistical delay in Tokyo, which led to the cease-fire order reaching Japan's field armies only on August 17, bought Stalin two more days, which was helpful, as by August 15 most of Manchuria's major cities— such as Harbin, Changchun, Kirin, Mukden, and Dairen—had not yet fallen. Marshal Vasilevsky won another two days by refusing to reply to the cease-fire request from Japan's Kwantung Army until August 19, which allowed him to issue directives on August 18 ordering the conquest of these cities. Even so, it was not enough time, as it took the Soviets two more weeks after agreeing to a cease-fire on August 19 to roll up the rest of Manchuria, even as the Soviet Pacific fleet, operating from Vladivostok, landed expeditionary forces on Sakhalin, the Kurile Islands, and on the Korean Peninsula, allowing Stalin to secure Pyongyang and the northern half of the peninsula above the thirty-eighth parallel. Not until September 5, seventeen days after the cease-fire and nearly three weeks after Hirohito's surrender broadcast, did the Soviet advance stop, at the Habomai Islands just off the Hokkaido coast.[24]

It was no accident that Hokkaido and the thirty-eighth parallel in Korea marked the boundaries of Stalin's new Asian empire. Giving the lie to Roosevelt's defenders who claim that there was little the British and Americans could have done to stop the spread of Communism, whether in Europe or Asia, because of the all-conquering Red Army, Stalin ordered his commanders to stop where they did because President Truman and his military advisers had drawn lines and said the Russians must not cross them. As Truman wrote Stalin on August 16, the day after Hirohito's surrender, US commanders had agreed that all Japanese forces "within Manchuria and Korea north of 38 degrees north latitude and Karafuto [Sakhalin] shall surrender to the Commander in Chief of Soviet Forces in the Far East." In fact, the Red Army arrived in North Korea before the Americans landed troops in the southern half of the peninsula at Incheon (on September 7), and the Soviets could probably have advanced past the thirty-eighth parallel had Stalin given the order. The same was true of Hokkaido, the northernmost of Japan's home islands, where neither side had yet landed troops when, in his reply to Truman on August 16, Stalin proposed, pursuant to the trial balloon he had floated with Hopkins back in May, to occupy and take the surrender of Japanese troops "in the northern half of Hokkaido," with a demarcation line to be drawn between Rumoi

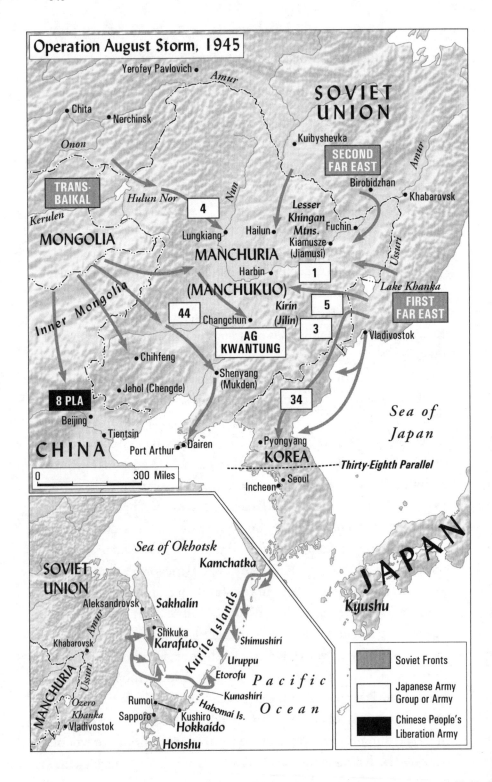

Operation August Storm, 1945

Yerofey Pavlovich

Amur

SOVIET
UNION

Chita • Nerchinsk

Kuibyshevka

Onon

SECOND
FAR EAST

Birobidzhan

Khabarovsk

TRANS-
BAIKAL

Hulun Nor

Nun

Lesser
Khingan
Mtns. Fuchin

Amur

Kerulen

4

Lungkiang • Hailun •

Kiamusze
(Jiamusi)

MONGOLIA

MANCHURIA

Harbin •

1

Ussuri

(MANCHUKUO)

Lake Khanka

Inner Mongolia

Kirin
(Jilin)

5

FIRST
FAR EAST

44 Changchun •

3

AG
KWANTUNG

Vladivostok •

Chihfeng •

Shenyang
(Mukden)

8 PLA

Jehol (Chengde) •

34

*Sea of
Japan*

Beijing •

Tientsin •

Port Arthur • Dairen

• Pyongyang

KOREA

Thirty-Eighth Parallel

0 ————— 300 Miles

CHINA

Incheon • • Seoul

Sea of Okhotsk

Kamchatka

SOVIET
UNION

Aleksandrovsk • *Sakhalin*

Kurile Islands

Shimushiri

Amur

Shikuka
Karafuto

Uruppu

Pacific

Khabarovsk

Etorofu

MANCHURIA

Ussuri

Kunashiri

*Ozero
Khanka*

Rumoi •

Habomai Is.

Ocean

• Vladivostok

Sapporo • Kushiro

Hokkaido

Honshu

JAPAN

Kyushu

Soviet Fronts

Japanese Army
Group or Army

Chinese People's
Liberation Army

on the western coast and Kushiro on the eastern coast. We know that Stalin was serious about Hokkaido, because on August 18 Vasilevsky ordered Meretskov, commander of the first Far Eastern front, to be ready to "to occupy the northern half of Hokkaido" by September 1, while awaiting final orders from Stalin. But Truman was not Roosevelt. On August 18, he said no. In retaliation, the Vozhd denied Truman's request for an air base in the Kurile Islands. The Soviet-American frontier in Asia was set.[25]

Truman's firmness saved about 3.5 million Japanese residents of Hokkaido and nearly 20 million Koreans living south of the thirty-eighth parallel from falling into Stalin's clutches in 1945. It is difficult to imagine Roosevelt, had he lived, taking a similarly strong stand on Soviet expansion. Nonetheless, Stalin's armies had still conquered 40 million new subjects for Soviet Communism in Manchuria alone, along with 640,000 Japanese war prisoners shipped off to Soviet labor camps in Siberia—of whom more than 62,000 would die in captivity—and nearly $2 billion worth of industrial property and assorted Manchurian war booty shipped back to the USSR in 50,000 railway cars. The story of the mass rapes of Japanese women in Manchuria by the Russian conquerors, including their use as what one military historian has called a "Soviet version of comfort women," is only now coming out.[26]

Given that the Soviet Far Eastern armies had been in a strong position vis-à-vis Japanese Manchukuo back in 1939, it is conceivable that some of Stalin's Asian gains might have been attained eventually even without the lend-lease aid lavished on the Red Army, if much more slowly and at a much heavier human and material price. The Soviet conquest was also made easier by the fact that, by the time Stalin entered the war in August 1945, Japan had already transferred more than a million troops from China and Manchuria back to the home islands. The combination of four years of the US Navy, Army, and Air Force softening up Japan while the USSR had been neutral and the massive amounts of armor, motor fuel, and warplanes shipped to Vladivostok (especially over the last fourteen months of the Pacific war) allowed Stalin to conquer an area larger than France and Germany combined in less than a month. Soviet gains in August Storm, like the cheap victories in Eastern Europe during the Molotov-Ribbentrop period, came at almost no cost to Stalin's treasury and with relatively light casualties (36,653 in all, of which 12,103 were deaths) compared to earlier Soviet campaigning in both Asia circa 1938–1939 and Europe from 1941 to 1945. In this way, Roosevelt's unilateral and unreciprocated generosity helped Josef Stalin plant the red flag over northern Asia, paving the way for Mao's triumph in China and the standoff in Korea that endures to this day.[27]

Epilogue

Stalin's Slave Empire and the Price of Victory

In Western Europe, VE Day is remembered fondly (if selectively) as a joyous time of liberation, with American GIs passing around cigarettes and candy while stealing kisses from the local beauties. In Eastern Europe and northern Asia, the Allied victory in the Second World War brought only more pain, as world war turned into a series of civil wars. In Poland, the NKVD and Red Army continued slaughtering or deporting AK fighters well into 1946. In November 1945, AK resistance in Liski, in former East Prussia, grew so intense that the Red Army sent in nine divisions to crush Polish rebels. In December 1945, six months after the war in Europe supposedly ended, the Soviets started bombing AK strongholds from the air. Lithuanian and other Baltic partisans killed at least twenty thousand Soviet troops between the "liberation" of the region in 1944 and the petering out of the last serious resistance in 1948. In Ukraine, as Khrushchev, the man overseeing the repression of partisan resistance, later admitted, "after the war, we lost thousands of men in a bitter struggle between the Ukrainian nationalists and the forces of Soviet power."[1]

These postwar wars allowed Stalin's empire to absorb another huge wave of forced-labor inmates. Stalin's Gulag camps had been massively reinforced in the period of "peaceful expansion" in 1939–1941 with Poles, Latvians, Estonians, Lithuanians, Finns, and Romanians. The camps had been fattened again in 1943–1944 with Crimean Tatars, Volga Germans, Circassian Muslims, and Poles; in 1944–1948 with an influx of conquered Ukrainians, Balts,

Hungarians, Romanians (again), Poles (again), and almost two million Germans; and, after August 1945, nearly a million Japanese, Mongolians, and Koreans. This was not even to reckon with the fate of millions of ex-Soviet POWs (many tens of thousands actually Cossack or White Russian émigrés who had never been Soviet subjects), who were sent home to certain imprisonment and forced labor, if not summary execution—with ancillary punishments meted out to their families as well. Thus began a renewed period of Soviet terror, fed by increasing paranoia about Jews and other pro-Western cosmopolitans, that would last until Stalin's death in 1953.

Terrible as the fate of Poland and Eastern Europe was, the most lasting consequence of Stalin's victories in 1945 was the impetus they had given to Communist expansion in Asia, above all in China. It is true that Stalin agreed to recognize Chiang's nationalist government in the Sino-Soviet agreement of August 14, 1945, and to give it formal political control over Manchuria—a deal initially seen by Mao and the Chinese Communists as a betrayal. On August 20, Stalin even ordered Mao to avoid armed confrontations with Chiang's forces. Chiang was confident enough of Stalin's good faith that he invited Mao to Chungking in September and coaxed a pledge out of him that the Communists would "stop the civil war" and "unite under the leadership of Chairman Chiang to build a modern China." With Chiang's government recognized by all the great powers and supported materially by the United States, it appeared that Stalin would have to settle for a sphere of influence in Manchuria, with a pro-American government south of it. Such, at any rate, was the hope of the Truman administration.[2]

With the stakes this high, Stalin was never likely to settle. Even while Stalin recognized Chiang's government, Red Army commanders in Manchuria and Outer Mongolia established contact with Mao's armies and began sharing arms with the Chinese Communists from stocks they had confiscated from the Kwantung Army after Japan surrendered. The Russians did not turn everything over, keeping much of the best equipment for themselves.

Nonetheless, Mao's armies received 700,000 rifles, 8,989 machine guns, 1,436 field artillery pieces, 11,052 grenade launchers, 3,078 trucks, 14,777 horses, 21,084 supply vehicles, 860 warplanes, 815 specialized vehicles, and 287 command cars. Stalin also agreed to let Mao's men take over Kalgan, a critical gateway in the Great Wall of China guarding the northern approaches to Beijing. It had been a key logistical hub of the Kwantung Army, who had left behind huge stores of weapons and vehicles. We now know that Mao's pledge of unity with Chiang on September 18 was phony, because the day before he had received orders from Stalin to "expand towards the north" into Soviet-occupied Manchuria, orders Mao passed on to his armies after returning to Yan'an on September 19. His statement in Chungking, Mao assured his generals, was "a mere scrap of paper." On October 4, 1945, Stalin ordered Mao to move his forces from southern China into the north and Manchuria, promising that Red Army commanders would provide arms for three hundred thousand of Mao's men. The idea was to lure Chiang's forces north, against the now lavishly supplied Maoist army.[3]

It worked. Although Chiang's American advisers, including Vinegar Joe Stilwell's successor General Albert Wedemeyer, urged him to avoid the trap, in October 1945 Chiang moved his troops north and resumed the Chinese Civil War. Stalin now showed his true colors, closing all Manchurian ports to nationalist forces. As an added insult, the Vozhd informed Chiang on October 17 that he would not share any captured Japanese war matériel with the Chinese government and that he would not be withdrawing Soviet troops from Chinese territory three months after the war as he had pledged to do in the Sino-Soviet agreement of August. The Soviet occupation of Manchuria lasted until April 1946, which gave Stalin's armies more than enough time to cart off nearly $2 billion worth of war booty—leaving one of Asia's key industrial areas in ruins—and to make sure that, by the time the Red Army left, Mao's armies were firmly in control. Stalin thus ensured that Manchuria, the richest region in China, would be controlled not

by the Chinese national government that had fought for it ever
since Japan invaded in 1931, but by a friendly Communist regime:
that of Mao, whose men had not fought there (or anywhere else in
China against Japanese forces, for that matter) and should therefore have had no claim on it.[4]

Had the US government been as devoted to Chiang's cause
as Stalin was to Mao's, the loss of Manchuria would not necessarily have been fatal to the Kuomintang. But the Truman administration, despite being less woolly minded about Stalin than
Roosevelt's had been, was snowed under in China just the same.
In a pattern similar to the British betrayal of Mihailović in Yugoslavia, US aid to Chungking was made conditional on Chiang
inviting Mao into his government, notwithstanding the fact that
the two men were fighting a civil war over China's future. On
September 15, 1945—when Mao was in Chungking pretending to
play nice—the US government instructed Wedemeyer to inform
Chiang "that military assistance furnished by the United States
would not repeat *not* be diverted for use in fratricidal warfare or to
support undemocratic administration." On November 10, a Joint
Chiefs of Staff directive stipulated that "American military aid to
China will cease immediately if evidence compels the U.S. government to believe that [Chinese troops] receiving such aid are using
it . . . to conduct civil war." In this vein, Truman sent General Marshall to Chungking in December 1945 to broker a coalition government between Chiang and Mao, two mortal political enemies
whose civil war had just resumed. Marshall even sent American
officers to Kalgan—the Great Wall gateway city Stalin had handed
over to Mao—to train Mao's Chinese Communist soldiers. On
Marshall's watch, US financial aid to Chungking was slow-walked
and arms shipments kept to a trickle and then cut off entirely in
September 1946. By 1947, the proxy conflict in China was wholly
one-sided, with Stalin providing Mao with whatever he needed,
including new Soviet tanks and artillery, and the United States
leaving Chiang to his own devices and forbidding him to use American arms against Mao's Communists. In view of the US cutoff of

Chungking in 1946 and Mao's ever-increasing arms intake from the Soviet Union by way of Communized Manchuria, the mystery is not that Mao won the Chinese Civil War, but that it took him three more years to do so.[5]

There is grim irony in the timing of the final US betrayal of Chiang, which coincided with the belated awakening of the United States and Britain to the Communist threat in Europe. Churchill's celebrated Iron Curtain speech, delivered at Truman's side in Fulton, Missouri, on March 5, 1946, helped sell the American heartland on the task of stemming Soviet expansion in Europe—a policy that took root with the so-called Truman Doctrine in March 1947, with the United States taking up the banner of supporting "free peoples" (in the first instance, Greece and Turkey) in their struggle against Communist totalitarianism. In the months after Churchill's speech, Washington cut off arms shipments to Chiang Kai-shek. There was no Truman Doctrine for China.

Had Churchill been at the helm in Washington, with the wealth and armed might Truman had at his disposal, it is possible to imagine a Cold War awakening occurring sooner. Churchill had road tested his "Iron Curtain" phrase with Truman as early as May 12, 1945, trying to convince the president to be firmer with Stalin on Poland. In that heady, anxious time after VE Day, Churchill had even instructed his Chiefs of Staff to prepare contingency plans for an attack on Soviet positions in Eastern Europe in order to win "a square deal for Poland," with a prospective launch date of July 1, 1945, a plan Churchill's generals dubbed Operation Unthinkable. Although these reckless plans remained mercifully secret at the time, now that we know about them, Britain's voters can perhaps be forgiven for voting Churchill's Tories out of office in the general elections of July 5, 1945, with the last votes counted while Churchill was in Potsdam.[6]

Veering from one extreme to the other, Churchill had moved from proactively assigning Baltic spheres of influence to Stalin in 1939—a time when the Soviet leader was allied to Hitler and had not yet occupied his Baltic neighbors—to preparing for all-out war

with Stalin over the latter's sphere of influence in Poland now that
Hitler was defeated and Stalin was already occupying that country.
The problem with this mercurial approach to statecraft was not
that Churchill's proposals were all misguided, but that they were
poorly timed. The time to confront Soviet aggression in Eastern
Europe was in 1939–1940, when Stalin was Hitler's odious partner
in crime and the Red Army was weak enough that Stalin did not
dare invade Poland until the Polish Army was already defeated. To
be sure, Britain and France would have been hard pressed to save
Poland then, but in truth they had not even tried. Taking a stand
in Finland would have given moral point to the European war,
possibly drawing the United States and other powers, including
pro-Axis Hungary and Fascist Italy, into a broad international coalition against totalitarian aggression. Even as late as the Teheran
conference in November 1943, a firmer stand could have made a
real difference, saving the Balkans and much of Eastern Europe
from Stalin's armies. Churchill's Mediterranean gambit is usually
dismissed as a fantasy, but it made far more strategic sense than his
other wartime inspirations. Of course, Roosevelt's decision to side
with Stalin and throw everything into Overlord doomed it. What
is more interesting is Churchill's abandonment of his own client
in Yugoslavia just weeks before Teheran, which consigned the
country to decades of Communist oppression. For all the postwar
claims of Fitzroy Maclean and Churchill that their backing of Tito
had created a Trojan horse in the Soviet camp in the Balkans, the
bitter fruit of their tag-team betrayal of the Chetniks came to harvest in August 1945 and June–July 1946, when Mihailović and his
officers were rounded up and condemned to death for treason in
a series of show trials,* on the basis of Communist talking points
Maclean and Churchill had adopted as their own in 1943.[7]

Viewed at a distance of three-quarters of a century, it seems
clear now that Churchill and Roosevelt became intoxicated with

---

* Mihailović's conviction was overturned by the Serbian government in
2015.

Stalin out of the emotional shock of the Barbarossa invasion, only to awaken with a painful hangover once Hitler's armies went down to defeat. Even Truman, although never as taken in as his predecessor, needed time to wake up to the mounting threat of Soviet expansion before he put his foot down in Asia. The peoples of South Korea and Hokkaido can be grateful that Truman realized it as soon as he did, although it was not soon enough for the peoples of Manchuria and, later, China, North Korea, Sakhalin, the Kuriles, and Europe east of the Elbe.

At least some of the Stalinophilia that overcame Washington and London between 1941 and 1945 can be attributed to Soviet agents of influence in the US and British governments. Purges of Russia hands in the US State Department carried out in 1937 and 1943 deprived Roosevelt of informed advice on Stalin and his foreign policy. Soviet agents in Cairo and the BBC helped ruin Mihailović's reputation, even as Harry Dexter White got his hands into everything from the "Hull note" ultimatum to Japan in November 1941 to the formation of the devastating Morgenthau Plan. Harry Hopkins, if not an NKVD asset like White then certainly an enthusiastic supporter of the USSR, almost single-handedly oversaw the Soviet lend-lease program that fed, armed, and provisioned the Red Army and Russian war industry for four years, arguably contributing more than any of Stalin's generals to the Soviet victories over Germany and Japan. Soviet agents in the State Department helped secure the dismissal of anti-Communist Asian experts such as Undersecretary of State Joseph Grew, purged in August 1945; Eugene Doonan, head of the Far Eastern division, purged alongside Grew; US ambassador to China Patrick Hurley, who resigned in November 1945 in protest of growing Communist influence over China policy; and Albert Wedemeyer, replaced as Chiang's top military adviser in December 1945 by George Marshall, who proceeded to sabotage the nationalist cause every way he could. Marshall's antipathy toward Chiang Kai-shek was, by then, the default position among policymakers in Washington, owing to the yearslong Communist smear campaign that had progressively ruined Chiang's (never sterling) reputation in the United States.[8]

All this is true. Nonetheless, it was Roosevelt and Churchill themselves who made the critical decisions that turned the conflict into Stalin's war, beginning with their unconditional pledges of armed and material support for the USSR after Barbarossa. The usual defense for this unreciprocated generosity is that supplying the Red Army was the best way of defeating Hitler and saving American and British lives. In Britain at least, at war with Hitler since 1939, there was a logical reason to respond to Barbarossa by supporting the Soviet war effort, paying the Red Army almost as a mercenary force to take pressure off the overmatched British armies. But this never made much sense in the American case, as the United States was not at war with Germany when Roosevelt extended Stalin his lifeline in 1941 and could just as easily have taken a neutral position on the German-Soviet conflict. Even after Pearl Harbor and Hitler's foolish declaration of war on the United States, Roosevelt's "Germany first" decision—prioritizing Stalin's war-fighting needs with shipping, production, and naval escorts over those of the war against Japan—was far from obvious and was deeply resented at the time by US Pacific commanders like General Douglas MacArthur.

Nor is there any evidence that the Red Army fought more efficiently than British or American soldiers would have done with the tens of millions of tons of war matériel sent to Stalin. Indeed, the lopsided loss ratios on the eastern front from 1941 to 1945 suggest the opposite. Had less lend-lease aid been sent to Stalin, or if shipments had been curtailed or stopped in 1943 following the sunset clause of the original statute, either on the June 30 cutoff date or after the Soviet victory at Kursk, the Red Army would surely have been slower to advance westward into Europe—an advance NATO was later expressly created to prevent. The idea that there was no choice but to send Stalin $11 billion in war matériel, industrial equipment and inputs, technology transfer, and intellectual property—the equivalent of well over $1 trillion today—without demanding anything in return, is refuted by the loan terms Roosevelt offered Churchill, from the extortionate bases-for-destroyers deal of 1940 to the steep interest charged for lend-lease and other war loans. It is also refuted by the treatment of China, which received barely a tenth the lend-lease aid Stalin did, and nearly all of that after the Burma Road was finally opened in January 1945, far too late to make an appreciable difference in the outcome of the Pacific war. When it counted, in 1943–1944, China received only 1 to 2 percent of what Soviet Russia received, despite Chiang having an infinitely greater moral claim to American aid than Stalin and just as strong a strategic claim, based on the huge number of Japanese divisions he was tying down despite being deprived of arms. Because "world peace"—the repayment condition applied in the master agreement of June 1942—remained out of reach, all Soviet wartime debts were written off for a song in 1951, at two pennies on the dollar. Britain paid its debts in full, with interest, until 2006.[9]

Of course, we cannot know what would have happened if Roosevelt had listened to American majority opinion and congressional critics in 1941 and let Hitler and Stalin fight it out without lend-lease aid tilting the balance on the eastern front. It is hard to imagine, however, that it could have been all that much worse than what did happen: from the jaw-droppingly horrendous Russian casualties and civilian suffering epitomized in the terrible nine-hundred-day siege of Leningrad; to the devastation of a continent through four years of intensifying land warfare and aerial bombardment; to the cascading atrocities and horrors on the eastern front bloodlands, culminating in the Nazis' destruction of European Jewry; to the mass rapes, deportations, and looting of Eastern Europe and the Balkans after the Red Army rolled in on American trucks to squat in the ruins.

To the extent the Western Allies liberated France, Italy, and the Low Countries from Nazi rule (and prevented Soviet incursions there) and freed survivors in German concentration camps located west of the Elbe (if not the very worst ones, which were mostly in occupied Poland and thus liberated by the Soviets), the war can be said to have accomplished something worthwhile in the end—if at a butcher's bill on all sides so high as to be almost unthinkable today. But even this comparatively positive aspect of the story raises the question of why the US-British coalition forces devoted so much war production, shipping tonnage, and naval escort strength to support the Red Army's inefficient and brutal march forward, rather than fighting their way into Europe sooner to liberate the Balkans and the death camps of Eastern Europe themselves, especially in view of the intelligence advantage conferred on the Western Allies by the breaking of the Germans' Enigma and other encryption systems by Britain's Ultra team at Bletchley Park in 1941, the story of which was first revealed to the world in 1974.[10]

Still more uncomfortable questions surround matters such as Britain's misleading promises to Poland in 1939, which encouraged Polish leaders to resist Hitler on the largely mistaken understanding that Britain and France would render them active armed assistance against Germany; the Allies' rejection of German peace feelers in October 1939, after the fall of Poland; Churchill's refusal to parley in June–July 1940, after the fall of Norway, France, and the Low Countries; his contemptuous treatment of the Hess mission in May 1941, however satisfying this was as a humiliation of Hitler at a time when Britain had not yet won a battle in the war; and Roosevelt's brusque dismissal of the negotiating offers coming in from Canaris and other German resistance figures in 1943. The pretext of all of these peace feelers, whether coming from Hitler or his would-be successors, was that Germany would renounce gains in Western Europe in exchange for a free hand in Poland and the East—or, in the Canaris version, Germany would give up Poland too. If the point of the war against Hitler was to save Western Europe from foreign subjugation, this could have been done at infinitely less human and material cost at the negotiating table. If the point was to save Poland and Eastern Europe from foreign subjugation, then the war was an abysmal failure.

In the greatest single injustice of the postwar settlement, to this day, Poland, the country most obviously deserving of reparations, has received none from Germany or Russia, even while Russia—the invader and conqueror—exacted reparations in cash or in kind from Poland and all the other countries Stalin occupied in 1945. As recently as 2017, Warsaw levied a reparations claim on Berlin, only to be informed by the chancellor's office that the Polish government waived its right to German reparations in 1953, when it was an occupied Soviet satellite state.[11]

We could say much the same about the war in Asia. If the Pacific conflict was about anything, it was about Manchuria and north China—Japan's successive invasions of which, in 1931 and 1937, resulted in the withdrawal of the country from the League of Nations, the imposition of sanctions, and so on. And yet the result of Roosevelt's wartime agreements with Stalin was to assign Manchuria and north China to the USSR. The United States then approved, funded, and armed the Soviet invasion that led North Korea, Manchuria, and ultimately all of China (except Taiwan) to come under Communist rule. This was a perverse outcome of a war fought to free these areas from oppression. Even the Asian countries liberated from Japanese rule that were outside Stalin's immediate reach—such as Thailand, Indochina, the Philippines, Malaysia, and Indonesia—though long coveted by Japanese imperialists and temptingly ill-defended after the collapse of France and the Netherlands in 1940, were only occupied by Japan after Pearl Harbor. That is, they were occupied after the United States had applied a de facto oil embargo on Japan in retaliation for its behavior in Manchuria and north China, culminating in the "Hull note" ultimatum we now know to have been authored by a Soviet agent trying to goad the United States into war with Japan. If the point of the Pacific war was to free these countries from occupation, this could have been accomplished more easily at the negotiating table in 1941, before they had been occupied, than with a yearslong war of attrition culminating in the detonation of two atomic bombs and a destructive Soviet invasion of northern Asia. If the point was to liberate Manchuria and north China, then, as in Eastern Europe, the war was a failure.

None of this is to cast shade on the heroism of the Soviet and Allied soldiers who fought, bled, and died in the wars against Nazi Germany, Fascist Italy (until 1943), and Japan. On all fronts, Allied soldiers fought under terrible conditions with courage and honor against enemies who showed them no mercy, who mistreated war prisoners, and who committed such grave and metastasizing atrocities between 1937 and 1945 as to salve the conscience of the men who killed and defeated them, despite uneasy Western memories about the firebombing of Hamburg, Dresden, and Tokyo and the atomic bombing of Hiroshima and Nagasaki (whether Soviet soldiers felt similar uneasiness about the atrocities they committed in Eastern Europe, Germany, and Manchuria is less clear). Still, in view of the disappointing returns, it is worth asking whether the sacrifices of millions of Poles, Britons, Frenchmen, Canadians, Australians, Russians, Americans, and others were necessary in the first place. Even once the struggle was joined, it is fair to ask whether it needed to be prolonged to the calamitous end with unconditional surrender, the Morgenthau Plan, and the inflexibility of both Truman and Stalin on Japanese surrender terms.

The roseate glow of the "Good War" has saved its victorious statesmen from the scrutiny applied to their World War I counterparts who led the men into the trenches. Perhaps the real reason why Stalin, Churchill, and Roosevelt, unlike Alexander Haig and David Lloyd George, were never seen as "donkeys leading lions to slaughter" is that they had better publicists. Stalin's opportunistic aggression in 1939–1940 and his lopsidedly offensive deployment of armor and warplanes near the German Reich in 1941 nearly led to the ignominious collapse of his empire after the Red Army's catastrophic defeats in 1941–1942, even while his cruel policies toward Soviet civilians, retreating soldiers, deserters, and prisoners of war exacerbated the already frightening losses of a war that cost the lives of tens of millions of his subjects, none of whom were

EPILOGUE   663

consulted at any point for their views. At least Churchill, in his "we shall never surrender" speech to the House of Commons in June 1940, was honest in demanding that Britons be willing to sacrifice their lives (and later, their empire) in order to avoid staining national honor by negotiating with Hitler. Roosevelt, by contrast, had promised Americans that October that their "boys are not going to be sent into any foreign wars," shortly before sending Wild Bill Donovan on a mission to recruit Balkan belligerents into a war the United States hadn't even joined yet and launching the lend-lease program for Britain and Soviet Russia, which amounted to belligerence in all but name. Whatever Americans voted for in 1940, it was not to finance, produce weapons for, and hire millions of Russians as (in effect) mercenaries, or to have their sons fight a global war to the death to make much of Europe and Asia safe for Communism.

Stalin, suspicious to the end, never really understood why the hated Anglo-Saxons threw him the lend-lease life raft, but he perceived quickly that their decision "to render aid to our country," as he noted in his July 1941 radio address, brought "tremendous political gain [to] the USSR" and would "form the basis for the development of decisive military successes of the Red Army." This capitalist lifeline allowed the Red Army to weather the crisis of October 1941, mount its first counteroffensive outside Moscow in December of that year, mount the mobile flanking operation that encircled the German Sixth Army at Stalingrad in 1942, see off the final German offensive at Kursk in 1943, mount the gigantic armored offensives of 1944 and 1945 into Poland and Germany, and, in a final crescendo, conquer most of northern Asia in a few weeks in August 1945.[12]

By objective measures of territory conquered and war booty seized, Stalin was the victor in both Europe and Asia, and no one else came close. The three Axis powers were crushed utterly. France, although restored after the humiliation of 1940, was a withered wreck and would soon lose its empire. Britain was bankrupt and moribund. The United States, relatively untouched by the conflict at home, emerged in a strong position, inheriting the infrastructure of the British Empire by financial default and seeing two industrial competitors, Japan and Germany, flattened. Even so, the proto-Keynesian fallback argument one sometimes hears—that the mobilization of the "arsenal of democracy" brought the United States (and later world) economy out of the Depression in a way Roosevelt's New Deal did not—rests ultimately on the broken-window fallacy identified by Frédéric Bastiat. It is true that people were put to work building weapons, trucks, tanks, ships, aircraft carriers, and warplanes, and that technological advances came rapidly, culminating in the Manhattan Project. Perhaps, absent this Keynesian war stimulus in Washington, the world might have been deprived, for a time, of the atomic age, including peaceful nuclear energy. But surely there were more constructive uses to which American economic energy, productivity, and ingenuity could have been harnessed between 1940 and 1945 than incinerating tens of thousands of factories and hundreds of cities from Hamburg to Tokyo, as well as supplying and fueling Stalin's marauding armies as they plundered prime economic real estate from Berlin to Beijing?

Roosevelt's admirers claim that the spirit of the Atlantic Charter lived on in the United Nations. As Serhii Plokhy argues in *Yalta*, Stalin, by agreeing to join the UN, unwittingly helped to "establish the foundations of a world order in which the United States would play a leading role." There is something to this, but the claim is weakened by Stalin's securing of a Soviet veto on the Security Council, which defanged the US-led bloc from the start, and of two extra votes in the General Assembly, which helped turn that body into a megaphone of anti-Americanism. Moreover, the idea that the United States needed Soviet endorsement of the UN to play a "leading role" in world affairs, and that this was a triumph of American diplomacy at Yalta, is dubious. With or without Yalta and the UN—with or without fighting in the Second World War, for that matter—the United States would have been an economic powerhouse and a world power.[13]

The notion that a great American victory was achieved in 1945 is hard to square with the strategic reality of the Cold War, which required a gargantuan expenditure over decades merely to hold the line at the Fulda Gap before the USSR finally collapsed in 1991. That Germany and Japan, supposedly mortal enemies of the United States in 1941, became crucial American partners in the Cold War, raises once more the question of what the point of the first conflict was. Two militaristic empires and would-be regional hegemons were defeated and turned into democracies (or one and a half, if we discount Sovietized East Germany). But another militaristic empire, after gorging on lend-lease aid and the war booty won with it, was transformed into a superpower with far greater global reach and influence than Germany or Japan had ever enjoyed. At home, the price Americans paid for this victory was the erosion of their own civil liberties, with an ever-expanding security state contrary to the country's founding principles and stated ideals, which bears increasing resemblance to the Soviet version they struggled against.

The thanks Americans received for their lend-lease generosity enabling Stalin's conquests was nicely illustrated in the addition of two new categories of "enemies of the people" to Article 58 of the Soviet legal codebook after the war: VAD, for "admirer of American democracy," and VAT, for "admirer of American technology"—this last category rich with irony after Stalin's purchasing agents in Washington had spent four years vacuuming up American war-industrial secrets and patents. To ramp up paranoia and xenophobia, a new agitprop campaign was launched, warning high-level Soviet operatives that, in the words of a secret policeman stationed in Budapest, "while for some people, possibly, the war is over, for us *Chekists* the real war, to bring about the final destruction of the capitalist world, has only just begun."[14]

The ultimate price of victory was paid by the tens of millions of involuntary subjects of Stalin's satellite regimes in Europe and Asia, including Maoist China, along with the millions of Soviet dissidents, returned Soviet POWs, and captured war prisoners who were herded into Gulag camps from the Arctic gold and platinum mines of Vorkuta to the open-air uranium strip mines of Stavropol and Siberia. For subjects of his expanding slave empire, Stalin's war did not end in 1945. Decades of oppression and new forms of terror were still to come.

Acknowledgments

WRITING ABOUT THE Second World War, after so many years wrestling with the First, feels like returning to an old friend. I first studied the Soviet-German clash on the eastern front in a summer research project sponsored by the National Endowment for the Humanities a quarter century ago. The impetus came from my high school history teachers, Debbie Doyle, who helped advise the project, and Brian Bell, who gave me a signed copy of Charles Mee's book on Potsdam to spur me on—a book I am proud to say I cite in the pages that follow. It was my great fortune that this project coincided with a Library of Congress exhibit in summer 1992 of *Revelations from the Russian Archives*, which sparked a decades-long fascination with the secrets of Soviet history now available to Western researchers. So let me salute two of the best teachers I know, who inspired my abiding love of history.

On a sadder note, it pains me deeply that I will not be able to share this book with Norman Stone, who passed away in June 2019. Norman was a teacher and mentor, a valued colleague, and above all a great friend, who gave me my first real job in academe and never stopped believing in me. I owe a great deal of my knowledge of the First World War, of Russia and Turkey and Central Europe and much else besides, to Norman, and I wish dearly that he could have read this book and let me know what he thought. I know that Norman's other colleagues from Bilkent and Koç, such as Ömer Koç, Ali Doğramaci, Sergei Podbolotov, Hasan Ali Karaşar, and Onur İşçi—colleagues whose counsel and support has been invaluable to me over the years—feel the same way as I do about our dear departed friend. Rest in peace.

I found more specific inspiration for *Stalin's War* from Nikolai Tolstoy, a fearless historian who unearthed many buried secrets in his pioneering studies of the *Victims of Yalta* (1977) and *Stalin's Secret War* (1981), both published at a time when the Soviet archives were still off limits to Westerners. Count Tolstoy has been kind enough to share his expertise and wisdom on this project, and I am grateful for his time and support.

There are many other courageous scholars who have probed the mysteries of Soviet foreign policy and military planning under Stalin before me, including a number of Russians who must now, sadly, write under pseudonyms. Of these, I must single out Mark Solonin, who generously shared some of his research, including archival references I was able to follow up on myself in Moscow. Slightly less anonymous is Richard Raack, an American scholar who now publishes mostly in obscure Polish and Central European journals, to the detriment of Western historians who pay much less attention to his work on Stalinist foreign policy than they should. Although Professor Raack's health issues have prevented us from meeting in person, he was game enough to write and speak by phone on numerous occasions, and I am grateful for his time and advice.

I have also received a great deal of practical help along the way. Getting into Russian archives, especially those run by government agencies such as the Foreign Ministry, is getting much harder these days. I would not have been able to manage it without guidance from Olga Pavlenko, Vladimir Pechatnov, and above all Yuri Rogoulev. David Reynolds and David Woolner provided the introductions to Yuri and Vladimir. Sam Hirst, Katia Prokopova, and Daniel Repko provided invaluable logistical help during my extended Moscow visits. Kasia Kalinowska was a wonderful guide to Warsaw and provided essential translation help in the Polish archives. Bogdan Musial shared some of his incomparable research on Poland and Eastern Europe in the war and on Stalin's looting operations. Professor Norihiro Naganawa invited me to a stimulating conference in Hokkaido, by way of Tokyo, and introduced me to professors David Wolff and Asahiko Shirakizawa, who kindly guided me through the splendid resources of the Slavic-Eurasian Research Center of Hokkaido University on Soviet-Japanese relations. Diana West shared tips from her own research in Washington. Mitchell Levinson tracked down an obscure Soviet Army manual in Saint Petersburg. Mike Neiberg introduced me to the wonders of the "Wild Bill Donovan" collection at the US Army War College in Carlisle, Pennsylvania. None of these generous souls, I should emphasize, bear responsibility for the conclusions I have drawn from the material they kindly helped me to exploit.

A book this ambitious, requiring archival work in a half dozen countries, including multiple extended visits to Russia, would not have been possible without generous financial support from Bard College, in particular the Bard Research Fund. For this I owe thanks to President Leon Botstein, former dean Rebecca Thomas, and the current dean, Deirdre d'Albertis. My Bard colleagues in Russian and Eurasian studies, Olga Voronina, Marina Kostalevsky, Oleg Minin, Liz Frank, Jonathan Becker, and Jonathan Brent, have been exceedingly generous with their time. My colleagues in history and politics, including Greg Moynahan, Rob Culp, Michelle Murray, and Omar Encarnacion, have indulged my teaching absences on recent research sabbaticals. Richard Aldous has been an invaluable friend and guide, a prince among colleagues.

At the Hoover Archives in Stanford, California, Linda Bernard, Carol Leadenham, and Elena Danielson have been advisers and friends since my undergraduate days. I hope to do them proud with another book drawing heavily on original material from their incomparable archive, which is a treasure trove of historical delights.

My agent, Andrew Lownie, has worked tirelessly for this book. Simon Winder, at Penguin in London, and Lara Heimert and Claire Potter, of Basic Books in New York, are the best editors a writer can hope for. Roger Labrie helped clean up my prose. My wife, Nesrin, and my lovely children, Ayla and Errol, have indulged my obsessive writing schedule. Nesrin also patiently read through a manuscript even longer than the ones I usually write. I do hope my children will understand someday why I spent so much time thinking and writing about Josef Stalin, who is much less cheerful and rewarding company than they are. For now, let me explain to them that writing history is what I love to do, and that I hope this passion carries through to them when, once these inveterate young readers are old enough, they give my book a try.

Abbreviations

AAN	Archiwum Akt Nowych w Warszawie (Archive of New or Contemporary Files). Warsaw, Poland.
AVPRF	Arkhiv Vneshnei Politiki Rossiiskoi Federatsii (Archive of the Foreign Policy of the Russian Federation). Moscow, Russia.
BA/MA	Bundesarchiv, Militärabteilung (Military Department of the German Federal Archives). Freiburg, Germany.
BSA	Bulgarian State Archives. Sofia, Bulgaria.
FDR Library	Franklin D. Roosevelt Presidential Library and Museum. Hyde Park, New York.
GARF	Gosudarstvennyi Arkhiv Rossiiskoi Federatsii (Government Archive of the Russian Federation). Moscow, Russia.
Hoover	Hoover Institution Archives. Stanford, California.
MSZ	Archiwum Ministerstwo Spraw Zagranicznych (Archives of the Polish Foreign Ministry). Warsaw, Poland.
NAA	National Archives Annex. College Park, Maryland.
PAAA	Politisches Archiv des Auswärtigen Amts (Political Archive of the German Foreign Ministry). Berlin, Germany.

PRO   National Archives of the United Kingdom. Kew
               Gardens, London, UK.*

QO   Archives of the Quai d'Orsay. Paris, France.

RGAE   Rossiiskii Gosudarstvennyi Arkhiv Ekonomiki
               (Russian Government Archive of Economics).
               Moscow, Russia.

RGASPI   Rossiiskii Gosudarstvennyi Arkhiv Sotsial-
               Politicheskii Arkhiv (Russian Government
               Archive of Social-Political History). Moscow,
               Russia.

RGVA   Rossiiskii Gosudarstvennyi Voennyi Arkhiv
               (Russian State Military Archive). Moscow,
               Russia.

SDA   Stalin Digital Archive. Yale University Press/
               RGASPI, fond 558.

TsAMO   Tsentral'nyi Arkhiv Ministerstva Oboronyi RF
               (Central Archive of the Ministry of Defense of
               the Russian Federation). Podol'sk, Moscow,
               Russia.

USAHEC   US Army Heritage and Education Center.
               Carlisle, Pennsylvania.

VSHD   Vincennes, Service Historique de la Défense
               (French Military Archives). Vincennes, Paris,
               France.

---

* Although it has been years now since the Public Record Office was
renamed the National Archives, for the sake of tradition, and to preserve
common currency, I continue to reference it in this book as the PRO.

Notes

Introduction: Whose War?

1. For an overview of the "Codification of World War II" under Putin, see Mark Edele, "Fighting Russia's History Wars," *History & Memory* 29, no. 2 (Fall/Winter 2017): 90–124. Putin himself has recently chimed in with a 9,000-word essay on the "75th Anniversary of the Great Victory: Shared Responsibility to History and Our Future," published on the Kremlin website on June 19, 2020, and available here: http://en.kremlin.ru/events/president/news/63527.

2. Victor Davis Hanson, *The Second World Wars: How the First Global Conflict Was Fought and Won* (2017). Antony Beevor, *The Second World War* (2012), 2. For mainstream versions that stick closer to the traditional line while still taking a global view of the conflict, see Gerhard L. Weinberg, *A World at Arms: A Global History of World War II* (1993), and Max Hastings, *Inferno: The World at War, 1939–1945* (2012).

3. Of special note are the volumes published by the Mezhdunarodnyi fond demokratiia from the 1990s until about 2008, when the vogue for revelatory tomes exposing Soviet misdeeds began to wane in the Putin era. The most astonishing was the two-volume *1941 God. Dokumenty* (The year 1941. Documents)—published in 1998, at the peak of the Yeltsin thaw, which collected documents from a half-dozen archives relating to Stalin's foreign policy and military build-up in 1940–1941, risking the third rail of Great Patriotic War mythology: the Soviet military posture in June 1941. These volumes are out of print today and difficult to find, but Russian libraries still carry them.

4. Among recent biographies, the most notable is Stephen Kotkin's *Stalin*, of which the first two volumes have appeared (2015 and 2017), with a third soon expected. Simon Sebag Montefiore's *Stalin: The Court of the Red Tsar* (2005) and *Young Stalin* (2008) remain essential reading. Popular Russian biographies translated into English include the revelatory if overwrought Dmitri Volkogonov, *Stalin: Triumph and Tragedy*,

trans. Harold Shukman (1991), and the better balanced Oleg Khlevniuk, *Stalin: New Biography of a Dictator*, trans. Nora Seligman Favorov (2015).

On the eastern front generally, the recent synthesis by Evan Mawdsley, *Thunder in the East: The Nazi-Soviet War, 1941–1945* (2006), incorporates post-Communist Russian archival research and specialist literature. David Glantz has written numerous specialized studies of specific campaigns; he synthesized much of this work, with Jonathan House, in *When Titans Clashed: How the Red Army Stopped Hitler* (2015). Antony Beevor has reached the biggest audience with his best-selling *Stalingrad* (1999) and *The Fall of Berlin 1945* (2003), both impressively researched though not comprehensive. David Stahel has made huge contributions, especially on the German side of the conflict, in *Operation Barbarossa and Germany's Defeat in the East* (2011) and *Retreat from Moscow: A New History of Germany's Winter Campaign, 1941–1942* (2019). John Erickson's *The Road to Stalingrad: Stalin's War with Germany* (1975) and *The Road to Berlin: Continuing the History of Stalin's War with Germany* (1983), though written before the Russian archives were opened, both remain informative.

Among recent general histories of the conflict, Beevor's *Second World War* stands out for the originality of its take, owing to the author's extensive work with Soviet sources. Although still German focused, Brendan Simms's new *Hitler: A Global Biography* (2019) also provides a fresh take on the war, as Simms challenges many reigning assumptions regarding Hitler's strategic thinking, taking seriously his periodic peace offers toward Britain, for example, and refusing to see Operation Barbarossa as inevitable for ideological reasons.

Prologue: May 5, 1941

1. "Vyistuplenie general'nogo sekretarya TsK VKP (b) I. V. Stalina pered vyipusknikami voennyikh akademii RKKA v Kremle," May 5, 1941, reproduced in the original Russian as no. 437 in *1941 God. Dokumenty*, eds. L. E. Reshin et al. (1998), vol. 1, 158–59. (The original of this document is in the Stalin file (fond 538) at RGASPI, opis' 1, del' 3808, list' 1–12.)

2. Ibid., 159.

3. Ibid., 160–61.

4. Ibid., 161–62. Some accounts claim that it was a different officer Stalin interrupted. In any case, the effect was the same. See Jürgen Förster and Evan Mawdsley, "Hitler and Stalin in Perspective: Secret

Speeches on the Eve of Barbarossa," in *War in History* 11, no. 1 (January 2004): 82n55.

5. Cited in Ernst Topitsch, *Stalin's War*, 100 (from the written account of Gustav Hilger, based on the debriefing of a captured Soviet officer who attended the banquet by Colonel Reinhard Gehlen of German Army Intelligence). As Förster and Mawdsley note in "Hitler and Stalin in Perspective" (84), the "Gehlen-Hilger" version of Stalin's speech is at best a secondhand account, but they also note that it is broadly consistent with both the official "Short Record" version in the Stalin fond at RGASPI ("Vyistuplenie general'nogo sekretarya TsK VKP (b) I. V. Stalina pered vyipusknikami voennyikh akademii RKKA v Kremle," May 5, 1941, op. cit.) and contemporary Russian eyewitness accounts of the speech now available, such as the diary entries of V. A. Malyshev and G. M. Dimitrov for May 5, 1941, which are reproduced in V. A. Nevezhin, ed., *Zastol'nyie rechi Stalina. Dokumentyi i materialyi*, 279–81.

6. "Vyistuplenie general'nogo sekretarya TsK VKP (b) I. V. Stalina pered vyipusknikami voennyikh akademii RKKA v Kremle," May 5, 1941, op. cit., 162. "The era of the peace policy is at an end . . .": cited from Gehlen-Hilger version in Förster and Mawdsley, "Hitler and Stalin in Perspective," 84. "Bourgeois and a fool": from the "Übersetzung des Berichtes des Generalmajors Naumow über ein Bankett in Moskau am 5.5.41 anläßlich des Abschlusses eines Kriegsakademie-Lehrganges," in PAAA, R 104585.

7. Ibid. After Stalin's interruption of Khozin, eyewitness accounts diverge. But all accounts agree on the thrust of Stalin's intervention, moving from defensive to offensive doctrine. "There's going to be war, and the enemy will be Germany": as cited in Stephen Kotkin, *Stalin*, vol. 2, *Waiting for Hitler, 1929–1941*, 862 (citing yet another version).

Chapter 1: World Revolution

1. Vladimir Lenin, "Left-Wing Childishness and Petty Bourgeois Mentality," May 1918, in *Selected Works*, vol. 7, 357.

2. Richard Ullman, *Anglo-Soviet Relations*, vol. 3, *Anglo-Soviet Accord*, 124–25. On the formation of the Red Army, see Jacob W. Kipp, "Lenin and Clausewitz: The Militarization of Marxism, 1914–21," in *Military Affairs* 49, no. 4 (October 1985): 188.

3. A. Rosemeyer, "Abschrift," sent from Moscow to Berlin, October 10, 1918, in DBB, R 901 / 86976, 84-87; report from the head of the German military commission in Petrograd, on November 19, 1918, in

PAAA, R 11207; and Franz Rauch's April 12, 1919, report to the German Foreign Office in Berlin after his return from Moscow, in DBB, R 901 / 82082, 22–25. On Soviet nationalities policy, see Sean McMeekin, *The Russian Revolution: A New History* (2017), chap. 15 and passim.

4. "Soviet Protest Against Allied Intervention," June 27, 1918, reproduced in Jonathan Daly and Leonid Trofimov, *The Russian Revolution and Its Global Impact: A Short History with Documents*, 107.

5. See Sean McMeekin, *History's Greatest Heist: The Looting of Russia by the Bolsheviks*, chap. 9. "If we are obliged": Vladimir Lenin, "Speech Delivered at a Meeting of the Moscow Organisation of the Russian Communist Party (Bolsheviks)," November 26, 1920, in *Selected Works*, vol. 8, 282–83.

6. Vladimir Lenin, "Speech Delivered at a Meeting of Nuclei Secretaries of the Moscow Organisation," op. cit., 288.

7. "The Conditions of Affiliation to the Communist International," July 1920, in Lenin, *Selected Works*, vol. 10, 200–205.

8. For details, see Jeremy Agnew and Kevin McDermott, *The Comintern: A History of International Communism from Lenin to Stalin*, 21; and Babette Gross, *Willi Münzenberg: A Political Biography*, 99.

9. Josef Stalin, "Two Camps," c. February 1919, in *The Essential Stalin: Major Theoretical Writings*, ed. Bruce Franklin, 85.

10. George Kennan, *Russia and the West Under Lenin and Stalin*, 225–27.

11. See Sean McMeekin, "Pre-Empting the Peace," in *The Red Millionaire: A Political Biography of Willy Münzenberg, Moscow's Secret Propaganda Tsar in the West, 1917–1940*, 193–203.

12. Josef Stalin, "The Foundations of Leninism" (1924) and "Concerning the Question of the Proletariat and the Peasantry" (January 1925), in *The Essential Stalin*, op. cit., 112–13, 189.

13. Josef Stalin, "Speech Delivered at the Plenum of the Central Committee of the R.C. P. (B.)," January 19, 1925, reproduced in Stalin, *Works*, vol. 7, 14.

Chapter 2: Stalin Makes His Mark

1. Montefiore, *Young Stalin*, 8 and passim.

2. Cited in Robert C. Tucker, *Stalin in Power: The Revolution from Above, 1928–1941*, 71.

3. Ibid., 47.

4. See McMeekin, *Red Millionaire*, chap. 13.

5. Citations in Tucker, *Stalin in Power*, 94–96.

6. The literature on Ukraine, at least, is now substantial. Although he did not enjoy access to Soviet archives, Robert Conquest's pioneering work in *The Harvest of Sorrow: Soviet Collectivization and the Terror Famine* (1986) is still worth reading. In more recent work drawing on archival documents, Timothy Snyder's *Bloodlands: Europe Between Hitler and Stalin* (2010) is a notable advance, although his slightly lower death figures occasioned protests from Ukrainian scholars and the Ukrainian government. There are now dozens of specialized monographs drawing on archival documents, many of which have been ably synthesized by Anne Applebaum in her recent work on the *Red Famine: Stalin's War on Ukraine* (2017).

7. Citation in Nikolai Tolstoy, *Stalin's Secret War*, 29. On the Siberian goldfields, see also Kotkin, *Stalin*, 2:133.

8. Anthony C. Sutton, *Western Technology and Soviet Economic Development*, 1, and, on nonferrous metals, 44–60. Freyn and Gipromez: Stephen Kotkin, *Magnetic Mountain: Stalinism as a Civilization*, 37. See also, "Russia Awards $110,000,000 Job to Chicago Firm," *New York Times*, November 12, 1929.

9. Stephen Kotkin, *Stalin*, vol. 1, *Paradoxes of Power, 1878–1928*, 700. *Moscow News*: David Caute, *The Fellow-Travelers: A Postscript to the Enlightenment*, 79. On Campbell's visits to the USSR: R. W. Davies and Stephen G. Wheatcroft, *The Years of Hunger: Soviet Agriculture, 1931–1933*, 337.

10. Svetlana Lokhova, *The Spy Who Changed History: The Untold Story of How the Soviet Union Stole America's Top Secrets*, xv, 262–71, and passim.

11. On the voluntary migration of Americans to Stalin's Russia in the early 1930s, there is an interesting study by Tim Tzouliadis, *The Forsaken: An American Tragedy in Stalin's Russia*.

12. Gerald Freund, *Unholy Alliance: Russian-German Relations from the Treaty of Brest-Litovsk to the Treaty of Berlin*, 96. Hans-Ulrich Seidt, *Berlin, Kabul, Moskau: Oskar Ritter von Niedermayer und Deutschlands Ostpolitik*, 150–153. Tukhachevsky: cited in Kotkin, *Stalin*, 2:51.

Chapter 3: Strategic Coup in Washington

1. Hirota to Tokyo: cited in Hiroaki Kuromiya, "Stalin in the Politburo Transcripts," in *The Lost Politburo Transcripts: From Collective Rule to Stalin's Dictatorship*, eds. Paul R. Gregory and Norman Naimark, 50. Stalin to Ordzhonikidze: cited in Khlevniuk, *Stalin*, 123.

2. Stimson to Senator William E. Borah, September 8, 1932, reproduced in *Foreign Relations of the United States. Diplomatic Papers. The*

Soviet Union 1933–1939 (henceforth "US-Soviet Diplomatic Papers 1933–1939"), 1–2. On the naval agreements, see S. C. M. Paine, *The Wars for Asia, 1911–1949*, 15–16.

3. Ibid., 85–89.

4. Stimson to Borah, September 8, 1932, op. cit.

5. The classic study of the illicit Soviet art dumping trade remains Robert C. Williams, *Russian Art and American Money, 1900–1940* (1980), although a number of recent works have expanded on his findings. See, for example, Anne Odom and Wendy R. Salmond, eds., *Treasure into Tractors: The Selling of Russia's Cultural Heritage, 1918–1938* (2009) and my own *History's Greatest Heist*, epilogue.

6. Memorandum by the Chief of the Division of Eastern European Affairs (Kelley) hand-delivered to President Roosevelt, July 27, 1933, "US-Soviet Diplomatic Papers 1933–1939," 6–7. Counterfeiting operation (and *New York Times* citation): Herbert Hoover, *Freedom Betrayed: Herbert Hoover's Secret History of the Second World War and Its Aftermath*, 26.

7. Kelley Memorandum, July 27, 1933, "US-Soviet Diplomatic Papers 1933–1939," 8.

8. Litvinov memorandum addressed to L. M. Kaganovich, secretary of the Russian Communist Party, "On the Questions Which President Roosevelt May Present During Negotiations," October 20, 1933, no. 351 in *Sovetsko-amerikanskie otnosheniya godyi nepraznaniya 1927–1933*, eds. V. I. Savchenko, G. N. Sevostyanov, and B. I. Zhilyaev, 707–9.

9. Cited in John Morton Blum, ed., *Roosevelt and Morgenthau: A Revision and Condensation of "From the Morgenthau Diaries*," 32–33.

10. Ibid., 33.

11. Litvinov memorandum, October 20, 1933, op. cit., 707.

12. "The Special Assistant to the Secretary of State (Bullitt) to President Roosevelt," November 15, 1933, and "Memorandum by President Roosevelt and the Soviet Commissar for Foreign Affairs (Litvinov)," November 15, 1933, "US-Soviet Diplomatic Papers 1933–1939," 25–27. For Litvinov's counterclaim: "Spravka narkomfina i NKID SSSR o Sostoyanii raschetov po kreditam SShA Vremennomu Pravitel'stvu, o pretensiyakh i kontrpretensiyakh SSSR i SShA," December 23, 1933, no. 374 in Savchenko, Sevostyanov, and Zhilyaev, *Sovetsko-amerikanskie otnosheniya 1927–1933*, 744.

13. Transcript of Stalin interview with Duranty, December 25, 1933, no. 375 in Savchenko, Sevostyanov, and Zhilyaev, *Sovetsko-amerikanskie otnosheniya 1927–1933*, 746–748.

14. The idea was that, instead of paying the prevailing market rate of 3 to 4 percent for a sovereign loan that size, the Soviets would instead pay 8 percent. Whatever the Americans believed they had negotiated, this deal of $75 million for recognition, payable via future loan interest, is what Litvinov and Stalin agreed to in exchange for recognition. See Litvinov to Stalin, December 25, 1933, no. 376 in Savchenko, Sevostyanov, and Zhilyaev, *Sovetsko-amerikanskie otnosheniya 1927–1933*, 748–749. In April 1934, Bullitt reported to Washington that, prior to any prospective Soviet agreement to pay anything at all, the Export-Import Bank would have to open a credit for Stalin of $150 million (if the agreed debt claim was $75 million), or $200 million (if it was $100 million). Bullitt to Hull, April 2, 1934, "US-Soviet Diplomatic Papers 1933–1939," 75–76.

15. Promise of noninterference: Litvinov memorandum to Roosevelt ("Dear Mr. President"), "US-Soviet Diplomatic Papers 1933–1939," 28–29. Haggling: see Moscow chargé d'affaires John C. Wiley to Washington, February 6, 1935, and chief of East European affairs (Kelley) memorandum regarding a conversation with the Soviet Ambassador, May 24, 1925, "US-Soviet Diplomatic Papers 1933–1939," 177–78, 189–90. "It's all in the bag": quoted in Hoover, *Freedom Betrayed*, 28.

16. Cited in Jonathan Haslam, *The Soviet Union and the Threat from the East, 1933–1941: Moscow, Tokyo, and the Prelude of the Pacific War*, 39.

17. Cited in ibid., 34–35. See also Greg Kennedy, *Anglo-American Strategic Relations and the Far East, 1933–1939: Imperial Crossroads*, 100.

18. "Communists Here Plan to Carry On . . . Only Abolition of Capitalism Will Solve World's Problems for Workers," *New York Times*, November 19, 1933. "Scrap of paper": Benjamin Gitlow, *The Whole of Their Lives: Communism in America, a Personal History of Its Leaders*, 265.

19. Ware and the baseball bat: English-language letter "Dear Comrades," circa summer 1922, in RGASPI, fond 538, opis' 3-4, del' 70. For placement and code names of Soviet agents: Christopher Andrew and Vasili Mitrokhin, *The Sword and the Shield: The Mitrokhin Archive and the Secret History of the KGB*, 106. For a table of party members and their dates of service in government: Hoover, *Freedom Betrayed*, 36–46.

20. Citations in Gitlow, *Whole of Their Lives*, 255–61.

21. Cited in Hoover, *Freedom Betrayed*, 34. On the Roosevelt administration's refusal to vet employees for foreign loyalties, see Andrew and Mitrokhin, *Sword and Shield*, 107.

22. For a useful summary of the state of the art on Venona and Hiss, see John Earl Haynes and Harvey Klehr, "Hiss Was Guilty," History News Network, 2007, http://historynewsnetwork.org/article/37456.

23. Vitalii Pavlov, *Operatsiya 'Sneg'* (1996). For a summary of archival revelations about the penetration of Washington by Soviet agents in the 1930s, see Andrew and Mitrokhin, *Sword and Shield*, chap. 7. On Harry Dexter White, see also Herbert Romerstein and Eric Breindel, *The Venona Secrets: Exposing Soviet Espionage and America's Traitors*, 29–44 and passim.

24. Cited in Thomas Fleming, *The New Dealers' War: Franklin D. Roosevelt and the War Within World War II*, 322. Tupolev's 1935 trip, and "agents in practically all American [aircraft] factories": citations in Lokhova, *Spy Who Changed History*, 233, 265. On Sorge, the most recent study is Owen Matthews's *An Impeccable Spy: Richard Sorge, Stalin's Master Agent* (2019).

Chapter 4: Behind the Popular Front

1. For a judicious weighing of the evidence, see Marin Pundeff, "Dimitrov at Leipzig: Was There a Deal?," *Slavic Review* 45, no. 3 (Autumn 1986): 545–49.

2. Edward E. Ericson, *Feeding the German Eagle: Soviet Economic Aid to Nazi Germany, 1933–1941*, 15–16.

3. Haslam, *Threat from the East*, 43–44.

4. Decree footnoted: cited in Robert Conquest, *The Great Terror: Stalin's Purge of the Thirties*, 86–87. The classic account of Western whitewashing of the Ukrainian famine and Great Terror remains Caute, *Fellow-Travelers*.

5. For a detailed discussion, see McMeekin, *Red Millionaire*, chap. 13.

6. See McMeekin, *Red Millionaire*, chap. 3.

7. See Anne Odom, "The Selling of Russian Art and the Origins of the Hillwood Collection," in *A Taste for Splendor: Russian Imperial and European Treasures from the Hillwood Museum*, 45.

8. Bullitt to Hull, July 19, 1935, "US-Soviet Diplomatic Papers 1933–1939," 224–25.

9. Transcript of Kremlin meeting of June 5, 1938, between Davies and Stalin, in RGASPI, fond 558, opis' 11, del' 375, list' 1–7.

10. Martin Weil, *A Pretty Good Club: The Founding Fathers of the U.S. Foreign Service*, 92–93.

11. Andrew and Mitrokhin, *Sword and Shield*, 58. For more on these recruits, see Andrew Lownie, *Stalin's Englishman: The Lives of Guy Burgess*, 51–57 and passim.

12. A copy of the original Franco-Soviet Pact of Mutual Assistance, with accompanying (mostly critical) commentary by the French General Staff, is available at Vincennes in VSHD, 7 N 3143.

13. "Note sur les repercussions possible du Pacte franco-soviétique," prepared by the French General Staff on January 27, 1936, in 7 N 3143. For the German objection citing Locarno: see Wilhelmstrasse memorandum submitted to the French and Soviet embassies in Berlin, May 25, 1935, in AVPRF, fond 5, opis' 15, papka 104, del' 3, list' 373–77.

14. See Litvinov to Potemkin in Paris, July 4, 1935, and again, November 4, 1935, in AVPRF, fond 5, opis' 15, papka 110, del' 94, list' 23–27, 30–31. Laval "basically alone": Transcript of discussion between Laval and N. Krestinsky at the Soviet embassy in Paris, July 8, 1936, in RGASPI, fond 82, opis' 2, del' 1346, list' 220–21. Soviet intelligence: "Dnevnik tov. Sokolina," from the Paris embassy, November 11, 1935, in AVPRF, fond 5, opis' 15, papka 110, del' 95, list' 196. Laval negotiates with Berlin: Litvinov to Aleksandrovskii in Prague, November 11, 1935, in AVPRF, fond 5, opis' 15, papka 111, del' 100, list' 11.

15. Cited in Tolstoy, *Stalin's Secret War*, 82.

16. Cited in ibid., 85–86. "Second imperialist war": Josef Stalin, *Stalin's Master Narrative: A Critical Edition of the History of the Communist Party of the Soviet Union (Bolsheviks), Short Course*, eds. David Brandenberger and Mikhail Zelenov, 333.

17. For examples of wishful thinking by Czechoslovak leaders, see the speech by Eduard Benes on July 10, 1937, where he faulted Czechs for not trying hard enough to "understand" the USSR. Excerpted in AVPRF, fond 138, opis' 14, papka 30, del' 11, list' 31. The mutual assistance pact was dubiously sold to the Czechoslovak public as part of a "united front against revision and war." See the Soviet press summary on Czechoslovakia in March 1934, in AVPRF, fond 138, opis' 11, papka 23, del' 11, list' 10. Benes's guided tour: Aleksandrovskii to Litvinov, July 1, 1935, in AVPRF, fond 5, opis' 15, papka 111, del' 101, list' 55–58.

18. Citations in Richard Raack, "His Question Asked and Answered. Stalin on 'Whither Poland,'" *Polish Review* 55, no. 2 (2010): 198–200, 207–8.

19. Tolstoy, *Stalin's Secret War*, 134–35; and William Trotter, *Frozen Hell: The Russo-Finnish Winter War of 1939–1940*, 12–13.

20. Citations in Raack, "His Question Asked," op. cit., 209–11. "Enemies of our enemies": cited in Kotkin, *Stalin*, 2:413.

21. Not everyone agreed about the purges' impact on Soviet army effectiveness. The Czechoslovaks reckoned that Soviet striking power

remained fully intact in 1938. Polish experts thought the Red Army had been irreparably weakened. The French agreed more with the Polish estimate. See French ambassador in Moscow, Robert Coulondre, to Foreign Minister Georges Bonnet, April 26, 1938, in VSHD, 7 N 3124. For different estimates on the Red Army purges, see Montefiore, *The Court of the Red Tsar*, 223–26; Mikhail Mel'tyukhov, *Upushchennyi shans Stalina: Sovetskii soiuz i bor'ba za Evropu 1939–1941*, 368; and Glantz and House, *When Titans Clashed*, 9. Not all of the purged officers were executed, and 11,500 were later reinstated. Nonetheless, the immediate effect on morale was surely negative.

22. Stanley Payne, *The Spanish Civil War, the Soviet Union, and Communism*, 153–56, 161. Gold shipped to Moscow: Tucker, *Stalin in Power*, 351. On Hitler and Mussolini financing Franco: see Pierpaolo Barbieri, *Hitler's Shadow Empire: Nazi Economics and the Spanish Civil War*.

23. Berzin ("Donizetti") to Stalin, December 12, 1936, in RGASPI, fond 558, opis' 11, del' 318, list' 35–36.

24. On the Glenn Martin deal: Sutton, *Western Technology*, 220–21. Douglas DC-3 deal: Lokhova, *Spy Who Changed History*, 270. Stalin's aircraft carrier: Kennedy, *Anglo-American Strategic Relations*, 106. French deals: "Commandes de materiel de guerre faites en France par l'URSS," summary by the French chargé d'affaires in Moscow, January 6, 1939, in VSHD, 7 N 3124.

25. Citations in Montefiore, *Court of the Red Tsar*, 228–29. On the ethnic focus of the deportations, see also Timothy Snyder, *Bloodlands: Europe Between Hitler and Stalin*, 111. For up-to-date documentation, see N. L. Pobol' and P. N. Polyan, eds., *Stalinskie Deportatsii 1928–1953*.

26. George Orwell, *Homage to Catalonia*.

27. Payne, *Spanish Civil War*, 270–71.

28. For details on the sale of the Manchurian railway: Haslam, *Threat from the East*, 47; and Paine, *Wars for Asia*, 89.

29. Ibid., 103, and Hans van de Ven, *War and Nationalism in China: 1925–1945*, 183–88.

30. Cited in Kennedy, *Anglo-American Strategic Relations*, 108.

31. Paine, *Wars for Asia*, 103, 132–33. On Soviet arms shipments, see Haslam, *Threat from the East*, 93-94. Sleeper agent: Beevor, *Second World War*, 58.

32. Paine, *Wars for Asia*, 141 and passim.

33. For a revealing rendition of this USSR-Japan frontier dispute, involving the violation of borders neither country pretended to actually

control, see the transcript of meeting between Molotov and Togo, May 19, 1939, in RGASPI, fond 82, opis' 2, del' 1386, list' 8–12.

34. For the armistice terms, see "Zapiska V. Dekanozova—O dokumente iz Rigi otnositel'no razgovora nashego Polpreda s yapontsami," September 15, 1939, in RGASPI, fond 82, opis' 2, del' 1383, list' 58. On the battle see Glantz and House, *When Titans Clashed*, 12; Paine, *Wars for Asia*, 146; and Alistair Horne, *Hubris: The Tragedy of War in the Twentieth Century*, 163–86. For more on Zhukov, see also Vladimir Karpov, *Marshal Zhukov*, 92 and passim.

35. The Japanese Army's "strike north" plan is cited in Paine, *Wars for Asia*, 148–49. See also Van de Ven, *War and Nationalism in China*, 236–27.

36. Bullitt to Hull, July 19, 1935, "US-Soviet Diplomatic Papers 1933–1939," 224–25.

37. Josef Stalin, *From Socialism to Communism in the Soviet Union: Report on the Work of the Central Committee to the Eighteenth Congress of the CPSU(B.) Delivered March 10, 1939*, 22–24, 28.

Chapter 5: Courting Hitler

1. "British blank check": see Stefan Scheil, *Polen 1939: Kriegskalkül, Vorbereitung, Vollzug*, 64–65. "Huge and hateful": Evelyn Waugh, *Sword of Honour*, vol. 1 *Men at Arms*, 10.

2. The Polish ultimatum to Prague, delivered on September 30, 1938, at 11:45 p.m., and the Czechoslovak acceptance of Poland's terms on October 1, 1938, are preserved in AAN, 2/322/0/-/24, list' 53–60.

3. "Tass Denial of the Report of Soviet Agreement to Supply Poland with Raw Materials in the Event of War," reproduced in Jane Degras, ed., *Soviet Documents on Foreign Policy*, 3:328. Maisky and Litvinov: citations in Adam Ulam, *Expansion and Coexistence: Soviet Foreign Policy, 1917–1973*, 268.

4. Weizsäcker "Aufzeichnung" of a conversation with Ambassador Merekalov on April 17, 1939, reproduced as no. 1 in Alfred Seidl, ed., *Die Beziehungen zwischen Deutschland und der Sowjetunion 1939–1941. Dokumente des Auswärtigen Amtes* (henceforth "Seidl Dokumente"), 1–2. "Leave the initiative to the British and French": cited in Jonathan Haslam, "Soviet-German Relations and the Origins of the Second World War: The Jury Is Still Out," *Journal of Modern History* 69, no. 4 (December 1997): 793.

5. Citations in Keith Feiling, *Life of Neville Chamberlain*, 403, 408.

6. Palasse to French General Staff, April 19, 1939, in VSHD, 7 N 3186. Placed under surveillance by Beria: Foreign Minister Bonnet to the French premier, war and defense ministers, July 27, 1938, in VSHD, 7 N 3124.

7. Cited in Haslam, *Threat from the East*, 129. Cosigned 3,167 executions with Stalin: Montefiore, *Court of the Red Tsar*, 232.

8. Cited in Felix Chuev, *Molotov Remembers: Inside Kremlin Politics*, ed. Albert Resis, 192 (interview conducted November 23, 1971).

9. Schulenburg to Weizsäcker from Moscow, May 22, 1939, no. 8 in "Seidl Dokumente," 9.

10. Mikoyan to Stalin, June 19, 1939, in RGASPI, fond 84, opis' 1, del' 146. See also Ericson, *Feeding the German Eagle*, 33–34, and Philipp W. Fabry, *Die Sowjetunion und das Dritte Reich: Eine dokumentierte Geschichte der deutsch-sowjetischen Beziehungen von 1933 bis 1941*, 71.

11. Cited in Ericson, *Feeding the German Eagle*, 54.

12. As noted in Fabry, *Die Sowjetunion und das Dritte Reich*, 72. On the Baltic: citations in Albert N. Tarulis, *Soviet Policy Towards the Baltic States, 1918–1940*, 106–107. Astakhov and Draganov: cited in Raack, "His Question Asked," 202.

13. Mole in the German embassy: Ericson, *Feeding the German Eagle*, 47.

14. Schnurre report on his conversation with Astakhov and Babarin, 27 July 1939, reproduced as no. 24 in "Seidl Dokumente," 37–41. For more on Schnurre's proposals, see Ericson, *Feeding the German Eagle*, 54–55.

15. Ribbentrop to Schulenburg, August 4, 1939, no. 166 in James Stuart Beddie and Raymond James Sontag, eds., *Nazi-Soviet Relations 1939–1941: Documents from the Archives of the German Foreign Office*, 37–39.

16. Schulenburg to Ribbentrop, August 4, 1939, no. 158 in Beddie and Sontag, *Nazi-Soviet Relations*, 39–41.

17. Joseph Doumenc, "Souvenirs de la Mission en Russie Aout 1939," in VSHD, 7 N 3186.

18. Ibid.

19. "Dnevnaya Zapis' zasedaniya voennyikh missii SSSR, Angliya i Frantsiya," August 14, 1939 (10:05 a.m. to 2:20 p.m.), in RGASPI, fond 558, opis' 11, del' 220, 57–60. Doumenc sends envoy to Warsaw on August 17: Doumenc, "Souvenirs de la Mission en Russie Aout 1939," op. cit. Stalin "will not consider": Doumenc to Gamelin, August 17, 1939 (at 9:45 p.m.), in VSHD, 7 N 3186 ("Missions militaires françaises 1935–1939").

20. "Dnevnaya Zapis' zasedaniya voennyikh missii SSSR, Angliya i Frantsiya," August 14, 1939, op. cit.

21. Schnurre to Schulenburg, August 14, 1939; Schulenburg to Weizsäcker, August 14, 1939, in Beddie and Sontag, *Nazi-Soviet Relations*, 47–48.

22. Schulenburg "Memorandum" on his conversation with Molotov on August 15, 1939, reproduced as no. 35 in "Seidl Dokumente," 60–63 (Molotov's "verbatim" remarks are on 62).

23. Ribbentrop to Schulenburg, August 16, 1939 (received on August 17, 1939), in Beddie and Sontag, *Nazi-Soviet Relations*, 58.

24. Schulenburg to Ribbentrop, August 18, 1939, reporting on his meeting with Molotov on the seventeenth, and same to same, August 19, 1939, in Beddie and Sontag, *Nazi-Soviet Relations*, 59–61, 65–66.

25. I have used the version cited in Carl O. Nordling, "Did Stalin Deliver His Alleged Speech of 19 August 1939?" *Journal of Slavic Military Studies* 19 (2006): 93–106. In *Stalin* (167–68), Oleg Khlevniuk notes that there is no record of a formal Politburo meeting held on August 19, 1939, which, even if true, does not prove that Stalin did not speak to Molotov on this critical day. Khlevniuk argues that the statement cannot be real as it "made it seem as if Stalin believed war was needed to weaken the West, expand the USSR's boundaries, and help spread communism in Europe." But Stalin believed exactly these things, as was plain in his statements on foreign policy dating back fifteen years—statements that drew on Lenin's oft-expressed views—and also in Stalin's subsequent actions (such as the Molotov-Ribbentrop Pact and everything in its wake). General Doumenc, the French envoy who was in Moscow while this took place, insisted in his own postmortem that there was "a secret session of the Politburo on August 19," at which Stalin made the decision to reject French-British overtures and come to an agreement with Hitler. Doumenc, "Souvenirs de la Mission en Russie Aout 1939," op. cit.

26. Stalin to Hitler (via Schulenburg), August 21, 1939, 7:30 p.m., answering Hitler (via Ribbentrop) to Stalin, August 20, 1939, in Beddie and Sontag, *Nazi-Soviet Relations*, 66–67, 69. Economic agreement of August 20: Ericson, *Feeding the German Eagle*, 57.

27. Hans-Heinrich Herwarth von Bittenfeld, *Against Two Evils*, 165. Swastikas: Roger Moorhouse, *The Devils' Alliance: Hitler's Pact with Stalin, 1939–1941*, 2.

28. For details on Ribbentrop's reception: Montefiore, *Court of the Red Tsar*, 314.

29. "Memorandum of a Conversation Held on the Night of August 23d to 24th, Between [Ribbentrop] and [Stalin] and [Molotov]," composed by Hencke in Moscow, August 24, 1939, in Beddie and Sontag, *Nazi-Soviet Relations*, 72–76.

30. "Treaty of Nonaggression Between Germany and the Union of Soviet Socialist Republics," August 23, 1939, in Beddie and Sontag, *Nazi-Soviet Relations*, 76–78. Libau and Windau: Ribbentrop to Hitler, 8:05 p.m. on August 23, 1939, in ibid., 71. "The Führer accepts": cited in Moorhouse, *Devils' Alliance*, 25. Shares of Polish territory and population: Norman Davies and Antony Polonsky, eds. *Jews in Eastern Poland and the USSR, 1939–46*, 1. "Buckets of shit": cited in Kotkin, *Stalin*, 2:665.

31. Cited in Kotkin, *Stalin*, 2:667. Beck petitions Soviet government for help: from Beck's memoir written while in Romanian exile in November 1939, in AAN, 2/1736/0/3/33, 101.

32. "Molotow-Rede vor dem Obersten Sowjet," August 31, 1939, in PAAA, R 261183.

Chapter 6: Gangster Pact, Part I

1. Gamelin: cited in Norman Davies, *God's Playground: A History of Poland*, 432. Déat: widely cited, including in André Larané, "4 mai 1939: Mourir pour Dantzig?," *Hérodote*, April 29, 2019, www.herodote.net/4_mai_1939-evenement-19390504.php.

2. "Agreement of Mutual Assistance Between the United Kingdom and Poland," August 25, 1939, Avalon Project, Yale Law School Lillian Goldman Law Library, http://avalon.law.yale.edu/wwii/blbk19.asp. Ironside: unpublished Beck memoir account written in Romanian exile in November 1939, op. cit., 87–89.

3. "Treaty of Nonaggression Between Germany and the Union of Soviet Socialist Republics," op. cit.

4. Cabinet minutes for August 27, 1939, in PRO, CAB/23/100.

5. Cabinet minutes for August 30, 1939, in PRO, CAB/23/100. Emphasis added. Roosevelt: Cabinet minutes for August 28, 1939, in PRO, CAB/23/100.

6. Cabinet minutes for August 30, 1939, in PRO, CAB/23/100.

7. Cited in Scheil, *Polen 1939*, 73.

8. "Hitler addresses his generals, 23 May 1939," reproduced by Anthony Adamthwaite, in *The Making of the Second World War*, 214–15. On the French and British ultimatums: Ibid., 94. "One possible, but very

distasteful explanation . . .": cited in Peter Hitchens, *The Phoney Victory: The World War II Illusion*, 43.

9. "W. Molotow über die Ratifizierung des Sowjetisch-deutschen Nichtangriffspaktes," speech delivered before the Supreme Soviet on August 31, 1939, in PAAA, R 104357.

10. Stalin to Dimitrov: Entry for September 7, 1939, in *The Diary of Georgi Dimitrov, 1933–1949*, ed. Ivo Banac, 115.

11. Ribbentrop to Schulenburg, September 3, 1939 (received in Moscow September 4, 1939), and Schulenburg to Ribbentrop, September 5, 1939, in Beddie and Sontag, *Nazi-Soviet Relations*, 86–87.

12. Davies, *God's Playground*, 437. One hundred and fifty-eight towns and cities bombed: Snyder, *Bloodlands*, 119.

13. Gerard Labuda and Waldemar Michowicz, eds., *The History of Polish Diplomacy X-XX c.*, 517–18.

14. Snyder, *Bloodlands*, 128–29; Davies, *God's Playground*, 437–39; Moorhouse, *Devils' Alliance*, 34–35; and Beevor, *Second World War*, 28–30.

15. Cited by Jan Gross, "The Sovietization of Western Ukraine and Western Byelorussia," in *Jews in Eastern Poland and the USSR*, eds. Norman Davies and Antony Polonsky, 61.

16. Report from "Fremde Heere / Ost" to Oberkommando des Heeres, September 13, 1939, in BA/MA, RW 6 / v. 98.

17. On the Japanese armistice request, see Hubertus Lupke, *Japans Russlandpolitik von 1939 bis 1941*, 20–21. For the erroneous communiqué about the fall of Warsaw: see Davies, *God's Playground*, 440.

18. Cited in Labuda and Michowicz, *History of Polish Diplomacy*, 519. For the meetings in Kolommy and Kuty, and their sad aftermath: Beck's unpublished memoir account written while in Romanian exile in November 1939, op. cit., 122–29.

19. Cited in Moorhouse, *Devils' Alliance*, 36–37.

20. Molotov speech to Supreme Soviet, October 31, 1939, translated (into German) by the Wilhelmstrasse, in PAAA, R 261183. Polish losses: Bogdan Musial, *Kampfplatz Deutschland: Stalins Kriegspläne gegen den Westen*, 411.

21. Ibid. For more on the ethnic breakdown in the Soviet zone, see Bogdan Musial, *Konterrevolutionäre Elemente sind zu erschießen: Die Brutalisierung des deutsch-sowjetischen Krieges im Sommer 1941*, 26. Forty armed clashes between Red Army and Poles: Moorhouse, *Devils' Alliance*, 38.

22. "Lagebericht Rote Armee 19.9.1939," in BA/MA, RW 6 / v. 98. "Germanski und Bolsheviki zusamm[e]n stark": cited in Moorhouse, *Devils' Alliance*, 39.

23. Gestapo report from Posen, passed on to the Wilhelmstrasse, November 17, 1939, in PAAA, Botschaft Moskau 495.

24. "Secret Supplementary Protocol" to the "German-Soviet Boundary and Friendship Treaty," September 28, 1939, in Beddie and Sontag, *Nazi-Soviet Relations*, 107.

25. Molotov speech to the Supreme Soviet, October 31, 1939, op. cit. Lloyd George in *Sunday Express* and Raczynski reply: both cited by Corbin in his dispatch from London, October 3, 1939, in QO, 92CPCOM/286, 24.

26. Ribbentrop to Molotov, "Confidential," September 28, 1939, in QO, 92CPCOM/286, 109. On the diplomatic ramifications of the Poland-for-Lithuania swap: Tolstoy, *Stalin's Secret War*, 98–99.

27. "German-Soviet Boundary and Friendship Treaty," September 28, 1939, in Beddie and Sontag, *Nazi-Soviet Relations*, 105.

28. Ibid., along with "Confidential Protocol" and "Secret Supplementary Protocols," all in Beddie and Sontag, *Nazi-Soviet Relations*, 105–7.

29. Moorhouse, *Devils' Alliance*, 41.

30. "Proekt polozheniya NKVD SSSR 'o spetsposelakh i trudovom ustroistve osadnikov, vyiselyaemyikh iz zapadnyikh oblastei USSR i BSSR," December 29, 1939, reproduced as no. 2.4 in Pobol' and Polyan, *Stalinskie deportatsii*, 112–14. Road construction: Beria order no. 315, September 25, 1939, reproduced as no. 24 in Rudolf Pikhoya et al., eds., *Katyn'. Plenniki neob'yavlenno voinyi*, 95–97. Politburo approval: Politburo protocol for October 1, 1939, point 260 ("o voennoplennyikh"), in RGASPI, fond 17, opis' 162, del' 26.

31. Cited in Tolstoy, *Stalin's Secret War*, 101.

32. Citations in Snyder, *Bloodlands*, 127.

33. Schulenburg from Moscow, March 21 and September 19, 1940, summarizing recent Soviet press reports from *Pravda*, in PAAA, Botschaft Moskau 495.

34. Politburo resolution of October 3, 1939, "O poryadke utverzhdeniya prigovorov voennyikh tribunalov v Zapadnoi Ukraine i Zapadnoi Belorussii," in RGASPI, fond 17, opis' 162, del' 25.

35. Gestapo report from Posen, November 17, 1939, op. cit. Litvinov on the Soviet-German commission: V. Ya. Birshtein, *Smersh. Sekretnoe oruzhie Stalina*, 145. On Ukrainian People's Republic, see John A. Armstrong, *Ukrainian Nationalism, 1939–1945*, 29–33. On Polish Jews fleeing into the Soviet zone, see Maciej Siekierski, "Jews in Soviet-Occupied East Poland, 1939," in *Jews in Eastern Poland and the USSR, 1939–46*, eds. Norman Davies and Antony Polonsky, 112–13.

36. For estimates of Poles and Jews deported east: Keith Sword, "The Welfare of Polish-Jewish Refugees in the USSR, 1941–43," in *Jews in Eastern Poland and the USSR, 1939–46*, eds. Norman Davies and Antony Polonsky, 145. Snyder, in *Bloodlands* (151), cites a lower figure of about 315,000. The Polish historian Daniel Bockowski has a middle estimate of about 750,000 to 780,000. For an assessment, see Alexander Watson, *The Fortress: The Siege of Przemysl and the Making of Europe's Bloodlands*, 267 and 331n45.

37. British war cabinet minutes, September 17, 1939, in PRO, CAB 65/1. Halifax was overstating France's agreement to ignore Soviet aggression, which was more Corbin being told he must accept what the British position was than affirmatively agreeing to it. See Corbin to Bonnet, September 20, 1939, in QO, 92 CPCOM/286.

38. British war cabinet minutes, September 18, 20, and 29, 1939 (on the blackmail of the crews at Archangel and Murmansk), in PRO, CAB 65/1.

39. Citations in Patrick Osborn, *Operation Pike: Britain Versus the Soviet Union, 1939–1941*, 11–13.

40. British war cabinet minutes, November, 16, 1939, in PRO, CAB 65/1.

Chapter 7: Gangster Pact, Part II

1. Cited in Tarulis, *Soviet Policy*, 150–51. See also Moorhouse, *Devils' Alliance*, 65–66; and Tolstoy, *Stalin's Secret War*, 118–19.

2. Tarulis, *Soviet Policy*, 155–56; and Moorhouse, *Devils' Alliance*, 66–67.

3. Cited in Tolstoy, *Stalin's Secret War*, 120.

4. Politburo resolution no. 18, dated November 3, 1939, in RGASPI, fond 17, opis' 162, del' 26. Order no. 001223: cited in Tolstoy, *Stalin's Secret War*, 130.

5. Tolstoy, *Stalin's Secret War*, 134–35; and Trotter, *Frozen Hell*, 12–13.

6. Cited in Trotter, *Frozen Hell*, 15–16.

7. Trotter, *Frozen Hell*, 15–16; and Eloise Engle and Lauri Paananen, *The Winter War: The Soviet Attack on Finland, 1939–1940*, 7–8.

8. Trotter, *Frozen Hell*, 13. Khrushchev: from Nikita Khrushchev, *Khrushchev Remembers: The Glasnost Tapes*, trans. and eds., Jerrold L. Schecter and Vyacheslav V. Luchkov, 152. For estimates of Soviet armor at the time: Bair Irincheev, *War of the White Death: Finland Against the Soviet Union 1939–1940*, 3–5; and Musial, *Kampfplatz Deutschland*, 322, 341.

9. Citations in Engle and Paananen, *Winter War*, 9–10.

10. Citations in ibid., 10–11; and Tolstoy, *Stalin's Secret War*, 138–39.

11. Cited in H. Montgomery Hyde, *Neville Chamberlain*, 152–53. In his new *Hitler*, Brendan Simms observes (356) that Hitler's peace offering was "sincerely meant," and argues (359) that Chamberlain's "refusal to compromise had . . . far-reaching consequences."

12. On Sir William Seeds, see Sidney Aster, "The Diplomat as Scapegoat?," in *Leadership and Responsibility in the Second World War*, eds. Brian Padair Farrell and Robert Vogel, 121 and passim.

13. Kalinin to Roosevelt, submitted by Molotov to US ambassador Steinhardt on October 15, 1939, no. 2 in A. N. Yakovlev et al., *Sovetsko-amerikanskie otnosheniya 1939–1945*, 12–13; and war cabinet minutes, October 31, 1939, in PRO, FO 371/ 24849. Molotov to the Supreme Soviet on October 31, 1939: reproduced in full as annex to rapport no. 69 of Colonel Palasse, the French military attaché in Moscow, dated November 15, 1939, in VSHD, 7 N 2790.

14. War cabinet minutes, October 31, 1939, op. cit.

15. Citations in Engle and Paananen, *Winter War*, 12–13.

16. Figures in Irincheev, *War of the White Death*, 5–9.

17. Cited in Trotter, *Frozen Hell*, 34.

18. Mekhlis to Voroshilov and Stalin, November 23, 1939, in RGASPI, fond 558, opis' 11, del' 449, list' 31–35. On Zhdanov's role in the Stalin terror apparatus, see Montefiore, *Court of the Red Tsar*, 137–41, 183n.

19. Citations in Trotter, *Frozen Hell*, 58–59.

20. Engle and Paananen, *Winter War*, 13–16. Thirty-five million Finnish markka for Kuusinen's puppet government: German army intelligence Lagebericht no. 4 ("Sowjetunion—Finnland"), in BA/MA, RH / 19 / III.

21. Snow to Halifax, December 14, 1939, in PRO, FO 371 / 24791.

22. Trotter, *Frozen Hell*, 72–73; and, for casualty estimates, Irincheev, *War of the White Death*, 26–27. Over in twelve days: cited in Birshtein, *Smersh*, 148. Voroshilov boast of four days and doctor treating four hundred wounded soldiers a day: Seeds to Halifax, December 7, 1939, in PRO, FO 371 / 24791.

23. Mekhlis and Zhdanov to Voroshilov, December 19, 1939, and follow-up field report from Thirteenth Army headquarters, dated December 28, 1939, in RGASPI, fond 558, opis' 11, del' 449, list' 44–46. Press reports ceasing on December 5, 1939: Seeds to Halifax, December 20, 1939, in PRO, FO 371 / 24791. Soviet use of chemical weapons: report of

Finnish General Staff headquarters (in French translation), December 7, 1939, in VSHD, 7 N 2790.

24. On Timoshenko's appointment: Kotkin, *Stalin*, 2:734; and Montefiore, *Court of the Red Tsar*, 328–29. Roast suckling pig: Tolstoy, *Stalin's Secret War*, 150.

25. From a series of reports collected by British army intelligence on February 15, 1940, in PRO, FO 371 / 24792. The Stalin decree of January 24, 1940, creating the punitive NKVD battalions is cited in Birshtein, *Smersh*, 149. For Mekhlis on self-wounding and making the terror battalions public, see German army intelligence Lagebericht no. 12, January 15, 1940, and no. 13, January 19, 1940, both in BA/MA, RH / 19 / III.

26. Reports collected by British army intelligence on February 15, 1940, op. cit.

27. Cited in Osborn, *Operation Pike*, 39.

28. British war cabinet minutes for January 17, 20, 23, 29, and February 1, 1940, in PRO, FO 371 / 24791; and Tolstoy, *Stalin's Secret War*, 119, 190–91. French propose landing at Petsamo: Gamelin, "Note Relative a la Participation des Forces Franco-Britanniques aux Operations en Finlande," March 10, 1940, in VSHD, 7 N 2790. French transshipments of Italian and Hungarian war matériel: "Transit en France de matériel italien pour Finlande," in VSHD, 7 N 2791. On Swedish volunteers fighting in Finland: see German army intelligence Lagebericht no. 12, January 15, 1940, op. cit. Soviet military intelligence reports on Romania and Turkey: cited in Kotkin, *Stalin*, 2:735.

29. Osborn, *Operation Pike*, 56. Vote in the House of Representatives: Snow to Foreign Office from Helsinki, February 1, 1940, in PRO, FO 371 / 24791.

30. Cited in Tolstoy, *Stalin's Secret War*, 191. Hoover, newspapers, and Congress aid appropriation: "Hoover. Finnish Relief Fund" collection, Hoover Institution Archives, box 1.

Chapter 8: Maximum Danger

1. Trotter, *Frozen Hell*, 121, 169–70.

2. Ibid., 171–73; and Irincheev, *War of the White Death*, 104–5.

3. Gamelin, "Note Relative a la Participation des Forces Franco-Britanniques aux Operations en Finlande," March 10, 1940, in VSHD, 7 N 2790. See also, T. C. Imlay, "A Reassessment of Allied Strategy During the Phony War, 1939–1940," *English History Review* 119, no. 481 (April 2004): 352–56.

4. British war cabinet minutes, January 6, 13, and 15, 1940; Maclean memorandum on the Soviet threat to Britain in the Middle East, c. early January 1940, forwarded to the British war cabinet by Le Rougetel, on January 11, 1940; and War Office memorandum copied to the war cabinet, Air Ministry, Admiralty, and India office, all in PRO, FO 371/ 24849.

5. Saraçoğlu: Report labeled "Views of Turkish Military Attaché on European Military Situation," February 15, 1940, in PRO, FO 371 / 24846. Iranian prime minister: W. C. van Cutsem to Foreign Office, February 13, 1940, in PRO, FO 371 / 24846. "The time had come": cited in Brock Millman, "Toward War with Russia: British Naval and Air Planning for Conflict in the Near East, 1939–1940," *Journal of Contemporary History* 29, no. 2 (April 1994): 274.

6. Taline Ter Minassian, "La neutralité de la Turquie durant la deuxième guerre mondiale," *Guerres mondiales et conflits contemporaines* 194 (December 1999): 120. For more on the Saadabad Pact, see also Dzhamil Gasanli, *SSSR-Turtsiya: Ot neutraliteta k kholodnoi voinyi (1939–1953)*, 41 and passim.

7. Transcript of meeting between Molotov, Stalin, and Saraçoğlu in the Kremlin, October 1, 1939, in RGASPI, fond 558, opis' 11, del' 388. In the final version of the Anglo-French-Turkish agreement signed in Ankara on October 19, 1939, a second protocol was added to satisfy Stalin. In VSHD, 7 N 3256, folder labeled "Mission Weygand à Ankara. Octobre 1939."

8. Citations in Osborn, *Operation Pike*, 52–54.

9. Report of the French military attaché in Ankara, October 27, 1939, in VSHD, 7 N 3227. Knatchbull-Hugessen from Ankara to Orme Sargent at Foreign Office, March 15, 1940; and Beaumont-Nesbitt to Mr. Nicholas at War Office, February 20, 1940, in PRO, FO 371 / 24846. On Saraçoğlu's visceral reaction to Stalin's bullying in Moscow, see Onur İşçi, "The Massigli Affair and Its Context." *Journal of Contemporary History* 55, no. 2 (2020): 5, http://doi.org/10.1177/0022009419833443. On Turkish foreign policy in the war generally, see İşçi, *Turkey and the Soviet Union During World War II* (London: Bloomsbury, 2019).

10. Citations in Osborn, *Operation Pike*, 83–84.

11. Stalin to Politburo on January 21, 1940: Nevezhin, *Zastol'nyie rechi Stalina*, 230; and Butler report of his conversation with Ambassador Maisky, February 24, 1940, in PRO, FO 371 / 24793.

12. Ibid.

13. These reports are referenced individually below.

14. "Report on the Political Conditions in the USSR," by Major R. O. A. Gatehouse and Captain C. H. Tamplin, February 22, 1940, in PRO, FO 371/ 24850.

15. Ibid.

16. Ibid.

17. Citations in Millman, "Toward War with Russia," 270–71, 273. After initial aerial surveillance was conducted, the estimate was that it would take "three or four Blenheim squadrons" almost three months to be certain of success. See British Air Ministry report dated April 2, 1940, in PRO, FO 371/ 24847. Churchill in *Le Petit Parisien*: noted in a Foreign Office dispatch from Campbell in Paris filed on April 2, 1940, in PRO, FO 371/ 24846.

18. Maclean memorandum, March 6, 1940, in PRO, FO 371 / 24846.

19. Knatchbull-Hugessen from Ankara to Orme Sargent at Foreign Office, March 15, 1940, op. cit. "Other places than the western front": cited in Millman, "Toward War with Russia," 271.

20. Tolstoy, *Stalin's Secret War*, 172; and, for Shamyl meeting with Maclean, "Compte rendu" of the meeting between "FITZROY MAC-LEAN and M. CHARVERIAT," May 13, 1940, in VSHD, 7 N 3227.

21. See report of the Bulgarian minister in Berlin to Sofia, February 14, 1940, in BSA, fond 176K, opis' 33, del' 66, list' 42. On agent 59, see Jeffrey Burds, "The Soviet War Against 'Fifth Columnists': The Case of Chechnya, 1942–1944," *Journal of Contemporary History* 42, no. 2 (April 2007): 284–87. Russian historian discovers: cited in Burds, "The Soviet War," 287.

22. Trotter, *Frozen Hell*, 206–9. Rumors of Allied intervention at Murmansk and Archangel: cited in Kotkin, *Stalin*, 2:740.

23. Trotter, *Frozen Hell*, 232–33, 242–45, 263. "If no relief comes": cited in Irincheev, *War of the White Death*, 171.

24. "Programme possible pour le transport du premier echelon français," circa February 22, 1940; and Gamelin's "Note Relative a la Participation des Forces Franco-Britanniques aux Operations en Finlande," in VSHD, 7 N 2790. That Stalin was following the Norwegian drama closely was proven by Molotov's behavior in April 1940. See below.

25. Knatchbull-Hugessen from Ankara to Orme Sargent at Foreign Office, March 15, 1940, op. cit. This report, delivered on March 15, must date back at least a week, if not earlier.

26. Pikhoya et al., *Katyn'*, 18–21. Steinhardt told Le Rougetel: cited in Steven Merritt Miner, *Between Churchill and Stalin: The Soviet Union, Great Britain, and the Origins of the Grand Alliance*, 21.

27. Cited by Tolstoy in *Stalin's Secret War*, 180. In his chapter "Forest Murmurs," Tolstoy first proposed the connection between Stalin's paranoia about imminent Allied intervention in March 1940 and what is now known as the Katyn Massacre. In view of the fact that Tolstoy had no access then to Russian archival material on the murders—which were carried out after the Finnish war ended, not before—it took an astonishing leap of imagination for Tolstoy to intuit Stalin's likely concerns at the time when Beria's orders were given. Soviet sources, precisely dated, now confirm the essentials of Tolstoy's brilliant argument.

28. Beria to Stalin, top-secret directive no. 794/B of March 5, 1940, reproduced in its entirety as no. 216 in Pikhoya et al., *Katyn'*, 384–90. The editors have reproduced a photostat of the original.

29. Mannerheim: Telegram from the French military attaché, March 12, 1940 (23h50), in VSHD, 7 N 2790 (Finlande 1929–1940). An English-language translation of the peace treaty is available online: Sami Korhonen, "The Moscow Peace Treaty," Battles of the Winter War, www.winterwar.com/War%27sEnd/moscow_peace_treaty.htm.

30. Tolstoy, *Stalin's Secret War*, 157 and passim. Stalin's rejection of a German mediation offer: reported by Mallet from Stockholm, passing on report from the US minister there, February 13, 1940, in PRO, FO 371 / 24792.

31. Molotov speech to Supreme Soviet, March 30, 1940, preserved in BA/MA, RH / 19/ III, 381.

32. Citations in Snyder, *Bloodlands*, 135–40; and in Moorhouse, *Devils' Alliance*, 45. For more gruesome details, see also Donald Rayfield, *Stalin and His Hangmen: The Tyrant and Those Who Killed for Him*, 378–79.

33. Snyder, *Bloodlands*, 141.

34. For a summary of this session in the Commons, see Osborn, *Operation Pike*, 117–20.

35. René Massigli telegram from Ankara, April 1, 1940, in both original and selectively edited German-stamped versions, in QO, 4GMII/126.

36. Osborn, *Operation Pike*, 144–46, 50.

37. As noted by Tolstoy, in *Stalin's Secret War*, 169, 183. The records from MacPhail's overflights of Baku and Batumi, carried out on March 30 and April 5, 1940, are preserved (including photographs) in PRO, AIR 34 / 717, and (in written form) in PRO, FO 371 / 24847.

Chapter 9: Stalin Strikes

1. "Aufzeichnung des Auswärtigen Amts vom 26. Februar 1940 über das . . . 11. Februar 1940 . . . deutsch-sowjetische Wirtschaftsabkommen," no. 118 in "Seidl Dokumente," 156–59. German mediation offers in Finland: Tolstoy, *Stalin's Secret War*, 117, 192.

2. Schulenburg to Ribbentrop from Moscow, April 11, 1940, in PAAA, R 104358.

3. Ibid. Schulenburg was not wrong about Allied plans either. See "Plan d'Action en Scandinavie," in VSHD, 7 N 2790.

4. Tolstoy, *Stalin's Secret War*, 176–77; and for more details on the Norwegian campaign, Andrew Roberts, *The Storm of War: A New History of the Second World War*, 38–45.

5. Details in Kotkin, *Stalin*, 2:758–59. For reforms on ranks and salutes, see Grigore Gafencu, *Prelude to the Russian Campaign, from the Moscow Pact (August 21st, 1939) to the Opening of Hostilities in Russia (June 22nd, 1941)*, 30. T-34 tank orders: TsK VKP (b) resolution no. 976-368cc of June 7, 1940, "O proizvodstve tankov T-34 v 1940 godu," no. 7, in Reshin et al., *1941 God. Dokumenty*.

6. H. L. Ismay, "Plan for Opening and Exercising Control in the Black Sea," April 8, 1940; Hollis to Sir Orme Sargent, April 9, 1940, both in PRO, FO 371 / 24846. Maclean's report, filed in the British embassy in Paris on May 15, is in PRO, FO 371 / 24850. Maclean memorandum on Stalin's foreign policy: cited in Miner, *Between Churchill and Stalin*, 38. For the French view of Maclean, see "Compte rendu," May 13, 1940, op. cit. Maclean's trip to Paris does not feature in *Eastern Approaches*.

7. Entry for September 7, 1939, in *Diary of Georgi Dimitrov*, op. cit.

8. Cited in Kotkin, *Stalin*, 2:768. Molotov to Schulenburg: Schulenburg to Ribbentrop, May 10, 1940, no. 133 in "Seidl Dokumente," 179. See also Tolstoy, *Stalin's Secret War*, 193.

9. *Daily Worker*: "Churchill Asked About Anglo-Soviet Relations," July 31, 1940. Russia Today Society: see letter from its chairman in PRO, FO 371 / 24847. Cripps: Transcript of his first audience with Stalin on July 1, 1940, in Reshin et al., *1941 God. Dokumenty*, 77. Maisky recommended Cripps: Kotkin, *Stalin*, 2:775. For Maisky's views about Churchill and Cripps, see also his recollection of a conversation with Butler reported in ciphered Maisky telegram from London, October 5, 1940, in RGASPI, fond 558, opis' 11, del' 216.

10. Cited in Tolstoy, *Stalin's Secret War*, 193–94. On dissension in the French Communist ranks against the Moscow line, see Moorhouse, *Devils' Alliance*, 111–12.

11. Figures in Musial, *Kampfplatz Deutschland*, 427; and Bogdan Musial, *Stalins Beutezug: Die Plünderung Deutschlands und der Aufstieg der Sowjetunion zur Weltmacht*, 29.

12. Citations in Tolstoy, *Stalin's Secret War*, 195–96. "Take other measures": cited in Moorhouse, *Devils' Alliance*, 85.

13. Molotov telegram to "Polpredam SSSR v Litve, Latvii, Estonii and Finlandii," June 14, 1940, no. 10, and transcript of Molotov meeting with Urbsys in the Kremlin, June 14, 1940, at 11:50 p.m., no. 11, both in Reshin et al., *1941 God. Dokumenty*, 29–32.

14. Transcript of Molotov conversation with the Latvian ambassador, 2 p.m. on June 16, 1940, and with the Estonian ambassador, 2:30 p.m. and midnight on June 16, 1940, document nos. 14, 16, and 18, in Reshin et al., *1941 God. Dokumenty*, 33–35.

15. Citations in Moorhouse, *Devils' Alliance*, 85.

16. Transcript of Molotov meeting with Schulenburg, June 17, 1940, no. 19 in Reshin et al., *1941 God. Dokumenty*, 40–41.

17. Ibid.; and Timoshenko, "Sluzhebnaia zapiska komanduyushchego voiskama BOVO [the acronym for the Red Army's new Baltic military district]," June 21, 1940, no. 23 in Reshin et al., *1941 God. Dokumenty*, 44–45. On the implications of this order, and Stalin's political appointments, see Birshtein, *Smersh*, 151–53.

18. Citations in Tolstoy, *Stalin's Secret War*, 200–201.

19. Ibid. Molotov protests American gold: Thurston from US embassy Moscow, August 1, 1940, in NAA, T 1248, Roll 1. German assets: see German military intelligence report labeled "Geheim! Umsiedlungsverhandlungen für die baltischen Staaten," November 20, 1940, passed on by German embassy Moscow on November 23, 1940, in PAAA, R 101388.

20. Citations in Tolstoy, *Stalin's Secret War*, 200–201.

21. Khristov' from Moscow, April 21, 1940, in BSA, fond 176K, opis' 33, del' 20, list' 5.

22. "Spravka o Bessarabii," September 9 and 19, 1939, and "Spravka o rumyinskoi provintsii Bukovine," October 7, 1939, and "Spravka o Bukovine," December 16, 1939, all in AVPRF, fond 125, opis' 21, papka 17, del' 15.

23. Transcript of Molotov conversation with Schulenburg, June 24, 1940, no. 26 in Reshin et al., *1941 God. Dokumenty*, 48–49.

24. Figures in Musial, *Stalins Beutezug*, 381 (table 2).

25. Transcript of Molotov conversation with Rosso, June 24, 1940, and accompanying Molotov written memorandum dated June 25, 1940, no. 27 in Reshin et al., *1941 God. Dokumenty*, 51–52. Massigli dangles idea of gains at Italy's expense if Turkey green-lights an Allied strike on Baku: Massigli telegram from Ankara, April 1, 1940, op. cit.

26. Transcript of Molotov conversation with Schulenburg, June 25, 1940, no. 28 in Reshin et al., *1941 God. Dokumenty*, 52–55.

27. Molotov ultimatum to Romania, handed over to Davidescu on June 26, 1940, and transcript of meeting between Molotov and Davidescu, June 27, 1940, nos. 32 and 34 in Reshin et al., *1941 God. Dokumenty*, 61–66. For Romanian railway property demanded in June 27 memorandum: Soviet protest filed with Romanian legation in Moscow on July 16, 1940, referencing the four "sovetsko-rumyinskogo soglasheniya ob evakuatsii Bessarabii i Severnoi Bukovinyi ot 28 iyunya c.g.," in AVPRF, fond 125, opis' 22, papka 18, del' 1.

28. Gafencu, *Prelude to the Russian Campaign*, 293. Soviet troops crossing frontier at 4 a.m. instead of 10 a.m.: clipping from *Kurentul*, July 8, 1940, excerpted in TASS summary of Romanian press reports on the invasion, in AVPRF, fond 125, opis' 22, papka 90, del' 35.

29. Molotov speech before the Supreme Soviet, August 1, 1940, translated by the German Foreign Office and preserved in PAAA, R 261183.

30. Citation in Moorhouse, *Devils' Alliance*, 90.

31. Kozlov to Molotov, August 15, 1940, in RGASPI, fond 82, opis' 2, del' 1302, list' 11. German property nationalized: German military intelligence report, November 20, 1940, labeled "Geheim! Umsiedlungsverhandlungen für die baltischen Staaten," op. cit. Estimate on number of Romanians deported: Tolstoy, *Stalin's Secret War*, 205–6.

Chapter 10: Showdown at the Danube Delta

1. OSS report No. 17 on the "Gains of Germany (and Her Allies) Through the Occupation of Soviet Territory," March 14, 1942, in USAHEC, Donovan Papers, box 32C.

2. Citations in Horst Boog et al., eds., *Das Deutsche Reich und der zweite Weltkrieg*, vol. 4, *Der Angriff auf die Sowjetunion* (henceforth Boog et al., *Angriff*), 4, 6.

3. Hitchens, *Phoney Victory*, 91–93.

4. Cited in David Dilks, ed., *The Diaries of Sir Alexander Cadogan, O.M., 1938–1945*, 317fn. For more on the Neutrality Acts and the destroyers, see Robert Dallek, *Franklin D. Roosevelt and American Foreign Policy*,

1932–1945, 244–245. On the gold shipments beginning in May 1939 and the extortionate terms of the destroyers-for-bases deal, see Hitchens, *Phoney Victory*, xvi, 110–11.

5. Cited in Gafencu, *Prelude to the Russian Campaign*, 46. Hitler to Halder: from Halder's war diary, no. 54 in Reshin et al., *1941 God. Dokumenty*, 115–16. Hitler remarks after France surrenders: cited in Stefan Scheil, *Die Eskalation des Zweiten Weltkriegs von 1940 bis zum Unternehmen Barbarossa 1941*, 46.

6. Schulenburg from Moscow, August 2, 1940, excerpting key passages from Molotov's speech of August 1 pertaining to Germany, in PAAA, R 104358. On the German press rollout of the "Massigli affair," see İşçi, "The Massigli Affair," 2.

7. Molotov speech before the Supreme Soviet on August 1, 1940, reproduced in German translation in PAAA, R 104358. Passages on the United States: as excerpted by US embassy counselor Walter Thurston, in his August 1, 1940, report to Washington in NAA, T 1248, Roll 1.

8. Churchill to Stalin, July 1, 1940, in RGASPI, fond 82, opis' 2, del' 1102. "Achieve hegemony in Europe": from the transcript of the meeting in RGASPI, fond 558, opis' 11, del' 278, list' 6. Orme Sargent and "formal and frigid": citations in Moorhouse, *Devils' Alliance*, 154. Stalin informs Hitler about conversation with Cripps: cited in Boog et al., *Angriff*, 7.

9. Maisky to Molotov, July 3–4, 1940, no. 38 in Reshin et al., *1941 God. Dokumenty*, 82–83. Churchill before the Commons: cited in Scheil, *Eskalation des Zweiten Weltkriegs*, 69. Emphasis added.

10. TASS communiqué of June 23, 1940, no. 25 in Reshin et al., *1941 God. Dokumenty*, 47.

11. Citation in Scheil, *Eskalation des Zweiten Weltkriegs*, 69–70. German spy report of June 19, 1940: in BA / MA, RW 5 / v. 353. Teil 1. (OKW / Amt Ausland / Abwehr).

12. Cited in Count Edward Raczynski, *In Allied London*, 58.

13. Cited in Scheil, *Eskalation des Zweiten Weltkriegs*, 71.

14. Draganov from Berlin, June 28 (twice) and 29 and July 1, 1940, in BSA, fond 316K, opis' 1, del' 273, list' 264, 260, 268, 272. Hitler asks Brauchitsch: Stahel, *Operation Barbarossa*, 34–35.

15. Transcript of meeting between Molotov and Schulenburg, July 29, 1940, no. 72 in Reshin et al., *1941 God. Dokumenty*, 136–37.

16. German troop movements east noted by Soviet military intelligence: Beria to Molotov and Stalin, August 13, 1940, and Beria again to same on August 17, 1940, document nos. 89 and 92, in Reshin et al., *1941 God. Dokumenty*, 169, 176–77. Hitler muses about invading the

Soviet Union: Halder war diary from the Berghof, July 31, 1941, no. 73 in Reshin et al., *1941 God. Dokumenty*, 137–38. Partial demobilization of Wehrmacht land forces: Boog et al., *Angriff*, 9 and passim.

17. Gafencu, *Prelude to the Russian Campaign*, 56–57. "Reasonable boundaries": Ribbentrop circular, c. July 26, 1940, in BSA, fond 176K, opis' 8, del' 554.

18. Gafencu, *Prelude to the Russian Campaign*, 297–98. Antonescu bans Soviet films and suppresses Russian-Romanian language dictionaries: see TASS press summary for April 25, 1941, in AVPRF, fond 125, opis' 23, papka 22, delo 19.

19. Cited in Gafencu, *Prelude to the Russian Campaign*, 58.

20. Transcripts of conversation between Molotov and Schulenburg, September 9, 1940, no. 111 in Reshin et al., *1941 God. Dokumenty*, 219–21. For Molotov's Danube commission proposal, see Gafencu, *Prelude to the Russian Campaign*, 67–68.

21. Ibid., 72–73. Ribbentrop to Stalin on October 13, 1940: no. 147 in Reshin et al., *1941 God. Dokumenty*, 305–10. Antonescu offers to pay: Clodius from Bucharest, November 14, 1940, in PAAA, R 30003.

22. Aide-Mémoires submitted by the Romanian legation in Moscow, September 19 and October 2, 1940, in AVPRF, fond 125, opis' 22, papka 18, del' 4.

23. Gafencu, *Prelude to the Russian Campaign*, 76–78. On the prisoner exchange: Soviet Foreign Ministry, "Pamyatnaya Zapiska," submitted to the Romanian legation in Moscow, December 27, 1940, in AVPRF, fond 125, opis' 22, papka 18, del' 1.

Chapter 11: Summit in Berlin

1. Cited in Wayne S. Cole, *Roosevelt and the Isolationists, 1932–1945*, 400.

2. Molotov commentary in *Pravda* on the "Berlinskii Pakt o troist-vennom soyuze," September 30, 1940, no. 131 in Reshin et al., *1941 God. Dokumenty*, 276–77.

3. Cited in Gafencu, *Prelude to the Russian Campaign*, 85. Agreements with Romania: see Clodius reports from Bucharest, October 21 and 26, November 12, and (on Antonescu's promises) November 14 and December 12, 1940, in PAAA, R 30003.

4. Steinhardt from Moscow, November 10, 1940 (at 11 p.m.), in NAA, Record Group 59, T1247, Microfilm Roll 13. Cripps's discomfiture about the Molotov summit was observed with schadenfreude by the Vichy

French ambassador, M. Eirik Labonne, in his dispatch of November 14, 1940, in QO, Etats-Unis 54, 159-6. Cripps's first audience with Stalin, on July 1, 1940, was his last until July 8, 1941—that is, until after Hitler had invaded the USSR. The Soviet transcripts of all of Cripps's audiences are in RGASPI, fond 558, opis' 11, del' 278. "Great and realistic statesman": cited in Gafencu, *Prelude to the Russian Campaign*, 107.

5. Schulenburg from Moscow, November 10, 1940, in PAAA, R 104359.

6. Details in Moorhouse, *Devils' Alliance*, 195–97; and Montefiore, *Court of the Red Tsar*, 337.

7. Montefiore, *Court of the Red Tsar*, 337–38; and Moorhouse, *Devils' Alliance*, 197.

8. Transcript of Molotov-Ribbentrop meeting on the afternoon of November 12, 1940, typed by V. Pavlov, no. 171 in Reshin et al., *1941 God. Dokumenty*, 356–61.

9. Ibid.

10. Transcript of Hitler-Molotov meeting on November 12, 1940, transcript by V. Pavlov and V. Bogdanov, no. 172 in Reshin et al., *1941 God. Dokumenty*, 361–66. The Soviet typescript makes no mention of the air-raid alarm, the most famous episode of the summit. "Intolerable and unjust": cited in Moorhouse, *Devils' Alliance*, 201.

11. Stalin to Molotov, 10:20 p.m. on November 12, 1940, replying to Molotov to Stalin, 4:20 p.m. on November 12, 1940, no. 173 and 174 in Reshin et al., *1941 God. Dokumenty*, 366–67. Berezhkov rebuked by Molotov: see Moorhouse, *Devils' Alliance*, 202–3.

12. Molotov telegram from Berlin, 5:10 a.m. on November 13, 1940, in RGASPI, fond 558, opis' 11, del' 216.

13. Stalin telegram to Molotov, 11 a.m. on November 13, 1940, no. 177 in Reshin et al., *1941 God. Dokumenty*, 374. "I got your message": Molotov to Stalin, November 13, 1940 (received in Moscow at 5 p.m.), in RGASPI, fond 558, opis' 11, del' 216, list' 54.

14. Transcript of Molotov meeting with Hitler, November 13, 1940, no. 179 in Reshin et al., *1941 God. Dokumenty*, 375–77. Luncheon menu: Montefiore, *Court of the Red Tsar*, 339.

15. Transcript of Molotov meeting with Hitler, November 13, 1940, no. 179 in Reshin et al., *1941 God. Dokumenty*, 378–80.

16. Ibid., 380–83.

17. Cited in Montefiore, *Court of the Red Tsar*, 340. There are reasons to doubt that this exchange was so perfectly turned out, as our source is

Molotov, who gave himself the winning line. Nonetheless, contemporary accounts agree that the bombing raid did occur.

18. A Russian-language translation of Ribbentrop's draft proposal of November 13, 1940, is reproduced as no. 182 in Reshin et al., *1941 God. Dokumenty*, 391–92. The handwritten original is preserved in PAAA, Botschaft Moskau 544.

19. Entry for November 15, 1940, in *The Goebbels Diaries, 1939–1941*, ed. and trans. Fred Taylor, 74.

20. Molotov to Stalin, November 14, 1940, at 1:20 a.m., received in Moscow at 4:50 a.m., in RGASPI, fond 558, opis' 11, del' 216, list' 56–58.

21. Schulenburg handwritten report of Molotov's reply to Ribbentrop's invitation to join the Tripartite Pact, November 25, 1940, in PAAA, Botschaft Moskau 544.

Chapter 12: Hitler Bars the Door

1. Cited in Gerhard Schreiber et al., eds. *Germany and the Second World War. Edited by the Militärgeschichtliches Forschungsamt*, 3:457. On the Tripartite Pact signing ceremonies: Gafencu, *Prelude to the Russian Campaign*, 122, 126–28.

2. Draganov from Berlin, December 3, 1940, in BSA, fond 316K, opis' 1, del' 273, list' 25. On the importance of Balkan nonferrous metals and ores for German war industry, see Jozo Tomasevich, *War and Revolution in Yugoslavia, 1941–1945: Occupation and Collaboration*, 633 and passim.

3. Cited in Georgi Markov, *Druga Istoriya na nai-goliamata voina*, vol. 1, *Razgarnyianeto na pozhara*, 288. A copy of the Bulgarian Foreign Ministry circular of November 20 is in BSA, fond 176K, opis' 33, del' 66, list' 69. Molotov summons Stamenev: Woermann from Moscow, November 22, 1940, in PAAA, Botschaft Moskau 541.

4. Entry for November 25, 1940, in *Diary of Georgi Dimitrov*, 135–36. For Filov's praise of Hitler, and the press jubilation in Sofia: BSA, fond 176K, opis' 8, del' 557, list' 48 and passim.

5. Entry for November 25, 1940, in *Diary of Georgi Dimitrov*, 136–37. Emphasis added.

6. Ibid., 137–38.

7. Richthofen from Sofia, December 15, 1940, reporting on a long conversation with Prime Minister Filov, in PAAA, Botschaft Moskau 541.

8. Cited in Gafencu, *Prelude to the Russian Campaign*, 129. Russians complain to German embassy: Richthofen from Sofia, December 19,

1940, in PAAA, Botschaft Moskau 541. Wire to Molotov declining offer: cited in entry for 20 December 1940, in *Diary of Georgi Dimitrov*, 139. On King Boris III and Filov quietly agreeing to let German troops into Bulgaria in December 1940: see Schreiber et al., *Germany and the Second World War*, 3:464.

9. Mackensen from Rome, April 23, 1941, collating a series of reports from regional consuls (Italian and German) in and around Romania's borders with the USSR, in PAAA, Botschaft Moskau 543. Fourteen aerodromes in Moldavia SSR planned for 1941: Lebedev report dated May 26, 1941, "Spisok odnopolosnyikh reshenii aerodromov," in GARF, fond 8437, opis' 1, del' 1, list' 20–21.

10. Politburo resolution no. 91 dated November 4, 1940 ("O peredache oboronitel'nogo stroitel'stva na poluostrove Khanko") in RGASPI, fond 17, opis' 162, del' 30. On the Hanko fortifications, see directive dated January 13, 1941, in RGVA, fond 25888, opis' 3, del' 189.

11. German embassy report from Helsinki, December 12, 1940, passed on to Ambassador Schulenburg in Moscow, in PAAA, Botschaft Moskau 541.

12. Tippelskirch from Moscow, December 9, 1940, in PAAA, Botschaft Moskau 543. "Not at all friendly to Germany": Schellhorn from Czernowitz (Chernivsti), February 9, 1940, in PAAA, Botschaft Moskau 495. Molotov to Kreve-Mickevicius: cited in Scheil, *Eskalation des Zweiten Weltkriegs*, 51. "The view is universally held in Soviet military circles": German military intelligence report, June 13, 1940, in BA/MA, RW 5 / v. 357.

For an example of Soviet intelligence on German troop movements in Eastern Europe in this period, see Dekanozov memorandum to Molotov on "German War Preparations," December 7, 1940, no. 204, and Red Army General Staff to Timoshenko on "the assembly of German troops in the Balkans," December 10, 1940, no. 206, both in Reshin et al., *1941 God. Dokumenty*, 440–41, 443.

13. "Führerweisung vom 18. Dezember 1940," no. 13 in Walter Post, *Unternehmen Barbarossa: Deutsche und sowjetische Angriffspläne 1940/41*, 390–92. "Fistfight breaking out between the Italian and Soviet delegations": cited in Moorhouse, *Devils' Alliance*, 216. On the breakup of the Bucharest conference and its significance, see also Gafencu, *Prelude to the Russian Campaign*, 82–83.

Chapter 13: Mobilizing the Proletariat

1. *Pravda* leader of December 31, 1940: cited in Gafencu, *Prelude to the Russian Campaign*, 128.

2. Third Soviet Five-Year Plan targets: cited in Lennart Samuelson, *Plans for Stalin's War Machine: Tukhachevskii and Military-Economic Planning, 1926–1941*, 191. Soviet warplanes operational by end of 1940: from "Postanovlenie soveta narodnyikh Komissarov Soyuza SSR 'O Voenno-Vozdushnyikh Silakh Krasnoi Armii,'" November 5, 1940, no. 165 in Reshin et al., *1941 God. Dokumenty*, 344. Figures for Soviet tanks by the end of 1940: cited Musial, *Kampfplatz Deutschland*, 322. Panzers prior to the Battle of France: figures in Boog et al., *Angriff*, 185. Luftwaffe and RAF: Beevor, *Second World War*, 131. Soviet warplanes deployed in Finland: Mark Solonin, "25 June. Stupidity or Aggression?," October 20, 2014, www.solonin.org/en/article_mark-solonin-25-june-stupidity3. Soviet submarine fleet: Mark Solonin, "Comrade Stalin's Three Plans," May 31, 2011, www.solonin.org/en/article_comrade-stalins-three-plans.

3. Cited in Mawdsley, *Thunder in the East*, 43–44.

4. Soviet manpower strength in peacetime by end of 1940: "Zapiska Narkoma Oboronyi i Nachal'nika Genshtaba Krasnoi Armii," c. October 11, 1940, no. 140 in Reshin et al., *1941 God. Dokumenty*, 298. Soviet mobilization plan for 1938: table 14 in Musial, *Kampfplatz Deutschland*, 304. Soviet mobilization plans for 1940 and 1941 (as of December 1940): table III.22 and accompanying text, in Bernd Schwipper, *Deutschland im Visier Stalins: Der Weg der roten Armee in den europäischen Krieg und der Aufmarsch der Wehrmacht 1941*, 122. German intelligence estimates: Boog et al., *Angriff*, 199. German soldiers under arms, as of May 1, 1941: Post, *Unternehmen Barbarossa*, 212.

5. Gosplan resolution, "O Gosudarstvennyikh Trudovyikh Rezervakh SSSR," ratified by President Kalinin on October 2, 1940, and Kalinin labor *ukaz* on the seven-day week, dated June 26, 1940, both in RGAE, fond 4372 (Gosplan), opis' 38, del' 1, list' 72 (and back), 133–35.

6. Figures in table 7 in Musial, *Stalins Beutezug*, 385. For the Politburo's order of 600 T-34s: "Postanovleniya SNK SSSR I TsK VKP (b) 'O proizvodstve tankov T-34 v 1940 godu," June 7, 1940, signed by Molotov and Stalin, no. 7 in Reshin et al., *1941 God. Dokumenty*, 1:26. On the "Christie suspension," see Horne, *Hubris*, 175. For more on the capacity of the T-34, see David Glantz, *Stumbling Colossus: The Red Army on the Eve of World War*, 119 and passim. Glantz makes no mention of the T-40 in

his chapter on Soviet tanks and other "mechanized forces" (116–145), which was such a huge priority in Soviet procurement in 1940–1941. It was clearly not mentioned in the Soviet General Staff "Collection of Combat Documents of the Great Patriotic War," published between 1947 and 1960, which furnishes Glantz's main source on Soviet procurement and logistics.

7. Table 7 in Musial, *Stalins Beutezug*, 385. For detailed production figures on the T-40 series tanks, see table 9 in Mel'tyukhov, *Upushchennyi shans Stalina*, 598.

8. Politburo resolution no. 93, November 5, 1940, in RGASPI, fond 17, opis' 162, del' 30.

9. *Pravda* headline: cited in Viktor Suvorov, *The Chief Culprit: Stalin's Grand Design to Start World War II*, 73. For more on the parachutists' role in the airborne brigades, see Glantz, *Stumbling Colossus*, 146–49. While Glantz's book was written to refute Suvorov's arguments about the Soviet deployment in 1941, and it tends to downplay offensive strategic intent behind Soviet decisions, it is striking how many points of common emphasis there are—the expansion of airborne assault brigades is a prominent example.

10. "Postanovlenie soveta narodnyikh Komissarov Soyuza SSR 'O Voenno-Vozdushnyikh Silakh Krasnoi Armii,'" November 5, 1940, op. cit. For numbers of Su-2s and Mig-3s ordered for 1941 in December 1940: "O programme vyipuska samoletov i aviamotorov v 1941," Politburo resolution, December 7, 1940, in RGASPI, fond 17, opis' 162, del' 30. Annual Soviet production figures of warplanes: table 10 in Mel'tyukhov, *Upushchennyi shans Stalina*, 600. Compare to figures in Glantz, *Stumbling Colossus*, 186–87 (although Glantz misses the Su-2 and the Mig-3). Glantz argues that the fighter-bomber balance by summer 1941 showed a heightened emphasis on "the role of air support for ground forces, in particular, tactically," and concedes that the speeches at a Red Army commanders' conference in Moscow in December 1940 emphasized "air support of offensive operations." Here, as elsewhere, Glantz is honest enough to provide evidence supporting the Rezun-Suvorov thesis, whether or not he means to.

11. Mark Solonin, *Na mirno spiashchikh aerodromakh . . . 22 iunia 1941*, 46–51 and passim. On the Su-2 and Il-2 see also Suvorov, *Chief Culprit*, 58–72. While Suvorov oversells the special qualities of the Su-2 (and exaggerates the number ordered, claiming that Stalin wanted one hundred thousand of them produced before the German invasion changed aviation priorities), he is not wrong that the Su-2 was a major priority of

Soviet procurement in the months before the German invasion, and he is still more right about the Il-2, production of which ramped up even further after the war started. The now-available Politburo records are full of excited talk about the Su-2, Il-2, and Pe-2 all through fall 1940 and winter 1941, with planned output (in the December 7, 1940, Politburo resolution cited above) of the Su-2 ramping up from 165 in the first quarter of 1941 to 485 by first quarter of 1942, and of the Il-2, from 45 to 805. So enamored was Stalin with the potential of the Su-2 that, in January 1941, he asked Factory No. 135 to produce three different versions of the Su-2 with slightly varying bomb-bay capacities, while ordering Sukhoi to design an even more lethal version, the Su-4, as soon as he could. See pt. 69 in the Politburo transcript for January 25, 1941, in RGASPI, fond 17, opis' 162, del' 32.

12. "Zapiska Narkoma Oboronyi SSSR i Nachal'nika Genshtaba Krasnoi Armii v TsK VKP (b) I. V. Stalinu i V. M. Molotovu ob osnovakh strategicheskogo razvertyivaniya vooruzhenyikh sil SSSR na zapade i na vostoke na 1940 i 1941 godyi," submitted by S. Timoshenko and B. Shaposhnikov on August 18, 1940, no. 95 in Reshin et al., *1941 God. Dokumenty*, 1:181–193.

13. "Zapiska Narkoma Oboronyi SSSR i Nachal'nika Genshtaba Krasnoi Armii v TsK VKP (b) I. V. Stalinu i V. M. Molotovu ob osnovakh strategicheskogo razvertyivaniya vooruzhenyikh sil SSSR na zapade i na vostoke na 1940 i 1941 godyi," submitted by Timoshenko and Meretskov on September 18, 1940, no. 117 in Reshin et al., *1941 God. Dokumenty*, 1:236–53.

14. "Zapiska Narkoma Oboronyi SSSR i Nachal'nika Genshtaba Krasnoi Armii v TsK VKP (b)—I. V. Stalinu i V. M. Molotovu," October 5, 1940, no. 134 in Reshin et al., *1941 God. Dokumenty*, 1:288–90. Emphasis added. For more on the meetings leading up to this document, see Mark Solonin, "Tri plana tovarisch' Stalina," February 25, 2009, www.solonin.org/en/article_tri-plana-tovarischa-stalina.

15. "Zapiska nachal'nika shtaba KOVO [eg Kiev military district] po resheniyu voennogo soveta yugo-zapadnogo front apo planu razvertyivaniya na 1940 god," prepared by M. A. Purkaev, c. December 1940, no. 224 in Reshin et al., *1941 God. Dokumenty*, 1:484–97.

16. "Spisok zashifrovannyikh aerodromov, naznachennyikh stroitel'stvom po Glavnomu Upravleniyu Stroitel'stva Aerodromov NKVD SSSR na 1941 god," April 1, 1941, in GARF, fond 8437, opis' 1, del' 1, list' 43–47 (and backs). On the cost of the new aerodromes, see Politburo resolution 171, "O meropriyatiyakh po obespecheniyu stroitel'stva 251

aerodroma dlya Narkomata Oboronyi v 1941 godu," March 24, 1941, in RGASPI, fond 17, opis' 162, del' 33.

17. On the re-gauging of the Polish railway net, see OSS report dated March 24, 1942, on the "Gains of Germany (and her Allies) Through the Occupation of Soviet Territory," 72, in USAHEC, Donovan Papers, box 32C. The dismantling of the Stalin line forms a huge part of the controversial Suvorov thesis about Stalin's offensive war plans in 1941. For a summing up of his argument, see Suvorov, "Destruction of the Stalin Line," in *Chief Culprit*, 171–77. Here, as elsewhere, Suvorov hurts his case by over-egging the pudding. The best evidence we have is that the old pillboxes were not torn down so much as neglected. Just as in France, the Germans were able to bypass what remained of the Molotov and Stalin lines without too much difficulty. The real problem was that the Soviet-German-Romanian frontier, stretching from the Baltic to the Black Sea, was far too long for effective fortification to cover. For a more balanced, and better sourced, discussion of this problem, see Solonin, "25 June. Stupidity or Aggression?," op. cit.

18. Solonin, "Tri plana tovarisch' Stalina," op. cit.

19. Ibid.

20. Ibid.

21. "Iz plana Genshtaba Krasnoi Armii o strategicheskom razverty-ivanii vooruzhenyikh sil sovetskogo soiuza na zapade i vostoke," submitted by Timoshenko and Zhukov on March 11, 1941, no. 315 in Reshin et al., *1941 God. Dokumenty*, 741–46. This is a truncated version of the plan. This document is also reproduced in German translation as document 17 in Post, *Unternehmen Barbarossa*, 408–12. "Commence the attack on June 12": cited by Solonin (who has seen the original), in "Tri plana tovarisch' Stalina," op cit. For discussion of this mobilization plan in relation to earlier ones: Mel'tyukhov, *Upushchennyi shans Stalina*, 372–74.

22. "Iz plana Genshtaba Krasnoi Armii o strategicheskom razverty-ivanii vooruzhenyikh sil sovetskogo soiuza na zapade i vostoke," op. cit.

Chapter 14: The Battle for Belgrade

1. See Gafencu, *Prelude to the Russian Campaign*, 135.

2. Johann Wuescht, *Jugoslawien und das dritte Reich*, 42–43.

3. Ibid., 37 and 37n40. See also Roberts, *Storm of War*, 116, 124.

4. Citations and context in Douglas Waller, *Wild Bill Donovan: The Spymaster Who Created the OSS and Modern American Espionage*, 60–61,

64–65. On Donovan's British liaison officer, see Bradley Smith, *The Shadow Warriors: O.S.S. and the Origins of the C.I.A*, 48–49.

5. Waller, *Wild Bill Donovan*, 65–66. For the version where Donovan gets burgled on the train, see "L'Odyssée du Colonel Donovan," in Archives Diplomatiques et Consulaires, February 1941, in USAHEC, Donovan Papers, box 66A. Filov's diary entry was published as part of his trial defense after Bulgaria switched sides in the war, forwarded on March 28, 1945, to Donovan by William Langer, in USAHEC, box 66A.

6. Cited in Anthony Cave Brown, *Wild Bill Donovan: The Last Hero*, 156.

7. Cited in Constantin Fotitch, *The War We Lost: Yugoslavia's Tragedy and the Failure of the West*, 46–47. Paul to Roosevelt: cited in Hoover, *Freedom Betrayed*, 179. "No halfway house in the war": Demaree Bess, "Our Frontier on the Danube. The Appalling Story of Our Meddling in the Balkans," *Saturday Evening Post*, May 24, 1941. "Yugoslavia would not permit the passage of German troops": cited in Brown, *Last Hero*, 157.

8. Umansky approaches Welles: see Mikoyan's instructions to Umansky, January 7, 1941, no. 34 in Yakovlev et al., *Sovetsko-amerikanskie otnosheniya 1939–1945*, 110. On the president trusting Welles over Hull, see Fleming, *New Dealers' War*, 15–16.

9. See the account of the lend-lease congressional debate submitted by Oscar Cox to Mr. Harry L. Hopkins, dated June 23, 1941, and letter from "Mr. Young" to Hopkins, headlined "Russian Clearance Problems Requiring Immediate Attention," March 1, 1941, both in the Harry L. Hopkins Papers (Sherwood Collection) at the FDR Library, box 305, book 4.

10. Citations (including the details footnoted here) in Hitchens, *Phoney Victory*, 66–67.

11. Miner, *Between Churchill and Stalin*, 113.

12. Bess, "Our Frontier on the Danube."

13. See, for example, the Yugoslav Communist Party pamphlet "Against Capitulation—In Favor of a Mutual Assistance Pact with the Soviet Union," submitted to Moscow for approval, no. 300 in V. V. Zelenii et al., eds., *Sovetsko-yugoslavskoe otnosheniya 1917–1941 gg.*, 358–60.

14. Churchill to Prince Regent Paul, March 22, 1941, reproduced in Winston Churchill, *The Grand Alliance*, 160. On Campbell's message to Prince Regent Paul on March 5, 1941: Churchill, *Grand Alliance*, 98. "Should bear in mind": cited in Jozo Tomasevich, *The Chetniks: War and Revolution in Yugoslavia, 1941–1945*, 43.

15. Fotitch, *War We Lost*, 60. Five hundred and fifty thousand German troops in Romania and Bulgaria: Soviet agent report from Budapest, March 15, 1941, no. 323 in Reshin et al., *1941 God. Dokumenty*, 1:771. "You talk of our honor": cited in Smith, *Shadow Warriors*, 52.

16. Ibid., 70–73.

17. Bess, "Our Frontier on the Danube." For more details on the coup: Fotitch, *War We Lost*, 77–81. For an account that gives more credit to General Bora Mirkovich and the SOE than Simovich, see Tomasevich, *The Chetniks*, 45–47. Detail about German and Italian shops being looted: Report of V. Z. Lebedev, the Soviet chargé d'affaires in Belgrade, March 28, 1941, no. 303 in Zelenii et al., *Sovetsko-yugoslavskoe otnosheniya*, 363.

18. Citations in Tomasevich, *The Chetniks*, 85.

19. Cited in Fotitch, *War We Lost*, 79–80. See also "Vozzvanie TsK KPYu s prizyivom borot'sya za zaklyuchenie Pakta a vzaimnoi pomoshchi s SSSR," no. 304 in Zelenii et al., *Sovetsko-yugoslavskoe otnosheniya*, 363–65. Soviet chargé d'affaires: Report of V. Z. Lebedev, March 28, 1941, op. cit. Golikov: cited in Kotkin, *Stalin*, 2:847.

20. Cited in Gafencu (to whom Gavrilovich reported this conversation), *Prelude to the Russian Campaign*, 148. Gafencu's version matches the one published recently in "Stalin's Table Talk" (*Zastolnye rechi Stalina*), 245–46, from the memoirs of N. V. Novikov. "Prevent Germany from attacking us" and request for Soviet arms on March 30, 1941: Lebedev to Molotov, March 30, 1941, no. 305 in Zelenii et al., *Sovetsko-yugoslavskoe otnosheniya*, 365–66. Shipments of anti-tank guns and warplanes: Kotkin, *Stalin*, 2:848. Bozich on Stalin's proposal of a military alliance: cited in Scheil, *Eskalation des Zweiten Weltkriegs*, 120.

21. Wuescht, *Jugoslawien und das dritte Reich*, 45–47. Germans informed: Schulenburg to Ribbentrop from Moscow on April 4, 1941, no. 217 in "Seidl Dokumente," 363–65. The Soviet-Yugoslav "Friendship and Non-Aggression Pact" is reproduced as no. 320 in Zelenii et al., *Sovetsko-yugoslavskoe otnosheniya*, 375. On Stalin backdating the pact with Yugoslavia, see Ivan Krylov, *Soviet Staff Officer*, trans. Edward Fitzgerald, 71.

22. Wuescht, *Jugoslawien und das dritte Reich*, 45–47. For details on the aerial campaign, see Brian Cull and Christopher Shores, *Air War for Yugoslavia, Greece, and Crete, 1940–41*, 222–29. On Mihailović and the early days of the Chetnik resistance, see Tomasevich, *The Chetniks*, 122 and passim.

23. Details in Beevor, *Second World War*, 154–65.

24. Stalin to Voroshilov: cited in Kotkin, *Stalin*, 2:849.

25. Luigi Villari, "Colonel Donovan's Mission," May 6, 1941, forwarded to Donovan on March 27, 1945, in USAHEC, Donovan Papers, box 2.

26. On the pushing back of the launch date for Barbarossa, see Andreas Hillgruber, *Hitlers Strategie: Politik und Kriegführung 1940–1941*, 505 and passim. Churchill to Stalin on April 3, 1941: cited in Kotkin, *Stalin*, 2:850.

Chapter 15: Operation Snow

1. George Lensen, *The Strange Neutrality: Soviet-Japanese Relations During the Second World War*, 8. "Adjust our relations": cited in Lupke, *Japans Russlandpolitik*, 79n2. Deal of October 3, 1940: cited in Paine, *Wars for Asia*, 178.

2. Lupke, *Japans Russlandpolitik*, 95; and Lensen, *Strange Neutrality*, 12.

3. Lensen, *Strange Neutrality*, 14; Lupke, *Japans Russlandpolitik*, 95; and Kotkin, *Stalin*, 2:851.

4. Schulenburg to Ribbentrop, March 25, 1941, no. 210 in "Seidl Dokumente," 322–23; and transcript of the Kremlin meeting between Matsuoka and Stalin, March 23, 1941, no. 333 in Reshin et al., *1941 God. Dokumenty*, 1:791.

5. Hitler's March 5, 1941, order is cited in Lupke, *Japans Russlandpolitik*, 96n26. For analysis, see also Gordon Prange, *Target Tokyo: The Story of the Sorge Spy Ring*, 368–69.

6. "Aufzeichnung über die Unterredung zwischen dem Reichsaußenminister und dem japanischen Außenminister Matsuoka," March 27, 1941, no. 211 in "Seidl Dokumente," 323–28.

7. "Aufzeichnung über die Unterredung zwischen dem Führer und dem japanischen Außenminister Matsuoka," March 27, 1941, no. 212 in "Seidl Dokumente," 332–42.

8. "Aufzeichnung über die Unterredung zwischen dem Reichsaußenminister und dem japanischen Außenminister Matsuoka," March 28, 1941, and "Aufzeichnung über die Unterredung zwischen dem Reichsaußenminister und dem japanischen Außenminister Matsuoka," March 29, 1941, nos. 213–14, in "Seidl Dokumente," 342–49.

9. "Aufzeichnung über die Unterredung zwischen dem Reichsaußenminister und dem japanischen Außenminister Matsuoka," March 29, 1941, no. 214 in "Seidl Dokumente," 347–49. For more on Matsuoka's thinking, see Lupke, *Japans Russlandpolitik*, 97.

10. Schulenburg protests: Transcript of Schulenburg meeting with Vishinsky, March 24, 1941, no. 334 in Reshin et al., *1941 God. Dokumenty*, 793–94. Turkish message intercepted on March 26, 1941, no. 338 in Reshin et al., *1941 God. Dokumenty*, 797–98. Beria's agents report to Molotov and Stalin on March 27, 1941, no. 340, in Reshin et al., *1941 God. Dokumenty*, 799–800. Schulenburg confronts Molotov: Schulenburg to Ribbentrop, April 4, 1941, no. 217 in "Seidl Dokumente," 364.

11. Transcript of the Stalin-Matsuoka meeting on April 12, 1941, no. 383 in Reshin et al., *1941 God. Dokumenty*, 69–71.

12. Ibid., 71–74.

13. Cited in Scheil, *Eskalation des Zweiten Weltkriegs*, 15. The terms of the Soviet-Japanese Neutrality Pact of April 13, 1941, are reproduced as no. 384 in Reshin et al., *1941 God. Dokumenty*, 2:74–75. On the implications of the key clauses, see Lupke, *Japans Russlandpolitik*, 100–101. *Japan Times and Advertiser*: cited in Lensen, *Strange Neutrality*, 18.

14. Citations in Lensen, *Strange Neutrality*, 18–19.

15. Dispatch from Jack Scott, a *News Chronicle* correspondent, forwarded by the British embassy in Moscow, April 18, 1941, in PRO, FO 371/29480. Gushing thank you footnoted: Matsuoka to Stalin, April 21, 1941, in RGASPI, fond 558, opis' 11, del' 404, list' 118–20.

16. Ibid., and Schulenburg to Ribbentrop (by wire), April 13, 1941, no. 224 in "Seidl Dokumente," 371–72.

17. US embassy report from Moscow, circa mid-April 1941, in NAA, Record Group 59, T 1248, Roll 1. "Diplomatic blitzkrieg": cited in Moorhouse, *Devils' Alliance*, 231.

18. See Romerstein and Breindel, *Venona Secrets*, 32–33.

19. Pavlov, *Operatsiya 'Sneg'*, 35–36.

20. Ibid., 36; and John Koster, *Operation Snow: How a Soviet Mole in FDR's White House Triggered Pearl Harbor*, 3.

21. Cited in Koster, *Operation Snow*, 7.

22. Cited (with dating and context) in Romerstein and Breindel, *Venona Secrets*, 41–42.

23. Cited with accompanying commentary in Koster, *Operation Snow*, 42–47.

Chapter 16: To the Brink

1. Cited in Miner, *Between Churchill and Stalin*, 129. Churchill shares Ultra intercept: David Murphy, *What Stalin Knew: The Enigma of Barbarossa*, 148.

2. Tippelskirch from Moscow, April 22, 1941, in PAAA, Botschaft Moskau 543. Molotov complains of overflights: Tippelskirch to Ribbentrop, April 22, 1941, no. 228 in "Seidl Dokumente," 376–77. German troop movements: Post, *Unternehmen Barbarossa*, 245.

3. Tippelskirch to Ribbentrop from Moscow, April 22, 1941, op. cit. Different dates reported: as cited in Post, *Unternehmen Barbarossa*, 280. For more intelligence reports from Helsinki, Sofia, Bucharest, and Tokyo: Constantine Pleshakov, *Stalin's Folly: The Tragic First Ten Days of World War II on the Eastern Front*, 86–87. Sorge changing his estimate to "by the end of June": cited in Owen Matthews, *An Impeccable Spy: Richard Sorge, Stalin's Master Agent*, 280.

4. NKVD reports about German failure to prepare for winter campaigning: cited in Suvorov, *Chief Culprit*, 249. Not all of Suvorov's claims stand up, but this one gels well with Stalin's sanguine attitude toward reports of the German arms buildup. Stephen Kotkin, in his multivolume biography of *Stalin* (2:856, 892), advances a similar argument about Stalin's likely rationale in allowing German overflights and visits to Soviet war production facilities.

5. Gafencu, *Prelude to the Russian Campaign*, 188.

6. Ibid., 194. "From defense to offense" (*ot oborony k nastupleniiu*): "Vyistuplenie general'nogo sekretarya TsK VKP (b) I. V. Stalina pered vyipusknikami voennyikh akademii RKKA v Kremle," May 5, 1941, op. cit., 162. "Era of the peace policy is at an end": from the Hilger-Gehlen version cited in Förster and Mawdsley, "Hitler and Stalin in Perspective," op. cit., 84.

7. Schulenburg to Ribbentrop (by wire), May 7, 1941, and again (via courier), May 12, 1941, nos. 235 and 236 in "Seidl Dokumente," 385–89.

8. "Zapiska Narkoma Oboronyi SSSR i Nachal'nika Genshtaba Krasnoi Armii Predsedatel'yu SNK SSSR I. V. Stalinu," May 15, 1941, no. 473 in Reshin et al., *1941 God. Dokumenty*, 2:215–20. For analysis of this plan, see also Mawdsley, *Thunder in the East*, 38. Schulenburg and other German diplomats ordered to counter rumors: see German Foreign Office Aufzeichnung dated May 7, 1941, in PAAA, Botschaft Moskau 543.

9. Cripps: op. cit. Hess treated as a prisoner of war: see Churchill to Eden, May 13, 1941, reproduced in *Grand Alliance*, 51. Soviet spies reported Hess carried genuine peace offer: "Spravka vneshnei razvedki NKGB SSSR," May 14, 1941, and "Spravka vneshnei razvedki NKGB SSSR," May 22, 1941, nos. 467 and 485 in Reshin et al., *1941 God. Dokumenty*, 2:200–201, 248–49. For an intriguing interpretation of the Hess

affair based on revelations from declassified British documents, see Martin Allen, *The Hitler/Hess Deception*.

10. Cited in Moorhouse, *Devils' Alliance*, 238.

11. Merkulov to Beria, Molotov, and Stalin, May 25, 1941, passing on Litzeist, May 19, 1941, no. 493 in Reshin et al., *1941 God. Dokumenty*, 2:259–60.

12. Report of "Kühlborn" to the German embassy in Moscow on April 3, 1941; report by the German military attaché in Stockholm, April 7, 1941; Mackensen to Ribbentrop from Rome, April 23, 1941; and German ambassador in Madrid, May 5, 1941, all in PAAA, Botschaft Moskau 543.

13. "Dokladnaia zapiska NKGB SSSR v TsK VKP (b)," signed by Merkulov for Beria, May 14, 1941, no. 474 in Reshin et al., *1941 God. Dokumenty*, 221; and Politburo resolution no. 117, May 14, 1941, in RGASPI, fond 17, opis' 162, del' 34. Serov's June 4 order: cited in Tolstoy, *Stalin's Secret War*, 221.

14. Reports filed on June 1, 3, 5, 6, 8, 11, and 12, 1941, in BA/MA, RH 2 / 312 (Tagesverlauf und Tagesmeldungen Bd III. 27 Mai 1941–4 Augt 1941). Romanian complaints about Soviet violations of Romanian airspace: "Notes Verbales" filed by the Romanian legation in Moscow on March 27, April 26 and 30, and May 2, 20, 22, and 29, 1941, in AVPRF, fond 125, opis' 23, papka 21, del' 2.

15. "Soobschenie TASS," June 13, 1941, in Reshin et al., *1941 God. Dokumenty*, 2:361. For more on the Cripps connection to this communiqué, see Solonin, "25 June. Stupidity or Aggression?"

16. "Spravka o razvertyivanii Vooruzhennyikh Sil SSSR na sluchai voinyi na zapade," June 13, 1941, in Reshin et al., *1941 God. Dokumenty*, 2:358–61, and Solonin, "Comrade Stalin's Three Plans," op. cit. Emphasis added. For more details on Soviet troop movements toward the western frontier, see Mel'tyukhov, *Upushchennyi shans Stalina*, 408–13 and passim. Timoshenko and Zhukov pointed out: cited in Pleshakov, *Stalin's Folly*, 80.

17. Cited in Moorhouse, *Devils' Alliance*, 247.

18. "O narushenii sovetskoi granitsyi inostrannyimi samoletami s 10 po 19 iyunya 1941 g.," no. 586 in Reshin et al., *1941 God. Dokumenty*, 2:396–97.

19. Figures in Post, *Unternehmen Barbarossa*, 248–53; and, for the foreign divisions, Stahel, *Operation Barbarossa*, 356–59.

20. Solonin, in "Comrade Stalin's Three Plans," places July 19 as the earliest possible launch date for a Soviet offensive in 1941, with late

August or early September as the latest, after which time, owing to the onset of wet fall weather, "it would be too risky to commence a large-scale offensive in southern Poland and in the Balkans." Mel'tyukhov, in *Upushchennyi shans Stalina*, pegs the earliest possible launch date—based on available data from Soviet troop concentration orders—at July 15, 1941.

Not all historians agree. The most strident cases against the "Suvorov thesis" have been mounted by Glantz in *Stumbling Colossus* and Gabriel Gorodetsky in *Grand Delusion: Stalin and the German Invasion of Russia*. Neither Glantz nor Gorodetsky, alas, has replied to more recent, well-documented work by Mel'tyukhov and Solonin, or the nuanced interpretation by Mawdsley in *Thunder in the East*, in chap. 1, "Preparations and Perceptions."

21. Mel'tyukhov, in *Upushchennyi shans Stalina*, 411; Solonin, "Comrade Stalin's Three Plans" and "25 June. Stupidity or Aggression?", op. cit., and *June 1941. Final Diagnosis*, in English at www.solonin.org/en /article_mark-solonin-june-1941-final.

22. Politburo resolution no. 171 of March 24, 1941, "O meropriyatiyakh po obespecheniyu stroitel'stva 251 aerodroma dlya Narkomata Oboronyi v 1941 godu," in RGASPI, fond 17, opis' 162, del' 33; and resolution no. 40 of May 5, 1941, in RGASPI, fond 17, opis' 162, del' 34. For other resolutions relating to weapons procurement, weapons systems, petrol depots and so on: open to almost any page at random from the Politburo files for the first six months of 1941, for example, resolution no. 1 of April 10, 1941 ("O reorganizatsii sistemyi aviatsionnogo tyila"), ramping up the production schedule for Mig fighters, in RGASPI, fond 17, opis' 162, del' 34.

23. Hitler's speech on June 22, 1941, as reproduced by the Bulgarian Telegraph Agency, in BSA, fond 176, opis' 8, del' 985, list' 1 and passim. Ribbentrop's explanation: Ribbentrop to Molotov, June 22, 1941, in Reshin et al., *1941 God. Dokumenty*, 2:417–19. Halder: from Franz Halder, *The Halder Diaries: The Private War Journals of Colonel General Franz Halder*, trans. Trevor N. Dupuy, 2:845 (entry for March 30, 1941). Hitler on June 16, 1941: *Goebbels Diaries*, 414.

24. Citation (and discussion of *vnezapnost'*) in Mawdsley, *Thunder in the East*, 37, 39. Emphasis added.

25. Politburo resolution no. 19, June 17, 1941 ("Ob otbore 3700 kommunistov na politrabotu v Krasnuyu Armiyu") in RGASPI, fond 17, opis' 162, del' 36. "German military preparations are complete": Merkulov passing on NKVD rezident Berlin to Molotov and Stalin, June 17, 1941,

in Reshin et al., *1941 God. Dokumenty*, 2:382–83. Stalin summons intelligence chiefs, and NKVD reports German preparations for evacuation and document burning: Gorodetsky, *Grand Delusion*, 297–98.

26. Cited in Gorodetsky, *Grand Delusion*, 299. "Tell the 'source'": cited in Montefiore, *Court of the Red Tsar*, 354.

27. Timoshenko/Zhukov memorandum to Stalin, June 19, 1941, no. 582 in Reshin et al., *1941 God. Dokumenty*, 2:392.

28. Ibid. A more detailed version of this resolution, including the assignment of responsibility to Beria on June 20, 1941, is also preserved in the "Special Politburo Files" at RGASPI, fond 17, opis' 162, del' 36.

29. Pleshakov, *Stalin's Folly*, 93. NKVD measures on the German frontier on June 19, 1941: Sazyikin, for NKVD Moldavia SSR, June 19, 1941, no. 584 in Reshin et al., *1941 God. Dokumenty*, 394–95; and "Prikaz nachal'nika Pogranvoisk NKVD belorusskogo okruga ob usilenii okhranyi granitsyi," June 20, 1941, no. 591 in Reshin et al., *1941 God. Dokumenty*, 399. Baltic deportations: cited in Tolstoy, *Stalin's Secret War*, 222.

30. Nikita Khrushchev, *Vospominaniia. Vremia, Liudi, Vlast'*, 1:233–34.

31. Cited by Mawdsley in *Thunder in the East*, 37. Phoned in reports from deserters: cited in Kotkin, *Stalin*, 2:895; and Montefiore, *Court of the Red Tsar*, 357.

32. "O khode vyipolnenii ukazanii tov. Stalina po vyipusku 50 samoletov v den'," from the Protocol of the State Defense Committee meeting on June 17, 1941, no. 565 in Reshin et al., *1941 God. Dokumenty*, 378–80; and (for specific factory production targets), Politburo resolution no. 84 from June 20, 1941, in RGASPI, fond 17, opis' 162, del' 36.

Chapter 17: Hitler Smashes Stalin's War Machine

1. Solonin, *June 1941. Final Diagnosis*, op. cit. Estimates of warplane losses on June 22 given by the Germans (1,489 on the ground, 322 in the air) and Russians (1,200/800) are compared in Leland Fetzer, trans., and Ray Wagner, ed., *The Soviet Air Force in World War II. The Official History. Originally Published by the Ministry of Defense of the USSR*, 35. See also Geoffrey Roberts, *Stalin's Wars: From World War to Cold War, 1939–1953*, 85.

2. Ibid., and Mawdsley, *Thunder in the East*, 59–63; Pleshakov, *Stalin's Folly*, 106–11 and 122–23. Cited in Montefiore, *Court of the Red Tsar*, 369. Rundstedt advances fifteen to seventeen miles: John Erickson, *Road to Stalingrad: Stalin's War with Germany*, 131.

3. "V. M. Molotov s poslom Germanii v SSSR F. Shulenbergom," June 22, 1941, no. 608 in Reshin et al., *1941 God. Dokumenty*, 431–32. Hitler speech on June 22, 1941: op. cit. For more on the timeline, see Moorhouse, *Devils' Alliance*, 252–54.

Details of the diplomatic exchange cited: Bulgarian Legation in Moscow reports dated June 27–28, July 6, and September 6, 1941, in BSA, fond 318K, opis' 1, del' 42.

4. An English-language translation of Khrushchev's Secret Speech is available online here: https://novaonline.nvcc.edu/eli/evans/his242/Documents/Speech.pdf.

5. For the most plausible versions of the story, see Volkogonov, *Stalin*, 412–13; and Beevor, *Stalingrad*, 9. In *Special Tasks: The Memoirs of an Unwanted Witness—a Soviet Spymaster*, trans. and eds. Anatoli Sudoplatov, Jerrold L. Schecter, and Leona P. Schecter, 428–29, Pavel Sudoplatov changes the date to July 25, 1941, which casts further doubt on his credibility. Sudoplatov interrogation in 1953: "Ob'yasnitel'noi zapiski P. A. Sudoplatova s Sovet Ministrov SSSR 7 Aug 1953," no. 651 in Reshin et al., *1941 God. Dokumenty*, 2:487. For an interesting discussion, see Richard Overy, *Russia's War*, 96.

6. "Fragment iz Zhurnala zapisi lits, prinyatyikh I. Stalinyim 22-25 iyunya 1941," reproduced in Sergei Kudriashov, ed., *Voina 1941–1945*. *Vestnik Arkhiva Prezidenta Rossiiskoi Federatsii*, 23–27. Stavka created on June 23, 1941: transcript of Politburo session of June 23, 1941, punkt 99 ("O Stavke Glavnogo Komandovaniya vooruzhennyikh sil Soyuza SSSR."), in RGASPI, fond 17, opis' 162, del' 35. Politburo resolution of June 25 signed by Stalin no. 1749–756cc, in RGASPI, fond 17, opis' 162, del' 36 (folder 2). Khrushchev overheard to say: Khrushchev, *Glasnost Tapes*, 49. On the context of directives 1 and 2, see Pleshakov, *Stalin's Folly*, 110.

7. The most detailed source for this episode is the unexpurgated version of Anastas Mikoyan's memoirs, published as *Tak bylo: Razmyshleniia o minuvshem (moi 20 vek)*, 389–91.

8. Mawdsley, *Thunder in the East*, 59–60.

9. "Spravka o razvertyivanii Vooruzhennyikh Sil SSSR na sluchai voinyi na zapade," June 13, 1941, no. 549 in Reshin et al., *1941 God. Dokumenty*, 2:358–61.

10. Stalin, "Direktiva voennyim sovetam severo-zapadnogo, zapadnogo, Yugo-zapadnogo i yuzhnogo fronta," June 22, 1941, no. 614 in Reshin et al., *1941 God. Dokumenty*, 2:439–40. Emphasis added. See also

Pleshakov, *Stalin's Folly*, 162–63. Soviet bombing raids into Romania: Wehrmacht intelligence summaries from the eastern front for June 24, 25, and 26, 1941, in BA/MA, RW 5 / v. 382. See also the debriefing of Konstantin Stefanesku, a Romanian infantryman captured at Stalingrad on September 29, 1942, on the Soviet bombing runs into Romania in summer 1941, no. 11 in I. I. Basik et al., *Stalingradskaia epopeia. Vpervyie publikuemyie dokumentyi: dnevniki i pis'ma soldat RKKA i vermakhta: agenturnyie doneseniya: protokolov doprosov: dokladnyie zapiski osobyikh otdelov frontov i armii*, 87–88.

11. Cited in Alexander Werth, *Russia at War: 1941–1945*, 148. For more details, see also Mawdsley, *Thunder in the East*, 76–77. On Riabyshev's offensive: Pleshakov, *Stalin's Folly*, 168–69 and passim.

12. Wehrmacht intelligence summaries from the eastern front for June 30 and July 12, 1941, in BA/MA, RW 5 / v. 382. Soviet bombs knock out Romanian railway between Ploeşti and Bucharest: from Romanian press summary compiled by the Soviet Foreign Ministry, circa September 1941, in AVPRF, fond 125, opis' 23, papka 22, del' 15, list' 6–9.

13. The most elaborate estimates of Soviet war matériel on the eve of the German invasion are in Solonin, *June 1941. Final Diagnosis*, op. cit.; Musial, *Stalins Beutezug*, 69–70; and Joachim Hoffmann, *Stalins Vernichtungskrieg 1941–1945: Planung, Ausführung und Dokumentation*, 29–32. Six hundred and twenty-five thousand horses to carry Wehrmacht supplies: Stahel, *Operation Barbarossa*, 118.

14. This is the theme of Glantz's *Stumbling Colossus*. Still, that the Red Army was woefully unprepared in June 1941 does not excuse Stalin's lopsidedly offensive deployment.

15. Cited in Roberts, *Stalin's Wars*, 80.

16. Photostats of these and similar Russian-language German leaflets are reproduced in A. V. Okorokov, *Osobyi Front: Nemetskaia propaganda na vostochnom fronte*, 30 and passim.

17. Mawdsley, *Thunder in the East*, 60. Soviet soldiers taken prisoner in 1941: Musial, *Stalins Beutezug*, 69 (citing the *Kriegstagebuch des Oberkommandos der Wehrmacht 1940–1941*, 1:1106). Soviet official estimates were naturally lower, although, even so, they were embarrassingly high, ranging from 2.3 to 3.3 million. See V. V. Litvinenko, *Tsena Voinyi. Lyudskie poteri na sovetsko-germanskom fronte*, 50.

18. Solonin, *June 1941. Final Diagnosis*. Not all Russian historians agree. In *Tsena Voinyi* (241–43), V. V. Litvinenko, using the lower Soviet estimate of prisoners taken in 1941 (2.335 million), estimates that the Red

Army was losing about 400,000 prisoners per month to the Germans, or fewer than Poland had lost in September 1939 (about 800,000) and France in six weeks in May–June 1940 (1.5 million in all). Solonin was therefore wrong that Soviet troops were "unwilling to fight for Communism." It is an interesting objection, but unconvincing. Most Poles and Frenchmen surrendered in a general capitulation, not while hostilities were still ongoing. Soviet soldiers continued surrendering in droves even after the debacle at the frontiers in late June–early July 1941, and well into 1942, 1943, and 1944.

19. "Extracts from a Broadcast Speech by Stalin on the German Invasion of the Soviet Union," July 3, 1941, reproduced in Degras, *Soviet Documents on Foreign Policy*, 3:491–92. Halder: cited in Mawdsley, *Thunder in the East*, 63.

20. "Extracts from a Broadcast Speech by Stalin on the German Invasion of the Soviet Union," July 3, 1941, op. cit. Churchill broadcast of June 22, 1941: reproduced in Winston Churchill, *His Complete Speeches, 1897–1963*, ed. Robert Rhodes James, 6:6429–30.

21. Politburo transcript for June 27, 1941, punkt 135 ("O poryadke vyivoza i razmeshcheniya lyudskikh kontingentov i tsennogo imushchestva"), in RGASPI, fond 17, opis' 162, del' 35. Lenin's body evacuated to Tyumen': Resolution 176 on July 2, 1941, in RGASPI, fond 17, opis' 162, del' 36 (folder 1). Resolution of July 3, 1941, on the evacuation of family members of regime elites: reproduced in V. P. Naumov et al., *Lubyanka. Stalin i NKVD -NKGB-GUKR 'Smersh'. 1939-mart 1946*, as no. 80, 293–94. Evacuation of skilled workers and families from Moscow and Leningrad: resolutions no. 196 and 197 on July 7, 1941, in RGASPI, fond 17, opis' 162, del' 36 (folder 1). But for a small trickle of resolutions in August and September 1941, this was the last major Politburo protocol before the end of the war. 9.3 billion rubles evacuated on June 28: Musial, *Stalins Beutezug*, 82.

22. Solonin, *June 1941. Final Diagnosis*, op. cit. "Mopping up" in Minsk: Erickson, *Road to Stalingrad*, 159. Stalin's son captured: Montefiore, *Court of the Red Tsar*, 379.

23. Solonin, *June 1941. Final Diagnosis*, op. cit. On the re-gauging of rail lines, see R. H. S. Stolfi, *Hitler's Panzers East: World War II Reinterpreted*, 1993, 175–77. Not a single Soviet warplane in the sky: "Bericht über eine Reise und die Lemberger Front," July 17, 1941, in BA/MA, RW 5 / 52.

24. "Poryadok evakuatsii vremenno priostanovlivaemyikh stroitel'stv aerodromov," June 28, 1941, in GARF, fond 8437, opis' 1, del' 1, list' 51–53.

25. "Bericht über eine Reise und die Lemberger Front," July 17, 1941, op cit. For more on the T-34's qualities, see also Andrei Aksenov et al., *Soviet Tanks in Combat 1941–1945*, 3 and passim.

26. Guderian: cited in Beevor, *Stalingrad*, 26.

Chapter 18: Terror at the Front—and in the Rear

1. Entry for March 3, 1941, in *Kriegstagebuch des Oberkommandos der Wehrmacht*, Band I, 341; entry for March 30, 1941, in Halder, *Halder Diaries*, 2:42. Führer edict of May 13, 1941, and commissar order of June 6, 1941: Boog et al., *Angriff*, 431–35. Hunger Plan / "many tens of millions of people": cited in Snyder, *Bloodlands*, 162–63.

2. On the implementation of the Commissar Order in the field, see Boog et al., *Angriff*, 1064 and passim. Two thousand, two hundred and fifty-two shot according to German military records: Snyder, *Bloodlands*, 182. On the Kaunas pogrom, see also Adam Tooze, *The Wages of Destruction: The Making and Breaking of the Nazi Economy*, 481. On the tangled issue of Jewish participation in the new Soviet occupation governments in Lithuania, the Baltic region, and Galicia, see Dov Levin, *A Lesser of Two Evils: Eastern European Jewry Under Soviet Rule, 1939–1941*, trans. Naftali Greenwood.

3. Germany military intelligence report, dated August 12, 1941 ("Zur russischen Kriegsführung"), in BA/MA, RW 5 / 52. Editorial board flooded with letters "expounding satisfaction with the collapse of Bolshevik rule" / locals hunt down those associated with Soviet government: citations in Vladimir Solonari, *A Satellite Empire: Romanian Rule in Southwestern Ukraine, 1941–1944*, 187–88, 207.

4. Cited in Musial, *Konterrevolutionäre Elemente*, 101.

5. Citation in ibid., 114–18.

6. "Gave the impression . . . nearly fainted": cited in Tolstoy, *Stalin's Secret War*, 248. "Decomposing corpses" / "recent traumas": "Bericht über eine Reise and die Lemberger Front," July 17, 1941, op. cit. For casualty estimates, see Musial, *Konterrevolutionäre Elemente*, 113.

7. Musial, *Konterrevolutionäre Elemente*, 127–28, 138.

8. Politburo resolutions of August 26 ("O pereselenii nemtsev iz respubliki Nemtsev Povolzh'ya i iz Saratovskoi i Stalingradskoi oblastei . . .") and (on Ukraine) August 31, 1941, in RGASPI, fond 17, opis' 162, del' 37. For more on the context and intent of these orders, see N. F. Bugai, *L. Beriya – I. Stalinu: 'Soglasno Vashemu ukazaniyu . . .'*, 27 and passim. On the *Schwarzmeerdeutschen*, see Solonari, *Satellite Empire*, 44–45.

9. Cited in Hoffmann, *Stalins Vernichtungskrieg*, 102.

10. Stamenov to Sofia, July 13 and 14 and August 8, 1941, in BSA, fond 318K, opis' 1 ('B'lgarska legatsiya v Moskva'), del' 42. Soviets ratify Geneva only in 1989: A. N. Mertsalov and L. A. Mertsalova, *Stalinizm i voina*, 357–58.

11. Citations in Hoffmann, *Stalins Vernichtungskrieg*, 102–4.

12. Ibid. Hull and Molotov exchange: "Memorandum of Conversation" in the White House on May 29, 1942, from 4:45 p.m. to 6:15 p.m., in the FDR Library, Hopkins Papers, box 311, book 5 ("Molotov Visit, 1942").

13. Cited in Mawdsley, *Thunder in the East*, 65. Yakov captured and his wife arrested: Montefiore, *Court of the Red Tsar*, 379–80.

14. Cited in Birshtein, *Smersh*, 190.

15. Cited in Montefiore, *Court of the Red Tsar*, 379n.

16. From reports of the "Wehrmacht-Untersuchungstelle für Verletzungen des Völkerrechts," in section labeled "Kriegsverbrechen der russischen Wehrmacht," November 11 and 26, 1941, and February 2 and 5, 1942, in BA / MA, RW / 2 / 151.

17. Solonin, *June 1941. Final Diagnosis*, op. cit. German prisoners by June 1942: Mawdsley, *Thunder in the East*, 237. Fueled by Pervitin: Norman Ohler, *Der totale Rausch: Drogen im dritten Reich.*

18. "Walking skeletons": cited in Beevor, *Second World War*, 209.

19. Ibid., 208–9; and Mawdsley, *Thunder in the East*, 102–5. As many as 1.5 million Osttruppen: Musial, *Stalins Beutezug*, 117–18. Linkage of food rations to willingness of Soviet prisoners to oppose Stalin: see pamphlets instructing Red Army troops on how to desert voluntarily or surrender shouting "Stalin kaputt!," in AAN, 2/1335/0/239/194, 148 and passim. Ukrainian prisoners released into Transnistria: Solonari, *Satellite Empire*, 52–53.

20. Snyder, in *Bloodlands* (178–82), estimates that five hundred thousand Soviet war prisoners had been shot by the Germans by war's end, with attrition rates of 2 percent per day in 1941. It is welcome that Snyder has brought the plight of these Soviet gentiles to light as fellow sufferers alongside Soviet Jews, who have received more attention. Nonetheless, in view of the million-plus Soviet POWs who volunteered to fight in the Wehrmacht between 1941 and 1945, one wonders if the German treatment of Soviet POWs can really have been quite this consistently brutal.

21. On the Babi Yar massacre and its meaning, see Snyder, *Bloodlands*, 201 and passim.

Chapter 19: War for Aluminum

1. Musial, *Stalins Beutezug*, 30–31.

2. Ibid; and, for data on how much was owed by each side on June 22, 1941, Ericson, *Feeding the German Eagle*, 173.

3. From a series of intelligence dispatches dated October 18, 25, and 27, 1941, in BA/MA, RW 4 / v. 889.

4. Stolfi, *Hitler's Panzers East*, 215 and passim.

5. Citations in Stahel, *Operation Barbarossa*, 260, 271.

6. Field report for July 11, 1941, in BA/MA, RW 5 / v. 382 ("Zusammenfassung wichtiger militärischer Ereignisse. 31.5.41 to 12.7.41.").

7. "Zusammenstellung wichtiger Meldungen über die Ostgebiete," August 28, 1941, in folder labeled "Russ. Beutematerial," ms dated September 23, 1941, in BA/MA, RW 4 / v. 329.

8. Ibid. On Nikolaev, see the OSS report dated March 24, 1942, appendix on "Condition of Cities in the Occupied Area," op. cit.

9. Musial, *Stalins Beutezug*, 86–87. On Tikhvin as "sideshow": Mawdsley, *Thunder in the East*, 91. In a similar vein, see also John Mosier, *Hitler vs. Stalin: The Eastern Front, 1941–1945*, 410n5. Interestingly, Mosier notes that Hitler justified the operation owing to the need to "seize the bauxite-producing area around Tikhvin," but dismisses this as "geologically dubious."

10. German intelligence summary dated November 24, 1941, in BA/MA, RW 4 / v. 329.

11. The most detailed and best-sourced estimates are in Musial, *Stalins Beutezug*, 82. See also Mawdsley, *Thunder in the East*, 48 and passim. Mawdsley cautions, sensibly, that "the success of *evakuatsiia* should not be exaggerated." For more inflated estimates and breathless claims, a kind of summary of the official Soviet story: Werth, *Russia at War*, 212–14.

12. Musial, *Stalins Beutezug*, 84–85.

13. "Zusammenstellung wichtiger Meldungen über die Ostgebiete," August 30, 1941, in folder labeled "Russ. Beutematerial," ms dated September 23, 1941, in BA/MA, RW 4 / v. 329. On Vilna (Vilnius) and its factories, see the OSS report dated March 24, 1942, appendix on "Condition of Cities in the Occupied Area," op. cit.

14. Transcript of "Conference held at the Kremlin on July 30, 1941 from 6:30 to 8:30pm, Between Harry L. Hopkins and Mr. Stalin," in FDR Archive, Hopkins Papers, box 306, book 4.

15. "Zusammenstellung wichtiger Meldungen über die Ostgebiete," August 30 and (for the updated production figures at Krivoi Rog) September 8, 1941, in folder labeled "Russ. Beutematerial," ms dated September 23, 1941, op. cit.

16. Mawdsley, *Thunder in the East*, 80–81.

17. "Orientierung über die wehrwirtschaftliche Bedeutung der besetzten und im Bereich der Kampfhandlungen liegenden russischen Gebiete," October 27, 1941, in BA/MA, RW 4 / v. 889.

18. "Geheim! Zusammenstellung wichtiger Meldungen über die Ostgebiete," December 1, 1941, in BA/MA, RW 4 / v. 889.

19. Aksenov et al., *Soviet Tanks in Combat*, 4; and Musial, *Stalins Beutezug*, 86. For allotted production figures in 1941, see Politburo resolution, "Ob obespechenii proizvodstva bronekorpusov i bashen tanka T-34," March 10, 1941, in RGASPI, fond 17, opis' 162, del' 32.

20. Politburo resolution, "Ob obespechenii proizvodstva bronekorpusov i bashen tanka T-34," op. cit.

21. Musial, *Stalins Beutezug*, 89 (production table) and 96 (for losses).

Chapter 20: On the Ropes

1. Cited in Glantz and House, *When Titans Clashed*, 97. For more details, see Mawdsley, *Thunder in the East*, 95.

2. "Orientierung über die wehrwirtschaftliche Bedeutung der besetzten und im Bereich der Kampfhandlungen liegenden russischen Gebiete," October 25, 1941, in BA/MA, RW 4 /v. 889.

3. Erickson, *Road to Stalingrad*, 216–17.

4. Cited in Mawdsley, *Thunder in the East*, 96.

5. Anatolii Voronin, *Moskva 1941*, 289. List of buildings to be destroyed: Rodric Braithwaite, *Moscow 1941: A City and Its People at War*, 218. For members of foreign press corps leaving: Alexander Werth, *Moscow War Diary*, 257–66. Werth, one of the most famous of war correspondents, left the morning of October 9. As for diplomats leaving, this was true even in the case of the Bulgarian ambassador, Ivan Stamenov, who was the principal conduit for back-channel negotiations between Molotov and Ribbentrop. See letter from Gergi Al. Tilev', the Bulgarian legation secretary in Moscow, to Stamenov (in Kuibyshev), November 8, 1941, in BSA, fond 318K, opis' 1, del' 42.

6. Mawdsley, *Thunder in the East*, 96; and Erickson, *Road to Stalingrad*, 218.

7. Erickson, *Road to Stalingrad*, 218–20.

8. Citations in Voronin, *Moskva 1941*, 29; and Montefiore, *Court of the Red Tsar*, 392, 396–97, and (for the details on Stalin and the generals in the Moscow Metro), 398–99. Mikoyan: Mikoyan, *Tak bylo*, 418.

9. A. A. Vetrov, "Moskva osen'yu 1941 goda," in *Moskva voennaya. Sbornik Vospominanii*, 66. "At the first sight of the enemy": cited in Erickson, *Road to Stalingrad*, 220. "Cowards and deserters": cited in Mertsalov and Mertsalova, *Stalinizm i voina*, 342–43.

10. Citations in Vetrov, "Moskva osen'yu 1941 goda," 66–67; and Montefiore, *Court of the Red Tsar*, 395.

11. Cited in Braithwaite, *Moscow 1941*, 227.

12. Citations in Vetrov, "Moskva osen'yu 1941 goda," 66–67; Braithwaite, *Moscow 1941*, 224–27; and Tolstoy, *Stalin's Secret War*, 243.

13. "Memorandum by Ronald Matthews, Daily Herald *Moscow Correspondent*," in PRO, CAB 66/54. "The Jews have sold Russia!": cited in Braithwaite, *Moscow 1941*, 225. "Lenin's tomb had been boarded over and the coffin removed": "Memoirs of Ivan D. Yeaton, USA (Ret.) 1919–1953," chap. 3, in the Hoover Institution Archives, Yeaton collection.

Chapter 21: Lifting the Moral Embargo

1. "Extracts from a Broadcast Speech by Stalin on the German Invasion of the Soviet Union," July 3, 1941, op. cit.

2. Figures in Musial, *Stalins Beutezug*, 70, 106; and Mawdsley, *Thunder in the East*, 47. On the decline in the second half of 1941, see Mark Harrison, *Accounting for War: Soviet Production, Employment, and the Defense Burden, 1940–1945*, 180 (table B1).

3. Lozovskii to Molotov, June 13, 1941, no. 41 in Yakovlev et al., *Sovetsko-amerikanskie otnosheniya 1939–1945*, 128–29, and (on the deportation order being rescinded), footnote 1.

4. Citations in Cole, *Roosevelt and the Isolationists*, 434–35, and in Hoover, *Freedom Betrayed*, 238–40.

5. Ibid.

6. Richard Norton Smith, *The Colonel: The Life and Legend of Colonel Robert R. McCormick, 1880–1955*, 411 and passim. Other citations in Cole, *Roosevelt and the Isolationists*, 434; and Hoover, *Freedom Betrayed*, 231–33.

7. Cole, *Roosevelt and the Isolationists*, 435; and Dallek, *Roosevelt and American Foreign Policy*, 278. July Gallup poll figure: cited in Robert Huhn Jones, *The Roads to Russia: United States Lend-Lease to the Soviet Union*, 55.

8.5 percent of Americans express strong preference for Stalin's regime over Hitler's: cited in Hemming, *Agents of Influence*, 242 and 354n2.

8. Cited in Susan Butler, *Roosevelt and Stalin: Portrait of a Partnership*, 197.

9. Hopkins memorandum, June 23, 1941, and Oscar Cox to Hopkins, June 23, 1941, in FDR Library, Hopkins Papers, box 305, book 3.

10. Stimson memorandum to "My Dear Mr. President," June 23, 1941, in FDR Library, Hopkins Papers, box 305, book 3.

11. Hopkins draft of Roosevelt speech, "To the Congress of the United States of America," in FDR Library, Hopkins Papers, box 305, book 3.

12. Citations in Dallek, *Roosevelt and American Foreign Policy*, 278–80. On the war matériel requested, the establishment of the special War Department office, and the Golikov mission: Jones, *Roads to Russia*, 37, 41–42. For more on the rules of engagement for US naval patrols and weapons shipments, see Cole, *Roosevelt and the Isolationists*, 425.

13. Citations in Butler, *Roosevelt and Stalin*, 196–97.

14. Lowell Mallett to Hopkins, July 26, 1941, and Katherine C. Blackburn, acting director of the Office of Government Reports, to Hopkins, August 10, 1941, summarizing reports from "our State Directors," August 10, 1941, both in FDR Library, Hopkins Papers, box 305, book 3. Soviet press summaries: see, for example, the fourteen-page "Spravka otdela amerikanskikh stran NKID SSSR 'k voprosu ob amerikanskoi pomoshchi SSSR,'" September 21, 1944, no. 48 in Yakovlev et al., *Sovetsko-Amerikanskie otnosheniya 1939–1945*, 141–54. Hopkins reassures Umansky: cited in David L. Roll, *The Hopkins Touch: Harry Hopkins and the Forging of the Alliance to Defeat Hitler*, 113–14.

15. James MacGregor Burns, *Roosevelt: The Soldier of Freedom*, 60. *Life* magazine profile: cited in Diana West, *American Betrayal: The Secret Assault on Our Nation's Character*, 130. Eleanor Roosevelt's patronage of Hopkins: Joseph P. Lash, *Eleanor and Franklin: The Story of Their Relationship, Based on Eleanor Roosevelt's Private Papers*, 657–58.

16. Robert E. Sherwood, *Roosevelt and Hopkins: An Intimate History*, 321–22.

17. Details in ibid., 323–27. For details on the stopover in Archangel, see Roll, *Hopkins Touch*, 123–24.

18. Sherwood, *Roosevelt and Hopkins*, 326–27.

19. "Memoirs of Ivan D. Yeaton, USA (Ret.) 1919–1953," chap. 3, in the Hoover Institution Archives, Yeaton collection. See also Roll, *Hopkins Touch*, 129–30. For more on Faymonville, see Romerstein and Breindel,

Venona Secrets, 218–19; M. Stanton Evans and Herbert Romerstein, *Stalin's Secret Agents: The Subversion of Roosevelt's Government*, 128; and West, *American Betrayal*, 211. For a contrary view, which takes Faymonville's side, see Butler, *Roosevelt and Stalin*.

20. "Memoirs of Ivan D. Yeaton, USA (Ret.) 1919–1953," chap. 3, op. cit.

21. "Priem tov. Stalinyim lichnogo Predsedatelya Ruzvel'ta g-na GOPKINSA 30 iyulya 1941 goda," in RGASPI, fond 558, opis' 11, del' 376.

22. Ibid. "Give us anti-aircraft guns and the aluminum": "Memorandum. Conference at the Kremlin on July 30, 1941. 6:30 to 8:30pm. Between Harry L. Hopkins and Mr. Stalin," in FDR Library, Hopkins Papers, box 306, book 4.

23. "Priem tov. Stalinyim lichnogo Predsedatelya Ruzvel'ta g-na GOPKINSA 30 iyulya 1941 goda," op. cit.; and on the Curtiss P-40s and Stalin's promise to make himself available to Hopkins, "Memorandum. Conference at the Kremlin on July 30, 1941. 6:30 to 8:30pm. Between Harry L. Hopkins and Mr. Stalin," in FDR Library, Hopkins Papers, box 306, book 4.

24. "Report of a Conversation Between General Yakovlev of the Russian Army and Mr. Hopkins, General McNarney and Major Yeaton," July 30, 1941, in FDR Library, Hopkins Papers, box 306, book 4.

25. "Memoirs of Ivan D. Yeaton, USA (Ret.) 1919–1953," chap. 3, op. cit.

26. Transcript of meeting between Molotov, Steinhardt, and Hopkins, from 3 p.m. to 4 p.m. on July 31, 1941, in FDR Library, Hopkins Papers, box 306, book 4.

27. Transcript of the Hopkins-Stalin summit from 6:30 p.m. to 9:30 p.m. on July 31, 1941, prepared "for the President only," in FDR Library, Hopkins Papers, box 306, book 4.

28. Ibid. Emphasis added. A photostat of the Russian original of this list is also reproduced in Sherwood, *Roosevelt and Hopkins*, 340. US entry into war as "the one thing that could defeat Hitler": cited in Roll, *Hopkins Touch*, 133.

29. Roosevelt memoranda, July 23 and August 19, 1941, in NAA, RG 169, box 176, folders labeled "Russia—Requirements," and "Russia—Exports" (as of November 26, 1941). One hundred transport vessels for Stalin: Hopkins to Churchill, during a conference at Downing Street on Thursday, July 24, 1941, 10 p.m., in FDR Library, Hopkins Papers, box 306, book 4. For more details: Robert W. Coakley and Richard M. Leighton, *Global Logistics and Strategy: 1940–1943*, 99.

30. Admiral Land, chairman of the US Maritime Commission, to Stettinius, November 27, 1941, in NAA, RG 169, box 176. Garden hose: cited in Jones, *Roads to Russia*, 12–13.

31. "Zapis' besedyi pervogo zamestitelya narodnogo komissara inostrannyikh del. Vyshinsky," with Steinhardt, "v svyazi s peredachei lichnogo poslaniya I. V. Stalina Prezidentu SShA. F. Ruzvel'tu," November 6, 1941, no. 54 in Yakovlev et al., *Sovetsko-amerikanskie otnosheniya 1939–1945*, 167–68.

32. Hopkins to Ambassador Umansky, September 22, 1941, in NAA, RG 169, box 176; Winant passing on Churchill to Hopkins, September 25, 1941, and "Minutes of Conferences Held by the Chief of the Army Air Forces with the Following British Representatives," October 21–22, 1941, both in FDR Library, Hopkins Papers, box 306, book 4. Valentine and Matilda tanks: Steven J. Zaloga, *Soviet Lend-Lease Tanks of World War II*, 6–7. British aluminum being delivered to Stalin: Harriman to Hopkins and FDR, October 10, 1941, in NAA, RG 169, box 176. British gift of Tomahawks: see also Alexander Hill, "British Lend-Lease Aid and the Soviet War Effort," *Journal of Military History* 71, no. 3 (July 2007): 780.

33. Air Marshal Archie Sinclair to Harry Hopkins ("Dear Harry"), September 21, 1941, in FDR Library, Hopkins Papers, box 306, book 4. Emphasis added.

34. Hopkins to Ambassador Umansky, September 22, 1941, in NAA, RG 169, box 176.

35. Ibid.; and Hopkins to Stettinius, October 22, 1941, in NAA, RG 169, box 176.

36. Ibid.

37. Transcript of Vishinsky-Steinhardt meeting, November 4, 1941, no. 53 in Yakovlev et al., *Sovetsko-amerikanskie otnosheniya 1939–1945*, 165–66.

38. Stettinius to William D. Wright, October 9, 1941, in NAA, RG 169, box 178, folder labeled "Russia. Motor Vehicles, Parts and Accessories." For more details on the Faymonville appointment, see "Memoirs of Ivan D. Yeaton, USA (Ret.) 1919–1953," chap. 3, op. cit., and Hopkins to Roosevelt, October 4, 1941, in FDR Library, Hopkins Papers, box 306, book 4.

39. Citations in Sherwood, *Roosevelt and Hopkins*, 1:376–77.

40. "Supplement Covering Balance of Conversation with Mr. Stalin at Meeting with Lord Beaverbrook and Mr. Harriman, Sunday, Sept 28, 1941, 7pm to 10:10pm," in FDR Library, Hopkins Papers, box 306, book 4.

Chapter 22: The Hinge of Fate

1. Japan's monthly oil consumption: cited in Paine, *Wars for Asia*, 182.

2. Cited in Hoover, *Freedom Betrayed*, 266. On the Japanese proposals for a summit, see R. J. C. Butow, "Backdoor Diplomacy in the Pacific: The Proposal for a Roosevelt-Konoye Meeting, 1941," *Journal of American History* 59, no. 1 (June 1972): 48–72.

3. "Donosenie R. Zorge ob otkaze yaponskogo pravitel'stva ot plana napedeniya na SSSR v 1941 g., o sostoyanii yapono-amerikanskikh otnoshenii i strategicheskikh planakh nemetskogo komandovaniya," September 14, 1941, no. 170 in V. A. Zolotareva et al., *Sovetsko-yaponskaya voina 1945 goda: Istoriya voenno-politicheskogo protivobortsva dvukh derzhav v 30-40 godyi*, 1:192–93. For more on Sorge's source and the context, see Matthews, *Impeccable Spy*, 315. Nomura's offer: cited in Koster, *Operation Snow*, 123–24. Hull's rejection: cited in Hoover, *Freedom Betrayed*, 271.

4. "Donosenie R. Zorge ob obostrenii yapono-amerikanskikh protivorechii i o podgotovke yaponii k vyistupleniyu v yugo-vostochnoi azii," October 3, 1941, no. 174 in Zolotareva et al., *Sovetsko-yaponskaya voina 1945 goda*, 1:196.

5. Mawdsley, *Thunder in the East*, 112–13. On Soviet armor transferred west from late September to mid-October 1941: Peter Herde, ed., *Die Achsenmächte, Japan, und die Sowjetunion: Japanische Quellen zum Zweiten Weltkrieg*, 43. On troops and armor transferred from Siberia earlier in 1941, with cumulative totals for the year: Stahel, *Operation Barbarossa*, 356.

6. On Ozaki's connections with Sorge and the "breakfast club," see Matthews, *Impeccable Spy*, 291–312 and passim. Clearly Sorge and Ozaki tried to influence Konoe toward an anti-American, Soviet-appeasing policy, but it seems doubtful this influence was decisive.

7. Proposals A and B are reproduced in full, in English translation, in Hoover, *Freedom Betrayed*, 285–87.

8. Cited in Dallek, *Roosevelt and American Foreign Policy*, 305.

9. On White's drafting of what became the "Hull note," and its resemblance to the Pavlov-White version typed up for Morgenthau on June 6, 1941, see Evans and Romerstein, *Stalin's Secret Agents*, 96–97. The White-Morgenthau memorandum of November 26, 1941, is cited in John Morton Blum, *Years of Urgency 1938–1941: From the Morgenthau Diaries*, 2:385. "Asian Munich" / "thirty blood-stained coins of gold": cited in Koster, *Operation Snow*, 136 and passim.

10. Tojo: cited in Koster, *Operation Snow*, 139. For details of the attacks, see Paine, *Wars for Asia*, 186 and passim.

11. Citations in Werth, *Russia at War*, 246–49.

12. Ibid., 247. Announcement of Roosevelt's legal finding: Jones, *Roads to Russia*, 68–69.

13. Hill, "British Lend-Lease Aid and the Soviet War Effort," 783–90; and Zaloga, *Soviet Lend-Lease Tanks*, 7–8. British instructors arrive: report submitted by Federenko, lieutenant-general of the Red Army tank forces, to Lieutenant-General N. V. Khrulev at the Soviet Ministry of Defense, November 14, 1941, in TsAMO, fond 38, opis' 11353, korobka 3799, del' 869, list' 102. On the Hurricanes: George Mellinger, *Soviet Lend-Lease Fighter Aces of World War 2*, 7–9 and passim.

14. Hayden Raynor to Hopkins, November 16, 1941, "For Your Confidential Information at the Request of Mr. Stettinius," and, for supplies scheduled by March 1942, report marked "SECRET. TOTAL EXPORTS TO THE USSR. Weekly Report of Exports as of March 28, 1942," both in NAA, RG 169, box 176. On the total number of trucks available on the Moscow front, circa December 1941: Erickson, *Road to Stalingrad*, 251.

15. Zaloga, *Soviet Lend-Lease Tanks*, 7–8. For real-time figures on British MK-2 and MK-3 tanks in action: "Svedeniya o nalichii i kachestvennom sostoyanii tankov zapadnogo fronta na 25 noyabrya 1941," "Vedomost' nalichiya boevyikh mashin tankovyikh chastei zapadnogo fronta na 10-11 dekabyra 1941," and "Dannyie o nalichii i sostoyanii tankov zapadnogo fronta na 25 dekabrya 1941 . . . MK-2 i MK-3 na khodu i v remonte," in TsAMO, fond 38, opis' 11353, korobka 3760, del' 12, list' 287 (and back), 317, 385.

16. Mellinger, *Soviet Lend-Lease Fighter Aces*, 9–13, 25–27.

17. Hill, "British Lend-Lease Aid and the Soviet War Effort," 790–91. The 108th Tank Division: Glantz and House, *When Titans Clashed*, 108.

18. Glantz and House, *When Titans Clashed*, 102. For an interesting interpretation, see also Mosier, *Hitler vs. Stalin*, 164–69.

19. Glantz and House, *When Titans Clashed*, 108–111. Chronologically speaking, the first German retreat happened in late November 1941, when Kleist's First Panzer Group pulled back outside Rostov-on-Don. But this maneuver attracted far less attention than Zhukov's Moscow counteroffensive of December. For more operational details: Boog et al., *Angriff*, 770–76; Mawdsley, *Thunder in the East*, 116–17 and passim; and Erickson, *Road to Stalingrad*, chap. 7.

20. For an intriguing argument that Roosevelt himself was the source, see Fleming, *New Dealers' War*, chaps. 1 and 2 ("The Big Leak" and "The Big Leaker").

21. As noted by Norman Rich, in *Hitler's War Aims: Ideology, the Nazi State, and the Course of Expansion*, 235 and passim.

22. Cited in Jones, *Roads to Russia*, 81. On POPPY and the decision not to reduce Soviet shipments by 30 percent, see Coakley and Leighton, *Global Logistics: 1940–1943*, 555–56.

Chapter 23: Capitalist Rope

1. Jones, *Roads to Russia*, 75.

2. Gromyko to Harriman, from the Soviet embassy in Washington, October 29, 1941, in folder labeled "Russia—Shipping. General & Miscellaneous," NAA, RG 169, box 176.

3. Harriman to Roosevelt, September 29, 1941, in FDR Library, Hopkins Papers, box 306, book 4.

4. Edward Stettinius to the "Strategic Shipping Board," Washington DC, December 31, 1941, in folder labeled "Russia—Shipping," and Land to Stettinius, November 27, 1941, passing on Lukashev's requests from the Soviet embassy, in folder "Russia, Shipping, Schedule of," both in NAA, RG 169, box 176. MacArthur: cited in West, *American Betrayal*, 47.

5. Brigadier General Spalding to Stettinius, February 6, 1942, in folder labeled "Russia—Shipping. General & Miscellaneous," NAA, RG 169, box 176. "Gray-cold, heavy Arctic seas": Jones, *Roads to Russia*, 100.

6. M. P. Komarov, *Lend-Liz dlya Voenno-morskogo flota SSSR*, 21–22.

7. Ralph A. Bard, assistant secretary of the navy, to President Roosevelt, "Personally," February 14, 1942, in folder labeled "Russia—Shipping," NAA, RG 169, box 176.

8. Transcript of Vishinsky-Steinhardt meeting, November 4, 1941, no. 53 in Yakovlev et al., *Sovetsko-amerikanskie otnosheniya 1939–1945*, 165–66.

9. Stettinius to Admiral Emory S. Land, chairman of US Maritime Commission, November 27, 1941, in folder labeled "Russia, Shipping, Schedule of," in NAA, RG 169, box 176.

10. Oscar Cox to Hopkins, Memorandum for the president, October 15, 1941, in folder labeled "Russia—to/from Port of Archangel," NAA, RG 169, box 176.

11. Thomas McCabe to Emory S. Land of the Maritime Commission, May 23, 1942, in folder labeled "Russia—to/from Port of Archangel," NAA, RG 169, box 176.

12. Cited in Barrie Penrose, *Stalin's Gold: The Story of HMS* Edinburgh *and Its Treasure*, 42–43.

13. Cited in Bernard Edwards, *The Road to Russia: Arctic Convoys 1942*, 69.

14. American officials were bewildered by Stalin's discovery of international law, but accepted that this meant Vladivostok was legally off-limits. See the discussion by James P. Baxter, director of research and analysis under the Coordinator of Information office (soon to become the OSS), in "Supply Routes from the United States to the Russo-German War Zone," December 22, 1941, in FDR Library, Hopkins Papers, box 310, book 5 ("Aid to Russia").

15. Oscar Cox to Stettinius, May 31, 1943, in folder labeled "Russia. Summary of Reports and Statistics," NAA, RG 169, box 178.

16. See, for example, K. I. Lukashev "requisitions" on letterhead of the "Pravitel'stvennaya Zakupochnaya Komissiya Soyuza SSSR v SShA" (Government Purchasing Commission of the Soviet Union in the USA), located at 3355 Sixteenth Street, NW, Washington, DC, dated September 13 and October 5 and 17, 1942, as compared to prior "requests" submitted via Amtorg and/or the Soviet embassy. The requisition forms were standard US Army issue. For the speeding up of processing times, report from C. L. Terrel to Thomas B. McCabe, February 7, 1942. All of these documents are in NAA, RG 169, box 176, in folder labeled "Russia. Requisitions."

17. Lokhova, *Spy Who Changed History*, 353 and passim. White proposes remaking US machine tool industry to Gromyko: Gromyko to Molotov, December 24, 1941, no. 70 in Yakovlev et al., *Sovetsko-amerikanskie otnosheniya 1939–1945*, 186–87.

18. Zaloga, *Soviet Lend-Lease Tanks*, 26–27. On Soviet tours of US steel and tube plants: A. A. Rostarchuk, to Stettinius via Mr. R. J. Lynch, July 13, 1942, in folder marked "Russia—Summary of Reports & Statistics," in NAA, RG 169, box 176.

19. Malyshev to Molotov, December 1, 1941, in RGASPI, fond 82, opis' 2, del' 1308, list' 66–67.

20. Stettinius to General Wesson, October 22, 1942, passing on Memorandum from Reeve Schley to Stettinius, dated October 20, 1942, passing on all "Pre-Protocol Projects" signed off on by President Roosevelt,

in folder labeled "Russia—Requirements," in NAA, RG 169, box 176. "Yes-man": Gromyko to Molotov, December 24, 1941, op. cit. Gromyko used the English word ("Eto chelovek 'yes'").

21. W. L. Batt to Stettinius, March 5, 1942, and J. N. Hazard to Hayden Raynor, March 19, 1942, passing on decision by the Lend-Lease Administration, both in folder labeled "Russia. Motor Vehicles. Ball Bearings," in NAA, RG 169, box 177.

22. W. C. Moore memorandum for Stettinius, February 9, 1942, and, for background and context, S. P. Spalding to Stettinius, January 27, 1942, and Stettinius to Lukashev, January 6, 1942, all in folder labeled "Russia—Chemicals & Explosives. NITROGLYCERINE," in NAA, RG 169, box 177.

23. These requisitions are preserved in the folders labeled "Russia—Requisitions" and (for black tea) "Russia—Foodstuffs," both in NAA, RG 169, box 176.

24. A. J. Walsh, for the procurement division of the Treasury Department, to the Westinghouse Electric International Company ATTN: Robert Russell, October 15, 1942, in folder labeled "Russia. Commodities General. 1941–1942," NAA, RG 169, box 177.

25. Stettinius to General Belyaev and Mr. Eremei at the Soviet Government Purchasing Commission on Sixteenth Street, October 16, 1942, in folder labeled "Russia—Requisitions," NAA, RG 169, box 176.

26. Report filed by Newman W. White, captain, JAGD, intelligence officer, on September 5, 1941, with the US Air Force, forwarded to the Lend-Lease Administration on September 16, 1941, in folder labeled "Russia—Summary of Reports & Statistics. Report of visit to March Field," in NAA, RG 169, box 176.

27. See Penrose, *Stalin's Gold*, esp. chap. 1. On the Norden-bombsight-for-radar exchange, see Joseph E. Persico, *Roosevelt's Secret War: FDR and World War II Espionage*, 22–23.

28. Hopkins to Stettinius, September 23, 1941, and Stettinius to Hopkins, September 30, 1941; and Stettinius to Mr. George C. McGhee, US deputy executive secretary, Combined Raw Materials Board, October 7, 1942, both in folder labeled "Russia. Commodities General. 1941–1942," in NAA, RG 169, box 177. Steel wire rope: Hopkins to Ambassador Umansky, September 22, 1941, in NAA, RG 169, box 176.

29. Major General C. M. Wesson to Stettinius, February 12, 1943, in folder labeled "Russia—Requirements," in NAA, RG 169, box 176.

Chapter 24: Just-in-Time Delivery

1. Jones, *Roads to Russia*, 89.

2. Roosevelt to Stalin (by way of Thurston in Kuibyshev and Molotov), February 11 and 13, 1942, in RGASPI, fond 558, opis' 11, del' 363, list' 86–87, 92–93. Standley: William H. Standley with Arthur A. Ageton, *Admiral Ambassador to Russia*, 129.

3. Churchill to Stalin, September 5, 1941, and Stalin to Roosevelt, February 18, 1942, both reproduced (the latter in English translation) in David Reynolds and Vladimir Pechatnov, eds., *The Kremlin Letters: Stalin's Wartime Correspondence with Churchill and Roosevelt*, 43–44, 85–86. "Silly, foolish, old dollar sign": cited in Jones, *Roads to Russia*, 95.

4. Citations in ibid., 95; and in Coakley and Leighton, *Global Logistics: 1940–1943*, 556.

5. Coakley and Leighton, *Global Logistics: 1940–1943*, 557–58; and Jones, *Roads to Russia*, 89.

6. Edwards, *The Road to Russia*, 67–77.

7. Hopkins to Harriman, September 24, 1941, FDR Library, Hopkins Papers, box 306, book 4. On the numbers of Poles in Beria's camps, and the numbers who agreed to serve, see Beria to Molotov, October 1, 1941, in RGASPI, fond 82, opis' 2, del' 1285, list' 80–84.

8. Stalin to Anders, March 8, 1942, in RGASPI, fond 558, opis' 11, del' 357, list' 1–15.

9. Churchill to Stalin, September 5, 1941, in Reynolds and Pechatnov, *Kremlin Letters*, 44.

10. Citations in Reynolds and Pechatnov, *Kremlin Letters*, 95–97, 116–17.

11. Citations in ibid., 118–19.

12. Jones, *Roads to Russia*, 104–7.

13. Ibid., 112–13.

14. Ibid., 107. On the Anglo-Soviet invasion of Iran, see Dzhamil Gasanli, *SSSR-Iran: Azerbaijanskii krisis i nachalo kholodnoi voinyi (1941–1946)*, 18–29. On the British offer to blow up Soviet Caucasian oil fields and refineries: see Foreign Office memoranda sent to Cripps in Moscow, August 12 and 15, 1941, in PRO, FO 371 / 29595.

15. Cited in Jones, *Roads to Russia*, 110–11.

16. G. K. Zhukov, *Vospominaniya i razmyishleniya*, 2:277. On this campaign generally, see Stahel, *Retreat from Moscow*.

17. Mawdsley, *Thunder in the East*, 139–41.

18. Ibid., 141–46.

19. "Orientierung über die wehrwirtschaftliche Bedeutung der besetzten und im Bereich der Kampfhandlungen liegenden russischen Gebiete," November 24, 1941, in BA/MA, RW 4 /v. 889.

20. Cited in Beevor, *Stalingrad*, 75. See also Mawdsley, *Thunder in the East*, 155–57.

21. "Prikaz Narodnogo Komissara SSSR o zapreshchenii otkhoda s zanimaemyikh pozitsii bez prikaza i merakh po ego obespecheniyu" (order no. 227), July 28, 1942, no. 101 in S. A. Gurov et al., eds., *Stalingrad 1942–1943: Stalingradskaia bitva v dokumentakh*, 75–77. For a discussion of the order and its meaning, see Mertsalov and Mertsalova, *Stalinizm i voina*, 339 and passim. Fifty-eight percent of cultivable land: Werth, *Russia at War*, 624. German officer writes his wife on August 7, 1942: Torsten Diedrich and Jens Ebert, eds., *Nach Stalingrad: Walther von Seydlitz' Feldpostbriefe und Kriegsgefangenpost*, 219.

22. Mawdsley, *Thunder in the East*, 157–59.

23. Ibid., 86–87, 224, 232–33, and appendix A, table 1. For more on the fulfillment of the first protocol, see Coakley and Leighton, *Global Logistics: 1940–1943*, 559–63.

24. "Svedeniya o khode formirovaniya ABT chastei i soedinenii pri Gor'komskom avtobronetankovom tsentre po sostoyaniyu na 1 iyulya 1942 g.," in TsAMO, fond 38, opis' 11353, korobka 3814, list' 290.

25. "Svedeniya o khode formirovaniya ABT chastei i soedinenii pri Gor'komskom avtobronetankovom tsentre po sostoyaniyu na 8 iyulya 1942 g.," in TsAMO, fond 38, opis' 11353, korobka 3814, list' 302.

26. Prepare for Boston-3s and B-25s: "NKO directive," June 22, 1942, in TsAMO, fond 13790, opis' 20191, del' 6, list' 383. Influx of British Hurricanes in July 1942: "Svedeniya o sformirovannyikh i otpravlennyikh na front aviapolkakh i o popolnenii chastei VVS frontov za iyul' mesyats' 1942 g"; of American warplanes in August 1942: "Svedeniya o sformirovannyikh i otpravlennyikh na front aviapolkakh i o popolnenii chastei VVS frontov s 1 po 31 avgusta 1942 g," both in TsAMO, fond 35, opis' 11285, korobka 1154, del' 516, list' 84–92, 164–68.

27. Stalin to Roosevelt, July 18, 1942, and Roosevelt to Stalin, July 23 and August 18, 1942 (all Russian-language versions), in RGASPI, fond 82, opis' 2, del' 1107, list' 893–94, 901.

28. "Secret" test report submitted by the Fourteenth Soviet Tank Division to Stavka, September 17, 1942, in TsAMO, fond 3212, opis' 2, del' 1, list' 60–61. For the American Stuart tanks: "Otchet 92 Tbr AVGUST 1942 goda o premenenii AMERIKANSKIKH tankov srednii i M-3 legkii," circa August 1942, in TsAMO, fond 3189, opis' 1, del' 5, list' 66.

29. Cited in Zaloga, *Soviet Lend-Lease Tanks*, 27.

30. Stalin to Roosevelt, August 22, 1942, and Churchill to Stalin, September 6, 1942, reproduced in Reynolds and Pechatnov, *Kremlin Letters*, 150-51. On the voyage of PQ 18: Jones, *Roads to Russia*, 145–50.

31. Jones, *Roads to Russia*,155–60. For Soviet request for Douglas transports: D. Kazlov, Shamanin, and Tolbukhin to Nachalniku Generalnogo Shtaba from Transcaucasian command in Tiflis, December 6, 1941, in TsAMO, fond 215, opis' 1185, del' 24, list' 42.

32. Citations in Reynolds and Pechatnov, *Kremlin Letters*, 155. On the fighting attributes of the Airacobra, see Blake Smith, *Warplanes to Alaska*, 106 and passim.

33. Stalin to Churchill, October 3, 1942, cited in Reynolds and Pechatnov, *Kremlin Letters*, 155–56.

34. Stalin to Roosevelt, October 7, 1942, in RGASPI, fond 558, opis' 11, del' 364.

35. Ibid. and, for second protocol, Jones, *Roads to Russia*, appendix A, table 1. Shipments to the Soviet Far East via Seattle, Portland, and San Francisco in November 1942: see Wesson to Stettinius, November 3, 1942, and Stettinius to Lukashev, November 7, 1942, in folder labeled "Russia—Foodstuffs," in NAA, RG 169, box 177.

36. Meisner to "Lieber Engel," December 1, 1942, in BA / MA, RW 8/5 (Zustandsbericht der 29. Infanterie Div. / 6 ArmeeKorps in Stalingrad). For second protocol estimates, see Jones, *Roads to Russia*, appendix A, table 1. For an interim estimate, which confirms that one hundred thousand trucks had been shipped by the end of April 1943, see Stettinius to Roosevelt, May 10, 1943, in folder marked "Russia—Commodities General. January–July 1943," in NAA, RG 169, box 177. The second protocol itself is preserved in FDR Library, Hopkins Papers, box 315, book 6.

Stalin's demand for eight thousand to ten thousand trucks per month: Stalin to Roosevelt, October 7, 1942, op. cit. For Soviet usage of Willys jeeps: see directive by Major Granovskii and battalion commissar Potryasaev, August 1, 1942, in TsAMO, fond 1257, opis' 1, del' 16, list' 171. Studebakers: see report of Podpolkovnik Svedshikov, November 26, 1942, in TsAMO, fond 10877, opis' 1, del' 46, list' 103. On the use of American all-wheeled vehicles more generally in supplying troops, David Glantz and Jonathan House, *To the Gates of Stalingrad: Soviet-German Combat Operations, April–August 1942*, 34. On the Germans appreciating captured American jeeps: Beevor, *Stalingrad*, 110.

37. David Glantz and Jonathan House, *Armageddon in Stalingrad: September–November 1942*, 53, 182. One hundred ninety-one of 200 tanks:

David Glantz and Jonathan House, *Endgame at Stalingrad: Book Two: December 1942–February 1943*, 44.

38. "Spravka o bezvozratnyikh poteriakh tankov v noyabre i dekabre 1942 g.," in TsAMO, fond 38, opis' 11353, korobka 287, del' 1172, list' 22. Fifteen percent: Glantz and House, *Endgame at Stalingrad*, 125. For more details, see Glantz and House, *Gates of Stalingrad*, 484.

39. Stalin to Roosevelt, October 7, 1942, op. cit. Nickel: see Soviet ambassador Umanski to Hopkins, February 11 and March 4, 1942, in the FDR Library, Hopkins Papers, box 315, book 6 ("Lend Lease to Russia, 1942"). The Americans could not meet the 800 ton per month requirement for nickel right away, but they did ship 1,600 tons immediately and agreed to send 800 tons per month in the second protocol. See copy of the second protocol in FDR Library, Hopkins Papers, box 315, book 6.

40. Exhibit C of memorandum (dated September 18, 1942) filed with Stettinius at the Lend-Lease Administration by Clifton Mack, director of procurement, Department of the Treasury, September 22, 1942, in NAA, RG 169, box 177; and Jones, *Roads to Russia*, 220.

41. Stettinius to Lukashev, October 23, 1942, in NAA, RG 169, box 177. For the Vistanex allocation, see also copy of the second protocol in the FDR Library, Hopkins Papers, op. cit.

42. Roosevelt to Stalin, October 9, 1942, in RGASPI, fond 558, opis' 11, del' 364.

43. Roosevelt to Stalin, October 12 and 16, 1942, in RGASPI, fond 558, opis' 11, del' 364.

44. The best account of the thinking behind Uranus is in Beevor, *Stalingrad*, 220–35.

45. The order for Operation Uranus is reproduced as document 284 in S. A. Gurov et al., *Stalingrad 1942–1943*, 210–15. On Uranus and its execution (including the German intelligence failure), see Beevor, *Stalingrad*, chap. 15. "Hedgehog defense": William Craig, *Enemy at the Gates: The Battle of Stalingrad*, 205. For a traditional Soviet account, see A. M. Samsonov, *Stalingradskaia bitva*, rev. ed.

46. "Svedeniya o postupleniya i peresleniya importnyikh tankov po sostoyaniyu po 15 noyabrya 1942 g." The December 1, 1942, *svedeniya* shows the total increased from 4,469 to 4,839, with 84 tanks sitting in port. In TsAMO, fond 38, opis' 11353, del' 1053, list' 209, 251.

47. Figures in Jones, *Roads to Russia*, 232–33.

48. Mellinger, *Soviet Lend-Lease Fighter Aces*, 40–43. For loss figures: "Vedomost' poter' samoletov VVS Krasnoi Armii po frontam i tipam,"

for June, July, and September 1942, all in TsAMO, fond 35, opis' 11285, korobka 1183, del' 11285, list' 14, 26, 93, 96, 171, 175–76.

49. As noted by Glantz and House in *When Titans Clashed*, 195–98. They downplay the effectiveness of US-British tanks and fighters, but admit they arrived in great quantities.

Chapter 25: Keeping Stalin Happy

1. Stalin to Churchill, November 27, 1942, reproduced in English translation in Reynolds and Pechatnov, *Kremlin Letters*, 182.

2. Citations in Dallek, *Roosevelt and American Foreign Policy* , 364; and in Fleming, *New Dealers' War*, 167–68.

3. Cited in Fleming, *New Dealers' War*, 170.

4. Roosevelt to Stalin, December 2 and 8, 1942, Stalin to Churchill, December 6, 1942, and Stalin to Roosevelt, December 14, 1942, all reproduced in Reynolds and Pechatnov, *Kremlin Letters*, 185–89.

5. Roosevelt to Stalin, November 19, December 10, 17, and 23, 1942, in RGASPI, fond 558, opis' 11, del' 364, list' 106, 134, 143, 151.

6. Transcript of JCS meeting, January 7, 1943, cited in Reynolds and Pechatnov, *Kremlin Letters*, 192.

7. On this sordid episode, see Standley and Ageton, *Admiral Ambassador to Russia*, chap. 13 ("The Tokyo Bomber Crew"), 221–34.

8. Roosevelt to Stalin, December 31, 1942, and Stalin to Roosevelt, January 5, 1943, in RGASPI, fond 558, opis' 11, del' 365, list' 3–4, 9.

9. Churchill's recollection of a conversation with Roosevelt in Casablanca, recounted to Soviet ambassador Maisky, cited in Reynolds and Pechatnov, *Kremlin Letters*, 186.

10. Transcript of JCS meeting, January 7, 1943, op. cit. "Was going to speak to Mr. Churchill": cited in Dallek, *Roosevelt and American Foreign Policy*, 373–74.

11. Roosevelt to Stalin, January 8, 1943, and Stalin to Roosevelt, January 13, 1943, in RGASPI, fond 558, opis' 11, del' 365, list' 14–15, 18–19.

12. Cited in Dallek, *Roosevelt and American Foreign Policy*, 374–75. Churchill: cited in Fleming, *New Dealers' War*, 174.

13. Cited in Roll, *Hopkins Touch*, 259. 1937 Gallup poll: cited in Hemming, *Agents of Influence*, 97.

14. Stalin to Roosevelt and Churchill, January 30, 1943, in RGASPI, fond 558, opis' 11, del' 365, list' 41–42. Churchill "dumbfounded": cited in Dallek, *Roosevelt and American Foreign Policy*, 375.

15. "Former Naval Person" to Roosevelt, February 2, 1943, in FDR Library, Hopkins Papers, box 309, book 5, folder 2, part 1.

16. Cited in Reynolds and Pechatnov, *Kremlin Letters*, 112.

17. Allen Paul, *Katyn: Stalin's Massacre and the Triumph of Truth*, 210–13.

18. Ibid., and, for queries lodged with the Soviets about the fate of the missing Polish officers, see "Sprawa jencow wojennych z 1939 g.," circa March 1942, and "Zasady zbierania informasyj od osob powracajacych z wiezien i obozow prasy," March 20, 1942, along with Polish-language queries by relatives of the missing officers, all in AAN, 2/2909/0/-/62.

19. Citations in Paul, *Katyn*, 217–22.

20. "Hitlerite lackeys" and "helpmates of Cannibal Hitler": cited in Jerrold Schecter and Leona Schecter, *Sacred Secrets: How Soviet Intelligence Operations Changed American History*, 64. Stalin to Roosevelt, April 21, 1943, in RGASPI, fond 82, opis' 2, del' 1107, list' 958–59; and Stalin to Churchill, April 21, 1943, reproduced in Reynolds and Pechatnov, *Kremlin Letters*, 237–38.

21. Ibid.

22. "Prime Minister to Premier Stalin," April 24 and 25, 1943, both telegrams shared by Churchill with the war cabinet on April 26, 1943, in war cabinet minutes, section on "Polish-Russian Relations, Note by the Prime Minister," in PRO, CAB 66/36.

23. Churchill to Stalin, April 24, Roosevelt to Stalin, April 26, and Stalin to Roosevelt, April 29, 1943, all reproduced in Reynolds and Pechatnov, *Kremlin Letters*, 241–42.

24. Cited in Paul, *Katyn*, 227. See also Laurence Rees, *World War II Behind Closed Doors: Stalin, the Nazis and the West*, 185.

25. Cited in Rees, *Behind Closed Doors*, 188. Churchill to Stalin, April 25, 1943: shared by Churchill with the war cabinet on April 26, 1943, in war cabinet minutes, op. cit. US Office of War Information broadcast: cited in West, *American Betrayal*, 203.

26. For a balanced overview of this contentious debate, see Richard Breitman and Allan Lichtman, *FDR and the Jews*. Churchill to Nicolson: cited in Andrew Roberts, *Churchill: Walking with Destiny*, 775. "German revelations are probably true": cited in David Carlton, *Churchill and the Soviet Union*, 105.

27. On the saga of American airmen being interned in the USSR, see John R. Deane, *The Strange Alliance: The Story of American Efforts at Wartime Co-operation with Russia*, 59–62.

28. Citations in Fleming, *New Dealers' War*, 175. Wedemeyer: "Untitled fragment on the Casablanca Conference," in the Wedemeyer Collection, Hoover Institution Archives, box 6.

29. For planning details of the March 13 plot, see Roger Manvell and Heinrich Fraenkel, *The Canaris Conspiracy: The Secret Resistance to Hitler in the German Army*, 138–43.

30. On the bomb plot and its failure, see Michael Mueller, *Canaris: The Life and Death of Hitler's Spymaster*, trans. Geoffrey Brooks, 224–25; Manvell and Fraenkel, *Canaris Conspiracy*, 143 and passim; and, for the most thorough exploration of the likely reason for the bomb's failure to detonate, Peter Hoffman, *The History of the German Resistance, 1933–1945*, 272–74, 282–83.

31. Although no transcript of this Istanbul encounter from late January 1943 has been found, Earle himself (after being told to keep it quiet) published an account after the war in *Confidential* as "FDR's Tragic Mistake," which has by now been thoroughly vetted against accounts by German resistance figures. The story checks out. See, for example, Heinz Höhne, *Canaris*, trans. J. Maxwell Brownjohn, 483–84; Mueller, *Canaris*, 220–21.

32. John Waller, *The Unseen War in Europe: Espionage and Conspiracy in the Second World War*, 280–85. For more details, see Fleming, *New Dealers' War*, 204–5, and Höhne, *Canaris*, 484–85.

33. Cited in Fleming, *New Dealers' War*, 465. Roosevelt to Churchill during the TRIDENT conference: Sherwood, *Roosevelt and Hopkins*, 791.

34. Höhne, *Canaris*, 479–80.

35. Cited in Weil, *A Pretty Good Club*, 136–37.

36. Citations in Carlton, *Churchill and the Soviet Union*, 101–2. "Soft underbelly"/"hard snout," and the five-minute tirade unrecorded by translators: citations in Reynolds and Pechatnov, *Kremlin Letters*, 141–42.

37. M. Lincoln Schuster to Stalin, January 18, 1943, in RGASPI, fond 558, opis' 11, del' 221, list' 58. This file is filled with dozens of now-embarrassing pitches from Western journalists to Stalin. Hundreds of American pilots interned by Soviet authorities: see Deane, *Strange Alliance*, 59–60. The Stalin cover on *Time* magazine, January 4, 1943, is preserved at http://content.time.com/time/covers/0,16641,19430104,00.html.

Chapter 26: Stopping Citadel

1. David Glantz, *Zhukov's Greatest Defeat: The Red Army's Epic Disaster in Operation Mars, 1942*, 199; and, for a concise summary, Glantz and House, *When Titans Clashed*, 181–82.

2. For an interesting counterargument to Glantz's view of Operation Mars, which argues that it was a feint designed to fail, see Beevor, *Second World War*, 370.

3. Details in Mawdsley, *Thunder in the East*, 249–59.

4. Ibid., and for a summary of these campaigns, Glantz and House, *When Titans Clashed*, 179–94.

5. Roosevelt to Stalin, June 2, 1943, reproduced in Reynolds and Pechatnov, *Kremlin Letters*, 257–59. Axis losses in Tunisia and north Africa: Douglas Porch, *Path to Victory: The Mediterranean Campaign in World War II*, 413–15.

6. Stalin to Roosevelt, June 11, 1943, translated and reproduced in Reynolds and Pechatnov, *Kremlin Letters*, 260–61.

7. Heinz Guderian, *Panzer Leader*, trans. Constantine Fitzgibbon, 299. Other citations in Dennis Showalter, *Armor and Blood: The Battle of Kursk, the Turning Point of World War II*, 46–50. For analysis with comparison to Soviet tanks, see Glantz and House, *When Titans Clashed*, 203–5.

8. For details: Showalter, *Armor and Blood*, 61–65; and David Glantz and Jonathan House, *The Battle of Kursk*, 31–50. On the electrified barbed wire, see K. K. Rokossovskii, *Soldatskii dolg*, 259.

9. For second protocol figures: Jones, *Roads to Russia*, 119 and passim. On Soviet tank production and loss figures, see Musial, *Stalins Beutezug*, 89–96. For specific Soviet losses in the winter battles of 1942–1943 (disaggregated by each battle; I have aggregated totals for the period from November 19, 1942, to March 25, 1943): Glantz and House, *When Titans Clashed*, appendix, table Q.

10. Cited in Tolstoy, *Stalin's Secret War*, 283. The targets for the second protocol are laid out in FDR Library, Hopkins Papers, box 315, book 6 ("Second Protocol"). For aluminum and steel: Chart of Lend-Lease Metals Exports, July 5, 1943, and Wesson to Mr. Booth, acting director of the Bureau of Service, Interstate Commerce Commission in DC, August 2, 1943, both in folder labeled "Russia—Metals and Minerals," NAA, RG 169, box 177. Stalin complained, and Roosevelt complied despite being warned about aluminum: J. H. Burns to Hopkins, January 5, 1943, and February 13, 1943, and minutes of the Soviet protocol committee, February 23, 1943, in FDR Library, Hopkins Papers, box 305, book 6. Nickel: Howard C. Sykes to Stettinius, June 9, 1943, in folder labeled "Russia. Metals—Nickel," in NAA, RG 169, box 177. Petroleum, industrial equipment, tire factories, and petroleum refineries: Minutes of the Soviet protocol committee, January 5 and February 23, 1943, in FDR

Library, Hopkins Papers, box 305, book 6. Aircraft: Minutes of the president's Soviet protocol committee, July 23, 1943, in FDR Library, Hopkins Papers, box 305, book 6. Cranes and hoists: W. Harnischfeger to Stettinius, March 18, 1943, in NAA, RG 169, box 178. Shovels and compressors: Minutes of the Soviet protocol committee, January 5, 1943, in FDR Library, Hopkins Papers, box 305, book 6. Anti-tank mines: Harriman to Roosevelt, September 29, 1941, in FDR Library, Hopkins Papers, box 306, book 4.

For summaries, see also Jones, *Roads to Russia*, 154–60 and appendix A, table 3 ("Second Protocol Period"), and Hubert P. van Tuyll, *Feeding the Bear: American Aid to the Soviet Union, 1941–1945*, 171, table 30 on "Deliveries to the U.S.S.R., October 1, 1941–July 31, 1943."

11. "Kratkii analiz boevyikh poter' i letnyikh proischestvii v chastiakh 6-go smeshannogo aviatsionnogo korpusa za period a 1 iyulya po 31 dekabrya 1943 g.," in TsAMO, fond 35, opis' 11285, korobka 1235, del' 1086, list' 13 and back. Stalin allows Bell and Douglas engineers to visit the front: Minutes of the Soviet protocol committee, September 30, 1943, in FDR Library, Hopkins Papers, box 305, book 6.

12. Stalin to Roosevelt, via Molotov, March 16, 1943, in RGASPI, fond 558, opis' 11, del' 365, 70–72. "Usual Russian runaround": cited in George C. Herring Jr., *Aid to Russia 1941–1946: Strategy, Diplomacy, and the Origins of the Cold War*, 92.

13. Cited in Herring, *Aid to Russia*, 92.

14. Cited in ibid., 117.

15. Figures in Musial, *Stalins Beutezug*, 97, and Glantz and House, *When Titans Clashed*, 216–17.

16. For Soviet manpower and "men under arms" figures, see Glantz and House, *When Titans Clashed*, appendix, table N. For German loss figures: Mawdsley, *Thunder in the East*, 404 (table 14.1). For Stalin's insistence on a French landing to draw off "forty divisions," see transcript of the exchange between Molotov and Roosevelt in the White House on May 30, 1942, in the FDR Library, Hopkins Papers, box 311, book 5 ("Molotov Visit, 1942"). The point about the comparative increase in military manpower is made by Mosier in *Hitler vs. Stalin*, 230.

17. On the kontrpodgotovka, see Erickson, *Road to Berlin*, 98–99.

18. Cited in Beevor, *Second World War*, 473. "We now have a better tank than the enemy": commander of the German 332nd Infantry Division, "Divisionsbefehl für den Angriff von 4.7.1943," in BA / MA, RH 26—332 / 20. For details of the first week, see Erickson, *Road to Berlin*,

99–105; Glantz and House, *When Titans Clashed*, 218–20; and Showalter, *Armor and Blood*, chaps. 3 and 4.

19. Erickson, *Road to Berlin*, 109. Stalin: Rokossovskii, *Soldatskii dolg*, 269.

20. Erich von Manstein, *Lost Victories*, trans. Anthony G. Powell, 448.

21. See Showalter, *Armor and Blood*, 217–18. For the legend, see Martin Caidin's *The Tigers Are Burning*.

22. For official Soviet estimates, see Glantz and House, *When Titans Clashed*, appendix, table Q. For German figures and different estimates for Soviet figures, see Musial, *Stalins Beutezug*, 97.

23. Musial, *Stalins Beutezug*; and Glantz and House, *When Titans Clashed*, appendix, table Q.

Chapter 27: Operation Tito

1. Tomasevich, *War and Revolution*, 61–63, 73.

2. "Die Lage in Kroatien," September 23, 1941, in BA / MA, RW 5 / 52 ("OKW. Amt Ausland / Abwehr"). Emphasis added.

3. "Die Lage in Serbien Anfang und Mitte August," August 28, 1941, in BA / MA, RW 5 / 52 ("OKW. Amt Ausland / Abwehr").

4. Tomasevich, *The Chetniks*, 142–45; and "Report on Mission to General Mihailović and Conditions in Yugoslavia. By Colonel S. W. Bailey, O.B.E.," circa April 1944, in PRO, HS 7/202.

5. See Hudson to Cairo command, November 14, 1941, in PRO, HS 5 / 967. For more on the Mihailović-Tito summit of October 27, 1941, see Tomasevich, *The Chetniks*, 147–48 and passim.

6. Cited in Evans and Romerstein, *Stalin's Secret Agents*, 161–62. On Klugmann's activities in MO4, see also Michael Lees, *The Rape of Serbia: The British Role in Tito's Grab for Power, 1943–1944*, 32–39.

7. "Miss Baker" of the BBC to the Foreign Office, March 12, 1943, in PRO, HS 5/969. Mihailović on the BBC: Bailey to Cairo command, March 1, 1943, in PRO, HS 5 / 967.

8. Citations in Tomasevich, *The Chetniks*, 150–51 and 246–48.

9. "Valter'" to Dimitrov, December 10, 1942, February 11, 1943, and, for slanders against "Kaptan Khudson," March 21, 1943, all in RGASPI, fond 82, opis' 2, del' 1369, list' 6–14, 20–22, 24. The Dimitrov radiogram to Tito, February 11, 1943, is reproduced as no. 210 in *Otnoshenii Rossii (SSSR) s Iugoslaviei 1941–1945 gg. Dokumentyi i materialyi*, 172. On press repeats of Tito's slanders, see Fotitch, *War We Lost*, 184. On Robertson's flight to the partisans, see "Report on Mission to General Mihailović and

Conditions in Yugoslavia. By Colonel S. W. Bailey, O.B.E.," in PRO, HS 7/202, and report circa early 1944 in PRO, WO 208 / 2018A.

10. Estimates of supplies sent to both Chetniks and partisans in 1943: "Report by Colonel S W Bailey on the Mission to General MIHAILOVIĆ and conditions in Yugoslavia—April 1944," in PRO, HS 7/202.

11. "Report by Colonel S W Bailey on the Mission to General MIHAI-LOVIĆ and conditions in Yugoslavia—April 1944," op. cit. Tito obtains arms from the Italians: "Valter" to Dimitrov, September 13, 1943, in RGASPI, fond 82, opis' 2, del' 1369, list' 27. On Tito's dealings with the Italians in 1943, see report of Kontre Admiral S. N. Ivanov', the Bulgarian liaison officer in Belgrade, August 5, 1943, in BSA, fond 176K, opis' 33, del' 24, list' 17–19.

12. "Report by Colonel S W Bailey on the Mission to General MIHAI-LOVIĆ and conditions in Yugoslavia—April 1944," op. cit. On the BBC misattributing the demolition of the Visegrad bridge, see Lees, *Rape of Serbia*, 75.

13. Maclean, *Eastern Approaches*, 294.

14. Ibid., 281, 402–3.

15. On the timeline of Maclean's first mission—a timeline nowhere given in his memoir *Eastern Approaches*, which is sloppy about dates—see Lees, *Rape of Serbia*, 209–10.

16. Lees, *Rape of Serbia*, 211–14. On Operation Weiss and the most accurate casualty figures, see "German Antiguerilla Operations in the Balkans (1941–1944)," CMH Publication 104-18, chap. 7 ("Operations (January–August 1943)").

17. Lees, *Rape of Serbia*, 218–19.

18. "Report by Colonel S W Bailey on the Mission to General MIHAI-LOVIĆ and conditions in Yugoslavia—April 1944," op. cit.

19. "Valter" to Dimitrov, September 1, 1943, no. 235 in *Otnoshenii Rossii*, 192.

20. Manuilskii to Molotov, January 27, Tito to Dimitrov, January 27, and Tito to Molotov and Stalin, February 5 and 8, 1944, all in RGASPI, fond 82, opis' 2, del' 1369. For earlier examples of these kinds of exchanges, see Tito to Dimitrov, October 2, 4, 7, 12, 13, and 30 and December 28, 1943. Many of these are also reproduced in *Otnoshenii Rossii* (for example nos. 243, 245, 247, 249, on pages 197–202).

21. "Report by Colonel S W Bailey on the Mission to General MIHAI-LOVIĆ and conditions in Yugoslavia—April 1944," op. cit.

22. Ibid.

Chapter 28: Teheran and Cairo

1. On the Faymonville-Burns-Standley affair, see Standley's report to Hull, June 1, 1943, in FDR Library, Hopkins Papers, box 309, book 5, folder 4.

2. "Memorandum on Luncheon at British Legation. Tehran, Iran. November 30, 1943," with Molotov, Eden, and Hopkins and their translators, in FDR Library, Hopkins Papers, box 332, book 8 ("Teheran").

3. "Profiles—House Guest," in the *New Yorker* in two parts, August 7 and 14, 1943. Clipped and preserved in FDR Library, Hopkins Papers, box 338, book 11. Marshall: as stated to his biographer, Forrest Pogue, on January 22, 1957; cited in West, *American Betrayal*, 138. Policy memorandum prepared for Roosevelt at Quebec: cited in Sherwood, *Roosevelt and Hopkins*, 748. "We are determined": cited in Evans and Romerstein, *Stalin's Secret Agents*, 22.

4. On Davies's latest mission to Moscow in May 1943, see Reynolds and Pechatnov, *Kremlin Letters*, 252.

5. Transcript of the conversation between Hopkins and Molotov in the White House, over drinks after dinner beginning at 7:40 p.m. on Friday, May 29, 1942, in FDR Library, Hopkins Papers, box 311 ("Book 5: Molotov Visit, 1942").

6. Cited in George Fischer, "Genesis of U.S.-Soviet Relations in World War II," *Review of Politics* 12, no. 3 (July 1950): 364–65.

7. As noted by Keith Sainsbury in *The Turning Point: Roosevelt, Stalin, Churchill, and Chiang Kai-Shek, 1943: The Moscow, Cairo, and Teheran Conferences*, 8.

8. Roosevelt to Stalin, May 5, 1943, in Reynolds and Pechatnov, *Kremlin Letters*, 248–49.

9. Stalin to Roosevelt, May 22, 1943, and accompanying analysis, in Reynolds and Pechatnov, *Kremlin Letters*, 253–54.

10. Roosevelt to Stalin, September 6 and 11 and October 14 and 27, 1943, and Stalin to Roosevelt, September 29 and October 20, 1943, all in RGASPI, fond 558, opis' 11, del' 366, list' 60–62, 87–89, 103, 106, 151–52, 161.

11. Roosevelt to Stalin, October 21, 1943, in RGASPI, fond 558, opis' 11, del' 366, list' 176–79, and Stalin to Roosevelt, November 5–6, 1943, in RGASPI, fond 558, opis' 11, del' 367, list' 1.

12. Weil, *A Pretty Good Club*, 134–39.

13. Cited in Burns, *Soldier of Freedom*, 398. On Karr and Older, the two Communists working for Drew Pearson, see Evans and Romerstein, *Stalin's Secret Agents*, 138–40.

14. On the Tashkent-Teheran airlift and the pledges of secrecy the other American internee-escapees were forced to agree to, see Deane, *Strange Alliance*, 59–61.

15. Sainsbury, *Turning Point*, 205–207 and passim. On the discussion of the Bay of Bengal operation and equipping ninety Chinese divisions: Burns, *Soldier of Freedom*, 404–5.

16. The Cairo Declaration is reproduced in Sainsbury, *Turning Point*, 321.

17. Evans and Romerstein, *Stalin's Secret Agents*, 147–49.

18. Burns, *Soldier of Freedom*, 406.

19. Montefiore, *Court of the Red Tsar*, 463.

20. Cited in Roll, *Hopkins Touch*, 314. For an interesting discussion of the possibility that Roosevelt knew he was bugged at Teheran, and used this knowledge to cultivate Stalin, see Warren F. Kimball, "A Different Take on FDR at Teheran," CIA Center for the Study of Intelligence, April 15, 2007, www.cia.gov/library/center-for-the-study-of-intelligence/csi-publications/csi-studies/studies/vol49no3/html_files/FDR_Teheran_12.htm.

Bohlen: Charles E. Bohlen, *Witness to History, 1929–1969*, 135–37. Bohlen notes that Hopkins viewed career diplomats as "cookie pushers, pansies—and usually isolationists" and was constantly trying to "provoke" Bohlen into saying something critical of Stalin so he could have him sent home.

21. Montefiore, *Court of the Red Tsar*, 465. "Servants who made their beds": Sherwood, *Roosevelt and Hopkins*, 776.

22. Montefiore, *Court of the Red Tsar*, 466.

23. "Memorandum of Conference 3pm, November 28, 1943," in the FDR Library, Hopkins Papers, box 332, book 8 ("Teheran (B). Meeting with Stalin"), folder 2.

24. Ibid.

25. W. Averell Harriman and Elie Abel, *Special Envoy to Churchill and Stalin, 1941–1946*, 263. For more on this bewildering exchange, see also Sainsbury, *Turning Point*, 219. Roosevelt's request to use Soviet air bases against Japan: "Advance Planning for Air Operations in the Northwestern Pacific," submitted to Stalin on November 29, 1943, in RGASPI, fond 558, opis' 11, del' 367, list' 36. Other Roosevelt memoranda: cited in Reynolds and Pechatnov, *Kremlin Letters*, 343.

26. For Molotov's positions laid down at the Moscow conference, see Sainsbury, *Turning Point*, 88–97.

27. Cited in Roll, *Hopkins Touch*, 314.

28. Sherwood, *Roosevelt and Hopkins*, 778.

29. "Minutes of Plenary Session Between the U.S.A., Great Britain, and the U.S.S.R., Held in the Russian Legation, Tehran, Iran, on Sunday, 28 November 1943, at 1600," in the FDR Library, Hopkins Papers, box 332, book 8 ("Teheran (B). Meeting with Stalin"), folder 2. On the discussion of Italy and the "Adriatic strategy" by Roosevelt's military advisers prior to the plenary session, and Brooke's remarks on the importance of Italian air bases for strategic bombing of Germany: Sainsbury, *Turning Point*, 222–24, 236. On the Allied Macedonian breakthrough in 1918, see Sean McMeekin, *The Ottoman Endgame: War, Revolution, and the Making of the Modern Middle East, 1908–1923*, 394–97.

30. "Minutes of Plenary Session Between the U.S.A., Great Britain, and the U.S.S.R., Held in the Russian Legation, Tehran, Iran, on Sunday, 28 November 1943, at 1600," op. cit.

31. Montefiore, *Court of the Red Tsar*, 467. Hopkins passes note: cited in Roll, *Hopkins Touch*, 318. See also Sainsbury, *Turning Point*, 231. Marshall dismissed on walking tour: Harriman and Abel, *Special Envoy*, 267.

32. "Memorandum of Marshal Stalin's Views as Expressed During the Evening of November 28, 1943," in FDR Library, Hopkins Papers, box 332, book 8 ("Teheran (B). Meeting with Stalin"), folder 2.

33. Montefiore, *Court of the Red Tsar*, 467. Stalin-Roosevelt exchange on the Baltic question (including mistranslation): cited in Sherwood, *Roosevelt and Hopkins*, 782.

34. Cited in Burns, *Soldier of Freedom*, 409. "The Devil's on my side": cited in Montefiore, *Court of the Red Tsar*, 467.

35. "Minutes of Plenary Session Between the U.S.A., Great Britain, and the U.S.S.R., Held in the Russian Legation, Tehran, Iran, on Monday, 29 November 1943, at 1600," in FDR Library, Hopkins Papers, box 332, book 8 ("Teheran (B). Meeting with Stalin.").

36. Cited in Sainsbury, *Turning Point*, 244–45, 247. For the full text: "Minutes of Plenary Session Between the U.S.A., Great Britain, and the U.S.S.R., Held in the Russian Legation, Tehran, Iran, on Monday, 29 November 1943, at 1600," op. cit. "Let's not waste our time here": cited in Montefiore, *Court of the Red Tsar*, 469.

37. A rough transcript of this exchange can be found in the transcript of "Dinner, November 29, 1943, at 8:30pm," in FDR Library, Hopkins Papers, box 332, book 8, folder 2. "British parliament and people": cited in Montefiore, *Court of the Red Tsar*, 470. This exchange is recalled, with slight differences, in Harriman and Abel, *Special Envoy*, 273–74; and

Bohlen, *Witness to History*, 147. "I would rather be taken out": cited in Fleming, *New Dealers' War*, 314.

38. Cited in Carlton, *Churchill and the Soviet Union*, 107. Stalin-Churchill exchange, and Elliott Roosevelt: citations in Montefiore, *Court of the Red Tsar*, 470.

39. Cited in Sainsbury, *Turning Point*, 259–60. Hopkins visit to Churchill: Bohlen, *Witness to History*, 148.

40. Sainsbury, *Turning Point*, 265–66; and Burns, *Soldier of Freedom*, 411. Stalin doodling: Montefiore, *Court of the Red Tsar*, 469.

41. Bohlen, *Witness to History*, 149.

42. Harriman and Abel, *Special Envoy*, 268. "Relying more and more on Hopkins, virtually to the exclusion of others": Bohlen, *Witness to History*, 148.

43. Cited in Burns, *Soldier of Freedom*, 412.

44. "Memorandum of conversation, 1 December 1943 at 3:20pm," with President Roosevelt, Averell Harriman, and Charles Bohlen, along with Stalin, Molotov, and Pavlov, in the FDR Library, Hopkins Papers, box 332, book 8, folder 2. For Harriman's recollection: Harriman and Abel, *Special Envoy*, 279–80. Bohlen, *Witness to History*, 151.

45. Summary of EUREKA decisions after the Teheran conference, prepared for the president and prime minister, in the FDR Library, Hopkins Papers, box 332, book 8 ("Teheran (C). Post-Teheran"). On the Italian fleet and merchant marine: "Meeting 6:00pm, December 1, 1943," in FDR Library, Hopkins Papers, box 332, book 8, folder 1.

46. Ibid.

47. Ibid.

48. Sainsbury, *Turning Point*, 289. "Caught with their pants down": Burns, *Soldier of Freedom*, 414.

49. "'SEXTANT' [i.e., Cairo] CONFERENCE. Minutes of Third Plenary Meeting, held at Villa Kirk, on Saturday, 4 December 1943 at 11:00," in the FDR Library, Hopkins Papers, box 332, book 8 ("Teheran (C). Post-Teheran"). Another hundred American airmen interned: Deane, *Strange Alliance*, 61–62.

50. Ibid., and, for "Suppose Marshal Stalin," "'SEXTANT' CONFERENCE. Minutes of Third Plenary Meeting, held at Villa Kirk, on Sunday, 5 December 1943 at 11:00," in the FDR Library, Hopkins Papers, box 332, book 8 ("Teheran (C). Post-Teheran"). "Stubborn as a mule": cited in Burns, *Soldier of Freedom*, 415.

51. Cited in Burns, *Soldier of Freedom*, 415.

52. Ibid. "After the monsoon": "SEXTANT Conference transcript, 4th plenary session, Sunday December 5, 1943, 11am," in FDR Library, Hopkins Papers, box 332, book 8 ("Teheran (C). Post-Teheran").

53. Citations in Evans and Romerstein, *Stalin's Secret Agents*, 149, 152. Stalin negotiates sanctuary for Mao with Japan and lend-lease spending on China: Paine, *Wars for Asia*, 181, 203, 228. Fifty to one hundred times as much aid: fifty in financial terms, one hundred in volume (e.g., Chiang had received ten thousand tons by May 1944, Stalin roughly ten million tons). On Soviet reexporting of lend-lease wheat to Iran: Stettinius to Hull, April 26, 1943, Stettinius to Faymonville, May 20, 1943, Faymonville to Stettinius, June 9, 1943, and Stettinius to Hopkins, July 23 and 24, 1943, in NAA, RG 169, box 177, folder labeled "Russia—Foodstuffs. WHEAT."

54. For Stilwell's epithets against Chiang: Anthony Kubek, *How the Far East Was Lost: American Foreign Policy and the Creation of Communist China, 1941—1949*, 205–6 and (for "rattlesnake"), 209. On the order to "prepare a plan for the assassination of Chiang Kai-shek," see Frank Dorn, *Walkout: With Stilwell in Burma*, 75–76.

Chapter 29: Second Front

1. The text of the original Lend-Lease Act can be viewed online here: "Transcript of Lend-Lease Act (1941)," Our Documents, www.ourdocuments.gov/doc.php?flash=true&doc=71&page=transcript.

2. "Lend-Lease and Victory," remarks by Honorable James A. Wright of Pennsylvania, February 1, 1944, in *Congressional Record: Proceedings and Debates of the 78th Congress*, vol. 90, part 8 (January 10, 1944–March 24, 1944), A528. For more on the political context of the vote, see Leon Martel, *Lend-Lease, Loans, and the Coming of the Cold War: A Study of the Implementation of Foreign Policy*, 7 and passim; and Herring, *Aid to Russia*, 93.

3. Citations in Standley and Ageton, *Admiral Ambassador to Russia*, 237.

4. Figures summarized in Herring, *Aid to Russia*, 115–16.

5. Figures on comparative German deployments are in Georg Tessin, *Verbände und Truppen der deutschen Wehrmacht und Waffen-SS im Zweiten Weltkrieg 1939–1945*, 17 vols. Tessin's lists of divisional deployments over the entire war have been aggregated by Ron Klages and John Mulholland, who compiled a summary of regional deployments each month from 1939 to 1945, available online here: Ron Klages and John Mulholland, "Number of German Divisions by Front in World War II," Axis History, last updated April 19, 2015, www.axishistory.com/books/134-campaigns

-a-operations/campaigns-a-operations/2085-number-of-german
-divisions-by-front-in-world-war-ii.

6. George Racey Jordan with Richard L. Stokes, *From Major Jordan's Diaries* (New York: Harcourt, Brace & Co., 1952), 22–25 and (for a photostat of the astonishing Newark Airport suspension order of June 12, 1942), 27.

7. Ibid., 44–45. Jordan reproduces the presidential order in full.

8. "Secret Addendum" to the minutes of the Soviet protocol committee, September 28, 1943, in the FDR Library, Hopkins Papers, box 305, book 6. "Cushion your crash": C. Margo Mowbray, *Havoc Red: Surviving the Alaska-Siberia Route, 1943*, xiv. On the fate of pilots who crashed in the Yukon, see Smith, *Warplanes to Alaska*, 129–30.

9. Cited in Alexander B. Dolitsky, ed., *Pipeline to Russia: The Alaska-Siberia Air Route in World War II*, 11–13.

10. Charles A. Sprague, of the *Oregon Statesman*, Salem, Oregon, to Stettinius, August 28, 1943. California: Stettinius responding to A. T. Welles of Los Angeles, January 18, 1943. Colorado: Mr. L. V. Alenviall of Denver, Colorado, to Stettinius, March 23, 1943. New Hampshire: W. S. Stowell of Henniker, New Hampshire, to Senator Styles Bridges, May 2, 1943. Pennsylvania: Knollenberg to Mr. John H. Foster of Pittsburgh, Pennsylvania, October 8, 1943. Massachusetts: Mr. Albert L. Mills to the Honorable Christian A. Herter of the House of Representatives, October 21, 1943. New Jersey: Knollenberg to Senator Hawkes of New Jersey, November 9, 1943. All in NAA, RG 169, box 177, folder labeled "Russia. Butter."

11. Marie Zgone to "Edward Stettinius, Lend-Lease Administrator," February 24, 1943, in NAA, RG 169, box 177, in folder marked "Russia. Butter." Women's apparel: cited in Jordan and Stokes, *Major Jordan's Diaries*, 135.

12. As cited in the letter from Senator Styles Bridges to Stettinius, June 9, 1943, in NAA, RG 169, box 177, in folder marked "Russia. Butter."

13. Bernard Knollenberg (from the Lend-Lease Administration) to Mr. John H. Foster of Pittsburgh, Pennsylvania, October 8, 1943, and Knollenberg again (making the same argument) to Senator Hawkes, November 9, 1943, both in NAA, RG 169, box 177, folder marked "Russia. Butter."

14. Stettinius to "the Honorable Warren Magnussen" of the US House of Representatives, June 7, 1943, in response to citizen complaints forwarded by the latter, in NAA, RG 169, box 177, folder marked "Russia— Commodities General. January–July 1943."

15. As explained by Stettinius to Senator Millard E. Tydings of Maryland, April 10, 1943, in response to Tydings's passing on of the usual round of constituent complaints (see below). In NAA, RG 169, box 177, folder marked "Russia—Foodstuffs."

16. Ibid., and E. D. Newman to Senator Millard Tydings of Maryland, in NAA, RG 169, box 177, folder marked "Russia—Foodstuffs."

17. Report OW-1736 of the Office of Lend-Lease Administration, prepared for the Office of War Information, May 3, 1943, in NAA, RG 169, box 177, folder marked "Russia—Butter." For estimates of US food production for the third protocol: Summary of minutes of Soviet protocol committee on February 23, 1943, in the FDR Library, Hopkins Papers, box 305, book 6. Wheat sold to Iran: Stettinius to Hull, April 26, 1943, Stettinius to Faymonville, May 20, 1943, Faymonville to Stettinius, June 9, 1943, and Stettinius to Hopkins, July 23 and 24, 1943, op. cit. Sugar supplying 70 percent of Soviet consumption: see OSS report No. 2321 ("Russian Import Requirements for Major Foods") in USAHEC, Donovan Papers, box 59B, book 5.

18. *Novyi vidi produktov, postupayushyikh na dovolstvie krasnoi armii.*

19. Ibid.

20. "Summary of Minutes of Soviet Protocol Committee on 23 February 1943," in the FDR Library, Hopkins Papers, box 305, book 6.

21. "Summary of Minutes of the Soviet Protocol Committee" for January 5, February 23, July 23, and September 1, 1943, with accompanying annexes and correspondence, in the FDR Library, Hopkins Papers, box 305, book 6.

22. W. Harnischfeger to Stettinius, March 18, 1943, in NAA, RG 169, box 178, folder marked "Russia. Motor Vehicles. Cranes."

23. Stettinius to General Wesson, July 10, 1943, passing on Clifton Mack (from Treasury) to Stettinius, July 7, 1943, and Stettinius to General Belyaev of the Soviet Purchasing Commission, June 8, 1943, all in NAA, RG 169, box 178, folder marked "Russia—Petroleum Products."

24. Lukashev to Stettinius, March 9, 1943, and Bradley Dewey to Stettinius, March 24–25, 1943, in NAA, RG 169, box 178, folder marked "Russia—Rubber."

25. Lukashev to Stettinius, November 24, 1942, Stettinius to Walsh at Treasury Procurement, November 4, 1942, Edsel B. Ford to Clifton Mack at Treasury, October 28, 1942, and supporting appendices, all in NAA, RG 169, box 178, folder marked "Russia—Rubber." The tire factory order was completed on schedule later in 1943.

26. Lend-lease policy memorandum dated October 8, 1943, written to be shared with correspondents questioning the legal propriety of technology transfer, in NAA, RG 169, box 178, folder marked "Russia—Rubber."

27. Ibid.

28. Jordan and Stokes, *Major Jordan's Diaries*, 93–95, 117. For more on Jordan and his postwar testimony to Congress, see Jones, *Roads to Russia*, appendix B ("Atomic Espionage and Lend-Lease"), 293–95.

29. Jones, *Roads to Russia*, 294–95.

30. Jordan and Stokes, *Major Jordan's Diaries*, 135–37. "Scientific papers by the thousands": cited in Smith, *Warplanes to Alaska*, 142.

31. Jordan and Stokes, *Major Jordan's Diaries*, 142 and passim, for another fifty pages.

32. For a sober discussion of the issues, see Jones, *Roads to Russia*, appendix B ("Atomic Espionage and Lend-Lease"). Jones was writing before many of the lend-lease records were declassified, which have only confirmed still further the veracity of the story Jordan told Congress. Ben Brown and other pilots: Smith, *Warplanes to Russia*, 142–43.

33. On the CKD truck reassembly plants, including the Soviet rejection of the US proposal to build one in Russia, see Stettinius to Litvinov, February 20, 1942, Faymonville to Stettinius, "Triple Priority," February 28, 1942, McCabe to Hopkins, March 28, 1942, and Willis C. Armstrong to Stettinius, November 18, 1942, all in NAA, RG 169, box 178, folder labeled "Russia—Motor Vehicles. Trucks." "Vast conveyer belt": cited in Herring, *Aid to Russia*, 115.

34. On the transfer of title and capacity of the "Soviet" vessels as of July 1943, see "Summary of Minutes of the Soviet Protocol Committee" for July 23, 1943, in the FDR Library, Hopkins Papers, box 305, book 6. "Deck lashings and turnbuckles": Willis C. Armstrong, principal liaison officer, to Lt. Commander Donald Watson, September 7 and 10, 1943, and (more diplomatically) to Golikov of the Soviet Purchasing Commission, September 29, 1943, all in NAA, RG 169, box 178, folder labeled "Russia—Watercraft." For totals shipped on the Pacific route by volume in the third protocol: Jones, *Roads to Russia*, appendix A.

35. Bascon N. Timmons in the *Chicago Sun*, September 17, 1943, clipped and preserved in NAA, RG 169, box 178, folder labeled "Russia—Petroleum Products."

36. Citations in Herring, *Aid to Russia*, 122. "Wartime emergency measure": cited in Martel, *Lend-Lease*, 10.

37. See Herring, *Aid to Russia*, 125–28.

38. Cited in Harriman and Abel, *Special Envoy*, 309. "Firm but friendly quid pro quo approach": see Herring, *Aid to Russia*, 139 and passim.

39. Cited in Harriman and Abel, *Special Envoy*, 309.

40. Roosevelt and Churchill to Stalin, April 19, 1944, received April 21, 1944, reproduced in Reynolds and Pechatnov, *Kremlin Letters*, 409. Emphasis added. Third protocol figures: Jones, *Roads to Russia*, 167.

41. Stalin to Roosevelt and Churchill, April 22, 1944, reproduced in Reynolds and Pechatnov, *Kremlin Letters*, 410. This was the last mention Stalin made of his reciprocal obligation regarding Overlord.

42. Antony Beevor, *D-Day: The Battle for Normandy*, 240. In his general history of the *Second World War*, Beevor derides Clark as "slightly deranged" in his obsession with taking Rome (571).

43. Beevor, *Second World War*, 522. On German regional deployment by divisions each month, see the Klages/Mulholland summary of Georg Tessin's research, op. cit.

44. Ibid.

45. "Spravka k svode o nalichii i tekhnicheskom sostoyanii avtomashin Krasnoi Armii po sostoyanii 15 iyula [1944] g.," in TsAMO, fond 41, opis' 11584, del' 175, list' 59. Tanks: "Svodka o nalichii tankov po frontam na 1 iyula 1944 goda," in TsAMO, fond 38, opis' 11353, korobka 291, del' 1316, list' 26. For the full order of battle on the eve of Bagration and operational details, see Glantz and House, *When Titans Clashed*, 265 (table 13-1) and passim.

46. Mawdsley, *Thunder in the East*, 299–301.

47. Ibid., 308, and for Soviet loss figures in Bagration and comparative German casualties inflicted, Glantz and House, *When Titans Clashed*, appendix, tables O and Q.

Chapter 30: Warsaw

1. Roosevelt to Stalin, February 7, 1944 (received February 11), and Stalin to Roosevelt, February 16, 1944, both in RGASPI, fond 558, opis' 11, del' 367, list' 83–85.

2. Stalin to Roosevelt, July 24, 1944, in RGASPI, fond 558, opis' 11, del' 368, list' 131–32. Stalin had assembled a Polish puppet government in spring 1943: see Norman Davies, *Rising '44: The Battle for Warsaw*, 152–53.

3. Citations in ibid., 134, 151. Soviets train Berling's army: see "Zapiska sotrudnika apparatata TsK VKP (b)," top secret, February 23,

1944, no. 2 in T. V. Volokitina et al., eds., *Sovetskii factor v vostochnoi evrope 1944–1953. Dokumentyi*, 49–50.

4. "Bekanntmachung zur Durchführung der vom SS. und Polizeiführer im Distrikt Krakau angeordneten Judenaussiedlung . . . ," August 22, 1942, and "Polizeiverordnung über die Bildung von Judenwohnbezirken in den Distrikten Warschau und Lublin," August 28, 1942, reproduced in Bogdan Musial, *Kto Dopomoze Zydowi . . .* , 290–91, 299–303. These decrees mandating the execution of anyone helping or sheltering Jews, as Musial notes, were unique to Poland—there were no such decrees in other occupied countries; the implication was that the Germans were punishing Poles for helping Jews too much. The effect was catastrophic, particularly after summary executions of entire gentile families began in October 1942, including children, to terrify other Poles into compliance. At least seven hundred Polish families were executed for aiding and sheltering Jews.

On Karski and the establishment of cooperation between the AK and Jewish Ghetto leaders, and the AK's sharing of arms with the latter and (limited) participation in the Ghetto Uprising, see Joshua D. Zimmerman, *The Polish Underground and the Jews, 1939–1945*, 170–72, 196–98, 219–27. On the origins of the AK, see also Davies, *Rising '44*, 171 and passim.

5. Snyder, *Bloodlands*, 291–92.

6. "Stavka Directive no. 220162" to Rokossovsky, commander on the First Belorussian front, July 27, 1944, reproduced as no. 34 in A. N. Artizov et al., eds. *Sovetskii Soyuz i pol'skoe voenno-politicheskoe Podpol'e. Aprel' 1943-dekabr' 1945*, vol. 2, part 1, *Varshovskoe Vosstanie iyul'-noyabr' 1944*, 94–95. For operational details: Mawdsley, *Thunder in the East*, 329.

7. For up-to-date accounts incorporating new evidence from Soviet and Polish documentary collections, see Mawdsley, *Thunder in the East*, 329–31; Snyder, *Bloodlands*, 300 and passim; and Zimmerman, *Polish Underground*, 382–85 and passim. Mikolajczyk to Molotov on July 30: cited in Reynolds and Pechatnov, eds., *Kremlin Letters*, 452. Posters on July 30: Davies, *Rising '44*, 227.

8. On the belligerent mood in the AK and in Warsaw generally on the eve of the uprising, see especially Davies, *Rising '44*, 226–33 and passim.

9. Snyder, *Bloodlands*, 302.

10. Churchill to Stalin, August 4, 1944, and Stalin to Churchill, August 5, 1944, reproduced in Reynolds and Pechatnov, eds., *Kremlin Letters*, 452–54. Estimates of RAF losses: Davies, *Rising '44*, 311, 380–81.

11. "Prikaz Komandovaniya 2-i tankovoi armiei o perekhode armii k ob-orone," August 1, 1944, 4:10 a.m., and "Dokladnaia zapiska zamestitelya verkhovnogo glavnokomanduyushchego krasnoi armiei G. K. Zhukova i komanduyuschego voiskami 1-go belorusskogo fronta K. K. Rokossov-skogo I. V. Stalinu o plane provedeniya varshavskoi operatsii," August 8, 1944, nos. 49 and 82 in Artizov et al., *Varshovskoe Vosstanie*, 102, 138. On the operational context, see Mawdsley, *Thunder in the East*, 330–31.

12. For details and casualty figures, see Davies, *Rising '44*, 323–30; and Snyder, *Bloodlands*, 302–305.

13. Churchill to Stalin, August 12, 1944, forwarded by Kerr on August 13, and Churchill to Eden, August 14, 1944, reproduced in Reynolds and Pechatnov, eds., *Kremlin Letters*, 456.

14. Stalin to Churchill, August 16, 1944, in RGASPI, fond 558, opis' 11, del' 368, list' 148.

15. Molotov to Harriman, "Sekretno," August 16, 1944, reproduced in Yakovlev et al., *Sovetsko-amerikanskie otnosheniya 1939–1945*, 581.

16. Roosevelt and Churchill to Stalin, August 20, 1944, in RGASPI, fond 558, opis' 11, del' 368, list' 150, and, for Harriman's report on his August 15, 1944, encounter with Vishinsky, Harriman and Abel, *Special Envoy*, 339–40. Vishinsky produced, in his diary, a real-time recollection of this exchange with Harriman, in which he repeatedly denounces the Warsaw uprising as an "adventure." "From the diary of A. Ya. Vishinsky," August 15, 1944, no. 129 in Artizov et al., *Varshovskoe Vosstanie*, 191–93.

17. Stalin to Churchill and Roosevelt, August 22, 1944, in RGASPI, fond 558, opis' 11, del' 368, list' 155. Stalin's order to NKVD on August 22, and Stavka to Rokossovsky: cited in Davies, *Rising '44*, 321–22. "Arrest all [AK] bands": Bulganin to Bierut, August 18, 1944, in AAN, 2/579/0/2/933, list' 18.

18. Cited in Davies, *Rising '44*, 321. Harriman's unsent letter of August 25: cited in Harriman and Abel, *Special Envoy*, 343–44.

19. Ibid., 341. Churchill: cited in Reynolds and Pechatnov, eds., *Kremlin Letters*, 462.

20. Cited in ibid., 462. State Department to Harriman: cited in Harriman and Abel, *Special Envoy*, 342.

21. For military details, see Mawdsley, *Thunder in the East*, 331–32.

22. Cited in Davies, *Rising '44*, 336.

23. Pamphlet addressed to "Pilsudski Followers," August 8, 1944, and German command communiqué, August 10, 1944, in AAN, 2/1335/0/239/194.

24. Mawdsley, *Thunder in the East*, 331–32.

25. See Davies, *Rising '44*, 358–61.

26. Ibid., 361–362, 369–70.

27. Ibid., 395–98.

28. Cited in ibid., 409–10.

29. Casualty, death, and other figures in the Warsaw Uprising are contested and by no means precise. For sober estimates based on recent research, see Musial, *Stalins Beutezug*, 221.

30. Bulganin to Bierut, November 17, 1944, in AAN, 2/579/0/2/933, list' 30.

Chapter 31: Soviet High Tide in Washington

1. "Dinner, November 29, 1943, at 8:30pm," in FDR Library, Hopkins Papers, box 332, book 8 ("Teheran (B). Meeting with Stalin"), folder 2.

2. From *The Morgenthau Diary: Germany*, 26.

3. John Morton Blum, *Years of War, 1941–1945: From the Morgenthau Diaries*, 3:354–55.

4. Cited in *Morgenthau Diary: Germany*, 13.

5. Blum, *Years of War*, 334. On White reporting to KOLTSOV: Romerstein and Breindel, *Venona Secrets*, 47–48. "Shattering violence": cited in John Dietrich, *The Morgenthau Plan: Soviet Influence on American Postwar Policy*, 34.

6. Cited in Blum, *Years of War*, 339.

7. Citations in ibid., 338–42.

8. Citations in Blum, *Years of War*, 354–55. "If you can move a million": cited in *Morgenthau Diary: Germany*, 29. On the Soviet agents in Morgenthau's inner circle at Treasury who worked on the Morgenthau Plan: Evans and Romerstein, *Stalin's Secret Agents*, 182 and 182n. The other four agents, not named in the text, were Harold Glasser, Irving Kapler, Josiah Du Bois, and Sonia Gold. On Glasser's contributions to the Morgenthau Plan, see *Morgenthau Diary: Germany*, 25.

9. Emphasis added. The full text of the Morgenthau Plan is reproduced online at: "Suggested Post-Surrender Program for Germany," Internet Archive (previously at Marist.edu), https://web.archive.org/web/20130531235410/http://docs.fdrlibrary.marist.edu/psf/box31/t297a01.html.

10. Ibid. For a more favorable interpretation of White's role in drafting this document, see R. Bruce Craig, *Treasonable Doubt: The Harry Dexter White Spy Case*, 166–67. Craig concedes that White added the parts about "the forced labor of German workers outside Germany." He also

notes that White asked only for "limited reparations," which is true, but does not tell us much. Still, though he misses the importance of the additions on restitution of German industrial property—a key Soviet aim—and the use of forced labor as "reparations," Craig is right that much of the harsh language came from Morgenthau, rather than White and "Soviet influence" as such.

11. Cited in Blum, *Years of War*, 350. Penrose and Mosely: cited in *Morgenthau Diary: Germany*, 15.

12. Cited in Dallek, *Roosevelt and American Foreign Policy*, 472–73. For Morgenthau's manipulation of Roosevelt on August 25 regarding the Handbook: Blum, *Years of War*, 349. For a sober assessment of Operation Valkyrie, see Hoffman, *German Resistance*, parts IX and X.

13. Citations in Blum, *Years of War*, 359–60. White proposes shootings without trial, and a transcript of the conversation between Morgenthau and Hopkins: *Morgenthau Diary: Germany*, 29–32.

14. Cited in Blum, *Years of War*, 352–53, 362–63. Clauses 10–12: "Suggested Post-Surrender Program for Germany," op. cit.

15. Blum, *Years of War*, 368.

16. Ibid., 369. "Unchristian": cited in Rees, *Behind Closed Doors*, 303.

17. Citations in Blum, *Years of War*, 373. "Beg like Fala": cited in *Morgenthau Diary: Germany*, 35–36. For the timeline of who met with whom when, the most thorough account is Dietrich, *Morgenthau Plan*, 58–69.

18. Blum, *Years of War*, 371–72.

19. Citations in Blum, *Years of War*, 371.

20. Cited in Lees, *Rape of Serbia*, 291. Soviet military mission gives Tito $2 million and appoints two Soviet officers to every partisan corps: Alekseev to Korneev, March 1 and 4, 1944, in RGASPI, fond 82, opis' 2, del' 1369, list' 78, 82. On the C-47s: see Astakhova and Nikitin to Molotov, July 10, 1944, in RGASPI, fond 82, opis' 2, del' 1370, list' 101.

21. Maclean, *Eastern Approaches*, 497–98 (on Tito's disappearance and Churchill's reaction) and 518–19 (on Churchill asking Stalin in Moscow about Tito's whereabouts). Tito denounces Maclean and thanks Stalin for "saving him from the English": Korneev passing on Tito to Stalin, July 31, 1944, in RGASPI, fond 82, opis' 2, del' 1371, list' 10.

22. Cited in Rees, *Behind Closed Doors*, 303. Churchill: cited in Roberts, *Churchill*, 838.

23. Cordell Hull, *The Memoirs of Cordell Hull*, 1616–17; and Thomas M. Campbell and George C. Herring, eds., *The Diaries of Edward R. Stettinius, Jr., 1943–1946*, 152. "Morgenthau business": Fleming, *New Dealers' War*, 432.

24. Cited in Forrest Pogue, *George C. Marshall*, vol. 3, *Organizer of Victory*, 467. Stimson on shooting German officers without trial: cited in Henry Lewis Stimson and McGeorge Bundy, *On Active Service in Peace and War*, 585. Other Stimson citations in Fleming, *New Dealers' War*, 431–32. Morgenthau on Stimson: Blum, *Years of War*, 376. The full text of the Atlantic Charter is available online here: "Atlantic Charter," August 14, 1941, Avalon Project, Yale Law School Lillian Goldman Law Library, https://avalon.law.yale.edu/wwii/atlantic.asp.

25. Citations in Dallek, *Roosevelt and American Foreign Policy*, 477, and Blum, *Years of War*, 377–78. For more on the leak war, see Craig, *Treasonable Doubt*, 174–75. Drew Pearson's Washington Merry-Go-Round column of September 21, 1944, is retrievable online at: "The Washington Merry-Go-Round (September 21, 1944)," American University Digital Research Archive, https://auislandora.wrlc.org/islandora/object/pearson%3A47833#page/1/mode/1up.

26. Cited in John H. Backer, *Priming the German Economy: American Occupational Policies, 1945–1948*, 22–23. "Grinned and looked naughty": Stimson and Bundy, *On Active Service*, 581. Eleanor Roosevelt: cited in Doris Kearns Goodwin, *No Ordinary Time: Franklin and Eleanor Roosevelt: The Home Front in World War II*, 544.

27. Citations in Dietrich, *Morgenthau Plan*, 79–81. Marshall: cited in *Morgenthau Diary: Germany*, 41. Goebbels: cited in Rees, *Behind Closed Doors*, 307. For more on opinion in the army on the Morgenthau Plan, see Earl F. Ziemke, *The U.S. Army in the Occupation of Germany 1944–1946*, 107–8.

28. Soviet radio broadcasts: cited in Romerstein and Breindel, *Venona Secrets*, 48. Dewey: cited in Dietrich, *Morgenthau Plan*, 79. Silvermaster: cited in Rees, *Behind Closed Doors*, 307. Gromyko meets White: cited in *Morgenthau Diary: Germany*, 42.

29. Citations in Dietrich, *Morgenthau Plan*, 81.

30. As noted by Koster in *Operation Snow*, 168.

Chapter 32: Moscow and Yalta

1. See Dimitrov to Molotov, September 6, 1944, in RGASPI, fond 82, opis' 2, del' 1130, list' 18–19. For details on the end of Finnish, Romanian, and Bulgarian resistance, see Mawdsley, *Thunder in the East*, 292–95, 338–45.

2. Maclean, *Eastern Approaches*, 506. SHAEF ban: "Bullseye" to Armstrong, April 27, 1944; "The Russians are treating our people as enemy

prisoners": Mitko to Cairo command, October 18, 1944. Both in PRO, HS 5 / 967. Tito bans British troops: Fotitch, *War We Lost*, 279.

3. The cabinet files launching Operation Manna are preserved in PRO, CAB 106/464. "Tito can be left to himself": cited in Lees, *Rape of Serbia*, 334.

4. Cited in Reynolds and Pechatnov, eds., *Kremlin Letters*, 482–83. "No, you keep it": cited in Roberts, *Churchill*, 843.

5. Churchill to Stalin, July 11, 1944, reproduced in Reynolds and Pechatnov, eds., *Kremlin Letters*, 438–39. For a historian defending Churchill's realistic approach with the "naughty napkin," see Paul Johnson, *Modern Times: The World from the Twenties to the Nineties*, 434.

6. On Churchill in 1939, see chapter 6. "Access to warm waters": "Zapis' besedyi tov. Stalina s Cherchillem," November 30, 1943, in RGASPI, fond 558, opis' 11, del' 234, 60–63.

7. Alekseev (for Stalin) to Tito via Korneev, October 7, 1944, in RGASPI, fond 82, opis' 2, del' 1372, list' 51.

8. On the Budapest campaign, see Mawdsley, *Thunder in the East*, 347–52.

9. Citations in Rees, *Behind Closed Doors*, 316–17. See also, for annotated transcripts of these meetings, Reynolds and Pechatnov, eds., *Kremlin Letters*, 487–92.

10. Mikolajczyk's message to Roosevelt on October 27, 1944, and Roosevelt's reply on October 30, are cited in Campbell and Herring, *The Diaries of Edward R. Stettinius, Jr.*, 162–63. Harriman: Harriman and Abel, *Special Envoy*, 359–60. On Roosevelt's cynical white lies to Mikolajczyk in June, see Rees, *Behind Closed Doors*, 318–19.

11. Report of N. A. Serov, NKVD commander on the "First Belorussian Front," from Lublin, submitted to Beria on October 16, 1944, reproduced in A. F. Noskova, ed., *Iz Varshavyi. Moskva, Tovarisch Beria . . . Dokumentyi NKVD SSSR o pol'skom podpol'e 1944–45 gg.*, 46–48.

12. Ibid., 48–49.

13. Cited in Rees, *Behind Closed Doors*, 310.

14. Bulganin to Bierut, November 17, 1944, in AAN, 2/579/0/2/933, list' 30.

15. "No plans to Sovietize Poland": Reynolds and Pechatnov, eds., *Kremlin Letters*, 487.

16. Citations in Fleming, *New Dealers' War*, 468, 472. Diagnosis of "severe hypertension and the early stages of congestive heart failure": David B. Woolner, *The Last 100 Days: FDR at War and at Peace*, 4–5.

17. Roosevelt to Stalin, October 25 and (including Churchill's suggestion) November 18, 1944, in RGASPI, fond 558, opis' 11, del' 369, list' 51–52, 61–63.

18. Roosevelt to Stalin, November 18, 1944, and Stalin to Roosevelt, October 29 and November 23, 1944, in RGASPI, fond 558, opis' 11, del' 369, list' 54–55, 61–63, 65–66.

19. Citations in S. M. Plokhy, *Yalta: The Price of Peace*, 36–37. On the impact of Roosevelt's medical condition on flight requirements: Woolner, *Last 100 Days*, 61.

20. Citations in Plokhy, *Price of Peace*, 45, 50; and Bohlen, *Witness to History*, 173.

21. Citations in Montefiore, *Court of the Red Tsar*, 480; and Plokhy, *Price of Peace*, 45, 50–51.

22. For operational details, see Mawsdley, *Thunder in the East*, 335–45.

23. Transcript of the Big Three plenary session held in Yalta at 4 p.m. on February 9, 1945, in RGASPI, fond 558, opis' 11, del' 235, list' 137–45. Expulsion of six million Germans: transcript of the Big Three plenary session at Yalta, 4 p.m. on February 7, 1945, in RGASPI, fond 558, opis' 11, del' 235, list' 93–101. Roosevelt agreed to "1939 borders" at Teheran: Soviet transcript of final plenary session of the Teheran conference, December 1, 1943, in RGASPI, fond 558, opis' 11, del' 234, list' 92–93.

24. Cited in Dallek, *Roosevelt and American Foreign Policy*, 515. Churchill and Stalin negotiate deal on Polish elections: "Zapis' beseda tov. Stalina i Cherchilla," with only Molotov, Eden, and translators present, February 10, 1945, late evening, in RGASPI, fond 558, opis' 11, del' 234, list' 157–62.

25. Transcript of the Big Three plenary session held in Yalta at 4 p.m. on February 7, 1945, in RGASPI, fond 558, opis' 11, del' 235, list' 93 and passim. "Bloodthirsty . . . make another toast": cited in Fleming, *New Dealers' War*, 486.

26. Plokhy, *Price of Peace*, 289–91 and 366–67. For praise of Roosevelt's "achievement" in getting the USSR to join "the world body," see also Dallek, *Roosevelt and American Foreign Policy*, 519 and passim.

27. Truman Smith letter to Brigadier General John Weckerling, July 3, 1951, in the Truman Smith Collection, Hoover Institution Archives, box 9, folder 10.3. Leahy: cited in Evans and Romerstein, *Stalin's Secret Agents*, 202.

28. Ibid., 203. On Marshall and the Yalta "briefing book," see also Plokhy, *Price of Peace*, 220–21.

29. Transcript of discussions between Roosevelt and Stalin at Yalta on February 8, 1945, in RGASPI, fond 558, opis' 11, del' 234, list' 118–23. For more on the Asian sphere of influence agreement, see Deane, *Strange Alliance*, 270, and Plokhy, *Price of Peace*, 224–25.

30. Cited in Deane, *Strange Alliance*, 248. For fourth protocol figures, January 1945 deliveries, and ALSIB deliveries to date: "Report on the Soviet Aid Program as of January 31, 1945," in the FDR Library, Hopkins Papers, box 309, book 5 ("Aid to Russia"), folder 2, part 2.

31. Hiss and Hopkins quotes: cited in Evans and Romerstein, *Stalin's Secret Agents*, 44 and 118–19. Roll, in *Hopkins Touch* (371) also cites Hopkins's intervention on Stalin's side on the German reparations issue, but generally downplays the significance of Hopkins's role at Yalta. As Roll notes (374), Hopkins was so sick that he did not even accompany Roosevelt on a ceremonial visit to Sevastopol at the conclusion of the conference.

32. From the Yalta conference protocol reproduced (as a photostat) in Evans and Romerstein, *Stalin's Secret Agents*, 192.

33. "Zapis' beseda tov. Stalina i Cherchilla," with only Molotov, Eden, and translators present, February 10, 1945, late evening, in RGASPI, fond 558, opis' 11, del' 234, list' 157–62. Molotov at Tolstoy conference: cited in Nikolai Tolstoy, *Victims of Yalta: The Secret Betrayal of the Allies, 1944–1947*, 75.

Chapter 33: Booty

1. "Ukaz Prezidiuma Verkhovnogo Soveta SSSR. O natsionalizatsii bankov, promyishlennyikh i torgovyikh predpriyatii, zheleznodoro-zhnogo i vodnogo transporta i sredtsv svyazi Bessarabii," August 15, 1940, in RGAE, fond 4372, opis' 38, del' 1, list' 106.

2. Soviet claims on Romanian territory: see Susaikov, Vinogradov to Molotov, August 18, 1944, in RGASPI, fond 558, opis' 11, del' 361, list' 40–44. Three hundred billion lei: Agreement of September 11, 1945, cited in Stalin to Gheorghiu Dej, 14 February 1947, in RGASPI, fond 558, opis' 11, del' 361, list' 72. Romanian deportation figures: Tolstoy, *Stalin's Secret War*, 267.

3. "Zapis' besedyi tov. Stalina" with Tito's representative, A. Khe-brang, on January 9, 1945, in RGASPI, fond 558, opis' 11, del' 397, list' 1–16. Hungarian deportations: Tolstoy, *Stalin's Secret War*, 268.

4. Bierut to Zhukov, March 8, 1945, and Zhukov to Bierut, March 15, 1945, in AAN, 2/579/0/2/933, list' 16–17, and Vasilevsky to Shatilov,

May 29, 1945, in AAN, 2/579/0/2/934, list' 20. British intelligence summary: cited in Gregor Dallas, *1945: The War That Never Ended*, 421–22.

5. Stalin to Churchill, May 4, 1945, referring to latter's letter of April 28, 1945, with note from Vishinsky, forwarded to Truman, in RGASPI, fond 558, opis' 11, del' 371, list' 45–50 and passim. Manifesto of the Lublin provisional government, Moscow radio broadcast, and Serov to Beria: cited in Davies, *Rising '44*, 457–58.

6. Tolstoy, *Victims of Yalta*; and, for the cited figure of "Soviet" prisoners deported: Tolstoy, *Stalin's Secret War*, 285. When Tolstoy, in his study *The Minister and the Massacres*, fingered British officials responsible for the betrayal of thirty thousand Cossacks in Austria, marked by triple-digit casualties, the full weight of British officialdom came down on his head in a 1989 libel lawsuit. Sentenced to silence while some principals remained alive, Tolstoy is now at liberty to retort, aided by revelations from the Russian archives. His forthcoming study *Stalin's Vengeance* is a devastating indictment.

7. US Army Handbook and "Operation Keelhaul": cited in Evans and Romerstein, *Stalin's Secret Agents*, 195. Mass suicide attempts in New Jersey, at Dachau, near Rome: Mark Elliott, *Pawns of Yalta: Soviet Refugees and America's Role in Their Repatriation*, 86–89, 90–97, 106–9, and passim.

8. "Zapis' beseda tov. Stalina i Cherchilla," with only Molotov, Eden, and translators present, February 10, 1945, late evening, in RGASPI, fond 558, opis' 11, del' 234, list' 157–62.

9. Roosevelt to Stalin, March 4 and 18, 1945, and Stalin to Roosevelt, March 6 and 22, 1945, in RGASPI, fond 558, opis' 11, del' 370, list' 35–36, 41–42, 44–45, 49–51. See also Deane, *Strange Alliance*, 194–99 and passim. On slow-walking and denying Americans access to camps in Eastern Europe, see also Elliott, *Pawns of Yalta*, 40–41 and chap. 3. The full text of the February 11, 1945, "repatriation agreement" is available online: "Agreement Relating to Prisoners of War and Civilians Liberated by Forces Operating Under Soviet Command and Forces Operating Under United States of America Command, February 11, 1945," Avalon Project, Yale Law School Lillian Goldman Law Library, https://avalon.law .yale.edu/20th_century/sov007.asp,.

10. Cited in Frank Freidel, *Franklin D. Roosevelt: A Rendezvous with Destiny*, 601. On Allied grievances with Stalin mounting from February to March 1945, see also David Reynolds, *Summits: Six Meetings That Shaped the Twentieth Century*, 148–51. Molotov confirmed: cited in Beevor, *Second World War*, 727.

11. Cited in Mawdsley, *Thunder in the East*, 387. Molotov and Stalin on the separate peace negotiations: citations in Reynolds and Pechatnov, eds., *Kremlin Letters*, 555–57. For Deane's side of the story: Deane, *Strange Alliance*, 162–65. On the Italian merchant marine, see Roosevelt to Stalin, February 18, 1944, and Stalin to Roosevelt, February 21 and 26, 1944, in RGASPI, fond 558, opis' 11, del' 367, list' 94, 96, 115.

12. Stalin to Roosevelt, April 3, 1945, in RGASPI, fond 558, opis' 11, del' 370, list' 93–95.

13. Cited in Freidel, *Rendezvous with Destiny*, 601. "Frankly I cannot avoid": Roosevelt to Stalin, April 5, 1945, in RGASPI, fond 558, opis' 11, del' 370, list' 103–105. Casualties in Italy: Porch, *Path to Victory*, 656.

14. Blum, *Years of War*, 416–419.

15. These are Glantz and House's estimates, in *When Titans Clashed*, 340. Losses of Soviet armor: Mawdsley, *Thunder in the East*, 392. For more, see Earl F. Ziemke, *Stalingrad to Berlin: The German Defeat in the East*, chap. 21.

16. For details on the looting of Berlin, including citations on NKVD estimates from the Reichsbank and Dahlem: Beevor, *Fall of Berlin 1945*, 324–25, 406–8. The SMERSH records on the recovery of the corpses of Hitler, Goebbels, et al., and their identification by dental records are in RGASPI, fond 82, opis' 2, del' 1166. This file is the Molotov fond, which indicates that Molotov, too, received these reports and was in the loop about Hitler's corpse, even though many Soviet generals, such as Zhukov, were not informed.

17. Mawdsley, *Thunder in the East*, 394–96.

18. "Zapis' Besedyi tov. I. V. Stalina s G. Gopkinsom, Lichnyim Predstavitelem Trumena," May 26, 1945, in RGASPI, fond 558, opis' 11, del' 376, list' 13–19. "Desire to continue President Roosevelt's policy": "Hopkins-Stalin Conference Record Moscow May 26–June 6, 1945," in FDR Library, Hopkins Papers, box 338, book 11.

19. "Zapis' Besedyi tov. I. V. Stalina s G. Gopkinsom, Lichnyim Predstavitelem Trumena," May 27, 1945, 8 p.m., in RGASPI, fond 558, opis' 11, del' 376, list' 23. Stalin's estimate of war dead, from the Soviet transcript, does not appear in the English-language transcript in the Hopkins papers.

20. "Zapis' Besedyi tov. I. V. Stalina s G. Gopkinsom, Lichnyim Predstavitelem Trumena, i Garrimanom, Poslom (USA) v USSR," May 26, 1945, in RGASPI, fond 558, opis' 11, del' 376, list' 18. Truman: cited in Johnson, *Modern Times*, 436.

21. Musial, *Stalins Beutezug*, 339.

22. Ibid., tables on 337–38 and, for the institutional organization of the looting operation, section on "Beuteorgane der roten Armee," 274–77.

23. Ibid., 338–39. Very similar figures, with slight variations depending on dates of estimates and countries of origin, can be found in "Spravka o tonnazhe obodurovaniya I materialov, vyivezennyikh iz Germanii v SSSR v schet reparatsiei I trofeev," in the Mikoyan files at RGASPI, fond 84, opis' 1, del' 27, list' 8.

24. Musial, *Stalins Beutezug*, 338–39 and 390–97 (tables 11–22). Musial's subtitle, *Die Plünderung Deutschlands und der Aufstieg der Sowjetunion zur Weltmacht*, summarizes his argument. The corporate files of Siemens, BMW, Allianz, and other German firms, along with much public archival material from Germany and occupied countries looted by the Germans, are housed in Moscow at the "Special Archive for Foreign Trophy Records" (first TsGOA, then TsKhIDK, now subsumed into RGVA), known colloquially as the "Osoby" archive.

25. Musial, *Stalins Beutezug*, 318–21.

26. Ibid., 318. Yalta zone of limitation and Dresden raid: Plokhy, *Price of Peace*, 214. On the looting of Museum Island in Berlin: Francine-Dominique Liechtenhan, *Le grand pillage: Du butin des Nazis aux trophies des Soviétiques*, 117–18.

27. Cited in Tolstoy, *Stalin's Secret War*, 268.

28. Cited in Norman Naimark, *The Russians in Germany: A History of the Soviet Zone of Occupation, 1945–1949*, 72. Goebbels on Ehrenburg: cited in Beevor, *Fall of Berlin 1945*, 25.

29. Citations in Tolstoy, *Stalin's Secret War*, 269–70. Solzhenitsyn: cited in Beevor, *Second World War*, 686–87.

30. Aleksandr Solzhenitsyn, *The Gulag Archipelago 1918–1956: An Experiment in Literary Investigation*, 1:21. "2 million of our children" / "often raped old women": cited in Beevor, *Fall of Berlin 1945*, 31. Montini and other eyewitness reports confirming rapes of elderly women: cited in Naimark, *Russians in Germany*, 81. Two million raped: Table labeled "Schätzung der Anzahl der vergewaltigten Frauen," in Helke Sander and Barbara Johr, eds., *Befreier und Befreite: Krieg, Verwaltigungen, Kinder*, 59.

31. Cited in Montefiore, *Court of the Red Tsar*, 479.

32. R. M. Douglas, *Orderly and Humane: The Expulsion of the Germans After the Second World War*, 1–2. "Frau ist Frau"/rape of Jewish camp prisoners: Beevor, *Second World War*, 750. On the broader aspects of this story, see also Keith Lowe, *Savage Continent: Europe in the Aftermath of World War II* (2012).

Chapter 34: Red Star over Asia

1. Cited in Lensen, *Strange Neutrality*, 263.

2. The original text of the G-2 estimate of April 12, 1945, is preserved in the Truman Smith Collection, Hoover Institution Archives, box 9, folder 10.3.

3. Citations in Tsuyoshi Hasegawa, *Racing the Enemy: Stalin, Truman, and the Surrender of Japan*, 76–78. On Hoover's visit to the White House, see also Hoover, *Freedom Betrayed*, 536–37.

4. "Top Secret Hopkins-Stalin Conference Record Moscow May 26–June 6, 1945," session on May 27 at 8 p.m., in FDR Library, Hopkins Papers, box 338, book 11. For background on the "cutoff" of lend-lease aid, see Herring, *Aid to Russia*, 202–7.

5. "Top Secret Hopkins-Stalin Conference Record Moscow May 26–June 6, 1945," session on May 27 at 8 p.m., op. cit.; and, for "to the end," "Zapis' Besedyi tov. I. V. Stalina s G. Gopkinsom, Lichnyim Predstavitelem Trumena," May 27, 1945, 8 p.m., in RGASPI, fond 558, opis' 11, del' 376, list' 23.

6. Figures in Jones, *Roads to Russia*, appendix A, table 1, parts 5–6, table 2 (for ALSIB deliveries), and Table 8 (for gross cargo shipped during the war). Wesson: "Hearings Before the Subcommittee of the Committee of Appropriations House of Representatives. Seventy-Ninth Congress First Session on the Second Deficiency Appropriation Bill for 1945," June 13, 1945, in Hopkins Papers, box 310, book 5.

7. Citations in Hasegawa, *Racing the Enemy*, 78–79.

8. "Paraphrase of Navy Cable May 30, 1945, Personal from Hopkins for the Eyes of the President Only," in the FDR Library, and transcript of conversation on May 28, 1945 at 6 p.m. in "Top Secret Hopkins-Stalin Conference Record Moscow May 26–June 6, 1945," both in Hopkins Papers, box 338, book 11 ("Hopkins in Moscow. (1945.))" Emphasis added.

9. On the Politburo discussion, see Hasegawa, *Racing the Enemy*, 115–16.

10. Citations in Hasegawa, *Racing the Enemy*, 66–67, 78. On Truman's love of poker and its impact on his thinking, see Charles L. Mee Jr., *Meeting at Potsdam*, 12 and passim.

11. On these Japanese peace feelers in Moscow and the Magic intercepts, see Hasegawa, *Racing the Enemy*, chap. 3 ("Decisions for War and Peace").

12. Ibid., 115–16, 137, 177–78. On the latest Soviet spy in the Manhattan Project (Oscar Seborer), see Harvey Klehr and J. E. Haynes, "On

the Trail of a Fourth Spy at Los Alamos," *Studies in Intelligence* 63, no. 3 (September 2019): 1–13.

13. Bohlen's notes of the critical July 17 encounter are cited in Mee, *Meeting at Potsdam*, 90–93. The Soviet transcript ("the United States expects assistance") is cited in Hasegawa, *Racing the Enemy*, 137.

14. Stalin's June 28, 1945, directives envisioning a late August offensive, and the updated orders, dated August 2 and 3, 1945, are reproduced as nos. 314–16 and 321–22 in Zolotareva et al., *Sovetsko-yaponskaia voina 1945*, 332–36, 337–38. On Stalin's demands for a base in Turkey or a leading role on the straits being denied: see Bohlen, *Witness to History*, 235. Stimson's diary entries: cited in Hasegawa, *Racing the Enemy*, 152–53. "Results seem satisfactory" and "unusual destructive force": citations in Mee, *Meeting at Potsdam*, 86, 221.

15. The text of the Potsdam Declaration is reproduced in Mee, *Meeting at Potsdam*, 313–15 (appendix I). "Formal request to the Soviet government": cited in Hasegawa, *Racing the Enemy*, 163.

16. Petroleum delivery: Mikoyan to Vasilevsky, commander of Soviet forces in the Far East, July 25, 1945, no. 304 in Zolotareva et al., *Sovetsko-yaponskaia voina 1945*, 311. Soviet order of battle in Far East as of August 9, 1945: David Glantz, *August Storm: The Soviet 1945 Strategic Offensive in Manchuria*, 44–47, tables 3–6. T-34 and Sherman tanks: "Iz spravki o nalichii i tekhnicheskom sostoyanii tankov na dal'nem vostoke na 5 avgust 1945 g.," no. 322 in Zolotareva et al., *Sovetsko-yaponskaia voina 1945*, 339. ALSIB deliveries: "Minutes of the Twenty-Third Meeting of the Protocol Subcommittee on Supplies Held May 16, 1945, at 3:00pm," in the FDR Library, Hopkins Papers, box 309, book 5 ("Aid to Russia"), folder 2, part 1. Fourth protocol figures: cited in Jones, *Roads to Russia*, 167.

17. On Suzuki's statement and how it was distorted: Hasegawa, *Racing the Enemy*, 165–70. Japanese peace feeler: Vishinsky to I. A. Malik, the Soviet ambassador in Tokyo, July 31, 1945, reporting on his conversation with Japanese ambassador Naotake Sato the previous day, no. 305 in Zolotareva et al., *Sovetsko-yaponskaia voina 1945*, 312. Soviets refuse to prolong neutrality pact: see Ambassador I. A. Malik to Molotov, April 21, 1945, reporting on his recent meeting with Togo, no. 295 in Zolotareva et al., *Sovetsko-yaponskaia voina 1945*, 302.

18. Cited in Hasegawa, *Racing the Enemy*, 181.

19. Ibid., 187.

20. Stalin to Vasilevsky, 4:30 p.m. on August 7, 1945, and Vasilevsky to the First and Second Far Eastern, Transbaikal, and Pacific Fleet

Commands at 22:35, 22:40, 23:00, and 23:10 on August 7, nos. 324–28 in Zolotareva et al., *Sovetsko-yaponskaia voina 1945*, 340–43.

21. "Boevoe donesenie komanduyushchego voiskami zabaikalskogo fronta . . . o perekhode gosudarstevennoi granitsu," 1:30 a.m. on August 9, no. 330 in Zolotareva et al., *Sovetsko-yaponskaia voina 1945*, 343–44. The frontier was crossed at 12:10 a.m. Transbaikal time, which was 6:10 p.m. Moscow time, or 1:10 a.m. Khabarovsk or Tokyo time. Sato-Molotov exchange: Cited in Hasegawa, *Racing the Enemy*, 190.

22. Glantz, *August Storm*, 120 and passim.

23. Dieter Heinzig, *The Soviet Union and Communist China 1945–1950: The Arduous Road to the Alliance*, 59–69.

24. Paine, *Wars for Asia*, 208–9. Vasilevsky's directives of August 18: nos. 345–47 in in Zolotareva et al., *Sovetsko-yaponskaia voina 1945*, 359–61.

25. Truman to Stalin, August 16 and 18, 1945, and Stalin to Truman, August 16 and 22, 1945, in RGASPI, fond 558, opis' 11, del' 372, list' 109–16. "Occupy the northern half of Hokkaido": cited in Hasegawa, *Racing the Enemy*, 271. See also Vasilevsky's "situation report" of August 20, 1945, 8 a.m., updating Stalin on Hokkaido preparations, no. 352 in Zolotareva et al., *Sovetsko-yaponskaia voina 1945*, 363–65.

26. On Stalin's Manchurian war booty, see Paine, *Wars for Asia*, 214–16. $2 billion: estimate cited in Frank Dikötter, *The Tragedy of Liberation: A History of the Chinese Revolution 1945–1947*, 15. "Soviet version of comfort women": Beevor, *Second World War*, 777.

27. For Soviet casualty estimates during August Storm: Glantz and House, *When Titans Clashed*, table Q (in appendix). Japan transfers a million troops from Asian theater back to home islands: cited in Paine, *Wars for Asia*, 215.

Epilogue

1. Cited in Tolstoy, *Stalin's Secret War*, 354. Soviets bomb AK positions from the air: see Red Army field report from occupied Poland, December 17, 1945, in AAN, 2/579/0/2/933, list' 57–58. Nine divisions: "Dlya Pamyati," November 23, 1945, in AAN, 2/579/0/2/934, list' 31–32.

2. Citations in Dikötter, *Tragedy of Liberation*, 12–14.

3. Paine, *Wars for Asia*, 238–39. "Mere scrap of paper": cited in Dikötter, *Tragedy of Liberation*, 13.

4. Paine, *Wars for Asia*, 240 and passim.

5. Orders forbidding the use of American arms against Mao's forces: cited in Kubek, *How the Far East Was Lost*, 321. US government to Chiang, September 15, 1945 (emphasis added), and US officers sent to Kalgan: documents reproduced in folder labeled "United States Forces China Theater. U.S.- Foreign relations. China / Military assistance, 1945," in Hoover Institution Archives, Wedemeyer Collection, box 91.

6. Citations in Reynolds and Pechatnov, eds., *Kremlin Letters*, 586–87. For a defense of the strategic thinking behind Churchill's order, see Roberts, *Churchill*, 879.

7. The first and less famous trial, of ten Chetniks, took place on August 9, 1945—the day Stalin declared war on Japan and the second US atomic bomb was dropped on Nagasaki, which buried the story. All were found guilty, with seven sentenced to death by shooting and three to fifteen or twenty years hard labor. See R. C. Skrine Stevenson to Ernest Bevin, from British Embassy Belgrade, August 10, 1945, in PRO, WO 208 / 2018A.

8. On the purges of Grew, Doonan, Hurley, and Wedemeyer, see Kubek, *How the Far East Was Lost*, 282–83 and passim.

9. In 1951, the USSR offered to settle all outstanding lend-lease claims for $240 million. Stalin firmly rejected the US request for international arbitration. See Jones, *Roads to Russia*, 261. On Chinese lend-lease, see Paine, *Wars for Asia*, 281.

10. Owing to the popularization of the "Bletchley Park" story in recent Hollywood films such as *The Imitation Game* (2014), the literature on the subject is now vast. Nonetheless, Frederick William Winterbotham's *The Ultra Secret*, the first historical account, remains an excellent place to begin.

11. "Deutschland lehnt Zahlung weiterer Reparationen an Polen ab," DW, September 8, 2017, www.dw.com / de / deutschland-lehnt-zahlung-weiterer-reparationen-an-polen-ab / a-40419869. West Germany did repay Polish individuals deprived of pensions they had contributed to in the 1970s, and compensation was offered after German unification in 1990 to individual Poles as part of the class-action settlements for victims of slave-labor camps. But to this day, no state-level reparations have been paid.

12. "Extracts from a Broadcast Speech by Stalin on the German Invasion of the Soviet Union," July 3, 1941, op. cit.

13. Plokhy, *Price of Peace*, 393.

14. Cited in Birshtein, *Smersh*, 633. New categories of VAD and VAT: Solzhenitsyn, *Gulag Archipelago*, 1:90–91.

Bibliography

List of Archives and Principal Collections Used

Archiwum Akt Nowych w Warszawie (AAN). Warsaw, Poland.

2/1736/0/3/33. Korespondencja Józefa Becka do Bolestawa Wieniawy-Dlugoszowskiego z zatacznikami 1939–1940 opracowania Jósefa Becka, 'Komentarze do dyplomatycznej historii wojny 1939 roku.'

2/131/0/2/34. Polocy w ZSRR. Liczebno´s´c i rozmieszczenie, transport, zdrowotno´s´c, rodziny wojskowe. 1940–1945.

2/2909/0/-/62. Kolekcja Katynska. Kserokopie dokumentów dotyszacych mordu w Katyniu . . . 1941–1943.

2/322/0/-/24. Gabinet Ministra (49c). Czechoslowacja. Stosunki polityczne z Polska w okresie 'kryzsu sudeskiego.' Noty, instrukcje, raporty, komunikaty. 1938.

2/503/0/8/1719. Wizyty w Warszawie ministrów spraw zagranicznych: Ribbentropa, Ciano, Gafencu. Raporty placówek polskich. 1939.

2/1335/0/239/194. Niemiecki wladze material propagandowy—'Premier Mikolajczyk odbyl konferencję ze Stalinem.' Bór Naczelny Dowódca Armii Krajowej. 1944.

2/273/0/7/1274. Sikorski Wladyslaw 'Polska opinia o rosyjskiej armii' 1939.

2/1320/0/-/197/10. Notatki z rozmow z Armia Krajowa.

2/579/0/2/ 933 and 934. Korespondencja z marszalkami: Koniewem, Rokossow-skim, Zukowem, z generalami: Bulganinemm Sawczenko, Szatilowem; Z KOMENDANTAMI ARMII CZERWONEJ W WARSZAWie; ze sztabemn glownym wojsk radzieckich w Polsce. 1944–1945.

Archiwum Ministerstwo Spraw Zagranicznych (MSZ). Warsaw, Poland.

Z. 27, W. 1, T. 5. Amb RP w Moskwie. Org. stosunkow dyplomaty-cznych. Org. Polskiej Misji Wojskowej.

Z. 27, W. 2, T. 17. Umowy polityczne: umowa polsko-radziecka 1941 r.

Z. 27, W. 2, T. 18. Umowy wojskowe. Notatka dot. Uregulowania oib-ytu i przemarszu wojsk radzieckich.

Z. 27, W. 3, T. 40. Powstanie Warszawskie. Oswiadczenia, wywiady, notatki, depesze, art. Prasowe, pomoc dla Warszawy. 1944.

Z. 27, W. 3, T. 41. Amb. RP w Moskwie. Umowy. Porozumienie miedzy PKWN I Rzadem ZSRR w spr. Stosunkow miedzy radzieckim Wodzem Naczelnym a polska administracja po wkroczeniu wojsk radzieckich na terytorium Polski z dn. 26.VII. 1944 r.

Z. 27, W. 10, T. 155. Ambassada RP w Moskwie. Umowy emigracyjne, repatriacyjne i reemigracyjne. Projekty, kopie, korespondencje. 1944–1945, 1951.

Z. 27, W. 9, T. 149. Stosunki polsko-radzieckie w swietle umow 1939–1947. Wykazy poszczegolnych umow z ZSRR a Rzadem RP zawarte w Moskwie. 1947.

Arkhiv Vneshnei Politiki Rossiiskoi Federatsii (AVPRF). Moscow, Russia.

Fond 5. Opis' 15. Sekretariat Litvinova, 1935–1938.

Fond 6. Opis' 1, 2, 3. Sekretariat Molotova, 1939–1941.

Fond 11. Opis' 2, 6. Iz Sekretariata Litvinova i Molotova, 1938–1945.

Fond 74. Papka 12. Referatura po Bolgarii.

Fond 125. Papka 17. Referatura po Rumanyii.

Fond 136. Frantsiya.

Fond 138. Papka 32. Referatura po Chekhoslovakii.

Bulgarian State Archives (BSA). Sofia, Bulgaria.

Fond 176, Opis' 7. Del. 791. Raporti ot BL v Moskva, Berlin i dr. za politich-eskite otnosheniya mezhdu SSSR i Germaniya, s'vetsko-yaponskiya konflikt v Mandzhuriya i dr. Aug. 9, 1938, to April 15, 1941.

Fond 176K. Opis' 8. Del. 1286. Prepiska s B'lgarekata legatsiya v Ankara. 1943 to 1944.

Fond 316K. Opis' 1. B'lgarska legatsiya v Berlin. Opisa vklyuchva material ot 1904 god do 1944 god.

Del. 189. Poveritelni pisma dc MVRI za germane-b'lgarskie otnosheniya, poseshcheniego na Molotov v Berlin, Dobrudzhanskia v'pros i dr.; Prepiski s MVRI vnos-iznos v B'lgaria; poveritelen protocol na germane-b'lgarska pravitel'stvena . . . i dr. 1938–1940.

Del. 273. Shifrovani telegram ot I do M-vo na v'nshnite raboti otnosno otkaza na B'lgaria ot s'vetskiya pakt za vzaimopomoshch I privlechaneto na B'lgariya v'v II svetovna voina na stranata na Tristranniya pakt. 1940.

Opis' 33.

Del. 24. Dokladi ot b'lgarskiya ofitser za svr'zka pri glavnokomandvashchiya voiskite v S'rbiya. May 25 to Dec. 18, 1943.

Del. 66. S.S.S.R. I B'lgariya.

Del. 854. Prepiska s B'lgarskata legatsiya v Moskva 1940–1941.

Del. 857. Prepiska (shifrovani telgrami I raport) s B'lgarskata legatsiya v Mosvka otnoso otnosheniyata mezhdu SSSR I Germaniya . . . 1940.

Del. 1008. Shifrovana telegramma ot B'lgarskata legatsiya v Moskva, 1941.

Fond 318K. Opis' 1. B'lgarska legatsiya v Moskva. 1907 to 1944.

Del. 5. Prepiska. Zashchita na germanskie interesi v SSSR ot b'lgarskata legatsiya v Moskva. June 27, 1941, to Dec. 13, 1942.

Del. 18. Noti ot M-vo na v'nshnite raboti na SSSR, podpisanii ot V. Molotov s koito dovezhda do znanie za grabezhite, gnusnite nasiliya, izdevatel'stvata i masovite ubiistva prechinenii ot nemskite okupatori v SSSR; prepiska s b'lgarskata misiya v Moskva i dr. izdirvaneto na germanski voenno-plennitsi i idr.

Del. 42. del. Prepiska s M-vo na v'neshnite raboti na SSSR, M-vo na v'nshnite raboti i dro. Otnosno priemaneto ot B'lgariya zashchita na germanskite interesi v SSSR; nota, podpisana ot V. Molotov otnosno zverstvata nad plennitsite-chervenoarmeitsyi ot strana na khitlerskiite voiski i dr.

Fond 1485. Opis' 1. Ministerstvo na V'nshnite Raboti (MVNR)—Komisarstvo prilozhenie s'glashenieto za primirie. 1945 to 1949.

Del. 3. Deklaritsiayata na B'lgarskata delegatsiya vr'chena pri oktrivane na konferentsiyata za primirie v Moskva na 26.X.44 g. Vst'pitelnata rech na prof. Stainov.

Del. 4. S'glashenieto za primirie mezhdu B'lgariya ot edna strana
I SSSR, SASch i Anglia . . . primirie s Ungariya I Rum'niya.
15.11.1944.

Del. 5, 8. Izzetite ot b'lgarskite okupatsionni vlasti imushchestva
ot Yugoslavii. Sept. 14, 1944 to April 20, 1945.

BUNDESARCHIV MILITÄRABTEILUNG (BA/MA). FREIBURG, GERMANY.

RH 2 / 312. Tagesverlauf und Tagesmeldungen 27. Mai 1941–4. Aug
1941.

RH 2 / 1983. Sowjetrussland.

RH 2 / 2106. Anschriften für Nachlässe militärischer Führer. Lagebericht
über die Sowjetunion, 1939–1941.

RH 2 / 3026. Lagebericht über die Sowjetunion (beginning with June
22, 1941).

RH 2 / 2411. Captured Files from Occupied Russia, 1941.

RH 19 / III. Oberkommando der Heeresgruppe Nord. Finnland.

RH 22 / 271. Geheim-Sachen der Abt. I für das Kriegstagebuch. 21.3.41
to 19.10.41.

RH 26–332 / 19. Kriegstagebuch, June 27 to Aug. 12, 1943. (Citadel).

RH 26–332 / 20–21. Befehle and Lageberichte. (Citadel).

RH 24–48 / 114. Operationsbefehle zum Unternehmen Zitadelle mit
Anlagen.

RM 2 / 2539. Entwicklung der Feindlage im Raum Stalingrad. Oct. 23,
1942–Feb. 8, 1943.

RM 2 / 2581. "Die Lage im Kessel von Stalingrad." Letters. Dec. 1942–
Jan. 1943.

RM 4 / 140. "Sonderbericht über den Fall von Stalingrad." 3.2.1943.

RW 4 / v. 329. Interrogations of Captured Soviet Officers, 1941–.

RW 4 / v. 889. Oberkommando der Wehrmacht / Wehrmachtführung-
stab, Abteilung Wehrmacht-Propaganda.

RW 5 / 52. OKW / Amt Ausland / Abwehr. 1941. (Balkans).

RW 5 / v. 29. OKW/ Amt Ausland / Abwehr. Rümanien. Aug.12, 1939,
to March 22, 1943.

RW 5 / v. 356. Aussen- und militärpolitische Nachrichten. July 21, 1940,
to May 26, 1942.

RW 5 / v. 357. OKW. Abteilung für Wehrmachtpropaganda. Geheim-
Akten. Laufende Informationen. Oct. 30, 1939, to Aug. 9, 1941.

RW 5 / v. 358. OKW. Abteilung für Wehrmachtpropaganda. Geheim-
Akten. Laufende Informationen. Aug. 14, 1940, to March 12, 1941.

RW 5 / v. 382. Zusammenfassung wichtiger militärischer Ereignisse. May 31, 1941, to July 12, 1941.

RW 5 / v. 383. Zusammenfassung wichtiger militärischer Ereignisse. July 13, 1941, to Sept. 8, 1941.

RW 5 / v. 384. Zusammenfassung wichtiger militärischer Ereignisse. Sept. 9, 1941, to Oct. 5, 1941.

RW 5 / v. 385. Zusammenfassung wichtiger militärischer Ereignisse. Nov. 6, 1941, to Jan. 20, 1942.

RW 5 / v. 351–52. Aussen-u. militärpolitsiche Nachrichten. Aug. 22, 1939, to Dec. 31, 1939.

RW 5 / v. 476. OKW / Amt Ausland / Abwehr. Yugoslawien. Oct. 1939 to May 1943.

RW 6 / v. 98. Teil: 1. Geheimakten über Polen. September 1939 bis Mai 1940.

RW 8/5. Zustandsbericht der 29. Infanterie Div. / 6 ArmeeKorps (Stalingrad).

DEUTSCHES BUNDESARCHIV BERLIN (DBB). LICHTERFELDE, BERLIN, GERMANY.

R 901. Auswärtiges Amt.

FRANKLIN D. ROOSEVELT PRESIDENTIAL LIBRARY AND MUSEUM (FDR LIBRARY). HYDE PARK, NEW YORK.

Harry L. Hopkins Papers. Sherwood Collection.
    Box 305.
        Book 3: Background of Lend Lease.
        Book 4: Russia Attacked. Early Political Decisions.
        Book 6: Lend Lease to Russia, 1943.
    Box 306.
        Book 4: Hopkins in Moscow, Beaverbrook Mission.
    Box 308.
        Book 4: Thoughts, December 6, 1941.
        Book 5: FDR and H.L.H[opkins] Actions, Post December 7.
    Box 309.
        Book 5: Aid to Russia.
    Box 310.
        Book 5 (Continuation): Aid to Russia.

Box 311.
Book 5 (Continuation): Aid to Russia. Molotov Visit, 1942.
Boxes 315–316.
Book 6. Notebook Plans for European Invasion—Lend Lease Russia 1943.
Boxes 317–319.
Book 6: Second Soviet Protocol (1942–1943).
Box 325.
Book 7: Lend Lease in Operation (1941).
Box 332.
Book 8: Teheran and Teheran (B). Meeting with Stalin. Conversations with Turks, Post Cairo. Teheran (C). Post-Teheran.
Book 9: Second Quebec Conference (Octagon).
Box 338.
Book 10. Post Election Problems.
Book 11. Hopkins in Moscow. (1945). Potsdam Conference. Miscellaneous. Newspaper Clippings
PPF (President's Personal File) 6558. Donovan, Gen. William J.
PSF (President's Special File). Confidential. Box 13. Lend Lease.

Gosudarstvennyi Arkhiv Rossiiskoi Federatsii (GARF). Moscow, Russia.

Fond 8418. Komitet Oboronyi pri Sovnarkome Soyuza SSR. Opis' 24. Za 1940 go. Sdannyikh na vechnoe khranenie v TsAUMVD SSSR.
Del. 2. Perepiska s Narkomatami: NKO, NKVMF I NKVD, Jan. 1940 to April 1941.
Del. 87. Perepiska po planu tekushchikh voennyikh zakazov na 1941 g. Feb 1940.
Del. 103. Perepiska po planu tekushchikh voennyikh zakazov na 1941 g. Po aviatsii. Nov. 1940 to April 1941.
Del. 117. O razrabotke mobplanov na 1940 i 1941 gg. July 1940 to Dec. 1940.
Del. 119. Delo zaklyucheniya narkomatov i SNK Soyuznyikh Respublik po Proektu Mobplana na 1941 g. po osnovnyim vidam vooruzheniya i boevoi tekhniki. Aug. 1940 to May 1941.
Del. 516. Raznaya perepiska po sudostroeniyu. April 1940 to April 1941.

Del. 766. Ob Aviatekhbyuro NKAP v SShA, Italii i Germanii. April 1939 to Dec. 1940.

Del. 1079. O meropriyatiyakh po chernomorskomu flout. April to Aug. 1940.

Del. 1170. O raspredelenii trofeinogo vspomogatel'nogo flota, portovyikh territorii, skladskikh i dr. pomeshchenii. Jan. 1940 to Aug. 1940.

Del. 1349. Raznaya perepiska 10-ogo otdela sekretariata komiteta oboronyi. May 1939 to March 1941.

Fond 8437. Opis' 1. Glavnoe upravlenie aerodromnogo stroitel'stva NKVD SSSR. Sekretariat.

Del. 1. Dislokatsiya, spiski i perepiski po stroit. Ob'ektam aerodromov. 1. Aprelya 1941 goda po 5 iyulya 1941 goda.

Del. 2. Glavnoe upravlenie aerodromnogo stroitel'stva NKVD SSSR. Sekretariat. Dislokatsiya, spiski i perepiska po str. ob'ektam aerodromov. July 6, 1941, to Dec. 31, 1942.

Del. 3. Polozhenie o rabote otdelov GUAS NKVD SSSR. 1942 g. March–Nov. 1942.

Fond P9401. Opis' 1a. Sbornik sovershenno sekretnyikh prikazov NKVD SSSR.

HOOVER INSTITUTION ARCHIVES, STANFORD UNIVERSITY, STANFORD, CALIFORNIA.

Collection: Drachkovitch, Milorad M.
    Box 150. Folder labeled "Ordeal of the Serbs."
Collection: Hoover. Finnish Relief Fund.
Collection: Sikorski, Wladyslaw. Miscellaneous Papers.
Collection: Truman Smith.
    Box 8.
        Folder 8-6. Army. G-2 Division. 1941–1952 and undated.
        Folder 10.3. Russian Declaration of War on Japan. 1943–1969.
Collection: Wedemeyer, Albert C.
    Box 6. Speeches and Writings.
    Box 25. Correspondence.
    Box 91. United States China Theater. Foreign Relations.
        Folder labeled "Southeast Asia Command. Correspondence, memoranda, messages August 1943–June 1944."

Folder labeled "United States Forces China Theater. U.S.-Foreign relations. China/Military assistance, Undated 1945."

Collection: Yeaton, Ivan D.

Box 1.

Folder labeled "Russia. Correspondence of I. D. Yeaton as Military Attaché, Moscow, 1939–1941."

Bound manuscript "Memoirs of Ivan D. Yeaton, USA (Ret.) 1919–1953." Published by the Hoover Institution, 1976.

Box 3. Folder labeled "Faymonville, Philip Ries, 1888–1962."

Box 6. Correspondence and Miscellaneous.

NATIONAL ARCHIVES ANNEX (NAA), WASHINGTON, DC.

Record Group (RG) 59.

T1247. Relating to Political Relations Between the Soviet Union and Other States, 1930–1939.

T1248. Relating to the Political Relations Between the Soviet Union and Other States, 1940–1944.

Record Group (RG) 169. Office of the Lend-Lease Administration. E. R. Stettinius Jr. File Geographic File of the Administrator. New Zealand–Russia.

Box 176.

Folder "Russia–Exports."

Folder "RUSSIA PRIORITIES."

Folder "Russia–Purchasing agent. Authorizations to Sign."

Folder "Russia, Shipping, Schedule of."

Folder "Russia–Requirements."

Folder "Russia–Requisitions."

Folder "Russia–Shipping, Difficulties in Completing."

Folder "Russia–to/from Port of Archangel."

Folder "Russia–shipping, status of."

Folder "Russia–Shipping. General & Miscellaneous."

Folder "Russia–Summary of Reports & Statistics Report of visit to March Field."

Box 177. Entry 9.

Folder "Russia. Commodities General. 1941–1942."

Folder "Russia–Commodities General. January–July 1943."

Folder "Russia. Chemicals and Explosives."

Folder "Russia. Chemicals and Explosives NITRO-GLYCERINE."

Folder "Russia. Arms & Ammunition. Trinitrotoluol (TNT)."

Folder "Russia–Foodstuffs."

Folder "Russia–Foodstuffs. WHEAT."

Folder "Russia–Butter."

Folder "Russia–Foodstuffs. Sugar."

Folder "Russia–Machine Tools."

Folder "Russia–Machinery."

Folder "Russia–Medical Supplies."

Folder "Russia–Metals and Minerals."

Folder "Russia–Metals and Minerals. Aluminum."

Folder "Russia–Metals & Minerals. Nickel."

Folder "Russia–Metals & Minerals. Steel."

Box 178. Entry 9.

Folder "Russia. Summary of Reports and Statistics."

Folder "Russia. Motor Vehicles. Ball Bearings."

Folder "Russia. Motor Vehicles. Cranes."

Folder "Russia–Motor Vehicles. Tanks."

Folder "Russia–Motor Vehicles. Trucks."

Folder "Russia–Petroleum Products."

Folder "Russia–Rubber."

Folder "Russia–Watercraft."

NATIONAL ARCHIVES OF THE UNITED KINGDOM (PRO).
KEW GARDENS, LONDON, UK.

AIR 34/717. Baku USSR. Report Number K 39/1. J.A.R.I.C. Intelligence Section.

AIR 40 / 2106. Operational Information. Russia.

CAB 21/849. Teheran.

CAB 21/860. Yalta.

CAB 65/1–2. War Cabinet. Conclusions W. M. (39) 1–W.M. (39) 66. 3rd Sept–Oct 1939.

CAB 65 / 5. War Cabinet. Conclusions W. M. (40)–W. M. (40) 55. Jan–Feb 1940. Vol III.

CAB 66/36. Cabinet Minutes and Papers, 1943.

CAB 66/54. Cabinet Minutes.

CAB 106 / 464. War of 1939–1945: Mediterranean and Middle East.

CAB 120/192–93. Conference. Operation 'Terminal.' Telegrams Target (Nos 1–335).

DO 35/1511. Meetings between Prime Minister and President of the United States. Meeting at Teheran with Marshal Stalin.

FO 181/965/4. Churchill/Stalin Messages (Original in Embassy).

FO 181/980/3. Secret. Military Operations. Part I. (incl. CHURCHILL-STALIN messages). Part I. Papers 1–50.

FO 181/983/1. Churchill-Stalin Messages. Part I. Papers 1–52.

FO 181/992/2. Most Secret Churchill-Stalin Messages. Part I. Papers 1–31. Part II. Papers 32–65. Part III. Papers 66–.

FO 371 / 24791–94. Political. Northern. Finland. Note: Folios 112–115 Extracted. (Closed until 2016.)

FO 371 / 24846–47. Political. Northern. Soviet Union.

FO 371 / 24849–52. Anglo-Soviet Relations. Political. Northern. Soviet Union.

FO 371/29480. More Northern. Political. Soviet Union. 1941.

FO 371/ 29498. Northern. Soviet Union. Soviet Union. File no. 114.

FO 1093/294. Yugoslavia, General.

HS 5/878. S.O.E. Yugoslavia. Missions. Determination of responsibilities of Brig. Maclean, Directives etc. from Aug. 1943 to Sept. 1944.

HS 5/966. S. O. E. Yugoslavia 100. Parts 1–4. Miscellaneous. Establishment of communications with TITO and MIHAILOVIC. Reports, Minutes & Appreciations.

HS 5 / 967. S. O. E. Yugoslavia 100. Parts 5–14. Aug. 1941 to Dec. 1944. Miscellaneous. Reports, Minutes, and Appreciations. Communications with TITO and MIHAILOVIC.

HS 5/969. SOE Yugoslavia. Volume 102. From 1942. To 1961. Notes on Maclean Mission. The First Mission to Tito & Copies of Telegrams.

HS 7/202. Report on Mission to General Mihailovic and Conditions in Yugoslavia. By Colonel S. W. Bailey, O.B.E.

    "Undated memorandum on SOE work with the Yugoslav guerrillas 1939–1944. Report by Colonel S W Bailey on the Mission to General MIHAILOVIC and conditions in Yugoslavia - April 1944."

HS 7/203. SOE History 146/A. Yugoslavia. Assorted Reports, 1943–.

WO 193 / 647. Secret. Russia. Soviet Aggression Against Finland or Other Scandinavian Countries. Dec. 1939–1940 March.

WO 202/138. F. Maclean letters Sept. 1943–Jan. 1944.

WO 208 / 2018A. The Cetnik Movement. Mihailovic - Historical Material 1941–1944. Closed Until 1972.

Politisches Archiv des Auswärtigen Amts (PAAA).
Berlin, Germany.

Akten betreffend: Ausw. Amt Pol. I M Geheim Akten. Abwehr Türkei.
  R 102028. Feb. 18, 1942, to Aug. 17, 1944.
Akten betreffend: Molotow.
  R 104359. Besuch des Vorsitzenden des Rats der Volkskommis-
  sare u. Außenkommissar's Molotow in Berlin im November
  1940.
Akten betreffend: Militärmission Rumänien, Sept. 1940 to Jan. 1941.
  R 101861. Abwehr.
  R 30003. Misc.
Akten betreffend: Politische Beziehungen Russlands zu Deutschland.
  R 104356. 15 Mai 1936 bis 31 Dez 1938.
  R 104357.
  R 104358. Vom 6 Jan 1940 bis 31 Dez 1940.
Akten betreffend: Politik Angelegenheiten Rußland.
  R 101388. July 10, 1939, to Dec. 31, 1940.
Akten betreffend: Politische Beziehungen zwischen Polen u. Rußland.
  R 104131. Nov. 16, 1940, to Jan. 3, 1941.
Akten betreffend: Politische Beziehungen zwischen Russland und der
  Türkei.
  R 104360. 25 Mai 1936 bis 15 Januar 1940.
Akten betreffend: Politische Abteilung Geheime Reichsakte. Türkei.
  R 261172. April 1, 1940, to Jan. 20, 1942.
  R 261183. 1936–1945.
Botschaft Moskau 402. "Poln. Umsiedl. Aus Lettland."
Botschaft Moskau 488. Polit. Beziehungen der Sowjetunion zu den Bal-
  kanpakt-Staaten (Bulgarien, Griechenland, Jugoslawien, Rumänien,
  Türkei) Balkanpakt, Mittelmeerfragen, Schwarzmeerpakt, Bessara-
  bien. Jan. 1940 to June 1940.
Botschaft Moskau 495. Politische Beziehungen der Sowjetunion zu Po-
  len (ukrainische Frage, Russisch-Polen).
Botschaft Moskau 507. Innenpolitik der Sowjetunion: Oberster Rat,
  Kommisariate, Personalien prominenter Staats- und Parteimänner
  Parteiwezen, Kongresse, Wahlen p p. Feb. 6, 1939, to May 24, 1941.
Botschaft Moskau 520. Politische Beziehungen Deutschlands zu Polen,
  auch Danzig. Jan. 1, 1939, to Aug. 31, 1939.
Botschaft Moskau 512. Innenpolitik der Sowjetunion, Militär, Marine,
  Luftfahre. April 14, 1939, to May 15, 1941.

Botschaft Moskau 514. Politische Beziehungen Deutschlands zu den Balkanstaaten: Bulgarien, Griechenland, Jugoslawien, Rumänien und der Türkei. March 20, 1939, to April 1, 1941.

Botschaft Moskau 521. Krieg. Sept. 1, 1939, to Dec. 31, 1939.

Botschaft Moskau 541. Akten betreffend: Geheime politische Akten. Nov. 1, 1940, to March 31, 1941.

Botschaft Moskau 542. Akten betreffend: Geheime politische Akten. April 1, 1941–

Botschaft Moskau 543. Geheim. Akten betreffend: Militärische Angelegenheiten. April 8, 1940, to May 19, 1941.

Botschaft Moskau 544. Akten betreffend: Politik, geheim. Vom 25. Nov. 1940 bis zum 3. März 1941.

QUAI D'ORSAY ARCHIVES (QO). PARIS, FRANCE.

Etats-Unis.
> File 54. Rapports avec l'U.R.S.S. et les pays de l'est. Jan. 31, 1940, to April 7, 1943.

Grand-Bretagne 1930–1940. Dossier général. Sept. 1, 1939, to June 8, 1940.

Grand-Bretagne 1930–1940. Politique Exterieure. Grande-Bretagne-Russie. Mars 1933–Décembre 1939.

Guerre 1939–1945. Vichy.
> File 815. U.R.S.S. Corps diplomatique et consulaire français. July 1940 to Aug. 1941.
>
> File 816. Attaché militaire. Attaché de l'air. U.R.S.S. July 1940 to Oct. 1942.
>
> File 817. Compte rendu et rapports de l'attaché militaire. March to May 1941.
>
> File 835. Allemagne-Russie. June 22, 1940, to June 21, 1941.

Guerre 1939–1945. Vichy. Levant.
> File 113. Turquie. Politique intérieure. Nov. 1941–Juillet 1944.
>
> File 117. Turquie. Relations avec la France. Dossier general. June 1940–Aug. 1944.
>
> File 126. Turquie. Attitude dans le conflit (en particulier rapports turco-allemand). Avril 1940–avril 1941.

Rossiiskii Gosudarstvennyi Arkhiv Ekonomiki (RGAE).
Moscow, Russia.

Fond 4372, Gosplan.
    Opis' 38.
        Del. 1. Ukaza Prezidiuma Verkovnogo soveta SSSR v 1940.
        Jan. 5 to Dec. 30, 1940.
        Del. 13. Vyipiski iz protokolov zasedanii Sovnarkoma SSSR za
        1940 g. No. 1–12. Jan. 21, 1940, to Dec. 6, 1940.
    Opis' 41.
        Del. 16. Protokol soveshchaniya Zamestitelei Predsedatel'ya
        Gosplana za 24 marta 1941 goda.
        Del. 30. Material k zasedaniyu Gosplana SSSR April 28, 1941.
        Del. 31. Material k zasedanii Gosplana SSSR 2 June 1941. April
        30, 1941, to June 2, 1941.
        Del. 32. Material k zasedaniyu Gosplana pri SNK SSSR 12
        maya 1941 goda.
        Del. 33a. Prikazyi Gosplana pri SNK SSSR za fevral'-dekabrya
        mstsyi 1941 g. 4. Feb. to Dec. 18, 1941.
        Del. 39. Kopii zaklyuchanii po porucheniem pravitel'stva
        . . . za 1941 g.
        Del. 343. Zaklyuchenie Gosplana SSSR v SNK SSSR po vo-
        prosu material'no-tekhnicheskogo obespecheniya po
        planu Narkomata aviatsionnoi promyishlennosti na 1941
        g., spravki Gosplana SSSR o material'no-tekhnicheskom
        obespechenii aviatsii v 1941 g. Aug. 7, 1940, to Aug. 23,
        1940.
        Del. 344. Ob'yasnitel'naya zapiska Gosplana SSSR k proektu
        mobilizatsionnogo plana na 1940 god i proekt plana pro-
        myishlennoi produktsii na 1940 voennyi god. Jan. 4 to
        April 22, 1940.
        Del. 354. Spravki mobilizatsionnogo otdela Gosplana SSSR,
        otcheta TsUNKhU Gosplana SSSR i Narkomatov po vo-
        prosu vyipolneniya plana kapital'nyikh rabot oboronnogo
        stroitel'stva po narkomatam za 1940 g. From Feb. 19, 1940,
        to Jan. 31, 1941.
Fond 8752, Opis' 1. Narodnyi Komissariat Tankovyi Promishchlennosti
SSSR.

Rossiiskii Gosudarstvennyi Arkhiv Sotsial-Politicheskii Arkhiv (RGASPI). Moscow, Russia.

Fond 17. Politburo TsK RKP (b) – VKP (b).

Opis' 162. Povestki dnia zasedanii. (Politburo Minutes and Resolutions, 1939–).

Del. 25 (March 1939 to 3 Sept. 1939).

Del. 26 (Sept. 4 to Oct. 3, 1939).

Del. 27 (Jan. 20 to June 23, 1940).

Del. 28 (June 25 to Aug. 24, 1940).

Del. 29 (Aug. 27 to Oct. 28, 1940).

Del. 30 (Oct. 29 to Dec. 13, 1940).

Del. 31 (Dec. 14, 1940, to Jan. 18, 1941).

Del. 32 (Jan. 20 to March 15, 1941).

Del. 33 (March 17 to April 9, 1941).

Del. 34 (April 10 to May 14, 1941).

Del. 35 (May 15 to June 12, 1941).

Del. 36 (June 14 to July 24, 1941).

Del. 37 (Aug. 26, 1941, to Dec. 29, 1945).

Fond 82. Opis' 2. (Molotov).

Del. 1102–5. Perepiska I. V. Stalina s Cherchill'om za 1940–1945 gg.

Del. 1107–9. Perepiska I. V. Stalina s Ruzvel'tom za 1941–43 gg. s zamechaniyami i pometkami V. M. Molotova, prilozheniya k zapiske MID SSSR ot 21 sentyabrya 1951 g.

Del. 1308. Soedinennyie Shtatyi Ameriki (sShA).

Del. 1161. Deyatel'nost' V. m. Molotova v kachestve narcoma, ministra inostrannyikh del.— o sovetsko-germanskom dogorove o nenapadenii, o berlinskom pakte o troistvennom soyuze, ob otklitkakh v zarubezhnyikh stranakh na visit V. M. Molotova v Berlin (1940).

Del. 1166. Germaniya (Germany). May 27, 1945, to June 22, 1945.

Del. 1285. Pol'sha. Zapiski, soobshcheniya, obzor materialov NKID, NK Finansov . . . ob otnosheniyakh SSSR s Pol'shei . . . pis'mo narodnogo komissara inostrannyikh del SSSR posle Pol'shi v SSSR ot 17 sentyabrya 1939 g. o prekrashchenii deistviya vsekh dogorovov, zaklyuchennyikh mezhdu SSSR i Pol'shei, i vyitekayushchikh iz etogo fakta posledstviyakh i dr. Aug. 1942.

Del. 1302. Rumanyiia. Sept. 14, 1921, to Aug. 18, 1947.

Del. 1329. Turtsiya (Turkey). Aug. 23, 1935, to May 29, 1952.

Del. 1330. Bolgariya (Bulgaria). 1925 to Nov. 24, 1945.

Del. 1339. Finlandiya. July 11, 1938, to Jan. 21, 1950.

Del. 1356. Czechoslovakia. April 6, 1929, to Aug. 6, 1941.

Del. 1369–73. Yugoslaviya. Feb. 27, 1942, to Feb. 3, 1953.

Del. 1386–88. Yaponiya (Japan). Sept. 7, 1931, to Aug. 13, 1952.

Fond 84. Opis' 1. (Mikoyan).

Del. 27. Voprosyi vneshnepoliticheskikh otnoshenii I vneshnei torgovli. Zapiski . . . o sokrashchenii razmera reparatsii s Germanii. Feb. 26, 1948, to May 16, 1950.

Del. 78. Voprosyi Krasnoi armii. Proektyi postanovlenii TsK VKP (b) i SNK SSSSR, zapiski NKVMF SSSR, NKO SSSR, NKVT SSSR na imya I. V. Stalina, V. M. Molotova i dr. po voprosam snabzheniya Krasnoi Armii boepripasami, perevoski voennyikh gruzov, pensionnogo obespecheniya lichnogo sostava Krasnoi Armii i dr., 25.X.39–14.6.41.

Del. 79. Kopii zapisok A. I. Mikoyana i dr. na imya I. V. Stalina, proektyi postanovlenii GOKO po voprosam snabzhenii Armii goryuchim, prodovol'stviem, obozno-veshchevyim imushchestvom I dr., . . . o voennoi obstanovke na otdel'nyikh uchastkakh. June 24, 1941, to Dec. 26, 1941.

Del. 80. Zapiski NKO SSSR Predsedatel'yu GOKO, spravochnyie dokumentyi o chislennosti Krasnoi Armii. Aug. 24, 1941, to Sept. 10, 1941.

Del. 81. Voprosyi Krasnoi Armii. Zapiski Narkomgoskontrolya na imya Stalina, V. M. Molotova, A. I. Mikoyana o rezul'tatakh I proverki sostoyaniya snabzheniya armii vooruzheniem, boepripasami goryuchim I dr. imushchestvom. Nov. 20, 1940, to Nov. 18, 1941. g.

Del. 82. Voprosyi Krasnoi Armii . . . Proektyi postanovlenii SNK SSSR I Ts VKP (b), GOKO, . . . Mikoyan, Stalin etc . . . snabzheniya Krasnoi Armii. Feb. 13, 1940, to Sept. 11, 1941.

Del. 96. Voprosyi Krasnoi Armii. Zapiski A. I. Mikoyana, N. A. Bulganina i dr. I. V. Stalinu, v GOKO, proektyi postanovlenii GOKO, SNK SSSR po voprosam snabzheniya Krasnoi Armii prodovol'stviem, material'nogo obespecheniya lichnogo sostava Krasnoi Armii, transportirovki voennyikh gruzov, o razvitii morskikh baz i torgovyikh portov na Dal'nem Vostoke i dr. Jan. 29, 1945, to Nov. 15, 1945.

Del. 146. Materialyi o peregovorakh s Germaniei v 1939–1941 g.g. po zaklyucheniyu i khodu vyipolneniya sovetsko-nemetskogo Khozaistvennogo soglasheniya.

Fond 558. Opis' 11. (Stalin).

Del. 215. Shiftelegrammyi NKID SSSR. Shiftelegrammyi polpredov i sovkinsulov s otvetami i rezolyutsiami Stalina I. V., chlenov Politbyuro TsK VK (b) i NKID SSSR za period s 3 iyunya 1938 g. po 27 iyunya 1940 g.

Del. 216. Shiftelegrammyi NKID SSSR. (Molotova V. M). o peregovorakh v Germanii, polpredov i sovkonsulov s otvetami i rezolyutsiami Stalina I.V., Molotova V. M. i NKID SSSR za period s 21 iyulya 1940 g. po 24 aprelya 1944 g.

Del. 220. Peregovoryi voennyikh missii Anglii, Frantsii i SSSR. Zapisi zasedanii voennyikh missii . . . June 16, 1939, to March 30, 1965.

Del. 234. Tegeranskaya konferentsiya (Teheran Conference) glav pravitel'stv SSSR, SShA I Velikobritanii. Zapisi 1-4 zasedanii konferentsii glav . . . Nov. 28, 1943, to Dec. 10, 1943.

Del. 235. Yalta. Feb. 4–11, 1945.

Del. 252. Bolgariya. Aug. 19, 1926, to Aug. 17, 1946.

Del. 297. Germaniya. Poezdka Molotova V. M. v Berlin. Zapis' besedy Pred. SNK SSSR i narodnogo komissara inostrannyikh del SSSR Molotova V. M. s reikhskantslerom Germanii Gitlerom A. i ministrom inostrannyikh del Germanii Ribbentropom I. v Berline. Nov. 12–13, 1940.

Del. 326. Kitai. Perepiska s Chan Kai-shi. March 27, 1940, to Jan. 17, 1946.

Del. 357. Pol'sha. Priem Stalinyim I.V. generala Andersa, perepiska s nim. Zapis' besedyi Stalina I. V. s komanduyushchim Pol'skoi armiei na territorii SSSR generalom Andersom . . . perepiska . . . March 8 to May 30, 1942.

Del. 361. Rumyiniia (Romania). Aug. 8, 1937, to Feb. 14, 1947.

Del. 363–70. SSha (USA: Stalin-Roosevelt Correspondence). Aug. 4, 1941, to April 12, 1945.

Del. 371–73. SSha (USA: Stalin-Truman Correspondence). April 13 to May 26, 1946.

Del. 375. SSha (USA). Priem Stalinyim I. V. Devisa D (Joseph Davies); perepiska s nim. June 5, 1938, to June 21, 1945.

Del. 376. SShA (USA). Priem Stalinyim I. V. Gopkinsa G. (Harry Hopkins), perepiska s nim. Zapisi besed Stalina I.V. s lichnyim predstavitelem Prezidenta SShA Ruzvel'tom (1941 g.), Prezidenta Trumena (1945 g.) Gopkinsom G., perepiska Stalina I.V. s Gopkinsom G. po povodu konchinyi Ruzvel'ta, vyipisk iz izdannoi v Londone knigi Shervuda 'Belyi dom. Dokumentyi Garri L. Gopkinsa." July 30, 1941, to March 17, 1951.

Del. 388. Turtsiya. Zapisi besed Stalina I. V., Molotova V. M. s Ismet-pashoi, s ministrom inostr. Del. Turtsii Saradzhoglu . . . zapis' bese-dyi Kemal' Atatyurka s Karakhanom . . . Oct. 8, 1921, to Feb. 18, 1946.

Del. 395–98. Yugoslaviya. Perepiska Stalina I. V. s marshalom Broz Tito o polozhenii v NOA Yugoslavii, po povodu osvobozhdeniya stolitsyi Yugoslavii Belgrada, s polozhenii v Yugoslavii, ob otdel'nyikh intsidentakh i oshibakh so storonyi otdel'nyikh ofitserov i boitsov Krasnoi Armii . . . 1938– 14 April 1948.

Del. 404. Zapiski Stalina I. V. i drugie materialyi o sovetsko-yaponskikh otnosheniyakh . . . June 1, 1922, to May 19, 1941.

Del. 449. Shifrtelegrammyi Genshtaba RKKA i VVS RKKA, NKVD i NKGB SSSR, narkomatov vneshnei torgovli i vooruzheniya SSSR s rezolyutsiyami Stalina I. V. i chlenov Politbyuro Ts VKP (b), s otvetami Narkomata vooruzheniya i VVS RKKA za period s 11 Marta 1939 g. po 11 sentyabra 1941 g.

Rossiiskii Gosudarstvennyi Voennyi Arkhiv (RGVA). Moscow, Russia.

Fond 4. Narodnyi Komitet Oboronyi SSSR.
Opis' 15-a. Prikazyi NKO.
Del. 505. Sekretnyi prikazyi NKO na 1940 g.
Opis' 15-b. Prikazyi NKO.
Del. 2. Sovershenno sekretnyie prikazyi Narodnogo Kommissara Oboronyi Soyuza SSR.

Fond 9. Opis' 29. Sekretariat Nachal'nika Politicheskogo Upravleniya RKKA. 1922–1941 gg.

Del. 390. Materialyi o partiino-politicheskoi rabote v Krasnoi Armii za 1938 i 1939 godyi. July 13, 1938, to July 31, 1940.

Del. 506. Dokladyi i materialyi chastei ob opyite partiino-politicheskoi rabotyi v period boevyikh deistvii v Zapadnoi Ukraine i Finlyandii. Oct. 4, 1939, to Aug. 6, 1940.

Fond 29. Opis' 57. N.K.O. Gl. Uprav. Aviatsionnogo Snabzhaniya Kr. Armii.

Del. 3. Perepiska s SNK, Upravl. VVS o sostoyanii i nalichii samoleto-motornogo parka VVS KA. May 25, 1940, to Dec. 3, 1940.

Del. 7. Svedeniya o vyipolnenii plana zakazov i plana snabzheniya po samoletam I motoram na 1940 g. (Otchetyi, vedomosti). Jan. 21, 1940, to April 3, 1940.

Del. 9. Perepiska s UVVS po mobilizatsionnoi rabote voennoi priyami po moshchnostyam samoletnyikh i motornyikh zavodov. Jan. 24 to Dec. 20, 1940.

Del. 18. Svedeniya a nalichii mob. (parachutnoi dessantnom), avtotransportom, sredstv mekanizatsii, aerodrome, sladkskomu. Jan. 4 to Oct. 21, 1940.

Fond 25888, Opis' 3. Dokumentyi po planirovaniyu oboronyi poluostrova 'Khanko'.

Del. 189. Jan. 13, 1941, to June 15, 1941.

STALIN DIGITAL ARCHIVE. YALE UNIVERSITY PRESS.

RGASPI, Fond 558. Available online at www.stalindigitalarchive.com /frontend/.

TSENTRAL'NYI ARKHIV MINISTERSTVA OBORONYI RF (TSAMO). PODOL'SK, MOSCOW, RUSSIA.

Fond 35, Glavnoe upravlenia VVS.

Opis' 11285.

Korobka 1154.

Del. 516. Direktivyi, planyi, otchetyi shtaba VVS Krasnoi Armii o formirovanii, ukomplektovanii, perevode na novyie shtatyi chastei VVS Krasnoi Armii, o formirovanii i otpravke na front aviatsionnyikh polkov, o

sostoyanii i dvizhenii samoletnogo parka v chastyakh
VVS Krasnoi ARmii na 1 iyula 1942 goda. June 1 to
Dec. 12, 1942.

Korobka 1183.

Del. 757. Svedeniya I spravki shtaba VVS Krasnoi Armii
o rezul'tatakh boevyikh deistvii, poteryakh lichnogo
sostava i material'noi chasti VVS. June 1, 1942, to Jan. 3,
1943.

Korobka 1186.

Del. 786. Otchetyi, dokladyi, opisaniya shtabov aviatsionnyikh soedinenii, vozdushnyikh armii, predstavitelei
General'nogo Shtaba Krasnoi Armii o boevom pri-
meenii aviatsii. May 2 to Sept. 22, 1943.

Korobka 1187.

Del. 806. Dokladyi shtabov vozdushnyikh armii s otsenkoi
kachestvennogo sostoyaniya material'noi chasti VVS
Krasnoi Armii i protivnika. Feb. 25 to Dec. 28, 1943.

Opis' 11287.

Korobka 1398.

Del. 1001. Otchet po spetsial'nomu letnomu ispyitaniyu
motora 'Allison' i vintomotornoi gruppyi na samolete
'Kertis Tomagauk-1' v zimnyikh usloviyakh. Jan. 7,
1942.

Fond 38. Opis' 11353. Upravlenia bronetankovyikh i mekhanizirovannyikh voisk.

Korobka 291.

Del. 1316. Spravki shtaba bronetankovyikh i mekhanizirovannyikh voisk Krasnoi Armii o nalichii soedinenii i
chastei, nalichii, vyipuske za 1941–1944 gg., remonte i
poteryakh otechestvennoi material'noi chasti, nalichii i
dvizhenii importnyikh tankov. July 1 to Dec. 31, 1944.

Korobka 3760.

Del. 12. Opersvodki ABTU Zapadnogo fronta; svedenia
fronta, armii, soedinenii i chastei o nalichii, sostoyanii i
poteryakh material'noi chasti I vooruzheniya; dokladyi
i doneseniya armii i soedinenii Zapadnogo i Briansk-
ogo frontov o boevyikh deistviiakh; donesenie 138-go
otdel'nogo tankovogo batal'ona o ego komplektovanii
angliiskimi tankami i ikh ispol'zovanii v boyu. Oct. 22
to Dec. 31, 1941.

Korobka 3789.

Del. 611. Informatsii I spravki GRU Krasnoi Armii, opisaniya, broshyuryi o proizvodstve, sostoyanii, ispol'zovanii material'noi chasti, organizatsii bronetankovyikh
i mekhanizirovannyikh voisk Yaponii, Anglii, SShA i
Germanii s prilozheniyami skhem; otchetyi predstavitelei SSSR o poseshchenii amerikanskikh predpriyatii
po Proizvodstvu material'noi chasti bronetankovyikh i
Mekhanizirovannyikh voisk. Jan. 5 to Oct. 2, 1944.

Korobka 3799.

Del. 869. Direktivyi i ukazaniya NKO, General'nogo shtaba
Krasnoi Armii i shtaba GABTU o sformirovanii, kom-
pletovanii, otpravke I peredislokatsii tankovyikh armii,
soedinenii i chastei i perepiska po etim voprosam. Oct.
20 to Dec. 31, 1941.

Korobka 3814.

Del. 985. Direktivyi zamestitelya narkoma oboronyi SSSR
o formirovanii otdel'nyikh tankovyikh i mototsikletn-
yikh batal'onov . . . March 2 to July 22, 1942.

Korobka 3830.

Del. 1053. Spravki shtaba i upravlenii GABTU Krasnoi
Armii o Formirovanii i gotovnosti chastei, o nalichii
i dvizhenii Otechestvennyikh i importnyikh mashin
(tanki, avtomobili, bronetransporteryi, bronepoezda).

Fond 41. Opis 11584. Glavnoe avtomobil'noe upravlenie.

Del' 175, list' 59. Tanks.

Fond 84. Opis' 12403. Upravlenia veshchevogo snabzheniya.

Korobka 3082.

Del. 372. Svedeniya voennyikh predstavitelei o postuplenii
i raskhode importnogo imushchestva. Feb. 12 to Dec.
24, 1943.

Korobka 3097.

Del. 538. Materialyi Upravleniya veshchevogo snabzheniya,
tekhnicheskogo komiteta, Glavnogo intendantskogo
upravleniya Krasnoi Armii po ustanovleniyu rostovki
angliiskoi obuvi i kachestvu obuvi, postupavshei iz
Irana . . . Aug. 27, 1941, to Nov. 30, 1942.

Digitized documents, retrieved individually:

Fond 215, opis' 1185, del' 24, list' 42. Online at: https://pamyat-naroda
.ru/documents/view/?id=130454165&backurl=q%5CДуглас:use
_main_string%5Ctrue:group%5Call:types%5Copersvodki:raspory
ajeniya:otcheti:peregovori:jbd:direktivi:prikazi:posnatovleniya
:dokladi:raporti:doneseniya:svedeniya:plani:plani_operaciy:karti:sh
emi:spravki:drugie

Fond 1257, opis' 1, del' 46, list' 103. Online at: https://pamyat-naroda.ru
/documents/view/?id=451285134&backurl=q%5Cанглийск:use
_main_string%5Ctrue:group%5Call:types%5Copersvodki:raspory
ajeniya:otcheti:peregovori:jbd:direktivi:prikazi:posnatovleniya:
dokladi:raporti:doneseniya:svedeniya:plani:plani_operaciy:karti:
shemi:spravki:drugie

Fond 3189, opis' 1, del' 5, list' 66. Online at: https://pamyat-naroda.ru
/documents/view/?id=134586035&backurl=q%5Cамериканские:
use_main_string%5Ctrue:group%5Call:types%5Copersvodki
:rasporyajeniya:otcheti:peregovori:jbd:direktivi:prikazi:posnatov
leniya:dokladi:raporti:doneseniya:svedeniya:plani:plani_operaciy
:karti:shemi:spravki:drugie:page%5C8

Fond 3212, opis' 2, del' 1, list' 60-61. Online at: https://pamyat-naroda.ru
/documents/view/?id=454731108&backurl=q%5Cанглийск:use
_main_string%5Ctrue:group%5Call:types%5Copersvodki:raspory
ajeniya:otcheti:peregovori:jbd:direktivi:prikazi:posnatovleniya:
dokladi:raporti:doneseniya:svedeniya:plani:plani_operaciy:karti
:shemi:spravki:drugie:page%5C6

Fond 10877, opis' 1, del' 46, list' 103. Online at: https://pamyat-naroda.ru
/documents/view/?id=455406899&backurl=q%5Cстудебеккер
:begin_date%5C1942:end_date%5C1942:fund%5C10877:use
_main_string%5Cfalse:group%5Call:types%5Copersvodki:raspory
ajeniya:otcheti:peregovori:jbd:direktivi:prikazi:posnatovleniya
:dokladi:raporti:doneseniya:svedeniya:plani:plani_operaciy:karti:sh
emi:spravki:drugie&static_hash=ad6990d086fcf52030e4dcee
a3ed2e7e

Fond 13790, opis' 20191, del' 6, list' 383. Online at: https://
pamyat-naroda.ru/documents/view/?id=454351842&back
url=q%5Cамериканские:use_main_string%5Ctrue:group%5Call
:types%5Copersvodki:rasporyajeniya:otcheti:peregovori:jbd
:direktivi:prikazi:posnatovleniya:dokladi:raporti:doneseniya
:svedeniya:plani:plani_operaciy:karti:shemi:spravki:dru-
gie:page%5C2

US Army Heritage and Education Center (USAHEC).
Carlisle, Pennsylvania.

William J. Donovan Papers.
Box 2B. Publications and Papers 1936–1945.
Folder "1941."
Box 32C. Germany, Economics, Volume II—Book No. 7. Gains of Germany. Occupation of Soviet Territory—Book No. 8.
Box 37A. Germany, Miscellaneous Studies, Volumes I and II. Books No. 1 and No. 2. Germany and Morale.
Box 57B. Book No. 6. USSR.
Box 58A. Russia, Administration, Labor, Religion—Book No. 1. And Russia. The Armed Forces and the War.—Book 2.
Box 59B. Russia, Geographic—Book No. 3. Russia, Industry— Book No. 5. Miscellaneous Studies—Book No. 7.
Box 66A.

Vincennes. Service Historique de la Défense (VSHD).
Vincennes, Paris, France.

(GR) 7 N 2790. Finlande. Attachés militaires, 1929–1940.
(GR) 7 N 2791. Finlande. Affaires Etrangeres. Finlande. 1919–1940.
(GR) 7 N 2819. Attaché militaire Grande Bretagne. 1939–1940.
(GR) 7 N 2820. Attaché militaire Grande Bretagne. Feb. 29 to April 29, 1940.
(GR) 7 N 3124. URSS. Documents diplomatiques. 1920–1940.
(GR) 7 N 3143. Renseignements sur l'armée 1930–1939.
(GR) 7 N 3186. Missions militaires françaises. 1935–1939.
"Mission du Général Doumenc en U.R.S.S. du 11 au 25 août 1939."
(GR) 7 N 3227. Turquie. Attaché militaire. 1939–1940.
(GR) 7 N 3256. Mission Weygand à Ankara. Octobre 1939.

Document Collections and Published Diaries

Artizov, A. N., et al., eds. *Sovetskii Soyuz i pol'skoe voenno-politicheskoe Podpol'e. Aprel' 1943-dekabr' 1945.* Vol. 2, Part 1, *Varshovskoe Vossta-nie iyul'-noyabr' 1944.* Moscow: Mezhdunarodnyi fond demokratiia, 2016.
Banac, Ivo, ed. *The Diary of Georgi Dimitrov, 1933–1949.* New Haven, CT: Yale University Press, 2003.

Basik, I. I., et al. *Stalingradskaia epopeia. Vpervyie publikuemyie dokumentyi: dnevniki i pis'ma soldat RKKA i vermakhta: agenturnyie doneseniya: protokolov doprosov: dokladnyie zapiski osobyikh otdelov frontov i armii.* Moscow: Zvonnitsa-MG, 2000.

Beddie, James Stuart, and Raymond James Sontag, eds. *Nazi-Soviet Relations 1939–1941: Documents from the Archives of the German Foreign Office.* Washington, DC: Department of State, 1948.

Blum, John Morton, ed. *From the Morgenthau Diaries.* 3 vols. Boston: Houghton Mifflin, 1959, 1965, 1967.

Bugai, N. F. *L. Beriya – I. Stalinu: 'Soglasno Vashemu ukazaniyu . . . '.* Moscow: Airo-XX, 1995.

Campbell, Thomas M., and George C. Herring, eds. *The Diaries of Edward R. Stettinius, Jr., 1943–1946.* New York: New Viewpoints, 1975.

Congressional Record: Proceedings and Debates of the 78th Congress. Vol. 90.

Dallin, Alexander, and F. I. Firsov, eds. *Dimitrov and Stalin 1934–1943: Letters from the Soviet Archives.* New Haven, CT: Yale University Press, 2000.

Daly, Jonathan, and Leonid Trofimov, eds. *The Russian Revolution and Its Global Impact: A Short History with Documents.* Indianapolis, IN: Hackett, 2017.

Degras, Jane, ed. *The Communist International, 1919–1943: Documents.* 3 vols. New York: Oxford University Press, 1956–1965.

———, ed. *Soviet Documents on Foreign Policy.* 3 vols. New York: Oxford University Press, 1951–1953.

Diedrich, Torsten, and Jens Ebert, eds. *Nach Stalingrad: Walther von Seydlitz' Feldpostbriefe und Kriegsgefangenpost.* Göttingen, Germany: Wallstein Verlag, 2018.

Dilks, David, ed. *The Diaries of Sir Alexander Cadogan, O.M., 1938–1945.* New York: Putnam, 1971.

Foreign Relations of the United States. Diplomatic Papers. The Soviet Union 1933–1939. Washington, DC: US Government Printing Office, 1952.

Gorodetsky, Gabriel, ed. *The Maisky Diaries: Red Ambassador to the Court of St. James's, 1932–1943.* New Haven, CT: Yale University Press, 2015.

Gregory, Paul R., and Norman Naimark, eds. *The Lost Politburo Transcripts: From Collective Rule to Stalin's Dictatorship.* New Haven, CT: Yale University Press, 2008.

Gurov, S. A., et al., eds. *Stalingrad 1942–1943: Stalingradskaia bitva v dokumentakh.* Kaliningrad, Russia: Minoboronyi Rossii, 2017.

Halder, Franz. *The Halder Diaries: The Private War Journals of Colonel General Franz Halder.* Translated by Trevor N. Dupuy. Boulder, CO: Westview Press, 1976.

Herde, Peter, ed. *Die Achsenmächte, Japan, und die Sowjetunion: Japanische Quellen zum Zweiten Weltkrieg.* Berlin: Walter de Gruyter, 2017.

Lih, Lars, Oleg Naumov, and Oleg V. Khlevniuk, eds. *Stalin's Letters to Molotov.* New Haven, CT: Yale University Press, 1995.

The Morgenthau Diary: Germany. Washington, DC: Senate Judiciary Committee, 1967.

Naumov, V. P., et al. *Georgii Zhukov. Stenogramma oktyabr'skogo (1957) plenuma TsK KPSS i drugie dokumentyi.* Moscow: Mezhdunarodnyi fond demokratiia, 2001.

———. *Lubyanka. Stalin i NKVD -NKGB-GUKR 'Smersh'. 1939–mart 1946.* Moscow: Mezhdunarodnyi fond demokratiia, 2006.

Nevezhin, V. A., ed. *Zastol'nyie rechi Stalina. Dokumentyi i materialyi.* Moscow: Airo-XX, 2003.

Nicolson, Nigel, ed. *Harold Nicolson. The War Years 1939–1945.* Vol. 2 of *Diaries and Letters.* New York: Atheneum, 1967.

Noskova, A. F., ed. *Iz Varshavyi. Moskva, Tovarisch Beria . . . Dokumentyi NKVD SSSR o pol'skom podpol'e 1944–45 gg.* Moscow/Novosibirsk: GARF, 2001.

Novyi vidi produktov, postupayushyikh na dovolstvie krasnoi armii. Moscow: War Publications of the People's Ministry of Defense, 1944.

Otnoshenii Rossii (SSSR) s Iugoslaviei 1941–1945 gg. Dokumentyi i materialyi. Moscow: Terra-Knizhnyi klub, 1998.

Pikhoya, Rudolf, et al., eds. *Katyn'. Plenniki neob'yavlenno voinyi.* Moscow: Mezhdunarodnyi fond demokratiia, 1999.

Pobol', N. L., and P. N. Polyan, eds. *Stalinskie Deportatsii 1928–1953.* Moscow: Mezhdunarodnyi fond demokratiia, 2005.

Reshin, L. E., et al., eds. *1941 God. Dokumenty.* 2 vols. Moscow: Mezhdunarodnyi fond demokratiia, 1998.

Reynolds, David, and Vladimir Pechatnov, eds. *The Kremlin Letters: Stalin's Wartime Correspondence with Churchill and Roosevelt.* New Haven, CT: Yale University Press, 2018.

Savchenko, V. I., G. N. Sevostyanov, and B. I. Zhilyaev, eds. *Sovetsko-amerikanskie otnosheniya godyi nepraznaniya 1927–1933.* Moscow: Izdatel'skaya firma Materik, 2004.

Schramm, Peter, ed. *Kriegstagebuch des Oberkommandos der Wehrmacht.* 8 vols. Munich: Bernard & Graefe, 1982.

Schreiber, Gerhard, et al., eds. *Germany and the Second World War. Edited by the Militärgeschichtliches Forschungsamt.* 9 vols. New York: Oxford/ Clarendon, 1990–2017.

Seidl, Alfred, ed. *Die Beziehungen zwischen Deutschland und der Sowjetunion 1939–1941. Dokumente des Auswärtigen Amtes.* Tübingen, Germany: H. Laupp, 1949.

Sovetsko-Germanskie Otnosheniia ot peregovorov v Brest-Litovske do Podpisaniia Rapall'skogo Dogovora. Moscow: Izdatel'stvo Politicheskoi Literatury, 1971.

SSSR i Germanskii Vopros 1941–1949. Moscow: Mezhdunarodnyie otnosheniya, 1996.

Stalingrad 1942–1943. Stalingradskaia bitva v dokumentakh. Moscow: Biblioteka, 1995.

Taylor, Fred, ed. and trans. *The Goebbels Diaries, 1939–1941.* London: H. Hamilton, 1982.

Volokitina, T. V., et al., eds. *Sovetskii factor v vostochnoi evrope 1944–1953. Dokumentyi.* Moscow: Rosspen, 1999.

Yakovlev, A. N., et al. *Sovetsko-amerikanskie otnosheniya 1939–1945.* Moscow: Mezhdunarodnyi fond demokratiia, 2004.

Zelenii, V. V., ct al., eds. *Sovetsko-yugoslavskoe otnosheniya 1917–1941 gg.* Moscow: Izdatel'stvo Nauka, 1992.

Zolotareva, V. A., et al. *Sovetsko-yaponskaya voina 1945 goda: Istoriya voenno-politicheskogo protivobortsva dvukh derzhav v 30-40 godyi.* 2 vols. Moscow: Terra, 1997, 2000.

Published and Online Works Cited or Profitably Consulted, Including Memoirs

Adamthwaite, Anthony. *The Making of the Second World War.* Boston: Allen & Unwin, 1977.

Agnew, Jeremy, and Kevin McDermott. *The Comintern: A History of International Communism from Lenin to Stalin.* London: Macmillan, 1996.

Aksenov, Andrei, et al. *Soviet Tanks in Combat 1941–1945.* Hong Kong: Concord Publications, 1997.

Allen, Martin. *The Hitler/Hess Deception.* London: HarperPerennial, 2004.

Allen, Robert C. *Farm to Factory. A Reinterpretation of the Soviet Industrial Revolution.* Princeton, NJ: Princeton University Press, 2009.

Andrew, Christopher, and Vasili Mitrokhin. *The Sword and the Shield: The Mitrokhin Archive and the Secret History of the KGB.* New York: Basic Books, 1999.

Applebaum, Anne. *Gulag: A History*. New York: Doubleday, 2003.

———. *Iron Curtain: The Crushing of Eastern Europe, 1944–1956*. New York: Doubleday, 2012.

———. *Red Famine: Stalin's War on Ukraine*. New York: Doubleday, 2017.

Armstrong, John A. *Ukrainian Nationalism, 1939–1945*. New York: Columbia University Press, 1955.

Aster, Sidney. "The Diplomat as Scapegoat?" In *Leadership and Responsibility in the Second World War*, edited by Brian Padair Farrell and Robert Vogel. Montreal: McGill-Queen's University Press, 2004.

Backer, John H. *Priming the German Economy: American Occupational Policies, 1945–1948*. Durham, NC: Duke University Press, 1971.

Ball, Alan. *Russia's Last Capitalists: The Nepmen*. Berkeley: University of California Press, 1987.

Barbieri, Pierpaolo. *Hitler's Shadow Empire: Nazi Economics and the Spanish Civil War*. Cambridge, MA: Harvard University Press, 2015.

Barthel, Max. *Kein Bedarf an Weltgeschichte*. Wiesbaden, Germany: Limes, 1950.

Baumgart, Winfried. *Deutsche Ostpolitik 1918: Von Brest-Litowsk bis zum Ende des Ersten Weltkrieges*. Vienna/Munich: Oldenbourg, 1966.

Bayer, Waltraud, ed. *Verkaufte Kultur: Die sowjetischen Kunst- und Antiquitätenexporte 1919–1938*. Frankfurt: Peter Lang, 2001.

Beevor, Antony. *D-Day: The Battle for Normandy*. New York: Penguin, 2010.

———. *The Fall of Berlin 1945*. New York: Penguin, 2003.

———. *The Second World War*. New York: Little, Brown, 2012.

———. *Stalingrad*. New York: Penguin, 1999.

Bell, Wilson T. *Stalin's Gulag at War: Forced Labour, Mass Death, and Soviet Victory in the Second World War*. Buffalo, NY: University of Toronto Press, 2019.

Bess, Demaree. "Our Frontier on the Danube. The Appalling Story of Our Meddling in the Balkans." *Saturday Evening Post*, May 24, 1941.

Birshtein, V. Ya. *Smersh. Sekretnoe oruzhie Stalina*. Moscow: Airo-XX, 2018.

Black, Conrad. *Franklin Delano Roosevelt: Champion of Freedom*. New York: PublicAffairs, 2003.

Blücher, Wipert von. *Deutschlands Weg nach Rapallo*. Wiesbaden, Germany: Limes, 1951.

Blum, John Morton, ed. *Roosevelt and Morgenthau: A Revision and Condensation of "From the Morgenthau Diaries."* Boston: Houghton Mifflin, 1972.

Bohlen, Charles E. *Witness to History, 1929–1969.* New York: W. W. Norton, 1973.

Boog, Horst, et al., eds. *Das Deutsche Reich und der zweite Weltkrieg.* Vol. 4, *Der Angriff auf die Sowjetunion.* Munich: Deutsche-Verlags Anstalt, 1983.

Braithwaite, Rodric. *Moscow 1941: A City and Its People at War.* New York: Knopf, 2006.

Braunthal, Julius. *Geschichte der Internationale.* 3 vols. Berlin: Dietz, 1961–1971.

Breitman, Richard, and Allan Lichtman. *FDR and the Jews.* Cambridge, MA: Harvard University Press, 2014.

Brent, Jonathan. *Inside the Stalin Archives: Discovering the New Russia.* Fayetteville, NC: Atlas, 2008.

Brown, Anthony Cave. *Wild Bill Donovan: The Last Hero.* New York: Times Books, 1982.

Buchanan, George. *My Mission to Russia, and Other Diplomatic Memories.* London: Cassell & Co., Ltd., 1923.

Buchanan, Patrick. *Churchill, Hitler, and "The Unnecessary War": How Britain Lost Its Empire and the West Lost the World.* New York: Crown, 2008.

Budnitsky, Oleg. *Russian Jews Between Reds and Whites, 1917–1920.* Translated by Timothy Portice. Philadelphia: University of Pennsylvania Press, 2012.

Burds, Jeffrey. "The Soviet War Against 'Fifth Columnists': The Case of Chechnya, 1942–1944." *Journal of Contemporary History* 42, no. 2 (April 2007): 267–314.

Burns, James MacGregor. *Roosevelt: The Soldier of Freedom.* New York: Harcourt Brace Jovanovich, Inc., 1970.

Butler, Susan. *Roosevelt and Stalin: Portrait of a Partnership.* New York: Knopf, 2015.

Butow, R. J. C. "Backdoor Diplomacy in the Pacific: The Proposal for a Roosevelt-Konoye Meeting, 1941." *Journal of American History* 59, no. 1 (June 1972): 48–72.

Byrnes, James F. *Speaking Frankly.* New York: Harper & Brothers Publishers, 1947.

Caidin, Martin. *The Tigers Are Burning.* Portland, OR: Hawthorne Books, 1974.

Carlton, David. *Churchill and the Soviet Union.* Manchester, UK: Manchester University Press, 2000.

Caute, David. *The Fellow-Travelers: A Postscript to the Enlightenment*. New York: MacMillan, 1973.

Charmley, John. *Churchill: The End of Glory. A Political Biography*. London: Faber & Faber, 2011. First published in 1993.

Chuev, Felix. *Molotov Remembers: Inside Kremlin Politics*. Edited by Albert Resis. Chicago: I. R. Dee, 1993.

Churchill, Winston. *The Grand Alliance*. Boston: Houghton Mifflin, 1950.

———. *His Complete Speeches, 1897–1963*. Edited by Robert Rhodes James. 8 vols. New York: Chelsea House Publishers, 1974.

Clements, Barbara Evans. *Bolshevik Feminist: The Life of Alexandra Kollontai*. Bloomington: Indiana University Press, 1979.

Coakley, Robert W., and Richard M. Leighton. *Global Logistics and Strategy: 1940–1943*. Washington, DC: Center of Military History, Department of the Army, 1955.

———. *Global Logistics and Strategy: 1943–1945*. Washington DC: Center of Military History, Department of the Army, 1968.

Cole, Wayne S. *Roosevelt and the Isolationists, 1932–1945*. Lincoln: University of Nebraska Press, 1983.

Conquest, Robert. *The Great Terror: Stalin's Purge of the Thirties*. New York: Macmillan, 1968.

———. *The Harvest of Sorrow: Soviet Collectivization and the Terror Famine*. New York: Oxford University Press, 1986.

Craig, R. Bruce. *Treasonable Doubt: The Harry Dexter White Spy Case*. Lawrence: University Press of Kansas, 2004.

Craig, William. *Enemy at the Gates: The Battle of Stalingrad*. Old Saybrook, CT: Konecky and Konecky, 2010.

Crisp, Olga. *Studies in the Russian Economy Before 1914*. London: Macmillan, 1976.

Cull, Brian, and Christopher Shores. *Air War for Yugoslavia, Greece, and Crete, 1940–41*. London: Grub Street Publishing, 2008.

Dallas, Gregor. *1945: The War That Never Ended*. New Haven, CT: Yale University Press, 2005.

Dallek, Robert. *Franklin D. Roosevelt and American Foreign Policy, 1932–1945*. New York: Oxford University Press, 1979.

Davies, Norman. *God's Playground: A History of Poland*. New York: Cambridge University Press, 1982.

———. *Rising '44: The Battle for Warsaw*. London: Macmillan, 2003.

Davies, Norman, and Antony Polonsky, eds. *Jews in Eastern Poland and the USSR, 1939–46*. New York: St. Martin's Press, 1991.

Davies, R. W., and Stephen G. Wheatcroft. *The Years of Hunger: Soviet Agriculture, 1931–1933*. London: Palgrave Macmillan, 2004.

Davis, Robert H., et al. *A Dark Mirror: Romanov and Imperial Palace Library Materials in the New York Public Library: A Checklist and Agenda for Research*. New York: Norman Ross, 2000.

Deane, John R. *The Strange Alliance: The Story of American Efforts at Wartime Co-operation with Russia*. London: John Murray, 1946.

Deutscher, Isaac. *The Prophet Armed: Trotsky, 1879–1921*. New York: Oxford University Press, 1954.

Dietrich, John. *The Morgenthau Plan: Soviet Influence on American Postwar Policy*. New York: Algora Publishing, 2013.

Dikötter, Frank. *The Tragedy of Liberation: A History of the Chinese Revolution 1945–1947*. London: Bloomsbury, 2013.

Djilas, Milovan. *Conversations with Stalin*. Translated by Michael B. Petrovich. New York: Harcourt Brace & Co., 1962.

Dolitsky, Alexander B., ed. *Pipeline to Russia: The Alaska-Siberia Air Route in World War II*. Anchorage: Alaska Affiliated Areas Program/National Park Service, 2016.

Dorn, Frank. *Walkout: With Stilwell in Burma*. New York: Thomas Y. Crowell Co., 1971.

Douglas, R. M. *Orderly and Humane: The Expulsion of the Germans After the Second World War*. New Haven, CT: Yale University Press, 2012.

DW. "Deutschland lehnt Zahlung weiterer Reparationen an Polen ab." September 8, 2017. www.dw.com/de/deutschland-lehnt-zahlung-weiterer-reparationen-an-polen-ab/a-40419869.

Edele, Mark. "Fighting Russia's History Wars: Vladimir Putin and the Codification of World War II." *History & Memory* 29, no. 2 (Fall/Winter 2017): 90–124.

Edwards, Bernard. *The Road to Russia: Arctic Convoys 1942*. Annapolis, MD: Naval Institute Press, 2003.

Elliott, Mark. *Pawns of Yalta: Soviet Refugees and America's Role in Their Repatriation*. Urbana: University of Illinois Press, 1982.

Engle, Eloise, and Lauri Paananen. *The Winter War: The Soviet Attack on Finland, 1939–1940*. Mechanicsburg, PA: Stackpole Books, 1992.

Erickson, John. *The Road to Berlin: Continuing the History of Stalin's War with Germany*. Boulder, CO: Westview Press, 1983.

———. *The Road to Stalingrad: Stalin's War with Germany*. New York: Harper & Row, 1975.

Ericson, Edward E. *Feeding the German Eagle: Soviet Economic Aid to Nazi Germany, 1933–1941*. Santa Barbara, CA: Praeger, 1991.

Evans, M. Stanton, and Herbert Romerstein. *Stalin's Secret Agents: The Subversion of Roosevelt's Government.* New York: Threshold, 2012.

Evans, Richard. *The Third Reich at War.* New York: Penguin Books, 2010.

Fabry, Philipp W. *Die Sowjetunion und das Dritte Reich: Eine dokumentierte Geschichte der deutsch-sowjetischen Beziehungen von 1933 bis 1941.* Stuttgart, Germany: Seewald, 1971.

Feiling, Keith. *Life of Neville Chamberlain.* London: Macmillan, 1947.

Fetzer, Leland, trans., and Ray Wagner, ed. *The Soviet Air Force in World War II. The Official History, Originally Published by the Ministry of Defense of the USSR.* Garden City, New York: Doubleday, 1973.

Fischer, George. "Genesis of U.S.-Soviet Relations in World War II." *Review of Politics* 12, no. 3 (July 1950): 363–378.

Fish, Hamilton. *FDR. The Other Side of the Coin.* New York: Vantage Press, 1976.

Fisher, Harold H. *The Famine in Soviet Russia, 1919–1923: The Operations of the American Relief Administration.* New York: Macmillan, 1927.

Fleming, Thomas. *The New Dealers' War: Franklin D. Roosevelt and the War Within World War II.* New York: Basic Books, 2001.

Förster, Jürgen, and Evan Mawdsley. "Hitler and Stalin in Perspective: Secret Speeches on the Eve of Barbarossa." *War in History* 11, no. 1 (January 2004): 61–103.

Fotitch, Constantin. *The War We Lost: Yugoslavia's Tragedy and the Failure of the West.* New York: Viking, 1948.

Freidel, Frank. *Franklin D. Roosevelt: A Rendezvous with Destiny.* Boston: Little, Brown, 1990.

Freund, Gerald. *Unholy Alliance: Russian-German Relations from the Treaty of Brest-Litovsk to the Treaty of Berlin.* London: Chatto and Windus, 1957.

Gaddis, John Lewis. *Strategies of Containment: A Critical Appraisal of American National Security Policy During the Cold War.* New York: Oxford University Press, 2005.

Gafencu, Grigore. *Prelude to the Russian Campaign, from the Moscow Pact (August 21st, 1939) to the Opening of Hostilities in Russia (June 22nd, 1941).* London: F. Muller, Ltd., 1945.

Gasanli, Dzhamil. *SSSR-Iran: Azerbaijanskii krisis i nachalo kholodnoi voinyi (1941–1946).* Moscow: Geroi Otechestvo, 2006.

———. *SSSR-Turtsiya: Ot neutraliteta k kholodnoi voinyi (1939–1953).* Moscow: Tsentr propagandyi, 2008.

The German Campaign in Russia: Planning and Operations (1940–1942). Washington, DC: Department of the Army, 1955.

Gitlow, Benjamin. *The Whole of Their Lives: Communism in America, a Personal History of Its Leaders.* New York: C. Scribner's Sons, 1948.

Glantz, David. *August Storm: The Soviet 1945 Strategic Offensive in Manchuria.* Fort Leavenworth, KS: Combat Studies Institute, 1984.

———. *From the Don to the Dnepr. Soviet Offensive Operations December 1942–August 1943.* London: Frank Cass, 1991.

———. *The Role of Intelligence in Soviet Military Strategy in World War II.* Novato, CA: Presidio, 1990.

———. *Soviet Military Deception in the Second World War.* London: Frank Cass, 1989.

———. *Stumbling Colossus: The Red Army on the Eve of World War.* Lawrence: University Press of Kansas, 1998.

———. *Zhukov's Greatest Defeat: The Red Army's Epic Disaster in Operation Mars, 1942.* Lawrence: University Press of Kansas, 1999.

Glantz, David, and Jonathan House. *Armageddon in Stalingrad: September–November 1942.* Vol. 2 of *The Stalingrad Trilogy.* Lawrence: University Press of Kansas, 2009.

———. *The Battle of Kursk.* Lawrence: University Press of Kansas, 1999.

———. *Colossus Reborn: The Red Army at War.* Lawrence: University Press of Kansas, 2005.

———. *Endgame at Stalingrad: Book Two: December 1942–February 1943.* Vol. 3 of *The Stalingrad Trilogy.* Lawrence: University Press of Kansas, 2014.

———. *To the Gates of Stalingrad: Soviet-German Combat Operations, April–August 1942.* Vol. 1 of *The Stalingrad Trilogy.* Lawrence: University Press of Kansas, 2009.

———. *When Titans Clashed: How the Red Army Stopped Hitler.* Lawrence: University Press of Kansas, 2015.

Gogun, Alexander. *Stalin's Commandos: Ukrainian Partisan Forces on the Eastern Front.* London: I. B. Tauris, 2016.

Goodwin, Doris Kearns. *No Ordinary Time: Franklin and Eleanor Roosevelt: The Home Front in World War II.* New York: Simon & Schuster, 1994.

Gorodetsky, Gabriel. *Grand Delusion: Stalin and the German Invasion of Russia.* New Haven, CT: Yale University Press, 2001.

Grinberg, Ilya, and Von Hardesty. *Red Phoenix Rising: The Soviet Air Force in World War II.* Lawrence: University Press of Kansas, 2012.

Gross, Jan. *Neighbors: The Destruction of the Jewish Community in Jedwabne, Poland.* New York: Penguin Books, 2002.

———. *Revolution from Abroad: The Soviet Conquest of Poland's Western Ukraine and Western Belorussia.* Princeton, NJ: Princeton University Press, 1988.

———. "The Sovietization of Western Ukraine and Western Byelorussia." In *Jews in Eastern Poland and the USSR, 1939–46*, edited by Norman Davies and Antony Polonsky, 60–76. New York: St. Martin's Press, 1991.

Grossman, Vasily. *Life and Fate: A Novel*. Translated by Robert Chandler. New York: Harper & Row, 1985.

Guderian, Heinz. *Panzer Leader*. Translated by Constantine Fitzgibbon. New York: Da Capo Press, 1996.

Hanson, Victor Davis. *The Second World Wars: How the First Global Conflict Was Fought and Won*. New York: Basic Books, 2017.

Harriman, W. Averell, and Elie Abel. *Special Envoy to Churchill and Stalin, 1941–1946*. New York: Random House, 1975.

Harrison, Mark. *Accounting for War: Soviet Production, Employment, and the Defense Burden, 1940–1945*. New York: Cambridge University Press, 1996.

———. *Soviet Planning in Peace and War, 1938–1945*. New York: Cambridge University Press, 1985.

Harrison, Mark, and John Barber. *The Soviet Home Front, 1941–1945: A Social and Economic History of the USSR in World War II*. New York: Cambridge University Press, 1996.

Hasegawa, Tsuyoshi. *The February Revolution: Petrograd, 1917*. Seattle: University of Washington Press, 1981.

———. *Racing the Enemy: Stalin, Truman, and the Surrender of Japan*. Cambridge, MA: Belknap, 2005.

Haslam, Jonathan. "Soviet-German Relations and the Origins of the Second World War: The Jury Is Still Out." *Journal of Modern History* 69, no. 4 (December 1997): 785–797.

———. *The Soviet Union and the Threat from the East, 1933–1941: Moscow, Tokyo, and the Prelude of the Pacific War*. Pittsburgh, PA: University of Pittsburgh Press, 1992.

Hastings, Max. *Inferno: The World at War, 1939–1945*. New York: Vintage, 2012.

Haynes, John Earl, and Harvey Klehr. "Hiss Was Guilty." History News Network, 2007, https://historynewsnetwork.org/article/37456.

Heinzig, Dieter. *The Soviet Union and Communist China 1945–1950: The Arduous Road to the Alliance*. Armonk, NY: East Gate, 2004.

Hemming, Henry. *Agents of Influence: A British Campaign, a Canadian Spy, and the Secret Plot to Bring America into World War II*. New York: PublicAffairs, 2019.

Herring, George C., Jr. *Aid to Russia 1941–1946: Strategy, Diplomacy, and the Origins of the Cold War*. New York: Columbia University Press, 1973.

Herwarth von Bittenfeld, Hans-Heinrich. *Against Two Evils*. New York: Rawson, Wade, 1981.

Hill, Alexander. "British Lend-Lease Aid and the Soviet War Effort." *Journal of Military History* 71, no. 3 (July 2007): 773–808.

Hillgruber, Andreas. *Hitlers Strategie: Politik und Kriegführung 1940–1941*. Munich: Bernard & Graefe, 1982.

Hitchens, Peter. *The Phoney Victory: The World War II Illusion*. London: I. B. Tauris, 2018.

Hoffman, Peter. *The History of the German Resistance, 1933–1945*. Montreal: McGill-Queen's University Press, 1996.

Hoffmann, Joachim. *Stalins Vernichtungskrieg 1941–1945: Planung, Ausführung und Dokumentation*. Stuttgart, Germany: F. A. Herbig, 2001.

Höhne, Heinz. *Canaris*. Translated by J. Maxwell Brownjohn. Garden City, NY: Doubleday, 1979.

Holquist, Peter. *Making War, Forging Revolution: Russia's Continuum of Crisis, 1914–1921*. Cambridge, MA: Harvard University Press, 2002.

Hoover, Herbert. *Freedom Betrayed: Herbert Hoover's Secret History of the Second World War and Its Aftermath*. Stanford, CA: Hoover Institution Press, 2011.

Horne, Alistair. *Hubris: The Tragedy of War in the Twentieth Century*. New York: Harper, 2015.

Hosking, Geoffrey. *Russia and the Russians*. Cambridge, MA: Harvard University Press, 2001.

Hull, Cordell. *The Memoirs of Cordell Hull*. New York: Macmillan, 1948.

Hyde, H. Montgomery. *Neville Chamberlain*. London: Weidenfeld & Nicolson, 1976.

Imlay, T.C. "A Reassessment of Allied Strategy During the Phony War, 1939–1940." *English History Review* 119, no. 481 (April 2004): 333–272.

Irincheev, Bair. *War of the White Death: Finland Against the Soviet Union 1939–1940*. Barnsley, UK: Pen and Sword Military, 2011.

İşçi, Onur. "The Massigli Affair and Its Context." *Journal of Contemporary History* 55, no. 2 (2020). http://doi.org/10.1177/0022009419833443.

———. *Turkey and the Soviet Union During World War II*. London: Bloomsbury, 2019.

Johnson, Paul. *Modern Times: The World from the Twenties to the Nineties*. New York: HarperPerennial, 1992.

Jones, Robert Huhn. *The Roads to Russia: United States Lend-Lease to the Soviet Union.* Norman: University of Oklahoma Press, 1969.

Jordan, George Racey, with Richard L. Stokes. *From Major Jordan's Diaries.* New York: Harcourt, Brace & Co., 1952.

Karpov, Vladimir. *Marshal Zhukov.* Moscow: Veche, 2017.

Keep, John. *A History of the Soviet Union, 1945–1991: Last of the Empires.* New York: Oxford University Press, 1995.

Kennan, George. *Russia and the West Under Lenin and Stalin.* New York: Mentor Books/New American Library, 1962.

———. *Soviet-American Relations, 1917–1920.* 2 vols. London: Faber & Faber, 1956 and 1958.

Kennedy, Greg. *Anglo-American Strategic Relations and the Far East, 1933–1939: Imperial Crossroads.* Oxfordshire, UK: Routledge, 2002.

Kershaw, Ian. *Hitler: 1936–1945. Nemesis.* New York: W. W. Norton, 2000.

Khlevniuk, Oleg. *The History of the Gulag: From Collectivization to the Great Terror.* Translated by Vadim A. Staklo. New Haven, CT: Yale University Press, 2004.

———. *Stalin: New Biography of a Dictator.* Translated by Nora Seligman Favorov. New Haven, CT: Yale University Press, 2015.

Khrushchev, Nikita. *Khrushchev Remembers: The Glasnost Tapes.* Translated and edited by Jerrold L. Schecter and Vyacheslav V. Luchkov. Boston: Little, Brown, 1990.

———. *Vospominaniia. Vremia, Liudi, Vlast'.* 2 vols. Moscow: Moskovskie novosti, 1999.

Kimball, Warren F. "A Different Take on FDR at Teheran." CIA Center for the Study of Intelligence, April 15, 2007. www.cia.gov/library/center-for-the-study-of-intelligence/csi-publications/csi-studies/studies/vol49no3/html_files/FDR_Teheran_12.htm.

Kipp, Jacob. "Lenin and Clausewitz: The Militarization of Marxism, 1914–21." *Military Affairs* 49, no. 4 (October 1985): 184–191.

Klehr, Harvey, and J. E. Haynes. "On the Trail of a Fourth Spy at Los Alamos." *Studies in Intelligence* 63, no. 3 (September 2019): 1–13.

Komarov, M. P. *Lend-Liz dlya Voenno-morskogo flota SSSR.* Saint Petersburg: Morskoe Nasledie, 2014.

Koshiro, Yukiko. *Imperial Eclipse: Japan's Strategic Thinking About Continental Asia Before 1945.* Ithaca, NY: Cornell University Press, 2013.

Koster, John. *Operation Snow: How a Soviet Mole in FDR's White House Triggered Pearl Harbor.* Washington, DC: Regnery, 2012.

Kotkin, Stephen. *Magnetic Mountain: Stalinism as a Civilization*. Berkeley: University of California Press, 1997.

———. *Stalin*. Vol. 1, *Paradoxes of Power, 1878–1928*. New York: Penguin Books, 2015.

———. *Stalin*. Vol. 2, *Waiting for Hitler, 1929–1941*. New York: Penguin Press, 2017.

Krylov, Ivan. *Soviet Staff Officer*. Translated by Edward Fitzgerald. London: Falcon Press, 1951.

Kubek, Anthony. *How the Far East Was Lost: American Foreign Policy and the Creation of Communist China, 1941–1949*. New York: Twin Circle Publishing Company, 1972.

Kudriashov, Sergei, ed. *Voina 1941–1945. Vestnik Arkhiva Prezidenta Rossiiskoi Federatsii*. Moscow: Arkhiv Prezidenta Rossiskoi Federatsii, 2010.

Kuromiya, Hiroaki. "Stalin in the Politburo Transcripts." In *The Lost Politburo Transcripts: From Collective Rule to Stalin's Dictatorship*. Edited by Paul R. Gregory and Norman Naimark. New Haven, CT: Yale University Press, 2008.

Labuda, Gerard, and Waldemar Michowicz, eds. *The History of Polish Diplomacy X–XX c.* Warsaw: Sejm Publishing Office, 2005.

Laserson, Max (M. J. Larsons). *Im Sowjet-Labyrinth: Episoden und Silhouetten*. Berlin: Transmare, 1931.

Lash, Joseph P. *Eleanor and Franklin: The Story of Their Relationship, Based on Eleanor Roosevelt's Private Papers*. New York: W. W. Norton, 1971.

Lebor, Adam. *Hitler's Secret Bankers: How Switzerland Profited from Nazi Genocide*. London: Simon & Schuster, 1999.

Lees, Michael. *The Rape of Serbia: The British Role in Tito's Grab for Power, 1943–1944*. Boston: Harcourt, 1990.

Lenin, V. I. "Left-Wing Childishness and Petty Bourgeois Mentality," May 1918, in *Selected Works*, vol. 7, 357.

———. *Sochineniia*. Edited by N. I. Bukharin, et al. Leningrad: Gosudarstevennoe Sotsial'no Ekonomicheskoe Izdatel'stvo, 1931.

———. *Socialism and War: The Attitude of the Russian Social-Democratic Labor Party Towards the War*. Geneva: Sotsial-Democrat, 1915.

Lensen, George. *The Strange Neutrality: Soviet-Japanese Relations During the Second World War*. Tallahassee, FL: Diplomatic Press, 1972.

Levin, Dov. *A Lesser of Two Evils: Eastern European Jewry Under Soviet Rule, 1939–1941*. Translated by Naftali Greenwood. Philadelphia: Jewish Publication Society, 1995.

Liechtenhan, Francine-Dominique. *Le grand pillage: Du butin des Nazis aux trophies des Soviétiques*. Rennes, France: Éditions Ouest-France, 1998.

Lieven, D. C. B. *Empire: The Russian Empire and Its Rivals*. New Haven, CT: Yale University Press, 2002.

————. *Towards the Flame: Empire, War, and the End of Tsarist Russia*. New York: Viking, 2015.

Litvinenko, V. V. *Tsena Voinyi. Lyudskie poteri na sovetsko-germanskom fronte*. Moscow: Veche, 2013.

Lloyd, Nick. *Hundred Days: The Campaign That Ended World War I*. New York: Basic Books, 2014.

Lokhova, Svetlana. *The Spy Who Changed History: The Untold Story of How the Soviet Union Stole America's Top Secrets*. New York: Pegasus Books, 2019.

Lowe, Keith. *Savage Continent: Europe in the Aftermath of World War II*. New York: St. Martin's Press, 2012.

Lownie, Andrew. *Stalin's Englishman: The Lives of Guy Burgess*. London: Hodder & Stoughton, 2015.

Lupke, Hubertus. *Japans Russlandpolitik von 1939 bis 1941*. Frankfurt: Alfred Metzner Verlag, 1962.

Maclean, Fitzroy. *Eastern Approaches*. London: Penguin, 2011. First published in 1949.

Madej, W. Victor. *The Russo-German War: June 1941–June 1943*. Allentown, PA: Game Publishing Company, 1983.

Malia, Martin. *The Soviet Tragedy: A History of Socialism in Russia, 1917–1991*. New York: Free Press, 1994.

Manstein, Erich von. *Lost Victories*. Translated by Anthony G. Powell. London: Methuen, 1958.

Manvell, Roger, and Heinrich Fraenkel. *The Canaris Conspiracy: The Secret Resistance to Hitler in the German Army*. New York: McKay, 1969.

Markov, Georgi. *Druga Istoriya na nai-goliamata voina*. Vol. 1, *Razgarnyianeto na pozhara*. Sofia: Zahariy Stoyanov, 2014.

Martel, Leon. *Lend-Lease, Loans, and the Coming of the Cold War: A Study of the Implementation of Foreign Policy*. Boulder, CO: Westview Press, 1979.

Marx, Karl. "Capital, Volume One" and "Manifesto of the Communist Party." In *The Marx-Engels Reader*, edited by Robert C. Tucker. New York: Norton, 1972.

Matthews, Owen. *An Impeccable Spy: Richard Sorge, Stalin's Master Agent*. London: Bloomsbury, 2019.

Mawdsley, Evan. *The Russian Civil War*. Boston: Allen & Unwin, 1987.

———. *Thunder in the East: The Nazi-Soviet War, 1941–1945*. London: Hodder Education Publishers, 2006.

McMeekin, Sean. *History's Greatest Heist: The Looting of Russia by the Bolsheviks*. New Haven, CT: Yale University Press, 2008.

———. *The Ottoman Endgame: War, Revolution, and the Making of the Modern Middle East, 1908–1923*. New York: Penguin Press, 2015.

———. *The Red Millionaire: A Political Biography of Willy Münzenberg, Moscow's Secret Propaganda Tsar in the West, 1917–1940*. New Haven, CT: Yale University Press, 2003.

———. *The Russian Revolution: A New History*. New York: Basic Books, 2017.

Mearsheimer, John J. *The Tragedy of Great Power Politics*. New York: W. W. Norton, 2003.

Medvedev, Roy. *All Stalin's Men: Six Who Carried Out the Bloody Policies*. New York: Anchor, 1984.

Mee, Charles L., Jr. *Meeting at Potsdam*. New York: M. Evans & Co., Inc., 1975.

Mellinger, George. *Soviet Lend-Lease Fighter Aces of World War 2*. New York: Osprey Publishing, 2006.

Mel'tyukhov, Mikhail. *Upushchennyi shans Stalina: Sovetskii soiuz i bor'ba za Evropu 1939–1941*. Moscow: Veche, 2000.

Menning, Bruce. *Bayonets Before Bullets: The Imperial Russian Army, 1861–1914*. Bloomington: Indiana University Press, 1992.

Merridale, Catherine. *Ivan's War: Life and Death in the Red Army, 1939–1945*. New York: Metropolitan, 2006.

Mertsalov, A. N., and L. A. Mertsalova. *Stalinizm i voina*. Moscow: Rodnik, 1994.

Mikoyan, Anastas. *Tak bylo: Razmyshleniia o minuvshem (moi 20 vek)*. Moscow: Vagrius, 1999.

Miller, Margaret. *The Economic Development of Russia, 1905–1914: With Special Reference to Trade, Industry, and Finance*. New York: A. M. Kelly, 1967.

Millman, Brock. "Toward War with Russia: British Naval and Air Planning for Conflict in the Near East, 1939–1940." *Journal of Contemporary History* 29, no. 2 (April 1994): 261–283.

Minassian, Taline Ter. "La neutralité de la Turquie durant la deuxième guerre mondiale." *Guerres mondiales et conflits contemporaines* 194 (December 1999): 117–148.

Miner, Steven Merritt. *Between Churchill and Stalin: The Soviet Union, Great Britain, and the Origins of the Grand Alliance.* Chapel Hill: University of North Carolina Press, 1988.

Montefiore, Simon Sebag. *Stalin: The Court of the Red Tsar.* New York: Vintage, 2005.

———. *Young Stalin.* New York: Vintage, 2008.

Moorhouse, Roger. *The Devils' Alliance: Hitler's Pact with Stalin, 1939–1941.* New York: Basic Books, 2014.

Morgan, Ted. *FDR: A Biography.* New York: Simon & Schuster, 1985.

Morgenthau, Henry, Sr. *Ambassador Morgenthau's Story.* Garden City, NY: Doubleday, Page, and Company, 1919.

Morley, James William. *The Japanese Thrust into Siberia, 1918.* New York: Columbia University Press, 1957.

Mosier, John. *Hitler vs. Stalin: The Eastern Front, 1941–1945.* New York: Simon & Schuster, 2011.

Moulton, Harold G., and Leo Pasvolsky. *Russian Debts and Russian Reconstruction: A Study of the Relation of Russia's Foreign Debts to Her Economic Recovery.* New York: McGraw-Hill, 1924.

Mowbray, C. Margo. *Havoc Red: Surviving the Alaska-Siberia Route, 1943.* Oklahoma City, OK: Clarity Communications, 2015.

Mueller, Michael. *Canaris: The Life and Death of Hitler's Spymaster.* Translated by Geoffrey Brooks. Annapolis, MD: Naval Institute Press, 2007.

Müller, Rolf-Dieter. *Das Tor zur Weltmacht.* Boppard, Germany: Harald Boldt, 1984.

Murphy, David. *What Stalin Knew: The Enigma of Barbarossa.* New Haven, CT: Yale University Press, 2005.

Musial, Bogdan. *Kampfplatz Deutschland: Stalins Kriegspläne gegen den Westen.* Berlin: Propyläen, 2008.

———. *Konterrevolutionäre Elemente sind zu erschießen: Die Brutalisierung des deutsch-sowjetischen Krieges im Sommer 1941.* Berlin: Propyläen, 2000.

———. *Kto Dopomoze Zydowi . . .* Poznan, Poland: Zysk i S-ka Wydawnistwo, 2019.

———, ed. *Sowjetische Partisanen in Weißrußland: Innenansichten aus dem Gebiet Baranovici 1941–1944. Eine Dokumentation.* Munich: R. Oldenbourg Verlag, 2004.

———. *Stalins Beutezug: Die Plünderung Deutschlands und der Aufstieg der Sowjetunion zur Weltmacht.* Berlin: Propyläen, 2010.

Naimark, Norman. *The Russians in Germany: A History of the Soviet Zone of Occupation, 1945–1949.* Cambridge, MA: Belknap, 1995.

Nation, R. Craig. *War on War: Lenin, the Zimmerwald Left, and the Origins of Communist Internationalism*. Durham, NC: Duke University Press, 1989.

New York Times. "Russia Awards $110,000,000 Job to Chicago Firm." November 12, 1929.

Nordling, Carl O. "Did Stalin Deliver His Alleged Speech of 19 August 1939?" *Journal of Slavic Military Studies* 19 (2006): 93–106.

Odom, Anne. "The Selling of Russian Art and the Origins of the Hillwood Collection." In *A Taste for Splendor: Russian Imperial and European Treasures from the Hillwood Museum*, by Anne Odom and Liana Paredes Arend, 45. New York: Antique Collectors Club Ltd., 1998.

Odom, Anne, and Wendy R. Salmond, eds. *Treasure into Tractors: The Selling of Russia's Cultural Heritage, 1918–1938*. Washington, DC: Hillwood Museum, 2009.

Ohler, Norman. *Der totale Rausch: Drogen im dritten Reich*. Cologne, Germany: Kiepenheuer & Witsch, 2017.

Okorokov, A. V. *Osobyi Front: Nemetskaia propaganda na vostochnom fronte*. Moscow: Russkii put', 2007.

Orwell, George. *Homage to Catalonia*. New York: Harcourt, Brace & Co., 1952.

Osborn, Patrick. *Operation Pike: Britain Versus the Soviet Union, 1939–1941*. Westport, CT: Greenwood Press, 2000.

Overy, Richard. *Russia's War*. London: Penguin, 1998.

Paine, S. C. M. *The Wars for Asia, 1911–1949*. New York: Cambridge University Press, 2012.

Patenaude, Bertrand. *The Big Show in Bololand: The American Relief Expedition to Soviet Russia in the Famine of 1921*. Stanford, CA: Stanford University Press, 2002.

Paul, Allen. *Katyn: Stalin's Massacre and the Triumph of Truth*. DeKalb: Northern Illinois University Press, 2010.

Pavlov, Vitalii. *Operatsiya 'Sneg'*. Moscow: Gaia interim, 1996.

Payne, Stanley. *The Spanish Civil War, the Soviet Union, and Communism*. New Haven, CT: Yale University Press, 2004.

Penrose, Barrie. *Stalin's Gold: The Story of HMS Edinburgh and Its Treasure*. Boston: Little, Brown & Co., 1983.

Persico, Joseph E. *Roosevelt's Secret War: FDR and World War II Espionage*. New York: Random House, 2001.

Pipes, Richard. *Russia Under the Bolshevik Regime*. New York: Vintage, 1995.

———. *The Russian Revolution*. New York: Alfred Knopf, 1990.

Pleshakov, Constantine. *Stalin's Folly: The Tragic First Ten Days of World War II on the Eastern Front*. Boston: Houghton Mifflin, 2005.

Plokhy, S. M. *Yalta: The Price of Peace*. New York: Penguin Books, 2010.

Pochtarev, A. N. *Morskie sekretyi vtoroi mirovoi voenno-morskie sotrudnichestvo SSSR i SShA*. Moscow: Veche, 2016.

Pogue, Forrest. *George C. Marshall*. 4 vols. New York: Viking, 1963–1987.

Pons, Silvio. *Stalin and the Inevitable War: 1936–1941*. London: Frank Cass, 2002.

Porch, Douglas. *Path to Victory: The Mediterranean Campaign in World War II*. New York: Farrar, Straus & Giroux, 2005.

Post, Walter. *Unternehmen Barbarossa: Deutsche und sowjetische Angriffspläne 1940/41*. Berlin: E. S. Mittler & Sohn, 2001.

Prange, Gordon. *Target Tokyo: The Story of the Sorge Spy Ring*. New York: McGraw-Hill, 1984.

Pundeff, Martin. "Dimitrov at Leipzig: Was There a Deal?" *Slavic Review* 45, no. 3 (Autumn 1986): 545–549.

Putin, Vladimir. "75th Anniversary of the Great Victory: Shared Responsibility to History and Our Future." Online at: http://en.kremlin.ru /events/president/news/63527.

Raack, Richard. "His Question Asked and Answered. Stalin on 'Whither Poland.'" *Polish Review* 55, no. 2 (2010): 195–215.

———. *Stalin's Drive to the West, 1938–1945: The Origins of the Cold War*. Stanford, CA: Stanford University Press, 1995.

Raczynski, Count Edward. *In Allied London*. London: Weidenfeld and Nicolson, 1962.

Rayfield, Donald. *Stalin and His Hangmen: The Tyrant and Those Who Killed for Him*. New York: Random House, 2004.

Rees, Laurence. *World War II Behind Closed Doors: Stalin, the Nazis and the West*. New York: Pantheon Books, 2008.

Reynolds, David. *Summits: Six Meetings That Shaped the Twentieth Century*. New York: Basic Books, 2007.

Reynolds, Michael A. *Shattering Empires: The Clash and Collapse of the Ottoman and Russian Empires*. New York: Cambridge University Press, 2011.

Rich, Norman. *Hitler's War Aims: Ideology, the Nazi State, and the Course of Expansion*. New York: W. W. Norton, 1973.

Roberts, Andrew. *Churchill: Walking with Destiny*. New York: Viking, 2018.

———. *The Storm of War: A New History of the Second World War*. New York: Harper, 2011.

Roberts, Geoffrey. *Stalin's Wars: From World War to Cold War, 1939–1953*. New Haven, CT: Yale University Press, 2008.

Rokossovskii, K. K. *Soldatskii dolg*. Moscow: Golos, 2000.

Roll, David L. *The Hopkins Touch: Harry Hopkins and the Forging of the Alliance to Defeat Hitler*. New York: Oxford University Press, 2013.

Romerstein, Herbert, and Eric Breindel. *The Venona Secrets: Exposing Soviet Espionage and America's Traitors*. Washington, DC: Regnery, 2000.

Sainsbury, Keith. *The Turning Point: Roosevelt, Stalin, Churchill, and Chiang Kai-shek, 1943: The Moscow, Cairo, and Teheran Conferences*. New York: Oxford University Press, 1986.

Samsonov, A. M. *Stalingradskaia bitva*. Moscow: Nauka, 1989. First published in 1960.

Samuelson, Lennart. *Plans for Stalin's War Machine: Tukhachevskii and Military-Economic Planning, 1926–1941*. London: Palgrave Macmillan, 2000.

Sander, Helke, and Barbara Johr, eds. *Befreier und Befreite: Krieg, Verwaltigungen, Kinder*. Munich: A. Kunstmann, 1992.

Schecter, Jerrold, and Leona Schecter. *Sacred Secrets: How Soviet Intelligence Operations Changed American History*. Lincoln: University of Nebraska Press, 2003.

Scheil, Stefan. *Die Eskalation des Zweiten Weltkriegs von 1940 bis zum Unternehmen Barbarossa 1941*. Berlin: Duncker & Humblot, 2011.

———. *Polen 1939: Kriegskalkül, Vorbereitung, Vollzug*. Schnellroda, Germany: Verlag Antaios, 2013.

Schwipper, Bernd. *Deutschland im Visier Stalins: Der Weg der roten Armee in den europäischen Krieg und der Aufmarsch der Wehrmacht 1941*. Gilching, Germany: Druffel & Vowinckel Verlag, 2015.

Seidt, Hans-Ulrich. *Berlin, Kabul, Moskau: Oskar Ritter von Niedermayer und Deutschlands Ostpolitik*. Munich: Universitas, 2002.

Service, Robert. *Lenin: A Biography*. Cambridge, MA: Belknap, 2000.

Shapiro, Leonard. *The Russian Revolutions of 1917: The Origins of Modern Communism*. New York: Basic Books, 1984.

Sherwood, Robert E. *Roosevelt and Hopkins: An Intimate History*. New York: Harper & Brothers, 1948.

Showalter, Dennis. *Armor and Blood: The Battle of Kursk, the Turning Point of World War II*. New York: Random House, 2013.

Siekierski, Maciej. "Jews in Soviet-Occupied East Poland, 1939." In *Jews in Eastern Poland and the USSR, 1939–46*, edited by Norman Davies and Antony Polonsky, 110–115. New York: St. Martin's Press, 1991.

Simms, Brendan. *Hitler: A Global Biography*. New York: Basic Books, 2019.

Slezkine, Yuri. *The House of Government: A Saga of the Russian Revolution*. Princeton, NJ: Princeton University Press, 2017.

———. *The Jewish Century*. Princeton, NJ: Princeton University Press, 2004.

Smith, Blake. *Warplanes to Alaska*. Surrey, Canada: Hancock House Pub Ltd., 1998.

Smith, Bradley F. *The Shadow Warriors: O.S.S. and the Origins of the C.I.A.* New York: Basic Books, 1983.

Smith, Richard Norton. *The Colonel: The Life and Legend of Colonel Robert R. McCormick, 1880–1955*. Boston: Houghton Mifflin, 1997.

Snyder, Timothy. *Black Earth: The Holocaust as History and Warning*. New York: Tim Duggan Books, 2015.

———. *Bloodlands: Europe Between Hitler and Stalin*. New York: Basic Books, 2010.

Sokolov, B.V. *Pravda o velikoi otechestvennoi voine*. Saint Petersburg: Izdatel'stvo Aleteiya, 1998.

Solomon, Georg. *Unter den Roten Machthabern: Was ich im Dienste der Sowjets persönlich sah und erlebte*. Berlin: Verlag für Kulturpolitik, 1930.

Solonari, Vladimir. *A Satellite Empire: Romanian Rule in Southwestern Ukraine, 1941–1944*. Ithaca, NY: Cornell University Press, 2019.

Solonin, Mark. "Comrade Stalin's Three Plans." May 31, 2011. www.solonin.org/en/article_comrade-stalins-three-plans.

———. *June 1941. Final Diagnosis*. Moscow: Eksmo Yauza, 2013. Available online and in English at www.solonin.org/en/article_mark-solonin-june-1941-final.

———. *Na mirno spiashchikh aerodromakh . . . 22 iunia 1941*. Moscow: Eksmo, 2007.

———. "Tri plana tovarisch' Stalina." February 25, 2009. www.solonin.org/en/article_tri-plana-tovarischa-stalina.

———. "25 June. Stupidity or Aggression?" October 20, 2014. www.solonin.org/en/article_mark-solonin-25-june-stupidity3.

Solzhenitsyn, Aleksandr. *The Gulag Archipelago 1918–1956: An Experiment in Literary Investigation*. 3 vols. New York: Harper & Row, 1973–1975.

Stahel, David. *Operation Barbarossa and Germany's Defeat in the East*. New York: Cambridge University Press, 2011.

———. *Retreat from Moscow: A New History of Germany's Winter Campaign, 1941–1942*. New York: Farrar, Straus & Giroux, 2019.

Stalin, Josef. *The Essential Stalin: Major Theoretical Writings*. Edited by Bruce Franklin. Garden City, NY: Anchor Books, 1972.

————. *From Socialism to Communism in the Soviet Union: Report on the Work of the Central Committee to the Eighteenth Congress of the CPSU(B.) Delivered March 10, 1939*. New York: International Publishers, 1939.

————. *The Great Patriotic War of the Soviet Union*. New York: International Publishers, 1945.

————. *Leninism*. 2 vols. London: G. Allen & Unwin, Ltd., 1928–1932.

————. *Selected Writings*. New York: International Publishers, 1942.

————. *Sochineniia*. Edited by Robert H. McNeal. 3 vols. Stanford, CA: Hoover Institution on War, Revolution, and Peace, 1967.

————. *Stalin's Master Narrative: A Critical Edition of the History of the Communist Party of the Soviet Union (Bolsheviks), Short Course*. Edited by David Brandenberger and Mikhail Zelenov. New Haven, CT: Yale University Press, 2019.

————. *Works*. 13 vols. Moscow: Foreign Languages Publishing House, 1952–1955.

Standley, William H., with Arthur A. Ageton. *Admiral Ambassador to Russia*. Chicago: H. Regnery, 1955.

Stimson, Henry Lewis, and McGeorge Bundy. *On Active Service in Peace and War*. New York: Octagon Books, 1971.

Stoler, Mark A. *The Politics of the Second Front: American Military Planning and Diplomacy in Coalition Warfare, 1941–1943*. Westport, CT: Greenwood Press, 1977.

Stolfi, R. H. S. *Hitler's Panzers East: World War II Reinterpreted*. Norman: University of Oklahoma Press, 1993.

Stone, Norman. *World War Two: A Short History*. New York: Basic Books, 2013.

Sudoplatov, Pavel. *Khronika tainoi voinyi i diplomatii 1938–1941 godyi*. Moscow: Algoritm, 2018.

————. *Special Tasks: The Memoirs of an Unwanted Witness—a Soviet Spymaster*. Translated and edited by Anatoli Sudoplatov, Jerrold L. Schecter, and Leona P. Schecter. Boston: Little, Brown, 1994.

Sutton, Antony C. *Western Technology and Soviet Economic Development*. Stanford, CA: Hoover Institution on War, Revolution, and Peace, 1968–1973.

Suvorov, Viktor. *The Chief Culprit: Stalin's Grand Design to Start World War II*. Annapolis, MD: Naval Institute Press, 2013.

Sword, Keith. "The Welfare of Polish-Jewish Refugees in the USSR, 1941–43." In *Jews in Eastern Poland and the USSR, 1939–46*, edited by Norman Davies and Antony Polonsky, 145–160. New York: St. Martin's Press, 1991.

Tanenhaus, Sam. *Whittaker Chambers: A Biography*. New York: Random House, 1997.

Tarulis, Albert N. *Soviet Policy Towards the Baltic States, 1918–1940*. Notre Dame, IN: University of Notre Dame Press, 1959.

Tessin, Georg. *Verbände und Truppen der deutschen Wehrmacht und Waffen-SS im Zweiten Weltkrieg 1939–1945*. 17 vols. Osnabrück, Germany: Biblio Verlag, 1965–1997.

Tolstoy, Nikolai. *The Minister and the Massacres*. London: Century Hutchison, 1986.

———. *Stalin's Secret War*. London: J. Cape, 1981.

———. *Victims of Yalta: The Secret Betrayal of the Allies, 1944–1947*. New York: Pegasus Books, 2012. First published in 1977.

Tomasevich, Jozo. *The Chetniks: War and Revolution in Yugoslavia, 1941–1945*. Stanford, CA: Stanford University Press, 1975.

———. *War and Revolution in Yugoslavia, 1941–1945: Occupation and Collaboration*. Stanford, CA: Stanford University Press, 2001.

Tooze, Adam. *The Wages of Destruction: The Making and Breaking of the Nazi Economy*. New York: Penguin Books, 2008.

Topitsch, Ernst. *Stalin's War: A Radical New Theory of the Origins of the Second World War*. London: Palgrave Macmillan, 1987.

Trotter, William. *Frozen Hell: The Russo-Finnish Winter War of 1939–1940*. Chapel Hill, NC: Algonquin Books, 1999.

Tucker, Robert C. *Stalin in Power: The Revolution from Above, 1928–1941*. New York: W. W. Norton, 1990.

Tzouliadis, Tim. *The Forsaken: An American Tragedy in Stalin's Russia*. New York: Penguin Books, 2009.

Ulam, Adam. *Expansion and Coexistence: Soviet Foreign Policy, 1917–1973*. New York: Praeger, 1974.

Ullman, Richard. *Anglo-Soviet Relations, 1917–1921*. 3 vols. Princeton, NJ: Princeton University Press, 1961, 1968, and 1972.

Van de Ven, Hans. *China at War: Triumph and Tragedy in the Emergence of the New China*. Cambridge, MA: Harvard University Press, 2018.

———. *War and Nationalism in China: 1925–1945*. Oxfordshire, UK: RoutledgeCurzon, 2003.

Van Tuyll, Hubert P. *Feeding the Bear: American Aid to the Soviet Union, 1941–1945*. Westport, CT: Greenwood Press, 1989.

Vetrov, A. A. "Moskva osen'yu 1941 goda." In *Moskva voennaya. Sbornik Vospominanii*, 62–74. Moscow: Rossiya molodaia, 1995.

Volkogonov, Dmitri. *Stalin: Triumph and Tragedy*. Translated by Harold Shukman. New York: Grove Press, 1991.

Voronin, Anatolii. *Moskva 1941*. Moscow: Pyatii Rim, 2016.

Waller, Douglas. *Wild Bill Donovan: The Spymaster Who Created the OSS and Modern American Espionage*. New York: Free Press, 2011.

Waller, John. *The Unseen War in Europe: Espionage and Conspiracy in the Second World War*. New York: Random House, 1996.

Watson, Alexander. *The Fortress: The Siege of Przemysl and the Making of Europe's Bloodlands*. New York: Basic Books, 2020.

Waugh, Evelyn. *The Sword of Honour*. 3 vols. London: Everyman's Library, 1994.

Wawro, Geoffrey. *A Mad Catastrophe: The Outbreak of World War I and the Collapse of the Habsburg Empire*. New York: Basic Books, 2015.

Weeks, Albert L. *Russia's Life-Saver: Lend-Lease Aid to the U.S.S.R. in World War II*. Lanham, MD: Lexington Books, 2010.

———. *Stalin's Other War: Soviet Grand Strategy, 1939–1941*. Lanham, MD: Rowman & Littlefield, 2003.

Weil, Martin. *A Pretty Good Club: The Founding Fathers of the U.S. Foreign Service*. New York: W. W. Norton, 1978.

Weinberg, Gerhard. *Germany, Hitler, and World War II*. New York: Cambridge University Press, 1996.

———. *A World at Arms: A Global History of World War II*. New York: Cambridge University Press, 1993.

Werth, Alexander. *Moscow War Diary*. New York: Knopf, 1942.

———. *Russia at War: 1941–1945*. New York: Skyhorse, 1964.

Werth, Nicolas. "The Iron Fist of the Dictatorship of the Proletariat," "The Red Terror," and "The Dirty War." In *The Black Book of Communism: Crimes, Terror, Repression*. Translated by Jonathan Murphy and Mark Kramer. Cambridge, MA: Harvard University Press, 1999.

West, Diana. *American Betrayal: The Secret Assault on Our Nation's Character*. New York: St. Martin's Press, 2013.

Wheeler-Bennett, John W. *Brest-Litovsk: The Forgotten Peace, March 1918*. New York: St. Martin's Press, 1956.

Williams, Robert C. *Russian Art and American Money, 1900–1940*. Cambridge, MA: Harvard University Press, 1980.

Winterbotham, Frederick William. *The Ultra Secret*. New York: Harper & Row, 1974.

Woolner, David B. *The Last 100 Days: FDR at War and at Peace*. New York: Basic Books, 2017.

Wuescht, Johann. *Jugoslawien und das dritte Reich*. Stuttgart, Germany: Seewald, 1969.

Zaloga, Steven J. *Soviet Lend-Lease Tanks of World War II*. London: Osprey, 2017.

Zhukov, G. K. *Vospominaniya i razmyishleniya*. 3 vols. Moscow: Novosti, 1992.

Ziemke, Earl F. *Stalingrad to Berlin: The German Defeat in the East*. Washington, DC: US Army Center of Military History, 2011.

———. *The U.S. Army in the Occupation of Germany 1944–1946*. Washington, DC: US Army Center of Military History, 1975.

Zimmerman, Joshua D. *The Polish Underground and the Jews, 1939–1945*. Cambridge: Cambridge University Press, 2015.

Index

Sean McMeekin is a professor of history at Bard College. The award-winning author of several books, including *The Russian Revolution, July 1914*, and *The Ottoman Endgame*, McMeekin lives in Clermont, New York.